Religion within the
Limits of History Alone

Religion within the Limits of History Alone

Pragmatic Historicism and the Future of Theology

DEMIAN WHEELER

Cover image: *In a Relationship* by Susan Cohen Thompson. Reprinted with permission.

Published by State University of New York Press, Albany

© 2020 State University of New York Press

All rights reserved

No part of this book may be used or reproduced in any manner whatsoever without written permission. No part of this book may be stored in a retrieval system or transmitted in any form or by any means including electronic, electrostatic, magnetic tape, mechanical, photocopying, recording, or otherwise without the prior permission in writing of the publisher.

For information, contact State University of New York Press, Albany, NY
www.sunypress.edu

Library of Congress Cataloging-in-Publication Data

Name: Wheeler, Demian, author.
Title: Religion within the limits of history alone: pragmatic historicism and the future of theology / Demian Wheeler, author.
Description: Albany : State University of New York Press, [2020] | Includes bibliographical references and index.
Identifiers: ISBN 971438479330 (hardcover : alk. paper) | ISBN 9781438479347 (pbk. : alk. paper) | ISBN 9781438479354 (ebook)
Further information is available at the Library of Congress.

Library of Congress Control Number: 2020937134

10 9 8 7 6 5 4 3 2 1

To Victoria and Shailer

Contents

Acknowledgments	ix
Introduction	1
Chapter 1 What Is Historicism? A Multileveled Definition	7
Chapter 2 Historical Particularity and the Problem of Insularity: Pragmatic Historicism as a Bigger Historicism	15
Chapter 3 Particularist Mutualism: Toward a Pragmatic Historicist Theology of Religions	61
Chapter 4 After Incommensurability: Pragmatic Historicism as an Impetus for Meaningful Interreligious Engagement	117
Chapter 5 Beyond Amnesia and Nostalgia: Pragmatic Historicism and the Authority of the Past	145
Chapter 6 Truth Reconsidered: Building Blocks of a Paleopragmatic Historicism	189
Chapter 7 Theological Truth Reconsidered: Four Traits of a Paleopragmatic Historicist Theology	251
Chapter 8 Sacred Conventions, Sacred Nature: Toward a Pragmatic Historicist Theology of the Divine	277

Conclusion	353
Notes	359
Bibliography	467
Index	491

Acknowledgments

If historicism is the notion that all phenomena are indelibly shaped by their histories and contexts, then acknowledging one's debts is a decidedly historicist activity.

Many thanks to the editorial staff at SUNY Press, especially Christopher Ahn, Amanda Lanne-Camilli, and James Peltz, as well as to the two anonymous reviewers who read an earlier draft of the manuscript and offered a number of helpful comments, criticisms, and suggestions. I am also grateful to Susan Cohen-Thompson for supplying the artwork for the book cover and to David Prout for preparing the index.

Religion within the Limits of History Alone is the culmination of several years of research, having originated as my dissertation at Union Theological Seminary. Thus, I want to express my deepest gratitude to the director of my dissertation, my PhD advisor, Gary Dorrien. I knew I wanted to work with Gary as early as 2002, the year I read the first volume of his magisterial trilogy on American liberal theology; and in 2007, he turned that dream into a reality and accepted me as his doctoral student. Since then, Gary has provided incomparable guidance, reassurance, wisdom, and support—both intellectual and personal. I have greatly benefited as well from his ongoing critical feedback—ever incisive, but always pastoral and genuinely constructive. Most of all, he has reminded me again and again that if I am going to call myself a historicist, I ought to grasp the history of the field I am entering. And, without a doubt, nobody has helped me grasp that history more than he has. Gary is, by far, the most learned and accomplished scholar I have ever encountered—John Thatamanil often quips that he is as close to omniscient as a fallible human being can get—and to have studied under him has been one of the highlights of my life.

I am also enormously indebted to the three other members of my dissertation committee: Paul Knitter, who became one of my primary mentors at Union and (persistently but gently) prodded me to wear my pluralist badge proudly; John Thatamanil, who is one of the most cutting-edge, groundbreaking, exciting, and constructively ambitious comparative and philosophical theologians on the contemporary scene; and Sheila Davaney, who was my MA advisor and teacher at the Iliff School of Theology and is one of the leading experts on and exponents of pragmatic historicism. It was profoundly humbling and gratifying to have scholars of such immense acuity, creativity, and luminosity read, critique, and evaluate my first book-length work.

Sheila Davaney was actually one of three historicist theologians with whom I closely worked while I was a master's student at Iliff. The other two were the late Delwin Brown, whose scholarship initially drew me to Iliff, and William Dean, whose steadfast mentorship, encouragement, and inspiration have sustained me for almost two decades. The "Iliff historicists" influenced my intellectual formation more than anyone else, introducing me to the Chicago school and, more broadly, to the traditions of American theological and philosophical thought that have become the focus of my own research and scholarship: empirical theology, religious naturalism, process philosophy, and, of course, pragmatic historicism. Deciding to move to Colorado to study with Sheila, Bill, and Del was one of the best decisions I ever made. I hope this book is a fitting tribute to them.

I have had the privilege of learning from several other exceptional teachers and scholars along the way, all of whom have played a significant role in my academic development. I wish to especially thank Antony Alumkal, Mary Boys, Euan Cameron, Roger Haight, Thomas Hall, Albert Hernández, Bruce Marino, Gregory Miller, Christopher Morse, Wayne Proudfoot, Hal Taussig, and the late James Cone.

In 2008, I joined the Institute for American Religious and Philosophical Thought (formerly the Highlands Institute for American Religious and Philosophical Thought), the institutional locus of most of my scholarly interests: the Chicago school, theological liberalism in America, and naturalist, empiricist, process, pragmatist, and historicist approaches to philosophy and theology. It has been an honor to share my work with this esteemed group of scholars, some of whom make an appearance in the pages to follow. I am particularly grateful to David Conner, Robert Corrington, Donald Crosby, Nancy Frankenberry, and Michael Hogue, who have become mentors, as well as to several other IARPTers who have offered indispensable criticisms, insights, and suggestions over the last few years, including Randy Auxier, Tom Byrnes, Linell Cady, Pamela Crosby, William Hart, Andrew

Irvine, Jennifer Jesse, Robert King, Bob Mesle, Barbara Hiles Mesle, Wade Mitchell, Les Muray (in memoriam), Robert Neville, Dan Ott, Creighton Peden (in memoriam), Karl Peters, Michael Raposa, Austin Roberts, David Rohr, LeRon Shults, Rob Smid, Jerome Stone, and Wesley Wildman. My conversations with these brilliant thinkers have helped hone many of the ideas fleshed out in this volume.

I met some of my closest intellectual companions during my time at Union, including Timothy Becker (in loving memory), Jason Von Wachenfeldt, and Thurman Todd Willison. My friendships with these three extraordinary individuals have pushed me and sharpened me beyond compare. Many other friends at Union also had a decisive impact on my thinking: Roberto Alejandro, Nkosi Anderson, Chris Ashley, Nick Astraeus, Joel Berning, Preston Davis, Jeremy Kirk, Celene Lillie, Jenn Lindsay, Rob Loring, Amy Meverden, David Orr, Elijah Prewitt-Davis, Nate Smith, A. J. Turner, Marvin Wickware, and Michael Wissa.

I would like to thank a few other friends as well, specifically, Art Bucher, Kevin Clark, Rich Eby, John Gray, Alfred Haase, Jeremiah Kitchen, Andrew Light, Caleb Maskell, Kathy Maskell, Clarissa Roberts, Chip Sprouse, and Mary Ward-Bucher. All of these remarkable people have enriched me in countless ways. I am profoundly thankful for my lifelong friendship with Andrew Arena, which has kept me grounded through this arduous but rewarding process.

I want to thank Terry Muck, Edwin Aponte, and the Louisville Institute for awarding me a postdoctoral fellowship in 2015. I am especially grateful for the other members of my postdoctoral cohort, Chris Hoklotubbe, Han-luen Kantzer Komline, David Turnbloom, and Sunggu Yang, and for our cohort leader, Grace Ji-Sun Kim. Without their urging and advice, I am not sure this project would have seen the light of publication.

A big thank you to the community of United Theological Seminary of the Twin Cities, which has become my academic and spiritual home. First and foremost, I want to thank Paul Capetz, who represents the very best of the liberal Protestant tradition and whose own scholarship embodies the spirit of nineteenth-century historicism. Paul is a treasured friend, colleague, and mentor and, as he often says, my closest theological *Gesprächspartner*. He read every word of this volume—endnotes included!—and provided extensive, substantive, and invaluable critical feedback. It was Paul who helped me revise my dissertation and turn it into a book, and his pointed queries, corrections, and reflections certainly made it a better book.

I feel extremely fortunate to work with so many talented and lovely faculty colleagues, among them: Jennifer Awes-Freeman, Dale Dobias, Eleazar

Fernandez, Gary Green, Cindi Beth Johnson, John Lee, Steve Newcom, Carolyn Pressler, Justin Sabia-Tanis, J. Samuel Subramanian, and Ayo Yetunde. I owe a huge debt of gratitude to Sharon Tan, who brought me to United as a Louisville Institute postdoctoral fellow, to Lewis Zeidner, who later invited me to join the faculty, and to Kyle Roberts, who keeps me mindful of one of the core convictions of historicism: the traditions we inherit, although utterly human and fallible, supply the basic resources out of which our theologies—and indeed our lives—take shape.

I am very thankful for my students, who energize me, challenge me, and make me a better theologian. A couple of them read this manuscript in its entirety: Andrea Johnson and Jeffrey Speaks. Eric Boehlke, United's "resident philosopher," also read the entire manuscript. Andrea, Jeff, and Eric have become three of my most cherished theological and philosophical interlocutors, and I have clarified and revised arguments in response to their probing questions and insights. I have profited considerably from conversations with other United students and coworkers, including John-Arash Adams, Brian Braskich, Max Brumberg-Kraus, Chris Eriksen, Jack Gaede, Barbara Holmes, Kyle Homstad, Karen Hutt, Arif Mamdani, Sam McConnell, Greg Meland, Kimberly McGlothlin, Vonda Pearson, Preston Price, Ken Reynhout, Phil Romine, and Sheryl Schwyhart, all of whom have contributed to the content of this book, even when they were not intending to do so.

There is nothing in this world that I am more appreciative of than my family, the extended members of which are too numerous to list but are all deserving of my most heartfelt thanks. My brother and sister-in-law, Matthew Wheeler and Jenna Wheeler, have especially been a constant source of joy, sustenance, and laughter. I have been blessed with wonderful in-laws, Al Ward and Marion Ward (in loving memory), who have nurtured, supported, and encouraged me and have truly been second parents. Neither this book nor the dissertation from which it arose would have ever reached completion were it not for my own mother and father, Nancy Wheeler and Robert Wheeler. During the final year of dissertation research, they trekked into the city week after week to look after their precious grandson, giving me the time and space to write. And in the years since, they have continued to support us in untold ways. More than anything else, my parents—both retired teachers and humanists in the true sense of the word—have taught me to value education and learning, to give curiosity full rein, to keep an open mind, to love the arts, to work hard, to respect history, to revere mystery, to cherish family, and to strive for excellence, compassion, fairness, and integrity in every aspect of my life. They have, akin to Whitehead's God, led me with tender patience by their vision of truth, beauty, and goodness.

Above all, I need to acknowledge Victoria Wheeler, my lover and partner of twenty-six years, the mother of our beloved son, Shailer James Wheeler, and the best human being I know. It is her undying love, provision, and sacrifice that have allowed me to find my calling and follow my bliss. She and I have journeyed together from the glorious beaches of the Jersey Shore, to the bucolic farmlands of Pennsylvania, to the breathtaking vistas of the Rocky Mountains, to the hustle and bustle of New York City, to the "Land of 10,000 Lakes" (actually, there are almost 12,000). Wherever the contingencies of history take us in the future, I am confident that my own historical existence will remain fulfilling simply because Victoria and our beautiful boy, Shailer, are at the center of it. I dedicate this book to them.

Demian Wheeler
January 2019
Saint Paul, Minnesota

Introduction

The rise of historical consciousness has been, and continues to be, one of the greatest challenges facing theologians in the modern age. And the overarching premise of this book is that any viable theology today needs to thoroughly historicize itself—its sources, its norms, its tasks, its claims, and even its contents. Put differently, religion must be conceived within the limits of history alone.

The historicizing of religion and theology is a byproduct of the widespread *historicism* that has come to dominate Western thinking over the past two centuries.[1] Historicism, which will be more fully defined in chapter 1, is the notion that, like anything else, human beings and all of their concepts, theories, communities, texts, and so on, are historical—that is, conditioned by contingent circumstances and tied to particular contexts. Historicism has a long, complex, and multifarious history.[2] The origins of an identifiably historicist worldview go back to the German *Aufklärung* and its effort to provide an alternative to the tradition-evading Franco-British Enlightenment. In the nineteenth century, reflection on human historicity assumed center stage in the intellectual life of Germany, largely thanks to the emergence of the modern academic discipline of history and to the historically focused philosophies of Georg W. F. Hegel, Ludwig Feuerbach, Karl Marx, David Friedrich Strauss, Wilhelm Dilthey, Ernst Troeltsch, and many other towering figures. And in the twentieth century, historicism found expression in the United States by way of classical pragmatism, the early Chicago school of theology, and the ideas of important thinkers like Mordecai Kaplan, W. E. B. Du Bois, and H. Richard Niebuhr. Historicism is also the underlying presupposition of much of what now passes as "postmodern" (deconstructionism, post-structuralism, etc.), and most of the major theological programs and movements of the last several decades, from radical or death-of-God theologies to black and Latin American liberation theologies, to feminist and womanist theologies, to postliberal and revisionist theologies, exhibit deep historicist assumptions about human situatedness, particularity, finitude, social construction, and the relation between knowledge and power.

This volume contends that contemporary theologians and religious thinkers must come to terms with historicism without reservation. And to illustrate what it means to tackle the historicist challenge head-on, this study delineates, develops, and defends a particular strand of historicist thought known as *pragmatic historicism*.[3] Pragmatic historicism, as Sheila Greeve Davaney has ably shown, grows out of the historicist traditions of nineteenth-century Germany.[4] Indeed, this project has one foot in German historicism,[5] and at least half of that foot stands in the long and formidable shadow cast by Ernst Troeltsch and the *religionsgeschichtliche Schule* (see especially chapters 3 and 5).[6] Be that as it may, the adjective "pragmatic" is meant to signal that the trajectory of historicism tracked and championed here is predominantly an American intellectual tradition.[7] In the United States, historicism is philosophically rooted in and nurtured by pragmatism[8] and its intellectual siblings, naturalism and radical empiricism. Thus, the philosophical genealogy of pragmatic historicism stretches back to the classical American pragmatists—Charles Sanders Peirce, William James, and John Dewey—and includes many of their neopragmatist descendants, most notably, Richard Rorty, Richard Bernstein, Cornel West, and Jeffrey Stout. Pragmatic historicism came to full flower theologically in the early twentieth century at the Divinity School of the University of Chicago, where George Burman Foster, Shirley Jackson Case, Shailer Mathews, and Gerald Birney Smith—all of whom were influenced by pragmatism as well as by Troeltsch and the history-of-religions school—developed an empirical, naturalistic, and sociohistorical approach to theology and the study of religion. The legacy of these first-generation Chicago schoolers lives on, however quietly, in the present-day pragmatic historicist theologies of Delwin Brown, Sheila Davaney, William Dean, Gordon Kaufman, and Sallie McFague. Davaney is responsible for coining the designation "pragmatic historicism," although she enlists Brown, Dean, Kaufman, and McFague (along with a few others) as fellow pragmatic historicists.[9] She is also historically conscious about her pragmatic historicism, mindful of the ways in which it has been shaped by earlier historicisms, "especially the positions of the early Chicago School and the first American pragmatists."[10]

The thesis of this book is that the liberal theologians of the early Chicago school and the first American pragmatists provide unparalleled resources for thinking through the conceptual problems posed by historicism as these were articulated in nineteenth-century German scholarship. They and their contemporary heirs have understood religion within the limits of history alone, all the while making bold affirmations about meaning, truth, tradition, pluralism, nature, and ultimate reality. For that reason, I want to lift up this oft-neglected but important pragmatic historicist tradition—not just as a rich and vital intellectual heritage in its own right but also as a new program for the future of theology. It is argued that pragmatic historicism is an underdeveloped resource for contemporary theology since it offers a model for normative religious thought that is theologically compelling yet wholly nonsupernaturalistic, deeply pluralistic, unflinchingly liberal, and radically historicist.

That argument, I acknowledge, is not entirely original. Brown, Davaney, Dean, Kaufman, and McFague spent the better part of their careers reimagining the theological enterprise along pragmatic historicist lines,[11] and this volume is, to a considerable degree, an exposition and vindication of their labors (and those of the earlier historicists on whom they rely, be it explicitly or implicitly—i.e., Troeltsch, James, and Dewey, as well as Foster, Case, Mathews, and Smith). Of course, from a historicist point of view, the quest for pure originality is futile, since human beings are historical creatures and, as such, always "live out of the heritages their histories have bequeathed to them."[12] Consequently, in good historicist fashion, I want to begin by historicizing my own project: the insights and claims I will put forward, far from emerging ex nihilo, are linked to, dependent on, and continuous with prior historicisms. Pragmatic historicists, though, also stipulate that we are both recipients and transformers of our inheritances (see chapter 5). And indeed, I will seek to both continue and change—that is, expand, recontextualize, reshape, build on, and occasionally amend—the extant pragmatic historicist canon, making this book a conscious exemplification of the very historicism for which it argues. This is evident in at least two ways.

First, on the analytical level, this volume, following Dean and Davaney,[13] will set out to offer a genealogically and descriptively thick account of pragmatic historicism, chiefly for the purposes of mitigating the ironic penchant among more postmodern historicists to neglect their own history and, even more importantly, of recovering what gets lost, philosophically as well as theologically, when pragmatic historicism's forebears (e.g., the early Chicago schoolers and the classical pragmatists) are forgotten (e.g., an openness to metaphysics and the natural world, a tool for combatting religious exclusivism and supernaturalism, a critically realist epistemology).

However, in contrast to Davaney's most recent monographs, this book is not a history or a map of historicism. On the contrary, I adopt Davaney's plotting of the historical and contemporary terrain as my point of departure and then set out to further explore and expound its constructive theological implications. Accordingly, my analysis proceeds more synthetically and thematically than chronologically, weaving together previous and current historicisms in the hopes of pinpointing common themes and emphases and constructively engaging specific theological topics and issues (e.g., religious diversity, the nature of authority, the doctrine of God) from a pragmatic historicist perspective.

Second, this book is not just descriptive, but prescriptive. That is, instead of merely summarizing the ideas of leading pragmatic historicists, I will advocate for pragmatic historicism and for the kind of theology it makes possible. In that sense, this volume can be seen as a sort of "sequel" to Davaney's *Pragmatic Historicism*, continuing to chart a course for the future development of pragmatic historicism as well as to draw out the fresh and exciting possibilities it augurs for the renewal of theological discourse in the twenty-first century. Without a doubt, Davaney and I often nudge pragmatic historicism in comparable directions. However, as will become abundantly clear in the last few chapters of the book, I end up holding out for a more critically realist, unashamedly metaphysical, and overtly theological historicism. I am also more interested in working *across* the historicist, pragmatist, empiricist, and naturalist lineages and accentuating and fortifying the intersections between them.

To be sure, most of the proposals advanced in this study rework arguments already ventured, in some manner or another, by Davaney, Dean, Brown, Kaufman, and McFague; James and Dewey; and Foster, Case, Mathews, and Smith. Still, I intend to travel even further down the trail blazed by these pioneering pragmatic historicists. At particular junctures, this volume will try to lead pragmatic historicism to some new frontiers. For instance, chapter 3 fleshes out the first pragmatic historicist theology of religions, while chapter 8 attempts to set forth a full-orbed pragmatic historicist theology of the divine. On occasion, I will necessarily part company with and push back on the different thinkers I am explicating. In some debates, I will side with certain historicists over others, and in a few cases, I will go my own way. For example, in chapter 6, I attempt to push pragmatic historicism away from the postmodern nominalism and relativism of today's neopragmatists (whom Davaney considers "philosophical fellow travelers"[14]) and toward the paleopragmatic realism of the classical pragmatists (especially

Peirce, whom pragmatic historicists tend to ignore or even impugn). And I look to pragmatism not only for its instrumentalist theory of truth, but also for its naturalist account of reality (see chapter 2). Indeed, throughout the book, I strive to strengthen the ties between pragmatic historicism and what might be termed its "sibling traditions" in American theological and philosophical thought: radical empiricism and religious naturalism (see chapter 8, in particular).

These sorts of critical and reconstructive efforts will frequently require looking to guides who do not necessarily identify as pragmatic historicists—for example, religious pluralists and comparative theologians, such as John Hick, Paul Knitter, and John Thatamanil; pragmatic realists, such as Charles Sanders Peirce, Robert Neville, and Wesley Wildman; radical empiricists and religious naturalists, such as Donald Crosby, Nancy Frankenberry, Michael Hogue, Jerome Stone, Ursula Goodenough, and Robert Corrington; and select representatives of the *later* Chicago school of theology, such as Henry Nelson Wieman, Bernard Meland, and Bernard Loomer. This volume invokes these and other voices—some sympathetic fellow travelers, some formidable critics—both to reinforce, augment, extend, and supplement central historicist intuitions and principles, and to occasionally blunt, even correct, a few of historicism's blind spots and limitations, excesses and exaggerations, thereby putting its own fallibilism into practice and, I hope, generating a richer and more robust pragmatic historicism.

Chapter 1

What Is Historicism?

A Multileveled Definition

The task of this brief opening chapter is to lay out a working definition of historicism. I already indicated in the introduction that historicism is the notion that, like anything else, human beings and all of their concepts, theories, communities, texts, and so on, are historical—that is, conditioned by contingent circumstances and tied to particular contexts. The dependent clause "like anything else" is particularly important here, because the American iteration of historicism set forth in this book is a *thoroughgoing* historicism. In other words, for pragmatic historicists, historicity is not limited to the human sphere. On the contrary, everything in reality, from protons and planets to plants and persons, is a product of history; it is history all the way down, as it were. Hence, my definition of historicism is multileveled, cutting across multiple domains of inquiry; it is an ontology and a cosmology as well as an anthropology and a methodology.

History All the Way Down:
Historicism as an Ontology and Cosmology

Ontologically, historicism is the idea that all of reality, including human existence, is historically constituted and conditioned. There is, according to pragmatic historicist thinkers like Richard Rorty, no escape from the contingencies of history; everything—from orchids and anthropoids to human beings and all our sundry languages, communities, and conceptualizations of selfhood—is "a product of time and chance."[1] The historical sphere is, for better or worse, the site, producer, and shaper of all meaning and value, the arena in which anything real lives and moves and has its being.[2] It is history that giveth and history that taketh away. As William James remarked in *A Pluralistic Universe*, "the only life we are at home in" is the "finite world *as such*," a world in which nothing "is great or static or eternal enough not to have some history."[3] To make this point a bit more modestly, all that is known and experienced (even items traditionally deemed ahistorical and transcendent) seems to be formed in and subject to the forces of history; hence, even if extrahistorical realities and realms do exist (and historicists are—or should be—genuinely agnostic about such a possibility), they lie beyond our ken.[4]

Yet a historicist would never diminutively characterize life as *merely* historical, for history is so much more than the scholarly discipline of describing something by reference to its past causes (although it is indeed partly that). More generally, it is an ontological catch-all term that represents the always intricate, gradual, varying, particularized, flowing, and creative spatial and temporal processes out of which things—all things—come to be and come to be what they are (and cease to be and cease to be what they are).[5] What historicists mean by *history* is roughly analogous to what religious naturalist Donald Crosby means by *nature*:

> Nature is not just an aggregation of particular entities but the established, as well as the dynamically evolving, *system* of things and their relations. . . . [This is] a holistic system that enables particular entities to come into being and to pass out of being, that maintains them throughout their existences, and that makes possible their distinctive characters, capacities, and functionings. . . . The term *nature* . . . suggests a dynamic, restless energy of growth, nurture, productivity, and change. It points to nature as the fruitful womb of all that is, has been, or ever will be.[6]

The concept *history*, like the concept *nature* (and, as I will indicate shortly, these concepts will function as near-synonyms in this book), is inclusive of every actual constituent[7]—that is, phenomena and their interconnections, perspectives, peculiarities, mutations, and potentialities within the complex, interlocking, and distinctive matrices (physical, biological, social, etc.) that house them. And *historicity* signals the fact that nothing in the cosmos is ahistorical—that is, devoid of context, conditioning, change, individuality, receptivity and reactivity, mortality, relationality, and so on. What is more, the components of history—objects and the spatiotemporal milieus in which they are located, interpreted, related, altered, and eventually extinguished— are coconstitutive; that is to say, the contingencies, variabilities, fluctuations, caprices, novelties, relativities, happenstances, interactions, and specificities of history's widely diverse and wildly shifting currents create, and are created by, the entities they environ.

On the ontological and cosmological levels, historicism can be categorized as a species of process philosophy. In fact, as Larry Axel keenly detects, the historicist line that stems from James and from the Chicago-school pragmatists (which includes Shailer Mathews, Shirley Jackson Case, Gerald Birney Smith, and George Burman Foster, as well as John Dewey) might even be deemed a proto-process tradition. Long before Alfred North Whitehead penned *Process and Reality* and Henry Nelson Wieman, Charles Hartshorne, Daniel Day Williams, Bernard Meland, and Bernard Loomer made Chicago the center of Whiteheadian process theology, James, Dewey, Foster, Case, Smith, and Mathews took leave of substance categories, defended "a relationism and an organicism in religious thought," rejected static or absolute truths in favor of a functional and evolutionary understanding of ideas and doctrines, conceived of ideological and theological developments "in terms of social processes of adaptation and adjustment," and highlighted the world's interconnections and "fluid and relational nature."[8] For instance, Dewey, like Whitehead, advanced an ontology of events, claiming that "every existence is an event" and "will eventually crumble before the gnawing tooth of time."[9] Likewise, James, also prefiguring Whitehead, denounced the Western philosophical and theological obsession with fixity and immutability and evoked, instead, a world of becoming, a world in motion, in flux, in time. "The essence of life," he enthused in *A Pluralistic Universe*, "is its continuously changing character."[10] That same year, Foster wrote that "the only thing that has not come to be is coming-to-be itself, and the only thing that does not change is change."[11] Case said virtually the same exact thing a few decades later: "Movement is constant. . . . Becoming and ending, ending and becoming, follow one another in perennial succession. . . . The most permanent thing that remains in our terrestrial world is the fact of perpetual change."[12]

In the contemporary period, a handful of pragmatic historicists, most notably Delwin Brown and William Dean, have explicitly identified as process thinkers (of a certain sort, at least[13]) and, more to the point, have regarded

Whiteheadian cosmological dynamism and historicism as of a piece. Brown believes that, thus far, there is no clearer, more fully worked out metaphysical base for a historicist worldview than process thought,[14] defending the Whiteheadian contention that "nature is vibrantly alive" and comprised of "minute, momentary quanta of energetic activity."[15] Every actual entity, writes Brown, "accepts and adapts the past, and imposes its adaptation of inherited data upon subsequent occasions, which in turn receive, synthesize, and project." Consequently, history is "dynamic, a creative synthesis," and "each quantum makes a difference, however infinitesimal, to the character of the cosmic process."[16]

More than Brown, Dean admits that Whitehead's philosophical system contains much that is ahistorical (e.g., an overemphasis on speculative reason, the concept of eternal objects and God's primordial nature). Regardless, there are, he opines, significant ontological parallels between historicism and process philosophy's "metaphysics of becoming." Essentially, Whiteheadians and historicists both maintain that reality (human as well as nonhuman) is undetermined, creative, fluctuating, relational, and made up of the temporal passage of events, of "the always-evolving interconnections of historical process."[17] According to Dean, Whitehead's cosmology is a "historicist cosmology," because all concrete things, all droplets of space-time, are composed entirely of their ever-changing, dynamic, historical relations with the world. That is, they are "derived from . . . the past," "interpreted from the standpoint of and, to some extent, with the freedom of the interpreting subject," and passed out of subjective existence and into the objective experience of future prehending and concrescing occasions.[18] As Whitehead himself exclaimed, "The historic character of the universe belongs to its essence."[19]

Dean, for his part, also thinks that Jacques Derrida's post-structuralist semiotics is useful for clarifying a historicist ontology. To say that reality is historical or marked by historicity is to assert, with Derrida, that it consists of "writing," of an endless series of what might be (metaphorically) termed "interpretations." For Derrida, as well as for Dean, it is historical interpretations all the way down, all the way back, and all the way out, present reconstructions of the past that, in turn, become the past to be reconstructed in the future, with the cycle repeating itself indefinitely. The "significations" of history's antecedents limit what contemporary "signifieds" are and can be, while contemporary "signifiers" determine what "signs" will and will not be bequeathed for subsequent "signification." Thus, behind the veil of history is not eternity, but more history—interpretations of earlier interpretations, which themselves were interpretations of still earlier interpretations, ad infinitum.[20] To quote Dean, "it is history that makes history," not something beyond, behind, or beneath it. It "testifies to nothing but that which works within history; it reinterprets nothing other than history; and it, and it alone, in human and nonhuman creatures, creates history."[21]

However, Dean, as I will demonstrate in chapter 2, goes on to postulate, over against the anthropocentric, linguisticistic, nature-neglecting historicisms of much post-structuralist and postmodern thought, a "naturalistic-humanistic historicism," identifying the ontological structures of historicity in *all* domains of being, both human and nonhuman:

> This historicism affirms that, whether in cultural *or natural* history, things come to be through a series of interpretations. . . . Working out of a Darwinian model, this historicism has the variant creature interpreting its environment and proposing that the environment of the future should receive this interpretation; at the same time, it has environmental selection interpreting the variant and determining whether in the future this variant will or will not survive.[22]

In sum, ontologically and cosmologically speaking, historicism is the claim that there is nothing more basic than history itself, because everything—without exception—emerges, becomes, and expires at particular moments of time, within discrete loci in space, and through contingent processes of interpretation.[23] Moreover, the conditions of historicality—for example, relationality, uniqueness, dynamism, perspectivalness, locatedness, finitude, particularity—are *universal* characteristics of reality, operative not only in human history but also in the innumerable natural histories (biological, geological, astronomical, etc.) to which it belongs.

Given the universality of historicism's ontological and cosmological reach, I need to quickly clarify the relationship between history and nature before proceeding any further. Human historicity, we will see in a moment, is unique largely by virtue of its cultural and linguistic situatedness. Culture and language are the bedrock of human distinctiveness. Be that as it may, American pragmatic historicists work assiduously to overcome any sort of nature-culture, human-nonhuman dualism; *Homo sapiens* and all its traits and inventions (including languages and cultures) are a part and product of the natural world.[24] What is more, nature itself is historical; it is "a history which is a succession of histories," to quote John Dewey.[25] One of the recurring refrains of this book is that nature is metaphysically ultimate; nothing lies above, beyond, or outside of it. However, *history is what nature consists of.* Expressed otherwise, naturalism is the metaphysic of which historicism is the ontology (and cosmology).

And so, because human beings are creatures of nature, and because no element of the natural realm is nonhistorical (cf. chapter 2), I will use the terms *history* and *nature* almost interchangeably.

Homo Historicus: Historicism as an Anthropology

But, once again, historicists do vehemently maintain that historicity is especially heightened in *Homo sapiens,* mainly because human beings not only inhabit natural environments, but highly advanced and particularized cultural and linguistic ones as well. For that reason, historicism is not just a theory about the historical nature of reality as such (i.e., an ontology) or the universe as a whole (i.e., a cosmology). It is also a theory about the historical character of human existence in particular (i.e., an anthropology), focusing more specifically on the ways in which women and men are circumscribed, conditioned, and funded—historicized—by the particularities of different cultures, languages, and contexts. As Rorty notes, historicists have been adamant that what defines the human is "socialization" and "historical circumstance," not something "prior to history."[26] I will strenuously insist in chapter 2 that any viable historicism today needs to offer a *holistic* account of our historicity and appreciate the natural historical developments (evolutionary, biological, geological, chemical, cosmic, etc.) that made—and make—human history possible. Nevertheless, in a historicist paradigm, the historicity of humanity is distinctive and intensified inasmuch as it is expressed in markedly specific, adaptable, diverse, and complex modes of cultural, social, linguistic, economic, religious, ideological, and political organization.[27] For historicists, it is not that we are not animals; it is that we are, in the words of cultural anthropologist Clifford Geertz, "incomplete or unfinished animals who complete or finish ourselves through culture—and not through culture in general but through highly particular forms of it."[28]

In short, anthropologically stated, historicism, I will contend, can be defined as the recognition that people, both individually and collectively, along with all of their ideas, symbols, stories, feelings, behaviors, rituals, worldviews, texts, projects, associations, self-understandings, hopes, and memories, are, first and foremost, influenced, limited, and even occasioned by the cultural-linguistic locales, social and political structures, and changing historical contexts in which they are situated.²⁹ The definition given by Ernst Troeltsch in *Der Historismus und seine Probleme* (1922) is as good as any: historicism is "the fundamental historicization of all our thinking about man, his culture and his values." Frederick Beiser plainly spells out what such historicization entails:

> Roughly, to historicize our thinking means to recognize that everything in the human world—culture, values, institutions, practices, rationality—is made by history, so that nothing has an eternal form, permanent essence or constant identity which transcends historical change. The historicist holds, therefore, that the *essence, identity or nature* of everything in the human world is made by history, so that it is *entirely* the product of the particular historical processes that brought it into being. In other words, among things human, there is no distinction between a permanent substance and changing accidents, because even the substance is a product of history. The particular causes that have brought human things into being make them what they are; and these causes are utterly historical, i.e., they depend on a specific context, a definite time and place. Hence the historicist is the Heraclitean of the human world: everything is in flux; no one steps twice into the river of history.³⁰

Or as Brown succinctly captures it, historicism "has been the effort . . . to take seriously the way the indelibly historical character of humanness qualifies our knowledge, our nature, our institutions, and our place in the larger scheme of things."³¹

Rediscovering the Sociohistorical Method: Historicism as a Methodology

If there are no actualities "that we can know, have experience of, or have access to" outside the historical sphere, nor any "extrahistorical principles to which we might have recourse as the basis for our understandings of reality,"³² then history itself is the ultimate key for unlocking the meaning and significance of everything. Put differently, historicism is not just an ontological and anthropological base from which to theorize the historicity of actuality and human subjectivity, respectively; it is also a *methodological* procedure for apprehending what something is and has been and for imagining what it could become. In point of fact, according to the philosophical historicist Jeffrey Stout, we will always need to historicize ourselves, to "locate ourselves meaningfully and realistically as human agents in space and time," *precisely because* "we are finite beings, shaped by history and capable of shaping it." That is, since human life and even existence itself are historically conditioned and constituted (historicism as an anthropology and an ontology), it follows that "historical insight" is essential to grasping anything (historicism as a methodology).[33] Indeed, according to Beiser, that has been the "fundamental principle of historicism" since its inception: "All human actions and ideas have to be explained historically according to their specific historical causes and contexts."[34] This is why historicists, as Dean specifies, make history both "a central category in principle" and "the central object of actual inquiry."[35]

In the spirit of the early Chicago school's "sociohistorical method," the historicist methodology I will employ in this book functions both descriptively and prescriptively. It declares that the best means of fathoming a concept (e.g., the doctrine of God), a religion (e.g., Christianity), a perspective (e.g., historicism itself[36]), or anything at all is to analyze the multivalent environmental conditions and particular social processes that gave rise and shape to it, as well as the ever-shifting circumstances, vicissitudes, and contextual factors that spurred its ongoing reconfiguration through history (the descriptive function). And appreciating its historical origins and evolution empowers us to further reconstruct it in congruence with the needs, experiences, and assumptions of our own age and milieu (the prescriptive function).[37]

Chapter 2

Historical Particularity and the Problem of Insularity

Pragmatic Historicism as a Bigger Historicism

With a preliminary definition of historicism in place, we can now begin to explore its philosophical and theological dimensions. Our first order of business will be to diagnose—and treat—one of the more vexing side effects of a historicist worldview: insularity.

This chapter examines how historicism's accent on the local, the contextual, the individual, and the particular often leads to separatism in one form or another (e.g., nationalism, ethnocentrism, human-nonhuman dualism, hard relativism, religious confessionalism). In short, historicism's contextual particularism potentially isolates and insulates human beings—both from each other and from the widest possible historical context: nature. This problem looms especially large in a global and ecological age, which is why it must be confronted before proceeding any further. To that end, I will reveal that the unique species of pragmatic historicism that has evolved in America over the last century is actually a *bigger* historicism, a *pluralistic* and *naturalistic* historicism. As such, it is optimally equipped to exorcize (or at least contain) the specter of insularity that has haunted historicists from the outset.

Contextual Particularism: Historicism's First Principle

Religious studies scholar, philosopher, and neopragmatic historicist, Jeffrey Stout, persuasively argues that modernity, and the Western (or Franco-British)

Enlightenment specifically, "was born . . . in a flight from authority"—or, more exactly, from "the problem of many authorities." Thinkers of the late Middle Ages put a lot of epistemic stock in *opinio*, that is, matters founded not on strict demonstration, but on the opinions and approval of authorities. However, in the wake of the Reformation and the horrendous religious conflicts that engulfed Europe during the ensuing century (e.g., the Thirty Years War, which was brought to an end by the Peace of Westphalia in 1648), those authorities, says Stout, "multiplied and began to diverge more and more sharply," giving rise to competing authoritative testimonies and thereby exposing "the unreliability of authority *per se*."[1]

In *Discourse on the Method* (1637), the father of modern philosophy, René Descartes, detected the same dilemma in the philosophical arena, befuddled at "how many diverse opinions learned men may maintain on a single question—even though it is impossible for more than one to be true." As a result, all that philosophers assert remains "disputed and hence doubtful." In response, Descartes challenged the very epistemological dependability of *opinio*, unwilling to trust "too firmly anything of which I had been persuaded only by example and custom" and even deeming "well-nigh false everything that was merely probable."[2] And no longer anchored to the shifting sands of probability, of convention, received opinion, prejudice, superstition, and clashing authorities, philosophy can then rebuild on a foundation of certitude, a foundation that is insusceptible to philosophical disputation, perspectival diversity, and skeptical opposition, a foundation that is grounded in reason and rationally demonstrable, infallible, indubitable, self-evident, immediately given and justified knowledge (*scientia*), a foundation that is, in the words of Sheila Davaney, able to "find a way beyond the impasse of conflicting voices."[3] As Descartes advised in *Rules for the Direction of Our Native Intelligence* (probably written in 1628, but published posthumously in 1684), we should "resolve to believe only what is perfectly known and incapable of being doubted. . . . *We ought to investigate what we can clearly and evidently intuit or deduce with certainty, and not what other people have thought or what we ourselves conjecture.*"[4] Thus, Stout concludes that, in essence, Cartesianism (and the Enlightenment more generally) "tried to make the inheritance of tradition irrelevant, to start over again from scratch, to escape history," hoping to discover an absolute foundation that attained "complete transcendence of situation," an unassailable, universal, historically unencumbered Archimedean point from which the philosophic quest could embark.[5] And for Descartes, that absolute foundation, that Archimedean point, is none other than the necessary existence of the autonomous thinking subject itself (*cogito ergo sum*) and its capacity to know with clarity and distinction, with the "self-evidence and certainty of intuition" and the precision of "certain deduction."[6]

Descartes, Davaney points out, set much of the agenda for the Enlightenment. For almost all post-Cartesian thinkers, "reason and the commitment to critical inquiry unencumbered by tradition and external authorities were the ideals. . . . Reason was to be autonomous, serving no master but reason alone, pursuing no goals but those dictated by rationality itself."[7] Written exactly a century after Descartes's *Rules for the Direction of Our Native Intelligence* appeared, Immanuel Kant's 1784 essay "Beantwortung der Frage: Was ist Aufklärung?" famously defined the Enlightenment as "man's release from his self-incurred tutelage." Kant explains:

> Tutelage is man's inability to make use of his understanding without direction from another. Self-incurred is this tutelage when its cause lies not in lack of reason but in lack of resolution and courage to use it without direction from another. *Sapere aude* [dare to know]! "Have the courage to use your own reason!"—that is the motto of enlightenment.[8]

Historicism emerged, to a significant degree, as a reaction against the pursuit of certain, incorrigible, traditionless foundations (I will further expound upon historicism's avid antifoundationalism in chapter 6) and tutelage-free, situation-transcendent, autonomy-seeking, history-independent reason. Indeed, German historicism grew out of the Enlightenment and remained indebted to it in many respects. Nevertheless, "the historical significance of historicism," according to Frederick Beiser, "is best measured by its *break* with the Enlightenment, which had dominated European intellectual life during the eighteenth century." He elaborates:

> All the thinkers of the Enlightenment . . . wanted to find some eternal and universal Archimedean standpoint by which they could judge all specific societies, states and cultures. One of the most profound implications of historicism is that there can be no such standpoint. . . . A characteristic doctrine of the Enlightenment was individualism or atomism, i.e., the thesis that the individual is self-sufficient and has a fixed identity apart from its specific social and historical context. . . . It is striking that almost all thinkers in the historicist tradition . . . questioned this

individualism. They insisted instead that human identity is not fixed but plastic, that it is not constant but changing, and that it depends on one's distinct place in society and history. . . . Against the Enlightenment's cosmopolitanism, they stressed the value of having local roots, of belonging to a particular time and place.⁹

Davaney recounts how the protohistoricists of the German *Aufklärung*, while preserving the critical, rational, and antiauthoritarian spirit of the Western Enlightenment, bristled against their Franco-British counterparts' "universalizing tendencies"—for example, their dehistoricizing and decontextualizing of reason, their presumption that an autonomous rationality furnished "nontradition-bound criteria" for arbitrating opposing viewpoints, their postulation of a "natural religion" supposedly shared by all human beings and untainted by the sectarian beliefs and divisive particularities of traditions, their efforts to ground religious freedom, tolerance, universal rights, and individual and secular autonomy in a nonlocalist European cosmopolitanism.¹⁰ The *Aufklärer* (and, later, the towering historicist intellectuals of the nineteenth century like Schleiermacher, Hegel, Marx, Dilthey, and Troeltsch, among others) actually envisaged "a different mode of modernity" in Germany,

> a form steeped in the recognition of human historicity and its implications for all areas of life. The negation of the past and of tradition prevalent in the Enlightenment was replaced by a profound sense of the role of the past in human experience. The general and universal were repudiated in the name of the particular and the individual; commitment to universal values was now replaced by adherence to the traditions and values of the nation and the *Volk*, and inhabitants of particular locales, languages, and histories replaced the cosmopolitan world citizen. The search for timeless truth and absolute certainty was increasingly foregone as the historicity and relativity of human claims to truth were acknowledged. And the methods of science were now complemented by the historical methods of the emerging disciplines of history and other social sciences.¹¹

What really distinguished Germanic historicism more than anything else was its *contextualist* and *particularist* outlook. To quote Davaney again, "In contrast to the Western Enlightenment's appeals to a more abstract reason and universal values as the means to avoid the pitfalls of particularism, in the German lands it was the recognition of historical particularities that was interpreted as challenging parochialism and sectarianism, undermining the imposition on others of what were really local values and commitments."[12] Among the numerous figures associated with the *Aufklärung* in Germany (Moses Mendelssohn, Gotthold Ephraim Lessing, Hermann Samuel Reimarus, and Johann Salomo Semler, to list but a few), it was Johann Gottfried von Herder (1744–1803) who, more than anyone else, paved the way for the rise of historical consciousness and historicist thought in the nineteenth century.[13] A student of both Kant (whose ambiguous place in the history of historicism will be very briefly explored in chapter 6) and Johann Georg Hamann (a Pietist and fellow protohistoricist), Herder called attention to the historicity and traditionedness of humanity and appreciated the distinctiveness, diversity, and integrity of different cultures, nations, and religions and the persons who inhabit them. Humans are historically situated and constituted beings; their thinking, behavior, morality, and very nature are indelibly and deeply shaped by the local circumstances, contexts, and traditions (*Bildung*) in which they are located. Accordingly, there is, in Herder's estimation, no such thing as "pure reason"—a sovereign rationality unaffected by the specificities of history and language. Reasoning—and every aspect of human life—is always contextual, socially, linguistically, and temporally conditioned, and, thus, irreducibly particular and diverse.[14]

Often hailed as the first major treatise on historicism, Herder's 1774 *Yet Another Philosophy of History* foregrounded the contextuality and particularity of human existence.[15] Here, Herder proclaimed that "no two moments in the world are ever identical." Nor are the "different worlds" in which men and women reside. Individuals, as well as cultures and nations, exhibit wildly distinctive characters and characteristics.[16] Throughout his corpus, Herder accounted for the distinctiveness of human beings in at least three ways.

First, humans are *traditioned* creatures. Herder's late-career work, *Ideas toward a Philosophy of History* (1784–1791), vehemently rejected the assumption that human reason (and human nature more generally) is completely "self-made," "pure," and "autonomous," developing independently of a cultural, national, and historical lineage and a highly specific and unique set of external conditions. Quite the reverse: "The history of humanity is necessarily a whole, that is, from the first link to the last it is a chain consisting of *social life* and of the *dynamic tradition* that shapes us." What we become, including our "minds" and "internal disposition," depends on "the means of our formation [*Bildung*]"—that is, the circumstances into which we are thrown, the place and time in which we are planted, and the heritages according to which we are fashioned.[17] As Herder powerfully put it in *On Human Immortality* (1791), "Our understanding along with its powers, the way in which we think, act, and exist, is, as it were, inherited."[18]

Second, and relatedly, humans are *linguistic* creatures. Anticipating (and influencing) modern linguistics, hermeneutics, and philosophy of language, Herder, especially in his *Treatise on the Origin of Language* (1772), argued that human consciousness, thinking, and identity are linguistically embedded and mediated. So is rationality: "I have demonstrated that not even the slightest use of reason, not even the most basic distinctions, not even the simplest judgment of human reflection is possible without language."[19] In short, Herder, as Marcia Bunge indicates, considered understanding and language "coterminous."[20] The latter is the "organ" of the former. An entirely natural phenomenon[21] and a distinguishing trait of the human species, language is the principal medium through and with which people conceptualize reality. It follows, then, that our conceptualizations are as heterogeneous and context-specific, as diverse and particular, as the languages in which they are conceptualized.[22] As Herder reasoned in *Fragments on Recent German Literature* (1767–1768), if the "limits and outline" of human cognition are wholly set by language, and each language "develops in accordance with the climate and region . . . [and] with the ethics and manner of thought of its people," then "the three goddesses of human cognition—truth, beauty, and virtue—[become] as national as language [is]."[23]

Third, humans are *malleable* creatures. Repeatedly, in *Yet Another Philosophy of History* and elsewhere, Herder maintained that the human self is like "pliant clay," taking on a multiplicity of shapes "under different circumstances, needs, and burdens." Who we are, in other words, depends on and changes with the "accidents of fate"—that is, the "context," "climate," "country," and "century" in which we happen to find ourselves. Consequently, every ideal, virtue, value, literary work, and notion of human perfection and happiness "is, in a certain sense, national, time-bound, and, most specifically, individual."[24] As Herder summarized in an early introduction to this text:

> Human nature had such a flexibility and mutability as to be able to form out [*ausbilden*] for itself in the most diverse situations of its efficacy also the most diverse ideals of its actions into what is called *virtue* and the most diverse ideals of its sensations into what is called *happiness*, and to be able to maintain itself therein

until circumstances change and further formation occurs [*man weiter bildet*].²⁵

Already by 1766, in *On the Change of Taste*, Herder had reflected that the "diversity," and even the "idiosyncrasy," of human beings extends rather far; perceptions, senses, fashions, governments and other sociopolitical structures, customs, feelings, and so on, differ—often quite radically and stubbornly—from time to time, place to place, nation to nation, family to family, and even individual to individual. Enlightenment philosophers, such as Hume and Voltaire, assumed that human beings are more or less identical across and within environments and eras. Herder, as Michael Forster aptly comments, insisted that the very opposite was the case: peoples from different societies, ages, and national locales "vary *tremendously* in their concepts, beliefs, and other propositional attitudes, perceptual and affective sensations, etc." Even in a *single* culture or period, "similar, if usually less dramatic, variations occur . . . between individuals."²⁶ To deny humanity's diverse forms, or to pridefully assert the universality and indispensability of one's own, is to betray a helpless historical ignorance, for history is the site of constant alteration and endless variety, the birthplace and eventual abattoir of *all* values and ideas.²⁷

Davaney cautions that, with Herder's "new particularism," a number of concerns that continue to bedevil historicists down to the present, most notably, nationalism and historical relativism, "began in full earnest"—a warning to which I shall return (and give heed) in the next section.²⁸ At the same time, though, Herder denounced the rampant Eurocentrism, colonialism, and militarism of the day, "disturbed by the inhumanity and arrogance of his 'enlightened' contemporaries who were oppressing and colonizing peoples of other countries."²⁹ And the basis of these denunciations was none other than his contextualism and particularism, which underscored, even celebrated, the fact that "nature has organized human beings as diversely as one human race could be organized on this earth."³⁰ While wanting to preserve the individuality of nations, Herder advanced a *cosmopolitan* nationalism, realizing that "one form of humanity" and "one region" could never "encompass the good."³¹ By his reckoning, the thoroughgoing variability that exists between nations is actually a positive and unifying thing, for the uniqueness and particularity of a nation's values, ideas, and literature impart a sense of local belonging, offer something distinct and inimitable for the benefit of humankind (*Humanität*) as a whole,³² and most importantly, undercut superiority complexes and the impulse toward homogenization, progressivism, and imperialism.³³ As he sardonically fumed in *Yet Another Philosophy of History*:

> The universal, philosophical, philanthropic tone of our century readily applies "our own ideal" of virtue and happiness to each distant nation, to each remote period in history. . . . In general, the philosopher is never more of a brute than when he most faithfully wishes to play God and when he confidently calculates the perfection of the world. He is wholly convinced that everything moves very nicely in a straight line and that every succeeding individual and every succeeding generation reaches perfection in a lovely progression according to *his* ideal! He alone is able to reveal the exponents of virtue and happiness in this progression. It so happens that everything always comes back to him: He is the final, the highest link in the chain of being in which everything culminates. "Look! To what enlightenment, virtue, and happiness the world has ascended! And look at me! I am atop the pendulum! The gilded tongue of the world's scales!"³⁴

Herder made comparable claims in regard to religion. A forerunner of the history-of-religions approach to the study of religion (which I will discuss in chapters 3 and 5), Herder treated religious heritages as natural and historical phenomena—that is, in relation to the different and evolving milieus in which they have been situated, the surrounding cultures and traditions by which they have been influenced, and the larger social and political structures to which they have been wed.³⁵ Moreover, as products of human history, religions are also vastly dissimilar and irreducibly multiple. *Concerning the Various Religions* (c. 1764) showcases just that: deep religious variety. The faiths of the world are "as disparate as heat is from cold, and as one pole from the other."³⁶ Their diversity is, of course, a consequence of their historicity. As Herder explained in *First Dialogue concerning National Religions* (1802): "Do not peoples differ from one another in every respect—in poetry and pleasure, in physiognomy and taste, in customs, morals, and languages? Does not religion, which participates in this 'everything,' also have to be distinguished nationally?"³⁷ And when the "national" and "most diverse characters" of humanity's religions are acknowledged and honored, religious tyranny, absolutism, and imposition are held at bay:

> The masquerade, the time of aping foreign peoples and times, is over. This would further peace on earth and the development

of every people out of its own trunk into its diverse branches. In this way no foreign language or religion will tyrannize the language and character of another nation.[38]

Stated otherwise, as a historicist and a contextual particularist, Herder was a type of religious pluralist and a proto-postcolonialist,[39] sympathizing with "all nations whose ancestral religion was torn from them," since "with the loss of their religion, they lost their spirit and character, indeed, their language, their heart, their land, their history."[40]

In brief, a contextualist and particularist perspective is historicism's birthright, introduced by the very first historicists as a counter-response to the universalism of the Western Enlightenment. The historian Georg Iggers seems to intimate that historicism—or, more precisely, the "radical form" of German historicism that surfaced in the eighteenth and nineteenth century—*is* contextual particularism: "Historicism . . . [is] a comprehensive philosophy of life which views all social reality as a historical stream where no two instances are comparable and which assumes that value standards and logical categories, too, are totally immersed in the stream of history."[41] With a little less dramatic flourish, Delwin Brown indicates that particularity is, at the very least, historicism's first principle.[42] To be sure, all of the historicists lifted up in this book—from Herder and Troeltsch to James and Dewey, to Case, Foster, Smith, and Mathews, to Brown, Davaney, Dean, Kaufman, McFague, Rorty, West, Stout, and Bernstein—agree that human beings do not exist in a vacuum. Rather, they always reside somewhere and somewhen, in some concrete historical locale. Ergo, there is no such thing as unconditioned, decontextualized, and nonparticular—in a word, ahistorical—reason and experience.

In actuality, contextual particularism is a fact of life. According to the biologist and religious naturalist, Ursula Goodenough, the planet's almost endless array of environmental parameters has generated stunning biodiversity. In other words, organisms are heterogeneous, fecund, unique, and specific because the niches that they fill and the surroundings to which they adapt are heterogeneous, fecund, unique, and specific.[43] As I stipulated in chapter 1 and will further clarify later in this chapter, historicists (especially the naturalistic and pragmatic historicists of the American tradition) maintain that all of reality—not just human existence—is historical; thus, for a pragmatic historicist, it is not surprising that particularity and diversity go all the way down. Yet, to reiterate one of historicism's driving themes, human particularity and diversity are especially pronounced due to the very particular and diverse cultural and linguistic settings people inhabit. As Davaney eloquently remarks, "human beings are neither residents of everywhere nor nowhere but are situated within particular locales demarcated by distinctive languages, worldviews, political and economic structures, and social, religious, and ethical configurations."[44] Thus, the human subject has, from top to bottom, been detranscendentalized and de-universalized—historicized.[45] In a historicist vision, the self is, to borrow a splendid image from Richard Rorty, "a tissue of contingencies."[46] Human identity, knowledge, and action, far from materializing out of nothing or out of history in general, are always molded and elicited by, given content and significance through, the spatiotemporal contexts in which they arise and evolve.[47] There are, in the Herder-esque words of Gordon Kaufman, "many different sorts of human nature, as various and variegated as the plurality of human cultures and subcultures." And in and through these cultures and subcultures, we "acquire a particular way of being human—particular ways of seeing and understanding ourselves, particular likes and dislikes, particular possibilities of thinking and experiencing, particular conceptions of the meaning of human life and the nature of the world in which we live."[48]

And in and through these cultures and subcultures, we also acquire a particular way of being *religious*. Pragmatic historicists such as Shailer Mathews give short shrift to the idea of "generic religion" and look, instead, to "the specific religions," each of which "has its own character and history" and is "relative to the culture and social mind-sets of those who practice" it.[49] I will come back to and expand upon this aspect of historicism in chapter 3.

To make the same point in slightly different terms, historicists are ontological, cosmological, anthropological, and religious *pluralists*. History, human as well as nonhuman, is "not of a piece, it is not everywhere the same."[50] It is, rather, populated and permeated by a diversity of intractable, irreducible particulars. As William Dean points out, there is nothing beyond the plurality of particularities experienced in nature. Generalizations are unavoidable and necessary (cf. my excursus on metaphysics at the end of chapter 6). But they must, insists Dean, be understood as "abstractions attempting to describe the particulars of one's world and never as things in their own right."[51] Likewise, James avowed, against absolute idealism, that reality is fundamentally many rather than one; we live in "a pluralistic universe," a putative "multiverse" in which there is no "all" because "there are only the 'eaches,'" only "the particulars of life."[52] And for historicism, every phenomenon (from galaxies, bacteria, maple leaves, and warthogs to human subjects, cultures, nations, and religions) is particular, is an "each," mainly by virtue of its contextuality, of its locatedness and relations within historically specific environments. As Davaney professes, the particularities of history "do not just emerge out of thin air but are deeply intertwined with the contexts within which they take shape; they are responses to, reflections of, and in turn, conditioners of those contexts."[53]

At this juncture, it is utterly critical to mention that contextual particularists do not have to turn a blind eye to the vital commonalities that obtain between humankind and other entities in nature.[54] Nor are they required to mulishly ignore those human universals that are undoubtedly the outcomes of historically contingent evolutionary developments but have, nonetheless, become species-wide, relatively stabilized, and transhistorical (albeit not *a*historical) attributes, common to all people in every time and place.[55] Rather, they should simply assert, as does Delwin Brown, that particularity itself is one such attribute, one of the more interesting universal characteristics of life, and "that the most informative things we can say about humans are rooted in, and reflective of, the particularities of our situations."[56] Accordingly, as will become more apparent in the concluding section of this chapter, the historicism for which I am pushing in this book is a bigger—dare I say, *universal*—historicism. A pragmatic historicist iteration of contextual particularism does not, in contradistinction to some varieties of postmodern/postliberal historicism, terminate in separatist communitarianism, radical incommensurability, or myopic humanism—in insularity or isolationism. But, as I now intend to show, that is exactly where historicism, and contextual particularism more specifically, too often ends up leading us.

The Short Distance from the Particular to the Insular: Historicism and the Many Faces of Isolationism

Oddly and paradoxically, for all its difference-loving contextualism, particularism, and pluralism, historicism, laments Davaney, frequently leaves us "ill-equipped to deal with the plurality and diversity of human communities and ways of being." To be sure, historicists from Herder on down have recognized the spectacular multiplicity and irreducible particularity of historical heritages as well as the uniqueness that marks each individual. But that very recognition, according to Davaney, "has led in turn to contentions that human communities and their inhabitants are profoundly separated, fated to exist in insularity from one another with little hope of significant communication or understanding."[57] In a parallel fashion, the historicist stress on localness and individuality, I submit, tends to cut human beings off from the various *natural* settings in which they are situated—biological, evolutionary, earthly, astrophysical, cosmic, and so forth. As McFague balks, historically conscious thinkers and theologians underline the contextuality of human claims and convictions (including theological ones), and yet often do so to the neglect of "the broadest as well as the most basic" context of all: "the context of the planet, a context which we all share and without which we cannot survive."[58] The distance from the particular to the insular is short indeed.

To start with what is perhaps the most troubling instance of particularism-turned-isolationism, the localism of Herder and other German historicists found expression in a kind of *nationalism*. To repeat, Herder's was "a cosmopolitan culture-oriented nationalism."[59] As Forster avers, he respected the national groupings of all peoples equally (not just Germany) and protested "military conflict, colonial exploitation, and all other forms of harm between nations."[60] With Forster, Davaney and Iggers both contend that Herder's nationalistic politics was supplemented, even undergirded, by a difference-preserving, diversity-based cosmopolitanism, where mutual cooperation, peaceful interaction, and free trade result not from the essential sameness of humans, but from the distinct contributions every nation makes to the worldwide community.[61] As Iggers clarifies: "Each nation contributes to the richness of human life. Nationalism links the nations to each other rather than separates them. Herder optimistically believes that the nationalization of political life contributes to international peace."[62]

But cosmopolitan nationalism is still nationalism. And that nationalism, as Iggers forebodingly chronicles, later morphed into "a state-centered exclusive nationalism." At the center of Herder's historicism was, again, the concept of contextual particularity. People, on both the personal and communal levels, are individual and diverse—radically so. And one of the primary sources of human individuality and diversity is, for Herder, the nation. Human historicity is marked by a rootedness in discrete national locales, and nations, like the persons who belong to them, have histories—that is, a finite lifespan and a distinctive language, spirit, and character.[63] As Herder affirmed in *First Dialogue concerning National Religions*, "Every nation blossoms like a tree from its own roots."[64] In addition, a nation's truths, principles, and scruples are locally—not universally—valid: "In a creation with various climates and temporal circumstances, there are bound to be virtues unique to a nation and a period that blossom and thrive almost untended in one place and die out or wither miserably in another."[65] And by alleging that all values, thoughts, rights, literary achievements, conceptions of beauty, and so on, are unique and nationally occasioned, colored, circumscribed, and particularized,[66] and more generally, by interpreting "the particular, contextual, and conditioned . . . in terms of collective and especially national identity," Herder, as Davaney notices, opened the door to a narrower nationalism (even if he himself did not walk through it).[67] Soon, educated opinion in Germany shifted to a decidedly anticosmopolitan, separatist mentality, which assumed that "alien" ideals, norms, sensibilities, and institutional structures "could not be transplanted to German soil," and eventually, Herder's "aesthetic, culturally oriented approach to nationality" gave way to the ideal of the power-interested nation-state and to what Iggers dubs "the German national tradition of historiography."[68]

Far from ideologically and politically innocent, German historicism, and the nationalistic fervor that accompanied it, arose in the context of the struggle against the French domination of Germany after the Revolution (1789–1799) and the ensuing Napoleonic Wars. Napoleon's invasion of Prussia in 1806 and the Wars of Liberation no doubt fueled Germanic nationalism and the historicist sentiments that underlay it: the defense of local rights, privileges, ideas, ethics, and traditions; the renewed appreciation for the uniqueness of a people's literature, art, poetry, mythology, and folk songs; the accent on "the intransferability of political institutions" and the "particular and inimitable spirit" of the "ethnic nation." In short, the revolt against France's quest for military and cultural hegemony, the anti-Enlightenment suspicion of universal truths, natural law, and the unity of humanity, the eventual solidification of German national identity and statehood under Bismarck, and the historicist contention that the historical realm is "the sphere of the unique" were all of a piece.[69] As Iggers shows, "German nationalism had become inextricably interwoven with the 'German' idea of history, which in turn now became closely and equally associated with the Bismarckian solution to the German question."[70]

Iggers thus concludes that historicism, with its emphasis on the individual, the contextual, and the national, "functioned as an ideology," supplying "a theoretical foundation for the established political and social structure of nineteenth-century Prussia and Germany."[71] And by the second decade of the twentieth century, "the celebration of the particular in the form of national cultures," Davaney ruefully reports, had "devolved into the ascendency of German nationalism and world war."[72]

Nationalism may be the most disquieting manifestation of historicism's insularity problem, but it is by no means the only one. The nationalization and individualization, the particularization and contextualization, of moral precepts and cognitions also bring about their *relativization*—an issue to which I shall give special and extended treatment in chapters 3 and 6. For now, suffice it to say that, with Herder and other German historicists (e.g., Troeltsch), historical relativism "entered the modern scene with real force."[73] To illustrate, in *On the Change of Taste*, Herder proposed that morals, reflections, social systems, and the like, are always localized and therefore relative to the contexts in which they are situated:

> As soon as it is shown that what I on the basis of reasons take to be true, beautiful, good, pleasant can likewise on the basis of reasons be regarded by another as false, ugly, bad, unpleasant, then truth, beauty, and moral value is a phantom that appears to each person in another way, in another shape: a true *Proteus* who by means of a magic mirror ever changes, and never shows himself as the same. . . . Let us observe . . . that manner of thought and taste change with climate, with regions of the earth, and with countries.[74]

Even *within* discrete milieus, "manner of thought and taste" undergo vast alteration through history: "propositions for which at certain times each person would have sacrificed his last drop of blood at other times get damned to the fire by precisely the same nation."[75] And if values (ethical, aesthetic, or religious) are location-particular, protean, and transitory, then so are the *criteria* deployed to evaluate them. There are no timeless, transnational, or ahistorical guidelines capable of adjudicating between the diverse truth claims and mores of different cultures, nations, and religions.[76] By late career, Herder sought to assuage the extreme relativistic ramifications of a historicist particularism. In *Ideas toward a Philosophy of History*, he spoke of a *Humanitätsideal*, wherein each individual nation, religion, and culture (and indeed each individual), instead of participating in a universal rationality (as the Western Enlightenment presupposed), cultivates its unique personality for the enhancement of a common, harmonious humanity: "All the different modes of life throughout the whole wide world have been established and all forms of society have been introduced for the benefit of humanity."[77] Even so, as Iggers qualifies, Herder's insistence that every idea and ideal is a "one-time event linked to a specific historical and cultural setting" prepared the way for relativism, the realization that the historicizing of knowledge, principles, and norms leads to the relativizing of knowledge, principles, and norms.[78]

Forster inveighs that Herder's relativism—the hypothesis that "different positions taken by different periods and cultures are equally valid, namely for the periods and cultures to which they belong, and that there can therefore be no question of any preferential ranking between them"—is undesirable, unsatisfactory, and unsustainable. To quote Forster: "We cannot in fact sustain such a relativist indifference vis-à-vis others' values. (Do we, for example, *really* think that a moral rule requiring the forcible burning of dead men's wives is no better and no worse than one forbidding it?)"[79] Iggers, too, refuses to suspend judgment and even goes so far as to postulate shared tenets of logic and ethics, a postulation that, in his estimation, is unequivocally "antihistoricist."[80] Whether or not there is such a thing as a nonrelativistic (or quasi-relativistic) historicism remains to be seen; as it happens, the "bigger" (i.e., pluralistic and naturalistic) historicist scheme for which I shall advocate later in the chapter, and even more in chapters 3, 4, and 6, substantially tempers historicism's relativistic proclivities, criteriological isolationism, and allergy to comparison. For the time being, I merely want to suggest that historicists, in giving theoretical prominence to contextuality and particularity, do tend to invite hard relativism, and hard relativism isolates human beings from each other, precluding cross-contextual appraisals and comparisons. For Herder, no "single ideal" can be "the sole standard for judging, condemning, or praising the customs of other nations or periods," which is why "all comparison is disastrous."[81] Accordingly, each group is bound to, and is to be assessed by, its own internal and parochial (read: insular) measures and criteria; none should bring down judgment upon another.[82] As he recommended in *First Dialogue concerning National Religions*, "Every religion" (or culture or nation) ought to "strive, according to and within its own context, to be the better, no, the best of its kind without measuring and comparing itself to others."[83]

Unfortunately, the passage from particularity to insularity is a road much traveled by historicists. In fact, iterations of relativism and even nationalism have continued to rear their heads in postmodern American historicisms, most famously in the neopragmatic historicist philosophy of Rorty. On the one hand, Rorty does not want to be called a "relativist," since such an epithet is usually deployed to denote (and mock) the self-refuting position that every belief is as good as any other (after all, most relativists, himself included, consider their views superior to—truer than—those of their antirelativist opponents). On the other hand, Rorty is willing to wear the relativist badge if relativism is defined as *ethnocentrism*. To be ethnocentric is simply to "work by our own lights." It is to divide the human race into those who share the sensibilities, language, narratives, interests, ideas, and norms of our *ethnos*, and those who do not. It is to "privilege our own group, even though there can be no noncircular justification for doing so." It is to humbly accept "that we are just the historical moment that we are," just "the networks we are." Unlike the Herder of *Ideas toward a Philosophy of History*, Rorty does not think that there is any such thing as "humanity as such," some ahistorical "supercommunity" with which we must associate; there is, in effect, "only *us*," only "one's family or tribe or nation." Put differently, it is merely the parochial communities with which we presently identify to which we are accountable.[84]

And Rorty makes no bones about identifying with the "postmodernist bourgeois liberalism" of "rich North Atlantic democracies" and the United States, in particular. Universities and academic departments are now "sanctuaries for left-wing political views," and left-wing political views, decries Rorty, are often "unpatriotic." In the name of a "politics of difference"—in a word, "multiculturalism"—the leftist academy exhibits a "vehement anti-Americanism," refusing to "rejoice in the country it inhabits" and, as a result, becoming increasingly self-involved and politically ineffective. Left-leaning academics usually equate American patriotism with the sanctioning of America's gravest transgressions: slavery, the genocide of Native Americans, class exploitation, imperialism, and so on. Rorty counters that we can think of the United States as having "a lot to be ashamed of" *and* "as having glorious—if tarnished—national traditions." We can condemn the greed, intolerance, and victimization that infect American history and culture *and* "be proud of being the heirs of Emerson, Lincoln, and King." We can be outraged at "the very slow extension of hope and freedom to marginal social groups" *and* fight for the local and contextually particular democratic ideals (e.g., universal equality and procedural justice) to which we are historically and nationally tied—and toward which we continually strive. A leftist himself, Rorty applauds the academic left for "doing a great deal of good for people who have a raw deal in our society: women, African-Americans, gay men and lesbians." But he is a *reformist*, not a radical, leftist, insisting that America cannot become "more decent, more tolerant and more civilized" unless its citizens identify with and participate in the nation's "self-invented, self-reforming, enduring constitutional democracy." To be sure, "arrogant, bellicose nationalism" must be jettisoned, but a sense of shared national identity, and even national pride, must not.[85]

Other pragmatic historicists, such as Davaney, worry that Rorty's inward-facing, ethnocentric, and patriotic historicism regrettably ends up separating human communities from each other. Indeed, it is one thing to "start from where we are," from our particular contexts; but it is quite another to acquiesce to a "lonely provincialism."[86] It is one thing to identify with and to take pride in our distinct heritages—cultural, religious, and even national; but it is quite another for a society to believe that "loyalty to itself is morality enough," that "it need be responsible only to its own traditions."[87] In Davaney's estimation, a navel-gazing, self-referential historicism, a historicism that traffics primarily with its own history, simply leaves out too much and dangerously "relegates us to isolated communities."[88]

To buttress this contention, Davaney looks to Clifford Geertz,[89] whose influential essay, "The Uses of Diversity," blanches at ethnocentrisms, historicist and otherwise. Geertz begins by targeting fellow anthropologist, Claude Lévi-Strauss, who plays up the impermeability and relative incommunicability of cultures and purports that a certain "deafness," or "insensitivity," to different systems of values is not only inevitable but also necessary for maintaining communal integrity in the global village. In the end, Lévi-Strauss turns our putative cultural "imprisonment" into a virtue and makes peace with the fact that "universal consensus—trans-national, trans-cultural, trans-class—on normative matters is not in the offing." This sort of "to-each-his-own," "relax-and-enjoy-it," "we-are-we and they-are-they *imperméabilité*," Geertz discerns, has been widely embraced by today's social scientists, historians, and philosophers, one of the most prominent of whom is Rorty. By Rorty's lights, since everyone's beliefs and principles are embedded in particular histories, we are required to simply "stand on our own feet and speak with our own voice." Thus, moral reasoning essentially entails narrating and refining the historical "self-image" of one's group (e.g., "the contemporary bourgeoisie"), which in turn involves "apotheosizing its heroes, diabolizing its enemies, mounting dialogues among its members, and refocusing its attention."[90]

For Geertz, such "an easy surrender to the comforts of merely being ourselves" simply will not do. For one thing, "we are living more and more in the midst of an enormous collage," on a globe that continues to grow increasingly crowded and interconnected. Accordingly, it is no longer possible, nor proper, to confine "people to cultural planets where the only ideas they need to conjure with are 'those around here.'" Besides, nothing is more impoverishing than "the sovereignty of the familiar." Furthermore, contemporary intellectuals often suppose that the social construction of meaning (which, as I will show in chapter 6, is a corollary of contextual particularism and a mainstay of historicism) implies *incommensurability*. That is to say, the widespread awareness that theories, practices, images, feelings, and so forth, are entrenched within historically constituted and culturally specific networks—"language games, communities of discourse, intersubjective systems of reference, ways of world making"—is taken to mean that human groups (cultures, subcultures, religions, nations, etc.) are (and should be) "semantic monads, nearly windowless." Geertz rejoins that this simply does not follow. We will probably remain committed "to our own commitments" and will most likely keep on "preferring our own preferences." Nevertheless, we humans can—indeed do—grasp "alien sensibilities" and "modes of thought." Sometimes, these "imaginative entries" even compel us to change our minds and to expand or refashion our symbolic forms and cultural traditions. Geertz concedes that one's worldview is, to a significant extent, linguistically limited. But that does *not* necessitate our entrapment "within the borders of our society, our country, our class, or our time." Rather, it merely indicates that "the range of signs we can manage to interpret . . . is what defines the intellectual, emotional, and moral space within which we live." And the greater our interpretive and semiotic reach is, "the clearer we become to ourselves, both in terms of what we see in others that seems remote and what we see that seems reminiscent, what attractive and what repellent, what sensible and what quite mad." For that reason, Geertz pits the ethnographer against the ethnocentrist. If the latter consigns human beings "to a realm of repressible or ignorable difference, mere unlikeness," then the former "places particular we's among particular they's, and they's among we's, where all . . . already are, however uneasily." Geertz has no illusions about unanimous agreement concerning what is decent, just, true, reasonable, or beautiful, nor is he endorsing an uncritical cosmopolitanism that tolerates anything and everything. But ethnography still struggles to comprehend the "irremovable strangeness" of the other, "not because it assumes people are all alike, but because it knows how profoundly they are not and how unable yet to disregard one another."[91]

To be fair, Rorty extols Western liberal democracies, such as the United States of America, precisely because these societies are *not* monolithic, tolerating a plurality of subcultures and willing to listen to neighboring cultures.[92] Moreover, there is some overlap between "we rich North American bourgeois" and the belief-systems of the communities with which we ought to talk, making possible a modicum of "conversation between nations."[93] As David Hall comments, Rorty's ethnocentrism does allow for "piecemeal, wholly experimental, and essentially nonprogrammatic, interactions."[94] But, for Geertz, construing the human populace as "turned-in social totalities" occasionally and accidentally interacting and "meeting haphazardly along the edges of their beliefs" is simply inadequate. What we need to do, instead, is to continually and deliberately engage others, endeavoring to understand them in all their immediacy and difference, in all their diversity and particularity.[95]

Davaney's brand of historicist particularism is, in this respect at least, Geertzian in character. The pragmatic historicism to which she aspires accentuates individuality without incommensurability, the "uniqueness of time and place without assumptions of disconnection" or confinement. It is a historicism that is "predicated both upon the recognition of difference . . . and upon the refusal to interpret such distinctiveness as an excuse for parochialism and isolation."[96]

And it is a historicism that refuses to isolate our particularized and diverse human cultures even further by severing them from the various *natural* locales in which they reside. Davaney goes on to condemn the *nature-human dichotomies* that vex narrower contextualisms, contextualisms that focus solely on humanity and the human context.[97] But even more than Davaney (or any other historicist, for that matter), it has been William Dean who has exposed historicism's lingering anthropocentrism, linguisticism, and antinaturalism. A good majority of contemporary American historicists, from neopragmatist philosophers like Rorty to postliberal theologians like George Lindbeck (cf. the following section), are so fixated on human history—and, even more narrowly, on the socially, linguistically, and narratively constructed particularities of very localized cultural or religious histories—that they disregard most of history: the history of nature.[98] In a similar fashion, historicisms of the Continental variety, such as Jacques Derrida's post-structuralism and Mark C. Taylor's postmodern a/theology,[99] are so preoccupied with human signifiers, textual chains, and hermeneutical methodologies that they say virtually nothing about the world beyond those signs, texts, and methods (a tendency that Dean terms "methodologism").[100] Derrida, for instance, dualistically divorces human behavior from the events of nature by limiting "deconstructive interpretation" to the former:

> Derrida's ideas, although they may move beyond the subject-object dualism of his critics, still appear to be imbued with a Kantian dualism of world and self, a dualism between fact and value, nature and human history, causally determined matter and freely developed meanings, scientific studies and human studies. The first member of the pair, the question of nature, is neglected, presumably given over to science. For Derrida, the second member of the pair, the question of human history, alone constitutes the arena for deconstructionist activity.[101]

In this, Dean echoes philosopher of religion, Robert Corrington. Standing in the classical pragmatist tradition (especially the philosophical pragmaticism of Charles Sanders Peirce), Corrington blasts so-called neopragmatists—Rorty as well as West, Bernstein, and others—for slipping back into a kind of idealism. Neopragmatism, in other words, restricts signifiers to linguistic signification, tries to free signs from their natural semiotic contexts, exaggerates "the sheerly manipulative dimension of experience" at the expense of a nature "that it neither created nor controls," and forgets that the human order is but one of innumerable others.[102] As for postmodern deconstructionism, "the concept of 'textuality' is held to pertain to anything whatsoever, ignoring domains that cannot, in any meaningful sense, be rendered as texts."[103] Corrington judges that Dean, in spite of his self-avowed "naturalistic historicism," construes pragmatism as a form of proto-postmodernism and, in so doing, ironically falls prey to an antinaturalism of his own. To be specific, Dean's project projects "the traits of human communal orders," such as "the self-interpretive process of historical horizons," onto all the complexes of nature, perpetuating the very humanism it hopes to supplant.[104] I will return to Corrington's partially valid critique a little later.

In the meantime, I want to submit that Dean, along with a number of other American pragmatic historicists, significantly allays historicism's otherwise anthropocentric, dualistic, and language-centered predispositions and, as I will show in the concluding section, opens up "a wider historicism."[105] One of the ways Dean accomplishes this is by allying historicism with a related heritage of American philosophical and religious thought: *radical empiricism*.[106] Stretching from James and Dewey to Alfred North Whitehead and the process empiricists of the later Chicago school of theology (e.g., Henry Nelson Wieman, Bernard Meland, and Bernard Loomer), to present-day philosophers of religion, such as Donald Crosby and Nancy Frankenberry, radical empiricism, like all empiricisms, is "a revolt against rationalism," unwilling to introduce "any nonempirical or a priori contents." However, radical empiricists excoriate eighteenth-century British empiricists (and their logical positivist and linguistic empiricist successors) for placing arbitrary limits on the experienceable, offering a much richer, thicker, and deeper—a more empirical—account of the totality and full breadth of experience.[107] Thus, to the visual, audial, olfactory, gustatory, and tactile senses, radical empiricist philosophers and theologians add, according to Dean, "certain other senses, such as the sense of beauty, the sense of a 'more,' the senses of aversion or attraction, and the senses of quality."[108] Sensation, consciousness, and language are epiphenomenal and selective, "late, clean, and anemic abstraction[s]" that arise from the more primitive, indistinct, ambiguous, penumbral, affective, unconscious, unmanageable, valuational, and physical recesses of experience.[109]

In Dean's telling, among the many things that radical empiricism offers that the historicisms of Jacques Derrida, Martin Heidegger, Michel Foucault, and Richard Rorty do not is a firmer grounding in the natural sciences and an unequivocal refutation of "the whole brood and nest of dualisms"[110] from which Western philosophy hatched—mind and body, subject and object, fact and value, and so on. And an especially persistent dualism that American radical empiricists dissolve is the one frequently erected between humanity and the rest of the natural realm, interpreting both as interrelated aspects of the "single reality that is experience." Dean exclaims that Whitehead, James, Dewey, Meland, Wieman, Loomer, and others were "polemically antibifurcated" and anti-isolationist, positing "a nature-history . . . continuum" and collapsing human-nonhuman dualities. For them, there is no "isolatable self" or "isolatable world." On the contrary, "the self is, in one way or another, comprised of its relations with the world."[111]

Like Dean, Delwin Brown also identifies as a radical empiricist, and does so for roughly the same reason: to surmount the "linguicentrism" and dualism of other historicists, such as Hans-Georg Gadamer. Brown's own historicist theory of tradition is part Gadamerian.[112] Be that as it may, Brown rebukes Gadamer for failing to acknowledge the fact that linguistic expression derives from and continuously interacts with an "inchoate mode of human interpretive inheritance," which is, in turn, "embedded in the larger sphere of the efficacies of the natural process." Resonating primarily with the Whiteheadian strain of radical empiricism, Brown claims that "we are bodies more than we are minds." As such, our most fundamental commerce with the environment occurs at the prelinguistic, intuitive, nonconscious level of *feeling*, in which the world is experienced—imprecisely, diffusely, tacitly—as causally efficacious, as a weighted and patterned vector physically impinging on us. Consciousness and cognition are but a "flickering in the closed circuits of our bodily and historical life." Accordingly, akin to all organisms, the human is, first and foremost, an embodied organism. And "this hypothesis," Brown concludes, "implying as it does a continuity between humans and nonhumans, is one way of overcoming the deleterious dualisms of mind and body and humanity and the rest of the natural order."[113] Radical empiricism, then, merges historicism with "a form of naturalism," placing the human historical context squarely in the context of nature.[114]

In brief, radical empiricists endeavor to account for the broadest possible range of empirical phenomena, for the whole of *human* experience (including nonsensuous, emotional, axiological, aesthetic, qualitative, bodily, and even religious experience) as well as the whole of historical experience *as such* (including nonhuman experience). As Dewey pleaded, the philosophical penchant to partition experience and nature is profoundly problematic, since "experience is *of* as well as *in* nature," and things in nature "interacting in certain ways *are* experience." Hence, a radical empiricism, in Dewey's assessment, is a "naturalistic empiricism" (or an "empirical naturalism").[115] This is precisely why Dean believes contemporary historicism ought to revisit Dewey and the entire radical empiricist lineage. Unlike the neopragmatists of today, who are more interested in articulating proper methodological procedures than in "establishing anything true about the world," the radically empirical "paleopragmatic"[116] historicists were naturalists first and pragmatists second. They began with the natural process, and their pragmatic methods were merely devices "for elaborating and testing their naturalism."[117] And that naturalism, Dean assures, can lend historicism a much-needed cosmological foundation.[118]

Yet, whether associating with radical empiricism or not, a healthy number of American pragmatic historicists opt for what I shall dub *holistic historicism*. Dean and Brown, as well as McFague, Kaufman, and Davaney, all disassociate themselves from the thinner, linguicentric, and mono-humanistic historicisms of many postmodernists and neopragmatists, endorsing "a holism not merely of words connected to words, but of the entire psychophysical web of words and bodies, and of natural and social histories."[119] A holistic historicism, I will soon demonstrate, calls for the "broadening and deepening of historicist assumptions," seeking to avoid dualistic, disembodied, and denaturalized forms of historicism, ones that (whether by commission or omission) abstract and isolate the particularities of human experience, language, and historicity from physical and natural reality.[120]

But before detailing what such a historicism might look like, I need to first describe the ways in which *religious and theological* historicisms succumb to insularity and, more specifically, parochialism and human-nonhuman dualism. I will zero in on one historicist theology in particular: postliberalism.

Religious and Theological Historicism in a Postliberal Key: Ghettoized, Confessional, and Mono-Humanistic

In his now-classic *The Nature of Doctrine: Religion and Theology in a Postliberal Age*, theologian George Lindbeck, after making very quick work of "cognitive-propositional" theories of religious belief (in which doctrinal propositions are "truth claims about objective realities"), attempts to steamroll the "experiential expressivism" that courses through the veins of the liberal theological tradition. An experientialist and expressivist outlook construes a religion's historically embedded and distinctive ideas, rites, ritual practices, and other outer and discursive features as objectifications of an internal, prereflective, and universal affection, as expressions of the "experiential depths of the self" or a shared "existential orientation." Therefore, the fine particularities of the world's faiths are, at bottom, "diverse symbolizations of one and the same core experience of the Ultimate," whether Schleiermacher's "sense and taste for the infinite" or Otto's *"mysterium tremendum et fascinans."*[121]

Lindbeck puts forward a "cultural-linguistic" alternative to—and inversion of—cognitive propositionalism, on the one hand, and experiential expressivism, on the other. Wedding the linguistic philosophy of Ludwig Wittgenstein and the cultural anthropology of Clifford Geertz to a type of neo-Barthian narrative theology, Lindbeck likens religions to cultures and languages. In the Lindbeckian model, culture and language precede rather than follow thoughts and affections, conditioning, even creating, the worlds in which men and women know, feel, and act. That is to say, cultural symbols and linguistic sign systems precondition and constitute, mold and make, understanding and experience. For that reason, there really is no such thing as uninterpreted or unschematized, nonlinguistic or transcultural, concepts and sensations, since the cognitive and emotive facets of human life are structured by culture and language, not the other way around. And because cultures and languages are heterogeneous and highly particular, so are the beliefs and behaviors they produce. A religion, Lindbeck alleges, is "a kind of cultural and/or linguistic framework or medium that shapes the entirety of life and thought," a "comprehensive interpretive scheme" that "makes possible the description of realities, the formation of beliefs, and the experiencing of inner attitudes, feelings, and sentiments." It is the external forms of a tradition—its myths, stories, ethical directives, liturgies, ritualized actions, and distinctive grammar—that give rise to religious passions and worldviews; the cultural-linguistic objectivities are constitutive, while the propositional and affective contents are derivative. For Lindbeck, this reversal of roles, as it were, rules out the thesis that there is "a single generic or universal experiential essence of which particular religions—or cultures or languages—are varied manifestations or modifications." Quite the opposite: there are "fundamentally divergent depth experiences of what it is to be human." And the reason why this is so, why there are no religious universals, is because the culturally situated narratives and language games that produced them are fundamentally divergent.[122]

As I will propose in the next chapter, pragmatic historicists, akin to Lindbeck, are bothered by the flattening out of the religions' deep particularities. Nevertheless, they are even more bothered by the ghettoization and isolating confessionalism that result from Lindbeck's version of particularism. Spiritual feelings and theological cognitions are indeed culturally and linguistically contextualized and, thus, irreducibly particular and multifarious. Lindbeck, however, goes on to infer that uniqueness implies a kind of parochialism and incommensurability. The faiths, that is to say, are self-sufficient, intracommunal, mutually untranslatable comprehensive frameworks. They can be understood only in terms of their own "emic categories" and "native tongue." Their meanings, experiences, and very realities are wholly "intratextual" and "immanent," constituted by their use in a specific language, by their function in a symbolic context, by their "place . . . in a story." Being religious ultimately involves learning the grammar, mastering the logic, following the rules, inhabiting the narratives, and interiorizing the dialect of a local heritage, letting a religion's "semiotic universe" and the authoritative "holy writ" in which it is "paradigmatically encoded" claim one's sense of identity and perception of reality, instead of vice versa. Barthian rather than Tillichian in sensibility, Lindbeck prefers "ancient catechesis" over foundationalist apologetics, maintaining that theological faithfulness requires "redescribing" everything from within the Bible's strange new world, not "translating" scripture into some extrascriptural idiom. "It is the text, so to speak, which absorbs the world, rather than the world the text."[123] At heart, then, Lindbeck's *post*liberal theology is a variant of the "Anselmic theological approach" of faith seeking understanding (an approach shared by the Reformers, Barth, von Balthasar, and others) rather than the Schleiermacherian (i.e., liberal) one of making religion intelligible to its cultured despisers.[124]

Lindbeck is admittedly worried about the relativistic and fideistic implications of intratextuality (and postliberalism, more generally); he does not wish to "balkanize" the traditions by cordoning them off into "self-enclosed and incommensurable intellectual ghettos," nor does he desire to make the choice between religious options a "purely arbitrary" one, "a matter of blind faith." And yet he does purport that religious truth is an "intrasystematic" affair, not an "ontological" affair, a question of "coherence," not "correspondence." "Christ is Lord," for example, is true only as a part of "a total pattern of speaking, thinking, feeling, and acting." In the end, religions are "all-embracing systems of interpretation" that, as such, possess "their own internal criteria of applicability," their own standards of judgment. Hence, Lindbeck may want to describe postliberalism as an "antifoundationalist" and "postmodernist" enterprise rather than a relativist or irrationalist one; but, in actuality, relativism, fideism, and arbitrariness—in a word, confessionalism—is exactly what his postliberal historicism engenders. As Linell Cady adroitly observes, Lindbeck co-opts elements of postmodernism (e.g., the historicist rejection of neutral, independently formulated, ahistorical norms of evaluation) for "confessional"—and premodern—purposes. In other words, the recognition that rationality is contextually located, that human beings "think in and through traditions of interpretation," and that the reasoning process is always shaped by specific interests, biases, and cultural assumptions, is appropriated by conservatively oriented postliberals to circumvent the Enlightenment marginalization of religion and "to legitimate a narrow identification with a particular community of faith." Lindbeck, Cady allows, acknowledges that humans "speak in and through multiple vocabularies," but then, without any rationale or argument, turns religions into "insulated" (i.e., intratextual, intrasemiotic, intrasystematic, intracommunal) enclaves and arbitrarily singles out Christianity's "biblicist worldview" as the totalizing lens through which to conceptualize reality.[125] This, I would contend, effectively isolates religious groups from one another, protecting them from outside influence and external criticism and making dialogue and comparison (at least *meaningful and transformative* dialogue and comparison) extremely difficult, if not impossible (cf. chapter 4).[126]

And, in a sense, it isolates them from *nature* as well. Analogous to American neopragmatic historicists (e.g., Rorty), postliberals and earlier narrative theologians (e.g., Hans Frei) are, as Dean points out, "heirs . . . to a Continental, mind-body, culture-nature dualism," emphasizing scriptural stories and semiotic systems to the exclusion of the natural realm and the natural sciences that investigate it. Consequently, postliberal historicism amounts to a *humanistic* historicism, a historicism that restricts "historical data to interpretations of human culture." And a humanistic historicism, in postliberalism's case, clears the way for a "group subjectivism," where human beings are bound to cultural-linguistic communes and solely gauged by the narrative logic, parochial authorities, doctrinal regulations, self-authenticating plausibility structures, and putatively unchanging and "nonoptional" grammar of a particular religious community. In Dean's account, such "communalism" finally limits theologians to "whatever is communally preferred," which, in turn, threatens to reintroduce into academic theology premodern theological notions (e.g., supernaturalism). Lindbeck, for instance, implies that the imaginative, narratively constituted worlds of religions do not necessarily refer to anything, but provide frameworks of meaning that are real in, of, and by themselves. Thus, doctrines are entirely self-referential, disconnected from any "naturalistic referent" and unconstrained by "the testimony of scientists about natural history." In point of fact, Lindbeck, overstating Thomas Kuhn's perspective, reduces scientific reason to "just another rhetorical gesture," to one interpretive scheme among others.[127] This, complains Dean, gives postliberals license to dismiss "the astounding accomplishments of science as simply a function of interpretation," leaving them with little or no ability to discard aspects of their traditions that are scientifically implausible (e.g., "supernaturalistic, biblically literal theological teachings"). To illustrate, Lindbeck professes faith in "a temporally and objectively future eschaton," a position that, he grants, will seem "mythological" from a scientific and philosophical point of view. Lindbeck's reply to this sort of incredulity exemplifies the subjectivistic, arbitrary, fideistic, and conservative quality of his culture- and language-centered historicism: "The sense of what is real or unreal is in large part socially constructed, and what seems credible or incredible to contemporary theologians is likely to be more the product of their milieu and intellectual conditioning than of their science, philosophy, or theological argumentation."[128]

As a historicist, Dean backs the postmodern denial of foundationalism, objectivism, and naive realism, but does so without undoing the gains of modern theology (e.g., the denunciation of the supernatural) or neglecting the natural sciences or the natural sphere beyond our own local religio-human histories. Rather than ignore (or "redescribe") that which is "extrascriptural and extraecclesiastical," theologians must appraise religious beliefs "before the bar" of nonhuman history and "incorporate the full scope of contemporary human opinion." If Lindbeck's postliberal historicism permits the scriptural universe to "absorb" the actual universe, then Dean's unapologetically liberal historicism allows science's (admittedly paradigm-laden, historicized, and ever-shifting, but observational, experimental, and well-tested) knowledge of nature to put restrictions on what counts as theologically admissible and, when necessary, to "veto" defunct concepts (including, as I will argue in chapter 8, a supernatural and anthropomorphic God).[129]

Indeed, one of the things that will slowly emerge over the course of this volume is a historicist theology that is openly *liberal*, not postliberal, a historicist theology that accepts contextual particularism, the culturally and linguistically mediated character of knowledge and experience, non-foundationalism, and the like, but that also champions religious pluralism (see chapters 3 and 4), antiauthoritarianism (see chapter 5), constructive realism, fallibilism, and a chastened correspondence theory of truth (see chapters 6 and 7), and a naturalistic metaphysics of ultimacy (see chapter 8). What I intend to do in the remainder of this chapter is to flesh out the *bigger*—that is, the nonisolationist, nonghettoized, nonparochial, nondualist, and nonanthropocentric—historicism in which that theology is grounded.

Historicity without Insularity: Prospects for a Bigger Historicism

To summarize, insularity is an unfortunate side effect of a historicist point of view, a point of view that puts a theoretical (and theological) premium on contextuality, individuality, uniqueness, and historical particularity. Be that as it may, the bigger American historicism to which I have repeatedly alluded is capable of alleviating the myriad symptoms of isolationism, narrowness, and seclusion diagnosed throughout this chapter: nationalism, confessionalism, ethnocentrism, nature-human dualism, and so on. This historicism is a *dynamic* and *holistic* historicism, a historicism that accounts for the plurality and hybridity of cultures and religions and for the expansiveness and interdependence of social and natural histories.[130]

The Diversity, Porousness, and Multitraditionedness of Cultural and Religious Histories: Toward a Dynamic Historicism

To begin, for pragmatic historicists, the particularities of human history are porous, pluralistic, fluctuating, and intersecting; they "do not exist in isolation from one another or in some sort of splendid self-enclosed purity or incommensurability," but "overlap, bump into each other, challenge each other and generally interact."¹³¹ Davaney goes a step further, however, describing how human identity is actually "composite" and "fragmented," "hybridized" and "hyphenated," wrought at the "crossroads" of multiple and interpenetrating contextual factors and forces—social, political, economic, national, biological, ideological, religious, geographical, and so on. Historicism, by definition, lifts up the ineluctable traditionedness of human existence (cf. the foregoing analysis of Herder as well as chapter 5). Davaney, though, scolds other historicists (e.g., Lindbeck) for consigning people to single, or at least dominant, traditions. Even Delwin Brown, she regrets, perpetuates a kind of "monotraditionalism." Brown, that is, probes (quite brilliantly) the internal diversity, fluidity, porousness, and malleability of cultural and religious inheritances (see chapter 5), yet fails to lay claim to the fact that human subjectivity takes shape not merely within the boundaries of an individual historical heritage, but several, arising from an *intermingling* of "different strands of interpretation." Drawing on contemporary developments in cultural theory and analysis, Davaney suggests that women and men are not just "traditioned," but "multitraditioned," molded by the combination and clash of varying conglomerations commingling in historically specific ways.¹³² More and more, she discerns,

> persons understand themselves as immersed within and defined by more than one religious or cultural tradition, racial or national identity, ideological or political set of commitments at once. They are Buddhist and Shinto, Catholic and practitioners of the Mayan Cosmo-vision, carriers of multiple passports, biracial persons who refuse to check off one box, and inheritors of multiple cultures; they are internally many, and in the face of their reality, traditional historicism seems too narrow and inflexible.¹³³

I will come back to the issue of multiple belonging in chapter 4.

Multitraditionedness is a feature not only of individuals but also of groups. Cultural, national, and religious traditions are, in a pragmatic historicist outlook, *multitraditions*, undergoing constant alteration and reconstruction through history, comprised of a vast and conflictual array of ideational, affective, and institutional permutations and offshoots, formed from a "composite" of multiple influences and historical interactions, and bereft of timeless grammars and pure, static, discrete, singular, or impenetrable essences and identities.¹³⁴

For example, religions, according to Brown, are "dynamic miscellanies, without clear and abiding centers, that splinter at their boundaries."[135] The borders of and between the world's faith traditions are real and particular enough to establish a tentative and proximate character and to differentiate one lineage from another but are, at the same time, malleable and porous enough to sustain a rich, ever-growing, and often factious plethora of resources, voices, and hermeneutical options and to "engage in transformative encounter and exchange." Succinctly stated, religions, for pragmatic historicists, are not self-contained universes—semiotic, narratival, cultural-linguistic, or otherwise—but distinct traditions with immense variety and blurry boundaries, specific heritages without unchanging essences or secure perimeters.[136]

Davaney agrees but, once again, criticizes Brown for underappreciating the "hybrid," even "syncretistic," quality of numerous traditions. Concrete lineages are created not only by the recovery and reconfiguration of indigenous resources or even by the incorporation of "alien" elements (cf. chapter 5). Sometimes, Davaney notices, heritages are "composite in origin and syncretic in development," emerging out of a conscious or unconscious *combination* of different historical movements and materials (e.g., "cultural, social, or political mechanisms").[137]

In short, pragmatic historicism hypothesizes that religious (and secular) heritages, along with the individuals who inhabit them, are *dynamic*. Far from staying hermetically sealed and secluded within tightly drawn national, cultural, linguistic, fabulational, confessional, or criteriological ghettoes, they remain responsive to others and permeable to outside influence and appraisal. Even more, they are "conjunctural," the products of the "constructive intermingling" ("bricolage") of varied historical phenomena and plural traditions.[138] And such multitraditionedness, as Gordon Kaufman realizes, is expressly heightened in today's pluralistic global village. Initially, as *Homo sapiens* migrated out of Africa and spread over the face of the earth, a multitude of sharply contrasting cultures, languages, social conventions, and theological beliefs appeared, each adapted to the climatic, topographical, and environmental conditions of its discrete locale. Yet, at the dawn of the twenty-first century, the neocapitalistic system of free enterprise, as well as improved communication technologies, the increasing ease of travel, the Internet and social media, and the disappearance of rigid geographical boundaries, have ushered in an era of economic, social, and religious globalization: "it is becoming apparent that the several great streams of civilization, each of which earlier had seemed to exist in relative independence from the others with its own quite proper integrity, are now rapidly flowing together and mingling with one another," increasingly becoming a "universal human civilization."[139]

I would point out that pragmatic historicism's resolutely anti-isolationist, insularity-resistant construal of cultural and religious histories lines up well with the most cutting-edge theories emanating from the academic study of religion. A host of recent genealogical and postcolonial interrogations of the term "religion" show that such a category is not a cross-cultural constant or an ontological given. Rather, as Talal Asad, David Chidester, Tomoko Masuzawa, Russell McCutcheon, Jonathan Z. Smith, Wilfred Cantwell Smith, and countless other scholars have collectively revealed, "religion" was (1) born on the frontiers of colonial conquest and expansion; (2) invented in the provincial imagination of the modern West through the analytic practices of comparison and generalization and then applied to cultures that, prior to colonization, lacked native equivalents to such a notion; (3) imbued with all sorts of Christian biases and criteria (e.g., the requirement of a written scripture) and established to demonstrate the normativity, truth, uniqueness, and incomparable superiority of Christianity vis-à-vis non-Christians; and (4) tied to the assumption that there is an independent, distinct, universalizable, and generic essence that can be cordoned off as "religious" and separated from other domains of cultural activity (e.g., the political).[140] Comparative theologian John Thatamanil indicates that the construction, exportation, and imposition of "religion" brought about, among many other things, the "idea of a singular religious identity," which, in turn, generated the assumption of discrete "religions," of heritages that are "neatly separated by clearly demarcated and impermeable borders." The discourses of "religion" and even "religions," in other words, "have been deployed to reify and thereby to separate peoples and traditions whose complex and intertwined histories hardly permit of essentialist disjuncture."[141]

A half a century ago, Wilfred Cantwell Smith demonstrated that religion is a "reified" notion, generalized and abstracted from concrete and historically particular phenomena and mistaken for a hypostasis, a thing. For Smith, there is no "objective systematic entity" out there called "religion" that "can be formulated and externalized into an observable pattern theoretically abstractible from the persons who live it."[142] What is more, many of the religions (e.g., Hinduism and Confucianism) were crafted and discriminated by Westerners to squeeze "prodigiously variegated" welters of cultural and religious data into misleadingly enclosed and artificially unifying taxonomic boxes.[143] What ends up getting labeled "Judaism" or "Jainism" is, in actuality, "not one thing but millions of things." The modern West, charged Smith, "has conferred names where they did not exist.... There are Hindus, but there is no Hinduism." The so-called religions are "growing congeries of living realities" rather than compartmentalized, insulated, fixed, uniform, or easily demarcated objects. Smith, therefore, recommended *replacing* the designation "religion" with "faith," and "religions" with "cumulative traditions."[144]

Pragmatic historicists, although conceiving of religion and religions in roughly similar terms, consider facets of Smith's argument slightly overstated. For one thing, along with a myriad of contemporary religious studies scholars, he presumes that just because "religion" and "religions" have a modern, Western, colonialist provenance, neither category is real.[145] Pragmatic historicism grants that religion and religions are, in fact, socially constructed—and sometimes misrepresentative, dehistoricizing, essentializing, isolating, and imbricated in the perpetuation of ideologies, the promotion of interests, and the operations of power. But, as Kevin Schilbrack provocatively insists, this does not entail that such labels refer to nothing "out there" in reality. Schilbrack takes a critical realist position with respect to religion and religions, seeing them neither as preexistent objects awaiting discovery (naive realism) nor as "chimerical" fabrications that have no existence outside the scholarly imagination (antirealism), but as "socially dependent facts." For Schilbrack and pragmatic historicists alike, "religion" and "religions" have the same ontological standing as, say, "sports" or "gender" or "economics," coming into existence through and continuing to depend on collective human thinking, speaking, and acting but, nevertheless, responding to and engaging *social realities* that subsist in the world, have historical and material effects, and are independent of both the investigator's criteria and the individual's preferences or beliefs. Religion, Schilbrack allows, is most definitely an impositional and nonnative, homogenizing and reifying abstraction that originated in the "European *imaginaire*" and often "hides differences and essentializes disparate ways of life." But it is an "abstract or general sorting term" that denotes the totality of embodied social realties describable as "religious" (just as the word "nations" signals "the set of inhabited worlds . . . that includes Japan, Ireland, and Senegal"). As Chidester modestly proposes, genealogies of religion rule out any "single, monolithic essence" or "genus" of which the particular religions are "species." Nonetheless, the concept may be redefined in a "polythetic" manner and, hence, support "ongoing inquiry into the 'family resemblances' through which identifiable aspects of religion might constellate."[146] Likewise, more than just a "taxon," the moniker "religions," suggests Schilbrack, identifies fluid and contested, but existing, historical entities, "inhabited" and "performed" worlds that shape and transform actual lives and bodies.[147]

Delwin Brown reaches a very similar conclusion. Religious (and cultural) traditions, he illuminatingly analogizes, are not like "constellations," which are arbitrary projections of human observers, or "planets," which are "precisely circumscribed heavenly bodies with fixed movements" and "brute givenness." Instead, they are comparable to "galaxies," which are "massively there," "distinguishable from other objects in the night sky," and held together by their own "gravitational pull" but are, nevertheless, "composed of a vast and varying multiplicity of elements" and delimited by approximate and inexact margins.[148] Brown concludes that religions are galactic in nature because, when beheld at a distance, they "seem to possess rough identities, but the closer we move in on them the more obvious their swirling internal diversity, and equally important, the raggedness of their edges." What follows from this "is not that there are not approximate things like Hinduism and Buddhism . . . but that they apparently do not have the structural unity, the neatness of being, we had thought."[149]

Moreover, Wilfred Cantwell Smith's prediction that "religion" and "religions" would disappear "from serious writing and careful speech within twenty-five years" has not come to pass.[150] Despite—or, rather, because of—their colonial legacies, they are now a part of the parlance, social and political structures, and thought patterns of nearly the entire globe. Hence, with Thatamanil and others, pragmatic historicists have no truck with quixotic attempts to remove the words from circulation. Instead of abandoning "religions" and "religion," Thatamanil would rather refine and reappropriate them with due care and deliberation, in ways that are more alert to "power asymmetries" and "conceptual violence."[151] The concept "religions," for instance, is retainable, so long as the traditions are understood as veritable "cacophonies" and "cornucopias," "marked by the widest and wildest kind of difference, even on central questions of soteriology and eschatology," and containing "hybrid and polyphonic" identities. This rules out any definition of "religions" that underplays the diversity *within* the traditions and embellishes the incommensurability *across* them, that views them as sites of consensus and homogeneity or as impermeable enclaves with uncontaminated and inoculated characters. Postliberals are notorious for such characterizations, turning each religion into "a world unto itself," into a "tightly woven, seamless, and integrated" unified system, with its own narrative logic (cf. the previous section).[152] Thatamanil lays out an alternative to postliberalism's cultural-linguistic model (and other Geertzian theological paradigms), arguing that cultures and religions always house multiple therapeutic regimes and interpretive schemes. Religious traditions are really "historically deep *conversations and contestations*" about how to employ "a shared *repertoire* of myths, symbols, founding narratives, motifs, practices, scriptures and histories" (I put forward an identical argument in chapter 5). And especially in pluralistic societies, components of religious repertoires constantly "move and float across boundaries," which makes any particular repertoire "always already a sedimented composite of resources accumulated from a variety of tributaries." Put differently, the lines that ostensibly demarcate the religions "are themselves always under construction and revision."[153]

Pertaining to this latter matter, there is, confessedly, a very subtle difference in emphasis between Thatamanil's viewpoint and pragmatic historicism's. Thatamanil underscores the absence of clear demarcation between the religions. Pragmatic historicists are generally in agreement with him, but still want to maintain that religious heritages are unique and particular. Thatamanil thinks that the world is not composed of discrete religious lineages that are completely "other to each other."[154] Even so, religions, says Davaney, do "have boundaries and characteristics that delineate them from other historical trajectories." However permeable its borders, jagged its edges, hybrid its identity, profligate its borrowing, and multitraditioned its traditions, a religion, according to Brown, has enough "gravitational force"—historical continuity, canonical specificity, and structural integrity—"to be one thing rather than another."[155]

Regardless, pragmatic historicists accept Thatamanil's basic claim: there are no "neat cartographies that affix hard-and-fast boundaries between communities and traditions," especially in "a time of persistent and multidirectional transnational flows of peoples, images, ideas, institutions, and practices."[156] In opposition to postliberalism, pragmatic historicism avers that religions, although contextualized and historically particular, are not homogenous, pure, incommensurable, cloistered, intratextual, or all-absorbing frameworks, but as Chidester states, "intrareligious and interreligious networks of cultural relations."[157]

In sum, the bigger historicism of Davaney, Brown, and other pragmatic historicists views nations, cultures, and religions as *dynamic, porous, hybrid, and multitraditioned*, thereby removing many of the barriers that divide human communities from one another: incommensurability, provincialism, impenetrability, and so forth. A bigger historicism, I now want to stipulate, is also *holistic*, incorporating all of history—human and nonhuman—into a historicist worldview and, in so doing, subverting the nature-culture dualisms that disconnect humankind from the natural world.[158]

The Breadth, Depth, and Interconnectedness of Human and Natural Histories: Toward a Holistic Historicism

Frederick Beiser notes that "historicism grew out of a naturalistic program in the eighteenth century." To a considerable extent, "historicism is the counterpart of naturalism":

> Just as naturalism states that everything in the *natural* world is in principle explicable according to science, so historicism states that everything in the *historical* world is in principle explicable according to science. Just as naturalism eventually led to natural history, the denial of stable species and eternal kinds, so historicism led to the denial of an eternal human nature or reason. Historicism simply took the lesson of natural history and applied it to the human world.[159]

However, Beiser goes on to point out that some later German historicists (e.g., Wilhelm Dilthey and Ernst Troeltsch) opposed historicism to naturalism.[160] Indeed, according to Georg Iggers, much of the historicism that pervaded Germany in the nineteenth century was decidedly humanistic, even antinaturalistic:

> The core of the historicist outlook lies in the assumption that there is a fundamental difference between the phenomena of nature and those of history, which requires an approach in the social and cultural sciences fundamentally different from those of the natural sciences. Nature, it is held, is the scene of the eternally recurring, of phenomena themselves devoid of conscious purpose; history comprises unique and unduplicable human acts, filled with volition and intent.[161]

In contrast to the antinaturalistic strands of the German historicist tradition (and in contrast to many of today's postmodern, deconstructionist, neopragmatic, and postliberal historicisms), the holistic historicism articulated by William Dean and other American pragmatic historicists is a *naturalistic-humanistic* historicism, a historicism that expands its gaze to include not only social scientific testimonies about the history of human cultures but also natural scientific testimonies about the history of nonhuman nature.[162] Such a "wider" historicism turns on three principal theses.

First, and most obviously, a holistic historicism is conversant with the natural sciences, from quantum mechanics and microbiology to evolutionary theory and cosmology. Historicists such as Rorty are rightfully critical of Enlightenment *scientism*, of the penchant to "divinize" science and to treat scientists as some sort of "quasi-priestly order." For Rorty, no vocabulary, scientific or otherwise, gives human beings ahistorical, objective, or theory-independent access to what is "out there."[163] Too often, however, efforts to historicize and humanize scientific inquiry and to place the sciences and the humanities on the same methodological and hermeneutical playing field allow historicists (especially of the postmodern/postliberal ilk) to compartmentalize or ignore science and its observations of nonhuman phenomena.[164] A holistic historicism, in contrast, consults science, not in the hopes of discovering unassailable truths or the panacea for the world's ills, but to simply "widen our view and locate us in the broadest possible context."[165] And in a holistic historicist *theology*, science's "hermeneutics of nature" is placed alongside of a religion's "hermeneutics of written texts," permitted to inform and contribute to traditions of religious interpretation—mainly by constraining the range of interpretive options and eliminating certain theological possibilities (e.g., supernaturalism—cf. chapter 8).[166] As Davaney urges, nature, and scientific understandings of it, must become "a testing site for our theological proposals."[167]

Second, a holistic historicism dissolves any bifurcation between culture and the rest of the natural world and recognizes the indelible embeddedness of human history in that of nature. "To be historical," writes Davaney, "means that humans exist within the complex and interrelated matrices of natural and humanly constructed history." We have been utterly decentered, "interpreted to be a small part of a much larger and ancient process."[168] Or, in the elegant and evocative words of Sallie McFague:

> All that make up our planet, from bacteria to coal, robins, water, iron, wildflowers, oak trees, deer, and human beings, have a common origin and are, at some stage, related. . . . All things living and all things not living are the products of the same primal explosion and evolutionary history and hence are interrelated in an internal way right from the beginning. We are cousins to the stars, to the rocks and oceans, and to all living creatures.[169]

Needless to say, for a holistic historicist, just as for any historicist, the historicity of *Homo sapiens* is distinctive, thanks to the human acquisition of symbolic language, abstract reason, self-conscious activity, and purposive agency, as well as humanity's locatedness in multifarious and highly sophisticated and individuated cultural and linguistic nexuses. Indeed, the historical givens that occasion, mold, and sustain us include not only our biology—the vast evolutionary ecosystem of which we are an infinitesimal part—but also our specific *culture*—"the roles we learn, the language we speak, the skills we acquire, the ideologies we accept, the values we cherish." "Without such historicocultural shaping," insists Gordon Kaufman, "we would have no form at all; we would not even be."[170]

Davaney adds that human life is also *materially* embedded. Our historically conditioned cultures and languages no doubt represent the primary media through and with which human beings engage, perceive, and interpret the world. Nevertheless, those cultures and languages are always bearers, conveyors, and perpetuators of *power*, "connected to its distribution and circulation." Davaney has little patience for "apolitical" and "truncated linguisticisms" that purport to "historicize" human existence while concomitantly abstracting it from the social structures, economic conditions, institutional networks, power dynamics, ideological commitments, and political systems in which it is nested. Hers, then, is a "materialist" and "politicized" historicism.[171] This is a page right out of Cornel West's playbook,[172] who upbraids Rorty for upholding a "thin," "bourgeois," and overly "academic" historicism, for neglecting the stuff of real, lived, material history. Similar to Rorty and the other American neopragmatists, West makes "historical consciousness" and the "historicist stress on human finitude and . . . agency" central to philosophical reflection and eschews all extrahistorical "quests for certainty." However, West's historicism is, like Davaney's, materially "thick," resisting the myopic obsession with language, epistemology, and textuality and, with Michel Foucault, concentrating on "the political gravity of various discourses" and on the (often surreptitious) ways in which rhetoric reinforces "structures of domination and subordination" and undergirds "multileveled operations of power" (e.g., "modes of production, state apparatuses, and bureaucratic institutions").[173]

Still, for all their distinctiveness—cultural-linguistic, material-political, and otherwise—human beings, as Kaufman proceeds to qualify, are "biohistorical" (or, better, socio-natural) animals. That is, we are *multiply* located, constituted not only by the intricate operations of power and ideology and the very specific cultures and languages in which we develop, but also by the larger natural, evolutionary histories (cosmic, astronomical, physical, chemical, biological, etc.) from which we arose, by which we are antedated, in which we are enfolded, of which we are comprised, and on which we continue to depend.[174] Here, holistic historicists second the sentiments of naturalists such as Donald Crosby: although "none is more astoundingly different from other kinds of organisms in its behavior, history, and accomplishments than the human species," *Homo sapiens* and all its emergent properties (consciousness, mind, culture, language, purpose, etc.) and complex, inimitable, and diversified creations are a part and product of nature.[175] Consequently, it is "not possible," to quote Kaufman again, "to understand human existence apart from its wider situatedness in the ecology of life on this planet," which, in turn, "can only be understood within the context of the solar system" and "the steadily expanding universe. We humans exist really as point-instants in a vast, complex ecosystem, hundreds of millions of light-years across and billions of years old."[176]

In brief, a holistic historicism is what Davaney terms an "expansive historicism," a historicism that resoundingly stresses the contextuality of historical experience, but places the historicity of humanity squarely in a broader natural context. "There is no human history that can be attended to outside the constraints and possibilities of the nonhuman world."[177]

Third, a holistic historicism not only thoroughly naturalizes human history; it also historicizes nature. Put differently, the natural realm in which humankind is wholly situated should itself be construed historically. The conditions of historicity—contextuality, change, finitude, perspectivity, spatiotemporality, contingency, and so on—are *universal* features of reality, obtaining not only in human history but also in the myriad natural histories (evolutionary, astrophysical, cosmological, etc.) of which it is a part. Accordingly, the "old dualism" between the natural and the historical must, as Dean beseeches, give way to a "new monism" that regards nonhuman nature as "one form of history."[178]

The historicality of nature was a predominant motif of classical pragmatism. James and Dewey (and Peirce) saw the universe as a historically indeterminate and contingent maelstrom, whose destiny is open to an unsettled range of possible futures and whose course is guided by an interchange between natural laws and chance happenings—and the often unintended consequences, accidental eventualities, and unanticipated outcomes that result therefrom.[179] As James shrewdly perceived, historical actualities "float in a wider sea of possibilities from out of which they are chosen." And for that reason, the future, far from being "foredoomed and settled," is genuinely *undetermined*. The events that come to pass, in other words, depend on the alternatives that get realized; things may really have turned out otherwise had different potentialities been actualized. Of course, what is possible is circumscribed by what is already actual, making James's indeterminism a kind of *soft* indeterminism. But it is an indeterminism nonetheless, because what is actual is always exceeded by what is possible and dependent on what is *made* actual (whether through intentionality or accident).[180]

According to both James and Dewey, such a position negates two competing conceptions of reality. Gone, on the one hand, are teleologically oriented views of history. Dewey's acceptance of Darwin's idea of evolution eventually compelled him to jettison his earlier Hegelianism (or, more precisely, to abandon the idealistic parts of Hegel's system and to naturalize the historicist parts).[181] Specifically, the Darwinian principle of natural selection, Dewey thought, stipulates that species emerge in and from the largely random, contingent, and survival-driven transitions of evolutionary history, which completely obliterates the teleological illusion that nature exhibits "purposefulness" or "design" or "follows . . . an ideal or rational force" or "a universal form."

> If all organic adaptations are due simply to constant variation and the elimination of those variations which are harmful in the struggle for existence that is brought about by excessive reproduction, there is no call for a prior intelligent causal force to plan and preordain them.[182]

In lieu of a teleology, Dewey emphasized the precariousness and perilousness of existence. "Man finds himself in an aleatory world. . . . The world is a scene of risk; it is uncertain, unstable, uncannily unstable. Its dangers are irregular, inconstant, not to be counted upon as to their times and seasons."[183] James concurred: "I find myself willing to take the universe to be really dangerous and adventurous, without therefore backing out and crying 'no play.' . . . I am willing that there should be real losses and real losers, and no total preservation of all that is."[184] Contingent, indeterminate, and rudderless—historical—the cosmos is a source of opportunity and threat, openness and vulnerability, surprise and tragedy.[185]

On the other hand, in defending a naturalistic metaphysics of radical indeterminacy and historical contingency, James and Dewey undercut notions of mechanistic necessity and hard determinism. James pitted Darwinian "variationism" against the leading spokesperson of nineteenth-century mechanism, Herbert Spencer.[186] Spencer, rued James, wrongly assumed that the progression of events is determined *solely* by environmental circumstances and "ancestral conditions." Darwin's great breakthrough was his discovery that historical change—in both human society and in nonhuman nature—happens, instead, through the *interactions* between the "accumulated influences," "initiatives," and "decisions" of individuals ("spontaneous variation") and the external environment that selects them ("natural selection"). In that way, the social revolution sparked by the "great man" is, in James's judgment, analogous to the impact nonhuman creatures have on their natural habitats.[187] He expounds:

> I affirm that the relation of the visible environment to the great man is in the main exactly what it is to the "variation" in the Darwinian philosophy. It chiefly adopts or rejects, preserves or destroys, in short *selects* him. And whenever it adopts and preserves the great man, it becomes modified by his influence in an entirely original and peculiar way. He acts as a ferment, and changes its constitution, just as the advent of a new zoological species changes the faunal and floral equilibrium of the region in which it appears.[188]

Likewise, Dewey pointed out that every creature, human and nonhuman, is both adapted to, and adapts, its surroundings. He realized, of course, that "experimental and re-adjusting intelligence" affords humanity with an extraordinary ability to exert "deliberate control" over its environment and, as a result, to effect colossal change in history.[189] Despite that, far from being "passive and inert," an organism acts on its habitat, and the resulting alterations that are produced in that habitat, in turn, "react upon the organism and its activities."[190] "Even a clam," Dewey observes, affects "the environment and modifies it to some extent. It selects materials for food and for the shell that protects it. It does something to the environment as well as has something done to itself. There is no such thing in a living creature as mere conformity to conditions."[191]

Contemporary holistic historicists, such as Dean, follow the early pragmatists in thoroughly historicizing nature.[192] For Dean, history, human and as well as nonhuman, is radically open. The future is truly nonactual and indeterminate, contingent on a "spontaneous" and "discontinuous train of events and decisions," making the natural sphere "wild," "untamed," and "essentially unplotted"—historical. Ultimately, "it is the creatures who must invent the plot and who must be responsible for what it yields," which means that they have "the power to send history off into directions it would not otherwise go." In this historical, teleless universe, so much hangs on how organisms play the hand history has dealt them (whether consciously or not), and a lot is left to chance and to contingencies that cannot always be controlled, foreseen, predicted, or knowingly and actively prepared for.[193]

Like James and Dewey, Dean also looks to Darwinism to support the historicity of nature. "Nature itself is a thoroughly historical state of affairs; it is not rigidly determined, but, as Charles Darwin has suggested, a chain of interpretations that organisms make of their organic environments and that environments make of organisms."[194] Dean is endorsing a "neo-Lamarckian" view of evolution over the mechanistic selectionism championed by some prominent neo-Darwinians (e.g., Richard Dawkins). If naturally selected, mutations (*some* of which are adapted "in response to environmental pressures and are heritable") enter history "as a living tradition" and alter the present and future order of a local environment, which, in turn, affects the evolutionary potentialities of the entities it subsequently environs. Therefore, nonhuman nature, like culture, is the product, not of "foreordained structures," but of "conventions," of "a sequence of prevailing social agreements" between the spontaneous (i.e., unpredictable) variations of life forms and the life-worlds that house and sometimes select them.[195] "Darwin," in short, "was the perfect nineteenth century preparation for an utterly historicist hearing of the world."[196]

Nature's historicality, Dean continues, has been further substantiated by recent developments in quantum physics, particularly, the research of John Wheeler. Deploying the Copenhagen explanation of the uncertainty principle, Wheeler, in Dean's account, hypothesizes "a participatory universe" that is established not by "blind physical chance," "predetermined law," or "subjective arbitrariness," but by the interactions between the unforeseeable, often chaotic, interpretive acts of present observers (macrophysical and microphysical) and the limits imposed by things observed, which themselves arose out of still earlier "random or decisional" observations. The regularities of nature are real temporary orders that set boundaries and restrict the range of possibilities, so much so "that there are scientific laws that do accurately generalize about the past and do have enormous predictive worth." But those laws, too, are historically contingent, not eternal or independent, emerging and passing out of existence at precise moments of time and being temporally shaped by each observational occurrence. So, for Wheeler, natural reality—its particularities and even its nomothetic constancies—is neither entirely given nor "whatever we subjectively make it," but *historical*. It is a slowly changing and indeterminate chain of *relations*, "literally created by a historical series of observer-observed, relational events, a series that could have taken a different course at innumerable junctures."[197] Whether in culture or in nonhuman nature, interpreting subjects *participate* in and *alter* what precedes them, as when preexisting photons in the delayed-choice experiment "become" either waves or particles depending on the apparatus used to register them.[198]

In Dean's telling, then, a significant minority of physicists and biologists intimate that nature exhibits a kind of conventionality. "They talk not primarily of objective worlds or of subjective readings but of how innovations initially 'proposed' by a nonhuman entity are then 'accepted' generally in a space-time location or in an environment. That is, they have understood the natural processes they study to be truly historical."[199]

Davaney applauds the attempt to formulate a "historicized naturalism," but reminiscent of Robert Corrington (see the discussion of nature-human dualism earlier in this chapter), suspects that describing the natural sphere as "a chain of interpretations" (or "conventions") anthropomorphizes nature and, ironically, reinscribes the very linguisticism Dean desires to overcome.[200] Davaney's (and Corrington's) charge, by my reckoning, is not without merit. After all, Dean, leaning on the historicist metaphysics implicit in Whiteheadian process philosophy, approves of Whitehead's form of panpsychism, according to which *all* entities, "from the present atom to the human thinker, are interpreting subjects."[201] A panpsychist cosmology is, as Corrington justifiably reproves, one more manifestation of "the perennial human tendency to magnify its own traits and to find them mirrored back from the heart of the world."[202] Yet, I would venture that Dean's naturalistic historicism, notwithstanding its problematic employment, embellishment, and extension of the category of "interpretation," is defensible for at least three reasons.

For one thing, it is very important to keep in mind that Dean is using "interpretation" *loosely and figuratively*, referring, as Davaney herself concedes, "not to the conscious elucidation of meaning" (which would restrict interpretive activity to human history), "but to creative and transformative engagement" with the givens of the environment (which takes place in every province of reality, including unconscious and nonhuman ones). To be sure, as Kaufman asserts, humanity's unique capacity to engage in culture-creating activity, to think in signs and highly abstract terms, to act with purposiveness, attentiveness, deliberateness, and intentionality, to imagine and decide between different possibilities, and to remember the past and project into the future significantly *amplifies* its agential creativity. Imagination, reflection, reason, symbolical cognition, and collective learning, as well as the ability to objectify themselves and refashion themselves according to culturally invented structures of meaning and patterns of action, afford humans with an unprecedented "power to transform their inherited conditions of existence"—to set their own goals, to take responsibility for their own lives and undertakings, and to guide their own historical course.[203] In addition to "free and responsible agency," women and men also have "self-reflexiveness" and "self-consciousness." Every creature possesses subjectivity, but only human beings are conscious of themselves and aware of their freedom to influence and choose their destiny. In short, the human species is, in a number of ways, a distinctively self-directing, history-making species.[204] As Kaufman (cautiously) remarks:

> We humans have gained—especially in and through our various symbolisms and knowledges, skills and technologies—a kind of transcendence over nature unequaled (so far as we know) by any other form of life. Consequently, for good or ill, humans have utterly transformed the face of the Earth, are beginning to push into outer space, and are becoming capable of altering the actual genetic makeup of future human generations. It is *qua* our development into beings shaped in many respects by historico-cultural processes like these . . . that we humans have gained these increasing measures of control over the natural order, as well as over the onward movement of history.[205]

Even so, as Dean, James, and Dewey all recognize, responsiveness or reactivity to environmental stimuli—which is roughly what the concept "interpreting subject" signifies in Dean's historicism—is operative everywhere in nature. And Dean forthrightly acknowledges that the responses and reactions of nonliving or nonconscious phenomena (e.g., when certain bacteria mutate and thereby transform their relation to the environment from an inhospitable to a hospitable one) are "*analogous to* observation and decision—that is, interpretation."[206] Thus, such statements as "nature is a convention" or "organisms at the simplest levels in some way experience and decide about how to react to environments"[207] are meant to be taken metaphorically, not literally. *Something like* interpretation occurs in physical and biological processes (although, with Davaney, I am wary of the anthropocentric connotations of the term).

What is more, a naturalistic, or holistic, historicism does comport with current scientific understandings of nature. For instance, the late evolutionary biologist and paleontologist, Stephen Jay Gould, shows that nature, far from being determined by mechanical and always predictable laws, is marked by radical historical contingency. The natural world evolves through the interplay between nomothetic regularities and the particularities, unforeseeable twists and turns, and chance occurrences of each moment, between the selection pressures of environments and the emergent internal structures of organisms, which, once established, influence and limit available evolutionary options and pathways. The developmental potentialities of evolution, then, are neither infinite nor foregone, but open, contingent, and indeterminate—in a word, historical. Things could have ended up *another* way, even if not *any* way. Ours is one possible world among many.[208] As Gould remarks in his national bestseller, *Wonderful Life: The Burgess Shale and the Nature of History*, "the 'pageant' of evolution [is] a staggeringly improbable series of events, sensible enough in retrospect and subject to rigorous explanation, but utterly unpredictable and quite unrepeatable. . . . Tiny alterations at the outset . . . could have sent evolution cascading down wildly different but equally intelligible channels."[209]

For Gould, as for Darwin, the "quirks, oddities, and imperfections" of nature lay bare the sheer historicity, randomness, and contingency of evolution's outcomes:

> Whales, with their vestigial pelvic bones, must have descended from terrestrial ancestors with functional legs. Pandas, to eat bamboo, must build an imperfect "thumb" from a nubbin of a wrist bone, because carnivorous ancestors lost the requisite mobility of their first digit. . . . If whales retained no trace of their terrestrial heritage [and] if pandas bore perfect thumbs . . . then history would not inhere in the productions of nature. But contingencies of "just history" do shape our world, and evolution lies exposed in the panoply of structures that have no other explanation than the shadow of their past.[210]

Indeed, humanity owes its very existence to the contingencies of "just history." Like every episode of evolution, the route that eventually led to the appearance of *Homo sapiens* was not an unavoidable or expected consequence, but a nonrepeatable and historically contingent possibility set in motion by a host of accidental, fortuitous, and auspicious happenings, most notably, the random—and, from our perspective, opportune—asteroid collision sixty-five million years ago that eradicated the dinosaurs and thereby created a niche for the ascendancy of mammals and, later, human evolution. Our mammalian ancestors were simply the beneficiaries of good fortune, surviving only because, earlier, they happened to have acquired features (e.g., a small stature) that originally arose "for reasons unrelated to their later (and lucky) use in seeing their possessors through the unanticipated debacle of mass extinction." Had the Cretaceous event never occurred and changed the "rules" for long-term evolutionary success, dinosaurs would have continued to dominate, mammals would have remained marginal, and humans would never have evolved. Not unlike everything else in nature, the human species is "an improbable and fragile entity," "an item of history," as opposed to "the predictable end result of a global tendency."[211] Gould thus concludes: "Darwin's revolution will be completed when we smash the pedestal of arrogance and own the plain implications of evolution for life's nonpredictable nondirectionality—and when we take Darwinian topology seriously, recognizing that *Homo sapiens* . . . is a tiny twig, born just yesterday on an enormously arborescent tree of life that would never produce the same set of branches if regrown from seed."[212]

The burgeoning interdisciplinary subfield colloquially known as "big history" further testifies to the historicity of the natural realm. Leading "big historians," such as David Christian,[213] begin by proposing that every single thing in nature—for example, human societies, planets, and photons, to list but a few—has, indeed *is*, a history, arising at a precise spatiotemporal juncture, altering over time, and eventually perishing. Darwin's revolutionary theory of evolution, in fact, essentially turns on the observation that plant and animal species are not designed or fixed, but contingent, changing, adaptive, and liable to extinction—historical.[214] And in the post-Darwinian era, *all* the objects, entities, and phenomena of our natural world, along with the natural sciences that investigate them, have been thoroughly historicized. Paleontologists, geologists, astronomers, biologists, and physicists now realize that they are, in effect, *historians*, "in the tricky business of constructing a vanished, and often highly contingent, past."[215] Even the universe itself, according to modern cosmologists, is historical, with "a clear and identifiable beginning" (approximately 13.7 billion years ago) as well as a finite future.[216] What big history does is analyze the past (and the present and future) across multiple disciplines (astrophysics, biology, anthropology, etc.) and at different and ever-widening spatiotemporal scales (up to and including the

Big Bang). The result is nothing less than a *history of everything*, a revisable but scientifically based "modern creation myth" that uses the best empirical evidence and methods available to elegantly and artfully weave the whole of human and nonhuman history into a coherent, unified history.

The historical narrative composed by David Christian and others spans enormous durations and sacrifices some detail in order to bring reality's general trends, slower changes, bigger objects, and new levels of complexity into focus. Admittedly, such grand, universalist ambitions may, on the surface at least, appear to undermine historicism. However, I would propose that just the opposite is the case: big history does not deny historicity, but *extends* it. That is, big historians demonstrate how the constituents of history, while unique and particular, are conditioned, elicited, and illuminated not only by the specificities of a local environment but also by the larger contexts, structures, and patterns in which they are situated. The manifold *cultural histories* of the last few millennia cannot be fully understood without mapping the *global history* of humanity, from its acquirement of "collective learning" in the Paleolithic era to its development of agrarian and urban civilizations, which cannot be fully understood without tracking the *evolutionary history* of the species, earlier hominines, multicellular organisms, eukaryotes and prokaryotes, and the biosphere, which cannot be fully understood without comprehending the *planetary history* of the earth's origins and formation, which cannot be fully understood without considering the *cosmic history* of the solar system, the elements, the stars, the forces of gravity and electromagnetism, and the universe itself. Hence, big history is, in effect, a big historicism: no part of history can be fully understood without understanding *all* the prior and broader histories that make it historically possible and contextually intelligible.[217]

Finally, and most importantly, by viewing every single component of nature as a member of "a common history dating back fifteen billion years, gradually emerging through transformations of enormous complexity into the billions of galaxies of the present observable universe, including our own tiny planet Earth,"[218] a wider, naturalistic-humanistic, holistic historicism enervates the various types of insularity that often characterize historicist modes of thinking. Holistic historicists are out-and-out historicists and, as such, never overlook the infinite particularities that make up the cosmos. As McFague appreciates, "No two things, whether they be two exploding stars or the veins on two maple leaves, are the same; individuality is not just a human phenomenon, it is a cosmic one."[219] Still, things, however distinctive, do not subsist in isolation from one another; "to be at all involves dependence upon the larger context and upon its constituent elements."[220] Frederick Beiser contends—rightly—that historicism balances the principle of individuality with the principle of holism; while laying stress on "this or that determinate person, action, culture or epoch which exists at a particular time and place," historicists insist that the individual "is not a self-sufficient and independent unit," since "its very identity and existence depends on its place within a whole, the wider social, historical and cultural world of which it is only a part."[221] The bigger historicism for which I am advocating in this book widens this holism to include the history of everything. And, as David Christian ventures, such a perspective—a *big* historical perspective—leaves plenty of room for specificity, difference, and diversity, while simultaneously locating everything in a *universal history* and, in so doing, providing "the framework within which we can create histories that can generate a sense of human solidarity or global citizenship as powerfully as the national histories once created multiple national solidarities."[222] I would add that it can generate a sense of *ecological* solidarity and *biological, planetary, and cosmological* citizenship as well, connecting humans not only to each other but also to "all else that exists."[223] Gone, to quote McFague once more, are "notions of human existence as separate from the natural, physical world." Rather, history is complexly interconnected, interdependent, and interrelated, a recognition that could utterly transform how we conceive of our relationships to and responsibilities toward our fellow human beings, other species, and the ecosystem.[224]

Chapter 3

Particularist Mutualism

Toward a Pragmatic Historicist Theology of Religions

Over the next three chapters, we will explore the impact historicism has on our conceptions of *the religious other* and *the religious past*. And the point of departure for both discussions is the *religionsgeschichtliche Schule* and, more specifically, the work of its most prominent exponent and theorizer, Ernst Troeltsch.

"A comparative history of religion," by Troeltsch's reckoning, "has shaken the Christian faith more deeply than anything else." For one thing, as I will spell out in chapter 5, it utterly historicizes and desupernaturalizes Christianity's origins. As Troeltsch soberly averred in 1898, the *"religionsgeschichtliche Methode"* has "almost destroyed" any "doctrine of authority and revelation," placing the beginnings of the movement squarely "within the framework of the history of religion and culture. . . . The rise of Christianity had to be related to the disintegration of Judaism, to the political movements and the apocalyptic ideas of the time; and the establishment of the Christian church had to be studied in the light of the interaction of primitive Christianity with the surrounding world of the Roman empire." In short, no different than any other religious tradition, Christianity has been "produced by the flow of history."[1]

But perhaps even more challenging still, the perception that Christianity is, like every other religion, the product of complicated historical forces completely emasculates its claims to "exclusive truth" and "decisive superiority." When examined comparatively, Christianity is seen as *relative*, not absolute, as one contingent development among others in the history of human religion.[2]

In his 1922 volume, *Der Historismus und seine Probleme*, Troeltsch referred to the problem of relativism as "the crisis of historicism."[3] And by the very end of his life, he resigned himself to the fact that cultures and religions, along with their ideals and values, norms and criteria, are particular and individual and, thus, only *locally* valid.[4] In the previous chapter, I suggested that such a relativistic mindset tends to insulate groups from one another, precluding the possibility of transcontextual judgments. And indeed, Troeltsch, not unlike Herder, Rorty, Lindbeck, and other historicists, eventually acquiesced to a kind of relativistic isolationism.[5]

This chapter forthrightly owns up to Troeltsch's shortcomings here, while simultaneously arguing that the basic Troeltschian mission of de-absolutizing, relativizing, and historicizing the world's faiths is utterly imperative in today's global religious landscape. I will also show that historicism, in the hands of contemporary American pragmatic historicists such as Gordon Kaufman and Sheila Davaney, leads not to a relativistic isolationism, but to a historically conscious, yet authentically pluralistic and dialogical, theology of religions. In a pragmatic historicist theology of religious pluralism, the thoroughgoing historicity (particularity, fallibility, diversity, relativity) of the faiths, rather than justifying their relegation to insular, sectarian, parochial, intrasystematic enclaves, renders their most venerable ideas and practices, and indeed their very identities and self-understandings, vulnerable to reformation; heightens their receptivity to difference and their obligation to converse, compare, co-criticize, cooperate, and even cross-pollinate (see chapter 4); and represents the very condition and apophatic basis of their unity (inasmuch as *all* of the world's religions are culturally distinctive, historically conditioned, and socially constructed traditions created to help human beings find orientation amid the contingencies of history, the exigencies of life, and the ultimate mystery of existence).

The Historicism of Ernst Troeltsch: The *Religionsgeschichtliche Schule* and the De-absolutizing of Christianity

The *religionsgeschichtliche Schule* was established in the late 1880s by a group of insurgent Ritschlians at the University of Göttingen. In 1897, Ernst Troeltsch, the school's leading representative, announced that a history-of-religions approach comprised a "grand new discipline," viewing "religion [as] a constitutive part of historical existence," and "Christianity . . . as only one of the great world religions, along with Islam and Buddhism." Gary Dorrien observes that Troeltsch and the other *religionsgeschichtliche* scholars (e.g., Hermann Gunkel, Wilhelm Bousset, Wilhelm Wrede, Alfred Rahlfs, and Johannes Weiss) chastised the more church-centered Ritschlian theologians for their belief in the superiority of Christianity. For them, "true historicism is not compatible with any religious claim to dogmatic absoluteness or finality."[6] As Troeltsch seared, by dint of the history-of-religions methods, "Christianity lost its exclusive-supernatural foundation." The Christian religion is on a par with all the other religions, occasioned and produced by the "maelstrom" of history and "clearly dependent on the situation and the conditions" in which it has arisen and evolved.[7]

At heart, Troeltsch was a pluralist. In the memorable words of the *Glaubenslehre* (derived from lectures Troeltsch delivered at the University of Heidelberg in 1912 and 1913): "When we see the great Light working itself out all over the earth, we will then no longer be able to understand why the great profusion of religions should be any cause for alarm. It remains an offense only to those who continue to see nothing but darkness in the non-Christian world. But these are the people for whom there will be no true joy in Heaven unless everyone who believes differently burns in Hell."[8]

A decade earlier, in *The Absoluteness of Christianity and the History of Religions* (1902), Troeltsch dispensed with the two strategies most commonly deployed to establish the absolute status and normative truth of the Christian faith. On the one hand, orthodox dogmatic theology tries to "isolate Christianity from the rest of history," basing Christian absoluteness, uniqueness, and superiority on miraculous interventions, subjective religious experiences, special revelations, and other extrahistorical phenomena. These tactics take for granted the "obviousness" of Christianity's revelatory source and "immediate divine causality," but refuse to treat the comparable claims of other religious traditions with equal seriousness. However, from a history-of-religions standpoint, it is purely arbitrary to accept the supernaturalist authorizations of Christians, while concurrently denying those of the non-Christian.[9] As he provocatively queried in a later essay, "Are we justified in tracing the Platonic *Eros* to a natural cause, while we attribute a supernatural origin to the Christian *Agape*?" Quite the opposite, "We should . . . be faced with the competition furnished by similar miracles in non-Christian religions, not to mention the negative results of historical criticism and the trouble attendant upon every theory of miracles."[10]

On the other hand, Troeltsch rejected the liberal "evolutionary apologetic," which discerns a single, universal principle (e.g., Hegel's *Geist*) unfolding linearly, progressively, and teleologically in history as a whole. Inhering within all religions "as their ground and goal," such a telos supposedly evolves in stages and reaches its climax and completion, its "untrammeled and exhaustive perfection," in Christianity. The Christian faith is unique, superior, and absolute, not by virtue of its supernatural foundation or miraculous genesis, but on account of its "realization of the idea of religion itself." In Troeltsch's estimation, though, there is no "gradual ascent to higher orientations." History does not admit of any "normative power actualizing itself by degrees," nor of any religious "essence" that "embodies a law governing the successive generation of individual historical realities." On the contrary, "the modern idea of history," insisted Troeltsch, "knows only concrete . . . phenomena, always conditioned by their context." And Christianity, far from being "the highest, ultimate . . . fulfillment" of some sort of "graded progression," is and always has been a creation of the particularities and contingencies of history, "interwoven with quite definite historical conditions."[11]

Strangely, however, Troeltsch *did* end up concluding that Christianity is the "convergence point" of the religions, albeit on somewhat different— that is, comparative—grounds. History's developmental evolution is not the "successive realization of an idea" and cannot be "calculated according to a strict law—the Hegelian dialectic." Even so, a history-of-religions approach, he assured, does uncover "a principle suggestive of tendencies toward a common goal."[12] As Georg Iggers comments, "Troeltsch saw a meaningful trend in history," even if not "a pre-imposed logical pattern."[13] He also believed that history divulges "criteria" that enable a "ranking" of the religious traditions from lowest to highest. His stalwart emphasis on relativity notwithstanding, Troeltsch never gave in to an "aimless relativism." The "roaring ocean" of historical relativities does not "swallow up" all meaning and purpose, but manifests a valuational undercurrent. Although "temporally conditioned" and "admittedly subjective," norms of value do exist within history and are discoverable—not by hovering "midair above the historical religions," but by *comparing* them. And Troeltsch confidently asserted that the values unearthed by careful and rigorous comparison establishes Christianity—and not Judaism, Islam, Hinduism, or Buddhism—as the apex of religion's ethical and spiritual development (though, as we will see, this was not his final position).[14]

Before crowning Christianity as the "high point" of religious history, Troeltsch took a number of preliminary steps. To begin, along with most Europeans of the day, Troeltsch simply dismissed polytheism and "the numerous religions of uncivilized peoples" out of court, limiting the options to the "really powerful religious world orientations," the ones of "ethical and spiritual greatness." That essentially leaves two choices: the Abrahamic faiths, on the one hand, or "the great religions of the East," on the other. Troeltsch then pronounced that, because "the higher goal and the greater profundity of life are found on the side of personalistic religion," the Western traditions are superior to Hinduism and Buddhism. And, finally, of the three heritages that embrace personalism, the "religions of law" (i.e., Judaism and Islam) are clearly inferior to the "redemption-religion of Christianity." Ergo, the Christian faith is "the purest and most forceful revelation," "the best and most profound truth," and "the freest and most universal" religion. After all, only Christianity makes a clean break with "the limits and conditions of nature religion," discloses "a living deity who is act and will," and looks to "a kingdom of pure personal values." To be sure, Christians need to discard the "artificial" type of absoluteness, which presumes that Christianity is true and saving "to the exclusion of everyone else." Nevertheless, as "the pinnacle of all religious development thus far," the Christian religion is absolute in a "naïve" sense, Troeltsch allowed.[15]

The attempt to hail Christianity as the "climax" (*Höhepunkt*) of the history of religions, as well as "the point of actual departure (*Voraussetzung*) of the religiosity of the future," is a manifestation of what Iggers calls the "tragedy" of Troeltsch's lifework, "the contradiction between his desire for intellectual honesty [i.e., the utter historicity and relativity of all faiths] and his inability to accept the full consequences of his thought [i.e., the utter historicity and relativity of the Christian faith]."[16] Comparative religion scholar Michael Pye agrees, observing that Troeltsch, while recognizing "the plurality of autonomous religious and cultural traditions in history," effectively subverts pluralism. The *religionsgeschichtliche* method serves merely to substantiate Christianity's superiority, proffering an interpretation of the religions that is "doomed to an 'us-them' dichotomy." What is more, the declaration that Christianity is the acme of religion's evolutionary development rests on a blatant circular argument. That is, Troeltsch begins by arbitrarily defining the criterion of religious truth in a manner favorable to Christianity (i.e., in overly personalistic and redemptionist terms), and afterwards, unsurprisingly "discovers" that the Christian religion satisfies such a criterion better than any other.[17] The *Glaubenslehre* succinctly encapsulates Troeltsch's question-begging logic: "Insofar as it embraces the most profound and comprehensive, and yet the most inner and personal, communion with God in Christ—a communion that powerfully triumphs over sorrow and sin—Christianity is the highest revelation."[18]

All that being said, by the time the second edition of *The Absoluteness of Christianity and the History of Religions* appeared (1912), Troeltsch had already begun to take much of this back. Here, Christianity's total historicity and relativity was indeed stressed: "Nowhere is Christianity the absolute religion, an utterly unique species free of the historical conditions that comprise its environment at any given time. Nowhere is it the changeless, exhaustive, and unconditioned realization of that which is conceived as the universal principle of religion." Rather, "the Christian religion is in every moment of its history a purely historical phenomenon, subject to all the limitations to which any individual historical phenomenon is exposed, just like the other great religions."[19] Troeltsch even questioned whether or not the Christian faith "will always remain the final culmination point" of religion. "However little one may speak of an actual eclipsing of Christianity to date," there is no definitive proof "that it will never be surpassed."[20]

The following year, in "The Dogmatics of the History-of-Religions School," Troeltsch once again targeted "the supernaturalist apologetic." In Troeltsch's view, assurances about "the sole, supernatural truth of one's own religion" are destabilized and relativized as soon as one realizes that other traditions make analogous declarations. The comparative methodology of the *religionsgeschichtliche Schule* expands one's "theoretical horizon . . . to include the totality of human religions," revealing a "pluralism" of "exclusive claims to revelation." Inevitably, these rival assertions of religious superiority "collide" and, in the process, cancel each other out. In addition, Troeltsch distanced himself even further from the Hegelian brand of Christian absoluteness, in which Christianity is construed as the "logically necessary result of the history of religion," the culmination of "the self-evolution of the Divine Spirit." *Pace* Hegel and Schleiermacher, Troeltsch grew increasingly wary of any and all efforts to acclaim the Christian faith as "the absolute religion" (in Hegel's case, as the perfect expression of the religious idea): "Indeed, the very thought of setting forth any one historical religion as complete and final, capable of supplanting all others, seems to us open to serious criticism and doubt." At best, Christians may proclaim "the fundamental and universal supremacy of Christianity *for our own culture and civilization.*"[21]

This about-face, as Wesley Wildman perceptively observes, came only after Troeltsch's mature philosophy of history was more or less fully worked out. Troeltsch judged that Hegel, in interpreting reality as a rational progression wherein *Geist* "attains to self-consciousness through self-expression in an infinitely varied succession of forms" (the climax of which occurred in the incarnation),[22] ultimately "transformed the whole of history into a preliminary state of the realization of the universal concept," thereby flattening out the *particularities* and *individualities* that make up historical events.[23] On Troeltsch's reading, Hegelianism is metaphysically monistic, failing to do justice to the contingencies and thick specificities of history's (and religion's) "various movements."[24] In contrast, the lynchpin of Troeltsch's later historicism was *Relativismus*, which required paying scrupulous attention to the empirical relativities and contingent singularities that actually constitute the historical process. Rather than imposing some preconceived philosophical superstructure—for example, "the logical necessity of the dialectic of the idea"—on the stubbornly particular and irreducible details of history, Troeltsch started with *historical facts*, in all their individuality, unrepeatability, adaptability, variability, uniqueness, unpredictability, concreteness, contextuality, conditionedness, and particularity—in a word, their relativity—and only then (in a limited and provisional fashion) extrapolated generalities and larger patterns of meaning from them.[25] Over time, Troeltsch became more and more circumspect about the existence and detectability of universal criteria within history and, eventually, began to articulate an alternative theory of *relative norms*.[26] As he later recalled:

> The subject to which I devoted most attention, however, was that of the relation of individual historical facts to standards of value within the entire domain of history in connection with the development of political, social, ethical, aesthetic, and scientific ideas. I have only lately published the results of these investigations in my new book on *The Historical Standpoint and Its Problems* (*Der Historismus und seine Probleme*, 1922). I encountered the same difficulties in each of these provinces—they were not confined to religion. Indeed, even the validity of science and logic seemed to exhibit, under different skies and upon different soil, strong individual differences present even in their deepest and innermost rudiments. What was really common to mankind, and universally valid for it, seemed, in spite of a general kinship and capacity for mutual understanding, to be at bottom exceedingly little, and to belong more to the province of material goods than to the ideal values of civilization.[27]

By late career, the philosophy of *Relativismus* compelled Troeltsch to revisit and revise the major theses put forward in *The Absoluteness of Christianity and the History of Religions*. In his posthumously published (and never delivered) Oxford lecture, "The Place of Christianity among the World Religions" (1923), he reiterated that history is not a process "leading to a single goal presented by nature," but a *sphere of contingent particulars*. Far from exhibiting "unity and universality," the historical realm is a "ceaseless flux" of ever-developing and "always-peculiar individualizations." As historically situated entities, the religions of the world neither possess a "common character" nor manifest a "natural upward trend," but contain "sharp distinctions" and "certain irresolvable contradictions." The Christian faith, then, is not the "most spiritual revelation," the "perfected expression of religion as such," or "the reconciliation . . . of all the forces of history," but one "purely historical, individual, relative phenomenon" among others. Even Christianity itself is "an immeasurable, incomparable profusion of always-new, unique, and hence individual tendencies," an internally diverse movement that "displays a different character in every age," each reflective of and dependent on—relative to—"the historical, geographical, and social conditions of the countries in which it has taken shape."[28]

If nothing in the world—including the religions—can be characterized as "anything else than a historical individuality," then it is no longer possible to claim *supreme or universal* validity for any of history's particularities. On the contrary, the "spectacle of bewildering diversity" that history generates has exposed "the relativity and transitoriness of all things, even of the loftiest values of civilization." And for Christians, the relativity and transitoriness of the Christian tradition and its loftiest values means that Christianity is, at most, *relatively* normative. In other words, "it is final and unconditional *for us*"—that is, for Europe and European culture. However, "other racial groups, living under other entirely different conditions, may . . . also possess a religion which has grown up with them, and from which they cannot sever themselves so long as they remain what they are. And they may quite sincerely regard this as absolutely valid *for them*."[29] Troeltsch, in other words, came to believe (quite paradoxically) that religious absoluteness is itself relative. As Tomoko Masuzawa explains, for the mature Troeltsch, the conviction that one's religion is absolute was "a matter of individual personal conviction" as well as "something intrinsic and interior collectively to a particular 'race.'"[30]

In brief, Troeltsch finally carried his historicism through to its logical conclusion and de-absolutized and de-universalized—historicized—Christianity. That is, he "cut Christianity down to size, relegating it to the status of just one of the many religions around."[31] As Paul Knitter remarks, by 1923 (the year Troeltsch died), the foremost historicist of the late nineteenth and early twentieth century had at last made peace with the fact that "all religions are relative—that is, limited, partial, incomplete, one way of looking at things. . . . The historical quality of all human achievements therefore excludes all absolutes, that is, all 'one and only' or unchangeable truth claims. . . . It is impossible to make any kind of judgment about the superiority of one religion over another."[32]

Nevertheless, as Dorrien importantly qualifies, Troeltsch was no hard relativist or nihilist.[33] Early on, he conceded to his Ritschlian detractors that critical historical consciousness does admittedly "relativize everything" (including Christianity). But relativistic thinking neither "eliminates every standard of judgment" nor "necessarily ends in a nihilistic skepticism," but simply entails that "every historical structure and moment can be understood only in relation to others and ultimately to the total context."[34]

One of the things that saved Troeltsch from hard relativism and nihilism was his unfaltering refusal to wed historicism to atheism.[35] Dorrien notes that, for him, the whole point of creating a historicist framework *for theology* "was to prevent atheistic academics from owning historical criticism." The young Troeltsch was deeply influenced by the Lotzean idea of a unified "spiritual ground" that exists within and behind history's individualities; and even in his 1922 volume, *Der Historismus und seine Probleme*, Troeltsch conceived of history as a collection of historical "totalities" or "wholes" (i.e., "integral unities of meaning and value") and adopted Leibniz's monadology, "in which every particular, conditioned, individual finite spirit 'participates intuitively' in the Divine Spirit."[36] Iggers suggests that this sort of theologically inflected objective idealism was Troeltsch's solution to "the problems of historicism," to "the apparent conflicts between subjectivity and objectivity, the relativity of all values and their validity, the variety of history and the basic unity of the world." The historical approach reveals that history is the domain of the particular and the relative, but these particularities and relativities are the manifold reflections, indeed revelations, of "one purpose," one "objective and living truth," one "divine order."[37] In "The Place of Christianity among the World Religions," Troeltsch went so far as to exclaim that every religious faith seems

> impelled by an inner force to strive upward toward some unknown final height, where alone the ultimate unity and the final objective validity can lie. And, as all religion has thus a common goal in the Unknown, the Future, perchance in the Beyond, so, too, it has a common ground in the Divine Spirit

ever pressing the finite mind onward toward further light and fuller consciousness, a Spirit Which indwells the finite spirit, and Whose ultimate union with it is the purpose of the whole many-sided process.[38]

Regardless, Troeltsch insisted that in the liminal space between "the divine Source and the divine Goal"—that is to say, *history*—"lie all the individual differentiations of race and civilization, and, with them also, the individual differences of the great, comprehensive religions." There are no transcontextual norms or universal truths and values—within the historical realm, at least—that enable human beings to make absolute comparative assessments across cultures and religions. Thus, Troeltsch held out for a kind of live-and-let-live pluralism, in which religious and cultural differences are tolerated, violence and domination are renounced, and missionary enterprises are mitigated (even if not entirely abolished). In such a climate, different groups certainly "influence" and "find contact with each other," effecting "a little shifting of their several territories at the fringes." Be that as it may, their primary duty is to fulfill their "own highest potentialities." In short, the various cultures, religions, and races of the world are "independent beings" that ought to "persist in their distinctiveness" and "only seek to purify and enrich their experience, each within its own province and according to its own standards."[39] Hence, although not a *hardcore* relativist, Troeltsch, as Sheila Davaney cautions, did summon "the specter of relativism that has haunted historicism ever since," intimating that judgments are, in the end, "intrasystematic affairs."[40] Ironically, in the midst of undercutting religious superiority complexes and de-absolutizing, historicizing, and particularizing—relativizing—the religions (including Christianity), Troeltsch's historicism, not unlike Herder's, Rorty's, and Lindbeck's (cf. chapter 2), tended to isolate traditions from one another, leaving them to till their own gardens and binding them to their own relative absolutes, to whatever is true and valid, valuable and normative, *for them*.

Dorrien recounts that Troeltsch, in his very last book *Der Historismus und seine Überwindung* (1924), relinquished the desire to compose a universal history and completely abandoned any concept of "humanity" in general: "He argued, with seeming finality, that we know nothing of . . . a Common Spirit. All that we know are particular groups, families, races, classes, schools, sects, and the like from the past six thousand years, a tiny fraction of the human experience." And what really mattered to him, adds Dorrien, "was the background to the *European* story" and *its* "best religion," namely,

Christianity.[41] Surely, personalism is too Christian to be supremely valid. But Christianity and its personalistic religiosity enjoy absolute validity "for us" (i.e., for Europe).[42] Troeltsch, then, did not jettison Christian absoluteness as much as he localized, relativized, and culturalized it, reinscribing it in the idiom of "Europeanism."[43] He is worth quoting at length:

> All our thoughts and feelings are impregnated with Christian motives and Christian presuppositions; and, conversely, our whole Christianity is indissolubly bound up with elements of the ancient and modern civilizations of Europe. From being a Jewish sect Christianity has become the religion of all Europe. It stands or falls with European civilization; while, on its own part, it has entirely lost its Oriental character and become hellenized and westernized. Our European conceptions of personality and its eternal, divine right, and of progress toward a kingdom of the spirit and of God, our enormous capacity for expansion and for the interconnection of spiritual and temporal, our whole social order, our science, our art—all these rest, whether we know it or not, whether we like it or not, upon the basis of this deorientalized Christianity. . . . We cannot live without a religion, yet the only religion that we can endure is Christianity, for Christianity has grown up with us and has become a part of our very being. . . . It is God's countenance as revealed to us; it is the way in which, being what we are, we receive, and react to, the revelation of God. It is binding upon us, and it brings us deliverance.[44]

Historian and postcolonial critic Tomoko Masuzawa alleges that Troeltsch's historicism amounted to little more than camouflaged exclusivism and "reconstituted European universalism," using the "presumably humbling" discourse of religious historicity and plurality to mask imperialist and supremacist pretensions.[45] This allegation is overstated, in my view. Admittedly, Troeltsch eventually embraced a kind of relativistic inclusivism (cf. the next section) in which cultures remain committed and bound to their own *relative* absolutes, to whatever religion is absolutely valid and normative *for them* (Christianity, in Europe's case).[46] Even so, Troeltsch was still way ahead of his time, anticipating the full-blown pluralism advocated by John Hick and other present-day theologians and philosophers.[47] Moreover, Masuzawa assumes that historicism is inexorably and forever "bewitched" by absolutist posturing and colonialist ambition; in Troeltsch's case, the recognition of historicity and plurality is precisely what enables "the transference and transmutation of a particular absolutism from one context to another—from the overtly exclusivistic hegemonic version (Christian supremacist dogmatism) to the openly pluralistic universalist one (world religions pluralism)."[48] However, the American historicist tradition lifted up in this volume shows that the linkage between historicism and pluralism and absolutism is hardly binding or necessary. As we shall see, contemporary pragmatic historicists follow Troeltsch in historicizing and relativizing every faith (including Christianity), but rather than settling for a global rivalry of relative absolutes,[49] adopt an approach to religious diversity that is at once "particularistic" and "mutualistic." A pragmatic historicist theology of religions—what I will call "particularist mutualism"—embraces the spirit and raison d'être of Troeltsch's pioneering historicism, but pushes it in a *fully* non-absolutistic, *explicitly* anti-imperialistic, and *radically* pluralistic direction.

Pragmatic Historicism and the Regnant Theologies of Religions: Toward a Particularist Mutualism

The theological subfield that endeavors to theorize—or, better, theologize—the meaning and implications of religious diversity is known as *the theology of religions*.[50] The theology of religions, as Perry Schmidt-Leukel succinctly defines it, "deals with the self-understanding of one's own religion in relation to other religions, and with the understanding of these other religions in relation to the self-understanding of one's own."[51] Theologians of religions take account of the plurality of the faiths from within the parameters of either their home tradition (Christianity, Islam, Hinduism, Buddhism, Jainism, Confucianism, etc.)[52] or a broader theoretical paradigm (e.g., Kantian philosophy, liberationist or feminist ethics, religious naturalism, Whiteheadian process thought).[53] And, typically, a theology of religions operates within the basic logic of one of three models.[54]

First, *exclusivism* regards a single religion (inevitably one's own) as the final and only mediation of divine revelation and salvific truth to the negation of other religious teachings. The rhetoric of exclusion exists in most religions. The Jewish people have traditionally considered themselves God's "chosen" people; the *Dhammapada* claims that "the purity of vision" is provided by the Buddhist dharma, and nothing else; and the first pillar of Islam is the *shahadah*, the profession that "there is no God but God and Muhammad is God's messenger." In Christianity, the exclusivist doctrine is perhaps best encapsulated by Cyprian's famous dictum, "*extra ecclesiam nulla salus*" (outside the church there is no salvation), and the Council of Florence's decree that pagans, as well as Jews, heretics, and schismatics, "will go to the 'everlasting fire which was prepared for the devil and his angels.'" Exclusivism is replete throughout the Bible, too, especially when testifying to the redeeming work of Jesus Christ. Acts 4:12 puts it pointedly: "There is no other name under heaven given among mortals by which we must be saved." And if Christianity alone was instituted by "God in person," the "only begotten Son" (John 3:16) and the "one mediator" between the eternal and the temporal (I Timothy 2:5), then adherents of Buddhism, Islam, Sikhism, Jainism, and so on, are, as John Hick decries, nothing more than "the unfortunate not-yet-Christianized portion of humanity," the "potential recipients of the divine grace which is coming through the evangelists whom we send out to them."[55] In brief, in an exclusivistic theology of religions (be it Christian, Muslim, Jewish, Buddhist, or whatever), one worldview, community, or tradition is taken as the supreme, unsurpassable, normative, and absolute way to the ultimate (and, thus, to ultimate human fulfillment), while the rest of the world's religious and spiritual paths are seen as inferior, lost, erroneous, or even demonic, needing to be "replaced" by the true faith.[56]

The second model, *inclusivism*, insists that the different faiths contain partial or general revelations of something that is completely and specially disclosed in a single religion. As Perry Schmidt-Leukel explains, inclusivists stipulate that "salvific knowledge of a transcendent reality is mediated by more than one religion (not necessarily by all of them), but only one of these mediates it in a uniquely superior way (which again will naturally be one's own)."[57] The other religions, then, are interpreted from within, and incorporated into, the theological framework and soteriological economy of one's home tradition.[58] To illustrate, according to the bishops of the Second Vatican Council (who, more than anyone else, helped push the Christian theology of religions in an inclusivistic direction[59]), non-Christian faiths are not so much "evil" or "wrong-headed" as they are incomplete "rays of truth" that are "fulfilled" in Christianity. Eternal life is accomplished and furnished solely by Jesus; but the redemptive benefits of Christ's atoning death and resurrection are available to all people and are operative, albeit in a hidden and fragmentary fashion, beyond the confines of the institutional church.[60] In the frequently quoted words of *Nostra Aetate*:

> The Catholic Church rejects nothing of what is true and holy in these religions. It has a high regard for the manner of life and conduct, the precepts and doctrines which, although differing in many ways from its own teaching, nevertheless often reflect a ray of that truth which enlightens all men and women. Yet it proclaims and is in duty bound to proclaim without fail, Christ who is the way, the truth and the life (Jn 1:6). In him, in whom God reconciled all things to himself (see 2 Cor 5:18–19), people find the fullness of their religious life.[61]

Roman Catholic theologian Karl Rahner[62] suggested that the religions, as one of the many embodied sites in which God's saving love is made manifest, may even function as vehicles of redemption, "preparing the way" for the good news of Jesus, in whom the fullness of salvation is found. Non-Christians who "implicitly" respond to the activity of the Spirit secretly at work in Buddhism, Islam, Hinduism, Native American traditions, and so on, are—unbeknownst to them—really "anonymous Christians." As Hick clarifies, "the salvific process is taking place . . . within each of the great world faiths and also outside them, but . . . Jews, Muslims, Hindus, Buddhists, and so on, who are saved are saved, and can only be saved, by Christ whether or not they know the source of their salvation."[63] Missionaries, therefore, simply help these "pre-Christians" become more consciously aware of what they already unknowingly are—children of God, redeemed by the grace of Christ and called to partake in the sacramental communion of the visible church, where the gospel is "tangibly" present, "explicitly" proclaimed, and "fully" revealed.[64]

Thirdly, *pluralist* theologies of religions accept the rough parity, depth, beauty, attractiveness, and autonomous legitimacy of the various faiths, none of which is universally plausible or binding.[65] To be sure, everyone nowadays acknowledges religious plural*ity*. After all, as Diana Eck observes:

> It is precisely the interpenetration, proximity, and interrelation of ancient civilizations, with both the conflict and the transformation inherent in such proximity, that is the hallmark of the late twentieth [and early twenty-first] century. This is our new "georeligious" reality. The map of the world cannot be color-coded as to its Christian, Muslim, Hindu identity. Each part of the world is marbled with the colors and textures of the whole.[66]

Plural*ism*, however, is a specific *interpretation* of religious plurality, a theory and evaluation of the diversity of religions.[67] It is a *prescriptive* and *normative* position, which views the pluralistic character of today's religious landscape as not just a "fact to be recognized, but a challenge to be achieved."[68] In a pluralist perspective, religious plurality is (1) a definite reflection of the ontologically dense, mysterious, and pluriform nature of reality as a whole; (2) a good reason for denouncing claims to finality, supremacy, normativity, and unsurpassability; (3) a positive value requiring active, reciprocal cultivation; (4) a clarion call for faith communities to refuse to live in "splendid isolation" from, "indifferent tolerance" towards, or "angry opposition" to one another and, instead, to engage in mutual learning and conversation; and (5) a special invitation for each religion to reform, albeit sometimes drastically and painfully, its own doctrines, mission, and self-understanding vis-à-vis the vitality, persistence, and teachings of the other religions.[69] Leading pluralists, like Paul Knitter and John Hick, describe pluralism as a "crossing of a theological Rubicon," as a movement away from the "myth" of Christian absoluteness (in both its exclusivist and inclusivist modalities) and "toward a recognition of the independent validity of other ways."[70] A pluralist flatly refuses, whether by exclusion or inclusion, to regard one religion "as the one and only 'true' faith and way of 'salvation,' uniquely superior to all others."[71] Rather, to quote Hick, the religious traditions of the world (though not necessarily all of them[72]) "now appear to many as different but, judging by their fruits in human life, equally authentic responses to God, the Divine, the Ultimate, the Real."[73]

To summarize, theological approaches to religious diversity range from the exclusivistic (one religion is "veridical" and the others are "delusory"), to the inclusivistic (the other traditions are "confused and inferior versions" of the one true faith), to the pluralistic (no religion has the only or fullest truth).[74]

Where on that spectrum does pragmatic historicism fall?

Beyond Exclusivism and Inclusivism: Pragmatic Historicism as a Type of Religious Pluralism

To state the obvious, pragmatic historicists are allergic to any and all exclusivist theologies of religions. As Gordon Kaufman plainly remarks:

> One of the problems in much traditional religion—Buddhist, Christian, and other—is that all too often it moves from highly

significant and illuminating insights into the human condition, and valuable therapies for certain failings of humankind, to universalistic claims that this is *the* (single, ultimate, and universal) truth about the human condition, *the* fundamental problem with which humans must deal, *the* only and ultimate solution to that problem. Human life and human problems are much too diverse for any such monolithic or totalitarian claims to be appropriate.[75]

From a pragmatic historicist point of view, religious exclusivisms are dubious for several interlocking reasons.

There is, first of all, the issue of arbitrariness. For instance, Karl Barth, in his *Church Dogmatics*, contended that religions (including the Christian religion when "taken by itself"), along with their attendant concepts of deity, are culturally manufactured creations of "human insight and constructiveness and energy." Nevertheless, divine grace and revelation ("God's self-offering and self-manifestation") confer upon Christianity an elevated status, "characterizing and differentiating it and not one of the others as the right and true religion." To be sure, its ultimate truth is a gift bestowed "from without," that is, "in virtue of a reckoning and adopting and separating which are foreign to its own nature and being, which are quite inconceivable from its own standpoint, which come to it quite apart from any qualifications or merits." But even so, the Christian church, Barth assured, is set apart and exalted to an exceptional and exclusive position.[76]

To pragmatic historicists like Davaney and Kaufman, the Barthian contention that the Christian tradition, and no others, somehow stands above the fray of historical relativity and conditionedness, possessing distinctive "knowledge given and guaranteed by God," seems like little more than "special pleading"—as do all efforts to deem one's faith the exclusively veridical or divinely revealed one. Indeed, the more one is exposed to the subtlety and sophistication of the various religions, and the more one comes to terms with the fact that one's own religion, no different than any other, is a product of history, the more arbitrary and fideistic assertions of exclusivity and supremacy will appear.[77] As the philosophical theologian Robert Neville similarly avers:

> The arbitrariness of fideism in Barth and other theologians has given rise to an uneasy conscience. Barth said, in effect, that Christianity is just the truth . . . and all other religions are just

cultural artifacts. This is difficult to maintain in serious dialogues with theologians from other traditions. . . . It is also difficult to maintain when the study of religions by so many disciplines shows that Christianity (or any other religion) is indeed a religion much like others. . . . Furthermore, the phenomenal growth of travel and cultural pluralism in Europe and North America have made it simply odd to affirm that one's own religion is the true revelation and way of life in the midst of so many alternatives *when there is no argument besides one's commitment for that superiority.*[78]

John Hick agrees, adding that people typically believe in the absoluteness or revelatory uniqueness of their particular religion, not because they have rational or evidential justifications for doing so, but because they happen to belong to one culture/tradition rather than another:

> When someone, anyone, is born to Muslim parents in Egypt or Pakistan or Indonesia that person is very likely to become a Muslim; when to Buddhist parents in Tibet or Sri Lanka or Japan, to become a Buddhist; when to Hindu parents in India, to become a Hindu; when to Christian parents in Mexico or Poland or Italy to become a Catholic Christian; and so on. The religion creates us in its own image, so that naturally it fits us and we fit it as no other can. And having been thus formed by one of these traditions it seems obvious to us that it is right/true/normative/superior to all others. But this obviousness does not usually depend upon evidences and arguments, nor will it easily be swayed by contrary evidences and arguments.[79]

I would also contend that even putatively apologetic, nonfideistic attempts to *argue for* the absolute and exclusive legitimacy of one's own tradition usually fall prey to arbitrariness and fall back on circular reasoning. For example, the evangelical philosopher of religion Harold Netland sets out to confirm the superiority of Christianity on the basis of "objective, nonarbitrary criteria," putting forward ten supposedly neutral principles with which to assess the religions:

P1   If a defining belief p of a religion R is self-contradictory then p is false.

P2   If two or more defining beliefs of R are mutually contradictory at least one of them must be false.

P3   If a defining belief p of R is self-defeating it cannot be reasonably accepted as true.

P4   If the defining beliefs of R are not coherent in the sense of providing a unified perspective on the world, then R cannot plausibly be regarded as true.

P5   Any religious worldview which is unable to account for fundamental phenomena associated with a religious orientation or which cannot provide adequate answers to central questions in religion should not be accepted as true.

P6   If a defining belief p of R contradicts well-established conclusions in other domains, and if R cannot justify doing so, then p should be rejected as probably false.

P7   If a defining belief p of R depends upon a belief in another domain (e.g., history) which there is good reason to reject as false, then there is good reason to reject p as probably false.

P8   If one or more defining beliefs of R are incompatible with widely accepted and well-established moral values and principles; or if R includes among its essential practices or rites activities which are incompatible with basic moral values and practices, then there is good reason for rejecting R as false.

P9   If the defining beliefs of R entail the denial of basic moral values and principles or if they entail the denial of the objective distinction between right and wrong, good and evil, then there is good reason for rejecting R as false.

P10 If R is unable to provide adequate answers to basic questions about the phenomena of moral awareness this provides good reason for rejecting R as false.[80]

Although commendably renouncing hard relativism, confessionalistic fideism, criteriological parochialism, and religious antirealism (renunciations that most of the pragmatic historicists analyzed in this book similarly make—

see especially chapters 2, 6, and 7), Netland overestimates our ability to establish universally recognized and binding foundations for determining the veracity and falsehood of competing religious worldviews. Bracketing the question of whether or not Christianity adequately satisfies all of the aforementioned criteria—for example, is the belief in Jesus's physical resurrection, miraculous powers, and virgin birth historically supportable and consistent with well-established scientific understandings of the world (P7 and P6)? Does the doctrine of the trinity remain immune to the law of noncontradiction and self-refutation (P1 and P3)?—the neutrality and nonarbitrariness of the principles themselves are far from apparent. As Gavin D'Costa bitingly illustrates, for a Zen Buddhist, a *koan* (e.g., "listen to the sound of one hand clapping") is religiously veritable and necessary for realizing *satori* precisely because it *"transcends* logical conceptuality and definition" (thereby undercutting P1 and P2).[81] Or take P9, which requires that right and wrong be objectively distinguishable. An Advaita Vedanta Hindu might use such a criterion as evidence *against* the finality of Christianity, since "it undermines the absolute undifferentiated nature of Brahman, which is . . . beyond the provisional duality of good and evil."[82] And, as far as Netland's appeal to a ubiquitously agreed-upon morality (P8) is concerned, D'Costa concludes:

> This unashamedly privileges western secular tastes and sensibilities in deeming religions true in accordance with their conformity to current notions of good taste and decency. . . . There are no sets of basic moral values which are neutral and acceptable to all people, and as soon as one tries to specify some their historical and tradition-specific nature becomes evident. Prohibition on suicide in one tradition amounts to martyrdom in another, avoiding meat only on a Friday in one tradition amounts to a six-day species-genocide in the eyes of another.[83]

In the end, Netland (akin to the *early* Troeltsch) corroborates the exclusive truth of Christianity by stacking the deck with Christian cards. Christianity comes out on top only because Netland gets to set the rules of the debate ahead of time, passing off prefabricated, loaded, unargued-for, and Christianly biased norms as objective measures, and then using them to "neutrally" appraise the different religions.[84] Later on in *Dissonant Voices*, he betrays the circularity and arbitrariness of his exclusivism by basing the absoluteness of the Christian faith on the uniqueness of Jesus:

> No other figure claimed to be able to forgive sin. Nor does any other major religious figure call all people to believe on himself and to find salvation in his person, as does Jesus. The Buddha, Confucius, Muhammad, and Jesus all died, but there is no reliable historical record of any of the others, apart from Jesus, being resurrected after death.[85]

This, of course, is equivalent to saying that Buddhism is absolutely true because only the Buddha underscored the inextricable link between desire and suffering, or that Judaism is better than Hinduism because the former is radically monotheistic, or that Islam is ultimate because no other religion has the Qur'an. In other words, any tradition can rig the game in advance by arbitrarily making its distinctive (and uncritically and unquestioningly accepted) presuppositions the benchmark of religious superiority. Netland professes to have successfully demonstrated that Christianity is the best religion, but what he has actually (and circularly) shown is that Christianity is the most *Christian* religion. Hick drives this point home with argumentative force: "If we define salvation as being forgiven and accepted by God because of Jesus' death on the cross, then it becomes a tautology that Christianity alone knows and is able to preach the source of salvation."[86]

Besides arbitrariness and question begging, exclusivist theologies of religions are riddled with a myriad of other problems, according to pragmatic historicists. For one thing, religious exclusivists are epistemologically overconfident. To allege to know which faith comes the closest to representing the world as it is in itself, which god is the real or supreme one, or which salvation satisfies the true end of human life is, for Kaufman, to pretend to know more than is humanly possible. Human knowledge (religious and otherwise) is simply too limited, perspectival, fallible, and socially conditioned, religion too historically diverse and culturally and linguistically particularized, and ultimate reality too fecund, deep, and mysterious, to deal in "dogmatic metaphysical certitudes." Historicism keeps us "humble about our every conviction and insight" and puts an epistemic check on our fanaticisms, literalisms, and exclusivisms, the collision of which can too "easily explode into utterly destructive conflagrations."[87]

Finally, exclusivist and absolutist presumptions fail to account for the fact that *all* religious communities, beliefs, and practices are, without exception, historically finite and surpassable, coming into being in a particular time and place and destined to eventually pass out of existence. What the early Chicago-school pragmatic historicist Gerald Birney Smith disclosed about the gods (cf. chapter 8) is applicable to the traditions as a whole: they are "human creations" that will eventually be "outgrown."[88] Indeed, for pragmatic historicists, religion has a way of outgrowing its *religions*, and it is conceivable—nay, inevitable—that Christianity itself (along with its triune god) will sooner or later be outgrown, engulfed by the ever-shifting currents of the historical process. And if every religion (and religious ultimate) that has ever been and ever shall be is fated to be surpassed, then none can claim finality.

Kenneth Rose helpfully points out that exclusivism and inclusivism are essentially stronger and weaker versions of the same outlook, namely, "the view that one particular body of religious teaching and practice is final and, therefore, exclusively binding on humanity."[89] For example, although more tolerant toward and open to the religious other, Christian inclusivists, no less than Christian exclusivists, declare that Christianity is "the locus of the only full divine revelation and the only adequate saving event."[90] And if inclusivism is, in effect, merely kinder and gentler exclusivism, then each of the critiques pragmatic historicism mounts against exclusivist theologies of religions (e.g., epistemological overconfidence, historical shortsightedness, arbitrary special pleading) applies equally to inclusivist ones. But two additional difficulties afflict inclusivistic attitudes toward religious diversity.

First, Kaufman rues that inclusivists fail to appreciate the other *as other*, assimilating the different religious and secular traditions into the categories, language, and worldview of one's own religion (e.g., the Vaishnava Hindu belief that all paths lead to Krishna or the Islamic conviction that anyone who submits to the will of the one God is really a muslim, with a small "m")[91] rather than honoring *their* self-understanding.[92] As Diana Eck likewise detects:

> The inclusivist viewpoint would be challenged by the independent voices of other people of faith, people who do not wish to be obliterated by being included in someone else's scheme and on someone else's terms without being heard in their own right. . . . For those on the receiving end of the inclusivist's zeal, it often feels like a form of theological imperialism to have their beliefs or prayers swept into the interpretive schema of another tradition.[93]

Admittedly, seeing the other faiths as incomplete truths is more benevolent and neighborly than regarding them as total falsehoods in need of replacement; but such a position is no less patronizing and impositional, for the home religion, as Langdon Gilkey rightly shows, transforms religious others "into something they are not" (e.g., anonymous Christians) and refuses to listen to what *they* have to say, incorporating them "into its own world" and viewing them "through its own eyes."[94] Even if, say, the non-Christian religions are approximations, as opposed to adversaries, of the gospel, Christianity still remains the criterion and completion of whatever is good, true, and holy in them, incapable of learning from any religious insight that might differ from, or even disagree with, the witness of Jesus Christ.[95]

Second, the idea that Confucius, Moses, Zoroaster, the Buddha, and so on, were covertly and unwittingly inspired by the cosmic Christ or the universal logos, or that Jainism, Hinduism, African indigenous religions, and so on, prepare the way for the gospel, is, to put it candidly, empirically baseless and historically unwarranted.[96] As Kaufman discerns, the other traditions "appear to express significantly different conceptions of the human condition and its salvation, conceptions which, in their profoundest formulations, seem to be alternatives to the Christian faith more than direct preparations for it."[97]

The implausibility of exclusivism and inclusivism, I want to propose, leaves some iteration of the pluralist model as the only viable option in the theology of religions. And, unequivocally, pragmatic historicists join pluralists such as Hick and Knitter on the voyage across the religious Rubicon, imploring the faiths to relinquish any pretense of finality, absoluteness, universal normativity, and the like, and to accept, even welcome, "the thoroughly pluralized character of human religious and cultural life."[98] As Davaney avers, "the realities of religious pluralism," along with the rising sensitivity to plurality in modern society, "mock" the presumption that one religion is truer than, superior to, or explanatory of the rest. Rather, pragmatic historicism recognizes that religious truths and ways of living and being are plural through and through.[99] According to Davaney, the pragmatic historicist who best epitomizes an explicitly pluralist stance is Kaufman.[100] In Kaufman's estimation, "What is greatly needed in the religions, especially today as we are growing together into 'one world,' are more pluralistic approaches, open to quite varied insights and to illumination from diverse perspectives on human nature, its problems and its possibilities."[101] Indeed, as the globe gets smaller and increasingly interdependent, and multifaith encounters, exchanges, and relationships become more and more commonplace, all the religions need to wrestle, both theologically and ethically, with the significance of ongoing religious diversity and to find fresh, creative ways of explaining and embracing the fact that different communities not only exist and thrive but also impressively interpret and orient human existence.[102] I would go so far as to argue that pluralism is the *sine qua non* of meaningful, responsible, and deep interreligious thinking and engagement in a global, interconnected age (notwithstanding its oft-berated past shortcomings, which I will discuss a little later).

That argument, and all the arguments pragmatic historicists set forth in opposition to exclusivism and inclusivism and in favor of the pluralist view, have been brilliantly articulated and reinforced by the recent work of religious studies scholar Kenneth Rose. The bold, and boldly refreshing, thesis of one of his latest books is implied in its title: pluralism is the future of religion.[103] That is, the movement toward pluralism is not simply a "vain hope," but an "unavoidable step." Put even more aggressively, a pluralistic interpretation of human religiousness is, and will forever be, "the only final truth in the theology of religions."[104] Rose sets forth three key defenses (all of which have been anticipated above) in support of such a proposition.

First, and most obviously, the irrevocable law of historical flux guarantees a "religiously pluralist future." Religions, not unlike cultures and biological species, are temporal and transitory, evolving through history and eventually disappearing in the relentless flow of time. And because no religion can "long remain in its current form" or hold out "against change and decay forever," declarations of finality, absoluteness, and universality are unjustifiable.[105] Stated otherwise, a tradition's historical finitude places considerable plausibility constraints on its claim to be the exclusively or maximally true religion.

"Departicularization" is the technical (and neologistic) term Rose assigns to the mechanism whereby presently "dominant religions . . . fade away or slowly morph into their successors." Actually, the departicularizing of a religion—its alteration and eventual extinction or mutation—is the last phase of the much larger phenomenon of syncretism, which begins with religious hybridity. On Rose's reading, the "syncretistic process of creativity and destruction" is neither an anomalous occurrence nor "a sign of faithlessness, shallowness, decadence, lack of commitment, inauthenticity, and contamination," but is "the natural state of human religiosity." Christianity, to illustrate, arose as an innovative reinterpretation and blend of Judaism, Zoroastrianism, Greco-Roman philosophies and religions, and perhaps "an undercurrent of ideas and practices from India communicated by wandering yogis and Buddhist monks." Other examples of religious syncretism include Japanese religion, which fuses (among other things) Shinto, Buddhism,

Daoism, and Confucianism, and more recently, South Korean varieties of Pentecostalism, which "syncretistically display 'shamanic tendencies' by developing a practical, this-worldly spirituality that focuses on salvation, prosperity, and health." Generally, syncretism starts with the emergence of hybrid religious identities, which then give rise to new religions. These traditions are, in turn, eventually transfigured, absorbed, or dismantled (in a word, departicularized) by the novel religious configurations that syncretize them.

Rose regards this ongoing syncretistic activity as "pluralism in action," demonstrating that no community or set of religious teachings "can preserve itself from inevitable supersession by the unpredictable religious forms arising now and in the future." Just as past heritages underwent adaptation or died out as innovators synthesized "formerly unrelated religious elements into new, hybrid expressions," so too will existing religions someday vanish from the scene as they are replaced by or mutate into their newly syncretized descendants. And if, given enough time, every religion, without exception, will be modified and surpassed, then exclusivistic "retreats" and inclusivistic "overextensions" are futile, desperate, last-ditch efforts to evade "the truth of pluralism" (i.e., the nonfinality and unceasing proliferation of new religious movements and meanings) and to save our faiths from the inexorable "transformations and dissolution of departicularization."[106]

Second, and relatedly, the historicity and inherent limitations of linguistic utterance (and human cognition in general) "sponsors the plurality of religions" and ensures that no faith "will be able to install itself as the one, true religion for all of humanity." In this connection, Rose, together with John Hick and "apophatic philosophers, theologians, and mystics of numerous traditions," contends that the pluralist vision is undergirded by "a lively sense of the ineffable but vital character of whatever is ultimately real." A "negative," or "apophatic," pluralism reveals that verbal formulas and doctrinal formulations, as products of finite human history and specific cultural contexts, are incapable of fully capturing the mysterious depths of reality. And precisely for that reason, no "body of teachings about the nature of being" can be declared "final or irreplaceable." Quite the contrary, the critical negation continually wrought by apophasis emasculates any and all absolutist fantasies about "the epistemic prowess, normativity, and ultimacy" of a religion, making the indefinite succession of "new cataphatic quests for ultimate meaning" inescapable. In brief, apophaticism and pluralism necessarily imply one another. Because the ultimate "eludes the power of language to express it exhaustively and definitively," the manyness, diversity, partiality, and transience of religions follow as a matter of both "simple logic" and "historical fact." And, conversely, the sheer variability and impermanence and multiplicity of humanity's faiths signal that whatever religion is attempting to name is finally unnamable.[107]

Of course, the ongoing and stubborn reality of religious plurality does not *prove* apophatic pluralism, any more than the historical finitude and inevitable departicularization of the religions do. Nevertheless, these empirical facts do seem to render apophatic pluralism more *plausible* than the alternatives. It is conceivable that salvific knowledge of ultimate reality is solely or supremely mediated by only one of humanity's innumerable religions, and it is even hypothetically possible that this religion will eventually die out (or already has). But is it likely?

Third, and finally, pluralism is the future of religion for the simple reason that "particularism," whether exclusivistically or inclusivistically rendered, cannot be.[108] That is, because there is no "generally accepted, non-tradition-specific method" of establishing which religion is the singularly or ultimately true one, no individual tradition or corpus of religious teachings, no matter how absolute it may seem to its convinced practitioners, will ever be able to "secure for itself universal assent that it is final and normative for all of humanity." For starters, exclusivist appeals to unique divine revelation or the "internal certainty" of a particular set of beliefs and symbols are undermined by parallel avowals in competing religions; and an inclusivist "offer by one tradition to fulfill another" will never be consented to by the adherents of the other tradition but will "more likely . . . be met with a similar [and similarly unconvincing and unacceptable] counteroffer." In short, Rose (reminiscent of Troeltsch) realizes that "religious exclusivism and inclusivism reduce to incoherence just as soon as more than one tradition makes exclusivistic or inclusivistic claims."[109]

What is more, in order to substantiate the absoluteness, unsurpassability, universality, supremacy, and culminating fullness of this or that religion, inclusivist theologies of religions in particular rely on what Rose refers to as "*ad hoc* and *ex post facto* interpretive strategies" (or what Hick once dubbed "epicycles"[110]), which "stretch the hermeneutical resources of a home tradition to account for religious others" from within its own conceptual, narratival, theological, or soteriological horizon. In Rose's judgment, such "makeshift devices" (e.g., the Jewish idea of a worldwide "Noahic Covenant," logos christologies, "the Hindu view that the Buddha is the ninth *avatāra* of Viṣṇu") are "flimsy," "obscurantistic," "self-serving," "improbable," "unverifiable," and "ultimately unworkable," remaining persuasive to the already persuaded but unpersuasive to the unpersuaded. Inclusivists, in a word, preach only to the choir. However ingenious and self-evident an "epicyclic adaptation" is to current converts and apologists of the home tradition, members of the target tradition(s) will tend "to be amused or appalled by its implausibility." In time, it will seem contrived, farfetched, and odious, not just "to those who are not predisposed to accept it," but even to the very community for which it was created (e.g., most present-day Christian inclusivists have dispensed with the Rahnerian notion of anonymous Christians). Thus, each and every inclusivism is really a "temporary refuge," a "halfway" house, a "stopgap measure that is the last but weakest defense against the inevitability of pluralism."[111]

Pluralism without Perennialism: Pragmatic Historicism as Particularist Mutualism

By the mid-1980s, a sizeable faction of eminent (and predominantly liberal) theologians appeared to have reached the other side the religious Rubicon. In 1987, John Hick and Paul Knitter coedited and published *The Myth of Christian Uniqueness: Toward a Pluralistic Theology of Religions*, which instantly became the classic statement of the pluralist position. This volume brought together a number of daring and trailblazing essays—including one by the pragmatic historicist Gordon Kaufman[112]—all of which set out to move decisively, unflinchingly, and programmatically beyond exclusivist and inclusivist interpretations of Christianity and toward a theological paradigm that acknowledged not only "the *reality* of so many other religious paths," but also their vivacity, profundity, desirability, and orienting power.[113]

Almost immediately, however, the field began to backtrack,[114] and after a promising and potentially momentous shift to pluralism more than three decades ago, the theology of religions, Rose regrets, has arrived at an impasse, retreating to and dead-ending in an "illiberal" and "parochial" antipluralism. As I will detail shortly, inclusivism (indeed quasi-exclusivism) has once again become the dominant and default model in the theology of religions.[115]

According to Rose, the triumph of antipluralist (i.e., neo-inclusivist or quasi-exclusivist) perspectives in contemporary theologies of religions has come about as a result of an "inclusivist caricature" of pluralistic views. A number of highly influential postmodern, or "particularist,"[116] theologians (Gavin D'Costa, S. Mark Heim, J. A. DiNoia, Paul Griffiths, Kenneth Surin, and Aimee Upjohn Light, among many others) satirize pluralism as a surreptitiously exclusivistic and ironically imperialistic outlook. Rose considers this accusation a rhetorically clever, but ultimately sterile, misreading of the pluralist standpoint, one that rests on several "failed reductio ad absurdum arguments."[117] I think so too, which is why I will try to exonerate pluralists of such a charge later in the section.

Be that as it may, these particularist theologians, I submit, *are* justified in criticizing modern-day religious pluralists for habitually falling prey to something else: *perennialism*. The particularists point out that Hick, Knitter, and a host of others, in the process of purging the traditions of exclusionary and absolutist proclamations, tend to run rough shod over the deep, real, and important variations between the religions. Religious differences, in other words, are reduced to phenomenal expressions of some generic—or perennial—essence, thereby diluting and rendering irrelevant the very concrete distinctions that make each faith special and unique. In the blistering words of Kenneth Surin, pluralist theologies of religions deploy a "comprehensive and homogenizing scheme which brackets . . . all the dense particularities, the fine specificities" of the faiths. The pluralist, therefore, "speaks well of the other but never to the other, and indeed cannot do otherwise because there really is no intractable other."[118]

Much pluralist discourse is, without a doubt, perennialist in orientation, construing the multifarious contents of the traditions as permutations of a lowest common denominator. Hick has been perhaps the staunchest exponent of a perennialistic pluralism. In the early 1970s, he began to (appropriately) chide exclusivists and inclusivists for navigating the religious cosmos with an outmoded "Ptolemaic" map, for presupposing that religions revolve around a single tradition (usually Christianity). Hick then called for a "Copernican revolution" in religion,[119] a paradigm shift from an "ecclesiocentric" or a "Christocentric" position to a decidedly "theocentric" one.[120] That is to say, the center of the "universe of faiths" is not Jesus or the church (or any individual faith), but God—or, to invoke the term Hick later coined, "the Real." The religions orbit God the *sun*, not God the *son*, reflecting—through vastly diverse historical lenses—an "originative source of life and light."[121] In the philosophically refined language of *An Interpretation of Religion* (and other late-career writings), the great religious paths "constitute different ways of experiencing, conceiving and living in relation to an ultimate divine Reality which transcends all our varied visions of it."[122] This is Hick's so-called "pluralistic hypothesis."

Why decenter Christianity (and all other faiths) and hypothesize that there is a singular and ultimately ineffable Real "whose universal presence is being differently conceived and experienced and responded to within the different human religious traditions?"[123] Hick gives several reasons. To begin with, the moral fruits of the various religions are, by and large, on a par. If, as traditional theology teaches, the Christian faith, alone among the religious traditions of the world, was divinely established, then Christians should exhibit greater virtues than other believers. But, alas, good and evil, saintliness and sinfulness, are spread fairly evenly among the faiths; no one religion produces better or worse human beings than any other. Christians are neither more nor less kindly, honest, honorable, loving, and compassionate than Hindus, Sikhs, Daoists, Jews, Confucians, and humanists.[124]

Moreover, the religions, according to Hick, each provide a distinct, but equally authentic, means for reaching a limitlessly better state of "salvation/liberation." Judaism, Christianity, Buddhism, Islam, and so forth, all seek to elicit a transformation from ego-centeredness, which educes "selfishness, greed, exploitation, cruelty, and injustice," to a life recentered in God or the Real.[125] And "it is this common soteriological process," Hick conjectures, "that suggests that the gods and the absolutes that produce it are different modes of presence of the same ultimate transcendent Reality."[126]

Lastly (and most compellingly), the ultimates of the religions are radically divergent and, hence, "cannot all be truly ultimate." Hick elaborates:

> If the ultimate Reality is the blissful, universal consciousness of Brahman, which at the core of our own being we all are, how can it also be the emptiness, non-being, void of Sunyata? And again, how could it also be the Tao, as the principle of cosmic order, and again, the Dharmakaya or the eternal Buddha-nature? And if it is any of these, how can it be a personal deity? Surely these reported ultimates, personal and non-personal, are mutually exclusive. Must not any final reality either be personal, with the non-personal aspect of divinity being secondary, or be impersonal, with the worship of personal deities representing a lower level of religious consciousness, destined to be left behind in the state of final enlightenment?[127]

Given that the religions evince a rough moral parity, a generically similar salvific aim, and a veritable pantheon of irreconcilable ultimates, Hick speculates that there is "one Ultimate Reality being humanly conceived and imaged or symbolized within the different major streams of religious life that we call Christianity, Islam, Hinduism, and so on."[128] To help flesh out this pluralistic hypothesis, Hick turns to Immanuel Kant's famous distinction between the *phenomenal* and the *noumenal* world, between an object as actively conceptualized and constructed through the categories of the mind and "the thing in itself" (*das Ding an sich*). Analogously, "the Real *an sich*"—which is ineffable and, thus, "cannot be said to be one or many, person or thing, substance or process, good or evil, purposive or non-purposive"—is distinguishable from the "range of divine phenomena" diversely expressed within the thought forms, mythologies, and cultural-linguistic constructions of the world's religions. The "noumenal ground" of which the gods (e.g., Yahweh, Allah, Vishnu, Shiva, the Heavenly Father) and metaphysical absolutes (e.g., the Brahman, the Dao, Sunyata, Dharmakaya) are "phenomenal appearances" is beyond all concepts and is never directly perceived in itself. Rather, the Real is always encountered *within* and *through* the historical and mythological media of the faiths and is only "experienced *as*"—*as* Adonai, *as* Trinity, *as* Nirvana, and so on. Nonetheless, the personal deities and nonpersonal ultimates catalogued by the phenomenology of religion are not "purely imaginary projections," but authentic manifestations of the same ultimate Noumenon, "the *personae* and the *impersonae* in terms of which the Real is humanly known" (on this score, Hick opts for a religious instead of a "naturalistic" interpretation of human religiosity).[129]

Like Hick, Knitter seeks a kind of *religio perennis*, a "common ground shared by all religions." However, the basis of religious unity is not the ineffable mystery of the divine, nor some sort of mystical center, but the willingness to "engage the pressing problems of the world today, including war, violence, poverty, environmental devastation, gender injustice, and human rights violations." In short, Knitter is a "soteriocentric" rather than a "theocentric" perennialist; the sun in his universe of faiths is not God or a mysterious Real, but a type of salvation (*soteria*), specifically, a cooperative commitment to promoting eco-human welfare and "removing the oppression that contaminates our globe." Knitter, then, crosses the religious Rubicon via an "ethical-practical bridge,"[130] merging a pluralistic theology of religions with a sociopolitical theology of liberation. Whether or not there is "one 'Ultimate' within or behind all the world religions," Hinduism, Christianity, Buddhism, Islam, Judaism, and so on, can still recognize suffering as a locus and arena of mutual concern and jointly exercise a "preferential option for the poor and the nonperson." The criterion of interreligious exchange, instead of resting on some foundation or essence known in advance of dialogue, would be determined in the midst of collaborative liberative praxis, after working together "with and for the victims of this world." Because "economic, political, and especially nuclear liberation is too big a job for any one nation, or culture, or religion," the faith communities of the world need to "reach across their incommensurabilities and differences" and unite in the struggle to bring about social justice for the world's vulnerable, disenfranchised, powerless citizens.[131]

As will become more and more evident in the pages to follow, the historicism for which this volume advocates—a pragmatic, naturalistic, and holistic historicism—is unapologetically allied with the pluralist, or "mutualist,"[132] project of Knitter and Hick, leaving ample room for religious commonality, both ethical-practical and theological, even while placing a good deal of emphasis on diversity and particularity. That being said, the particularist critics of pluralism are not unfair in pointing out that pluralistic theologies of religions are frequently, and ironically, *nonpluralistic*. With slight exaggeration, J. A. DiNoia insists that Hick is actually more of a monist than a pluralist, diverting the diverging spiritual aims of the religions (nirvana, eternal life with the blessed trinity, etc.) onto a converging soteriological pathway ("salvation/liberation"), and alleging that religiously distinctive ultimates, such as Brahman, Allah, and Yahweh, point to the *same* amorphous, mysterious, and indeterminate Ultimate. The significant dissimilarities between different doctrines of salvation (e.g., whether the final state involves gaining or losing personal identity) and particular conceptions of ultimacy (e.g., polytheism, monotheism, nontheism) are minimized and, effectively, rendered vacuous and otiose, neutered, absorbed, and flattened out by a uniform, generalized, and undifferentiated salvific structure (i.e., the transformation from self-centeredness to Reality-centeredness) and a singular reality beyond and behind the diverse objects of religious worship (i.e., the Real).[133] Comparative theologian John Thatamanil captures the spirit of DiNoia's gripe with crispness and clarity: if there is "but one mountain to climb," then

> we need not be religiously interested in the concrete disciplines and practices of other religious traditions. The Christian who partakes in the Eucharist is generically doing the same thing as the Buddhist who engages in vipassana meditation or Zen. Each is but a tradition-specific way of moving from self-centeredness to reality-centeredness. The means differ but the end is the same. Hence, Hick fails to offer reasons for serious interest in the richly textured differences between traditional practices or between Christian conceptions of God and Buddhist accounts of Buddha-nature. . . . His commitment to one unknowable ulti-

mate reality trumps the importance of diversity. There is but one ultimate reality and just one worthwhile religious end. Strangely, Hick's pluralism turns out to be not so pluralistic at all."[134]

S. Mark Heim agrees. Although purporting to propound a pluralistic model, Hick, in actuality, undermines genuine pluralism, espousing "a metaphysical dogma that there can be but one religious object" (i.e., the Real) as well as "a soteriological dogma that there can be but one religious end" (i.e., an existence centered in the Real). In Hick's account, the transcendent Noumenon wears the masks of many gods and absolutes, and the conversion from self-centeredness to Reality-centeredness takes place in a multiplicity of religions, yet neither, in the end, directly bears the indelible mark of any of the traditions. Univocally and homogenously understood, both the Real and salvation/liberation are abstractions, divorced from the historical particularities of the actual religions. The divine *personae* and *impersonae* and soteriological processes of the extant faiths are necessary phenomenological (and mythological) vehicles for, but not really constitutive determinants of, the Real and salvation/liberation, respectively, essentially making the "differential experiential content" of the concrete religious traditions empty and extraneous.[135] As Heim admonishes: "Pluralists relegate specific individual elements in a tradition and its concrete historical texture to secondary status; these are the culturally variable forms in which we encounter what is truly ultimate for religion. Their truth or falsity, their integral uniqueness, are both beside the point."[136]

Knitter's soteriocentric mutualism does not fare much better, in Heim's telling. By making the preferential option for the poor and oppressed the "supervening agenda" for interfaith relations and the perennial "key to validity in all religious traditions," Knitter universalizes and essentializes a blatantly Western conception of justice, Marxist sociopolitical theory, and Christian liberation theology, unable to deal with the fact that the religions offer "stubbornly . . . distinctive alternatives" both in matters of doctrine *and* at the level of social engagement and praxis.[137] Heim goes for the jugular:

> To make "justice" the compulsory subject of dialogue . . . is unjust. It is unjust on its own terms for not wanting to hear what any of the poor and oppressed it claims to privilege may have to say about anything they might think important and ultimate besides their oppressed status as we have defined it. It is unjust for ruling out of dialogue the very kind of interchange

that could reveal our commitment to "justice" as particularistic and limited rather than universal. . . . Liberation has many meanings in various religious traditions. "Liberation" in "the liberation theology of religions" would appear to deal distinctly with structural organization in a modern secular state. It presupposes economic and political analysis that itself makes little sense without reference to such societies.[138]

In sum, according to DiNoia and Heim, the "pluralistic" theology of religions touted by Hick and Knitter is somewhat of a misnomer, because the many faiths are considered different cultural embodiments of one perennial essence, whether an "ineffable Real" (Hick) or an ethical, this-worldly "*soteria*" (Knitter). To quote Heim, "There is no diversity in the religious object (Hick) . . . or the primary religious function (Knitter)."[139]

Particularists profess to be *true* pluralists, accepting the fact that the faiths of the world are really and radically diverse and particular.[140] In the main, particularist theologians are not Enlightenment modernists who imperialistically squeeze all of reality into a grand metanarrative or feign a bird's-eye and universal perspective. On the contrary, Heim and DiNoia (along with D'Costa, Griffiths, Surin, and Light) are nonfoundationalists who reject ahistorical truths and accent the *postmodern* qualities of multiplicity, plurality, fragmentation, and indeterminacy. If knowledge and experience are always shaped by history, and if the historical filters through which people perceive and engage the world are local, specific, and varied, then everything human—from selfhood and rationality to morality and religion—is marked by unmitigated uniqueness and particularity. The other traditions, therefore, are exactly that—other—unable to be boiled down to a singular essence or reconstituted within some homogenized, unified, all-encompassing, perennial framework—philosophical, ethical, or otherwise. Even if exhibiting certain "family resemblances," the religions, each deeply embedded within the mythos and ethos of a distinctive lineage, are more dissimilar than alike, presenting true religious alternatives—spiritually, theologically, and even soteriologically. The variations between the religions are not minor disagreements that can be explained away or dismissed as inconsequential, but cultural and linguistic differences that are real, deep, vital, serious, valuable, and irreducible.[141]

The cornerstone of most particularist theologies of religious pluralism is George Lindbeck's postliberalism, which I critically assessed in chapter 2.[142] To very quickly recap, for Lindbeck, a cultural-linguistic theory of religion disqualifies the notion that the religions are different "expressions or objectifications of a common core experience," since it is the historically particular "objectivities" of a religious community—its language game, symbol system, doctrinal formulae, scriptural narratives, grammatical rules, liturgical practices, institutional forms, moral directives, and so on—that shape, condition, and even create the "subjectivities of individuals," rather than vice versa:[143]

> There can be no experiential core because, so the argument goes, the experiences religions evoke or mold are as varied as the interpretive schemes they embody. Adherents of different religions do not diversely thematize the same experience, rather they have different experiences. Buddhist compassion, Christian love, and . . . French Revolutionary *fraternité* are not diverse modifications of a single fundamental human awareness, emotion, attitude, or sentiment, but are radically (i.e., from the root) distinct ways of experiencing and being oriented toward self, neighbor, and cosmos.[144]

Heim makes essentially the same point with respect to religious fulfillments. Bristling against conservative exclusivists, for whom "what is contrary cannot be true," and liberal pluralists, for whom "what is different cannot be important," Heim develops the "more pluralistic hypothesis" of multiple religious ends—or *salvations* in the plural. The distinctive salvific aim heralded by each faith is neither the only possible end of human existence (traditional exclusivism) nor a diverse means to a common end (classical pluralism), but a genuine, yet dissimilar, end. To invoke Stephen Kaplan's imagery, there is not one path to one summit, nor are there different paths to one summit; there are different paths *and* different summits.[145] Exclusivist and pluralist theologies of religions both "denature" the cultural uniqueness and soteriological integrity of the traditions and assume that "salvation is an unequivocal, single reality." The various religious soteriologies are treated as either unreal or ancillary, as leading either away from the one true salvation (e.g., heaven) or toward an identical endpoint or *soteria* (transformation from self-centeredness to Reality-centeredness, liberation, etc.). Contrary to the former, Heim affirms the plurality and diversity of real—and realizable—religious fulfillments. Nirvana, moksha, Torah holiness, and the like are not the destiny Christians long for (i.e., communion with God in Christ), but they are authentic, if alternative, religious possibilities. They are valid pathways to the fates they seek and bring "persons to the distinctively varied states they advertise." And contrary to the latter, Heim appreciates these salvations, not for their ubiquitous telos, but for their thick empirical peculiarities, taking seriously the terms in which they are specifically described and the ways in which they are concretely embodied by the adherents of the actual traditions rather than imposing some generic, ersatz soteriological structure on them.[146]

Particularist theologians, in short, speak of religions, of religious experiences, of salvations *in the plural*. Each is tied to a distinct historical community, located within a particular social context, and fashioned out of the rich specificities of a culture and language. As Heim evocatively concludes:

> There is too much particularity in the wisdom, truth, and human transformation in the differing religious paths, seamlessly woven into the concrete, unique textures of these traditions, to ignore. . . . It is not some abstract common truth "behind" the religion, some vague universal revelation, that explains the tradition's power. It is the specific convictions the believer takes to define the nature of things, and the specific practices undertaken on those assumptions that are crucial.[147]

The particularists, it seems to me, offer a necessary corrective to pluralist theologies of religions. From a historicist point of view, perennialism is a chimera; there are no easily discernable essences, no singular religious experiences, objects, or ends, lurking beneath, behind, or beyond the accidental or secondary cultural differences of the actual religions.[148] As I indicated in chapter 2, a robust and carefully nuanced particularism is at the heart of what historicism is all about. And as particularists, historicists maintain that religious life, not unlike any other facet of human life, is molded by a vast array of historical contexts and heritages and is, therefore, pluralized through and through. The palpable and recalcitrant empirical fact is, in Kaufman's judgment, that the faiths "really do make different sorts of claims; and that, in the various parts of the world where they have been able to shape human living and acting, they have each brought into being (over many generations) significantly different forms of human existence." Accordingly, "what is needed," Kaufman opines, "is an approach to human religiousness that begins in and with this enormous diversity and difference itself . . . instead of playing down its significance."[149] Heim, then, is absolutely right to save as many of the "particulars," as much of the "phenomenal content," as possible.[150] As Rose properly grants, "the strength of Heim's proposal"—and indeed the particularist, or acceptance, model in general—"is its stressing, against overly generalized theories of religious similarity, the irreducible particularity of religious traditions, movements, and bodies of teaching and practices."[151]

Regardless, I want to suggest that the particularist critique of perennialism, however incisive and imperative, has come at a great price, opening the door to new iterations of antipluralism and religious absolutism. As Rose likewise reproves, postmodern particularists have undone many of the crucial gains made by pluralist theologians over the past several decades and have led the theology of religions back to a "renewed inclusivism" (or, more perniciously still, a quasi-exclusivism), stalling "efforts to move beyond religious chauvinism" and, more specifically, blocking "the inevitable movement of . . . Christian theologies toward embracing as a settled truth the nonabsoluteness of Christianity and of all other religions."[152]

Case in point, DiNoia reckons that a vital part of each tradition's concrete proclamation is its "particularist claim to universality." Pluralists reprimand orthodox theologians for upholding the "unique definitiveness, absoluteness, normativeness of Christianity," but in truth, *every* faith, DiNoia declares, purports to offer the practices required to attain and enjoy "life's true aim," approaches the ideas of nonmembers with caution, and repudiates any notion of "relative parity" between the religions:[153]

> Each of the world's major religious communities seems to combine a claim to the universal applicability of its teachings with an insistence on their privileged and unique embodiment in the community's authentic doctrines. Thus, for example, Buddhists believe that the Dharma—the truth about the way to Nirvana—describes the route for anyone who wants to escape the round of rebirths. Yet, the Buddha is the historically unique "discoverer" of the Dharma. The Dharma is at once universal (in its relevance to the conditions of human existence across time and cultures) and particular (uniquely discerned and taught by Gautama the Buddha). . . . The Christian community possesses a similar kind of claim, centered on the person and work of Jesus Christ. In Christ's teaching, there is the definitive revelation of the way to salvation. In his passion, death, and resurrection, the salvation of all humankind is accomplished.[154]

Fellow Catholic particularist, Paul Griffiths, ups the ante, announcing that religions, *by definition*, impart "comprehensiveness, unsurpassability, and centrality." An authentic religion, that is, has "universal scope," includes and explains everything, elicits total commitment, answers life's most fundamental questions, and possesses "essential characteristics" that are nonnegotiable and unable to be changed, abandoned, surpassed, superseded, or "replaced by or subsumed in a better account."[155]

What, given this view of religion, is "the properly Christian response to religious plurality?" To begin with, since upholding the veracity of any claim necessarily requires "affirming the falsity of those claims that . . . contradict it or . . . stand contrary to it," devotion to Christianity unavoidably entails rejecting incompatible beliefs as false. Alien religious teachings that are different from, yet congruent with, basic Christian doctrines may be considered true, but should be "wrenched . . . from their metaphysical, ritual, and epistemological moorings" and "baptized, read in Christ." Concerning the salvation of the unevangelized, Griffiths adopts an agnostic, nonjudgmental posture and defers to the providence and grace of God. Still, if one accepts the Christian worldview, then the exclusive availability of redemption in Jesus, and even the old adage "outside the Church no salvation," are not up for debate. While needing to listen carefully "for the *logos spermatikos*, the traces of the divine word sown in all human hearts," Christians ought to consider religious others the objects of Christian love and witness, which sometimes necessitates boldly confronting and prophetically denouncing elements of other faiths that appear "mistaken, damnable, improper, or simply very puzzling."[156]

Heim strikes a more amicable, but no less absolutist, tone. For him, preserving "the particularist features a religious tradition itself values" includes witnessing to its "exclusivity," to "its 'one and only' quality, indeed . . . its superiority in relation to others."[157] Heim defends—simultaneously—the existence of multiple religious ends *and* the appropriateness of maintaining "the universal value of one's own convictions." Religious conceptions of human destiny, far from emanating from a common source, are really manifold, taking shape within divergent cultural and linguistic locales and reflecting the concrete experiences of a specific community. Yet, the acknowledgment of radical soteriological alterity, of salvations, never prohibits fundamental religious commitments nor prevents members of the various traditions from elevating their own image of redemption to a central, decisive, and normative status. Succinctly put, Heim posits a "pluralistic inclusivism." On the one hand, the sheer manyness of religions and salvific possibilities enable believers to see another faith as an effective, transformative, and authentic route "to the religious fulfillment it seeks" (Heim's "more pluralistic hypothesis"). On the other hand, the "one and only" aspects of the traditions "appear inevitable, almost tautological," since each faith, although recognizing the diversity of perspectival orientations, conceives of reality through a very particular perspective, each of which is capable of accepting *only one* theological position, religious soteriology, or spiritual path—inevitably its own—as right, supreme, or veridical ("we are all inclusivists," according to Heim). For example, nothing other than Christianity makes fully possible the aim to which Christians aspire, namely, reconciliation in Jesus Christ. Naturally, then, Christians do, and should, assert that Christianity, *in their view*, presents the best, truest, and most universally valid salvific option and that other religious aims offer "lesser," albeit actual and achievable, goods, so long as every other faith is afforded the same opportunity to make similar inclusivistic judgments from *its* own vantage point. Accordingly, confessing "the decisive and universal significance of Christ" and respecting the "particularistic integrity" and "independent validity of other ways" are not "mutually exclusive." The pluralism of religions and salvations renders moot the question, "Which religion alone is true?" Nevertheless, as an inclusivist, Heim thinks that religious practitioners will naturally ask, "What end is most ultimate, even if many are real." And, inescapably, each will regard "the other's ultimate as penultimate."[158]

From the standpoint of a pragmatic historicist theology of religions (which I will soon describe as a "particularist mutualism"), particularism's reclamation of "the myth of religious superiority" is fallacious and misguided for at least two reasons.

First, the particularists' arguments for absoluteness, unsurpassability, universality, and finality—for the "one and only" properties of religions—resort to problematic inclusivistic tactics. Grounded in postmodern critical theories, these current inclusivisms, or neo-inclusivisms, usually manage to avoid the imperialistic assimilationism endemic to classical fulfillment theologies, conceding much more autonomous legitimacy to the other religious traditions.[159] However, as I already insinuated in my examination of Lindbeck in chapter 2, the fashionable discourse of postmodernism, when adopted by confessionally interested theologians, really serves to give cover to a more sophisticated and hospitable, but no less dubious and deleterious, parochialism. For instance, Lindbeck himself takes issue with the "religious pretentiousness" and "imperialism" implicit in Rahner's notion of anonymous Christians. "There is something arrogant about supposing that Christians know better what nonbelievers experience and believe in the depths of their beings better than they know themselves, and that therefore the task of dialogue or evangelism is to increase their self-awareness." Nevertheless, Lindbeck's universe-absorbing, or "intratextual," theological method requires "describing everything as inside, as interpreted by the religion." And the only nonimperialistic, particularity-preserving, difference-respecting way to include other religious traditions within Christianity's cultural-linguistic paradigm is to propose that "non-Christians can share in the future salvation even though they, unlike those with living Christian faith, have not yet begun to do so" (anonymously, implicitly, or otherwise).[160] DiNoia very similarly claims that a prospective theory of non-Christian redemption, according to which every human being is eventually afforded the chance to acknowledge Jesus—whether in this life or in purgatory—enables Christians to affirm the universality of God's salvific will, without needing to "sublate the distinctive soteriological programs of other religions in the Christian scheme of salvation" or to attribute "an implausible implicit faith in Christ to the members of other religious communities."[161] D'Costa pretty much concurs with DiNoia, with the caveat that "righteous non-Christians," before undergoing purgation and continuing "their pilgrimage into the community of the saints and the blessed," enter into limbo, where the just receive a postmortem opportunity to hear and respond to the gospel (although it is possible that non-Christians with "startling righteousness" will bypass purgatory's purifying fires and go straight to heaven).[162]

Heim is less focused on how adherents of other religions or persons who never heard of Jesus might gain access to what Christians understand as salvation. Even so, he calls himself "a convinced inclusivist" and, as such, endeavors to interpret religious diversity within a Christian—and, more specifically, a trinitarian—framework, hypothesizing that the distinctive fulfillments and ultimates of the different faiths are rooted in apprehensions of and connections with "real," "permanent," and "coequal" aspects of the trinity.[163] For example, Biblical and Qur'anic traditions alike speak of humanity's historical encounter with a "Thou," which is an intimation of the *personal* dimension of the triune God. Other religions "tune into" trinity's *impersonal* features, particularly, "the constant exchange of immanence and emptiness" by which the three members relate to one other and to the creation. The perception of Brahman in Vedanta Hinduism, of "the one unshakable reality" that "sustains all things by pervading all things," is an expression of God's presence in the world and of the way that the Father, Son, and Spirit are each fully present in all the others. Conversely, the Buddhist insight into Nirvana reflects "the 'withdrawal' in which God makes space for creation's own being and freedom," as well as "the continual process in which each triune person continually empties itself . . . within the divine life for the unique identities of the others to be expressed."[164]

In short, because the particularists' theological point of departure is the Lindbeckian one of "redescribing reality within the scriptural framework"[165] (or, as Griffiths characterizes it, "reading the world in Christ"[166]), inclusivism is the best they can do. And, as Rose rightly inveighs, these new-fangled inclusivisms, while "increasingly self-consistent," are just as "labored," "offensive," and "dialogically barren" as the fulfillment theologies of a generation ago, relying on epicycles (wild and unverifiable speculations about the "prospective salvation" of non-Christians, the squeezing of other religious traditions into "certain preassigned slots" within the multidimensional Christian trinity,[167] etc.) that "spin inwardly in self-justificatory spirals" and remain untenable, irrelevant, artificial, and ridiculous to people outside the inclusivist's hermeneutical circle.[168] Heim all but admits to the epicyclical character of his—and every—inclusivistic account, confessing that it is "plainly a Christian description: the faithful in these traditions do not understand themselves and their practice in trinitarian terms."[169] This is another way of acknowledging that no inclusivist—himself included—will ever be able to sway anyone other than the already swayed.

Second, particularist theologians fail to comprehend that the particularity, relativity, perspectivity, diversity, and plurality—the historicity—of the faiths entails *non*absoluteness and *non*finality. Heim feels that appreciating "the religions as they actually exist," in all their irreducible specificity, requires conserving their unique witness to exclusivity vis-à-vis the other faiths. Each and every religion, that is, continues to proclaim the ultimacy of its own perspective and "to have its own 'inclusivist' means" (e.g., a complex triune deity) of assimilating and affirming the "penultimate" truths of other religious testimonies, while accepting that other faiths will reach comparable decisions about the superiority and universal validity of their salvific ends and ultimate realities.[170] Accordingly, just as Troeltsch envisioned "a kind of global competition and battle" of "culture-specific absolutes,"[171] so too Heim leaves the traditions' "pluralistic inclusivisms" (their "particularist claims to universality," to invoke DiNoia's phrase) in unresolved tension with one another. Rather than satisfactorily explaining how every religion can justifiably and simultaneously profess to be the exclusively or inclusively superior one, or how mutually exclusive ultimates can all be construed as truly ultimate (a conundrum that Hick's pluralistic hypothesis attempts to solve[172]), Heim and the particularists (akin to Troeltsch) simply settle for a *relativism* that allows the different religions "to stand as they are in their own self-presentation as final and absolute"—or, to use Troeltschian jargon, as "absolutely valid *for them*."[173] This situation, as Rose woefully warns, "results in an unavoidable stalemate where apologists for competing absolutes meet in conflict and contradiction." Worse, because absolutisms, universalisms, and exclusivisms/inclusivisms become incoherent and implausible when "multiplied beyond one absolutist religious movement," the practitioners of those movements tend to double down on "inadequate or indefensible measures, including custom, nostalgia, narrowly interpreted religious experience, fideism, authority, fundamentalism, or, in the worst instances, force."[174] Heim, in fact, practically owns up to (though rationalizes) the arbitrariness and fideistic, subjectivistic, and even tribalistic quality of his position. Some pluralists, he anticipates, will "disparage exclusivist and inclusivist religious commitments on the grounds that they amount to little more than tribalism, privileging a faith or judgment for the arbitrary reason that it happens to be mine. At one level this point is well taken; conclusions reached on limited evidence are always fallible. No one can make good the claim to have a 'God's-eye view.' On another level the objection is ludicrous: Whose basis of judgment am I to privilege if not my own?" For that reason, "the conviction that one follows the most inclusive true religion is," Heim concludes, "not only defensible but inescapable."[175]

I would retort that Heim's own particularistic (indeed quasi-historicist) premises warrant another inference. If the religions' proclamations of absoluteness are culturally particular, radically diverse, and mutually exclusive, if the very conception of multiple absolutes is a contradiction in terms,[176] and if humans are "fallible" creatures, shorn of a "God's-eye view," then nobody—not Christians or anyone else—can, or should, insist that its god or salvation is the absolutely true one. Knitter's logic seems sound: "To suggest that there are many absolute expressions of truth is to imply that there are no absolute expressions of truth."[177] Hence, the two central postulates of particularism, the existence of multiple historically specific (and often diametrically opposed) religious possibilities, and the nonexistence of a tradition-free, nonparticular, perspective-neutral vantage point from which to objectively perceive ultimate reality,[178] support the foundational principle of the *pluralist* (or mutualist) model, namely, the finitude and nonfinality—the penultimacy, as it were—of *all* religions, without exception. In other words, the diversity of the traditions and their diverging absolutisms has a kind of de-absolutizing effect on the religions. The particularists, in contrast, rightly recognize the relativity of the faiths, but then contradict themselves by trying to absolutize a relative (once again, much like Troeltsch).[179] Pluralism, not inclusivism (or exclusivism), is the modal corollary of particularism.

In the last chapter of *Introducing Theologies of Religions*, Knitter wonders whether a "merger" between the mutuality and the acceptance models is possible. Is there a way of acknowledging that the faiths of the world are "distinctive, special, unrepeatable"—that is, really different and particular—without presuming that any of them "has to stand out, or end up, as the final, clearest or absolute expression of divine truth and revelation?"[180] I want to propose that this "particularist mutualism," so to speak, is the signal contribution of pragmatic historicism to the theology of religions. The particularist mutualist *par excellence*, Gordon Kaufman, critiques fellow pluralists, such as Hick, Knitter, Wilfred Cantwell Smith, and Marjorie Suchocki, for attempting to dig "beneath all the 'accidental' and 'historical' differences among the religions" in order unearth "some supposed 'essential oneness' we all share." He champions, instead, a dogged particularism, appreciating the "special historicity" of every faith community and trying to "take seriously its integrity and unique claims." Certainly, "similarities, parallels, and overlappings" exist between cultures and groups. Nevertheless, he realizes that "every religious (or secular) understanding and way of life we might uncover is a *particular* one, that has grown up in a particular history, makes particular claims, is accompanied by particular practices and injunctions, and hence is to be distinguished from all other particular religious and secular orientations." We humans are incapable of leaving behind these concrete "symbolic, linguistic, and conceptual frames of reference" and getting to some universal, ahistorical point of view.[181]

Be that as it may, over against Lindbeck, Griffiths, Heim, DiNoia, and others, Kaufman maintains that the particularity, diversity, and historicity of human and religious existence utterly *relativize* each and every faith (including Christianity) and weaken "the sense of *absoluteness*" that accompanies most religions. The brand of historically conscious theology to which Kaufman is tethered (the contours of which will be gradually delineated as this book continues to unfold) is more full-sweeping, modern, and naturalistic than that of the particularist theologians, informed by a historical and comparative view of human religiousness, a view now widely accepted in the academic study of religion. This historicism sees the faiths, along with their dogmas, institutions, creedal formulas, myths, liturgies, scriptures, ethical prescriptions, and ideas of the sacred, as "the product of human imaginative creativity in the face of the great mystery that life is to us all."[182] No different than any other religion, Christianity is a humanly and socially created tradition, constructed (and perpetually reconstructed) for the purposes of helping specific women and men, living in specific eras and places, confronting specific circumstances and difficulties, find orientation, meaning, and direction in the world. The religions each represent *one* relative perspective, *one* contingent worldview, *one* distinct vision that has developed in a particular cultural locale and through a long history alongside many others. And precisely for that reason, "none of us—Christian or non-Christian—possesses absolute or final truth," much less the path that is "ultimately salvific for all of humanity" and "directly and uniquely authorized or warranted by divine revelation." What we do have is the profound, but profoundly limited, finite, revisable, fallible, local, and all-too-human, wisdom of our forebears, "formed under the influence of their own experience and of the problems they faced in their time," and handed down and reformed from generation to generation. Kaufman ventures that such a "historicist self-interpretation," insofar as it requires us to take ownership of and responsibility for the traditions and religious teachings that we ourselves have made, can counteract the authoritarian, fanatical, and absolutist "self-idolatry" that has prohibited healthy interaction between Christians and others.[183]

According to Heim, pluralists surmise that religious plurality leaves only three alternatives: all are illusory (naturalism), one is reliable and the others are false (exclusivism), or each is a specific instantiation of a shared core (perennialism).[184] Heim sees a fourth option, of course: there are many true religions, and each is the one and only way.[185] I have been arguing that pragmatic historicism's "particularist mutualism" envisages a fifth—and much more coherent—possibility: there are many true religions, and each is one—but not the only—way. To regard the religions as manifestations of the same *religio perennis* (theological, soteriological, ethical, or otherwise) is to underestimate the alterity and distinctiveness of the traditions; each faith has its own discrete (though not isolated) history, its own distinguishable (though not untranslatable) language game and culture, and its own unique (though not intrasystematic) beliefs and practices. Every religion, in brief, is genuinely *one* way among numberless others. Nevertheless, in a pragmatic historicist theology of religions, this very particularity, this oneness, actually *forecloses* the absoluteness, the "onlyness," of any tradition. For particularist theologians like Heim, conserving the exclusivist and inclusivist dimensions of the religions "is the necessary correlative of respect for the diversity of faith traditions in their concrete, historical actuality."[186] For pragmatic historicists like Kaufman, historicizing, contextualizing, and particularizing the religions takes absolutist and exclusionary pretentions out of the equation, enabling the faith traditions to retain their variety and thick specificity (*pace* perennialists), even while surrendering their finality and universal normativity (*pace* particularists). As Davaney summarily notes, "Neither the attempt to reduce the multiplicity of traditions to a common essence nor the repudiating of the value of the many in the name of the superiority of one, invariably our own, tradition, is finding compelling support among historicists in our era."[187]

To sum up, in contradistinction to postliberal or particularist theologies of religions, pragmatic historicism refuses to throw the pluralist baby out with the perennialist bathwater, foregrounding the unique specificities and constitutive differences of the traditions without turning the clock back and regressing to new forms of religious absolutism and sectarianism. In this, pragmatic historicists are aligned with process theologians David Ray Griffin and John Cobb, who supplely differentiate between "religious pluralism in the generic sense" and "identist" versions of it. The latter is roughly what I have been designating "perennialism," the notion that "all religions are oriented toward the same religious object . . . and promote essentially the same end." The former, on the contrary, is simply the assertion that there is no single tradition which "has been divinely established as the only legitimate religion" or as the absolute and exclusive source of salvation, and that "there are indeed religions other than one's own that provide saving truths and values to their adherents."[188] According to Griffin and Cobb, one can be generically pluralistic without subscribing to the "pseudopluralism" of identism, and thoroughly particularistic without abandoning "religious pluralism as such." Put another way, there is such a thing as "deep" or "differential" pluralism, a pluralism that accepts the real diversity of religious experiences, soteriologies, and ontologies *and* rejects the presumption that one religion is "intended to replace [or fulfill] all others" (classical exclusivism and inclusivism) or is the most inclusively true one (the position of Heim and the other particularists).[189] I have been arguing that pragmatic historicist thinkers like Davaney and Kaufman are pluralists of this ilk, propounding a non-identist—that is, a historically conscious and particularist—mutualism. I have even suggested that affirming the historicity, relativity, and particularity of the faiths, far from supporting Heim's "post-pluralistic" (or, better, antipluralistic) model, bolsters—nay, compels—the Copernican revolution launched by Hick, Knitter, and other intrepid religious visionaries. Or to employ another favorite metaphor of the pluralists, pragmatic historicism can enable mutualist theologians of religions to *recross* the religious Rubicon, this time from the postmodern desert of quasi-exclusivisms and neo-inclusivisms, and now with the hard-learned (and perhaps over-learned) lessons of particularism firmly in tow.

What the Religions Have in Common: Historicity and Nature as the Ground of Mutuality

Pragmatic historicism's particularist mutualism, however, is as much *mutualistic* as it is particularistic. To be sure, pluralism and particularism, I have repeatedly insisted, are practically synonyms; to be a pluralist is to recognize that reality (human and nonhuman) is made up of a multiplicity of richly textured particulars. Still, as I indicated in chapter 2, a pragmatic historicism is a bigger, holistic historicism, situating these particulars—including, presumably, the particular religions—in a common, universal, interdependent history. The historicist, to quote Delwin Brown, "is oriented to the particular but not the parochial, i.e., not to the particular in isolation, and thus she is attendant to the common as well as the specific."[190] Ergo, from a pragmatic historicist perspective, the driving maxim of Paul Knitter's mutualism is basically correct: "Greater unity amid abiding diversity."[191] On the one hand, although usually lumped in with the other ironically nonpluralistic perennialists, Knitter realizes that pluralists *qua* pluralists give "ontological priority" to "manyness." And *religious* pluralists stipulate that there is, and always will be, many religions, the dissimilarities and distinctions of which are not "secondary," but "primary," "irreducible," and "irradicable," never to be subsumed in a "final state of integration" or "ultimate oneness."[192] On the other hand, "there is," Knitter persists, "something within and beyond" the faith traditions that "functions as the ground or matrix of their connection. . . . There is something common, something universal, something more than just our differences."[193]

Pragmatic historicists such as Kaufman agree, hypothesizing that the ground or matrix of religious mutuality is the religions' very historicity, their historical and natural origins and function.[194] To repeat, Kaufman has no truck with the assertion "that at bottom all religions are one." Rather, religious diversity "cuts deeply," going all the way down, all the way out, and all the way up, as it were; the objectives, and even the objects, of the traditions are multiple and multifarious.[195] Be that as it may, Kaufman puts forward a thoroughly historical and nonessentializing, but cross-culturally and cross-religiously adequate, theory of religion. He describes how humans, in the course of evolution, gradually acquired language and culture and, in respects unprecedented in the animal kingdom, became aware of both themselves and the environment around them. The establishment of distinctively sociocultural modes of living and the capacity for linguistic expression eventually enabled people, in virtually every civilization and tribe on the earth, to develop "comprehensive" or "unifying" ideas. Drawing on the scholarship of the sociologist of religion Peter Berger and of the cultural anthropologist Clifford Geertz,[196] Kaufman contends that human beings are essentially *world-making* beings, creating general, large-scale frameworks through which a society interprets the nature of the cosmos, comprehends humanity's place in the grander scheme of things, and adapts to and deals with the difficulties, threats, promises, tragedies, limits, possibilities, and enigmas of existence. Embedded in the institutions, practices, beliefs, rituals, values, sacred writings, and mythologies of concrete peoples, these overarching and orienting world-pictures and elaborate symbolic frames of reference are what get identified and earmarked as "religions." Thus, the great religious traditions that have appeared in human history are, more or less, the all-encompassing and irreducibly diverse worldviews and imagistic and performative systems, imaginatively constructed and reconstructed by men and women over several generations, through and within which individuals and communities have found direction and meaning in life and have oriented themselves to the vicissitudes, exigencies, and utter mystery of reality.[197] Kaufman waxes existential and theological:

> For we who live and think, experience and act, continually in terms of purposes and meanings, values and significances, cannot help but wonder—especially in moments of crisis or calamity or suffering, or of overwhelming tedium and boredom—what kind of sense it all makes, whether it makes any sense at all. In face of this ultimate mystery the various religions (and in modernity, quasi-religions like Marxism and humanism) have presented a variety of visions of the Whole within which human life falls, each providing its own interpretation of the meaning (or the lack of meaning—which is also a meaning) of human existence, each thus suggesting how life should be understood and lived.[198]

And because human religiosity has taken root and developed in an immense multiplicity of milieus, situations, and epochs, "there are many quite distinct ways of being religious and of being human."[199]

In brief, Kaufman's pragmatic historicism is capable of accounting for religiousness in all its stunning plurality and particularity, and yet is able to explain—naturalistically and historically—why religiosity is a species-wide, universal, common feature of human experience. Religion, always and everywhere, (1) is produced through the imaginative creativity of highly evolved, symbol-using, culture-inhabiting, self-conscious, world-constructing creatures; (2) is based in the need to conceptualize and offer norms, tasks, and forms of action appropriate to the wider and ultimate setting of human existence (i.e., nature as a whole and the gods, God, or other divine powers); (3) is shaped by the specific historical settings in which it finds itself; (4) is constructed to solidify group cohesion and comportment, to confront the vexing and varying problems facing people in particular times and places, to facilitate meaningful participation in an overall symbolic order, and to provide orientation amid the contingencies of history and the awareness of death; and (5) is provoked and nourished by the "ultimate mysteriousness of things" and the necessity of establishing "bulwarks against the void."[200]

I would go a step further, however, and hazard that religious unity lies not just on the *subjective* (or anthropological) end of religion (e.g., its imaginative genesis, its orienting purpose and comprehensive scope, its cultural conditionedness and diversity), but on the *objective* end of religion as well. I want to venture (contrary to Kaufman[201]) that pragmatic historicism is able to affirm the basic Hickian intuition that the religions are reaching toward a common metaphysical ultimate, but without gutting the traditions' deep specificities and ineradicable differences and reintroducing perennialism/identism. This nonperennialist/nonidentist—that is, historicist—reimagination of "the Real" can be accomplished in three moves.

First, against Cobb and Griffin,[202] and with Thatamanil, Hick, and Heim, pragmatic historicism ought to rule out any conception of *multiple ultimates*. As Thatamanil plainly avers, the postulation of many ultimate realities seems "self-contradictory" and "runs contrary to the very idea of ultimacy."[203] Or to quote Hick, there cannot be "a plurality of ultimates, because none of them would then be *truly* ultimate."[204] Heim concurs: there can only be one *actually* ultimate religious reality.[205] Nonetheless, Heim and Thatamanil both justifiably call Hick to task for painting an ironically nonpluralistic picture of ultimacy, for positing an "undifferentiated" Noumenon or a "monomystery" and restricting diversity to "the subject side" of religion.[206] That is, the particularities of religious knowledge and experience only disclose "where people were coming from when they met mystery."[207] In Hick's own words, "The noumenal Real is experienced and thought by different human mentalities, forming and formed by different religious traditions."[208] In order to avoid identism and to do full justice to "the real variety of religious goods," Heim and Thatamanil believe it is more cogent and fruitful not only to acknowledge the plurality of the phenomenological, cultural, and human facets of religion, as does Hick,[209] but also to think of *ultimacy itself* as having "diverse aspects" or "plenitude."[210]

Second, with Hick and against Heim (and, to a lesser extent, Thatamanil), pragmatic historicism dissuades the traditions from identifying the one complex, multiaspected, plentiful ultimate reality with their particular god or absolute, however enlarged (e.g., Heim's multidimensional Christian trinity), or even with a divinity resourced by several of the extant religions (e.g., Thatamanil's "polydoxic" trinity, which is informed by a "Buddhist-Christian-Hindu trialogue"[211]). Heim, to reiterate, is in agreement with Hick that conflicting religious ultimates cannot all be *really* ultimate. However, unlike Hick, he thinks that this means each will—and should—regard "the other's ultimate as penultimate," as an actual but "lesser power or entity."[212]

From a pragmatic historicist viewpoint, Hick's approach is the more judicious, credible, and nontribalistic one: since no more than one of the religions' ultimates can be objectively or ultimately ultimate, it is more probable that *all* of them are penultimate. To Hick, it seems flatly arbitrary and irredeemably exclusivist to affirm the ultimacy of one's own ultimate and the penultimacy of the others (in Heim's case, to reconceptualize other ultimates as dimensions of the Christian trinity), which is why he "downgrades" *everyone's* ultimate to "a lesser power or entity," so to speak. What is more, these lesser powers and entities are, for Hick, historically conditioned myths, metaphors, or symbols, not straightforward, literal, or supernatural realities. Heim overestimates the explanatory capaciousness of the religions, their ability to adequately and accurately reconcile, in their own native metaphysical categories, the mutually exclusive soteriological possibilities and religious ontologies of the religions. In point of fact, although his intended desire is to acknowledge the "truth in the convictions of these other traditions *in the terms concretely stated and believed by those within those traditions*,"[213] his trinitarianism, in actuality, requires him to contort (if not distort) both his home religion (the triune economy needs to be radically renovated in order to accommodate the destinies and ultimates of the various faiths, in all their difference and particularity) and, even more, the non-Christian religions. As Thatamanil regrets, the faiths are "understood entirely on Christian theological terms" and are made to "fit within a given trinitarian scheme that is formulated *prior to dialogue* with other religious traditions."[214] Consequently, it is much more economical, even particularistic, to follow Hick's lead and to "reduce" the religions' deities and nonpersonal absolutes to a "relative, mythic, metaphorical, or symbolic" ontological status, to view them as "human responses" to something that is finally ineffable and incomprehensible, something that surpasses the conceptualities and experiences of any single tradition or the traditions en masse.[215] As pragmatic historicists would very similarly put it, they are culturally distinct and historically shaped ways of engaging, through the "social patterns" (Shailer Mathews),[216] "metaphorical elaborations" (Sallie McFague),[217] "sacred conventions" (William Dean),[218] or "imaginative constructions" (Gordon Kaufman)[219] of particular traditions, with that which is ultimately mysterious and inexhaustible.

In short, in concert with Hick, pragmatic historicists, such as Kaufman, recognize that the sheer plurality and historical diversity of religious objects and ends force us to call into question the ultimacy, literalness, and epistemic straightforwardness of any of them—including our own—and to accept that they are, in all probability, humanly created, culturally mediated, and linguistically constituted symbols that, at best, "lamely and abstractly" point to a "profound mystery."[220] Just as opposing absolutisms de-absolutize all the religions' absolutes (see the previous section), so too opposing ultimate realities de-ultimatize and demythologize all the religions' ultimates. Heim and the particularists, on the contrary, leave us with an irresoluble rivalry of ultimacy claims, a veritable war of the gods.

Third, with Hick and Thatamanil, pragmatic historicism can profess that sacred conventions, theological symbols, and metaphorical elaborations, while historically relative, socially patterned, linguistically funded, and humanly constructed, are responsive to, engaged with, and even potentially disclosive of something real and nonhuman. However, against both Hick, who posits a Noumenal ultimate beyond the phenomenal world, and Thatamanil, who speculates that the religions tap into "intraworldly signals" of a triune (and presumably extrawordly) divinity, pragmatic historicists accord ultimacy to *the natural, historical world itself.*

As I will stipulate in chapter 7, a pragmatic historicist theology is open to what Hick terms "critical realism," which hypothesizes that the "human, and therefore culturally conditioned," ultimates of the religions are, nevertheless, "responses to a transcendent reality."[221] But as I will argue at great length in chapter 8, pragmatic historicists are *religious naturalists* for whom such a transcendent reality is a superhuman and noncultural,[222] but fully empirical, natural, and historical reality[223]—e.g., what James refers to as "a more," what Dewey refers to as "that imaginative totality we call the Universe," what Case refers to as "the mysterious power generating and sustaining the physical world and its life," what Kaufman refers to as "creativity," what Dean refers to as "mystery," or what I will summarily refer to as the sacred depths of nature itself, nature in all its complexity and incalculable density of meaning, its aesthetic and axiological fecundity, its wonder and ambiguity, its splendorous diversity and near-infinite potentiality, its mysteriousness and multidimensional, multiaspected richness.[224] Religious naturalism is not to be confused with the reductive and materialistic naturalism that Hick properly abjures,[225] although it does consider the natural sphere both metaphysically and religiously ultimate. In other words, the pluralistic, inexhaustible, and historically constituted matrix of nature is not the vehicle through which the ultimate is manifested, but is the very locus of ultimacy and indeed of the sacred. Thatamanil correctly declares that the deep differences between and within humanity's faith traditions not only signify "phenomenal cultural variations," but also register different facets of the one (mutual) Real—that is, its "isness," "contingency," and "relationality." Still, for pragmatic historicists, this "ontological threefold,"[226] rather than pointing to a divine trinity that transcends nature, signal plural dimensions *within* nature, and nature alone. Pragmatic historicism is Thatamanilian inasmuch as the metaphors, myths, and imaginative constructs of the various religions are (fallibly, perspectivally, tentatively, relatively, historically) oriented to particular and distinctive aspects of the divine life and are relativized by the divine life in its spiritually breathtaking and utterly mysterious fullness—its "plenitude," to use Heim's term.[227] Yet, according to religiously naturalistic pragmatic historicists, the "intraworldly" mysteries of existence are not pointers to the divine life; they *are* the divine life.

What, in sum, do the religions have in common? For one thing, each religion is a unique, historically conditioned way (or, better, pastiche of ways) of orienting men and women to the exigencies of specific circumstances and to the enigmas of life and death. Moreover, the culturally particular and radically diverse ultimates (and salvations) of the world's faith traditions are all, without exception, mythological and metaphorical, finite and fallible, provincial and provisional, historical and human responses to a universal ultimate reality, an ultimate reality that is deeply mysterious and wholly natural and is itself pluralistic and multidimensional.

I will revisit—and unpack—a pragmatic historicist model of ultimacy in chapter 8. However, I want to devote the remainder of the present chapter to addressing a lingering question: is pluralism, and more specifically a pragmatic historicist construal of it, a Western imposition and covert exclusivism?

A Lingering Question: Is Pluralism a Western Imposition and Covert Exclusivism?

Particularist theologians of religions have made a virtual pastime out of branding pluralists "closet exclusivists and imperialists." Gavin D'Costa instigated the name-calling,[228] indicting the "anonymous exclusivism" of Hick and Knitter. Hick's pluralistic hypothesis, D'Costa jibes, "cannot tolerate alternative claims and is forced to deem them as mythological. The irony about tolerant pluralism is that it is eventually intolerant towards most forms of orthodox religious belief, Christian or otherwise. Hence, Hick . . . reveals that he is an exclusivist and not a pluralist." Likewise, Knitter's "practical pluralism" remains "committed to a doctrine of 'God' or the Divine which entails certain social actions and sustaining beliefs and presuppositions, which in turn exclude other forms of social actions and their sustaining beliefs." Ergo, "pluralism operates within the same logical structure of exclusivism."[229] Recently, D'Costa has exposed and chided the unacknowledged "triumphalism and imperialism" of Hick and Knitter's putatively "pluralistic" theology, charging that it "erases the self-understanding of the religions to which it is trying to relate" and "provides a meta-solution that is finally framed and based outside any traditional religion—betraying its possibly secular presuppositions: in Hick's case, his Kantianism; in Knitter's, his Marxism."[230] Aimee Upjohn Light levels the same criticism: pluralism is a supposedly neutral "meta-position" that purports to respect and "represent the world religions" but, in actuality, "contradicts them all."[231]

Heim is quick to gang up as well, chastising pluralists for perpetuating an inadvertent *inclusivism*. Religious practitioners, while intending to relate to Krishna or Jesus or Allah or the Dao, in actuality, unknowingly worship a transcendent noumenal mystery, a "Real" explicitly available only to privileged academics like Hick. And even though the different religions are salvific in a certain sense, "those without a pluralistic understanding of their faith stand urgently in need of fulfillment and enlightenment. Without such conversion they and their traditions are at least latent threats to world peace and justice, morally dangerous as well as theologically wrong."[232] In addition, Hick imposes a totalizing *metatheology* on the religious world, attempting to neutrally and omnisciently explain *religion* from above the *religions* and refusing to take the actual traditions seriously *on their own terms*. But far from enjoying an impartial, nonparticular starting place, Hick's pluralism embodies "very particularistic Western assumptions" (Enlightenment structures of plausibility, critical historical thought, etc.). Similarly, Knitter takes a this-worldly and liberal Christian notion of salvation—for example, liberation theology's "preferential option for the poor"—and a blatantly Westernized and modern theory of equality and justice—for example, Marxist analyses of poverty and structural oppression—as the criterion of "validity in all religious traditions." What pluralist theologians fail to grasp, however, is that each perspective—including pluralism—is one value-laden, historically situated, and culturally conditioned viewpoint among others. Heim is a postmodernist for whom there are no tradition-free, ahistorical, or universal metaperspectives from which to perceive or judge the faiths. That makes pluralists, by contrast, *imperialists*, expecting "the religions to play a consultative role in an unequivocally Western theological project" and even commodifying the traditions as "forms or 'brands' of a common product."[233]

Dismissals such as these—what S. Wesley Ariarajah aptly describes as "ritual Hick-bashing"[234]—have become almost a rite of passage for admittance into interreligious circles. Be that as it may, it seems to me that pluralists have really been outwitted, outzinged, and outnumbered, not outargued. As Rose demonstrates, the particularist parody of pluralism as Western imperialism and "crypto-exclusivism" (or inclusivism) fails on a number of levels.[235]

To begin with, D'Costa, Light, Heim, and others misconstrue the pluralistic hypothesis as a "first-order," or "substantive," position, when in actual fact, it is predominantly a "second-order," "critical," "regulative," or "nonsubstantive" activity of evaluating and purifying theological constructions and cataphatic discourses. Like the Mahāyāna notion of Sunyata and the Jewish, Christian, and Islamic practice of negative theology, pluralism, Rose clarifies, is a fundamentally *apophatic* enterprise, underscoring the inability of human language to generate an unsurpassable and definitive body of teachings about ultimate reality and, in so doing, undercutting "inclusivistic illusions" about the absoluteness, superiority, and universality of any religious doctrine, practice, institution, or tradition.[236]

Additionally, particularists assume that the pluralist view is merely a modern, Enlightenment, Western imposition. But pluralists find precedent for pluralism—and, more particularly, "the apophatic unsaying of cataphatic symbolic landscapes"—in the religions themselves. As Knitter likewise points out, *all* of the world's major religious traditions, in various ways and to varying degrees, "recognize that the ultimate reality or truth that is the object of their quest . . . is beyond the scope of complete human understanding. Here, then, is one of the most evident and effective resources within each of the religions to counteract free-wielding claims of superiority."[237]

For example, Mahāyāna Buddhism refers to the ultimate as "emptiness" (Sunyata), and even the Buddha's own silence on metaphysical and theological matters is a skillful performance of apophasis. Advaita Vedanta defers to the Upaniṣadic method of speaking of ultimacy negatively, as *neti, neti* ("not this, not this"), and the overriding tendency of the Upaniṣads in general is pluralistic, striving to "move beyond naming" and "the limits of any tradition or sect." The New Testament, which is largely inclusivistic (and in a few cases, exclusivistic) by contrast, "only rarely reaches the peak of mystical unknowing that is the beginning of postsectarian religious wisdom." Even so, pluralism, presses Rose, is an opportunity for the Christian faith to live up to its own "kenotic" impulses: "Just as Jesus was said to have renounced the prerogatives of divinity (Phil. 2.6–8), so Christianity ought also to divest itself of its claims to religious sovereignty."[238] Mystical theologians, such as Gregory of Nyssa, have picked up on "the implicit apophaticism" of the Christian scriptures, claiming that the divine remains "beyond the reach not only of the human but of the angelic and all supramundane intelligence, unthinkable, unutterable, above all expression in words."[239] Similarly, fellow mystic Thomas Merton cultivated, according to Rose, an "inward sense . . . of brilliant darkness," a "protopluralist stance of apophatic openness to an inscrutable reality beyond the machinery of institutional religion and the ordinary economy of theology and Christian redemption."[240] Perry Schmidt-Leukel contends that this longstanding tradition of apophatic or negative theology laid one of the major foundations for the development of a pluralist theology of religions, namely, "the awareness that divine ineffability leaves room for a plurality of . . . images. . . . Traditional belief in divine transcategoriality corresponds to the insight that there can (and has to) be a legitimate diversity of approaches ('names') to the divine mystery."[241]

In truth, a full-orbed pluralism became a live option within Christian theology only at the end of the nineteenth century as a result of improved knowledge about the world religions and increasing dialogical encounters with adherents of other faiths. However, the seeds of a Christian pluralism were planted earlier. Schmidt-Leukel points to small groups of Christians who lived among the major non-Christian religions and exhibited pluralist leanings—for instance, the Nestorians in India and China—as well as to the protopluralistic outlook of a number of late medieval and early modern thinkers, from Nicholas Cusanus and Herbert of Cherbury to Gotthold Ephraim Lessing, Immanuel Kant, and Friedrich Schleiermacher.[242]

Hick, Rose, and Schmidt-Leukel maintain that even the distinction between the ineffable, mysterious Real, on the one hand, and humanity's incomplete, finite, symbolic conceptions of it, on the other, exists in most traditions—for example, within Hinduism, in the distinction between *nirguṇa* Brahman (i.e., "Brahman without attributes, exceeding the grasp of human language") and *saguṇa* Brahman (i.e., "Brahman with attributes, known within human religious experience as Ishvara, the personal creator and governor of the universe"); within Daoism, in the distinction between the eternal Dao and the expressible Dao; within Kabbalist Judaism, in the distinction between En Soph ("i.e., the absolute divine reality beyond human description") and the deity of the Bible; within Sufic Islam, in the distinction between "the abyss" of Al Haq and the self-revelation of Allah; and within Christianity, in the distinction between the "hidden depths" of the *gotheit* and the *got* of "conventional piety" (Meister Eckhart) or between "the God above the God of theism" and the God of theism (Paul Tillich).[243]

In short, "apophatic pluralism," Rose concludes, surfaces "*within* and *not in opposition to* the practice of a religious tradition." It is not a mere "novelty,"[244] but a "spiritual discipline"—and a quite ancient one at that—which shows each faith "to be a limited indicator of that which it serves: the divine ground of life that both inspires and transcends the numberless languages that arise in its honor." It can be discerned in any attempt to "improve upon, supersede, overthrow, reinterpret, fulfill, or replace earlier forms of religion. Every cry of the reformer, heretic, or prophet, and every innovation of the theologian and religious thinker is . . . evidence for pluralism."[245]

This is to say nothing of the fact that religions are capable of being *reinterpreted* pluralistically. Particularists presume that exclusionary (or inclusionary) proclamations and claims to absoluteness and universal normativity belong to the unchanging and authoritative "grammar" of a religion. Taking up Lindbeck's postliberal methodological approach,[246] Griffiths asserts that religions embody "essential features" that remain constant, unalterable, regulative, and unforsakeable. Christianity's *norma normans non normata* (its "norm that norms but has not itself been normed") is the Bible, which functions as the syntactic and semantic structure through which Christians "read the world in Christ."[247] And, according to Griffiths, an integral part of the enduring "syntax and semantics" of the biblical witness, and thus of the Christian life, is "a uniqueness that includes both universalism and exclusivism."[248]

As I will establish in chapter 5, however, pragmatic historicism deflates essentialist and authoritarian theories of tradition. Religious essences, unassailable authorities, lexical cores, normative rules, orthodox purities, narratival constants, and so on, simply do not exist. Traditions, rather, are fluid and unstable, contentious and contestable, multifarious and developmental. Hence, for pragmatic historicists, Griffiths's insistence that universalism and exclusivism are inviolable, essential components of Christianity's abiding grammatical structure is untrue, for there is no such thing. As products of history, religions change over time and undergo reinvention and reconstruction in each new context. And in the global and increasingly pluralistic context of the twenty-first century, the faiths (Christian and non-Christian) can, do, and must reinvent and reconstruct themselves in nonabsolutistic and nonexclusivistic ways.

Without a doubt, pronouncements of superiority, as Griffiths indicates, inhere in most, if not all, religions, be it Islam's proclamation of the Qu'ran as Allah's last and supreme revelation, Buddhism's judgment about the "salvific inefficacy of Hindu doctrine," or the traditional Jewish prayer in which the Jew praises God "for not having been made a non-Jew."[249] Knitter, though, poses a very fair question: "Must each religion *continue* to insist on being 'the best' or having the 'final word'?"[250] Pragmatic historicists, conceiving of religious traditions in strenuously antiessentialist and antiauthoritarian terms (again, see chapter 5), emphatically answer, "No!" Encountering the wisdom and distinctive genius of the world's various faiths ought to drive the religions, not to obstinately and deferentially cling to absolutist or exclusivist assertions made in the past, but to reject (or at least radically reform) beliefs and practices that reinforce pretentions of supremacy, absoluteness, and supernatural uniqueness (e.g., "Christological maximalism"[251]) and to dialogically confront "the possibility (if not probability) that other religious figures or events may also bear truths—very different perhaps—that are also really and universally important."[252]

Pluralism, then, is not an imperialistic bludgeon inflicted upon a religion, but a sign of faithfulness to that religion's creative transformation. With Knitter and the pluralists, pragmatic historicists assume that most religions possess the gumption, wherewithal, and inner resources needed for moving beyond holier- and better-than-thou presumptions and unleashing the pluralistic promise of their religious inheritances.[253] Indeed, Knitter's own efforts to refashion the superlatives attributed to Jesus in the New Testament ("no other name," "one mediator," etc.) as devotional and praxic rather than ontological or dogmatic in nature, and to understand Christ as "truly savior," but not the "only" savior, serve as apt examples of a tradition's immense malleability, revisability, plurivocity, and Rubicon-crossing potential.[254]

What is more, imposition is, to a certain extent, unavoidable. As Heim allows, "We are *all* inclusivists." That is, *everyone* interprets reality from within one's own perspectival horizon, not from some "God's-eye," "objective," "neutral," or "non-doctrinal" vantage point. And, indisputably, pluralist theologies of religions (pragmatic historicist ones included), no less than the faiths themselves, "are religious commitments and perspectives among others," not nonparticular or tradition-free positions (i.e., "meta-positions")—a fact that pluralists sometimes forget or fudge.[255]

Despite that, *every* religious commitment and perspective, whether a generalized framework *or a religion*, naturally imposes itself on the other. But pragmatic historicism, which accents the ways in which human knowledge is socially constructed, historically occasioned, perspectivally meditated, and implicated in the perpetuation of ideologies, the promotion of interests, and the operations of power (cf. chapter 6), is internally wired to be self-aware and critical of its own limits, fallibility, nonneutrality, biases, particularity, material and political consequences, and impositional dangers—much more so than the religions themselves, with their inbuilt claims to absoluteness, superiority, and revelatory definitiveness.

In addition, *no* theology of religious diversity—be it pluralistic, inclusivistic, or exclusivistic—can be consonant with *all* of the religions. Admittedly, pluralism violates the self-understanding of the different faiths by assigning each of them a nonabsolute, nonuniversal, nonfinal status. But exclusivism and inclusivism are only capacious enough to be consistent with *a single religion*, since they affirm the absolute truth of a home tradition and the falsity or inferiority of the rest. In some respects, theologies of religions that are based in a broader conceptual or philosophical model are *less* hegemonic than ones derived from the theological categories and belief system of an individual religion, for the exclusivistic or inclusivistic apparatus of each faith "can only accommodate other traditions *by subordinating them to itself*, whether as total errors or partial truths," whereas pluralistic views (including pragmatic historicism) endeavor to give an intelligible, global account of religious phenomena in all their stunning plurality and sheer breadth.[256] I would go so far as to contend that a pluralist like Hick is actually able to save *more* of the empirical data—more of the "phenomenal content," more of the "particulars"—than a particularist like Heim. The concrete particularities and divergences of the religions' ultimates and salvific options can be preserved precisely by construing each as a limited, fallible, mythological, and symbolic response to a mystery that transcends and exceeds them all. Heim, by contrast, is only able to account for the multiplicity of salvations and ultimate realities by inclusivistically (epicyclically) cramming them into the metaphysical, soteriological, and eschatological economy of a singular tradition, which is *more* disingenuous and *more* misrepresentative of what the other religions believe about themselves—in a word, *more imperialistic*. Heim, then, is guilty of the very sin he accuses Hick of committing, namely, imposing "a generic construct" on the religions. But Heim's generic construct (i.e., Christian trinitarianism) seems *less* true to "the religions as they actually exist" than Hick's (i.e., pluralism), which strives to conserve, in a coherent and nontribalistic explanatory scheme, "the range of gods and absolutes which the phenomenology of religion reports."[257] Surely, the faiths will be reluctant to let go of the ultimacy of their ultimates. Still, I would guess that they are probably more likely to view their ultimates as human, historical engagements with an utterly mysterious and multidimensional Real (an instinct that, as I demonstrated above, is present in most religions) than as penultimate aspects of Christianity's triune deity.

Finally, pluralism, according to Hick, "is arrived at inductively, from the ground level," attempting to explain the phenomenological data furnished by historians of religions.[258] This is especially true of a historicist iteration of the pluralist model, which, as Troeltsch observed in 1897, arises out of a "comparative history of religion."[259] Thus, the conclusion towards which this chapter has been moving—that is, that every faith is particular rather than universal, relative rather than absolute, finite rather than unsurpassable, human rather than supernatural, historical rather than transhistorical—is not a metatheory being imposed on the traditions from above, but a provisional, *a posteriori* hypothesis that strives to take account of and theorize the actual, concrete religions in all their specificity, historicity, and irreducible plurality.

Chapter 4

After Incommensurability

Pragmatic Historicism as an Impetus for Meaningful Interreligious Engagement

The last chapter argued that pluralism is the only defensible and healthy option in the theology of religions, even a necessary precondition for "being religious interreligiously."[1] After all, as Perry Schmidt-Leukel declares, only pluralism truly *values* religious plurality:

> Neither exclusivism nor inclusivism is able to see any genuine value in religious diversity. If one is honestly convinced that one's own religion is in an objective sense uniquely true or uniquely superior, and if one honestly wishes one's neighbour only the best, one will inevitably harbour the wish that ideally all people in the world should embrace this uniquely true or uniquely superior religion. . . . But if ideally all people should join the one and only true or superior faith, all other religions would disappear. For someone who is a convinced exclusivist or inclusivist, religious uniformity—a global religious monoculture—will thus be quite naturally the religious ideal. In contrast, a religious pluralist can and does appreciate, within limits, the value of religious diversity.[2]

This does not mean that pluralism is problem-free. Most glaringly, the "pluralistic hypothesis" advanced by John Hick and others is almost certainly wrong about perennialism. Nevertheless, I have attempted to show that

American pragmatic historicists, standing on the shoulders of Ernst Troeltsch, open up a *nonperennialistic* variant of a pluralist theology of religions—a *particularist mutualism*. A particularist mutualism (i.e., a pragmatic historicist theology of religions) resists the penchant to reduce religious differences to vague generalities, while also affirming the major tenets of pluralism, namely, (1) that plurality lays bare the humanness, historicity, and nonabsoluteness of our traditions; (2) that certain undeniable commonalities exist between human beings and across cultures and religions; (3) that the spiritual quest is, always and everywhere, relativized—and energized—by the metaphysical plenitude and impenetrable mystery of ultimate reality; and (4) that encountering others compels us to check our presumptions of superiority and finality and even to reformulate our deepest convictions, including our soteriologies, missiologies, and doctrines of ultimacy.

This chapter is a continuation—and a practical application—of the previous one. Pragmatic historicism, I will suggest, supports and even fortifies yet another central principle of pluralism: the insistence that people of faith can, do, and should build bridges across lines of difference. The historicizing, particularizing, and relativizing of the religions is, in a word, a bracing invitation to engage the other.

Of course, as I pointed out in chapter 2, historicisms, particularisms, and relativisms, more often than not, lead to insularity and incommensurability rather than engagement, presupposing that difference and particularity entail isolation. To recall the most (in)famous example, Lindbeck's postliberal historicist theology effectively consigns the religions to "self-enclosed" communes. Every faith, in other words, is bound to its own provincial community, its own "mutually untranslatable" language game, its own "unsubstitutable memories and narratives," and its own grammatical rules and "intratextual" and "intrasystematic"—confessional and fideistic—criteria.[3] Most of the particularist theologians analyzed in the preceding chapter work out of a Lindbeckian framework and, as a result, envision the various religions, not as a universe of faiths (à la the pluralists), but as a *multiverse* of faiths, as *separate universes* governed by distinctive laws, by incommensurable pluralistic inclusivisms (Heim)—or, to hark all the way back to Troeltsch, locally valid (i.e., relative) absolutes. Griffiths puts it extremely: differing religious accounts simultaneously proclaim "comprehensiveness, unsurpassability, and centrality" and, thus, remain completely "alien to one another," displaying an "otherness of noncompossibility."[4] Needless to say, such an approach all but disqualifies significant cross-religious and cross-cultural communication. As Lindbeck himself cautions, construing uniqueness as incommensurability and untranslatability (or as alienness and noncompossibility) makes interreligious dialogue and other forms of multifaith exchange difficult (even if not impossible).[5]

Contrary to postliberal/postmodern particularists (and even to Troeltsch, who advised the religions to "increase in depth and purity by means of *their own interior impulses*"[6]), pragmatic historicists such as Sheila Davaney and Gordon Kaufman encourage deep, meaningful, and transformative interreligious engagement. Expanding upon the argument I began in chapters 2 and 3, I submit that the pragmatic historicism/particularist mutualism of Davaney and Kaufman is one that views the fine particularities of our cultural and religious traditions not as a prohibition against mutual understanding, influence, and criticism, but as a summons to undertake "the disciplined practice of challenge, exchange, and reconstruction."[7] That is, our dissimilarities, limitations, relativities, and unique historical textures should *enervate* the instinct to hunker down in self-protective, parochial enclaves and *motivate* the religions to engage one another through dialogue, comparison, the sharing and blending of resources, and joint ethical ventures.

Shared Limits, Emergent Truths: The Goad and Goal of Interreligious Dialogue

In *The Nature of Doctrine*, George Lindbeck grants that "a shrinking world makes it more and more imperative that religions no less than nations learn to communicate." And a cultural-linguistic theory of religion, precisely by challenging presumptions of an agreed-upon essence or an underlying sameness, actually permits "a strong case for interreligious dialogue." Fundamentally dissimilar, the faiths will inevitably have varying motivations and rationales for conversation and cooperation; but in a postliberal scheme, "they can regard themselves as simply different and can proceed to explore their agreements and disagreements without necessarily engaging in the invidious comparisons that the assumption of a common experiential core make so tempting."[8]

Although Lindbeck's call for particularity-preserving interfaith discussions is commendable, postliberal historicism, and particularist theologies of religions more generally, seem to *attenuate* what can actually be gained—or lost—from dialogue. For starters, the idea that traditions are self-contained and untranslatable semiotic systems (Lindbeck), or alien and noncompossible religious accounts (Paul Griffiths), considerably curbs cross-religious understanding and exchange. As Knitter fairly protests, the accent on untranslatability and incommensurability imprisons religions within cultural-linguistic cells: "Every religious person is confined only to his/her own text or language or religious community. That looks like a prison." And if we are locked into our particular "intratextual" worlds, then "it becomes impossible to truly talk with and understand another person from another language or tradition," much less to receive and benefit from her/his criticisms.[9] Moreover, how can a religion be significantly changed and transformed by an interreligious conversation if it regards itself as the "most ultimate" and "inclusively true" one (Heim), as "including or explaining everything but not able to be included or surpassed by anything else" (Griffiths)?[10] Surely, as Lindbeck allows, practitioners of one tradition might help others "to purify and enrich *their* heritages, to make them better speakers of the languages *they* have."[11] But what about *our* heritage, the language *we* have? At most, dialogical encounters with other religious believers, J. A. DiNoia stipulates, may enable people of a particular faith (e.g., Christians) to become "open to possible developments of *their own doctrines*."[12] As Terrence Tilley comments: "DiNoia finds that we can learn more deeply *what we already know*. While it is not clear that other traditions give us truths, they can and do provide the context for new *Christian* insights."[13] Griffiths (like Lindbeck[14]) does think that other traditions might give us truths. But since our religion (e.g., Christianity) is taken to be "totally comprehensive" and "unsurpassable," those truths can only be "transferred to a new, Christian harbor" and "written into the margins of our account."[15]

Elsewhere, Griffiths declares that the most preferable and fruitful form of communication between faiths is "interreligious polemics." Significant multifaith exchange, in other words, depends not on a pledge to dissolve assertions of superiority, unsurpassability, and universal normativity in a nebulous mire of contrived spiritual cohesion, but on a willingness to engage in "apologetics," to make a "reasoned argument in defense of what one takes to be true." The pluralist project of tempering and downplaying absolutes in the name of tolerance, politeness, and understanding is inane and trivial, amounting to little more than "mutual congratulation." As Griffiths sneers, pluralism "produces a discourse that is pallid, platitudinous, and degutted. Its products are intellectual pacifiers for the immature: pleasant to suck on but not very nourishing."[16] Hence, against nonargumentative and nonconfrontational—"irenic"—types of "dialogue" (practiced by organizations like the World Council of Churches and well-meaning liberal Christians riddled with "postcolonialist guilt"), Griffiths envisions an arena in which competing metaphysical worldviews clash and vie for the loyalty of all claimants. Here, "universalistic aspirations" and "awkward questions about truth" are upheld rather than averted, and reciprocal learning and self-correction are ancillary to debating successfully, refuting falsehoods, winning converts, and achieving victory.[17]

Pragmatic historicism conceives of the dialogical task somewhat differently. To begin, with Lindbeck, Davaney warns that leaving aside the "elements that make a tradition distinctive" and imagining an amorphous uniformity across the religions does not fuel dialogue, but eviscerates it. Meaningful interreligious conversations occur "not in spite of our historical particularity but because of it."[18] Yet, against Lindbeck, DiNoia, and Griffiths, Davaney and Kaufman insist that religious absoluteness, superiority, unsurpassability, comprehensiveness, and so on, are the antitheses of historicism and particularism, not their corollaries. On the contrary, interpreting the religions as particular "entails an acknowledgement of their partiality, contingency, fallibility, and need for correction and revision."[19] And acknowledging that each religion is partial, contingent, fallible, correctable, and revisable, in turn, invites interreligious encounters and permits religious believers to gain (and lose) a great deal from them. Above all, our historicity and limits goad us to leave the "safety of our local enclaves"—our incommensurable grammars, our untranslatable narratives, our cultural-linguistic ghettos, our intrasystematic standards of assessment—and to open ourselves "to insights, criticism, and correction from other points of view, including other religious and secular perspectives and worldviews."[20] For pragmatic historicists like Kaufman, there is so much more at stake in dialogue than, say, setting the conditions for the development of our own doctrines (DiNoia) or helping Buddhists become better Buddhists (Lindbeck). Interreligious dialogue provokes what Raimon Panikkar dubs "intrareligious dialogue," which allows us to "discover the 'other' in ourselves" and to discern the internal diversity and profound richness of our own tradition.[21] Dialoguing with others, in Kaufman's view, also involves entering into an "open marketplace" of religious experiences, ideas, and ways of life in the hopes of "learning from each other whatever we can" and "exposing the weaknesses and problems of our own perspectives to each other." Pragmatic historicism provides a powerful incentive for these sorts of transformative dialogical encounters (interreligious as well as intrareligious), reminding us that all of the religions—including our own—are relative rather than absolute, particular rather than universal, human rather than divine, fluid rather than fixed, incomplete rather than comprehensive, plurivocal rather than monolithic.[22] The humbling—and historicist—realization that theological beliefs and religious visions, ours and everyone else's, "are always made by *particular finite human beings*, with their idiosyncratic limitations of . . . understanding, and their propensities to prejudice and self-interested falsification," is precisely what prods us to seek out the challenge and input of others and to perceive the various faiths not as threats, but as conversation partners, critical interlocutors, and potential resources.[23] As Catherine Cornille has recently contended, the first condition for *genuine* dialogue—dialogue that includes "the possibility of change and growth"—is "doctrinal or epistemic humility," that is, "a certain degree of admission of the finite and limited ways in which the ultimate truth has been grasped and expressed within one's own religious teachings, practices, and/or institutional forms."[24]

Furthermore, with Griffiths, Davaney refuses to reduce relations among traditions to a "superficial exhibition of our 'religious wares.'"[25] As I will set forth in chapter 7, a pragmatic historicist theology is committed to the candid search for truth in religious matters, which means that interreligious conversation sometimes entails getting polemical, even apologetical, as proponents of particular beliefs strive to give persuasive, public reasons for them and to build a case for their plausibility and relevance. Griffiths is spot-on: real discussion often requires taking part in "serious and argumentative engagement." Instead of trivializing religious commitments and practices by avoiding or inhibiting "the airing of intellectual differences," participants in interfaith discussions ought to come to the table *as they are*, in all their messy diversity, without feeling pressured to check their particularistic baggage at the door or to rush too hastily or glibly to warm, fuzzy agreement. Dialogue involves risk and vulnerability, as each tradition allows itself to be challenged, changed, and even converted by others. And people of faith—especially of the progressive persuasion—should not let the allure of the exotic or the embarrassment over Western imperialism prevent them from seeing, naming, and criticizing superstition, cruelty, anti-intellectualism, fanaticism, intolerance, and closed-mindedness in other religions.[26]

That being said, against Griffiths, Davaney insists that the goal of dialogical exchange is not "to defeat the other or to prove that one tradition is superior to all others."[27] For Griffiths, while "revision, alteration, and abandonment of passionately held religious views must be a possibility,"[28] the whole point of multifaith encounters is to triumph. As Knitter observes, "when the final bell sounds, there can be only one winner," since no more than a single religion can be *actually* comprehensive (even though all inexorably *claim* comprehensiveness).[29] Davaney, in contrast, asserts that the true end of interchange is for everyone to be transformed and for "new possibilities to *emerge* both within and beyond the confines of the historical traditions humans have inherited."[30]

In this, Davaney is drawing directly on Kaufman's notion of *emergent* truth. Kaufman maintains that shared and legitimately novel religious wisdom may appear organically and corporately, as noncoerced agents converse with and critique one another in an egalitarian, nonhierarchical, democratic forum. Truth is not an unchanging absolute or a property that belongs exclusively to one party,[31] but a creative, collective, pluralistic pursuit among (formal) equals, a living, ever-becoming reality that develops over time and comes into being spontaneously, unpredictably, and dialogically in the midst of a never-ending mutual deliberation between different voices and particular points of view (*none* of which, *pace* Griffiths, is comprehensive or "complete in itself").[32] As Kaufman synopsizes:

> None claims possession of final religious insight or understanding; each wishes to contribute whatever it can from the riches of its own tradition to the ongoing conversation, and will be listened to respectfully and attentively; all expect to learn from the others, through appropriating with appreciation what they have to offer, and through opening themselves willingly to probing questions and sharp criticism. . . . Through such a process . . . it may be hoped that deeper religious truth than that presently known in any of our traditions will in due course emerge.[33]

Comparative Theology in a Pragmatic Historicist Perspective: How a Particularist Mutualism Facilitates Deep Learning across Religious Borders

Besides interreligious dialogue, pragmatic historicism makes possible, indeed demands, the practice of theological comparison. As A. Bagus Laksana notes, the historical particularities and thick distinctions that obtain between different religious traditions "should not be taken as a hindrance, but rather as an invitation to further comparative probing, assuming that real differences, when read back and forth, can yield to unforeseeable fruits of understanding."[34]

Francis Clooney and James Fredericks define comparative theology as a mode of interreligious reflection that endeavors to interpret and enhance the meaning and truth of one's own religion by "learning deeply across religious borders." Comparative theology, akin to comparative religion, relies on focused, learned, and specific acts of comparison between two or more religions. However, unlike comparative religionists, who are disciplinarily located within the academic field of religious studies and are, for the most part, unconcerned with what comparison implies religiously, theological comparativists are typically *believers* who are interested in doing *theology* comparatively, in deepening their own faith commitments by making themselves vulnerable to the insights and wisdom of others. Comparative theologians often blanch at overly generalized theories of religion (both ones that reduce the religions to "more of the same" and ones that construe the traditions as "incommensurate") and prefer, instead, to engage in actual—and patient and persistent, meticulous and methodical—studies of other faiths (which in some instances reveal similarities, and in others dissimilarities). In brief, a comparative theologian assumes that religions are different, but not insurmountably so, and comparable, but not reductively so, and on that basis, conducts rigorous, small-scale, concrete experiments in comparison, placing two (or more) realities—usually texts, but sometimes works of art, liturgical practices, doctrines, and the like—side by side in order to uncover "dimensions of ourselves that would not otherwise, by a non-comparative logic, come to the fore."[35] Concomitantly committed and open, a comparative theology is one that is informed by and significantly changed through the serious back-and-forth engagement between more than one religious and theological tradition. Comparative theologians begin by slowly, painstakingly, and critically investigating the particularities of another faith—on their own terms and in their own language—and, afterwards, return to the home religion in order to reflect on the import and creative implications of that comparison.[36] As Clooney remarks, "As we learn another tradition in some depth, we will then begin also to re-read our own in light of that other."[37]

Adamantly, polemically, and controversially, many theological comparativists demarcate comparative theology as an *alternative* to theology of religions:

> All theologies of religions . . . think of religious diversity as a problem to be solved. Comparative theology, in contrast, is a process or practice, not a theory. Before Christians can fully understand themselves and the role of their religion in the history of the world's many religions, we must first learn *about* non-Christians. Even then, the job of comparative theology

has only begun. After learning *about* non-Christians and their religions, we will then be ready to learn *from* them.[38]

Fredericks recommends actually abandoning theology of religions, at least for the time being, because understanding the various faiths in keeping with the doctrinal requirements of a home tradition or in accordance with some metareligious theory of religion "usually leads to systemic distortions" of religious others and even to a "domestication of difference," whereby "the threat of the Other, as well as its transformative power, are muted." In addition, when the construction of overarching theological interpretations of religious diversity is prioritized, "comparative procedures that require the careful and detailed study of other religious traditions" are delayed and given a secondary status. In so doing, "the apriorism of theologies of religion" ironically "hobbles interreligious dialogue by allowing Christians to talk to themselves and place in abeyance" the necessity of learning from and being engaged—and changed—by the actual, concrete teachings of the different faiths.[39] Clooney agrees, charging that theologians of religions endlessly defer real interchange with incessant theologizing and theorizing about the meaning of religious plurality or the salvation of non-Christians, strangely leaving the field "in a space where nothing is ever studied in particular."[40]

Many of the complaints comparative theologians lodge against regnant theologies of religions are registered by pragmatic historicism as well: the perpetuation of metatheories or grand narratives constructed at a distance from the thick specificities of the faiths or merely in conversation with Christian theologians; the hollowing out of religious diversity and particularity in the name of a feigned common essence; the embellishment of either similarity or incommensurability; the forcing of the traditions into a generic mold or into the categories and doctrines of the home religion; the unwillingness to step out of the comforts of one's own community in order to be challenged and transformed by the teachings of another faith; the avoidance of actual study and deep, disciplined learning.[41] Even so, taking a cue from Kristin Beise Kiblinger and others, I want to suggest that none of these understandable grievances warrants a so-called moratorium on the theology of religions.[42]

For one thing, Kiblinger indicates that many contemporary theologies of religions (of both the inclusivist and pluralist variety) manage to avoid, even temper, the difficulties that plague earlier models—for example, the "snuffing out" of distinctiveness and the overstressing of agreement, insensitivity to imperialism and the political ramifications of taking account of other traditions or appropriating resources from them, "armchair theorizing," the penchant to spend more time "talking about dialogue" than actually "practicing it," the seeing of ourselves in others rather than respecting their voices and self-descriptions.[43] And, as I lengthily demonstrated in chapter 3, pragmatic historicism is one such theology.

Moreover, theology of religions, as Kiblinger refreshingly argues, "is properly prior to comparative theology," because comparisons are always motivated and shaped by our theological perspectives on religious diversity. Even more, a theology of religions, according to Stephen Duffy, "is the condition grounding the very possibility" of comparison, validating and giving direction to "comparative analysis and synthesis."[44] The way a comparison is carried out and, later, theologically integrated, and even the selection and gathering of the materials to compare, are affected by our attitude toward and interpretation of the world's religiously pluralistic landscape. In short, there is no such thing as theology-of-religions-free comparative theology.[45] Accordingly, Kiblinger urges that "we cannot skip getting clarity on our theological presuppositions about the other and just jump into the practice of reading, because so much hangs on *how* we read, which is determined by our theology of religions in the first place."[46] Comparativists, therefore, need to disclose their "theology of religions leanings" upfront rather leave them unacknowledged or implicit.[47] As Clooney himself realizes, if comparative theology can encourage the theology of religions to pay "closer attention to specific traditions," then "the theology of religions can usefully make explicit the grounds for comparative study" and "help correct biases that may distort or impede comparative work."[48]

Finally, Kiblinger is absolutely correct: "One's theology of religions makes a significant difference in one's comparative theology, and getting the former right is essential to doing the latter well and to framing what one is doing properly."[49] And I submit that pragmatic historicism's particularist mutualism is uniquely and optimally positioned to facilitate the deep interreligious learning that theological comparativists themselves envision, removing perennialist presumptions of *sameness* that render comparison negligible, confessionalistic presumptions of *untranslatability* that render comparison impossible, and absolutist presumptions of *superiority* that render comparison unnecessary. Stated positively, theologians are driven and poised to compare precisely because the faiths are, on the one hand, constitutively different but not incommensurable, and on the other, revisable, capable of being influenced and enriched by others, and in possession of humanly constructed, historically relative and conditioned, incomplete, and contestable beliefs, not absolute and unsurpassable ones.

In fact, I would hazard that the mutualistic, or pluralistic, dimension of a pragmatic historicist theology of religions gives theoretical sanction to the more adventurous, risky, experimental, and constructive comparative projects undertaken by younger theological comparativists, such as John Thatamanil.[50] I have already analyzed Thatamanil's very recent attempts to formulate a trinitarianism from a "Buddhist-Christian-Hindu trialogue" (see chapter 3).[51] Elsewhere, he puts the Protestant theologian Paul Tillich in conversation with Hinduism's eighth-century master teacher Sankara, exploring how a "Christian nondualism" might *emerge* (in the Kaufmanian sense) out of a comparison between a Tillichian ground-of-being theology and the Hindu idea that "the true self is just Brahman." Thatamanil concludes that Sankara, and Advaita Vedanta more generally, "challenges Christian theologians to carry the antidualistic impulses found in Tillich further," inviting them "to consider an absolute divine presence that goes so far as to make possible an affirmation of nonduality between humanity and divinity"—all while still preserving "creaturely freedom" and even "a realistic assessment of the depth of estrangement."[52] In short, a Thatamanilian comparative theology is willing to engage concepts that are plausible and yet unavailable within (and perhaps at loggerheads with) the home tradition (e.g., the strict identity of Atman and Brahman) and to radically rethink and reconstruct fundamental theological convictions (e.g., the nature of ultimate reality) in light of them.[53] And it is my contention that pragmatic historicism, with its emphasis on the utter historicity, relativity, fallibility, contingency, provisionality, partiality, adaptability, and nonfinality of religious traditions and teachings, can stimulate the enormous theological returns that Thatamanil and others get on their comparative investments.

The comparative theologies of Fredericks and Clooney, by contrast, operate within the loose parameters of a Catholic inclusivism and, precisely for that reason, yield much more modest gains.[54] By Clooney's own admission, "rarely, if ever, will comparative theology produce new truths." At most, theological comparativists will "achieve fresh insight into the creeds and doctrines precious to their community."[55]

To illustrate, in *The Truth, the Way, the Life*, Clooney studies three mantric devotions to Narayana, a revered name for God in the tradition of Srivaisnava Hinduism. Focusing especially on the exegesis of these mantras in the commentary of the fourteenth-century Hindu theologian Desika, Clooney describes the one hundred and eight perfections attributed to

Narayana—for example, "protector," "the person for whom all exists," "the one who enables conscious beings to be responsible agents," "the one who is the destiny of the self," "the one in whom lies our ultimate bliss." At the end of the book, Clooney comes to the seemingly radical conclusion that Narayana could possibly be invoked in Christian prayer—but *only because* Christians "can really have no objection to praising God in most of these 108 ways" and may "hear and utter anew prayers central to the bible and Christian tradition."[56] But, hypothetically speaking, what if some of these attributions *were* objectionable to Christians? What if the mantras *ran counter to* prayers central to the Bible and Christian tradition? Theologians engaged in Clooney- and Frederick-style (read: inclusivistic) comparative theology would be unable to deal with them—or at least theologically (and spiritually) profit from them. After all, how can comparativists truly "go beyond their own religious tradition" and be receptive to "teachings that may be strange, unsettling, or even disturbing,"[57] when Christ is still heralded as "the universal savior" and the founder of "the one universal religion?"[58] As Knitter fairly queries: theological comparisons appear to provide Christians "only with new ways to come to a deeper understanding of what they already have and implicitly know. But is there the possibility for Christians to learn something they really did not know before, something that was not contained in Jesus' revelation? Yet how could that be possible if Christian revelation is full and final?"[59] For pragmatic historicists, Christians can indeed learn something that is uncontained in—and even at odds with—the Christian revelation, precisely because that "revelation" is *not* full and final, but fallible and finite. A pragmatic historicist comparative theology, then, would be a completely vulnerable, radically revisionistic, and genuinely multireligious comparative theology, looking to the other not only to unlock what is tacit within our traditions, but also to supplement what is missing from them, to access what is inaccessible to them,[60] and to correct what is wrong with them.

And it would be an embodied, materialistic, and political comparative theology, too. Like the academic study of religion in general, comparative theology, at least as it is presently practiced, consists almost exclusively of *textual* comparisons. As Clooney rationalizes, "Texts are only a part of religion but . . . remain the single best resource . . . for knowing religious traditions deeply and subtly."[61]

On the whole, pragmatic historicism, as I signaled in chapter 2, ardently denounces mind-body and nature-culture dualisms and accentuates the materiality and politically embedded character of human existence. As a result, pragmatic historicists reject the widespread tendency to reduce religions to systems of beliefs, sacred writings, narratives, dogmas, and the like (a tendency, I would add, that is reflected in comparative theology). Davaney, for example, tries to positively account for so-called popular religion, which focuses on the everyday lives and activities of ordinary people and on the ways in which communities on the ground not only passively consume but also creatively appropriate and reconfigure religious meanings, heritages, and identities. Moreover, neither religions nor cultures are merely discursive, "theater[s] of ideas and symbolic forms." Rather, religious life, Davaney contends, is fundamentally a nonlinguistic, nonliterary, and nonideational production and is always enmeshed in the material and social dynamics of a cultural locale—for example, in the exchange of capital, in the valuation and regulation of bodies, in the politics of domination and resistance, and so on.[62] Delwin Brown refers to this as "the materialist principle of radical historicism," which attempts to incorporate the "non-discursive dimensions" of a tradition and its entanglement in the varied "concrete realities of the material environment"—for example, "political and economic processes and institutions and the structures of power that pervade them." More emphatically and explicitly than most historicists, Brown also grounds a historicist materialism in a robust philosophy of human embodiedness.[63] Drawing on Merleau-Ponty's "phenomenology of lived existence," which proposes that the subject is a *body* immersed in a context of natural and cultural relationships, and even more on Whitehead's radical empiricism, which postulates that humanity's connectedness with nature is massively, even primarily, physical and felt, Brown infers that "our habitation of religious traditions, too, is largely a non-conscious, bodily habitation." And in Brown's view, ritualized rites and behaviors are perhaps the most powerful and significant avenues through which embodied, material beings "express" and "register," as well as "enliven" and "alter," the dynamic patterns of their religions. "Feelings" and "affective vitalities of communal practice," in other words, are just as indispensable to religion as doctrines, myths, and literary canons are, and ritual enactment, in particular, plays a crucial role in the transmission and transformation of a faith.[64]

A comparative theology that is based in pragmatic historicism's materialist, embodied, and ritualized understanding of human and religious existence would require comparativists to do more than read scriptures and other theological classics "back and forth across religious borders."[65] In a pragmatic historicist mold, comparative theology would also need to compare religions' nondiscursive features—their spiritual affections, spatial habitations, ethical injunctions, ritual actions, popular rites, artistic creations, and so on—and maybe even engage in a comparative pursuit of justice. Fortunately, a few comparativists of the "next generation" like Michelle Voss Roberts have already begun to nudge the field in a more post-textual, nonelitist, and unapologetically political direction, attending not just to the reflections of theologians, contemplatives, commentators, and other elites, but also to the religious lives of "ordinary practitioners,"[66] making topics like "desire" and "institutional power" and "gendered constructions of the body" subjects of comparison, and pointing to "the wealth of ways comparative theology can work toward liberative ends." To quote Voss Roberts: "Comparative theologians might . . . consider what forms oppression takes in different settings, whether terms such as 'oppression' and 'patriarchy' apply across contexts, and who is permitted to name oppression. We can inquire how marginal subjects accommodate, survive, and resist hegemonies; and we can bear witness to the theological implications of their practices."[67] Indeed, this is just the sort of comparative theology that a pragmatic historicism inspires.

Hybrid Histories, Porous Particularities: From Multitraditionedness to Multiple Religious Belonging

Thatamanil argues that comparative theology, when conceived as a truly conversational, constructive, and collaborative task—that is, as a mode of theological reflection that seeks to learn from and with other religions and risks reimagining deeply held convictions in light of such encounters—sometimes leads us "into the relatively uncharted waters" of "hyphenated" or "double inhabitation" (Hindu-Christian, Jewish-Buddhist, etc.).[68] Indeed, a number of contemporary comparativists and theologians of religions are beginning to explore and debate the religious ramifications of simultaneously incorporating the theological beliefs, moral principles, ritual practices, and so on, of more than one tradition. As Catherine Cornille observes, "A heightened and widespread consciousness of religious pluralism has presently left the religious person with the choice not only of *which* religion, but also of *how many* religions she or he might belong to."[69] Already the rule rather than the exception in Asia, believers throughout the world (including the West) are increasingly attempting to form reciprocally enriching, even mutually corrective, symbiotic bonds across traditions (even if such complementarity often remains "asymmetrical"). While surely not for everybody,[70] many people of faith today desire not only to understand but also to integrate the stories, customs, and teachings of religious others.[71] In what follows, I want to propose that pragmatic historicism also gestures toward the possibility, even the inevitability, of dual or multiple religious belonging.

Of course, according to several present-day theorists, the very notion of "multiple religious belonging" is somewhat redundant, since "to belong is already to multiply belong."[72] Jeffrey Carlson, Jeannine Hill Fletcher, Devaka Premawardhana, Michelle Voss Roberts, and John Thatamanil, to name just a few, all insist that there really is no such thing as an individual, a culture, a society, *or a religion* that is not inherently complex, plural, fluid, and crossbred.[73] Carlson goes so far as to suggest that double religious participation is a "tautology." To "belong" to Christianity or Buddhism, for example, is to inevitably amalgamate certain components traditionally identified as "Christian" or "Buddhist" with "practices and beliefs drawn from other places and times." And those faiths are *themselves* "mixed," "pluralistic," and "syncretic"—that is, made up of "diverse elements that have been drawn together into the current amalgam" by those who came before. Thus, any religion is "an ongoing process of selective reconstruction," a "blending of . . . impermanently related bits and pieces."[74]

Similarly, Fletcher demonstrates that personal, communal, and even spiritual identities are "constructed out of the intersection of multiple fundamentally defining features—religion, race, class, gender, nationality, ethnicity, profession, sexual orientation, and so forth."[75] Both personal selves and human collectivities are "multifaceted," "dynamic," and "relational," perpetually remade in different circumstances and situations and altered afresh as a result of new interactions. Each individual, indeed each tradition, far from possessing a monolithic or insular character, is always a "hybrid," a "web" spun from the particularities of *many* communities and categories of identity. All over the world, practices of religious cross-fertilization occur regularly. Even Christianity is (and always has been) a permeable, syncretistic religion, forged in conversation with, not in isolation from, "so-called 'non-Christian' communities."[76] Thatamanil concurs, surmising that a straightforward reading of the historical development of Christianity reveals "not only that many of the central categories, practices, and symbols of Christian life are borrowed from Hellenistic philosophical schools, mystery religions, and, of course, most vitally from what we now call 'Judaism,' but that for long stretches of history, no clearly defined and rigid boundaries existed between 'Christianity' and those traditions we now take to be Christianity's others."[77] Or as Premawardhana pithily puts it, "The Christian identity *is* a multiple religious identity."[78]

For pragmatic historicists, multiplicity is characteristic of *all* identities, religious or otherwise. Davaney, as I pointed out in chapter 2, maintains that human existence is not only traditioned (as Delwin Brown, along with every historicist, rightly claims), but also *multitraditioned*. Both individual and communal subjectivities are porous, overlapping, interactive, multilayered, migratory, composite, hyphenated, hybridized, and syncretistic, constituted by endless recombinations of diverse, interpenetrating, and ever-shifting particularities. It is simply untrue that human beings receive orientation in life from only one language or dialect, one nation or ethnos, one conversation or culture, one grammar or narrative. Nor do humans (especially today) merely live out of singular, or even dominant, faith traditions. Like the religions themselves,[79] the spiritual lives of many persons are constructed out of the intermingling and syncretizing of several religious sources and theological/philosophical perspectives. On occasion, legitimately new heritages *emerge* (again, in the Kaufmanian sense) out of the creative fusion of multiple influences, possibilities, and religious traditions.[80]

Davaney is acutely sensitive to what Delwin Brown negatively refers to as "the bee and nectar" view of religious habitation, where individuals derive "symbolic nourishment by flitting from flower to flower, drawing rather indiscriminately from the fruit of one tradition, then another, and another, and so on."[81] Much too often, the processes of interreligious "borrowing" and cross-pollination amount to "cultural plundering," as other religions get "raided for the benefit of the powerful" (perhaps the most flagrant and nefarious example being the white appropriation of Native American traditions and practices). Be that as it may, although vigilant about the ways in which dialogue, multiple belonging, and the like sometimes become "covert mechanisms of control, plunder, and domination," Davaney refuses to settle for Brown's more "monotraditionalist" approach (cf. chapter 2).[82] Instead, religious practitioners, now more than ever, ought to renounce lingering hang-ups about "purity of lineage" and (responsibly, self-consciously, and critically) open themselves and their traditions to any "instrument" that enables them to respond to the complexities and challenges facing humanity in the twenty-first century. Inhabiting more than one religion does not automatically make us "perpetrators of cultural or religious imperialism and theft." It can also signal that we are good historicists, humbly recognizing that "no group or thought or value system is fully adequate on its own but requires the wisdom and insight of others both as a corrective and a resource."[83]

Griffiths confidently asserts that "no one can offer more than one religious account at a time. Bilingualism is possible, but bireligionism is not."[84] However, the compositeness, hyphenatedness, hybridity, and multitraditionedness of human and religious identity, especially in the global village, seem to suggest otherwise, offering yet another reason why particularism's penchant for insularity and incommensurability is flatly misguided and wrong.

Naturalism, Empiricism, Pragmatism: Pragmatic Historicist Pillars for the Ethical Bridge

Lastly, pragmatic historicists stand with Paul Knitter on "the ethical-practical bridge," imploring the faiths to keep global responsibility at the forefront of interreligious exchange. Knitter's landmark text, *One Earth, Many Religions*, actually pushes back on the perennialist notion that the religions co-inhere in some sort of timeless essence or overarching metanarrative. Still, there is a common *context* impinging on every culture, faith, and believer, namely, "a world in agony, torn by starvation, dehumanizing living conditions, unjust distribution of wealth, ecological deterioration."[85] Knitter, therefore, continues to promote the pluralist ideal of religious unity, except the factor unifying the traditions exists outside of rather than above, beneath, or within them. After all, the religions are probably less likely to come together around some "theocentric" philosophy of religion (however plausible) than around a joint concern for "our endangered globe and all its inhabitants," which is simply much more "identifiable and immediate and pressing."[86] Because of the universality and urgency of, say, deforestation and the overconsumption the environment's precious resources, of dehumanization, victimization, and oppression, of abject poverty and hunger, of militarism and the threat of nuclear war, eco-human plight deserves a position of primacy on the dialogical itinerary. Crises of such magnitude and ubiquity, Knitter passionately and prophetically pleads, demand a merging of "the religious Other and the suffering Other," a cooperative response by a globally responsible multifaith community.[87]

That being said, Heim and the particularists, as I indicated in chapter 3, scorn Knitter for presupposing "the universality of a particular Western standard" and attempting to "scaffold religious cooperation" upon it.[88] The radical orthodox theologian, John Milbank, likewise chides the ethical pluralists for falsely (and imperialistically) universalizing a contingent (and ideological) construction of reality (i.e., secular modernity, along with its attendant "liberal values") and presuming that "a politico-legal discourse about justice and liberation" is a foundation "that the religious traditions can now all share in common." Milbank's ruling is just as harsh as Heim's: "The uncritical embrace of modern norms of politics and legality leads [Knitter as well as Langdon Gilkey, Marjorie Suchocki, and Tom Driver] to gloss over, and even try to deny, the obvious fact that religions have differed over political and social practice quite as much as anything else."[89]

Milbank and Heim are not entirely off base; Knitter and the others do tend to downplay the sharp (and sometimes violent) disagreements that obtain between (and even within) the religions over the nature of liberation, justice, and social and political practice.[90] Be that as it may, pragmatic historicists wholeheartedly concur with Knitter that interreligious engagement is a moral imperative and that the most appropriate meeting place for dialogue and collaboration, especially in an era of vast globalization and interdependence, is the "pain-ridden and crisis-strewn state of the world."[91] A pragmatic historicist iteration of ethical pluralism, however, is less susceptible to most of the objections raised by the particularists.

For starters, pragmatic historicists are not soteriocentrists, but what I would term *hamartiocentrists*. In a hamartiocentric realignment of ethical pluralism's religious universe, the center is not a global *soteria*—that is, a totalizing (and notoriously Western) metastrategy for eco-human salvation—but a shared awareness of the *hamartia*, or the "sin" (i.e., the problem and undesirability), of eco-human suffering. Of course, Knitter himself intimates that human and planetary anguish is a negative instead of a positive common ground; the religions can accept it as a unifying *locus* and *situation*, even when they are in conflict about its *diagnosis* and *alleviation*.[92] Yet, to Knitter's postmodern detractors, soteriocentrism's universalization of "the preferential option for the poor" or "the liberation of the oppressed" is still too redolent of a modern, Western, and even Christian imposition.[93] For that reason, the ethical pluralist cause, in my view, would be better served by hamartiocentrism than soteriocentrism. After all, as Anselm Min perceptively notices, even if all the traditions hold divergent conceptions of justice, no religion "defends the reality of such gross *injustices* as genocide and outright exploitation."[94] Or to quote Catholic theologian Francis Fiorenza, there is enough agreement "about the evil of suffering" to sustain quite a bit of "disagreement over how to ameliorate suffering."[95]

Kaufman, I would contend, can be classified as a kind of hamartiocentrist. In his view, what unites people and their religions is not "a universally human position" (sociopolitical, soteriological, or otherwise), but "the enormous problems now threatening humankind worldwide"—environmental overreach, weapons of mass destruction, warring ideologies, terrorism, poverty, pandemics, white supremacy, widespread starvation, and so on. Human existence is deeply and radically diverse. Nevertheless, the globe is rapidly becoming a single, interconnected global village, and the crises we face today impact humankind on a universal scale, thereby binding the species together in one shared fate. Thus, the various religions, Kaufman beseeches, need to contribute their unique and irreducibly particular insights, salvations, practices, and hopes "to the building of a world in which we, in all our differences, can live together productively and in peace." The ethical rallying point of interfaith conversation and cooperation, then, is not so much to apply some sort of ready-made metasolution (a *soteria*, as it were) to eco-human suffering, as it is to "take collective responsibility for our common situation" and to bring the totality of humanity's multifarious religious wisdom to bear on the "calamities that could destroy us all."[96]

In defending hamartiocentrism, I do not mean to imply that everyone is equally responsible for or affected by the injustices and catastrophes that imperil the planet. With respect to the ecological crisis in particular, there is surely a disparity of culpability and impact—and, thus, a differentiation of moral obligation. Hamartiocentrists must attend to these sorts of asymmetries.[97] The *hamartia* of eco-human suffering infects and affects humanity disproportionately, placing different responsibilities on us; some are obliged to make reparations, while others are owed it, some are called to repent of their sin, while others are the "sinned against." Still, even if our responsibilities differ (in terms of both blame and burden), the problems confronting the planet today—for example, nuclear armament, the population explosion, environmental and economic instability—remain universal. And if there are solutions to be had, they must be reached collectively. As Sallie McFague urges, "the times are too perilous and it is too late in the day" not to cooperate and pool our ethical and theological resources. Each has an inimitable perspective to offer and a distinctive role to play, but humanity's cultures and religions must work together "to create a planetary situation that is more viable and less vulnerable."[98]

What is more, even though a metasolution is not in the offing, a hamartiocentric approach to ethical pluralism by no means precludes the possibility of finding agreed-upon values and fostering joint programs of action. But for pragmatic historicists, these will arise out of an ongoing dialogue between the religions' historically specific and diversely textured ethico-socio-political visions, between their "concrete prescriptions . . . of what it means to love, or what freedom is."[99] Like religious truths in general, mutual moral norms and guidelines (analogous to the Universal Declaration on Human Rights and the Millennium Development Goals ratified by the United Nations) are *emergent* (yet again, in the Kaufmanian sense) rather than given, piecemeal and provisional achievements that come into being (spontaneously and often surprisingly) in the course of interreligious exchange and activism and develop in unpredictable ways as the conversation continues.[100]

If hamartiocentrism can serve as a more historically conscious foundation on which to rebuild the ethical bridge, then perhaps *naturalism, empiricism, and pragmatism*—historicism's "sibling traditions" in American religious and philosophical thought—may function as the pillars with which to prop it up.

The First Pillar: (Religious) Naturalism

First, I argued in chapter 2 that a pragmatic historicism is a *holistic* or *naturalistic* historicism, a historicism that obliterates nature-culture binaries and attends to the entirety of historical reality, human and nonhuman. To repeat, Brown, Davaney, Dean, Kaufman, and McFague, along with their predecessors, are full-on historicists, giving theoretical priority to the individualities that constitute existence and, even more, to the pluralities, relativities, and particularities that exist both among and within humanity's cultural and religious heritages. But pragmatic historicists are also naturalists, locating every single thing in nature (including humans) in what McFague calls "the common creation story."[101] However pluriform and culturally, linguistically, and religiously particular, all human beings, according to Kaufman, come from "one original genetic stock" and belong to the same species. And although settling down in vastly different settings and creating a plethora of languages, cultures, societies, and religions, the human race is now rapidly reconverging.[102] "What had been quite distinct histories is today becoming one history, one world, one overarching universal civilization—doubtless with many subdivisions, many unique local colors and smells, many distinctive local practices, institutions, and traditions, but all interconnected and interrelated in the on-moving all-inclusive tide of human history."[103] Moreover, *Homo sapiens* is emergent from, sustained by, and related to "the whole complex system of life" that gradually emerged on this planet, and the earth itself is "determined largely by its situatedness in the solar system and ultimately in the steadily expanding universe."[104]

Such a bigger, naturalized historicism, I believe, is able to inculcate the global (but pluralistic) sensibilities that an ethical mutualism requires, obliging the religions to move beyond their "provincial traditions," "particular values and customs," and "limited loyalties" and to develop a truly *universal* consciousness.[105] Biologist and religious naturalist, Ursula Goodenough, alleges that "the epic of evolution" recounted by contemporary science "has the potential to unite us" and to lay the groundwork for a "planetary ethic," even as "we continue to orient our daily lives in our cultural and religious contexts."[106] After all, as Knitter eloquently writes, "Before we are located in our separate, diverse cultural-religious houses, we are located, more deeply and decisively and responsibly, in the cosmic neighborhood, in the one world in which we all share and which connects us with each other and which, today, pleads with us for its own salvation."[107] Pragmatic historicists like McFague agree with Knitter and Goodenough: the fact that everything—from stars, black holes, and photons to oceans, bacteria, and human societies—is a part and product of "the same primal explosion and evolutionary history" and is "woven into a seamless web" ought to "have immense significance in transforming how we think about ourselves and our relations and responsibilities toward other human beings, other species, and our home, planet Earth."[108] At the very least, our modern, scientific awareness of the thoroughgoing interdependency and interrelatedness of the natural sphere, Kaufman advises, should compel religious (and secular) traditions to work together to construct the ideas, practices, narratives, and forms of life suitable for averting a nuclear or environmental catastrophe and for living in ecological balance both with our fellow humans and with the broader ecosystem on which we all depend.[109]

In the last chapter, I suggested that pragmatic and naturalistic historicists (from James and Dewey to Foster, Case, Mathews, and Smith, to Kaufman, Dean, and McFague) espouse varying versions of *religious* naturalism, too. Religiously inclined naturalists are polemically antisupernaturalistic but are, at the same time, confident that *this* world contains enough sublimity, beauty, grace, splendor, depth, grandeur, value, and mystery to be "called religious without stretching the word beyond recognition."[110] The outsideless, all-inclusive realm of nature itself, be it in whole or in part, is that which is holy, sacred, and even divine and is, thus, the most appropriate object of ultimate concern, devotion, and reverence.[111]

I want to venture that pragmatic historicism's *religiously* naturalistic outlook (which I will flesh out in great detail in chapter 8) might further nurture an ethically grounded pluralism. As Michael Hogue avows, religious naturalism has much to commend in an age of both environmental peril and ever-increasing plurality, since it is consonant with "expressions of faith and piety organized around commitments to valuing and respecting nature" and is able to cultivate the "interreligious moral solidarities" necessary for adequately responding to globally scaled ethical predicaments (e.g., climate change).[112] Religious naturalist Loyal Rue expects "the day to arrive when religious naturalism will prevail as the most universal and influential religious orientation on the planet."[113] Such a prediction strikes me as unlikely and somewhat triumphalistic. Nonetheless, I do agree with Rue that the presence of religious naturalism is already "noticeable *within the precincts of established religious traditions*," and will become even more so with the passing of time, as supernaturalism is shown to be irrelevant, unpalatable, and out of harmony with reality.[114] Indeed, as Ursula Goodenough assures, religious naturalism provides a way of being religiously and morally oriented within, across, and between the living faiths. Religious naturalism, in Goodenough's telling, anchors the "search for planetary consensus," even as it beckons believers to eventually return to their "religions of origin" and to reflect on and revere the depths and dynamics of nature from within "their own cognitive, experiential, and religious perspectives."[115] She elaborates:

> Once we have our feelings about [and conceptions of] nature in place, then I believe that we can also find important ways to call ourselves Jews, or Muslims, or Taoists, or Hopi, or Hindus, or Christians, or Buddhists. Or some of each. The words in the traditional texts may sound different to us than they did to their authors, but they continue to resonate with our religious selves.[116]

Pragmatic historicism's dynamic, antiessentialist, and developmental conception of tradition (see the next chapter) indeed allows the religions to be reconstructed naturalistically; and, fortunately, a host of thinkers have shown that the existing historical religions are, in fact, reinterpretable along naturalist lines.[117] Wesley Wildman points out that the religions of the world "encode much wisdom about sacred nature."[118] Donald Crosby agrees, arguing that most faiths possess "underlying motifs of fascination and awe directed at nature as the context within which the powers of the sacred or divine operate and manifest themselves," and some traditions share deep resonances with religious naturalism (e.g., Daoism, Shintoism, and Native American religions).[119] However, whereas Crosby draws on these motifs and resonances to develop ideas, evocations, precepts, and so on, appropriate to a *new* religion of nature, Wildman insists that religious naturalism is already "widely woven into the tapestry that is religion on planet Earth," especially in its more mystical and intellectual subtraditions. Thus, rather than viewing religious naturalism as a novel movement, Wildman underscores its venerable theological and philosophical pedigree. He prefers to dwell with the mystics and the iconoclasts on the "undersides" of the historic religions, pushing back against and demythologizing the supernatural legends and myths that have hardened into literal metaphysical descriptions and searching for traces of the "Whence of religious naturalism," the "abysmal and creative depths of nature" (e.g., the West's "God Beyond God" and the "Daodejing's conception of a deeply patterned dynamical structure in reality").[120]

On this score, pragmatic historicists are closer to Wildman than Crosby. Kaufman, for example, sees religious naturalism (as well as the ecological ethics it demands) as a call to reform—and bring together—the religions we already have.[121] After all, in a pragmatic historicist paradigm, humans are irrevocably traditioned and historically situated beings, which is why the most effective and enduring innovations (e.g., religious naturalism) are *re*constructions of dominant (though not necessarily singular) historic inheritances and their symbolic landscapes and affective repositories of ritual practice.[122] Religious naturalism, as Crosby admits, has "no practicing communities, no institutional structures, no duly constituted cadre of leaders, no body of traditional beliefs, no rituals or ceremonies, no revered founders or scriptures, no stories, myths, and symbols," making it religiously and culturally impotent in, of, and by itself.[123] However, as a common theological and ethical orientation within, across, and between the religions, religious naturalism might empower the traditions to recover and reformulate aspects of their heritages that respect and honor the powers and numinous mysteries of nature and to come together around a mutual concern for our endangered planet and its inhabitants. Perhaps humanity will witness the *emergence* (yes, in the Kaufmanian sense) of new religions of nature (note the plural) in due course.[124] But, in my view, they can only emerge out of creative interactions between and innovative reconfigurations of the existing historical traditions, as adherents of the different religions unite around a common reverence for nature and seek to reconstruct their inherited beliefs, myths, pieties, rituals, spiritualties, and ethical practices in markedly naturalistic and ecocentric ways.

The Second Pillar: (Radical) Empiricism

In addition to being metaphysical and religious naturalists, a few of the pragmatic historicists featured in this book (most notably, James, Dewey, Dean, and Brown) are *radical empiricists*. In chapter 2, I mentioned that radical empiricism endeavors to overcome every form of dualism and to register all that enters experience (i.e., not only the five senses, but also aesthetic and religious affections, felt penumbra and adumbrations, the perception of causal efficaciousness, etc.). According to Dean, one of the more intractable dualistic gaps radical empiricists close is the so-called fact-value distinction, seeking to empirically describe a relationally and valuationally rich natural environment. In contradistinction to the relativistic, subjectivistic, methodologistic, textualist, and linguisticistic historicisms of contemporary postmodernists (e.g., Rorty), the "classical American historicists" (i.e., the early pragmatists and the theologians of the Chicago school), on Dean's reading, adopted a "fuller"—a radically empirical—historicism, adamant that "history is important not only as the stage and judge of facts, but of relations, qualities, and values as well."[125] Dewey testified that "esthetic and moral traits," far from reducing to "groundless whims" or "arbitrary preference," are "realistic," "objective," and "natural," signifying "something that belongs to nature as truly as does the mechanical structure attributed to it in physical science. . . . They are *found*, experienced."[126] Similarly, James claimed that "affective phenomena" and the "appreciative attributes" of objects ("their dangerousness, beauty, rarity, utility, etc.") are objectively, physically, and empirically given, producing "visceral" and "immediate bodily effects upon us."[127] For James and for the entire radical empiricist lineage, the world comes to us with a certain directedness, with a value-laden (and sometimes resistant) thrust and tendency.[128] As Brown summarizes: "What is inherited are not innocent, indifferent buzzes; they are forces, values that incline us, influence us, move us. Like strong winds they bend us in particular directions."[129] In short, radical empiricists hypothesize that the relational, qualitative, and valuational facets of reality are, in some sense, resident and ingredient in, and not simply imposed and projected on, the world.[130] To again quote Dewey: "The live animal does not have to project emotions into the objects experienced. Nature is kind and hateful, bland and morose, irritating and comforting, long before she is mathematically qualified."[131]

A radical empiricist axiology, I submit, is capable of undergirding Knitter's call for "global, coordinated action based on commonly recognized truths or values."[132] To be sure, historicists like Davaney cringe at the suggestion that "history yields criteria,"[133] pointing out that the "deeper context of value" to which radical empiricists refer is, at best, dimly and vaguely experienced and, thus, unable to provide "clear or usable norms." Besides, the historical world is the progenitor of *all* values, "including conflicting ones," which leaves the problem of adjudication unsolved (a dilemma that also dogged Troeltsch).[134] Complicating matters further, in a pragmatic historicist outlook, moral obligations, human rights, and so on, are, as Rorty asserts, social constructions. They do not have "a source . . . different from tradition, habit and custom."[135]

These are legitimate—but allayable—concerns. To begin with, radical empiricists themselves recognize that history is the bearer of *all* values, including conflicting and even negative ones.[136] James emotes that there is "something really wild in the universe which we, with all our idealities and faithfulness, are needed to redeem,"[137] Dewey acknowledges that "there exists a *mixture* of good and evil,"[138] Crosby (a contemporary proponent of radical empiricism) contends that nature is pregnant with "disvalues" as well as values,[139] and Bernard Loomer (an empirical theologian of the later Chicago school) insists that life is metaphysically and valuationally "ambiguous."[140]

Radical empiricists also realize that morality, ethical convictions, and the like are social constructions. As Crosby explains: "Nature provides a context for moral deliberation and the construction of moral principles, but it does not give us those principles. As free beings with the gifts of language, reason, and reflective experience, we must develop those principles on our own and in light of our shared historical experiences."[141]

But Crosby persists that values are not *merely* constructed. Radical empiricism adopts an *interactionist or constructive realist* axiology,[142] according to which value is fashioned out of the interactions between creaturely evaluators and the real valuative features of nature. Crosby surmises that values are neither purely subjective nor purely objective, neither merely invented nor strictly antecedent, but are emergent from the relations between the interpretations, decisions, responses, and discriminations of valuers (human as well as nonhuman) and the axiological possibilities of the natural order.[143] As Dewey very similarly resolved, values (whether aesthetic, ethical, or religious) are not created "*de novo*" or "attributed exclusively to the human subject," but are generated from the collaborations between creature and environment, between "criticism" and the "immediate" and "intrinsic qualities of things," which "are what they are." In other words, "critical judgment" and "intelligence" must "clarify, liberate and extend" the "causal goods" that ontologically inhere in nature, working to "bring them to consciousness," to "criticize," "valuate," and "recreate" them, and to (pragmatically) determine which among them "will do more in the way of security, liberation and fecundity for other likings and values."[144]

And yet, even if the determination of value is partly (maybe mostly) a constructive, interpretive effort, even if reality is shot through with ambiguity, even if history does not quite yield "criteria" or "clear norms" (a Deanian overstatement, in my estimation), even if "explaining where . . . values come from" is not the same as "giving a justification" for them, and even if, as I will argue in a moment, evaluation is ultimately a human, fallible, and pragmatic process,[145] radical empiricism stipulates that decisions about what is or is not religiously or ethically valuable (e.g., the eradication of eco-human suffering) are not as arbitrary, relative, subjective, local, or incommensurable as some historicists and postmodernists—including many particularist theologians—seem to imply.[146] Undoubtedly, the measures religious communities deploy to arbitrate good and evil, justice and injustice, are, as Heim correctly declares, never neutral and always perspectival, particular, and enmeshed in diverse "textures of belief, narrative, and ritual."[147] Even so, radical empiricism accounts for the ways in which the ethical imagination, while historically contextualized, conditioned, and constituted, nevertheless seizes upon an empirically real (albeit morally ambiguous) field of axiological potentialities. Perhaps when Knitter entreats the religions to express collective moral outrage over air pollution, over social injustice, over preventable death, over economic exploitation, over sectarian violence,[148] he is not simply inflicting his own Western, liberal, Christian standards on the religious other, but is responding to values—or, more exactly, disvalues—that are, to some extent, inherent in the world. As James would put it, "The man is really hateful; the action really mean; the situation really tragic—all in themselves and quite apart from our opinion."[149]

The Third Pillar: (Criteriological) Pragmatism

Of course, in order to bring evaluative judgments to bear on "the buzzing, blooming confusion" (James) of the world's axiological milieu, some sort of methodology and criteriology is required.[150] And for James and Dewey, for Case, Foster, Mathews, and Smith, and for Brown, Davaney, Dean, Kaufman, and McFague, that method and criterion is *pragmatism*. Pragmatism purports (1) that knowledge is one of the many *instruments* or *tools* devised and utilized by *Homo sapiens* to adapt to and cope with specific environmental circumstances and (2) that the formal norm for adjudicating disputes is *functional* and *prospective*, determined by ascertaining which beliefs bring about "more satisfactory historical consequences."[151] Dewey sums it up well:

> *If* ideas, meanings, conceptions, notions, theories, systems are instrumental to an active reorganization of the given environment, to a removal of some specific trouble and perplexity, then the

test of their validity and value lies in accomplishing this work. If they succeed in their office, they are reliable, sound, valid, good, true. If they fail to clear up confusion, to eliminate defects, if they increase confusion, uncertainty and evil when they are acted upon, then they are false. Confirmation, corroboration, verification lie in works, consequences. Handsome is that handsome does. By their fruits shall ye *know* them.¹⁵²

I will devote a fair amount of time to elucidating (and problematizing) historicism's relationship to and employment of the pragmatist tradition in chapter 6. For now, I simply wish to recommend that pragmatism become the final pillar for the ethical bridge, serving as the criteriological gauge for evaluating interreligious praxis and dialogue. The particularists are right: there is no transhistorical moral law or absolute, no uniform benchmark of justice to which the religions have access, no unanimously agreed-upon panacea to the world's ills, and no global *soteria* toward which each tradition is moving. Regardless, Davaney opines that people of different faiths can—and should—pose a whole gamut of *pragmatic* questions to each other:

> What are the repercussions of thinking, acting, organizing life in one way or another? What kinds of life are made possible by living out one vision of reality rather than another? Who benefits from one set of practices or way of organizing our social lives and institutions? What is historically inhibited and what is nurtured and supported? How does one set of beliefs or practices cohere with another, and what are the ramifications of such cohesion or dissonance? On the most basic levels, what persons, values, and possibilities get to survive and flourish, and who dies, what possibilities are lost, and which values disappear?¹⁵³

Needless to say, since religions tend to invoke *internal* norms when distinguishing truth from falsehood, right from wrong, quarrels about what counts as a pragmatically favorable, beneficial, and preferable outcome are liable to ensue.¹⁵⁴ As Dean fairly inquires: "What . . . is the criterion for . . . pragmatic or functional tests? . . . On what grounds [is] something . . . declared valuable in [one's] own history or in any history?"¹⁵⁵ At this juncture, it would behoove ethical pluralists to turn once again to Kaufman. On Kaufman's account, even though there are no universal criteria for resolving disagreements, there are at least two "quasi-universal" criteria that make cross-cultural and interreligious judgments possible, namely, *humanization* (traditionally referred to as "salvation") and *historicity*.

First, precisely because religious believing is—always and everywhere—a humanly constructed and historically situated activity, all the religions ought to be appraised in terms of the *human* needs they fulfill and the *historical* lifeways they elicit. Do our practices and programs bode well for our children and our children's children? What are the repercussions of our doctrines for the common good? Which elements of our traditions are, in a word, humanizing,[156] contributing to the establishment of a "humane order in this world" (as opposed to distracting us with supernaturalistic assurances about the next life), instilling a sense of collective responsibility for "humanity-as-a-whole" (as opposed to confining us to our parochial communities), and portending a sustainable tomorrow for the earth and its human and nonhuman residents (as opposed to ushering in a nuclear or environmental apocalypse)?

Second, Kaufman avers that a biohistorical understanding of the human has *normative* implications for assessing the faiths. Our modern knowledge of "the increasing development of well-ordered freedom in individuals and societies," coupled with the realization that all our traditions are the products of we "culture-creating" and "in some respects self-determining beings," empowers *us* to take ownership of and accountability for our institutions, ideas, and actions and the wider biological and cosmic networks to which they belong. More than ever before, ecological volatility, globalization, growing interdependence, religious extremism and terrorism, and the ever-looming menace of nuclear annihilation have made us all painfully aware that the decisions humans make today impact the globe and the species as a whole, not just shaping future generations but even determining whether there will be any future generations. And it is "our awareness of our historicity and its significance" that might compel us to assume much greater responsibility for our religions, our neighbors, and our planet.[157]

Chapter 5

Beyond Amnesia and Nostalgia

Pragmatic Historicism and the Authority of the Past

The previous two chapters contended that the historicizing of the religions significantly weakens their claims to superiority and absoluteness, unsurpassability and comprehensiveness, incommensurability and self-sufficiency. The present chapter will show that it also undercuts their belief in a supernaturally revealed, stable, and authoritative tradition.

A pragmatic historicist theory of tradition—which, again, takes its rise from Ernst Troeltsch and the *religionsgeschichtliche Schule* as well as from the early Chicago school of theology—avoids both amnesia and nostalgia, simultaneously accounting for the ineradicable traditionedness of human existence and for the utter humanness of religious traditions. What is more, pragmatic historicism explains—as well as invites—theological change and innovation. Its historically conscious but thoroughly antisupernaturalist, antiessentialist, and antiauthoritarian understanding of the religious past reveals that the lineages we inherit are formative yet fallible, dynamic, diverse, contestable, and in need of ongoing revision. Our historic faiths have always been, and ever ought to be, interrogated and interpreted afresh, in light of the best available knowledge, in conversation with culture, and in response to contemporary problems and the incessantly shifting currents of history.

Give the Historical Method an Inch and It Will Take a Mile: The Historicizing, Humanizing, and Desupernaturalizing of Religious Traditions

I indicated in chapter 2 that historicism arose in the German *Aufklärung* as a response to the Enlightenment abandonment of history and tradition and, from the outset, fervently maintained that human beings are, in the words of Delwin Brown, "inescapably traditioned and traditional beings."[1] In point of fact, whatever else historicism is, it is the conviction that women and men always live in and out of the various heritages bequeathed to them by prior generations. As Sheila Greeve Davaney remarks: "Language, culture, interpretations of reality, practices, institutions, and so forth do not spring *de novo*, or from nothing. . . . Any particular moment is always in some way the reworking, repetition, transformation, or creative departure from what has come before."[2]

However, while placing renewed emphasis on the *traditionedness* of human life, historicists since the late nineteenth and early twentieth centuries have also contributed to the broad-based modernist assault on *traditionalist* construals of the religious past, especially in the form of critical historiography and biblical criticism. Precisely as the importance of origins and historicity was rehabilitated by historicism, misgivings about the religions' historical authenticity, revelatory status, and (as I will expound later) unquestionable authority were voiced with greater regularity and rigor.[3] In short, historicists in both Europe and the United States went to painstaking lengths to wholly historicize, humanize, and desupernaturalize our faith traditions and their founding documents, figures, and events. Our religions have—indeed *are*—histories, emerging in particular times, places, and cultures and undergoing ceaseless alteration through complex processes of historical development.

In Germany, historicism and modern historical consciousness in general found expression above all in the burgeoning scholarly discipline of history (for instance, in the German historiographic tradition represented by Wilhelm von Humboldt, Leopold von Ranke, Johann Gustav Droysen, and Friedrich Meinecke, among others).[4] "Underlying this new science," states the religious studies scholar Van Harvey, "was an almost Promethean will-to-truth. The aim of the historian, it was declared, was to 'tell what really happened.' The magic noun was 'fact,' and the honorific adjective was 'scientific.' Description, impartiality, and objectivity were the ideals."[5] Harvey goes on to describe how efforts to investigate the origins of Christianity critically and historically conflicted with the "supernaturalistic metaphysics" of traditional Christian theology:

> If the theologian regards the Scriptures as supernaturally inspired, the historian must assume that the Bible is intelligible only in terms of its historical context and is subject to the same principles of interpretation and criticism that are applied to other

ancient literature. If the theologian believes that the events of the Bible are the results of the supernatural intervention of God, the historian regards such an explanation as a hindrance to true historical understanding. If the theologian believes that the events upon which Christendom rests are unique, the historian assumes that those events, like all events, are analogous to those in the present.[6]

Perhaps no German historicist wrestled more indefatigably, aggressively, and candidly with the radical and unsettling repercussions of critical historiography, and biblical criticism in particular, than Ernst Troeltsch. "Give the historical method an inch and it will take a mile," he cautioned. "Like the modern natural sciences, it represents a complete revolution in our patterns of thought vis-à-vis antiquity and the Middle Ages." And when applied to the study of the Bible and church history, it "acts as a leaven, transforming everything and ultimately exploding the very form of earlier theological methods."[7]

The "earlier theological methods" to which Troeltsch was referring included the "dogmatic" ones employed by prominent Ritschlian theologians of the day. Of course, while at the University of Göttingen, Troeltsch came under the influence of Albrecht Ritschl's neo-Kantian historicism, which regarded religious knowledge and theology as postulates of moral rather than metaphysical or scientific reason (i.e., as value judgments about the way things should be as opposed to descriptions of the way things are or appeared to be) and refashioned Christianity as a historical—i.e., a this-worldly, outward-moving, socio-ethical, kingdom-building—movement. But Troeltsch, as I pointed out in chapter 3, really belonged to a mostly younger group of renegade Ritschlians, the *religionsgeschichtliche Schule*. According to Gary Dorrien, this Göttingen-based, academy-centered, post-Ritschlian, history-of-religions offshoot, whose ranks numbered not only Troeltsch but also Hermann Gunkel, Wilhelm Bousset, Wilhelm Wrede, Alfred Rahlfs, Johannes Weiss, and, a little later, Rudolf Otto, Ulrich von Wilamowitz-Moellendorff, and Albrecht Dieterich, alleged that the Christian dogmatism and absolutism of Ritschl and the church-oriented Ritschlians (most notably, Adolf von Harnack and Wilhelm Herrmann) ultimately "compromised the critical spirit of historical criticism."[8]

Troeltsch, for his part, rebuked the Ritschlian School for seeking to bypass the results of historiographical methodologies. Foreshadowing the Barthians and neo-orthodox thinkers of the early and mid-twentieth century,

Julius Kaftan, Friedrich Niebergall, and other Ritschlians took "the doctrine of a supernaturalistic authority" for granted. They deferred to dogmatically established truths that are not "analogous to other happenings," but are "safeguarded . . . by a miraculous transmission," "sealed by an inward testimony in the heart," "authenticated by their supernatural mode of revelation," and "apprehended by faith." They laid claim to "the 'historical' character of Christianity," as all historicists do. However, the "history" to which they appealed "is not the ordinary, secular history reconstructed by critical historiography" (*Historie*), but "a history of salvation (*Heilsgeschichte*), a nexus of saving facts, which, as such are knowable and provable only for the believer." At best, this, rejoined Troeltsch, amounted to a quasi-historicism, to a set of bad (i.e., "essentially non-historical") immunizing strategies that, in effect, placed Christianity beyond "the flux, the conditioning, and the mutability of history" and, thus, beyond the reach of historical inquiry.[9]

Refusing to elevate anything above the relativities, vicissitudes, and conditions of history or to protect any text, person, institution, or heritage from the probabilistic and uncertain findings of critical historiography ("the habituation on principle to historical criticism"), Troeltsch was more than willing to subject "the Judaeo-Christian tradition to all the consequences of a purely historical method," however devastating.[10] Dorrien comments that if Ritschlian theology "started with Christianity," then "the post-Ritschlian historicists started with religion, of which Christianity is one among others." Put somewhat differently, the Troeltschian starting point was "the real world of empirical and historical experience," of which every religion, without exception, was a product.[11]

For Troeltsch, investigating the Judeo-Christian lineage critically, scientifically, and historically (i.e., with the tools and criteria of historiographical analysis instead of the parochial norms of a particular religious community) involves, first and foremost, locating it within the interconnected matrix of historical relations and influences ("correlation") and situating its emergence and evolution within the larger history of religion and culture (the *religionsgeschichtliche Methode*). The beginnings of Israelite religion, for example, must be elucidated in relation to both "the religions of other Semitic peoples" and "the general conditions prevailing in Western Asia." Similarly, "the rise of Christianity" must be "related to the disintegration of Judaism" and "to the political movements and the apocalyptic ideas of the time," and the establishment of the primitive church must be studied in light of its interactions "with the surrounding world of the Roman empire."[12] In brief, the Christian faith must not be treated as isolated or unique. Rather, it too "must be regarded as an entity to be explained and evaluated in relation to the total context of which it forms a part."[13]

Troeltsch also highlighted the indispensability of analogical thinking for historical knowledge. Though singular and distinctive, occasions in history exhibit a certain similarity, consistency, and homogeneity across time and space, which permits historians to make informed judgments about other periods and cultures. To quote Troeltsch:

> The illusions, distortions, deceptions, myths, and partisanships we see with our own eyes enable us to recognize similar features in the materials of tradition. Agreement with normal, customary, or at least frequently attested happenings and conditions as we have experienced them is the criterion of probability for all events that historical criticism can recognize as having actually or possibly happened.[14]

In other words, we are able to determine what may or may not have taken place within a range of possibilities, since what is recognized as true and plausible from the perspective of our present experience and ken bears some analogy with the past.

For example, if "Jewish and Christian history" is "analogous to all other history"—that is, if our modern scientific sense of what is and what is not historically possible provides a standard for "imputing probability" to occurrences recounted in scripture, and if scholars are able to compare the literature of the Bible with comparable and contemporaneous "vestiges of antiquity"—then its accounts about Christ's miracles more likely belong to the genre of mythology than literal historical fact, since (1) a miracle contradicts science's well-established understandings of the normal mechanisms of nature and (2) ancient religious texts are replete with miracle stories.[15] As Harvey, commenting on the criterion of analogy, explains, "a *prima facie* case exists" for miraculous reports *not* being historically probable, because such phenomena are incompatible with the known laws of physics and biology, and because "the comparative study of religion" (which, again, is the bread and butter the history-of-religions approach) discloses that "myth and legend are the almost natural forms of expression for the veneration of extraordinary founders, teachers, and saints of religion."[16] To Troeltsch, to exempt, say, the resurrection, Jesus's moral character, or any of Christianity's originating occurrences from "the exigencies of the analogical principle" smacked of arbitrariness, protectionism, and special pleading.[17]

Troeltsch, in a nutshell, judged that "the spirit of historical criticism, analogy, and relativity" virtually "destroyed" the dogmatic assumption that the Christian religion is somehow exceptional, superior, or supernatural—i.e., founded on "a special revelation" or on anything "outside of and contrary to history."[18] As he remarked elsewhere, "It is . . . evident that Christianity in every age, *and particularly in its period of origin*, is a genuinely historical phenomenon—new, by and large, in its consequences, but profoundly and radically conditioned by the historical situation and environment in which it found itself as well as by the relations it entered into in its further development."[19]

Troeltsch's impact was felt on the other side of the Atlantic, particularly by the Chicago-school historicists.[20] On the whole, the *religionsgeschichtliche* and Chicago schoolers shared a decidedly post-Ritschlian orientation. Reminiscent of Troeltsch, Shailer Mathews and George Burman Foster, says Dorrien, began as proponents of "Ritschlian historicism" and "left-Ritschlian personalism," respectively, but eventually endeavored to move liberal theology away from "a gospel-centered Ritschlianism" and towards a "modernist-centered naturalistic empiricism."[21] Foster, though, was directly influenced by Troeltsch, Bousset, and the other history of religionists,[22] upbraiding "the orthodox-apologetic isolation of Christianity over against the rest of historical reality."[23] In fact, his 1906 book, *The Finality of the Christian Religion*, owes its title, in part, to the Troeltschian "recognition of the historicalness and consequent relativity of Christianity."[24] Foster elaborated:

> The religio-historical method employed by the science of comparative religion, puts, *a priori*, Christianity on a stage with other religions and strips it of its character as a unique religion. It investigates, for example, the kinship between any given Christian phenomenon and the parallel phenomenon in other religions, and determines what "moments" Christianity has borrowed from other religions. Formerly, the finality of the Christian religion was based upon its isolatedness and singularity. But, from the point of view of comparative religion, the very fact that Christianity is a historical religion involves its relationship and interaction with other religions, as against its supposed isolatedness; and the fact that it has drawn thoughts and ideas and values from other religions raises doubt as to its supposed singularity.[25]

In addition, Foster utilized analogical reasoning to bring to light the mythological and legendary—that is, unhistorical—quality of the Bible's miraculous narratives. "Authority-religion" tries to prove the revelatory origins of Christianity by citing the "evidential value" of the virgin birth and the resurrection of Christ, for example. Without using the term, Foster retorted by invoking the principle of analogy (and, more explicitly, the rationalist criticism of thinkers like Spinoza and Hume). Simply and succinctly but sharply stated, "Today we witness no miracles." The supernatural happenings and wondrous occurrences recounted in the scriptures frequently express profound *poetic* truths, Foster allowed. Be that as it may, accepting miracle stories as "actual facts" is an affront to "science," "common-sense," "intellectual honesty," and even "true faith," for such events deviate from "everything we know" about "the relations and laws of nature"—that is, from "the scientific understanding of the world."[26]

Shirley Jackson Case, too, was familiar with and sympathetic to the *religionsgeschichtliche Schule*:[27]

> The representatives of the so-called religio-historical school . . . affirmed not only the varied content of early Christianity's ideas and practices, but declared that many of its features were by no means original to the new religion. It was not so alarming to be told that much had been taken over from the later Judaism of the post-Biblical era, but when Babylonia, Egypt, and the Hellenistic environment were alleged to have been the original home of certain notions and rites that once we had thought distinctive of Christianity, the problem of defining the nature of our religion and justifying our confidence in its worth became still more difficult.[28]

As a matter of fact, Case's sociohistoricism and the history-of-religions approach performed essentially the same methodological function, helping historians realize that the Christian movement, from New Testament times onward, was formed, even funded, by the Jewish and Greco-Roman milieu in which it evolved.[29]

That sobering, and perhaps unnerving, realization was the thesis of Case's 1914 work, *The Evolution of Early Christianity*, which, according to William Hynes, was "the first example of the socio-historical method in nearly full form."[30] Dorrien comments that, in Case's estimation, all religions, including Christianity, are "social and historical without remainder."[31] As a result, comprehending the genesis (and success) of the primitive Christian church, as well as the literature it produced (e.g., the New Testament), requires attaining a thorough knowledge of the society from which it arose, in which it took shape, and to which it was genetically linked.[32] In other words, students of Christian beginnings must undertake "a careful study of the vital forces dominating the first believers' immediate environment," mainly because Christianity was generated in and by that environment. On this score, Case sounded a lot like Troeltsch:

> An interpretation of religion, whether Christian or non-Christian, which does not proceed from a close examination of, and a sympathetic touch with, the total surroundings in which its adherents lived cannot be truly historical in the fullest sense of that term.[33]

Most Christians mistakenly presume that the religion is "supernaturally given," as if "human experience and historical circumstances contribute nothing to its making." But Case, as Dorrien observes, "was a straightforward sociohistoricist who insisted that history is the golden key to unlocking whatever is worth knowing about religion."[34] For him, Christianity is "an affair of real life," and has been so "from the outset." The movement did not "start out full grown," appear "*de novo*," or come into being simply as a result of its own independent and internal (much less revelatory) resources, but was "stimulated," "nourished," and "influenced" by a host of environmental factors—cultural, political, economic, and religious. To be specific, it "was rocked in a Jewish cradle and . . . grew to maturity in a gentile home." Without a doubt, Christianity, Case allowed, "may be called original" inasmuch as it reacted to its "several worlds of reality" with a modicum of creativity and vitality. But it is also "derived" insofar as it emerged out of its historically particular and constantly changing "social relationships," out of its ongoing adjustment to "new situations" and "the religious language and thought-forms of the age." First-century Christianity is "Mediterranean," not "other-worldly," in origin, Case noticed, germinating from the soil of Second Temple Diaspora Judaism and, over time, incorporating ideas and practices from Greek philosophy and pagan traditions, imperial and mystery cults, and Hellenistic religions of redemption.[35] Its spatiotemporal, sociohistorical context provided the "stimuli" of its "richest spiritual developments" and indeed the very "materials" out of which its most revered theological teachings were constructed:[36]

> Since its advocates lived in a world already full of competing religions, since they were in close contact with other faiths and

even contended with them for territory already occupied, since many aspects of developing Christianity were determined under the pressure of these conditions, and since the membership of Christian communities was drawn largely from other communions, the importance of consulting the religious situation in the contemporary Graeco-Roman world is self-evident.[37]

Later, Case argued that supernaturalism, far from a distinctive trait of early Christianity, was a product of its historical locale:

The sky hung low in the ancient world. Traffic was heavy on the highway between heaven and earth. Gods and spirits thickly populated the upper air, where they stood in readiness to intervene at any moment in the affairs of mortals. And demonic powers, emerging from the lower world or resident in the remote corners of the earth, were a constant menace to human welfare. All nature was alive—alive with supernatural forces.[38]

In fact, virtually every aspect of Christianity's supernaturalistic "veneer" had Jewish or gentile analogues. To mention the most striking—and perhaps disconcerting—example, Mediterranean civilization abounded with savior figures, heroic individuals, divine mediators, and miraculous healers. There were other human beings of great stature (e.g., Hippocrates, Homer, Plato, Pythagoras, Alexander the Great, Romulus) and epic heroes (e.g., Achilles, Agamemnon, Hector, Hercules) who were revered and honored, even worshipped and deified. Many demigods (e.g., Asklepios) were accorded healing powers and credited with a godly ancestry and a supernatural birth. Roman emperors like Augustus were often deemed saviors, gods, and sons of god. A plethora of deities, from the Greek Dionysus, to the Syrian Adonis, to the Egyptian Osiris, were said to have been resurrected and exalted into a heavenly realm. In Persia, Mithra celebrated a last supper (subsequently commemorated by disciples) and promised to return to earth to raise the departed and destroy the forces of evil. Accordingly, to the Greco-Roman culture whose conversion the first Christians sought, the affirmation of Jesus as the only Son of God, who entered history through the womb of a virgin, marveled crowds with wisdom and wonders, cured the sick, attracted followers, promised immortality, celebrated a final meal, rose from the grave, ascended into heaven, and vowed to come again to judge the living and the dead, would have been neither unfamiliar nor unprecedented.[39]

In a word, Christianity's supernaturalist worldview surfaced for wholly historical, contingent, and provisional reasons, namely, "to serve a functional need in the course of the new religion's expansion within its particular environment and in relation to the characteristic modes of thinking prevalent in that day."[40] Christianity became the "prevailing faith" of the Roman Empire, not by rejecting supernaturalism, but by co-opting, transforming, supplementing, and intensifying the otherworldly beliefs, rites, and motifs of both its Jewish ancestors and its pagan rivals and demonstrating that its "supernatural credentials" surpassed everyone else's. In particular, Christian missionaries proclaimed that the Lord Jesus Christ was the "superior supernatural being," who alone offered "protection from the machinations of evil spirits," restored heath to the infirm, brought "the dead to life," and released "the spirit from its bodily imprisonment," thereby convincing potential converts of Christianity's supremacy.[41]

Of course, such a proclamation, rather than factually portraying "the real Jesus of history," stemmed from the interpretive imagination of the early Christians. Case resolved that "neither the prestige of canonicity nor the hypothesis of apostolic authorship" ensures the accuracy of any ancient depiction of Jesus, mainly because the Christs of the New Testament (and *all* the christological formulations, creeds, and dogmas of the primitive church) do not represent "any reality beyond the sincere efforts of Jesus' ancient admirers to phrase their estimates of him in imagery and categories conformable with their social and cultural interests."[42] Or as he more cynically put it five years later, "Whatever one imagines the ideal Christian to be in one's own area of experience and activity, it is thought natural and proper to make Jesus the supreme example of that person." There are "serious discrepancies," then, "between the idealized Jesus portrayed in the history of Christianity and the actual Jesus of Palestine who lived and died in that remote part of the world hundreds of years ago."[43] As for "the actual Jesus," the first-century, flesh-and-blood Jew from Galilee, Case concluded that he, too, was fully, indeed only, human and decisively affected by the contingencies, conditions, and colorations of his time and place. "He was connected with a past which played its part in the process of his development, he was surrounded by definite historical circumstances, and he had his own personal inclinations, his own characteristics, his own intellectual life and his own spiritual experiences."[44] Therefore, historians are able to tentatively construct a "biography of Jesus" only by critically and painstakingly sifting through the extant sources (canonical and noncanonical) and separating data that are consonant with *his* historical context and socioreligious world from those that reflect the theological assumptions, concerns, problems, and agendas of the earliest Christian communities:[45]

> Every statement in the records is to be judged by the degree of its suitableness to the distinctive environment of Jesus, on the one hand, and to that of the framers of gospel tradition at one or another stage in the history of Christianity, on the other. When consistently applied, this test will prove our safest guide in recovering from the present gospel records dependable information regarding the life and teaching of the earthly Jesus.[46]

Thus, Case (emblematic of the early Chicago school in general) completely humanized and historicized every element of the Christian past—the Bible, the supernatural doctrines of the early church, and the historical Jesus and the Christs of faith. Gone, for Case, is any "sphere of alleged revelation lying outside the realm of specifically human history."[47] The writers of scripture and progenitors of the religions (ours and everyone else's) were fallible human beings. They were influenced by "local circumstances" and "the time and place and conditions under which they lived"; they were driven by "personal likes and dislikes," "the allurements of a vivid imagination," and "zeal for a favorite cause"; they were shaped by a specific language and culture and a particular set of purposes; and they were bound by "every other weakness or limitation to which human flesh is heir," such as the "lack of knowledge," inadequate "opportunities for assembling correct information," and a "sincere or perverse desire to shape the thinking of posterity." And precisely for that reason, religious traditions reflect all the limits of their human creators—for example, partial, derivative, socially conditioned, and interest-laden points of view, historically unreliable sources and inaccurate or incredulous depictions of events, factual mistakes and theological misjudgments, and so on.[48]

In sum, according to Case, Troeltsch, and all the pragmatic historicists featured in this project, our religious inheritances are exactly that—ours. Our spiritual forebears—including the authors of sacred writ and even the architects of the world's religions—were human beings, and nothing more. And as human beings, they engaged in the same sorts of constructive and reinterpretive activities, manifested the same proneness to error, shortsightedness, historical exaggeration, and ideological bias, and bore the same characteristics of fallibility and partiality, cultural relativity and social conditionedness, as contemporary people do. Consequently, the past is on a par with the present. Our traditions did not fall from heaven and do not impart truths removed from the particularities, relativities, limitations, contingencies, and natural workings of history.

Givenness, Agency, and the Flux of Historical Process: Why Religions Lack Essences

Nor are our traditions in possession of essences impervious to temporal change and contextual reconstruction. Quite the opposite: they are as adaptive, mutable, porous, and heterogeneous as the histories that made them. Produced in and by particular historical environments, our religious heritages, pragmatic historicism stipulates, evolve with those environments. Their historicity, in other words, is not just a sign of their humanness; it is also a guarantor of their dynamism and a stimulus of their perpetual reconfiguration.

In chapter 1, I defined a historicist ontology (and cosmology) as a kind of process philosophy. To very briefly review, the universe, in a process and historicist outlook, is fluid, dynamic, and on the move, continually developing along time's irreversible, noncircular, ever-advancing arrow.[49] Moreover, pragmatic historicism (again, not unlike certain iterations of Whiteheadianism) understands the processive nature of existence historically, describing how actuality "is grown in a historical chain," with each link both hinging and building on the links that precede it. With most historicists, William Dean maintains that everything that exists is "a construction on— based on and limited by—what is inherited from the past."[50] However, the present "interpreter," in some sense, always "newly perceives" or makes an "imaginative contribution" to that historical inheritance, thereby tweaking and "add[ing] to the reality that once was." Dean thus surmises: "History grows. And any historicism must deal with that fact."[51]

Such a fact is what Brown refers to as historicism's dialectic of *givenness* and *agency*.[52] Brown avers that these principles are "polar" in nature. On the one hand, the myriad particularities in which our lives take shape— our cultural locales; our genetic, biological, and evolutionary legacies; our religious, national, and political affiliations; our material conditions; our linguistic conventions; our natural, ecological, and geographical environments; our social statuses and classifications into systemic hierarchies and power structures, such as race, class, gender, and sexual orientation; our family upbringings; and so on—all place considerable restrictions on, and in part demarcate, what we can think, know, feel, do, see, or be. Yet, on the other hand, we (and, to some extent, all living entities) are *self-determining* beings, possessing the freedom to affect and alter the further development of our particularities, which become, in turn, the given particularities to which later agents (whether us or others) will contribute. We are who we are because of the particular givens we inherit, but we agentially transform our historical inheritances in light of our current situations and in anticipation of ones to come. As Davaney explains, "Human historicity entails being both constituted by our past and context and being agential contributors to new historical realities."[53] Stated otherwise, we are both the objects and subjects of history, the products of our surroundings and the producers, and reproducers, of them. To quote Brown, "We are actors who impact and are impacted by the diverse streams of life within which we find ourselves."[54] Hence, history (human as well as nonhuman) is at once partially given and partially made, partially closed and partially open, partially fated and partially free, partially determined and partially indeterminate (cf. the treatment of "holistic historicism" in chapter 2). For process-oriented historicists, the world is constantly changing, and change is, by and large, historical in character; the present literally creates the not-yet-actualized future out of the contents and within the limits of the past it receives, which itself was created by the recreation of its past, and so on in perpetuity.[55]

Three implications follow from pragmatic historicism's historical processism. First, because history is a dynamic, restless, interrelated, ever-changing process, so is everything *in* history. Ours is simply a world without "essences" that are unchanging and everywhere the same, without timeless, dehistoricized, form-like, universal, transcendentalized, immutable, independent "substances" of which the fleeting objects of history are mere accidents, appearances, properties, qualities, copies.[56] Put differently, historicist dynamists are, to employ Richard Rorty's labels, "antiessentialists" or "panrelationalists," regarding *all* historical phenomena—tables, stars, electrons, human beings, academic disciplines, social institutions, quarks, and even numbers—as "a flux of continually changing relations."[57] Rorty rightly attests that we never quite reach something—some "substantial" essence or "intrinsic" nature—that is not just one more "forever expandable . . . web of relations."[58]

Second, a changing world must be, as I insinuated earlier, a world that is capable of *being changed*, a world open to the interpretive and creative agency of historical creatures. According to John Dewey, existence is "relatively malleable and plastic," able to be shaped "for this end *or* that."[59] For that reason, he (along with most pragmatic historicists) prized the "experimental empiricism" of modern science, which treats reality as both given and "taken." The scientific spirit of experimentalism—which, Dewey pleaded, ought to permeate all areas of social practice and every sphere of inquiry and activity, including philosophy, ethics, aesthetics, and religion—compels people not to submissively acquiesce to what the universe is "experienced as," but to submit everything to critical investigation, "active experimentation," and ongoing revision; to induce "definite changes in the environment"; to "bring nature still further into actual and potential service of human purposes and valuations"; and, through "directed practice" and "overt doing," to facilitate "the construction of a new empirical situation."[60] "We do not merely have to repeat the past, or wait for accidents to force change upon us," assured Dewey. "We *use* our past experiences to construct new and better ones in the future."[61]

Third, to highlight history's dynamism is to gesture toward its bewildering capacity for *novelty* and *emergence*. Indeed, the whole premise of historicism, I have repeatedly insisted, is the claim that things are not created ex nihilo, but in the context of preexistent continuities.[62] Yet history, Davaney, Dean, Kaufman, McFague, Brown, and other pragmatic historicists marvel, is emergent; it is both "conditioned and self-constituting," delineated by certain givens but capable of real newness and increasing complexity.[63] As McFague indicates, the cosmological image emanating from astrophysics, biology, ecology, and the other sciences is not of a deterministic, stagnant, and closed system, but of a cosmos "still in process," where "time is irreversible, genuine novelty results through the interplay of chance and necessity, and the future is open. This is an unfinished universe, a dynamic universe."[64] When the conditions are optimal, history astonishingly crosses "thresholds," constantly giving birth to the "unexpected," the "unprecedented," and the "surprising"—to "unpredictable novelties." Somehow, heretofore nonexisting forms and organizational patterns come to be, displaying properties and potentialities that are absent in, different from, and often more complex than those from which they emerged.[65] In brief, according to Kaufman, "More happens than one would have expected, given previously prevailing circumstances. . . . The new, the novel, the unforeseeable, the previously unheard of, break forth roundabout us and in our midst."[66] Brown makes the same basic point in Whiteheadian terms. Out of the material of their prehensions, "atomic unities" create (albeit often at the level of unrealized possibility) "something more than the sum of the elements synthesized," a novelty,[67] which is then projected "into the subsequent processive flow, into the future as a factor in and influence on" later becomings.[68]

Turning now to the topic at hand, Brown proceeds to suggest that historicism—especially its processive worldview and its historical rendering of reality's unfolding processes—is the theoretical perspective best equipped to account for the dynamic and essenceless quality of religious traditions.[69] Humankind's cultures and religions, I proposed in the final section of chapter 2, are not static, reified essences, but living movements. They have character, to be sure. Nevertheless, they develop over time, display unimaginable richness and diversity of opinion, and overlap with one another in a myriad of interesting, unpredictable, and mutually transformative ways.[70]

But the question is, *why*? According to pragmatic historicists, historicism itself is the answer: religions lack essentialized and pure identities and fixed and homogenous meanings chiefly because they are, everywhere and always, emergent in and created by history. And like everything historical (e.g., stegosauruses, sycamore trees, rocks, the United States, cancer cells, protons, Jupiter, shopkeepers), they are simultaneously given and made, determinative and undetermined, inherited and reinvented, formative and in-process, continuing and changing, conservative and ever-novel. Troeltsch made the point eloquently:

> So long as Christianity is a living religion, people will be constantly quarreling with one another concerning what it is and what it ought to be; and they will constantly seek through new syntheses to meet present conditions and to adapt it to future exigencies. . . . *An unchangeable Christianity never has been and never can be so long as it genuinely belongs to history.* . . . Everywhere the dams that attempted to halt change through eternal, changeless truths are breaking.[71]

Indeed, *all* religious traditions, in a pragmatic historicist paradigm, are circumscribed and molded by the received givens and continuities of particular historical lineages, yet are unremittingly transmuted through the interpretive, experimental, and constructive imagination of human agents and adapted and augmented as a result of the circumstances encountered, the vicissitudes faced, the knowledge acquired, and the relations forged in new and ever-changing contexts.

Brown's own "constructive historicism" tenders one of the most sophisticated, even-handed, and compelling theories of tradition (religious and otherwise) on the contemporary scene. Brown leans heavily on recent post-Geertzian developments in cultural analysis and criticism, and in particular on the "new ethnography" of James Clifford, which question the assumption, widely held by anthropologists since the nineteenth century, that cultures are organically unified wholes or systematic and settled structures of meaning. Clifford and other theorists (e.g., Roy Wagner, Raymond Williams, Marshall Sahlins, and Paul Rabinow) view cultures, instead, as arenas of conflict and struggle, as those fractured and complex processes wherein individual and collective identities are continually "being bartered and bargained for." Cultural spaces bear "sharp mutations, persisting contradictions, radical displacements, and stark breaks," demanding that persons and communities constantly negotiate and re-create character in open-ended dialogue and amid both "order" and "chaos." Stabilities and continuities do emerge but, nevertheless, endure continual contestation, transgression, subversion, amendment, and sublation.[72] As Brown concludes:

> A culture is not a tightly coherent system; its components are diverse, always in some tension with each other, often in stressful opposition. The unity of a culture is light, vulnerable to challenge, always more or less unwieldy, continuously in need of re-formation. Thus a cultural process is not like the growth of a plant; it is like a labor/management dispute. Culture is a continuous negotiation.[73]

If cultures are contests of "varied visions and voices," veritable "debating grounds" and "fertile jungles of sources," then a tradition, as a specific form of cultural activity, is an incessantly "reformed and formative milieu, . . . a dynamic stream of forces in which we live (or die), move (or stagnate), and gain (or lose) our being."[74] Brown adduces that traditions exhibit, at one and the same time, "apparent constancies" and "enormous variety," unfolding through history in an interminable dialectic of "continuity" and "novelty," "limitation" and "ingenuity."

On the one hand, taking a cue from and building on the hermeneutical philosophy of Hans Georg Gadamer, Brown realizes that "to be is to be traditioned." Human beings, in other words, are situated and formed within particular horizons of language and culture. In Gadamer's words: "History does not belong to us; we belong to it. Long before we understand ourselves through the process of self-examination, we understand ourselves in a self-evident way in the family, society, and state in which we live."[75] The pasts we inherit, in one sense, function as an "other," calling the present into question (and indeed into being) and providing the raw material "upon which" and "with which" the future is made. But what Gadamer fails to adequately address, Brown opines, is that men and women are not only "played by" but also "play" tradition, receiving *and revising*, taking in *and improvising on* the inheritances given by preceding generations. Human beings are "recipients" as well as "transformers" and "transmitters" of historical lineages; they claim and challenge, create and construct us, and we them. And for that reason, the traditions in which our lives take shape, Brown insists, change—constantly—even if almost always unintentionally and gradually.

Historical lineages are, for one thing, internally plurivocal. Although certainly not "amenable to any and every adaptation," they harbor a rich and ambiguous "multitude of possibilities," some beneficial and others deleterious. What is more, the boundaries of our habitations are pliant and permeable, undergoing adaptation as a result of interactions (and sometimes clashes) with other heritages and the broader sociopolitical environment. Yet, while provoked from external influences and occasionally involving the adoption and integration of foreign elements, efficacious reformation, most of the time at least, occurs through the recovery of materials—both cognitive repositories of doctrines and argumentations and affective reservoirs of rituals, feelings, and embodied practices—internal to the tradition.[76] Practitioners, put otherwise, generally "recontextualize" heretofore suppressed, forgotten, or buried attitudes, tenets, experiences, and customs and, in turn, pass off that recontextualization as a rediscovery of something ancient and indigenous.[77]

Moreover, the transformation of traditions (both religious and nonreligious) frequently happens through rearrangements within or of *canons*—that is, socially and historically constructed complexes of narratives, myths, practices, dogmas, writings, symbols, associations, rites, affections, evocations, and so forth, which get handed down and amended from generation to generation and give form and shape to a particular heritage. In fact, that is precisely what a tradition *is*, according to Brown; it is a type of cultural negotiation that "takes place within, and with, a canon." A canon is that "diverse and dynamic space within which, through which, and sometimes against which" personal and communal identity is pragmatically brokered and rebrokered. Inhabitants of a tradition live within a canonical locus; they "enter its stories, enact its rituals, play its roles, explore its visions, try its arguments, feel its sensibilities." Such a canon, stipulates Brown, is *bounded*, containing relatively clear (albeit loose) parameters: "It is this collection and not that one. It has these elements and not those."[78] In a word, it has a character. However, its character is *curatorial*. That is to say, it is a "multilith, not a monolith," a "ragged and fractious" assemblage that, while certainly not capable of sustaining all tendencies and permutations, is shorn of an "abiding essence" and is generative of a multiplicity of possible construals and configurations. "A canon is not an answer, a point of view, a truth, a way of life. It is many answers, points of view, claims to truth, ways of life."[79] Even a canon's boundaries are negotiable; they are "not only what we negotiate within, but also what we sometimes negotiate with and about."[80]

With Jacques Derrida and other post-structuralists, Brown is deeply cognizant of the plurality, undecidability, and alterity of interpretation and of the disruptions, heterogeneities, instabilities, cracks, traces, surprises, and hermeneutical surpluses inherent within texts, corpuses, language games, and the like. Still, Brown does not share the deconstructionist suspicion that canonicity automatically entails closure, the illicit attempt to fix and pin down meaning. Although not quite an *endless* or *infinite* play of differences (a Derridean overstatement, in Brown's judgment), a canon is fecund and ever-shifting, a "pluralistic ensemble" of constant renegotiation, debate, and interchange as opposed to a static enclosure with a univocal core, an unassailable orthodoxy, or rigid borders. While providing existential "negotiating spaces" in which "people work out who they are" and even proffering norms for belief and action, canons are always *contestable* and *contemporaneous* rather than closed and antiquarian, requiring ongoing renovation within the morass of concrete life and in relation to other discourses, ideas, and criteria, "both inside and outside their canonical home." And the appropriation of canons is inevitably selective, as each community tentatively decides which resources and themes it will accent and promote and which ones it will subordinate or denounce; "every establishment is at the same time an invitation to disestablishment."[81]

In short, similar to everything in history, traditions (religious as well as other kinds), along with the canons they harbor, are given inheritances *and* sites of agential renovation, identity-shaping pastiches *and* endlessly renegotiated processes. We relate to a tradition much like we relate to life itself—as both "gift" and "task." To indwell a heritage, in other words, is to "contribute to its perpetual doing and undoing—to receive and give, honor and challenge, accept and create, continue and change."[82] As Brown observes in a later article, whether bringing a hitherto marginal component of the canonical repertoire into a sharper focus or a more hermeneutically centralized position, redrawing a tradition's boundaries, or completely metamorphosing one lineage by incorporating and assimilating elements from another, religions, at any particular moment, "are continuing in some respects and changing in others."[83]

Much of what Brown says about the dynamic, ever-changing, reconstructible, and variegated character of traditions was already anticipated by the Chicago-school historicists in the early decades of the twentieth century. In general, Foster, Mathews, Case, and Smith advanced what Dean dubs "an improvisational theory of religious history," contending that institutions, creeds, ceremonies, ideas, and so on, emerge and develop in response to "the mismatch between a community's old theological heritage" and the complexities and problems of the current historical era. Their sociohistorical method revealed that Christians throughout the ages—including the writers of the New Testament and the fathers of the early church—continually and creatively revised (even if often unconsciously) received traditions in congruence with the vicissitudes, resources, understandings, sensibilities, and conundrums of different and shifting cultural environments. Consequently, there are, for the liberal theologians of the early Chicago school, "many Christianities, each relative to its social context, none representative of what might be called an essential meaning of Christianity."[84]

Mathews, to illustrate, discerned that religions are, from top to bottom, developmental. Every time the "felt tensions" between a religious tradition and the broader external environment increases, and old beliefs subsequently become stale, problematized, irrelevant, obsolete, ineffective, outgrown, vestigial, unadapted, or simply unresponsive to the intellectual assumptions, practical needs, and moral concerns of the day, practitioners seek to reconstruct inherited symbols in innovative ways and in fresh "terms and formulas." And because they are continually forced to give reasons for their existence and to acclimate themselves to new spatiotemporal settings and "social minds," religions (e.g., Christianity) are not invulnerable to historical flux and fluctuation.[85]

The same holds true for theological teachings, Mathews assured. *The Atonement and the Social Process* and *The Growth of the Idea of God* demonstrate that the doctrines of redemption and deity, respectively, far from exhibiting monolithic consistency, took on novel, and sometimes competing and contradictory, interpretations through history, recurrently adjusted to confront the specific conditions and quandaries of different times and locations. There is no "correct" theory of the atonement or "right" idea of God, only the staggering multiplicity of efforts to pragmatically decipher the soteriological import of Jesus and the nature of divine reality for each people, period, and place. Whenever circumstances alter, and a concept of salvation or divinity no longer speaks to the realities and mindsets of the moment (thus becoming "a sort of ghost of a previous social order"), the cultural "patterns" in which such notions get couched undergo renovation, expansion, or sometimes even replacement.[86] In short, whether evolving or devolving, progressing or regressing, neither Christian dogmas nor Christianity itself has ever stopped changing.[87]

That, according to Case, is because *nothing* in history is "stable, permanent and unchanging." And insofar as Christianity is historically located and conditioned, "thoroughly at home in a changing world," it has, since its inception, been a "plural," not a "singular," phenomenon, evincing a vast plethora of manifestations, characteristics, and expressions both within and across historical epochs and locales.[88] Case reasoned:

> Christianity is a constantly changing religion. This is true because it is the religion of real people. They have lived at different periods of history, they have resided in many different parts of the world, and they have sought in different environments to work out their own salvation with fear and trembling. . . . In an ever-evolving society they faced a wide range of new problems with each new generation of mankind. In the last analysis Christianity is, always has been and always will be, a way of religious living in a complex and changing world. It ever remains a quest rather than a finished attainment.[89]

Case's classic, *Jesus through the Centuries*, uses christology to demonstrate this very point: images of Christ (e.g., the triumphant martyr, the new messiah, the deified hero, the lord of the cult, the incarnate God, the model pacifist) have differed from age to age and culture to culture, sometimes radically, each shaped by the contextual circumstances from which it arose. Over the last two millennia, Christians have taken enormous interpretive liberties with Jesus, stripping him of "his Palestinian robes" and reclothing him "with garments that were in style among new peoples far removed by time and distance from him and the scenes of his earthly activity." Therefore, the meaning and significance of Jesus's "conduct," "teaching," "personality," and "status in the universe," far from remaining unaltered and univocal, have been constantly reinterpreted in keeping with varied situations, perspectives, crises, and interests and in light of developing knowledge and experience. And frequently, such christological reappraisals were "seriously out of harmony with earlier opinions or with views that Jesus himself had entertained."[90]

The negative upshot of Christianity's historicity and changeability is, Case went on to show, the rejection of any so-called Christian "essence."

To try to mine "one uniformly consistent statement satisfactory to all communities" from among "the variant dogmas" and "divergent creeds" of Christendom is ultimately "doomed to failure," Case portended. Gone is any permanent storehouse of doctrine or "divine deposit of truth preserved unaltered in a fixed corpus of Christian beliefs perpetuated throughout the centuries." One cannot peel away Christianity's historical trappings and "excrescences" in order to extract "a God-given quantum of revelation, original in content, complete at the outset, and historically unconditioned."[91] Even liberalism's different candidates for Christianity's essence—for example, Adolf von Harnack's reduction of the Christian religion to Jesus's ethical teachings about "the fatherhood of God and the brotherhood of man"—are attempts to discover something "undevelopmental" and "immutable" in Christianity, something that holds steady amidst the raging and restless torrents of history. However, there is no "essential nature of Christianity," nor is there a surefire way to "distinguish between essentials and non-essentials." Quite the opposite: "Christianity can be ultimately and comprehensively conceived only in the developmental sense, as the product of actual persons working out their religious problems in immediate contact with their several worlds of reality, the process being renewed in the religious experience of each new generation."[92] Every effort to isolate "the true faith" is abstractive and arbitrary, "making the whole equal to only one of its parts" and neglecting "other features which may have been equally important . . . at certain periods and within particular circles."[93] Still, the fact that the tradition's pluralism and heterogeneity persist despite the various tactics employed to establish and occasionally enforce uniformity (e.g., ecclesial fiat, claims to inerrancy and inspiration, heresy trials, councils, excommunication, pogroms, kernel-and-husk differentiations) intimates that essentializing strategies are not only undesirable but also futile. The question, "What is Christianity?" (the title of Harnack's most famous book[94]), cannot be answered ahead of time, but must be readdressed again and again in each new milieu and with "the free play of fresh creative energy focused upon [the] pressing interests of the hour."[95]

Mathews concurred. What Christianity "is" is always perspectival and fluid, reflecting the idiosyncrasies, frameworks, angles, agendas, and needs of the particular Christian group doing the specifying (e.g., Protestant or Catholic, Eastern or Western, Pauline or Gnostic, Johannine or Markan, liberal or conservative); a generalized, all-encompassing definition is simply unavailable, as is "some alleged theological 'essence.' "[96] As Mathews recalled in a late-career autobiographical essay, "My studies have convinced me that Christianity was the religion of people who called themselves Christian; that is to say, who believed themselves loyal to Jesus Christ, but that there was no static body of truth which was a continuum to be accepted or rejected or modified."[97]

Some years earlier, Foster came to a similar conclusion. Christianity, he alleged, is simply too internally pluriform, too theologically diverse, too institutionally conflictive, too culturally specific, too doctrinally elastic, and too environmentally adaptive to boast any "common denominator," whether a universal norm, changelessly and unvaryingly intact, or some ecclesial authority, "confessionalistic standpoint," or portrait of Jesus, arbitrarily elevated. On the contrary, the ascertainment of Christianity's (or any religion's) putative "essence" is not a passive, objective, impartial, one-time induction of "trivial generalities" or some "fixed and self-identical core," but a socially located, irreducibly multifaceted, spatiotemporally particularized, historically open-ended, and humanly constructed accomplishment:[98]

> Finally, determination of essence is *construction* of essence, since the task is personally conditioned. That is, it is not simply a datum to be received, but a reality to be created ever anew. Hence the significance of the influence of personal subjective presuppositions. But if the conception of Christianity is conditioned by the personal attitude toward it, this personal attitude is conditioned in turn by the age of the world in which one lives, the type of civilization of which one is a member, the stage of culture to which one belongs, and the local and temporal currents or drifts from which one, try hard as one may, cannot hold himself aloof. All in all, therefore, the task is not simply scientific, but moral, and thus belongs to man's larger vocation of forming an ethical personality through pain and struggle, perplexity and sorrow. Once personal, man must be free—free lord of the essence of the Christian religion.[99]

In jettisoning dehistoricized religious essentialisms, Foster not only presaged Mathews and Case but also took a cue from Troeltsch.[100] "If we are to speak of the essence at all," uttered Troeltsch, "it cannot be an unchangeable idea given once for all" or derived from one doctrine or source, be it the Bible, a creed, an ecclesiastical confession, or the life of Jesus. Rather, the essential meaning of Christianity, inasmuch as it has one, must include all the "flexibility and richness"—all the inner tensions and ambiguities, all the historical colorations and mutations, all the offshoots, adaptations, reformations, incongruities, contestations, disagreements, contradictions, and novel developments—that have actually characterized the movement from the get-go. What is more, *Das Wesen des Christentums* is not forever settled and purely given but involves "subjective and creative interpretation and construction:"[101]

> To define the essence is to shape it afresh. It is the elucidation of the essential idea of Christianity in history in the way in which it ought to be a light for the future. . . . The definition of the essence for a given time is the new historical formulation of Christianity for that time. . . . There is within the definition of the essence a living new creation, related afresh to new circumstances, and since it is a question of the re-creation of the highest religious revelation it is a new vouchsafing of revelation in the present.[102]

The antiessentialist torch has been passed down from Troeltsch and the early Chicago schoolers to present-day pragmatic historicist theologians, like Davaney and Brown. In the preceding chapters, I have contended that pragmatic, empiricist, and naturalistic historicists seek to refute several assumptions of "postliberal" theological historicisms. Among them is the claim that religions possess unified grammars, nonnegotiable rules, and immovable boundaries. In Lindbeck's schema, every religious lineage contains a "lexical core."[103] Even if its "vocabulary of symbols, concepts, rites, injunctions, and stories is in part highly variable," its grammatical and narratival essence is not, "persist[ing] down through the centuries and subsist[ing] within the different and usually competing traditions that inevitably develop." Lindbeck continues:

> There is nothing uniquely Christian about this constancy: supernatural explanations are quite unnecessary. This is simply the kind of stability that languages and religions, and to a lesser extent cultures, observably have. They are the lenses through which human beings see and respond to their changing worlds, or the media in which they formulate their descriptions. The world and its descriptions may vary enormously even while the lenses or media remain the same.[104]

Davaney declares that "a truly historicist orientation" (*pace* "the Lindbeckian version of historicism") quells "the desire for purity of traditions" and recognizes that religious lineages "are not the bearers of abiding meanings or values" but are "simply what they have historically come to be." In a word, religions do not have pristine origins or "common cores, centers, or essences." They do not contain "Platonic-like" substances "capturable in a singular moment, claim, or person," in an originating event or historical artifact, or "in one self-same story." They do not exhibit grammatical, doctrinal, and narratival consistency through history, "variations on unchanging themes," or fixed, identifiable points of sameness that appear "complete in all essentials, in some instantaneous moment of birth." On the contrary, religions, according to Davaney, actually evolve over time and, even from the very beginning, elicit multiple, disputed, unstable, and contradictory understandings of ultimate reality, human nature, soteriological fulfillment, and the like.[105] "Every tradition is in reality many traditions, conglomerations of distinctive and even heterogeneous interpretations, sets of meanings and practices that cannot be assimilated to or reduced to any universally present factor."[106]

Brown also critiques Lindbeck (and other conservatives, such as the evangelical theologian Clark Pinnock) for pretending that religions (e.g., Christianity) have syntactical stabilities, authoritative teachings, regulative doctrines, and unitary narratives. Such "pious possessiveness" stultifies the possibilities of a tradition's permutations, underestimates its capacity to redefine itself in each new setting, and forgets that "often what is altered was once thought basic." Yet, when it comes to essentializing religions, liberals do not fare much better than postliberals, Brown laments. Be it Schubert Ogden's identification of the "Jesus-kerygma" as the "canon within the canon," or Rosemary Radford Ruether's elevation of the "prophetic-liberating" strand of scripture, or John Cobb's postulation of Christ as the normative principle of "creative transformation" for Christians, liberal theologians tend to isolate some "interpretive center" of the faith. Brown protests: "The supposedly authentic core of the inheritance is elevated, and the remainder drops from view. The quaint, presumably misguided voices within tradition are shunted aside like an odd uncle at a family wedding." But, he persists, "no interpretation—whether a construal of the whole or a summation of its core—finally 'gets it right,' not simply because of the inevitable deficiency of the interpreter but also, and far more important, because canons are not the kind of things that can be gotten right."[107] Religions are intrinsically polyphonic, even cacophonic. As such, theologians, rather than entertaining only what is taken to be "essential" and "pure" (and usually "good"),[108] need to first contend with "the full range of the canonical inheritance," including "its problematic forms," and then attempt to make a religiously, intellectually, and ethically compelling case, within "the arenas of its contemporary communities of discourse," for why a certain rendering or reordering of the tradition ought to be preferred and privileged.[109]

Of course, from a pragmatic historicist standpoint, the rejection of tightly drawn perimeters and static essences does not mean that religious heritages are bereft of distinguishing marks and real (even if fuzzy, permeable, and ever-moving) borders. No different than any other historical object, each religion is funded and constituted by the differing contexts from which it has emerged and evolved, and as a result, displays attributes that are specific and distinctive and that differentiate it from other lineages.

In order to prevent antiessentialism from entirely dissolving the boundaries and characteristics that render the religions historically particular, Davaney looks to Jonathan Z. Smith's "polythetic" conception of tradition. Smith finds debates within the biological sciences surrounding competing classificatory systems instructive for the study of religion. Over against "taxonomic" approaches, which determine the identity of something by ascertaining a singular "item of discrimination," and "evolutionary" paradigms, which make ancestral origins and descent the basis of a description, polythetic classifications locate, through thick historical analysis, a sprawling and manifold panoply of properties, each of which is possessed by "a large (but unspecified) number" of individuals, but none of which is definitive or exhibited "by every member of the class." Polythetically conceived, a religion is not defined by its founding narratives nor by "a single trait which is held to reveal the 'essence' of that tradition," but by a messy and motley "hotch-potch" of ever-shifting qualities. There is no "normative Judaism," for example, only "a variety of . . . Judaisms, clustered in varying configurations." Hence, Smith rebuts essentialist "impulses toward totalization, unification, and integration," surrendering "perfect, unique, single differentia" as well as some "historical *primordium*" that persists in every "given descendent" (thereby stripping religions of essences), even while affirming that a tradition has an array of multiple identity markers, "the possession of any one of which is sufficient for admission to the taxon" (thereby giving religions historical characters, albeit multifarious, contested, loose, and tangled ones).[110] Davaney surmises that a polythetic view reminds us that religions have "a plurality of identifying elements," which enables us to distinguish one faith from another and "to attend to a wide variety of continuities without making any one characteristic or set of elements the sole determining factor for inclusion in a group. . . . It directs our attention to the widest range of historical realities in all their diversity and resists the exclusion of certain features through definition or appeal to nonhistorical authoritarian norms. Traditions are simply all they have ever been."[111]

To summarize, along with antisupernaturalism, antiessentialism is a staple of a pragmatic historicist conception of the religious past. Religious identities and boundaries exist, but enduring religious essences do not, whether between traditions or within them. That religions are bereft of univocal, unchanging, essentialized characters is, in part, simply a historical observation made by pragmatic historicists. To quote Case: "Christianity . . . is a hydra-headed religious movement within which unity has never prevailed for any considerable length of time. On the contrary, throughout the entire course of its development variety has been a conspicuous feature at every period of its history."[112] More than that, though, pragmatic historicism endeavors to theoretically accommodate this fairly obvious empirical fact, to explain *why* religions lack essences—common denominators, grammatical constants, self-identical narratives, hermeneutical nuclei, abiding substances, doctrinal cores, and so on.[113]

Firstly, akin to all cultural and historical products, faith heritages are "plural, diverse, and contentious to the core" and, consequently, are "internally weighted toward change."[114] Even a relatively closed canonical domain, such as the Judeo-Christian scriptures, "does not present uniform positions on God, Christ, or human nature." Indeed, "even if we did turn to the Bible for 'the' answer, what we would find instead are 'answers.' "[115] And, for pragmatic historicists, it is precisely their tension-ridden and conflict-filled diversity, their "inherent plurivocity," "structural fluidity," and "inescapable contestability," that make cultures, traditions, canons, and religions averse to essentialist reductions and revisable when faced with novel situations and challenges.[116]

Secondly, Mathews, Case, Foster, Troeltsch, Davaney, and Brown all realize that a religious lineage frequently changes as a result of *external* pressures, "constantly being called into question, its adequacy for the time challenged from without." Religions are not "hermetically sealed." They are neither unaffected by the world around them nor cut off from other historical trajectories and traditions. Rather, their contents are "always vulnerable to intrusions and enlargements," and their borders, although extant and identity-forming, are malleable and porous, providing continuity *and* inviting amplification, exhibiting conservation *and* prompting innovation, providing character *and* igniting imagination. In brief, whether coming from another culture, another religion, or another discipline, the "introduction of novelty from the outside" continually incites the transformation of our faiths. "Alien contributions" can be repudiated or integrated, critically or creatively engaged. They can be responded to as "threats or resources." They can be used to release what has been unrealized within our heritages, to supplement what has been missing from them, or even to correct what has been errant about them. But they cannot, according to pragmatic historicists, be ignored or entirely "shut out." Present circumstances and conditions, modern knowledge and experience, changing contexts and relationships, new interactions and encounters, always drive people of faith to reinterpret (be it actively or reactively, consciously or unconsciously, incrementally or radically) religious beliefs and customs afresh, even the so-called "essentials" typically considered immutable and set.[117]

Thirdly, finally, and most demonstrably, religious traditions are essenceless and developmental because they are artifacts of history. To summon Case once more, "Nothing remains permanently stagnant in the ever flowing historical stream of life, and religion necessarily partakes of this fluidity."[118] Like the universe in which they are situated, every faith that has ever existed and ever will exist is pluralistic, not singular; in the making, not ready-made; fluctuating, not static; relational, not isolated; hybrid, not uncontaminated. They are ever-growing and ever-becoming, malleable and mercurial, dynamic and processive. They are received and revised, given and made, continued and changed. They are historical.

From Antisupernaturalism and Antiessentialism to Antiauthoritarianism: Rethinking the Normativity of the Past

Pragmatic historicism declares that the repudiation of supernaturalism and essentialism carries far-reaching consequences for understanding the status and normativity of the religious past. For pragmatic historicists, the fact that religions are deprived of divine revelations and everlasting essences and are malleable, ever-altering, contestable, internally multilithic, permeable to outside influences, and reconstructible from top to bottom is not only empirically and historically descriptive but also theologically and methodologically prescriptive (cf. my discussion of historicism as a methodology in chapter 1), inciting us to treat our traditions not as sacrosanct authorities that demand deference, conformity, and replication, but as formative habitations that require reappraisal and reformation for each new time, place, and cultural situation. That is, antisupernaturalism and antiessentialism, I now want to submit, are powerful rationales for *antiauthoritarianism*. Utterly human and constantly changing, our religious inheritances do not deserve to be repeated merely for posterity's sake or elevated simply by virtue of their ancientness and supposed venerability. They must not—indeed cannot—be discarded; but neither should they be romanticized, ossified, repristinated, or, worse, deified.[119]

Yet again, the early Chicago-school liberals set the stage for pragmatic historicism's uncompromisingly antiauthoritarian theology. Foster asserted that authoritarianism rests on a fundamental misconstrual of religious heritages. Whether proclaiming the church as the "warranty" of salvation or viewing scripture as the revealed and inerrant "Word of God," Christians, even today, typically presume that the Christian tradition houses absolute, supernatural truths "authoritatively communicated" to humanity from on high. The critical methods of modern historiography, however, swiftly rule out presumptions of scriptural revelation, papal infallibility, and the like. In the vein of Troeltsch, Foster pronounced that "sacred history has been sucked into the stream of history, and hence has become something relative and conditioned, and the kind of dogmatic finality and absoluteness predicted of it by the religion of authority has suffered irrevocable dissolution. The pseudo-history of miracle yields to the real history of criticism."[120] For instance, the notion that God is the Bible's "real author" is simply "untrue historically." On the contrary, scripture "has all the marks of a deliberate human composition," contains ideas that are "not unmixed with error," reflects the cultures of its varied writers, and exhibits sharp disagreements not only about "external and incidental" issues but also about "basic questions of the religious life." And if the biblical witness is not divinely inspired, infallible, or superhuman in origin, but is "burdened with the burdens, good and bad, of all our humanity," then requiring "assent to its thoughts and commandments" or making it binding "in all matters of faith and practice" are no longer viable theological options.[121]

In fact, *all* "authority-religion" needs to go, Foster entreated. As Dorrien points out, Foster "swept the house of authority clean," insisting that theological modernism was tantamount to nothing less than "a new Reformation."[122] A modernized theology must be ready to jettison "dead dogmas, injurious survivals, meaningless customs, moribund churches," and be willing to "make a new future," to "re-create life," to "release the spirit," and to think of the tradition as "inspirational rather than regulative, dynamic rather than static, creative and nourishing rather than statutory and repressive." Foster wanted modern theologians to look forward as opposed to backward, to privilege the affirmation of what "shall be" over the impotent acceptance of what "once was," to appeal to conscience, reason, and science rather than external authorities or "the antiquity of an ecclesiastical past," and to found contemporary Christianity on the principles of "true spontaneity and free development" instead of "blind obedience" and passive resignation.[123]

Gerald Birney Smith followed suit. Smith noted that, before the advent of modernity, theological assertions were, by and large, predicated on acquiescence to some kind of final norm, external authority, or "revelation from above"—a divinely authored and inspired Bible, the apostolic traditions, hierarchy, and creeds of the ecclesia, the "Christocentric ideal," and so on. The principal test of theology was "scripturalness," and the primary duty of the theologian "exegesis," faithfully preserving, obediently submitting to, and logically expounding on a revelatory deposit, which was handed down, unaltered, from era to era and granted immunity from "adverse criticism." Modern critical historical scholarship, however, has utterly humanized and historicized, desupernaturalized and de-exceptionalized, the religious past:

> It insists on the historical relativity of biblical doctrines, thereby contradicting the theory that these doctrines have a super-historical origin. It is progressively recognizing that Christianity did not come into existence and grow up in quarantine from all pagan influences; but that, on the contrary, it felt and responded to the same historical exigencies which contributed to the making of pagan religions. Little by little it is coming to be seen that there is not so wide a gulf between the religion of the Bible and the kindred religions of biblical times as was presupposed in the traditional interpretation of scripture; and that there is not so absolute a difference as has been commonly assumed between the way in which the men of the Bible arrived at their convictions and the way in which men in later times achieved their faith.[124]

In a word, ancient expressions of faith, no different from modern-day ones, are humanly and historically constructed; no religious text (e.g., the New Testament), personage (e.g., Jesus Christ), institution (e.g., the church), or dogma (e.g., hypostatic union), however hoary, is interpretable apart from the cultural processes that produced it, the "function it performed" and the dilemmas it encountered at any given moment of its development, and the wider social, political, economic, and religious contexts in which it has been situated over time. And precisely for that reason, we need to proceed without recourse to "sacredly guarded" creeds, "the 'essentials' of the 'faith once delivered,'" or an "authoritative religious system." Rather than paying uncritical allegiance to scripture or the magisterium or striving to build a theological system on "super-empirical" truths putatively imparted by God in the "distant past," the theologian today ought to "focus attention on the immanent forces of this world" and on the urgent concerns and conditions of this age, "willing to make changes in traditional doctrine if such changes serve to make religion more vital in the life and thought of his day."[125]

That, in actuality, is exactly what theologians have always done, whether wittingly or not. With Case, Foster, and Mathews (cf. the previous section), Smith realized that the history of Christianity displays "an interesting variety of interpretation" and an often antagonistic "diversity of opinion," not a stable essence or a "static body" of doctrinal principles. No generation ever simply clones the tradition it receives, but modifies it in order to address new predicaments and historical circumstances.[126] Even when conservatism holds court, and "religious sentiment is on the side of unchanging dogma, the change comes."[127] In point of fact, merely parroting "what has been prescribed in the Bible" is not just unmodern, but also ironically unbiblical. "Religious non-conformists," the authors and characters of scripture, far from lauding "the good old-time religion," open-mindedly and experimentally refurbished the faith in accordance with the social realities, assumptions, and quandaries of *their* epochs and environments.[128] Smith wondered:

> If the apostle Paul, for the sake of a more vital religious life among the Gentiles, refused to make obligatory on them the rite of circumcision, although it was repeatedly commanded in his Bible and had all the sanction of centuries of usage, what would he say of a church which is more concerned with conformity to ancient customs than with the new demands of a new age? If Jesus considered the need of living man more sacred than the scriptural law of the Sabbath, how would he judge a church which systematically subjects the thinking of living men to the compulsion of agreement with prescribed doctrines?[129]

To be sure, as a proponent of historicism, Smith declared that the very first task of theology involves gaining "a clear and accurate conception of the reasons for the rise and growth of fundamental ideas and institutions in the history of the religion" the theologian sets out to interpret. Even so, the purpose of acquiring a historical understanding of a religious inheritance is neither to make "any one period . . . normative for the rest" nor to encourage "helpless dependence on antiquity," but "to know just the extent and the nature of our relation to the past out of which we have grown, and to appeal to that past with critical intelligence."[130] The ancients, without a doubt, often provide "stimulus and help" by supplying models for creative revision. Despite that, "tradition," for Smith, is "a servant of the present and not its despot." Our ancestors are able to offer "counsel," not because they came into possession of "superhuman knowledge which sets them metaphysically apart from us," but because they "shared completely with humanity the perplexities and struggles which all must experience." And they did (albeit often unintentionally) what people in all times and places need to do, striving to reinterpret inherited symbols and practices in culturally compelling, socially meaningful, and intellectually convincing ways.[131]

Smith, when all is said and done, repudiated any authority that stymies the free flow of theological construction:[132] "To the man of really scientific temper, it makes little difference whether theology defer to the pope or to the Bible or to a superhuman Christ or to certain *Heilstatsachen* or to a religious a priori as the ultimate court of appeal. So long as any *absolutum* whatever is erected as an exception to the 'natural' order, the theologian will seem like an advocate rather than an investigator."[133]

Nowhere is the early Chicago school's antiauthoritarianism more clearly, fully, and succinctly expressed than in the work of Case. Like Smith, Case spurned both modernist dismissals of our inheritances and conservative idealizations of them. To begin with, as a historicist, Case thought that making a clean break from our historical lineages was impossible: "We cannot cut ourselves adrift from the world that has made us what we are."[134] The present, while never tethered to "ancient norms" and "outgrown heritages," is "deeply and widely rooted in the past." And the past, Case permitted, retains *didactic*, even if not normative, import. Learning from the achievements—and the mistakes—of our forebears enables contemporary people to find solutions to present-day problems, to anticipate the "probable outcome of a particular line of action," to plan the future much more intelligently and carefully, and to sometimes even rediscover values that continue to efficaciously meet the needs of society today. Unfortunately, though, human beings, especially when religion is involved, tend to treat "the voice of antiquity" as "the voice of authority," allowing the "right of tradition," "ancestral practice," or "historical attestation" to substantiate a position. The ancient world gets regarded as some sort of idyllic paradise vis-à-vis "the decadent present," and the unfolding of history as a tale of loss, where humanity, instead of progressing toward an uncertain future, moves farther and farther away from a primordial Eden.[135] In Christianity, the universal human penchant for golden-ageism is exacerbated by the belief in the divine revelation of scripture. Christians are called to faithfully surrender to the truths vouchsafed in the Bible, which becomes "the infallible source of inspiration," the "ultimate court of appeal," and "the authoritative guide in all matters of religion." However, with the other Chicago schoolers (and indeed all pragmatic historicists), Case purported that, by tracing "the concrete circumstances under which the different books of the Bible came into existence," the historical-critical method exposes the utter historicity and humanness of the scriptural canon. Accordingly, Christians ought to remove the authoritative "halo" from the testimonies of the ancients, including those of the biblical writers. "The past," for Case, "was simply the past."[136]

Moreover, because history is always "in the making" and "in the process of becoming," and every generation is confronted with facts and issues unknown and unforeseen by prior eras, each new community is responsible for treading novel "paths of exploration" and for constructively and creatively interpreting the tradition afresh. While change is no guarantee of improvement, our religions ought to be continuously revamped in congruence with the ever-shifting "conditions of life and thinking." Without a doubt, in the course of renovation, the past cannot be gotten rid of and may even lend inspiration, stimulate and instruct the imagination, supply correction, and open up innovative possibilities for future belief and action. Still, modern believers are under no compulsion to repeat it. We are its successors, persisted Case, but never its "bondservants."[137]

Apropos of the nature, standing, and authority of the religious past, contemporary pragmatic historicists march pretty much in lockstep with the Chicago-school theologians. To illustrate, Kaufman recognizes, with Foster, Smith, and Case, that the "authoritarian approach" to the theological enterprise—the idea that theology consists of the rehearsal, exposition, and passing on of tradition—is based on the (no longer tenable) belief in revelation. If "the very 'word of God' " is located and available in the Bible and the creeds, then the proper job of the theologian is simply to extract, translate, and hand on that "divine truth," which is "otherwise inaccessible to women and men." However, the assumption that God "definitively deposited" a "self-revelation" in the scriptures, in the person of Jesus Christ, or in subsequent Christian writings and dogmas is difficult to justify, Kaufman inveighs. Besides, even the most facile reading of the history of doctrine reveals that theology has *always* been a critical and constructive work; it has *never* been the mere citation, translation, and transmission of inherited wisdom, even when it has purported to be so. Theologians—including the writers of the biblical texts and the fathers of the church—have continually *reconstructed* received notions of God, Christ, salvation, and so on, "in the face of ever new problems and crises arising in life" and "in terms of their own best understanding or insights." As a result, Kaufman, like the Chicago schoolers before him, beseeches fellow theologians to quit according historic "formulations and conceptions" a "normative status for the present and the future," to "take full responsibility for our definitions, our interpretations and our conclusions," and to self-consciously conceive of theology as imaginative construction. As Linell Cady observes, at the heart of Kaufman's theological method "is the desacralization of the Bible and its dethronement as arbiter of divine truth."[138] Theologians, of course, never start from scratch or create ex nihilo, but always theologize *in media res*, in the midst of "a world already in certain respects defined in and by . . . [their] religious traditions." Contemporary theology, in other words, is "always a qualification and development of notions inherited from earlier worshipers and prophets, poets and thinkers."[139] Regardless, our modern knowledge (e.g., our scientific conceptions of the universe or our awareness of religious diversity), along with the "radical novelty" of our current historical situation (e.g., the unprecedented power to blow ourselves up in a nuclear holocaust), may compel us "to depart in important ways from dominant traditional views."[140] As he later put it:

> At any given time it is always an open question whether the conceptions and values and perspectives inherited from the past remain suitable for orienting human existence in the new present: this is a question to be investigated, never a position which can simply be taken for granted. . . . Only if and as we are able to show that [a theological] symbol, properly constructed, can and does have important significance and use in modern life, are we justified in continuing to advocate its employment.[141]

Davaney takes a similar position. Historically conditioned, shot through with ambiguity, and indelibly "contentious," "multileveled," and "complex"—in a word, human—religious heritages, according to Davaney, neither provide "uncontested norms for thought or guidelines for action" nor confer "self-evident present-day legitimacy."[142] While enabling people of faith to map the identity of the community and ascertain the historical causes of certain beliefs and practices, the past never obviates the necessity of theological debate or establishes whether or not a viewpoint is religiously true and ethically justifiable today. It tells us where we have been, but not necessarily where we must go. Undeniably, our ancestors contribute to and have a voice in the process of contemporary theological deliberation. Even so, they never dictate it. In this connection, Davaney cites the Jewish theologian Mordecai Kaplan: "We should accept the past as no more authoritative than the present. It should have the right to vote but not the right to veto."[143] Human historicity entails that our histories should not, indeed cannot, be disregarded. Nonetheless, contending with an inheritance, Davaney states, is not synonymous with conforming to it, whether in whole or in part. It demands our attention, but not necessarily our allegiance. Modern theologians turn to antiquity, not to forestall argument or to legitimate the status quo or to invoke divine authority, but to struggle with and reform the historic roots to which we are inextricably tied.[144] But, ultimately, the locus of normativity lies in the here and now: "Contemporary persons forge visions for today that we are responsible for and whose adequacy is determined not by whether they embody the depth grammar of a past age or the classic answers of a bygone era, but whether they offer a way of interpreting reality and a vision for living that meet our present needs."[145]

Brown is more invested than Davaney (and Kaufman) in helping theologians, especially of the liberal variety, recover their pasts,[146] but is, nonetheless, no less critical of authoritarianism in theology. Referencing an early essay by the political theorist and philosopher Hannah Arendt,[147] Brown castigates the "authorization" model of authority, which originated in Roman law and government. For the Romans, authority—*auctoritas*—belonged to the ancestors, who, by establishing sacred and eternally binding foundations, stood as exemplars of "greatness for each successive age." And in the Roman world, religion, according to Arendt, "meant *religare*: to be tied back, obligated," to the "cornerstone" laid by the authorities, the "founders." Christianity, Brown decries, ended up adopting the Roman paradigm of *auctoritas*, presuming that the past supplies "objective" guidelines or prescriptions requiring repetition from age to age. "The Apostles became the 'founding fathers' of the Church," and the Bible the singular "standard" for belief and practice. A theological claim, in other words, was legitimized insofar as it conformed to the apostolic and scriptural witness. Fortunately, from Brown's vantage point, the Judeo-Christian heritage itself provides alternate conceptions of authority. In Judaism, for example, a "dynamic interplay" has always existed between Tanakh and Talmud, Moses and Midrash, Torah-teaching and rabbinic commentary—in short, between the received tradition and the contemporary community provoking its ongoing reformulation. Similarly, in the New Testament, the *exousia*, or authority, given to Christ by God and extended to the disciples by Jesus (see Mark 1:21–28, 6:7) connotes "the right or power to act or respond creatively. . . . It does not command conformity; it commends freedom."[148]

Brown goes on to suggest that the authority of a lineage resides in its capacity not to "authorize," but to "author" (*auctor*), that is, to give identity to a people. The present is woven from the fabric of the past, "constituted by what has gone before." Yet, "the making of the future," Brown qualifies, "is always a *remaking* . . . of what has been inherited."[149] Therefore, tradition does not so much regulate and validate theology as it does elicit and fund it. It is authoritative, in other words, not because it tells us, like some inviolable dictator, what to think and do, but because it continues to supply the basic resources out of which our lives take shape and to "speak to us with a power and challenge that will not let us be content with who we are and will not let us change glibly."[150] The canons, confessions, teachings, narratives, practices, and scriptures furnished by our religious heritages by no means offer any infallible "criterion of truth," much less some direct, revelatory, inerrant line of communication with ultimate reality. Neither are they "inherently good." On the contrary, traditions and every aspect thereof are human, fallible, and ambiguous through and through, capable of building up and tearing down, liberating and oppressing. They display "blindness on some occasions and brilliance on others."[151] Accordingly, our religious inheritances, Brown implores, require "metamorphosis," not "mimesis." They should not (and cannot) be simply "replicated" or "uncritically embraced," but must be imaginatively transfigured, critiqued, reordered, and adjudicated "in our ever-changing and varied arenas of contemporary discourse," where they "are entitled to full but unprivileged participation." Yet, even when we disagree with them, problematize them, repudiate them, agonize over them, and transform them, they are still authoring our religious characters and theological constructions. They remain "formative," even if not "normative."[152]

In short, traditions are neither, as conservative theologians profess, rules to be obeyed nor, as Enlightenment modernists and deconstructionist radicals maintain,[153] limits to be overcome, but are "dynamic and diverse streams of being and meaning that mold and are molded, conserve and create, save and destroy." Brown calls for a "constructive historicist" construal of the religious past, where inherited rituals, doctrines, texts, symbols, feelings, creeds, and so on, are not put on a pedestal or tossed aside, but are "rearranged and recontextualized, and debated and tested, in an effort to provide a more adequate habitation for the present and anticipated future." Constructive historicism evinces both "evangelical" and "progressive" theological sensibilities; it avoids both "nostalgic antiquarianism" and "faddish modernism," refuses to give uncritical preference to either conservation or difference, and approaches the faith as "artist" and "caretaker" as well as "analyst" and "critic." Theology, in a constructive historicist mode, is careful not to "stultify imagination" or to "valorize novelty" and, instead, identifies the varying potentialities (conceptual and affective, dominant and repressed, orthodox and heterodox, life-giving and death-dealing) embedded in a religion, evaluates each element according to "the needs of the community" and the multiple fields of contemporary knowledge and experience, and then advocates for "some variants over others."[154] As Brown synopsizes:

> Theology accepts as a starting point what a tradition has been and is, accepts as a goal what it might be and should become, and accepts as an obligation the advocacy of that potential realization. If a tradition is right for the time, theology will sustain and enhance it. If a tradition becomes shallow, its hidden depths will be uncovered, explored, and proclaimed. If it becomes silent, the tradition will be made to say what it can. If it feigns uniformity, the tradition's diversity, actual and potential, will be held up to view. And whenever a tradition is wrong, consent means to condemn it, to challenge it, and to work for its transformation. Theology is the creative reconstruction of inherited symbols, the construction of a tradition's future from the resources of its past.[155]

To recapitulate, the truth and value of a theological outlook, in a pragmatic historicist model, is not established by citing an external authority, be it a sacred text (e.g., the Rig Veda or the Qur'an), an ancient teacher (e.g., Rumi or Sankara), or even a movement initiator (e.g., Muhammad or Buddha). Of course, the very premise of historicism is that "the past is not something alien to us" but something that "lies deep inside us; it does not disappear but remains present with us here and now, for it is the past that has made us who we are."[156] The same goes for our *religious* pasts. In religion, as in life, the past occasions, gives birth to, and shapes—"authors"— the future. In Davaney's words, "Humans are constituted by the mass of historical inheritance that has preceded every present moment, including strands we have heuristically designated religious traditions."[157] Regardless, our historical inheritances and religious traditions are not authoritative, pragmatic historicists insist. As Kaufman remarks, "In a methodologically self-conscious constructive theology" no religious question "can be settled simply by noting that 'the Bible says . . .' or 'tradition holds . . .' or 'Jesus said . . .'"[158]

Postliberal historicists are theologically authoritarian by comparison. Lindbeck, for instance, views church doctrines as those "communally authoritative teachings" that constitute "faithful adherence to a community" and remain "essential to the identity or welfare of the group in question." Ancient confessions, such as the Nicene Creed, are "not formulas to be slavishly repeated," Lindbeck assures. Nevertheless, the "rules" they "paradigmatically instantiate"—for example, "the monotheistic principle" and "Christological maximalism"—are. They are, in other words, "unconditionally and permanently necessary" components of the "self-identical story" and "indispensable grammar or logic of the faith." As such, they have "authority." A postliberal (read: conservative) species of historicism, then, sees theology as essentially faithfulness to the "abiding" and "doctrinally significant grammatical core" of a religion—again, not to particular doctrinal formulations, but to "the same directives that were involved in their first formulation."[159]

Pragmatic historicism is a completely different animal. For pragmatic historicists, religions simply do not embody timeless essences to which we can return or regulative norms to which we should conform, any more than they possess supernatural revelations to which we must surrender.[160] In chapter 7, I will hazard that this thoroughly historicist, but unequivocally antiauthoritarian, sentiment is one of the principal reasons why the theological proclivities of a pragmatic and naturalistic historicism are fundamentally and unapologetically *liberal* (as opposed to *post*liberal). But before moving on, I want to conclude the present discussion by applying pragmatic historicism's antiauthoritarianism to perhaps the most highly venerated aspect of the Christian past: Jesus.

The Authority of Jesus: A Case Study on the Benefits of an Antiauthoritarian Theology

In her most recently published article, Davaney illustrates a nonnormative construal of religious traditions by examining the significance of historical Jesus research for modern theological construction. On the one hand, Christianity's past "includes a man named Jesus and all the interpretations and uses of that person." And the so-called "quests for the historical Jesus" are useful exercises in "genealogy," constructing a (provisional) sketch of a figure to whom Christians are historically linked and by whom they are constantly inspired. On the other hand, theologians ought to engage the scholarship of the questers not to discover a "blueprint" for contemporary thinking and acting or "an original event that somehow explains or legitimizes Christianity," but because the Jesus of history continues to form our practices, commitments, and worldviews and still "moves us forward in our present world." As Davaney advises elsewhere, what renders Jesus's program of "radical solidarity" persuasive and deserving of adoption "is not that Jesus proposed it but that it made possible for him and others a life worth living and commending."[161] In the end, the quests—and the Jesus for whom they quest—can help us "understand better who we *have been*" and who we *might* become, but do "not tell us what we *should* be today or in the future." "The question for theology at least is not who Jesus was but who we will be," Davaney boldly enthuses.[162] None of this is to insinuate that the historical Jesus (or the Christ of faith, for that matter) is unimportant. Quite the reverse: for most pragmatic historicists, he is formative, albeit not normative, for Christian belief and praxis today. Even so, it is we who must figure out his role and meaning for our context, not the other way around. The book of Hebrews (cf. 12:2) got it only half-right: Jesus may be the "author" of the faith, but *we* are its finishers.

As with so many other theological subjects, the early Chicago schoolers were way ahead of their time when it came to the authority of Jesus. Prefiguring Davaney by almost a century, Case likewise averred that the historical Jesus ought to play a stimulative rather than an imitative role in contemporary theology. Jesus, while a great "source of help and inspiration for a profitable life," remained acutely "engrossed in issues integral to the life of [his] own age and of a Palestinian society" and entertained ideas about the universe that moderns no longer consider valid, relevant, or suitable (the existence of angels and demons, a looming apocalypse, etc.). Christians, therefore, must approach him in a spirit of "freedom and selective valuation." Negatively put, no religious teaching, social action, or ethical norm of Jesus has "to be pursued to the letter . . . by all persons who should come after him" or ought to be considered "automatically authoritative" for each subsequent era.[163] Case explains:

> His way of life is not necessarily to be our way of life, nor are we to treat the injunctions he delivered to his contemporaries

as though they were a legal code regulative for our conduct and belief. The new type of appreciation abandons outright the dogma of normativeness. . . . Creative religious living must strive not to imitate but to transcend all past and present standards, not excepting even the example and precepts of Jesus.[164]

Besides conferring theological liberty, jettisoning "the dogma of normativeness" engenders other advantages as well. In particular, Case and the rest of the Chicago-school theologians realized that divesting the past of final authority also mitigates the penchant—especially among Christian liberals—to fashion Jesus in our own image and likeness. "The representatives of the 'liberal' school of Christology," according to Case, "have always been able to convince themselves that the New Testament writings, or at least their more genuine and earlier portions, when correctly understood, yield one's favorite views as to Jesus' significance, and thus show his thought to have been in conformity with modern opinions."[165] In this, Case obviously echoes Albert Schweitzer, whose 1906 masterpiece, *Von Reimarus zu Wrede: Eine Geschichte der Leben-Jesu-Forschung*,[166] famously lambasted liberal Protestant questers for retrojecting contemporary ideals and values back onto the historical Jesus. Schweitzer did not mince words: "The Jesus of Nazareth who came forward publicly as the Messiah, who preached the ethic of the Kingdom of God, who founded the kingdom of Heaven upon earth, and died to give His work its final consecration, never had any existence. He is a figure designed by rationalism, endowed with life by liberalism, and clothed by modern theology in an historical garb."[167] Liberal theology, thus, set out in search of the Jesus of history but, in actuality, found itself. It "finds its own thoughts . . . in Jesus, and represents Him as expressing them." Schweitzer countered that the real Jesus "comes to us as One unknown," as an enigma and a scandal to the twentieth-century mind, as a stranger from a vastly different eon and culture.[168] His ministry, as a matter of fact, was characterized by something categorically *un*modern: a world-negating eschatology. With a nod to Johannes Weiss (among others), Schweitzer hypothesized that the historical Jesus was really a failed and relatively insignificant apocalypticist, who wrongly anticipated and announced the imminence of the Day of Judgment.[169] Liberalism, contrariwise, followed a "Jesus of its own making," regretfully presupposing that he could "mean more to our time by entering into it as a man like ourselves."[170]

The early Chicago-school liberals, though, actually made peace with the views of Schweitzer and Weiss, and I would venture that it was their historicist antiauthoritarianism that enabled them to do so. A prominent social gospeler, Mathews, early on, confidently asserted that the Jesus unearthed by historical-critical scholarship essentially embodied the spirit of modern Protestant liberalism. His 1897 book, *The Social Teaching of Jesus: An Essay in Christian Sociology*, instantly became a movement classic, assuring that Christ exhibited a "superb optimism" and "saw the possibilities of infinite good in humanity." The kingdom of God, moreover, referred not to an "apocalyptical . . . post-mortem or post-catastrophic condition," but to "an ideal (though progressively approximated) social order in which the relation of men to God is that of sons, and (therefore) to each other, that of brothers." Accordingly, the liberal mission of "Christianizing" the government, society, and the world was based on nothing less than "the principles of fraternity and love that underlie the entire social teachings of Jesus."[171]

But gradually, and with certain reluctance, Mathews made concessions to Weiss's "thoroughgoing eschatology." Mathews's book, *The Messianic Hope in the New Testament*, which appeared one year before *The Quest of the Historical Jesus* took the world of liberal theology by storm, reached a strikingly Schweitzerian conclusion: "Any strict definition of the kingdom of God must be eschatological. With Jesus as with his contemporaries, the kingdom was yet to come. Its appearance would be the result of no social evolution, but sudden, as the gift of God; men could not hasten its coming; they could only prepare for membership in it."[172] By 1905, then, Mathews came to unreservedly accept something he tacitly sensed all along, namely, that "the first century . . . was . . . not the nineteenth."[173]

Most liberals of the day (rightfully) worried that the apocalypticism of Weiss and Schweitzer undermined the very foundation of the social gospel. As even Foster recognized, "The hour struck for the knowledge that the historical Jesus was much farther from us and much stranger to us than we had believed, and that we could not count upon him off-hand to play a leading part in our social program."[174] Mathews, however, was also a historicist, conceiving of Christianity as a reconstructible and growing organism, not as a "fixed" phenomenon that remains forever identified with an "authoritative orthodoxy," an "alleged theological essence," or "the behavior and beliefs" of the New Testament.[175] And precisely because he stressed a developmental rather than an essentialist or authoritarian notion of theology, he managed to simultaneously confront the historical truth about Jesus's eschatological message and to celebrate the genuine gains of a progressive and democratic Christian community. As Dorrien reflects, what was "misleading as a characterization of the kingdom faith of early

Christianity" was, for Mathews, "true as a description" of modernity's "own Sprit-moved religious witness" and grafting of "the ideals of Jesus into the ongoing social process."[176] We can come to frank and realistic terms with the fact that Jesus was more concerned with preparing his disciples for the "catastrophic" and "speedy end of the world" than with reforming the state or subverting the status quo, even while still trying to make his values the basis for our social life.[177] In brief, by freeing modern Christianity from the authority of the past—including Jesus of Nazareth—*Mathews* could firmly believe in the social gospel without needing to pretend that *Jesus* did, rebuilding the movement on a *historicist* rather than a *historical* foundation. While the social gospel was not Jesus's gospel, it can—indeed, should—be ours; the Christian gospel has *evolved into* the social gospel.[178]

The lesson to be learned from Mathews (and the Chicago school in general) is not that apocalypticism accurately captures who Jesus really was, but that antiauthoritarianism allows contemporary Christians to become both more theologically innovative and more historically candid. Gerald Birney Smith sums it up well: when the locus of theological normativity is transferred to the present, it is no longer necessary or even desirable "to make the Bible teach everything which the modern theologian wishes to affirm." An equivalent "honesty of attitude" obtains with respect to Jesus:

> We may still continue positively to affirm all that a vital religious faith requires without feeling compelled to validate the entire content by explicit reference to the person of Christ. If once this broader [read: antiauthoritarian] conception of the nature of Christianity shall come to prevail, we shall be in a position to find out honestly the real significance of Jesus for our faith and to construct a doctrinal statement in the person of Jesus compatible with historical accuracy.[179]

In many ways, the impulse to "project [modern notions and standards] back into history and make them speak to us out of the past"[180] is as rife in our own time as it was in Schweitzer's. One of the leading contemporary defenders of the eschatological thesis, Paula Fredriksen,[181] complains that many self-styled "third questers,"[182] especially members of the Jesus Seminar,[183] are still bent on resisting the "awkward and unwelcomed stranger" of Schweitzer and Weiss, the apocalyptic prophet of "the impending end of days." Their "wandering cynic sage" and "social revolutionary" does not bear an exact resemblance to the ethical teacher of the liberal lives of Jesus, but he is, nonetheless, "his twentieth-century avatar: radically egalitarian, anti-elitist, anti-nationalist, anti-racialist, anti-patriarchal." They try to expunge, or exegete away, the "offending awkwardness" and "embarrassment" of a first-century Jewish apocalypticist who performed wondrous deeds, drove out unclean spirits, and (incorrectly) predicted a looming and cataclysmic eschaton. But what they end up with is a past exclusively of their "own imagining" and liking, not the Jesus of history—"miracles without cures, time without end, resurrections without bodies. The kingdom does not come, it is present as an experience, a kinder, gentler society, mediated, indeed created, by Jesus."[184]

Pragmatic historicism, I submit, is able to at least quell these ongoing retrojective tendencies, one of the primary (albeit mostly unconscious) causes of which is deferring to antiquity—in this case, Jesus—as an authority. New Testament scholar Luke Timothy Johnson astutely observes that many liberal third questers, ironically similar to the traditionalists and fundamentalists they impugn, erroneously suppose (as did their lives-of-Jesus forebears, I would add) that "historical knowledge is normative for faith, and therefore for theology." Their assumption is that "origins define essence," that the "first understanding of Jesus was necessarily better than any following." However, as liberals, they tend to be turned off by orthodox Christian teachings. For that reason, their strategy is to completely dichotomize the pre-Easter sage and the post-Easter Christ and cavalierly contrive an alternative history of "the original form of the Jesus movement," which was supposedly obscured and distorted by Paul, John, and the church fathers. Jesus is still regarded as authoritative, but now it is "the real Jesus," the Jesus uncorrupted by later theological (and sociopolitical) developments. And, seen as the pristine, pre-Nicene norm for a progressive, post-Constantinian Christian vision, Jesus ends up, once again, inevitably becoming awash in anachronisms, except it is the ideas and sensibilities of the twentieth and twenty-first century, rather than the christological confessions of the first, second, third, fourth, and fifth, that are retrojected. These "historical" Jesuses are nothing of the kind, Johnson harshly judges. They are, rather, politically correct platitudes, "mirror reflections" of their creators' "own social location in the liberal academy." Although claiming to be based on sober, fair-minded, and unbiased historiographical research, the results of such investigations—the "proper image of Jesus"—are first "determined ahead of time" and then read eisegetically, retrojectively, back into the sources.[185]

Pragmatic historicists, on the contrary, do not have to retroject, because they follow through on their liberalism and renounce authoritarianisms and essentialisms of all stripes. That is, they can be more *historically* open to Jesus since they are not compelled to *theologically* accept everything he said, accomplished, and was. For a resolutely antiauthoritarian historicist, christological controversies are not resolved by answering the question, what would—or did—Jesus do? Instead, she asks, what do we need? And remembering that we, and not Jesus, are the deciders should make us less prone to historically downplay or ignore repellant, odd, irrelevant, or specious aspects of his message (e.g., his apocalypticism) or, worse, turn him into who we want him to be (whether a deity who ascended into heaven and is seated at the right hand of God the Father or a Mediterranean peasant Cynic[186]). Pragmatic historicists, in other words, do not have to write revisionist *histories*, because they espouse revisionist *theologies*. With Johnson, Fredriksen, and others, they do not think that the best way to challenge the adequacy, cogency, and morality of Jesus's millenarianism, Rome's imperialism, and Paul's patriarchalism is to invent a life of a radical egalitarian whose teaching is suspiciously congenial to modern-day left-wing politics and whose revolutionary movement was ostensibly corrupted by the whims and machinations of an increasingly world-denying, dogmatic, antisapiential, power-hungry, and hegemonic early church. Instead, in the spirit of Mathews's reconciliation of the social gospel and the eschatological hypothesis of Weiss and Schweitzer, contemporary pragmatic historicist liberals can argue for an anti-apocalyptic, pro-liberation, countercultural, nonhierarchical, this-worldly, post-Constantinian christology on the basis of what Christians *today* consider religiously viable, valuable, and veritable. If we presume that we need the past to authorize our present beliefs, we will inexorably "discover" our present beliefs in the past. But if we take ownership of and responsibility for our present beliefs, being openly selective about, critical of, and constructively engaged with the traditions to which we are heirs, we can let the past be the past and Jesus be Jesus.

Chapter 6

Truth Reconsidered

Building Blocks of a Paleopragmatic Historicism

I want to shift gears and turn to a more philosophical question, the question of truth. Pragmatic historicism's epistemology considerably limits the human capacity to make truth claims about reality. To be specific, pragmatic historicists hold that human knowledge is (1) perspectival (i.e., conditioned by our particular historical perspectives); (2) constructed (i.e., largely made rather than found); (3) foundationless (i.e., bereft of any sort of Archimedean point); (4) fallible (i.e., tentative and vulnerable to correction); and (5) instrumental (i.e., adjudicated by utility and results). Perspectivism, constructivism, nonfoundationalism, fallibilism, and instrumentalism are well-founded, in my estimation.

Yet, however compelling, these very same epistemological tenets sometimes tempt pragmatic—especially neopragmatic—historicists to embellish human construction at the expense of reality's epistemic circumscriptions and sheer givenness and to reduce the true to "whatever works." Accordingly, taking a cue from Robert Neville, who coined the moniker "paleopragmatism" to distinguish the classical (especially the Peircean) strand of the pragmatist tradition from postmodern, or neopragmatist, reappropriations of it,[1] I will gesture towards a *paleopragmatic historicism*, a historicism that is rooted more in the truth-seeking, correspondence-preserving, and metaphysics-wielding pragmatic realisms of James, Dewey, and Peirce (and some of their successors in contemporary American philosophy) than in the nominalistic, relativistic, and putatively "postmetaphysical" neopragmatism of Richard Rorty and others. The next two chapters will make a fresh case for such a paleopragmatist mode of historicist thought—and for the kind of theology that flows from it.

Perspectivism, Constructivism, Nonfoundationalism, Fallibilism, Instrumentalism: Historicist Checks on the True and the Real

The preceding chapters have already intimated that historicism significantly curbs claims about the true and the real. After all, historicism is, by definition, an ontologically and epistemologically limiting doctrine, postulating that all phenomena—including, ipso facto, human beings and their perceptions of things—are emergent from and subject to the vicissitudes of a finite, ever-shifting, open, and contextually circumscribed historical process (cf. chapter 1). Chapters 2 and 3 argued that human reason, experience, and religiosity are always historically situated and particular—relative to place and time, conditioned by culture, language, and material circumstances, and embedded in and funded by the resources of a past and tradition (or, more precisely, multiple traditions); there are, therefore, no nontemporal or unmediated, objective or universal, neutral or innocent vantage points or viewpoints, no ahistorical perch from which to view reality. And chapter 5 added that the universe, and everything in it, is in flux. To quote William James, "what really *exists* is not things made but things in the making," things that "bud" and "burgeon," "change" and "create."[2] In *Pragmatism*, James insisted that truth is no different. New beliefs are constantly grafted onto previous ones, as men and women reform their "stock of old opinions" in light of fluctuating, and sometimes contradicting, experiences. So, truths, like anything else, are not "complete and ready-made from all eternity." Rather, they alter, grow, and vary over time (albeit slowly and conservatively), arising, evolving, and dying in the transitions and movements of history.[3]

But in addition to historical contextualism, particularism, and dynamism, there are several other philosophical principles inherent in a historicist worldview that check what humans are able to affirm about truth and reality.

The First Check: Perspectivism

There is, firstly, historicism's thoroughgoing *perspectivism*. Philosopher of religion, Donald Crosby, defines perspectivism metaphysically, as the notion that existence as such is perspectival. That is, every single thing in the world without exception—a neutrino, an atom, a star, an inorganic entity, a cell, a human mind—has a distinctive take on everything else and "experiences what is 'there' from its own 'here.'"[4] A bigger, or holistic, historicism (cf. chapter 2) is certainly consistent with a metaphysical perspectivism. If all phenomena (and not just human beings) are historical, residing somewhere and somewhen amid the flow and fluidities of history's dynamic processes, and becoming particular somethings[5] through their relations with, responses to, and influences on the contingent givens of diverse contexts, then every object and occasion of experience (including nonhuman, nonconscious, and even nonliving ones) occupies a unique perspective relative to the rest of reality.

On the whole, however, historicists tend to emphasize and champion an *epistemological* perspectivism, describing the ways in which *human knowledge* is shaped by and filtered through culturally and linguistically mediated, ideologically and politically vested, and interest- and theory- and paradigm- and interpretation- and power-laden perspectives. As is typical, James captures a perspectivist epistemology with unequalled clarity, contending that what we human beings make of reality "depends on the perspective into which we throw it." For example, our most basic philosophical orientations (e.g., whether we are "tender-minded" rationalists or "tough-minded" empiricists), far from resting strictly on "objective premises," are almost always biased by the theories "to which we are already partial," as well as by our "temperament," which "loads the evidence" for us. "Wanting a universe that suits it," we believe "in any representation of the universe that does suit it."[6] And even what counts as true, James alleged in his "sequel" to *Pragmatism*, is affected by one's "standpoint" and, consequently, varies from person to person.[7]

In embracing (epistemological) perspectivism, historicism is actually tapping into a lineage that runs quite deep in modern—and now postmodern—philosophy. At the end of the nineteenth century, the perspectivist par excellence was Friedrich Nietzsche. If perspectivism has a dictum, it is found in Nietzsche's posthumously compiled notebooks (published under the title *The Will to Power*): "It is precisely facts that do not exist, only *interpretations*."[8] What Nietzsche meant by this rhetorical overstatement is simply that there is no way of grasping a "thing-in-itself," since knowledge is inescapably interpretive (obviously harking back to Kant). That is, we unavoidably interpret the world, and do so through our "needs" and "drives," our "lust to rule" and "will to power." Therefore, "evaluations," "values," "moral distinctions," "norms," "truths," and even projections of human subjectivity are always made from and conditioned by "a definite perspective (that of the . . . individual, a community, a race, a state, a church, a faith, a culture)."[9] The notion of a "pure, will-less, painless, timeless knowing subject," Nietzsche declared in *On the Genealogy of Morals*, is a "conceptual fiction." Observers, along with the observations they make and the things they observe, are inherently perspectival.[10]

Approximately two decades earlier, and on the other side of the Atlantic, the founder of American pragmatism, Charles Sanders Peirce (on whom I will draw repeatedly in the present chapter), already propounded a type of perspectivism. In 1868, Peirce published two important articles in the *Journal of Speculative Philosophy*, "Questions concerning Certain Faculties Claimed for Man" and "Some Consequences of the Four Incapacities," taking aim, specifically, at Descartes. For starters, the Cartesian presumption that philosophy "begins with complete doubt" is dubious. Inquiry always commences *in media res*, in the middle and midst of all sorts of initial, nondispellable "prejudices" and reflection that is already underway—that is, a perspective.[11] As he expounded in 1905, "In truth, there is but one state of mind from which you can 'set out,' namely, the very state of mind in which you actually find yourself at the time you do 'set out,'—a state in which you are laden with an immense mass of cognition already formed, of which you cannot divest yourself if you would."[12] Furthermore, Peirce put forward several refutations of Descartes's idea that human beings possess "intuitions," knowledge that "refers immediately" or directly to its referent. On the contrary, there is no cognition "that is not determined by a previous cognition of the same object." Even awareness of "the internal world" and "self-consciousness" are not known intuitively or through "the power of Introspection," but are the outcomes of "hypothetical reason" and inferences drawn from "external facts" and "evidence." Accordingly, "every thought" is "interpreted in another," and all thinking "must necessarily be in signs." This is Peirce's semiotics, according to which there is no noninferential or sign-less (perspective-less) knowing. Reality is inescapably interpreted through an endless sequence of signs. And the things that signs signify are themselves signs (in that they are able to be signified "*in* some respect or quality"), as are the "interpretants" that do the signifying.[13] It is signs all the way down, for Peirce.[14]

Over the course of the twentieth century, philosophers took up the perspectivist mantle. In the second part of *Philosophical Investigations*, the mature Ludwig Wittgenstein argued for the perspectivalness of human perceiving, employing the psychologist Joseph Jastrow's famous duck-rabbit figure to demonstrate that all seeing is really "seeing-as"—that is, aspectual, interpretive, and shaped by "custom and upbringing," previous experiences, background concepts, and language.[15]

Nearly a decade later, Thomas Kuhn (who was heavily influenced by Wittgenstein as well as by the psychology of perception and "B. L. Whorf's speculations about the effect of language on world view"[16]) called attention to the perspectival character of what many consider the paragon of scholarly objectivity: science. According to Kuhn, the beliefs held by scientists at any given time and place are, in large part, colored by distinctive and historically constituted "paradigms," the regnant conceptual models that produce and delineate coherent traditions of scientific discourse and conduct. Divergences between various schools of scientific opinion often boil down to divergences in competing paradigms, to the divergent—even "incommensurable"—ways scientists behold the world and do science within it.[17] He illustrates:

> An investigator who hoped to learn something about what scientists took the atomic theory to be asked a distinguished physicist and an eminent chemist whether a single atom of helium was or was not a molecule. . . . For the chemist the atom of helium was a molecule because it behaved like one with respect to the kinetic theory of gases. For the physicist, on the other hand, the helium atom was not a molecule because it displayed no molecular spectrum. Presumably both men were talking of the same particle, but they were viewing it through their own research training and practice.[18]

Scientific revolutions, Kuhn then claims, happen when something analogous to a "gestalt switch" occurs. When the field's up-and-coming generation of scientific practitioners hails one theoretical competitor as superior to the community's previous (and often time-honored) theories, a "paradigm shift" takes place, and scientists begin to perceive their environment in another way. Converted to a new paradigm, they "adopt new instruments and look in new places" and, even more tellingly, "see new and different things when looking with familiar instruments in places they have looked before."[19] In other words, their perspective has changed, and with it, their data and results. It is almost as if they are "responding to a different world," Kuhn surmised.[20]

In recent years, perspectivism has become a mainstay of so-called postmodern thought. As Steven Best and Douglas Kellner comment, postmodernism, first and foremost, jettisons "totalizing macroperspectives on society and history" and, instead, takes the "perspectivist" position "that theories at best provide partial perspectives on their objects, and that all cognitive representations of the world are historically and linguistically mediated."[21] And for a number of postmodernists, theories and cognitive representations of the world provide, in particular, power- and interest-laden perspectives on their objects and ideologically mediated representations of the world.[22] In a succession of provocative studies on insanity, sexuality, criminality, and several other topics, the philosopher Michel Foucault unmasked the ways in which ideas, practices, institutions, and discourses are "profoundly enmeshed in" the "political and economic structures of society." The formation of knowledge (and, for that matter, every domain of human activity, from the normalizing of behavior and the regulation of bodies, to the infliction of punishment and the maintenance of prisons) is always constituted by a "whole series of power networks." Even "truth," far from being "outside power," is inextricably linked with "multiple forms of constraint" and with those "who are charged with saying what counts as true." Truth and knowledge are, in a word, "already power."[23] As Foucault wrote in *Discipline and Punish*:

> We should admit rather that power produces knowledge (and not simply by encouraging it because it serves power or by applying it because it is useful); that power and knowledge directly imply one another; that there is no power relation without the correlative constitution of a field of knowledge, nor any knowledge that does not presuppose and constitute at the same time power relations. These "power-knowledge relations" are to be analyzed, therefore, not on the basis of a subject of knowledge who is or is not free in relation to the power system, but, on the contrary, the subject who knows, the objects to be known and the modalities of knowledge must be regarded as so many effects of these fundamental implications of power-knowledge and their historical transformations. In short, it is not the activity of the subject of knowledge that produces a corpus of knowledge, useful or resistant to power, but power-knowledge, the processes and struggles that traverse it and of which it is made up, that determines the forms and possible domains of knowledge.[24]

Fellow postmodernist and preeminent deconstructionist and post-structuralist Jacques Derrida famously derided the Western philosophical fixation on "speaking," on "reflecting" in an "immediate" and "essential" manner the "logos"—that is, some "eternal verity" or "being," some "infinite understanding of God" or "substance/essence/existence [ousia]," some "consciousness" or "so-called 'thing itself,' " some "metaphysics of presence" or "self-presence of the cogito." This "logocentric" tendency, which marks the "epoch of onto-theology," ultimately desires to "transgress the text toward something other than it, toward . . . a reality that is metaphysical, historical, psychobiographical, etc."[25] However, there is, for Derrida, no "outside-text" (*il n'y a pas de hors-texte*), no disinterested, unmediated, transcendent, perspective-free vantage point above the "the play of signifying differences that constitute language." There is, in contrast, only "writing," nothing but "supplements" or "substitutive significations which could only come forth in a chain of differential references."[26] As John Caputo comments, human beings, in Derrida's estimation, are always already immersed in a variety of "social, historical, linguistic, political, sexual networks." For that reason, no one is able to perform "an act of absolute transcendence by means of which one lifts oneself out of one's textual boots or peeks around behind the text to some sort of naked, prelinguistic, *hors*-textual, ahistorical, uninterpreted fact of the matter called the thing-in-itself, or Real Being, or the 'transcendental signified.' "[27]

Notably, Derrida is not, Caputo clarifies, denying linguistic referentiality, much less objective reality, the widespread misrepresentations of him notwithstanding.[28] He is, similar to Peirce[29] and the other aforementioned perspectivists, merely advancing the view that there is no way of referring to objective reality nonperspectivally—that is, without language, signs, and interpretation. It is not that there is no signified; it is that there is no "pure signified," a signified that "leaps over the text" and "could rightly be separated from the signifier," that is, from a perspective.[30]

Such is the venerable legacy of perspectivism in which pragmatic historicism participates. And, of all the pragmatic historicists presently under discussion, Richard Rorty is perhaps the most connected to his perspectivist roots. Exceptionally proficient at spotting subtle overlaps between pragmatism (the "chief glory" of America's intellectual heritage[31]) and comparable sensibilities, projects, sympathies, developments, and trends in analytic and Continental philosophy,[32] Rorty alludes to (and identifies with) the shared perspectivism of Peirce and Wittgenstein, Derrida and Foucault. In Rorty's mind, when Peirce says that human beings "can think only by means of words or other external symbols," when Wittgenstein says that "one can mean something by something" solely through linguistic utterance, when Derrida says that signs always refer to previous signs, and when Foucault says that "man is in the process of perishing as the being of language continues to shine ever brighter on our horizon," they are all saying something roughly equivalent, namely, that there are no "natural starting-points"—that is, no nonperspectival starting-points—"which are prior to and independent of the way some culture speaks or spoke."[33] This veritable perspectivist "chorus" is saying, in effect, that it is impossible "to step outside our skins—the traditions, linguistic and other, within which we do our thinking and self-criticism—and compare ourselves with something absolute." As a result, "the regress of interpretation" cannot be stopped, whether by Cartesian "intuition," a "transcendental signified," "Nature's Own Vocabulary," "Philosophical truth," or anything else.[34]

The monograph that launched Rorty into academic stardom (and notoriety), *Philosophy and the Mirror of Nature*, can be regarded, to some extent, as a treatise on perspectivism—or, more precisely, as a polemic against "representationalism." The book endeavors to dispel the long-standing philosophical image of "the mind as a great mirror," the "polishing" of which, according to Descartes, Kant, and their successors, enables knowledge to more accurately reflect, or "represent," reality. In place of the ahistorical "ocular metaphors" that have dominated Western epistemology (especially from the seventeenth century onwards), Rorty substitutes the "historicist sense" that is common to Wittgenstein, Dewey, Heidegger, Gadamer, James, Santayana, Quine, Sellars, and others, particularly, the sense "that words take their meanings from other words rather than by virtue of their representative character" or "their transparency to the real."[35] Rorty exhorts philosophers to "drop the notion of correspondence," to relinquish their hang-ups with "how things are," and to make peace with the fact that human beings see "as in a glass darkly"—that is, through a perspectival lens or, in his words, a "potential infinity of vocabularies." And once we let go of the picture of "an unclouded Mirror of Nature," which presumably allows "reality to be unveiled to us . . . with some unimaginable sort of immediacy," we can get on with more important business, above all, "continuing the conversation of the West." The purpose of philosophy would then become edification instead of representation, the never-ending endeavor to find better "descriptions" and "more interesting, more fruitful ways of speaking" and "expressing ourselves." It would aim to "cope" with the world, not copy it, to "strive for" truth, not "discover" it.[36]

For Rorty, antirepresentationalism and perspectivism are really two sides of the same coin. It is hard to determine if and when our ideas have correctly represented the world—that is, have gotten it "right," "corresponded" to it, or described it "as it would describe itself if it could"[37]—because there is no way to "contrast the world with what the world is known as." And there is no way to contrast the world with what the world is known as because "we can never compare human thought . . . with bare, unmediated reality."[38] We cannot, in other words, disentangle the objects we contextualize from the contexts in which they are contextualized, phenomena from our construals of them. To quote Rorty: "Between ourselves and the thing judged there always intervenes mind, language, *a perspective* chosen among dozens, one description chosen among thousands. . . . If all awareness is a linguistic affair, then we are never going to be aware of a word on the one hand and a thing-denuded-of-words on the other."[39] Things, then, are what they are only perspectivally, with respect to their "position in a web." They cannot be perceived "as they are in themselves," apart from their relation to other things and the "marks and noises" we use to depict them. There are no "skyhooks" that could hoist us out of our interpretations to a noninterpretive, "God's-eye" standpoint, a standpoint from which we "see reality plain, unmasked, naked to our gaze."[40] Instead, "interpretations, recontextualizations, go all the way down."[41]

Rorty, as I hope to establish later, is not rejecting objective *reality* (although he admittedly teeters dangerously close to the edge of antirealism), only objective *knowledge*. He is promoting the fairly obvious and relatively noncontroversial claim that we are "finite," incapable of rising above the historical "contingency of having been acculturated as we were" and reaching some theory- and mind- and context- and culture- and language-independent—that is, nonperspectival—point of view.[42] As he puts it in *Contingency, Irony, and Solidarity*, we cannot transcend "the various vocabularies we have employed and find a metavocabulary which somehow takes account of *all possible* vocabularies."[43]

In short, for Rorty, and indeed for all the pragmatic historicists upon whom this book focuses, there are no advantageous angles from which to observe things in a direct, transparent, detached, value-free, disinterested, unmediated, impartial, or pure manner. As William Dean plainly avers, the renunciation of naive realism in epistemology entails that events in space and time cannot "be known, without bias, as objective correlatives."[44] Nor do we have, according to Sheila Greeve Davaney, any "nonhistorical" and "nonperspectival" means of testing our various accounts of the world against the world as it is in itself—an "uninterpreted" world, as it were—in order to ascertain (definitively or absolutely) whose version "has it right."[45] More impressively, Davaney's perspectivism manages to couple the linguistic awareness of a Wittgenstein, a Peirce, a Derrida, a Rorty, with a Foucauldian, Nietzschean, and Westian[46] vigilance about the mechanisms of power. As I briefly mentioned in chapter 2, Davaney upholds a *thick*—that is, a materialist and politically discerning—historicism, spotlighting the "ideological commitments" to which our historical perspectives are tied, the "social relations" of which they are reflective, and the "specific values" to which they are partial.[47]

To summarize, historicism's perspectivism puts serious restraints on what we can say about the true and the real, underscoring the fact that "all of our linguistic and conceptual forms of thought, our assertions of knowledge and truth about . . . historical reality," are "localized, contextualized, and relative" and are "situated and conditioned by their perspective."[48]

The Second Check: Constructivism

But pragmatic historicists go a step further: our knowledge claims are not just perspectives; they are also human constructions. Pragmatic historicism, that is to say, advances a species of *constructivism*, realizing that one of the upshots of historicizing everything is that so much of what customarily gets passed off as discovered—including truth, meaning, selfhood, and even reality—turns out to be created, constructed.[49]

James's constructivism found expression in a type of humanism, especially with regard to the concept of truth. The whole notion of the Truth ("with a big T") is "a perfect idol of the rationalistic mind," James resolved. What we have, instead, are "truths in the plural," approximations, not literal duplications or transcriptions, of the world. More to the point, true propositions are additions to both the "subject" and the "predicate" parts of reality, humanly created sentences or tools that actually contribute to and "carve" up experience. "Truths emerge from facts; but they dip forward into facts again and add to them; which facts again create or reveal new truth (the word is indifferent) and so on indefinitely."[50] Accordingly, the empirical realm, far from being "ready-made," is "what is made of it," so much so that "faith in a fact can help create the fact."[51] The world is "plastic" and "malleable" to the constructions humans "engender" upon it, "waiting to receive its final touches at our hands."[52]

In brief, although "the stubborn fact remains that there *is* a sensible flux" (cf. the following section), "what is *true of it* seems from first to last to be largely a matter of our own creation."[53] Or as James elegantly stated in his very first philosophical essay, "Remarks on Spencer's Definition of Mind as Correspondence" (1876):

> The knower is an actor, and co-efficient of the truth on the one side, whilst on the other he registers the truth which he helps to create. Mental interests, hypotheses, postulates, so far as they are bases for human action—action which to a great extent transforms the world—help to *make* the truth which they declare. In other words, there belongs to mind, from its birth upward, a spontaneity, a vote. It is in the game, and not a mere looker-on; and its judgments of the *should-be*, its ideals, cannot be peeled off from the body of the *cogitandum* as if they were excrescences, or meant, at most, survival.[54]

Dewey also believed that "the knower is an actor" and that the mind has "a vote," famously abjuring "the spectator theory of knowledge," which equates understanding with passive correspondence to "the antecedently real," with a "reduplication in ideas of what exists already in the world." In contrast, Dewey "naturalized" intelligence, highlighting its capacity to experiment with and to readjust that which is given in experience. Ideas "have a constructive office," able to "change" the "state of things" and to "rearrange and reconstruct in some way . . . the world in which we live." And thought has a "positive function," capable of "*re*constituting the present stage of things instead of merely knowing it."[55] Put another way, knowing is essentially "one mode of doing," organically related to, not dualistically separate from, action, practice, and problem-solving. Additionally, the things that *are* known are actually things "*to be* known." Reality is neither intrinsically rational nor intrinsically irrational, but "intellig*ible*" and "understand*able*," becoming an object of knowledge after *we* subject it to the processes of knowing and use it to satisfy human needs. Our observations, therefore, do more than "register" what is real; they help make and mutate it. Likewise, the knower is not an outside bystander in the epistemological act, but "a part and partner" who has an effect on "what is finally known," who shapes and reshapes it through "initiative, inventiveness and intelligently directed labor."[56]

More than any other pragmatic historicist on the contemporary scene, Rorty emphasizes (maybe overemphasizes) Jamesian and Deweyan constructivism, playing up the constructive capacities of human beings and the constructed character of human products. For instance, he maintains that meaning is a social construction: "Humans have to dream up the point of human life, and cannot appeal to a nonhuman standard to determine whether they have chosen wisely."[57] In fact, everything is a social construction, according to Rorty—from morality, human rights, law, and communal commitments, to selfhood, language, conscience, and even atoms.[58] Truth, too, is socially constructed, is "made rather than found."[59] Rorty argues for the "madness"—the constructedness and humanness—of truth almost syllogistically:

(Premise 1) Truths are properties of sentences.

(Premise 2) Sentences are components of languages.

(Premise 3) Languages are creations of human beings.

(Conclusion) Therefore, truths are human creations.[60]

His constructivism notwithstanding, Rorty chafes hard against accusations of "linguistic idealism." He has no doubt that there are objects that exist independently of "human beliefs and desires." He has no doubt that "there were trees and stars long before there were statements about trees and stars." He has no doubt that "most things in space and time are the effects of causes which do not include human mental states," and that when we talk we are "talking mostly about things to which [we] stand in real cause-and-effect relations."[61] Rorty is even enough of a realist to affirm a relationship of "aboutness" and "causation," albeit not "representation,"[62] between human knowledge and "other items in the universe." That is, there is a real cosmos outside of ourselves, and it "may cause us to be justified in believing a sentence true," which means that our constructions are not completely "arbitrary." Still, acknowledging, "with common sense," that there is an external reality that is "not our creation," and that it sometimes pressures us to hold certain views, is one thing; imagining that it contains "self-subsistent," "sentence-shaped chunks called 'facts'" waiting to be discovered or a language of its own waiting to be spoken is something else altogether. "The world is out there, but descriptions of the world are not."[63] The world, persists Rorty, is mostly "indifferent to our descriptions of it."[64]

To summarize, pragmatic historicism's second check on the true and the real—constructivism—posits that our knowledge and rationality, our conceptualizations of who we are, why we are here, and what we should be doing, our scientific theories and artistic expressions, our moral, philosophical, religious, and cultural systems, our truths and conceptions of reality, are exactly that—ours. They are not absolutes that are "out there" awaiting human recognition. They are not objective facts that are reflective of something extrahistorical, something beyond the trappings of time and chance (e.g., Plato's forms, Descartes's indubitable foundations, God's revelation). They are, rather, social constructions that we clever and imaginative, yet finite and fallible, animals have ourselves built in order to predict, control, explain, describe, influence, and modify what happens and to deal, in a tentative and pragmatic fashion, with the exigencies and vicissitudes of existence.[65]

The Third Check: Nonfoundationalism

That we (at least partly) construct reality, and do so within the boundaries of a particular past, place, and perspective and inside a natural, empirical realm that is itself ever-evolving, historically contingent and conditioned, imperfect, pluralistic, and finite, entails that those constructs do not—and cannot—furnish incontrovertible epistemological foundations. Pragmatic historicism is, in a word, *nonfoundationalistic.*

Foundationalism is typically traced back to Descartes. In the opening passage of *Meditations on First Philosophy* (1641), Descartes wrote:

> Some years ago I was struck by the large number of falsehoods that I had accepted as true in my childhood, and by the highly doubtful nature of the whole edifice that I had subsequently based on them. I realized that it was necessary, once in the course of my life, to demolish everything completely and start again right from the foundations if I wanted to establish anything at all in the sciences that was stable and likely to last.[66]

Descartes went on to portray such stabilized and lasting epistemological foundations as a kind of "Archimedean point":[67]

> Anything which admits of the slightest doubt I will set aside just as if I had found it to be wholly false; and I will proceed in this way until I recognize something certain. . . . Archimedes used to demand just one firm and immovable point in order to shift the entire earth; so too I can hope for great things if

I manage to find just one thing, however slight, that is certain and unshakeable.[68]

To state the extremely obvious, pragmatic historicists are profoundly suspicious of the modern Cartesian enterprise, of what Jeffrey Stout describes as the effort to purify "thought of historical contingency."[69] Dean goes so far as to make nonfoundationalism the very first principle of "the new historicism."[70] In point of fact, historicism has been nonfoundationalist from the outset. As I recounted in chapter 2, the historicists of the German *Aufklärung* (along with their nineteenth-century heirs) set forth a modern alternative to Enlightenment universalism and foundationalism, that is, to the postulation of "pure reason" and the pursuit of certitude-bestowing and tradition-independent Archimedean points.[71] Nonfoundationalism also blossomed in the fertile soil of early American pragmatism. Peirce got the ball rolling by making short work of Descartes's presupposition that certainty can be reached by instituting indubitable foundations, and that the human mind is able to ascertain those foundations through some a priori "fountain of true principles" (i.e., clear and distinct ideas secured by "the individual consciousness"), some special faculty of insight (i.e., noninferential intuitions undetermined by prior cognitions or signs), or some incorrigible, prejudice-free point of departure (i.e., the method of "universal doubt").[72] In short, Peirce participated in what Cornel West splendidly refers to as "the American evasion of philosophy," circumventing the "epistemology-centered" outlook of Descartes and his ilk.[73]

James quickly followed suit. As West again observes, Peirce and James, although often at loggerheads, each shunned "the Cartesian problematic" and turned "away from foundations, certainties, and bases and toward effects, consequences, and practices."[74] In *The Will to Believe*, James lamented that human beings are "absolutists" by nature, appealing to "objective evidence and certitude" to shore up their perspectives. In actual fact, though, there are no such things on "this moonlit and dream-visited planet." There are no propositions "ever regarded by any one as evidently certain" that have not eventually been called "absolutely false" or at least "sincerely questioned by some one else." There are no definitive, foundational criteria that can be deployed to infallibly adjudicate between humanity's "contradictory array of opinions," whether "revelation," "the *consensus gentium*," "the instincts of the heart," "common-sense," "synthetic judgment *a priori*," or "clear and distinct ideas, guaranteed by the veracity of God." There are, in a word, no beliefs that are not "reinterpretable or corrigible."[75]

Like Peirce and James, Dewey wanted to bring an end to "the quest for a certainty which shall be absolute and unshakeable," a quest that predates even Descartes. The West's "most enduring philosophic tradition" has sought to transcend the limits of nature and experience, swearing fealty, instead, to what Dewey labeled "the really real"—timeless realms, eternal objects, unchangeable deities, necessary principles, ideal forms, sure foundations:

> Whatever names were used, they had one thing in common: they were used to designate something taken to be fixed, immutable, and therefore out of time. . . . Philosophical doctrines which disagreed about virtually everything else were at one in the assumption that their distinctive concern as philosophy was to search for the immutable and ultimate—that which *is*—without respect to the temporal or spatial.[76]

The "search for the immutable and ultimate" has actually been spurred by a basic historicist intuition, namely, that a historical world, a world of ceaseless "becoming" and "perishing," is a world of "absence," "incompleteness," "finitude," "imperfection," "multiplicity," and "strife." In reaction, philosophy has sought, dualistically, to take shelter in realities that are fundamentally ahistorical and, hence, infallible—"unshakeable," "permanent," "total," "all-comprehensive," and "one." And for Western philosophers since Socrates, it was rational thought and pure understanding that presumably allowed human beings to rise above the empirical, natural sphere, to escape from the perils of "vicissitude and uncertainty," "chance and change," and to mentally grasp, or correspond to, universal, essential, perfect being and fixed, certain, antecedent truths. Dewey, however, hoped modern philosophy might muster the pragmatic wherewithal to abandon the "cognitive quest for absolute assurance" and its resulting "spectator theory of knowledge," foregoing "over-pretentious" (i.e., foundationalist) claims to conclusiveness.[77]

Present-day American neopragmatists and historicists are just as critical of foundationalism. For them, any and all efforts "to achieve sure and certain knowledge," knowledge that is "applicable for all times and places" and "predicated upon unquestionable foundations," appear "misguided and illusory."[78] For example, West approves of the "move toward antifoundationalism in epistemology." In West's account, Quine, Goodman, and other prominent postmodern American philosophers pick up where Nietzsche left off, undermining the Western philosophical struggle to found human understanding on solid, secure, and certain epistemological grounds.[79] The repudiation of foundationalism is perhaps best exemplified by Wilfrid Sellars, West points out. In particular, Sellars debunks "the Myth of the Given," the assumption that there is "a given element—a self-justifying, intrinsically credible, theory-neutral, noninferential element—in experience that provides the foundations for other knowledge claims and serves as the final terminating points for chains of epistemic justification."[80]

Another postmodern American nonfoundationalist with whom West allies himself is Rorty.[81] Rorty suggests that foundationalism ultimately—but futilely—strives to "end the potentially infinite regress of propositions-brought-forward-in-defense-of-other-propositions." It attempts to take us "outside language, history, and finitude" in order to put us in touch with "the atemporal," with "immutable structures" that are "so compelling that their accuracy cannot be doubted."[82] Essentially, the historicist move in philosophy is the post-Cartesian willingness to stop trying "to answer the epistemological skeptic," to tame the "desire to find 'foundations' to which one might cling, frameworks beyond which one must not stray, objects which impose themselves, representations which cannot be gainsaid."[83] In Rorty's estimation, we need neither a "transcultural, transhistorical order of reasons," nor an "ultimate source of evidence" (e.g., scripture, tradition, sense experience, common sense), nor a special mental faculty (be it Plato's eye of the soul, which perceives the realm of being, or Descartes's eye of the mind, which intuits clear and distinct ideas) to validate our truth claims; it is enough simply "not to believe anything which cannot be justified to the rest of us." Being "rational," in other words, requires that we argue publicly and subject our convictions to the judgment of our peers, not that we establish certitude, that we make "an airtight case" before "our interlocutors," not that we build on "an unshakeable foundation."[84]

In short, pragmatic historicism limits the true and the real by repudiating foundationalism, the notion "that there is or must be some permanent, ahistorical matrix or framework to which we can ultimately appeal in determining the nature of rationality, knowledge, truth, reality, goodness, or rightness."[85]

The Fourth Check: Fallibilism

The epistemological alternative to foundationalism, in a pragmatic historicist perspective, is not relativism, nihilism, subjectivism, or skepticism, but *fallibilism*. Fallibilism asserts that all our conceptions of what is true and real (and good, beautiful, valuable, etc.) are fallible—uncertain, incomplete, interpretive, experimental, tentative, conjectural, selective, hypothetical, revisable, and falsifiable—and, consequently, open to constant interrogation, reformulation, correction, and rejection.[86]

Along with pragmatism, Peirce invented fallibilism, "the doctrine that our knowledge is never absolute but always swims, as it were, in a continuum of uncertainty and of indeterminacy."[87] In other words, having exorcized the foundationalist "spirit of Cartesianism," Peirce pointed to the correctability, modifiability, questionability, and rejectability of every claim to truth and habit of thought. A fallibilist is not the same as a skeptic, he clarified. There is a huge difference between "knowing outward things as they really are" (which skepticism precludes) and "being *absolutely certain* of doing so in any special case" (which fallibilism precludes). An unabashed realist (see the ensuing section), Peirce recognized that human beings might actually acquire knowledge of an external reality, that is, of an "object of a well-founded hypothesis." But in Peirce's fallibilistic scheme, "well-foundedness," as Robert Neville explains, involves criticizing that "hypothesis in all respects, testing it in all ways, which requires an infinite amount of time because at no finite stage of probation is it ever infallible."[88] For that reason, inquiry—which struggles to "settle opinion" and "attain a state of belief"—ought to be modeled on the self-corrective procedures of scientific investigation. Here, an indefinitely extended community of critical inquirers interminably assesses and refines warranted and reasonable, but utterly fallible and provisional, hypotheses:[89]

> Philosophy ought to imitate the successful sciences in its methods, so far as to proceed only from tangible premises which can be subjected to careful scrutiny, and to trust rather to the multitude and variety of its arguments than to the conclusiveness to any one. Its reasoning should not form a chain which is no stronger than its weakest link, but a cable whose fibres may be ever so slender, provided they are sufficiently numerous and intimately connected.[90]

Or, as Peirce wrote a number of years later, the philosophical enterprise needs to emulate the experimentalist practices of the natural sciences,

> where investigators, instead of contemning each the work of most of the others as misdirected from beginning to end, cooperate, stand upon one another's shoulders, and multiply incontestable

results; where every observation is repeated and isolated observations go for little; where every hypothesis that merits attention is subjected to severe but fair examination, and only after the predictions to which it leads have been remarkably borne out by experience is trusted at all, and even then only provisionally.[91]

James and Dewey followed in Peirce's fallibilist footsteps. James claimed that there are only fallibilized ideas, ideas that are "man-made," "mutable," uncertain, possibly untrue, and susceptible to error, adjustment, growth, and replacement. For James, all understanding is "incomplete," "insufficient," and "subject to addition" (or subtraction, as it were), continuously altered alongside and in light of new knowledge and novel experiences.[92] Even our principles of "common sense," as well as our "most assured conclusions concerning matters of fact," are nothing more than "extraordinarily successful hypotheses" that, while remaining modifiable, have stood the test of time and have come to be "used by everybody."[93]

Reminiscent of Peirce, Dewey opined that philosophy ought to come to terms with the fact that every idea and idealism is a "hypothesis," not a "finality." As "hypothetical" and "experimental," philosophical, ethical, and religious conceptions, no less than scientific ones, are utterly fallible—that is, "conditional" and "provisional," vulnerable to "unremitting observation," "scrupulous development," and "thoroughgoing testing," reliant on "the most dependable methods of inquiry," formed out of judgments of "probability" rather than certitude, reconstructed in accordance with "actual need," and evaluated by "the consequences of the operations they define and direct."[94] "They are hypotheses to be worked out in practice, and to be rejected, corrected and expanded as they fail or succeed in giving our present experience the guidance it requires."[95]

For pragmatic historicists of both yesterday and today, epistemic fallibility is an inexorable upshot of the historicalness of human life. Expressed otherwise, knowledge is fallible precisely because people remain circumscribed and constituted by the particularities of their historical contexts, cultures, and circumstances, live in a changing universe, and perceive reality through perspectivally mediated and socially constructed frames of interpretation. As Cornel West reasons, to acknowledge the "historicity of our claims"—the fact that "our background prejudices, presuppositions, and prejudgments" always lie in between our thoughts and the external world—is "to give up the all-too-human quest for certainty and indubitability" and to accept an "inescapable fallibilism."[96] Davaney puts it even more dramatically, suggesting that fallibilism is a corollary of the very nature of historical reality:

> The original American pragmatists [had] . . . a profound sense of the fallibility and limitation of historical existence. I believe pragmatic historicism . . . shares that tragic sense. . . . Historicism . . . concedes that the options concretely offered up by history are never as inclusive as they could be. History grants to each people and place the option of addressing some dilemmas, but not others. The decisions made by earlier communities result in some possibilities while closing off others for those that come later. The limitations of mind and imagination, of heart and conscience, of physical ability and natural resources all contribute to the limited possibilities that are available in any concrete historical moment, giving us options but constricting them as well. Future generations will certainly wonder, as we have done concerning our forebears, whether we could have done better. And of course we always could have to some degree. But a tragic historicism knows that while history is open and malleable it can also be stingy.[97]

In brief, there is something about history per se—its finitude, its contingency, its mutability, its fragility, its impermanence, its spatiotemporality, its localness, its potentiality-constraining givenness, its inherent ambiguities, tragedies, and limits, its "stinginess"—that compels us to thoroughly fallibilize our ventures, to admit that "they will not gain us a new certitude, promise of moral rightness, or guarantee of positive outcomes" but will, instead, be most assuredly "criticized and left behind by some future generation."[98] Such fallibilism, to say the least, has a chastening, humbling effect on our truth claims. After all, to be a fallibilist is, as Rorty announces, to concede that "what is rational for us to believe" today may not always be so. It is to realize that "somebody may come up with a better idea." It is to acknowledge "that there is always room for improved belief, since new evidence, or new hypotheses, or a whole new vocabulary, may come along."[99]

The Fifth Check: Instrumentalism

The fifth and final pragmatic historicist constraint on the true and the real is *instrumentalism*, which is the centerpiece of a pragmatist philosophy. In fact, whatever else pragmatism is, it is the conviction that beliefs are, first and foremost, instruments people concoct for solving certain problems and adapting to particular environmental conditions (social as well as natural), and that evaluating those beliefs finally comes down to determining how efficaciously they execute the instrumental functions for which they were created—that is, whether or not they *result in* a viable solution to a problem or a successful adaptation to the environment.

Pragmatism's pragmatic instrumentalism is, in a way, an outgrowth of its underlying commitment to naturalism, especially Darwinian evolution.[100] To be sure, Darwin's influence on classical pragmatism was second to none.[101] Essentially, Peirce, James, and Dewey, as Louis Menand chronicles, extrapolated from Darwin the notion that ideas are no different than any other natural trait, evolving to assist a particular organism (i.e., *Homo sapiens*) in adapting to its environmental surroundings.[102] To quote James, "The pragmatistic view [is] that all our theories are *instrumental*, are mental modes of *adaptation* to reality, rather than revelations or gnostic answers to some divinely instituted world-enigma."[103] Nearly twenty years earlier, in the concluding chapter of *The Principles of Psychology*, James used Darwin's "quite convincing" theory of "accidental variation" to show that all "the features of our organic mental structure"—instincts, innate ideas, conceptualities of time, space, number, resemblance, and causation, mathematical relations, a priori or necessary truths, metaphysical, aesthetic, and moral principles, and so on—have a "naturalistic . . . *cause*." They are "spontaneous variations" that have been naturally selected because they are "fitted by good luck (those of them which have survived) to take cognizance of objects (that is, to steer us in our active dealings with them)" and, as such, "help [us] and [our] progeny to survive."[104] In a word, for the early pragmatists, concepts, thoughts, beliefs, and so on, are what Peirce called "habits" or "rules of action," or what Dewey called "instruments." Their "origin," averred Dewey, is "in biological adaptive behaviour," and their "ultimate function" is "a prospective control of the conditions of the environment."[105] Menand elaborates:

> [Peirce, James, and Dewey] all believed that ideas are not "out there" waiting to be discovered, but are tools—like forks and knives and microchips—that people devise to cope with the world in which they find themselves. . . . They believed that ideas do not develop according to some inner logic of their own, but are entirely dependent, like germs, on their human carriers and the environment. And they believed that since ideas are provisional responses to particular and unreproducible circumstances, their survival depends not on their immutability but on their adaptability.[106]

Contemporary neopragmatists, such as Rorty, continue to play up the indelible link between pragmatism and Darwinism. The point of departure for pragmatism is, according to Rorty, Darwin's "animalization" of the human. In a Darwinian account, people are, "like everything in the universe, accidentally produced assemblages of particles," utterly natural creatures "doing their best" to "deal with" the world. And knowledge and language as a whole are among the many "tools which these clever animals have developed" for the purposes of "manipulating" that world and addressing the various problems it poses. Accordingly, sentences, belief systems, theories, and so forth are, Rorty declares, nothing more than "a set of gimmicks for keeping a certain species alive and healthy," a series of "noises and marks" that enable us *Homo sapiens* not to "copy" what is out there, but to "master" and "adapt ourselves to" what is out there. At no stage of biological evolution did human beings "stop just coping with reality and start representing it," which means that an idea is akin to a spearhead or a hammer or a stethoscope, is a "part of the interaction of the organism with its environment," and is a device for "coordinating the activities of individuals" and, more generally, for making life more pleasurable and less painful.[107]

If human ideas are instrumental in nature, then the standard for assessing the meaning and truth of those ideas, the pragmatists surmise, lies in their function and utility, in the results that ensue from acting on them and putting them to work. "This," proclaimed James, "is the principle of Peirce, the principle of pragmatism."[108] Indeed, the pragmatic criterion—the hallmark of American philosophical pragmatism—was introduced in Peirce's 1878 essay "How to Make Our Ideas Clear." Here, Peirce suggested that achieving clearness and distinctness in thought involves ascertaining the different "practices" and "modes of action" to which rival notions give rise. We know what an idea means when we understand the tangible "habits it produces" and "how it might lead us to act." Peirce went on to spell out the maxim of pragmatism: "Consider what effects, which might conceivably have practical bearings, we conceive the object of our conception to have. Then, our conception of these effects is the whole of our conception of the object."[109]

James considered Peirce's "principle of practicalism—or pragmatism" a helpful method for settling otherwise intractable intellectual debates (design versus chance, freewill versus determinism, materialism versus theism, etc.). In both *Pragmatism* and the earlier essay "Philosophical Conceptions and Practical Results" (1898), James alleged, with Peirce, that ideas are, in effect, "rules" or "habits" that inspire "conduct," and that interminable and theoretically irresolvable disagreements, therefore, are best resolved by tracing the concrete ramifications each perspective bodes for "somebody, somehow, somewhere, and somewhen." James wants to know what "difference" it would make in "anyone's actual life" if one "world-formula" instead of another gets accepted. And if the differences are negligible, and "the alternatives mean practically the same thing," then the quarrel is "specious and verbal" and "unworthy of further contention"—in a word, "idle." "There can be no difference," he quipped, that does not "make a difference."[110] So, for James, establishing whether or not assenting to an outlook is warranted boils down to verifying its *effects*. A pragmatist asks, what is the concept in question "*known as*? In what facts does it result? What is its *cash value* in terms of particular experience?"[111] Thus, to determine meaning and truth, the pragmatic criterion looks toward "last things" rather than "first things," toward "actions" rather than "principles," toward consequences rather than "necessities," toward the "fruits" rather than the "roots" of our thoughts. The true, particularly, is not what mirrors or transcribes or copies the way the world "really" is in and of itself, but is "the name of whatever proves itself to be good in the way of belief." It is, that is to say, what "leads to consistency, stability and flowing human intercourse." It is what "works," "guides," and "fits." It is what "pays" and is "profitable" over time and "in the long run." It is what saves labor and is satisfactory, "instrumentally" speaking. It is what assimilates new information and old opinions with as much conservation and as little disturbance as possible.[112] The false, by implication, is the exact opposite, denoting anything that is "instable" and "useless," "lying and unreliable," "unverifiable and unsupported," "inconsistent and contradictory," "artificial and eccentric," and "unreal in the sense of being of no practical account."[113]

For the most part, Dewey resonated with the pragmatism of Peirce and James.[114] Knowledge, insisted Dewey, is a "tool," an "instrumentality of direction." As a result, the truth—or, better, "warranted assertibility"[115]—of any belief is substantiated by demonstrating what can be "done with it," by specifying the upshots of its usage and gauging its workability and functionality.[116] All concepts, however time-honored, noble, and venerable, must justify themselves by virtue of their effects, "present or potential." Dewey cared less about their "conformity" with reality and more about their ability to "control" and "cope" with it. As a matter of fact, the very "function of intelligence . . . is not that of copying the objects of the environment, but rather of taking account of the way in which more effective and more profitable relations with these objects may be established in the future."[117] For that reason, Dewey shifted the measure of judgment from "what precedes to what comes after, from the retrospective to the prospective, from antecedents to consequences," praising James for "looking forward instead of backward," toward "what the world and life might become" as opposed to "what they have been." Intellectual viewpoints, social structures, and moral teachings are appraised in light of what lies ahead, not "what is said to be antecedently known," pragmatism teaches. What matters is that which they "will do," the repercussions that follow from living them out. An authentic and worthwhile belief is a "weapon" for facing "the unknown," bringing about a "successful outcome," and "removing the undesirable, the inconsistent," not "a bare transcript or duplicate of some finished and done-for arrangement pre-existing in nature." Even scientific hypotheses are "good and sound" only if they work well, that is, "if they do what is wanted of them," yield certain "observable results," and satisfy "the conditions set by the nature of the problem in hand." Pragmatists, then, favor the adverbs "truly" and "falsely" over the nouns "truth" and "falsehood" and the adjectives "true" and "false." The latter stand as intellectualist "fetishes," wrongly reputed to be a priori or intrinsic qualities, whereas the former connote "way[s] . . . of acting" or "propert[ies] of use and employment," consequences of leading either to or away from desired ends.[118]

Rorty, while putting a more relativistic spin on pragmatism than Dewey, James, and especially Peirce (an observation about which I shall say more momentarily), nonetheless captures the spirit of the pragmatic criterion:

> Pragmatists hope to make it impossible for the sceptic to raise the question, "Is our knowledge of things adequate to the way things really are?" They substitute for this traditional question the *practical* question, "Are our ways of describing things, of relating them to other things so as to make them fulfill our needs more adequately, as good as possible? Or can we do better?"[119]

For Rorty, all ideas are vetted not by referring to some ahistorical standard or standpoint, but by trying them out and seeing what happens. Galileo's discovery that things are "masses of particles blindly bumping each other" is true not because it "fits" reality as a key to a lock, but because it allows us to make "much better predictions" than Aristotle's teleological and anthropomorphic stance does. Modern science's description of the cosmos as "infinite and cold and comfortless" is true not because it enunciates "Nature's Own Vocabulary," but because it gives us "a better handle on the universe" than "thinking of it as finite, homey, planned, and relevant to human concerns." Democracy's vision of a government founded on the principles of "toleration," "free inquiry," and "undistorted communication" is true not because it mirrors a universal moral law, but because, given the choice, nobody would prefer the inverse—that is, a fascist society based on intolerance, censorship, and propaganda. So, when it comes to justification, Rorty, following the classical pragmatists, defers to the *future*, "to the substance of things hoped for," to the "detailed practical advantages" of holding one position rather than another.[120] Deciding "what propositions to assert, which pictures to look at, what narratives to listen to and comment on and retell," are finally decisions "about what will help us get what we want (or about what we *should* want)."[121]

To sum up, Dean notes that pragmatic historicists, having repudiated representationalism, naive realism, and foundationalism, "are driven to accept pragmatism."[122] And pragmatism places yet another check on truth, naturalizing its origins and instrumentalizing its character and criterion.

In Defense of Getting Things Right: Toward a Paleopragmatic Historicism

In my view, pragmatic historicism's perspectivism, constructivism, nonfoundationalism, fallibilism, and instrumentalism are assets, accounting for the perspectival, constructed, uncertain, provisional, and instrumental nature of human understanding (a sentiment that is becoming more and more widely accepted in our "postmodern" age), without devolving (as some other likeminded philosophies do) into deleterious forms of subjectivism, skepticism, or nihilism. Richard Bernstein enthuses that pragmatists (and, I would add, pragmatically inclined historicists) "provide a philosophical orientation that is truly *beyond* the sterile opposition (and oscillation) between objectivism and relativism," beyond the Scylla of a knowledge that objectively mirrors (Rorty) or directly spectates (Dewey) the world, and the Charybdis of a nominalism that denies truth, objective facts, and universal validity claims altogether.[123] In short, pragmatism, as well as a pragmatic historicism, put considerable constraints and checks on the true and the real, *but without obliterating them*. As Dean (commenting on Bernstein) assures, "No longer do we think that, if something is not established objectivistically, then it is merely relativistic and, for that reason, meaningless."[124]

That being said, pragmatic historicists, especially those of the postmodern or neopragmatic variety, do sometimes flirt with nominalism and relativism. Rorty, we will see, is perhaps the most glaring offender, tantalizingly proclaiming that "the world is well lost,"[125] and that "corresponding with reality" and "getting things right" are "empty metaphysical compliments" or "rhetorical pats on the back."[126] To counteract this more nominalistic, antirealist, and relativistic—and seductive—neopragmatism, I will attempt to tease out a *paleopragmatic* historicism. A paleopragmatic historicism is two-pronged. The first prong is what I will term *constructive realism*, according to which truths arise out of the collaborative interactions between humanity's contingent, fallible, interest-laden, and culturally, ideologically, semiotically, and linguistically mediated social constructions, on the one hand, and an ontologically real and epistemologically constraining objective environment, on the other. The second prong is a reclamation of classical pragmatism's sophisticated and refurbished view of correspondence, where "correspondence" designates (1) the ideal and regulative *end* of inquiry (as opposed to the capability of objectively mirroring things as they are in themselves, without the media of language, tradition, culture, ideology, theory, semiosis, context, perspective, etc.), and (2) the *meaning* of true knowledge (as opposed to the means of evaluating it). In order to push pragmatic historicism in a more paleopragmatist—that is, a more realistic and nonrelativistic—direction, I will recover the often neglected, downplayed, underappreciated, and misconstrued realisms of James and Dewey as well as their empirically robust, anti-anti-intellectualist, nonsubjectivistic, and correspondence-amenable versions of pragmatism. Ultimately, however, I will need to look beyond James and Dewey, to pragmatists who do not explicitly identify as historicists, specifically, to the father of the pragmatist school, Charles Sanders Peirce, as well as to a small sampling of contemporary American philosophers[127] who have followed in his wake: Robert Neville, Douglas Anderson, John McDowell, Donald Crosby, Nancy Frankenberry, John Ryder, and Wesley Wildman.[128]

Historicist Epistemology as Constructivist and Realist:
Balancing the Social Construction of Reality

Earlier, I suggested that historicism regards truth, reason, value, meaning, and so on, as made, invented, constructed. But even the most humanistic of historicists suspect that truth, reason, value, meaning, and so on, are not *merely* made, *merely* invented, *merely* constructed. Delwin Brown generalizes that the relationship between the self and its given environment (both social and natural) "is best described as interactive, codeterminant, or reciprocal," so that "neither is simply 'causing' (creating, imagining, constructing) nor 'being caused' (receiving, picturing, corresponding). Each is to some degree creative subject and to some degree created object, plastic or malleable coparticipants in an interconnected process."[129] The subsequent analysis attempts to apply such a "constructive realism" to a historicist epistemology. True knowledge, I submit, emerges from and consists of the collaborations between creaturely interpreters and a world that is extant, external, and exerting—empirically as well as epistemologically. I shall argue that pragmatic historicism's constructivist instincts, although inevitably dominant, are (or should be) balanced, and sometimes even tempered, by a realist seriousness about history's constraints and ineradicable overagainstness. The historicist stress on agency, contextuality, creativity, novelty, perspectivity, and so on, implies that the phenomenon sociologists of knowledge and postmodern theorists refer to as "the social construction of reality" is real;[130] but so is the reality on which our social constructions are heaped, toward which they are directed, to which they are receptive, and by which they are gauged. As Bernstein acknowledges, "Regardless of the many errors of those who have been wedded to the concept of representation . . . [and] the doctrine that the function of the mind is to mirror nature, we cannot avoid the 'primordial intuition' that there is a world that is independent of our beliefs and fancies that forces itself upon us willy-nilly and constrains what we can think, say, and do."[131]

One way of making the constructive realist argument is to say, with William Dean, that historicism is (or should be) a *tertium quid* that coalesces Kantian and Lockean sensibilities, while avoiding the excessive subjectivism of the former and the excessive objectivism of the latter. First of all, akin to Immanuel Kant, historicists, Dean declares, are deeply aware of the processes by which the human subject actively "fabricates the world."[132] In his recent book about the enormous impact Kantian and Hegelian idealism had on the founding of modern theology, Gary Dorrien observes that Kant managed to repel "extreme subjectivism" (à la Descartes and Berkeley) by alleging that the "universal forms of experience" are the "intersubjective" and "*necessary conditions* of ideas" and by asserting, in good realist fashion, that the empirical world and the external entities perceived by the senses, "whatever they are, are real." Yet the fulcrum on which Kant's philosophy hinged was, Dorrien allows, "subjective idealism."[133] Since sense data are always received, organized, and synthesized through—and, hence, affected by—"*a priori* categories of understanding,"[134] humans have no direct comprehension of "reality per se" or of "things in themselves" (*Dinge an sich*). On the contrary, the perceiving, transcendental subject knows phenomena only as constructs of the mind or as "representations."[135] Kant put it starkly: "Everything intuited in space or time, and hence all objects of an experience possible for us, are nothing but appearances. I.e., they are mere presentations that—in the way in which they are presented, viz., as extended beings, or as series of changes—have no existence with an intrinsic basis, i.e., outside our thoughts."[136]

Dean notices that the logic of Kantian constructivism is implicit in present-day narrativist, neopragmatic, deconstructionist, and postmodern thought, except narrativists, neopragmatists, deconstructionists, and postmodernists regard narratives, cultures, languages, theories, symbols, paradigms, group identities, and interpretations (rather than Kant's "pure concepts") as the primary funders and shapers of consciousness.[137] And, in Dean's reading, historicists, too, are Kantians (or, better, half-Kantians) inasmuch as they recognize that knowledge is cognitively, culturally, perspectivally, and historically constructed and "laden with the personal and social bias of the knower."[138] As Davaney verifies:

> Kant has . . . played a substantively positive role in influencing both the historicism that emerged in the nineteenth century and the historicism of our current scene. . . . While the ahistorical categories structuring the knowing process have given way to interpretations of reason that are less universal and more contingent and localized, the recognition that the human knower is not only a passive recipient but an active participant in the construction of knowledge contributed immensely to the eventual historicizing of knowledge itself.[139]

But, Dean continues, historicism's constructivist, or Kantian, pole is (or should be) counterbalanced by its realist pole, its Lockean pole. As an empiricist, John Locke talked about the reality outside "language and symbol" and the "actual real existence" to which ideas should refer. In their Lockean mode, historicists stress that what is experienced and known, while subjectively "constituted," is "more than subjective." The world may be narratively, semiotically, socially, and linguistically constructed, but *pace* radical varieties of postmodern neo-Kantianism, there is a natural, physical world beyond "narrative," "signs," "conversation," and "literate figuration." And "any authentic belief" must be "first suggested and then . . . corroborated by some weak experience" of that world, "the world beyond the subject."[140]

Dean rues that in current academic discourse "the Lockeans have been muted, and the battle has gone to the Kantians." There is a very fine line between rigorous constructivism and narrow subjectivism, and Kantianism too frequently crosses it, Dean opines. The Kantian rightly deconstructs naively objectivistic realisms yet, in the process, repeatedly leaves people confined to subjective constructs and untethered from the objects of those constructs.[141]

I would point out that historicists (especially, though not exclusively, neopragmatic historicists) are also wont to let their Kantianism overpower their Lockeanism, their constructivism outpace their realism. Cornel West, to illustrate, looks favorably upon "the move toward antirealism in ontology," which completely disavows "the correspondence theory of truth" and the "distinctions" on which it depends (disavowals, we will discover later, *not* made by the classical pragmatists): "ideas and objects, words and things, language and the world, propositions and states of affairs, theories and facts, schemas and contents." West quickly qualifies that historicists are not "closet idealists." Rejecting "theory-free" and "value-neutral"—nonhuman, nonperspectival, nonconstructed—truths is not the same as rejecting the real, objective, external environment. West is sure that ideas do not create objects, or words things, or language the world, or propositions states of affairs, or theories facts, or schemas contents, any more than they mirror or copy them. However, might not objects impinge and exert pressure on ideas, things words, the world language, states of affairs propositions, facts theories, contents schemas? Even if reality is not the "ultimate standard" for adjudicating between competing "reality-claims," might not our reality-claims at least be epistemically constrained by reality? Remaining within the limits of Kant alone, West's construction-heavy historicism is simply incapable of affirming anything about "sense-independent" phenomena save that they "exist"—a rather commonplace and philosophically trivial observation, to say the least. Reality and our interpretations of it live in a kind of one-way relationship, where the latter "mediates" the former, but the former contributes very little to the latter (except evidence that it is out there and is something with which we must "cope").[142]

Even more than West's, Rorty's constructivism and antirealism tend to run amok. Whatever realist inclinations Rorty has are usually drowned out by his overemphasis on social construction, his often flippant, insouciant, and reductionistic handling of the true and the real, and his insinuation that it is "words all the way down."[143] Like West, he balks at the thought of being branded a "linguistic idealist" or a "relativist,"[144] and yet he declares that truth is "what our peers will . . . let us get away with saying,"[145] and that attributions of reality are nothing more than "compliments we pay to entities . . . that have won their spurs, paid their way, proved themselves useful, and therefore been incorporated into accepted social practices."[146] He shrugs off the charge of "irrationalism,"[147] and yet he pronounces that scientific breakthroughs, like Galileo's, are merely a matter of "lucking out" and stumbling on the "right jargon," and that philosophical and intellectual progress comes down to "changing the subject," "speaking differently," or switching "metaphors," as opposed to "arguing well."[148] At times, Rorty even advises pragmatic historicists to leave behind "realism" and to become "sufficiently historicist and nominalist"—or, at a minimum, to quit worrying about "objectivity."[149]

Certainly, as noted before, Rorty is no *hard* (i.e., ontological) antirealist. "Most of the world," he grants, "is as it is whatever we think about it."[150] Even so, he strangely judges that it is unnecessary for human inquiry to be "guided" or "constrained" by the world; our only constraints are "conversational ones," those "provided by the remarks of our fellow-inquirers."[151] This is why Bernstein insists that Rorty, for good or for ill, is a "deep humanist," a self-proclaimed defender of "self-reliance."[152] In Rorty's own words: "We human beings are answerable only to one another. We are answerable only to those who answer to us—only to conversation partners. We are not responsible to the atoms or to God, at least not until they start conversing with us."[153]

To be very clear, it is not Rorty's (or West's) antirepresentationalism with which I find fault; indeed, human beings cannot untangle themselves from their cultural-linguistic "webs" and represent the way things intrinsically are. Nor do I take issue with his adroit and forthright analysis of the mechanisms by which *Homo sapiens* put human words in the world's mouth, "capitalize" Truth and Goodness, and forget that our cultures, our communities, our intellectual heritages, our moral, religious, and sociopolitical traditions, and the like are human constructs—"*ours* rather than *nature's*, *shaped* rather than *found*, one among many which men have made."[154] On the contrary, Rorty's problem, in my estimation, is that he thinks describing reality as "causally independent of us" is enough "to satisfy our realist intuitions."[155] In other words, he supposes that we can recognize the world's *ontological* existence without assuming that it administers any *epistemological* controls. As he baldly remarks in *Philosophy and the Mirror of Nature*, knowledge is "a matter of conversation between persons, rather than a matter of interaction with nonhuman reality." Ergo, there is no need to get "beyond argument to compulsion from the object known."[156]

To be sure, Rorty is right to state that the world "does not speak. Only we do."[157] But he is wrong to proclaim that it does not constrain, that it does not check—and sometimes even correct—what we say and think about it. He is right to reject the assumption that "anyone gripped by the object in the required way will be *unable* to doubt or to see an alternative." But he is wrong to deny "a power, not ourselves, which compels us."[158] Just because reality is perceived and, to a considerable extent, actively constructed through our interpretations and languages, our social customs and personal predispositions, our interests and desires, our ideologies and historical perspectives, does not entail that reality is passive or uninvolved in the acts of perception and construction.[159] As Rorty himself confesses, a constructivist should be able to admit that there are "lots of objects . . . continually causing her to have new and surprising beliefs. . . . She is no more free from pressure from outside, no more tempted to be 'arbitrary,' than any one else."[160] However, arbitrariness (i.e., relativism, subjectivism, nominalism, radical constructivism, etc.) is precisely what results when we hastily give up on the *ideal* of "correspondence," of "getting reality right" (see the next subsection), when we stop trying to be as "adequate" as possible to a world that is "out there" and ever-encroaching—empirically and epistemically.[161]

In this, I ally myself with a whole gamut of philosophical critics, from Robert Neville to Douglas Anderson to John McDowell, who all locate themselves within the pragmatist heritage but who worry that Rorty, and the neopragmatists more generally, threaten to cut us off from what is real. Robert Neville agrees with Rorty (and with nearly every pragmatist) that philosophizing is a mode of conversing, of inquiring "within a community of inquirers." But, over against Rorty's "default nominalism," Neville urges that the "conversation itself," however edifying, is not the point; what matters is the *content* of that conversation, namely, "our actual engagement with realities about which we might be wrong." Perhaps philosophy is best "thought of as a work of art that allows new things to be envisioned, heard, or danced, than as a scientific theory that conceives itself to map its subject matter." Even so, "envisioning, hearing, and dancing," Neville presses, "are not mere subjective activities. They are responses to reality by which reality is engaged and its importances registered in human experience."[162]

Fellow Peirce scholar, Douglas Anderson, likewise judges that Rortian neopragmatism amounts to a "nominalistic historicism" and, even worse, advocates for "a sort of twentieth-century gnosticism—a knowing without constraint." Peirce feared that some of the more subjectivistic pragmatisms of his time threatened to make "inquiry a matter of sheer creativity with no element of discovery." And thanks to Rorty and his ilk, pragmatism, Anderson laments, has become exactly what Peirce hoped it would not: a "degenerate" form of "full-blown constructivism."[163] Fortunately, as John McDowell reassures, we can follow Rorty in disposing of foundationalism, representationalism, and the like without slipping into a "full-blown constructivism." We can admit that our norms and our truth claims are internal to our worldview without failing to keep "the world in view." We can "face up to contingency" and to the "limitations of reason" without reducing justification to convincingness to one's particular audience or to whatever "linguistic performances will pass muster in our present practice." We can expose the pretentiousness and hypocrisy of "philosophy as priestcraft" without acquiring a "phobia of objectivity" or abandoning the aspiration "to get things right." We can, in short, "share Rorty's conviction that we ought to try to get out from under the seeming problems of epistemology in the Cartesian and British-empiricist vein . . . and still dissent from his suggestion that, in order to avoid entanglement in that familiar unprofitable epistemological activity, we need to discard the very idea of being answerable to something other than ourselves."[164]

Rorty claims James and especially Dewey as philosophical ancestors.[165] Nevertheless, unlike Rorty, both James and Dewey defended a kind of realism, a constructive realism. James, to repeat, was an out-and-out humanist. In a Jamesian framework, concepts and theories are instruments produced and wielded by human beings for a variety of purposes, and the mind, rather than passively or absolutely transcribing a given, external environment, actively and inventively interacts with it. What is more, reality itself exhibits a thoroughgoing plasticity and malleability, molded, constructed, and even augmented by our creative undertakings.[166] "The trail of the human serpent is thus over everything," James believed.[167]

But this does not mean that the human serpent *is* everything. In *Pragmatism* and especially *The Meaning of Truth*, James worked assiduously and tirelessly to dissociate pragmatic humanism from antirealism. Caricatures notwithstanding, he was not a solipsistic subjectivist who denied the existence of an objective, ever-impinging universe outside of ourselves, much less a sophomoric, crude relativist for whom anything goes. He was, rather, a self-avowed realist—metaphysically, ontologically, and even epistemologically.[168]

The nature and extent of Jamesian realism is a hotly debated issue in the secondary literature. For my part, I side with analysts like Michael Slater, who lifts up both the humanist and the realist strands of James's philosophy. Slater observes that, for James, "there is a real, mind-independent world that is distinct from, and irreducible to, our conceptions of it." And reality, according to James, serves as "a necessary condition" for an idea being true and useful.[169] Of course, James was no naive realist.[170] The real, mind-independent world may be glimpsed, but never grasped; "what we grasp is always some substitute for it which previous human thinking has peptonized and cooked for our consumption."[171] However, even if the *what* of the world "depends on us," on the perspectives, purposes, and questions that humans beings bring to bear on it, "the *that* of it is its own." Put differently, truths are "man-made products," but that which truths are "about" and endeavor to "take account of" (i.e., "facts") are "*found*, not manufactured."[172] James illustrated the point by considering constellations (e.g., "the great bear"), which to some degree are the constructions of human perceiving, organizing, and arranging: "But the stars (once the mind has considered them) themselves dictate the result. The counting in no wise modifies their previous nature, and they being what and where they are, the count cannot fall out differently. It could then *always* be made. *Never* could the number seven be questioned, *if the question once were raised*."[173] James, in other words, took for granted that there are externalities—for example, "other men's minds," "independent physical realities," "past events," "external logical relations"— which are what they are irrespective of our subjective wishes or preferences (an echo of Peirce, as I shall suggest below).[174] These actualities "are not *true*, they *are*; and beliefs are true *of* them."[175] And, added James, beliefs are true of them if, and only if, they "fit" them.[176] Experience exerts not only empirical but also epistemic "pressure" on us, and "the more of it a man has the better position he stands in, in respect of truth."[177] Thus, when it came to truth, James was a constructive realist, not a pure constructivist or a pure realist: "If there is to be truth . . . both realities and beliefs about them must conspire to make it" (see the next prong).[178]

Dewey, too, was a constructive realist. To be sure, Dewey, as I observed previously, put the epistemological stress on the instrumental, transformative, and constitutive quality of knowledge. In the words of *The Quest for Certainty*:

> The organs, instrumentalities and operations of knowing are inside nature, not outside. Hence they are changes of what previously existed: the object of knowledge is a constructed, existentially produced, object. The shock to the traditional notion that knowledge is perfect in the degree in which it grasps or beholds without change some thing previously complete in itself is tremendous.[179]

Be that as it may, Dewey was *not* an extreme constructivist. With a nod to James, he alleged that experience "is 'double-barrelled' in that it recognizes in its primary integrity no division between act and material, subject and object, but contains both of them in an unanalyzed totality."[180] As Jerome Stone comments, Dewey's epistemology was not just transformational, but "transactional," seen as "a continuing interaction or transaction between knower and known," between that which is experienced "and the stock of ideas used to understand and transform it."[181]

Douglas Anderson goes so far as to note that this interactionism/transactionism places Dewey squarely within the tradition of Peirce's "dynamic realism" (a tradition from which Rorty has completely "degenerated"). On the one hand, Dewey did espouse a form of constructive historicism. Our "morals, religion and politics . . . reflect the social conditions which present themselves. . . . We believe many things not because things are so, but because we have become habituated through the weight of authority, by imitation, prestige, instruction, the unconscious effect of language, etc." More radically yet, "knowledge or science, as a work of art like any other work of art, confers upon things traits and potentialities which did not previously belong to them."[182] On the other hand, Dewey was adamant that the "subject-matter experienced" is not simply experience (or to employ the Rortian locution, "the web of beliefs and desires"[183]), but the external and exertive natural environment—"stones, plants, animals, diseases, health, temperature, electricity, and so on." And such an environment possesses intrinsic features that knowers come to know: "Unless nature had regular habits, persistent ways, so compacted that they time, measure, and give rhythm and recurrence to transitive flux, meanings, recognizable characters, could not be." Even "the striving of man for objects of imagination is a continuation of natural processes; it is something man has learned from the world in which he occurs, not something which he arbitrarily injects into that world."[184] Thus, *pace* Rorty's self-styled "Deweyan" neopragmatism, Dewey himself, Anderson concludes, resisted "a thoroughgoing nominalism" and "subjectivism" and evinced a deep "affinity for Peircean realisms." That is, he never relinquished the view that "inquirers are constrained by the real" and that experiencing and knowing involve both interpretation (what Peirce termed "thirdness") and constraint (what Peirce termed "secondness"), an interactive, "mutually affecting" collaboration between an experiencer and the experienced environment.[185]

In brief, any historicism that is truly grounded in a Deweyan and Jamesian pragmatism would have to be not simply a constructive historicism, but *a constructive realist historicism*. As Anderson recognizes, pragmatism is, at root, a via media, such that "experiencing and knowing are transactions between an experiencer and an environment." And yet many pragmatically inspired historicisms (e.g., Rorty's) instead fall prey to the fallacy of the "excluded middle,"[186] placing so much emphasis on human construction that reality's circumscriptions and sheer thereness almost disappear from view—an occupational hazard, perhaps, of a worldview that gives theoretical prominence and priority to history's indeterminate, dynamic, open, moldable, and perspectival character. Anderson admits that even Dewey focused primarily (albeit not singularly) on the "transformative dimension" of knowledge, making his pragmatism "once removed" from Peirce's pragmaticist realism (by implication, James's pragmatic humanism would be at least twice removed).[187] Accordingly, in order to help keep their constructivist side from completely taking over, pragmatic historicists, I now want to propose, should follow the lead not only of James and Dewey but also of several other American pragmatists, none of whom directly self-identifies as a historicist, but all of whom strike a healthy balance between constructivism and realism, a balance that lies at the heart of the pragmatist tradition. I will zero in on five thinkers, in particular: Donald Crosby, Nancy Frankenberry, John Ryder, Wesley Wildman, and Charles Sanders Peirce.

To begin, Donald Crosby gainsays both "direct realisms" that discount the ways in which "concepts, models, and theories . . . guide and give intelligibility to [i.e., construct] our experiences of the world" and "radical constructivisms" that pay little attention to how our experiences of the world are capable of "challenging and correcting" those concepts, models, and theories. As a perspectivist, Crosby appreciates that human beings never comprehend reality "just as it is." There is no "in-itself nature," only "nature for us," nature as it is conceptualized by and experienced through particular "interpretive schemes." Regardless, the "mediating" lenses with which humans perceive things, although unable to furnish absoluteness, certainty, and finality, do not have "a mere silvered surface" that reflects back "arbitrary inventions" or "purely subjective" constructions, inventions or constructions that are "projected willy-nilly upon a chaotic world." Rather, they are "significantly testable hypotheses" that potentially put us in touch with a real universe with real "structure." All of these hypothetical interpretations, Crosby presses, are "debatable," "tentative," "changeable," "partial," and "fragmentary"—fallible; but some of them account for reality, for the stubborn "facts of experience," more amply, adequately, and accurately than others, and many of them allow us to "interact meaningfully with the world and to explore the intricacies of our relationships to it."[188]

Similar to Crosby, Nancy Frankenberry navigates between "naive realism," where the human reads structures of meaning "off the face of experience, finding whatever is there to be found," and "personal idealism," where the world is simply cast "into patterns of our own choosing." Sounding very Rortian, she undercuts the tendency in "classical thought" to inflate "the discovery of truth by the mind (as if reality were somehow, 'out there,' waiting)." At the same time, she is equally critical of postmodern-types (like, presumably, Rorty), who have "erred on the side of imposition (as if, in a faceless facticity, every shred of meaning were the creation of human intentionality)."[189] Human constructs, for Frankenberry, are derived from experience just as much as they are projected onto it. On the one hand, interpretive models are surely not "pure givens" that are imparted "in pre-packaged units with labels," ready to be "realistically reflected" or "mirrored and matched by nature." Quite the opposite, they "originate as social constructions," as human attempts to organize and interpret the world through particular "conventions," linguistically mediated schemes, and "systems of signification." In a Deweyan vein, Frankenberry even lifts up the "active" dimensions of knowledge, describing how knowers "intervene" in the world to produce their "own objects of investigations, including empirical 'facts.' " On the other hand, the datum of experience, although never "self-evident" or "uninterpreted," does exist independently of us and enjoy a certain "givenness," a "distinctive objectivity," and, as such, "imposes limits on what humans can sensibly say about it." Frankenberry's radical empiricism, then, is a kind of constructive realism—or to use her own chosen designation, an *interactionism*. All constituents of experience (including human formulations of truth and value), and indeed experience itself, are conceived as "semiotically and historically constructed in an interactive process between organisms and their environment."[190]

John Ryder has also recently insisted that there is a philosophical third way between "objectivism and constructivism"—or, more broadly, "modernism and postmodernism." That tertium quid is "pragmatic naturalism," a lineage that runs from Dewey to the "Columbia naturalists" of the mid-twentieth century (F. J. E. Woodbridge, John Herman Randall, and Justus Buchler, among others). Ryder prefers classical pragmatism to Rortian neopragmatism, chiding the latter for giving up too precipitously on objectivity. Unlike Rorty, Peirce, James, and Dewey, on Ryder's reading, managed to affirm that experience is "constitutive of that with which it interacts," without presuming that "we 'make the world up' in any simplistic sense." Human beings always inquire and think within a history, tradition, context, and point of view, and for a multiplicity of reasons, ends, intentions, and interests. What is more, reality is shaped, even reconstructed, "as a consequence of its complex relations with us." Nevertheless, "there are aspects of nature that are real and significantly independent of us." Ryder, then, believes it "possible and desirable" to endorse all of the following propositions simultaneously:

1. Natural phenomena have objectively determinate traits.

2. The traits of natural phenomena are knowable.

3. The process of inquiry is necessarily conditioned and perspectival.

4. Human interaction with the rest of nature, cognitive or otherwise, is active and creative.[191]

A pragmatic naturalist, in short, is part modern and part postmodern, part constructivist and part realist, asserting that the world is found *and* made, known *and* interpreted, independently existing *and* altered by our purpose-driven, culture-specific, and perspective-laden inquiries.[192]

Wesley Wildman advances a critical pragmatic realism in which reality is understood as "the whence of correctability in rational inquiry." As a pragmatist, Wildman, like Crosby, Frankenberry, and Ryder, thrashes naive realism and its pretenses of "direct perception." Indeed, he is as mindful as any historicist of the ways in which human inquiries, perceptions, and cognitions are "tradition-borne," "socially contextualized," "interest-driven," and "thoroughly mediated through layer upon layer of categorization, symbolization, and interpretation." Be that as it may, the world, Wildman posits, possesses what he calls "feedback potential," an "impressive yet uneven power to correct hypotheses."[193] Admittedly, reality's "awesome and mysterious" capacity to supply correction is frequently inhibited, in some cases by humanity's "cognitive and social limitations," and in others by the "multivocal" or even "relatively weak corrective resources" available within certain domains of experience (for instance, aesthetic and moral judgment, metaphysical speculation, and religion—a point to which I shall return later in the chapter). Even so, reality is that resistant "other" that is "external to human experience" and "presses back against our physical and conceptual self-assertion, forcing us to adjust our behavior and refine our ideas." Wildman is careful to distinguish his pragmatic realism from excessive rationalism, where reality is presumed to furnish "clear and distinct ideas" (Descartes) and render "soluble every problem regardless of topic or difficulty." But just as dubious, according to Wildman, are "extreme forms of post-structuralist critical theory," which treat the real as "exhaustively a social construction" and the true as "nothing but relative patterns of agreement." Wildman, instead, strives to traverse a middle territory in which inquiry is governed by the "regulative" goal of "long-run consensus among qualified inquirers" in an "idealized" and always receding "distant future"[194] and is rooted in "the biological encounter of organism with environment," in the interactions between the constructive faculties of "human minds" and "social contexts" and the variegated gradations of feedback potential that reality offers.[195]

Critical pragmatic realism sets Wildman up to interpret the true, the good, and the beautiful as "collaborative achievements of organism-world engagement." Neither merely "imposed on" nor "simply read off" the surface of nature, truth, value, and beauty both are products of "human appraisal" and "creative response" and are "constrained and informed by" real, objective qualities of the external world:

> When we write $F=ma$ we must understand *both* that nature displays mathematizable regularities *and* that we have the cognitive capacity and social inquiry skills necessary to detect the regularity and model it. When we feel guilty for being needlessly cruel to another living being we must understand *both* that the other being possesses a wondrous integrity that obliges us *and* that our cognitive-emotional capacities register this in the form of guilt and remorse. When we lie beside the magnificent body of a precious lover we must understand *both* that nature contains beauty in its shapes and angles, shadows and light, movement and warmth, *and* that we are primed to sense and respond to those features of beauty.[196]

Epistemologically, axiologically, and even aesthetically, Wildman is, in a word, a constructive realist.[197]

The doggedly realist orientation of Wildman's pragmatism stems, most of all, from Charles Sanders Peirce.[198] Peirce resonated deeply with the Scholastic realism of Duns Scotus, spurning modern nominalism and idealism and acknowledging the existence of empirical realities that are independent of the "opinions" and "vagaries of me and you," that are what they are regardless of what any finite number of people presumes them to be. "That is *real* which has such and such characters, whether anybody thinks it to have those characters or not." For example, redness "is relative to sight, but the fact that this or that is in that relation to vision that we call being red is not *itself* relative to sight; it is a real fact."[199] If truth is the opinion which an indefinite community of investigators agree upon over the infinite long run (see the next subsection),[200] then "the real," Peirce asserted, is the *object* of that imagined agreement—that is, "that which, sooner or later, information and reasoning would finally result in."[201]

Moreover, real things—those nonhuman, "external permanenc[ies] . . . upon which our thinking has no effect"—actually "affect our senses according to regular laws" and even exist in a causal relationship with our beliefs,[202] a point Peirce reinforced by describing the *secondness* of phenomena. In Peirce's categorical scheme, "secondness" denotes "the rough-and-tumble of this world" and the element of "struggle," "resistance," "otherness," and "surprise" in our interactions with it. At the level of secondness, reality is encountered as "brute compulsion," as the "Outward Clash" that is intractably there and is even "forced upon us." Experience thus becomes our "great teacher," constraining, chastening, compelling, and often correcting what we believe.[203] Peirce, to repeat, had no truck with the intuitionism and foundationalism of Cartesianism, giving short shrift to the modernist quest for epistemic certainty, for incorrigible, necessary starting points, and for some "discriminable first cognition, undetermined by earlier cognitions."[204] In fact, Peircean philosophy, by Lawrence Cahoone's reckoning, offers "the canonical formulation" of "the critique of immediacy," undermining the presupposition that judgments are immediately related to what they judge and are, as such, infallible, complete, settled, insusceptible to criticism, and able to "give inquiry a resting place, a self-satisfying sense of accomplishment, an anticipated 'end' not in the sense of a goal but a termination."[205] Indeed, Peirce's category of *thirdness* indicates that cognition always involves inference and semiotic—constructive—mediation; thoughts are connected to their objectively real referents via their "triadic relation" to interpretations, habits, symbols, and representations—signs.[206] All that being said, there is such a thing as "hard facts," Peirce announced. "That hardness, that compulsiveness of experience, is Secondness."[207]

Rorty opines that there is "a tendency to overpraise Peirce," crediting him merely for naming pragmatism and for inspiring James.[208] I have reached a much different conclusion: contemporary pragmatic historicists need to incorporate Peirce into their pragmatist hagiography, to wed Jamesian humanism, Deweyan experimentalism, and Rortian constructivism to Peircean realism. Such a (plural) marriage, I have suggested, could potentially prevent historicism's constructive realist scale from tipping too far in the direction of construction (which, in a postmodern era of constructivist exaggerations, seems more vital than ever). As Frankenberry keenly discerns, "At issue, finally, is not simply the question of the relativity of worlds to words, a harmless assumption, generally granted [by historicists, postmodernists, and many others], but the question of *how far are we to take this assumption?*"[209] Of course, as I indicated above, James and Dewey, and to a lesser extent even West and Rorty, should be characterized as constructive realists, not radical constructivists. However, Peirce, along with Wildman, Ryder, Frankenberry, and Crosby, model a somewhat more balanced constructive realism, in my judgment, able to teach historicists how to take thirdness seriously without underplaying secondness, how to appreciate the social construction of reality without losing sight of the world's power to constrain and correct. This is why I want to include them among pragmatic historicism's band of "philosophical fellow travelers."[210]

Before moving on to the second of paleopragmatic historicism's two prongs, I need to quickly mention a further sense in which pragmatic historicists are (or should be) realist. Along with a constructive realism, some pragmatic historicists champion a *realist constructionism*, recognizing not only the social construction of reality but also *the reality of social constructions*. As sociologists Peter Berger and Thomas Luckmann observe, social constructions become "institutionalized" and eventually "objectivated":

> An institutional world . . . is experienced as an objective reality. It has a history that antedates the individual's birth. The history itself, as the tradition of the existing institutions, has the character of objectivity. . . . The institutions are *there*, external to him, persistent in their reality, whether he likes it or not. . . . They have coercive power over him, both in themselves, by the sheer force of their facticity, and through the control mechanisms that are usually attached to the most important of them. . . . The relationship between man, the producer, and the social world, his product, is and remains a dialectical one. . . . The product acts back upon the producer.[211]

Historicists like Dean up the ontic ante, however, defending an even more full-throated realist constructionism known as "conventionalism." Similar to Berger and Luckmann, Dean is cognizant of "reification," of the processes by which men and women "forget" their own "authorship" of socially constructed phenomena and treat them as something other than human creations (e.g., "manifestations of divine will").[212] However, whereas Berger and Luckmann assume that "the objectivity that marks the social world . . . does not thereby acquire an ontological status apart from the human activity that produced it,"[213] Dean hypothesizes that many of our constructions do, in fact, become independent realities by developing into "conventions." Undoubtedly, conventions are "social products," made from "the stuff of historical interpretation" and arising, evolving, living, and perishing within local environments. And yet conventions, insofar as they have concrete, material effects and are "able to innovate," are as real as any empirical reality can be. They eventually "take on a life of their own" and turn into "active" heritages, acting back on the communities that birthed them and accomplishing for a society what it cannot accomplish for itself. Neither purely subjective nor purely objective (the two ontological options Berger and Luckmann envisage), they have a third kind of actuality, constructed (and reconstructed) from growing constellations of historical influences but irreducible to the totality of those influences. Social constructions, in short, begin as social fictions yet, sooner or later, can become "social facts"—partially autonomous and entirely real conventions that change lives, impact the world, and often behave spontaneously and uncannily.[214]

A good example of a construction-turned-convention is the United States Constitution. Dean elaborates:

> It is, first, the object as it was, with exact language that is its own and with the original intent of the constitutional framers to express. Yet it is also what it is interpreted to be, founded at the beginning by the human imagination and re-founded, or re-created, with the establishment of every new court precedent. But, finally, the constitution, like any living tradition, is not the sum of those objective and subjective identities. It acts in unpredictable ways, admonishing in turn both court supporters and court critics, astonishing courtrooms, surprising strict constructionists and legal deconstructionists alike.[215]

The human person, Dean further illustrates, is also a convention, so to speak. She is "constructed" out of a historically contingent and unique sexual encounter that takes place between two particular people in a passing and unrepeatable moment of time and is constituted by the complex interactions of her "genetic and environmental inheritances." However, she acquires "an organic integrity," freely contributes to her own development, affects others, and "does things that no geneticist, social scientist, or parent could conceivably predict." Biological species and human cultures, too, are conventions, starting out as innovative constructs that correspond to "nothing previously found" in the natural or social world but, after being selected by their environment, "become actual, history-making realities."[216] In chapter 8, I will examine Dean's contention that even the sacred is, in some measure, a convention.

To summarize, then: a paleopragmatic historicism would need to steer clear of a one-sided constructivism, contending that the true, the beautiful, the good, and so on, are cooperative accomplishments, interpretive dances between the constructive agency of historical creatures and an objective world that delivers pushback and feedback. And the constructions that result are themselves real, sometimes even blossoming into independent, universe-altering conventions.

Beyond Whatever Works: Reevaluating the Correspondence Theory of Truth

A paleopragmatic historicism would also need to steer clear of an intellectually lazy relativism, where the true is reduced to "whatever works" in a particular context. And in my (perhaps unfashionable and seemingly unhistoricist) estimation, the best way to avoid an intellectually lazy relativism is to reclaim yet another crucial (and controversial) feature of the classical pragmatist heritage: a (pragmatically reformulated) correspondence theory of truth.

Pragmatic historicists would do well, once more, to consult Wesley Wildman, who carefully differentiates between the *meaning* of truth, on the one hand, and the *means* by which we adjudicate it, on the other. Usually, truth, urges Wildman, "means correspondence." But the standards we deploy to *evaluate* truth claims are "many and varied," including practicality, coherence, and in some cases "straightforward confirmation or disconfirmation."[217] The failure to make such a fine yet necessary distinction is, as Robert Neville inveighs, extremely problematic, leaving pragmatism unable to account for practically meaningful and satisfactory, but fallacious, ideas.[218]

In this connection, Wildman prudently distances himself from Rorty's more relativistic neopragmatism, which regards pragmatic "coping" and word-world correspondence as conflicting objectives. "What matters," emotes Rorty, "is our loyalty to other human beings clinging together against the dark, not our hope of getting things right."[219] However, what if the "hope of getting things right" is itself a way of coping with the environment, of "clinging together against the dark?" To reiterate, pragmatic historicism is incompatible with any and all representationalist epistemologies and naive realisms; if corresponding involves representing the "intrinsic nature" of objects or knowing "how things are in themselves," shorn of historical perspective and constructive interpretation,[220] then historicists are most definitely anti-correspondence theorists. Nevertheless, with Wildman, I see no reason to jettison the conception of truth as correspondence with reality, provided that we, like Peirce and James, construe truth and reality as *convergent*.[221] For Peirce, truth is the judgment "which is fated to be ultimately agreed to by all who investigate," while the reality to which it is (fallibly) striving to correspond is the hypothesized object of an "ideal state of complete information" in a future that is infinite and always retreating.[222] James concurred with Peirce: the true is "an ideal set of formulations towards which all opinions may in the long run of experience be expected to converge."[223] Of course, such convergence never *actually* occurs, but forever remains out in front of us as an *imagined possibility*. James demonstrated that we can think of correspondence as an "ideal vanishing-point," as "a regulative notion of a potential better truth to be established later," while still challenging "the pretense on anyone's part to have found for certain at any given moment what the shape of that truth is."[224] Or, making the same basic argument in Peircean terms, corresponding with—or converging upon—reality is something that happens to an "indefinite community" of inquirers in the "hereafter." It is a never fully realized, collective, and ever-ebbing potentiality that regulates inquiry and keeps it going.[225] It is, to use Rorty's phrase, the *hope* of getting things right. To quote Peirce:

> We cannot be quite sure that the community ever will settle down to an unalterable conclusion upon any given question. Even if they do so for the most part, we have no reason to think the unanimity will be quite complete, nor can we rationally presume any overwhelming *consensus* of opinion will be reached upon every question. All that we are entitled to assume is in the form of a *hope* that such conclusion may be substantially reached concerning the particular questions with which our inquiries are busied.[226]

Wildman's blistering criticism of the pragmatist penchant to "rule out the commonsense meaning of truth as correspondence" is directed not only at Rorty but also at the "relativizing view" of James. Here, Wildman unequivocally aligns himself with Peirce, who famously coined the term *pragmaticism* ("which is ugly enough to be safe from kidnappers") to distinguish his own correspondence-friendly[227] pragmatic realism from ostensible misappropriations of pragmatism, including the more nominalistic and humanistic version touted by James.[228] But I think Wildman and even Peirce (ironically much like Rorty[229]) misread James on this score. James, as I already touched on previously, went to painstaking lengths to show that "a pragmatist can be a realist in his epistemology." And a key assumption of an epistemological realism is that "with some such reality any statement, in order to be counted true, must agree."[230] The conventional wisdom is that James conceived of pragmatism as an *alternative* to the correspondence theory of truth. In actuality, though, James put forward a *pragmatic account* of the correspondence theory of truth.

On this point, I stand, yet again, with Michael Slater. In Slater's telling, James refused to interpret truth as a property distinct from usefulness. Even so, "what *makes* a belief instrumentally useful," what gives it "cash value," so to speak, is its "agreement with a real world."[231] In James's own words, "That . . . ideas should be true in advance of and apart from their utility, that, in other words, their objects should be really there, is the very condition of their having that kind of utility."[232] In point of fact, pragmatists, according to James, realize that truths, by definition, "agree" with reality. Beliefs are true of their referents, that is, *only if* they "point to" and "correspond with" them "in perfectly definite and assignable ways." James even went so far as to deem "copying . . . one genuine mode of knowing." Hence, in a Jamesian mold, pragmatism is not so much a novel hypothesis about what truth *means* as it is a *criteriology* for detecting, understanding, and assessing it. James, akin to Peirce and Wildman, actually accepted the standard meaning of truth as "agreement" and saw pragmatism simply as a *method* for clarifying how, when, and in what manner a signifier can be said to agree with its signified. For the pragmatist, agreement or correspondence—truth—is attained at the *end* of the verification process.[233] It is not, as "intellectualists" suppose, a "static," "prior," or "stagnant property" that is "inherent" in an idea, but an *effect*, something which "happens to" it. There is, James asserted, no "inert static relation" between the mind and the world. There is no "*absolute* correspondence of our thought with an equally *absolute* reality." There is no "storage-vault" of "discarnate" or "timeless 'agreements' [that] had never been embodied in any panting struggle of men's live ideas for verification."[234] Rather, our notions "become" true, are "*made* true by events," realized "*in rebus*" as opposed to "*ante rem*." They *come to* agree and correspond with an object *after* "guiding" and "leading" us to it and helping us "handle" it, *after* demonstrating their adaptational advantages and "functional possibilities." In short, truth is agreement or correspondence, for James, but agreeing or corresponding is taken "to mean certain ways of 'working,' be they actual or potential," and workability is discerned and evaluated pragmatically, by examining the degree and extent to which concepts and knowledge claims "yield satisfaction as their result." And "satisfaction" is not achieved unless those concepts and knowledge claims "fit" the mind-independent world in some form or another.[235] As Slater comments, "While not *all* practically useful beliefs are true, [James] explains, *in most cases* practically useful beliefs are those that really acquaint us with, or lead us to, their objects, and it is precisely their capacity to do so which makes them useful."[236]

James was not exactly the paragon of philosophical consistency, however. Slater notices that James, when speaking of religious or metaphysical convictions, frequently regressed to a "truth-as-mere-utility" functionalism.[237] No good pragmatist, James thought, rules religion out ahead of time, but first finds out whether or not "consequences useful to life flow from it." Though embodying an "empiricist temper," pragmatism "has no *a priori* prejudices against theology. *If theological ideas prove to have a value for concrete life, they will be true, for pragmatism, in the sense of being good for so much*."[238] Indeed, the very thesis of *The Varieties of Religious Experience* is that the truth and import of conversion, saintliness, mystical encounters, and the like lie in the "results" and "effects" borne by them.[239] "By their fruits ye shall know them, not by their roots," effused James.[240]

Even the divine is predominantly "used" instead of "known."[241] As *Pragmatism* put it, "if the hypothesis of God works satisfactorily in the widest sense of the word, it is true."[242] And the hypothesis of God works satisfactorily (i.e., is true) insofar as it guarantees "an eternal moral order" (which is "one of the deepest needs of our breast"). Materialism, on the contrary, is inferior to theism precisely because it cannot fulfill "our remotest hopes," predicting that death has the last word, that humanity and its "ideal interests" will "go down into the pit" and ultimately "perish."[243] Of course, as a radical empiricist and pragmatic naturalist, James wanted a God relevant to human experience and fully at home in the natural, historical, pluralistic universe and, for that reason, ended up replacing the necessary, unalterable, simple, immaterial, self-sufficient, omnipotent, omniscient, and infinite "metaphysical monster" of classical dogmatic theology with a finite "more."[244] Despite that, every divinity has been effectively chosen

> for the value of the fruits he seemed to them to yield. So soon as the fruits began to seem quite worthless; so soon as they conflicted with indispensible human ideals, or thwarted too extensively other values; so soon as they appeared childish, contemptible, or immoral when reflected on, the deity grew discredited, and was erelong neglected and forgotten. . . . The gods we stand by are the gods we need and can use, the gods whose demands on us are reinforcements of our demands on ourselves and on one another.[245]

The same goes for "the Absolute." James faulted its "intellectual inconsistencies" and even doubted its existence but, nevertheless, affirmed its *practical* veracity (i.e., "its bare holiday-giving value").[246]

Slater is right: cases such as these fly in the face of James's epistemological realism and correspondence theory of truth.[247] And in the next chapter, I will advise pragmatic historicist theologians not to invoke this Jamesian double standard, demanding that theological claims, no less than the claims of science or common sense, "agree with reality."

On his better days, though, James resisted crude utilitarianism. He stipulated that, in order to count as valuable or workable or satisfactory (i.e., true), ideas must not only be "pleasant," but also move us "away from foiled and barren thinking" and "metaphysical paradoxes that are inacceptable" and lead us towards "useful verbal and conceptual quarters . . . and sensible termini." We must be able to "assimilate, validate, corroborate, and verify" them, and they must square both with "other parts of our experience" and with "our whole stock of previously acquired truths." Indeed, that which "immediately feels most 'good' is not always most 'true,' when measured by the verdict of the rest of experience," and "the greatest enemy of any one of our truths may be the rest of our truths."[248] In brief, truth is what enables people to "deal, whether practically or intellectually," with "reality's whole setting," which is why the concrete "differences" and "consequences" that the pragmatist looks for include coherence,[249] as well as the "theoretic" and "logical" operations of "analysis, deduction, comparison," and so on.

For instance, "emotionally considered," absolute monism, James confessed, "has a high pragmatic value." Even so, its affective and functional merits are canceled out by its rational and experiential difficulties, particularly, by its irreconcilability with the intractably many and "imperfectly unified" world. James had no choice, then, but to turn his back on the monistic stance and, instead, "follow pluralism's more empirical path."[250] In *The Varieties of Religious Experience*, he rendered a similar verdict on "the religion of healthy-mindedness," surmising that it "is splendid as long as it will work," but that it "is inadequate as a philosophical doctrine, because the evil facts which it refuses positively to account for are a genuine portion of reality."[251] Evidently, for James, a position cannot be branded "pragmatic" if it "derange[s] common sense" and "clashes with" everything else we know about existence. Surely, it is valid only if it produces "expedient" effects, but its effects are expedient only if they are factual and accord with experience. James would, therefore, no doubt back Peirce's claim that pragmatism (or pragmaticism) should not elevate "doing" and "action" at the expense of "thought" and "rational purport," endeavoring, instead, to "dismiss make-believes" and to ensure that every proposition is "true of a certain real individual object, often the environing universe."[252] Hence, the all-too-common tendency—both in his own day and in ours—to glibly dismiss James as a hard relativist amounts to little more than a straw man.[253] As Slater observes, James knew full well that without an epistemological realism and an accompanying correspondence theory of truth, pragmatism "would be unable to account for what true beliefs and statements are true *of*, and similarly unable to explain why certain beliefs and statements about reality 'work' and others do not."[254] Notwithstanding his occasional backsliding (which is undoubtedly regrettable), James's pragmatism was *not* relativistic or subjectivistic, anti-intellectual or anti-correspondence, nonrealist or nonempirical.

Neither was Dewey's. For one thing, while denouncing the conviction that truths are one-to-one replications of "full and ultimate Reality" or fixed, preexistent, a priori "properties of things themselves," Dewey sought, with James, to pragmatically reformulate, not replace, the correspondence conception of truth. A true thought, Dewey allowed, is one that agrees with existence, but agreement is a *consequent* rather than an antecedent, something that comes into being "after ideas have worked"—that is, after they have been "tried out" and proven fit, after they have led us to the phenomena to which they were intended to correspond, after they have answered a question, made sense of experience, disposed of a difficulty, rendered a previous inconsistency coherent, assuaged doubt or obscurity, cleared up confusion, mastered a perplexity, settled a dispute, adequately explained the cosmos, or gotten things right:

If a notion or a theory makes pretense of corresponding to reality or to the facts, this pretense cannot be put to the test or confirmed or refuted except by causing it to pass over into the realm of action and by noting the results which it yields in the form of the concrete observable facts to which this notion or theory leads. If, in acting upon this notion, we are brought to the fact which it implies or which it demands, then this notion is true. A theory corresponds to the facts when it leads to the facts which are its consequences, by the intermediary of experience.[255]

Pragmatism, then, is essentially an activity of "looking ahead, toward the eventual, toward consequences," and beliefs are legitimated and substantiated when *satisfactory* consequences eventuate. But Dewey was no hedonist, subjectivist, or antirealist. Far from functioning as a "mere tool of private ambition and aggrandizement," the pragmatic criterion of satisfactoriness is accorded only to principles that pass experiential muster and meet "public . . . conditions," that adapt the human organism to "some empirical, extra-mental situation," that relate and respond to the real world, and that emanate from hypotheses that are logical, scientifically warranted, reasonable, rigorously tested, and obtained through "unremitting observation" and experimentation. To quote Dewey, "The satisfaction upon which the pragmatist dwells is just the better adjustment of living beings to their environment effected by transformations of the environment through forming and applying ideas."[256] Thus, what pragmatism means by "practical" is not simply whatever is "agreeable." Rather, practicality—utility, profitability, and so on—obtains only if a concept engenders "esthetically admirable, intellectually acceptable and morally approvable" outcomes. For Dewey, the "desirability" of our systems, opinions, philosophies, practices, and so on, never "overrides the question of the meaning of the ideas involved in them and the existence of objects denoted by them," nor is "personal preference" a license to "run rough-shod over all objective controls" and to arbitrarily assert anything we want.[257]

To summarize, following Wildman, I want to counsel pragmatic historicists to subtly discriminate between the meaning and the convergent, regulative end of truth, which is typically correspondence with reality, and the means by which a truth claim is assessed, which are multiple and include not only practical efficaciousness but also coherence and, in certain instances, empirical confirmation.[258] But following the early pragmatists (the paleopragmatists), I would add the caveat that (1) correspondence is ascertained, approximated, and measured pragmatically, that is, by observing the comportment a belief dictates, the outcomes it engenders, the uses it has, the work it does, the experiences it generates, and the future it portends; and (2) practical efficaciousness, coherence, and even empirical confirmation are all pragmatic criteria inasmuch as they are *instruments* that the human organism wields for the purposes of environmental adaptation and *results* that the pragmatist tests for.

Taking the Highroad around Modernism: An Excursus on Historicism and Metaphysics

Besides the development of a constructive realist epistemology and a pragmatic reconstruction of the correspondence theory of truth, there is one additional and related aspect of classical American pragmatism that neopragmatists tend to disregard or discard: an unblinking willingness to make metaphysically meaningful inquiries into the nature of reality. For the paleopragmatists, one can be a nonfoundationalist and a fallibilist *and* probe what Dewey labeled "the generic traits of existence."[259] For Rorty, in contrast, to be truly postfoundationalist is to be "postmetaphysical."[260] In what follows, I will suggest, against Rorty and with a number of different historicists, that the early pragmatists were wise not to dispense with metaphysical speculation, and that any viable pragmatic historicism today needs to be just as unwavering, both substantively and methodologically, in its commitment to a fallibilistic, nonfoundationalist, and thoroughly historicist metaphysics of nature and history.

Rorty is not the only philosopher to assert that historicism, along with its efforts to undermine the quest for timeless and incorrigible foundations, "has helped free us, gradually but steadily, from . . . metaphysics."[261] Among other things, the so-called "postmodern turn" turns on the denunciation of foundationalism, or what the French philosopher Jean-François Lyotard in his 1979 *La Condition postmoderne: Rapport sur le savoir* (published in English in 1984) famously referred to as "the metanarrative apparatus of legitimation." The adjective "modern," in Lyotard's usage, designates "any science that legitimates itself with reference to a metadiscourse of this kind making an explicit appeal to some grand narrative, such as the dialectics of Spirit, the hermeneutics of meaning, the emancipation of the rational or working subject, or the creation of wealth."[262] And postmodernism is *post*modern insofar as it exhibits "incredulity" toward the Enlightenment yearning for such "metanarratives," for "totalizing" (i.e., foundation-laying and metaphysical) worldviews that violently vitiate "differences" and homogenize "the heterogeneity of language games" in the name of "the whole and the one."[263]

John Caputo concurs, more or less equating postmodern deconstructionism with nonfoundationalism and antimetaphysics. Indeed, the raison d'être of Derrida's project of deconstruction, says Caputo, is to "pull the plug on" any "firm foundation or perfectly enclosed system," to prevent some "metaphysics of presence" or "logocentrism," some "*ousia*" or "*hors-texte*," some "cogito" or "thing itself," from closing the ongoing play of meaning or feigning the absolute and final word. The deconstructive method, rather, exposes the multiplicity, plasticity, instability, alterity, discursivity, historicity, and debatability of texts, institutions, traditions, beliefs, practices, philosophies, societies, laws, languages, and scientific theories. It keeps them open to radical "otherness" (*tout autre*), to the "trace" (*trace*), to that which "differs" and "defers" (*différance*) and is always "to come" (*à venir*). It points out their own internal tensions, fissures, contradictions, abjections, anomalies, deviations, disseminations, loose threads, novel possibilities, and multivalent hermeneutical layers.[264] In a word, it fallibilizes them, insisting that they remain "open-ended, porous, experimental, nonprogrammable, vigilant, self-questioning, self-revising, exposed to their other." It continuously unmasks their thoroughly constructed and, thus, deconstructible character, reserving "the *right* (*droit*) to ask any question, to think any thought, to wonder aloud about any improbability, to impugn the veracity of any of the most venerable verities."[265]

Of course, the paleopragmatists already said a lot of this a hundred and fifty years ago. Davaney complains that there is a tendency, especially among scholars who describe the present historical moment as peculiarly postmodern, to simplistically conflate the entire modern period with the Enlightenment and its ideals and assumptions. But in actuality, modernity was "culturally and cognitively pluralistic." Without question, it gave rise to the Cartesian presumption that "universal claims to knowledge and truth" can be established on "sure and indubitable grounds" and that "the autonomous individual" is the locus of such knowledge and truth. Even so, within modernity can also be "found a celebration of history and the natural" as well as "a growing sense of the historicity of human existence and knowledge."[266] As Wesley Wildman also notices, the modern world "produced both the foundationalist epistemological project *and its criticism*," boasting "a steady stream of nonfoundationalist, holist, fallibilist, biosocial theories of knowledge."²⁶⁷ And, as I have already established, Peirce, James, and Dewey were nonfoundationalists and fallibilists a century before postmodernity made it cool, a fact that postmodern critics rarely acknowledge when mounting their otherwise appropriately directed criticisms of metanarratives, transcendental signifieds, oppressive binaries, and the like.²⁶⁸

The early pragmatists, as well as a host of other thinkers in America, from process philosophers, such as Alfred North Whitehead, to the historicists, empiricists, and naturalists of the Chicago school of theology, all travelled what Robert Neville aptly calls "the highroad around modernism."²⁶⁹ They were "late or advanced modern" thinkers who, nevertheless, managed to avoid modern*ism* and its putatively "wicked 'onto-theo-logocentrism.'" They were post-Enlightenment and postfoundationalist, but not postmodern; nonmodernist, but not nonmodern. Sadly and ironically, postmodern thinkers end up totalistically reducing the whole modern Western tradition to its ostensible "center" (i.e., "the Enlightenment concern for certainty" and the post-Cartesian preoccupation with epistemic foundations) and, in so doing, miss or misinterpret "many of that tradition's most interesting parts," parts that long "anticipated the postmodernists in most of their valid points" (including nonfoundationalism and fallibilism).²⁷⁰ Bernstein, reflecting back on his own intellectual journey, echoes Neville's sentiments:

> The late 1980s were a time when so-called "postmodernism" seemed to be the rage in many circles. Foucault, Derrida, Lyotard, Deleuze (and other French thinkers) were the "theorists" that excited the imagination of many young intellectuals. At first I found the talk about the novelty of "postmodern" discourse perplexing. For when I examined closely what was being attacked—foundationalism, the metaphysics of presence, grand narratives and systems—I felt that I had seen all this before. This was the starting point for the classical pragmatists in the nineteenth century.²⁷¹

The point of mentioning postmodernity's "remarkable amnesia"²⁷² concerning the paleopragmatist "highroad around modernism" is not to snidely brag about how pioneering, cutting-edge, and ahead of its time pragmatism was, or to expose postmodernism as a Johnny-come-lately in the deconstruction of foundationalism, or to snub the many crucial and unique insights a Lyotard, a Derrida, a Caputo, and a Foucault contribute to philosophical discourse in the contemporary age. Rather, I bring up nonfoundationalism's *late modern* beginnings mainly because a lot of postmodernists, in eschewing foundations, give up something the early pragmatists did not, something I (along with several present-day pragmatic historicists) regard as utterly indispensable: metaphysics.

For a good number of postmodernists, metaphysical reasoning and the foundationalist pursuit of certainties and centers are inseparable. As Derrida pronounces:

> The history of metaphysics, like the history of the West, is the history of these metaphors and metonymies. Its matrix . . . is the determination of Being as *presence* in all senses of this word. It could be shown that all the names related to fundamentals, to principles, or to the center have always designated an invariable presence—*eidos, archē, telos, energeia, ousia* (essence, existence, substance, subject), *alētheia*, transcendentality, consciousness, God, man, and so forth.[273]

What Derrida and other postmodern theorists fail to consider, though, is whether metaphysics is *exhausted by* the "metaphysics of presence," whether nonfoundationalism, fallibilism, and historicism rule out metaphysical inquiry as such. Peirce, James, and Dewey did not think so. As Wildman points out, the original pragmatists "deliberately rejected epistemic foundationalism and worked hypothetically within a fallibilist epistemological framework," all while pursuing "the whole range of philosophical questions, including the big questions of metaphysics and morality and religion."[274]

For instance, Peirce, as we discovered earlier, thoroughly fallibilized human knowledge and deemed the Cartesian aspiration for certainty a dead end. Neville goes so far as to classify Peirce as a kind of historicist:

> Peirce knew that all philosophy is situated in its historical context, and is limited by the perspectives of its situation. He had many discussions of the historical limitations of ancient philosophy, medieval philosophy, early modern philosophy, and of the philosophical arguments in his own nineteenth century. This historicism was a reflection of the basic point of Peirce, namely, that all thought is hypothetical and fallible, perhaps justified so far as we can tell but limited in its truth claims to what can be known or tested in its historical context.[275]

And yet, while repudiating "big-deal, logo-centric modernist pretensions" and envisaging "a new form of late modernism free of foundationalism, mirroring, and all that," Peirce, Neville continues, never presumed that metaphysics was thereby *verboten* or that philosophers could not proffer provisional hypotheses about "overarching cosmological structures."[276] In fact, Peirce advanced speculatively daring arguments in favor of "absolute chance" and "evolutionary love" (the doctrines of "tychism" and "agapism," respectively) and maintained that the categories of firstness, secondness, and thirdness are metaphysically real and operative in nature.[277]

Likewise, James's radical empiricism and pluralism and Dewey's empirical naturalism,[278] although "not foundational" or "born of the quest for certainty," still provided an axiological, epistemological, and metaphysical basis for plumbing "the valuational depths of the world," for giving non-subjectivistic, empirically grounded reasons for normative judgments and actions, and for exploring a whole range of abstract philosophic topics, from the existence of consciousness and the nature of experience (e.g., as "precarious and stable") to the subject-object relation and the function of qualities, interests, and contexts in the thinking process.[279] Dewey, for his part, panned any and all dualistic metaphysical systems, which pit an ostensibly inferior realm of being, "variously called appearance, illusion, mortal mind, or the merely empirical," against "what really and truly is." Nevertheless, he unapologetically considered *Experience and Nature* a work of metaphysics, where "metaphysics" is simply defined as "a detection and description of the generic traits of existence."[280]

So, as far as Peirce, James, and Dewey were concerned, one can metaphysically generalize about reality without forgetting that such generalizing is wholly fallible and historical—hypothetical, open to dispute and reconsideration, exploratory, contextual, never certain, and embedded in, conditioned by, constructed from, and related to the particularities of nature and history.[281] As James clarified, pragmatism objects to "bad *a priori* reasons," "fixed principles," "closed systems," and "pretended absolutes and origins," but not to the "realizing of abstractions," inductively assembled from history's particulars. "The pragmatist clings to facts and concreteness, observes truth at its work in particular cases, and generalizes."[282] This paleo-pragmatic conception of metaphysics, as both Neville and Dean rightly surmise, deflects the antimetaphysical assaults of today's postmodernists, deconstructionists, and neopragmatists (as well as the arguments Kant leveled against metaphysics in *The Critique of Pure Reason*), for Peirce, James, and Dewey all regarded metaphysical theories as (1) "large hypotheses" that are, nevertheless, "vulnerable to correction" and even replacement; and (2) "generalizations" about the most basic features of *this* world, the world of "becoming rather than being," of "history rather than substance."²⁸³

Rorty does not deny the metaphysical ambitions of the early pragmatists as much as he frowns on them. He completely dismisses Peirce's assumption that "a general theory of signs" could provide "an all-embracing ahistorical context in which every other species of discourse could be assigned its proper place and rank" and chides, as well, "the bad ('metaphysical') parts of Dewey and James," that is, "the Dewey of *Experience and Nature*" and "the James of *Radical Empiricism*."²⁸⁴ In particular, Dewey's effort to compose a "naturalistic metaphysics" is, on Rorty's reading, basically an unfortunate aberration and a "contradiction in terms." The "good Dewey" asserted that philosophy is "an instrument of social change" and cultural criticism and, in noble Hegelian fashion, urged that "the starting point of philosophic thought is bound to be the dialectical situation in which one finds oneself caught in one's own historical period—the problems of the men of one's time." But Dewey "wanted to have things both ways," rues Rorty. He hoped to displace the Platonic image of the philosopher as "a spectator of all time and eternity" *and* to spell out the "generic traits manifested by existences of all kinds," thereby offering "an 'empirical' account of something called 'the inclusive integrity of experience'" and imbuing "harmless-sounding naturalistic phrase[s]" like "transaction with the environment" and "adaptions to conditions" with "the same generality," transcendentality, and air of mysteriousness as Kant's notion of the "thing-in-itself." In short, Dewey rightly set out to overcome traditional philosophical dualisms, and yet, by presuming that such a task required a metaphysic, he ended up occasionally contracting "the disease he was trying to cure."²⁸⁵

The historicist allergy to the metaphysical is, of course, nothing new. Johann Herder, in *Yet Another Philosophy of History*, discussed "the weakness of generalizing."²⁸⁶ A century and a half later, Shailer Mathews, who ended up putting forward a naturalistic theism (see the next chapter), curiously exclaimed that religious reflection on "the ultimate nature of being . . . does not rest upon metaphysics."²⁸⁷ And, most famously, the protohistoricist Kant, as Neville points out, imposed considerable limitations on metaphysical knowledge by positing that "we know things only as they appear to us, as structured by our cognitive apparatus."²⁸⁸ These antimetaphysical predispositions notwithstanding, I want to exhort contemporary pragmatic historicists to retrieve the metaphysical sensibilities of classical pragmatism. If a neopragmatic historicism is (or at least purports to be) postmetaphysical, then a paleopragmatic historicism is (or at least strives to be) post-postmetaphysical. This recommendation is spurred by three primary factors.

First, metaphysics is unavoidable. Everybody, whether wittingly or not, is in possession of a metaphysic, an overarching conception or, at the very least, an intuitive sense of what existence is like, of what sorts of patterns and features and characteristics and values and potentialities it has, broadly and generally construed. As Davaney admits, all our positions, without exception, "are the bearers of operative assumptions about what it means to be human and to exist in a certain kind of world."[289] When Derrida announces that "there is nothing outside the text," or when Rorty speculates about "the ubiquity of language," they are making unmistakable metaphysical claims.[290] It is naive and disingenuous, then, to pretend to be somehow postmetaphysical, to presume that large generalizations about the import of our lives and the nature of the universe in which we live can be suspended or averted by simply "changing the way we talk."[291] We should, therefore, be self-conscious and deliberate, frank and explicit, about the basic cosmological, anthropological, and ontological presuppositions and premises that inevitably undergird our thoughts and practices. We ought to develop plausible worldviews, not deny that we have them, demanding that our comprehensive, encompassing philosophies of human life and the wider cosmos—our metaphysics—are as coherent, desirable, sound, valid, inclusive, omnidisciplinary, and justifiable as possible.[292]

Second, historicism itself is a metaphysical interpretation of existence. In fact, throughout this book, I have endeavored to demonstrate that a very particular anthropology, cosmology, and ontology underlie a pragmatic historicist world-picture, wherein the human, nature, and being itself are historically constituted, circumscribed, and conditioned.[293] As Brown discerns, historicists require—and indeed already possess—a kind of empiricist and process-relational metaphysics (cf. chapters 1 and 5), an "expanded, speculative conceptuality," derived and "generalized" from "experience," that "indicates why both the social and historical are intrinsic to being human" and characteristic of reality as such.[294] Kaufman concurs, arguing that historicism pivots on "the metaphysical significance of . . . temporality." A historicist, that is, "sees historical development in time as central. In this view change is more fundamental than structure: all structures come into being in the course of time and eventually pass away again in time."[295] Even Rorty's brand of historicism depends on a few (unstipulated and latent) anthropological and cosmological suppositions. Impishly, he alleges that historicists "have denied that there is such a thing as 'human nature' or the 'deepest level of the self.' Their strategy has been to insist that socialization and, thus historical circumstance, goes all the way down—that there is nothing 'beneath' socialization or prior to history which is definatory of the human."[296] However, Rorty, as Jerome Soneson observantly comments, does say something positive and general about "human nature" and the "deepest level of the self," namely, that who we are is, deep down, a matter of "socialization," that we are products of our histories, cultures, and circumstances.[297] In addition, Rorty's pragmatic method works and makes sense only if the cosmos is metaphysically configured in one way rather than another. To quote Dean:

> To claim that we are capable of freely, deliberately, and purposively coping with environments to get a better outcome or of freely, deliberately, and purposively conversing with people holding opinions incommensurable with our own . . . is to affirm: that the world, while not completely determined, is ordered enough for acts to yield predictable consequences; that the world, while not completely random, is disordered enough to allow room for choice; that the world, while not completely indifferent to human intention, is indifferent enough to override unrealistic intentions.[298]

In short, historicism cannot avoid metaphysics because it *is* a metaphysic, an expansive theory about the thoroughgoing historicity of the universe and everything in it, including human beings.

Third, the classical pragmatists were dead-on: a nonfoundationalist, fallibilistic, historicist metaphysic, far from being oxymoronic, is conceivable. Rorty believes that historicism is necessarily a turn away from the metaphysical because he associates metaphysics with "the temptation to look for an escape from time and chance,"[299] or as he describes it in a later book, with "the traditional theologicometaphysical belief that Reality and Truth are One—that there is One True Account of How Things Really Are."[300] Likewise, Mathews assumes that metaphysical speculation is necessarily antithetical to the empirical method and the "data given by science."[301] For many other pragmatic historicists, though, metaphysics is incompatible with historicism *only if* metaphysics is reducible to an ahistorical, nonempirical, foundationalist delineation of it. As Robert Corrington very similarly avows:

If metaphysics is polemically reduced to onto-theology and its search for an ultimate genus or first principle, then it will indeed have no role to play in ordinal phenomenology [or, I would add, in pragmatic historicism]. If, however, metaphysics is seen in its less imperial guise as the search for general features that themselves locate and honor difference, then it is clearly indispensable to any sustained form of human query.[302]

Metaphysics no more has an unchanging essence than truth or goodness or beauty or human identity do. Thus, however it has been carried out in the past, it must be capable, at least potentially, of being rehabilitated along nonfoundationalist, fallibilistic, and historicist lines. And, alas, it has, not only by the original pragmatists, but also by several pragmatic historicists.

To illustrate, Jerome Soneson construes what Rorty terms "final vocabularies" as both decidedly historicist and functionally metaphysical, created by finite people in order to meet the urgent "needs of the present contingent historical situation," and yet still able to regulate larger patterns and connections and meanings.[303] A pragmatic historicist, Soneson finds affinity especially with Dewey's understanding of metaphysics, where the metaphysician brings fundamental and often implicit philosophical presuppositions out into the open. Soneson avers that, in a Deweyan scheme, metaphysical generalizations, like all meanings, are unequivocally human and, hence, wholly fallible, formulated by men and women for particular purposes and interests, in a definite social setting, under a certain set of "limiting conditions." They "have the status of hypotheses" and a "self-correcting," "unfinished," and "uncertain" character, remaining "bound to the specific contexts of their use," "subject to further criticism," "growth," "adjustment," and "reconstruction," and amenable to "novel possibilities," alternate viewpoints, and shifting historical circumstances.[304]

Like Soneson, Davaney regrets that Rorty's fear (I would say repression) of "platonic urges" makes him reluctant "to engage in any general reflection about the nature of reality or the cosmos or human nature."[305] But abstract generalities are not, in Davaney's judgment, "de facto ahistorical" and, as such, precluded by historicism. Even if there are no "unlocated and unattached beliefs," there may be "generalized" ones. Undeniably, human historicity requires a healthy dose of epistemological and metaphysical humility. However, there is no reason why we cannot propound full-orbed cosmological and anthropological worldviews, and yet still recognize that those worldviews are emergent in history, human, perspectival, temporally and spatially bounded, fallible, embedded in traditions, interpretive and tentative, hypothetical, socially constructed, disputable, predicated on a good deal of guesswork, speculation, and probability, and in need of constant critique, reappraisal, improvement, and feedback from others. In brief, although never using the word, Davaney intimates that we can do metaphysics "without betraying historicist commitments," feigning "absolute certitude" and "unassailable foundations," or engaging in "totalitarian adventurism." Historicism's nonfoundationalism and fallibilism, then, lead not to theoretical chastity, but to theoretical modesty. It calls us not to suppress our metaphysical curiosities, but to build "our pictures of reality" in a piecemeal, dialogical, interdisciplinary, and provisional fashion.[306]

Kaufman is more or less on the same page as Davaney. He resists both the foundationalist ambitions of "dogmatism" *and* the metaphysical austerity measures taken by "modern positivism." What we need, recommends Kaufman, is to develop metaphysical conceptions that are "hardheaded" and scientifically cogent, on the one hand, and historically conscious, on the other. In other words, we should strive to rigorously comprehend "the objects and structure" of the cosmos "which environs us," even as we concede that every metaphysic is a product of "our own imaginative construction," fashioned to make sense of our experiences and to orient ourselves to reality. Our metaphysical speculations and cosmic visions are never entirely "objective," but nor are they simply "arbitrary." Rather, they are humanly constructed and utterly metaphorical "world-pictures" that, nevertheless, "attend as carefully and completely as possible to the actual place of human life in the world as we today understand these matters."[307]

Even the neopragmatist Cornel West is not entirely averse to metaphysics. In one sense, West has little time for metaphysics, lauding the pragmatists' efforts to reconceive philosophy "as a form of cultural criticism" (as opposed to a series of "solutions to perennial problems in the Western philosophical conversation initiated by Plato").[308] In a review of *The American Evasion of Philosophy*, Robert Corrington chafes against this characterization of pragmatism, upbraiding West for "sliding too far down the road of a mere historicism," for overplaying "epistemic relativism and linguistic play," and for "ignoring the role of metaphysics in securing and furthering the full pragmatic program of radical social reconstruction." As Corrington puts it elsewhere, West and the neopragmatists in general remain "unfaithful to the more profound metaphysical insights of the classical [pragmatist] tradition."[309] With respect to Peirce, West focuses on his anti-Cartesianism and his theory of inquiry but completely overlooks the ways in which his naturalistic metaphysics opens up "the possibility of radical novelty and qualitative emergence within the world as a whole." Even Dewey, the patriarch of West's genealogy, is stripped of his mature metaphysics, which locates human and cultural interaction within larger, natural orders of relevance and roots the freedom of the self in an event-governed universe that allows, even encourages, "novel configurations in time." For all his biting censures of Rorty, West ends up capitulating to the erroneous Rortian notion that "Dewey was not fundamentally a metaphysician but was a critic of American culture who happened to say a few things about nature." Evading the metaphysical naturalism of the early pragmatists carries not just intellectual but political ramifications, Corrington warns, for the emancipatory power of a prophetic pragmatism "loses much of its force if it fails to remember that it is enabled by nature's plenitude."[310]

And yet, despite these antimetaphysical predilections, West maintains that historicism—"an acceptance of our finitude and fallibilism"—only necessitates the rejection of "old-style," totalizing, certainty-craving, metanarrative-spinning Metaphysics (with an uppercase "M"), not metaphysics as such. While always colored by certain "background conditions" and "relative to specific traditions" and "particular sets of social practices," ontological and metaphysical thinking "will and must go on." And West holds out for a less "grand" and more temperate—that is, a nonfoundationalist and fallibilistic—mode of metaphysics, where "self-critical inquirers" deploy "synoptic narratives and overarching vocabularies" in the hopes of accomplishing various tasks and aims. A pragmatic historicist form of metaphysical reason recognizes the "theory-laden," purpose-driven nature of *all* "reality-claims" (whether scientific, religious, or otherwise) without falling prey to a "vulgar relativism," confident that there are "rational standards" for adjudicating "between better and worse . . . interpretations" and even that some discourses engage reality more adequately and truthfully than others (e.g., science's capacity to predict and control phenomena far exceeds that of numerology and magic).[311] Therefore, there is nothing wrong, according to West, with redescribing nature and experience (à la Dewey) or proposing "metaphorical versions of what one thinks the way the world is in light of the best available theories," so long as we own up to "the needs and interests" which motivate such metaphysical endeavors.[312]

In sum, Soneson, Davaney, Kaufman, and even West reveal that it is possible to be a nonfoundationalist, a fallibilist, a historicist, and a metaphysician, all at the same time. For Rorty, on the other hand, it is an either-or proposition. West is right to call attention to the "thinness" of Rorty's neopragmatic historicism. But it is thin not only because it disregards "the realities of power" and "remains relatively silent about forms of political, economic, racial, and sexual privilege" (glaring and troubling omissions, to be sure),[313] but also because it refuses any and all metaphysical inquiries into the nature of reality.[314]

In order to further mitigate the antimetaphysical impulse inherent within pragmatic historicism and to deepen what Soneson deliciously dubs "historicist metaphysics,"[315] I want to close the chapter by turning, once again, to Wildman, whose recent book, *Religious Philosophy as Multidisciplinary Comparative Inquiry*, presents an extraordinarily elegant, expert, and even-handed case for a nonfoundationalist, fallibilist approach to metaphysical analysis.

Wildman recounts that at some point in the midst of admirably undercutting the medieval reliance on authority and revelation, the modern world became infatuated with certainty. Modernity's philosophers, as a result, drastically inflated the powers of human reason, embellishing the penetrability of "the ontological, moral, aesthetic, and epistemological depths of reality" and making overblown and overreaching, artless and aggressive, claims about axiomatic deductions, universal, self-evident truth, sure foundations, decontextualized argumentation, and clear and distinct ideas. In the main, therefore, the postmodernist deconstruction of modernism is well-aimed and justified, in Wildman's estimation. Postmodernists are spot-on in insisting that rationality and knowledge are limited, that indubitability and pure objectivity are illusions, and that interpretations are always tied to historical and social contexts, enmeshed in intricate power complexes, and driven by (often covert) ideological interests and (often colonialist) political aspirations. Be that as it may, postmodern critical theory, Wildman discerns, is so "haunted by shame" (over imperialistic, paternalistic, and expansionist politics; over foundationalism, structuralism, and scientism; over Western chauvinism and economic hegemony; over the deleterious ecological consequences of technological innovations; over patriarchy, racism, and oppressive and repressive constructions of sexuality) that it has developed a severe antipathy toward systems, toward metaphysics, toward "big-question philosophy," and toward generality in general. Like Kant and A. J. Ayer before them,[316] postmodernists tend to be epistemic "watchdogs," policing the borders of the knowable. Not unreasonably, they worry that generalizing and abstract theorizing risk underestimating pluralism, legitimating centers and delegitimating peripheries, assimilating the finely textured details, variations, and particularities of history into "empirically flat footed" patterns (as Hegel did when tracking the dialectical logic of *Geist*), and even committing grave social injustices. However, akin to Soneson, Davaney, Kaufman, and West, Wildman underscores the "inevitability" of generalizations for human cognition, and so would rather "generalize skillfully," in full recognition of its "moral and political and intellectual dangers," than shirk generalizing altogether or, worse, "hide" or "sublimate it within criticism in a pitiful pretense at being theory free."[317]

According to Wildman, it is nonfoundationalism and fallibilism that facilitate such skillful generalizing, that enable us to "produce large-scale, existentially orienting, and intellectually satisfying conceptual interpretations of the world," while concomitantly remaining conscious of and sensitive to the mechanisms by which those interpretations sometimes mask ideology, rationalize the status quo, ignore difference, dominate the other, evade history, and simulate certitude. A pragmatist, Wildman shares postmodernism's sociohistorical consciousness, antifoundationalism, and fallibilism. But, on Wildman's account, accepting the thoroughgoing contextuality of human existence and thinking, the futility of the "modern quest for certain foundations," and the fact that all our beliefs are fallible—that is, born in uncertainty, prone to error, hypothetical, and in need of ceaseless refinement—is grounds for multidisciplinary, comparative theory-building, not speculative "paralysis," postmodern "asceticism," assertional "self-restraint," or crippling "relativism." Nonfoundationalist fallibilism, in other words, is not simply "a set of warnings." It "is a bracing invitation to allow curiosity full rein and to formulate hypotheses freely," cautiously, and publicly, where they can be "discussed, debated, corrected, and improved." Fueled as opposed to disappointed by ideology- and context- and framework-dependence, and expecting rather than fearing oversights and missteps, it is inclined to hazard wide-ranging propositions and then actively look for and "leverage" the "corrective resources" that would modify, rectify, or falsify them. It holds "the morality of assertion" and "the morality of correction" in creative tension, at once "fearlessly adventurous and humbly aware of its inescapable limitations." It is a "boon," not an impediment, to metaphysics and "big-question philosophy," goading us to generate "inference-to-best-explanation arguments" and to test "abstract generalizations" and "highly theoretical constructions" as rigorously and exhaustively as possible, instead of allowing Kantian antinomies, Ayerian positivism, or Foucauldian power/knowledge to prematurely delimit the bounds of human reason and experience before inquiry even begins.[318]

And, like Peirce and Dewey, Wildman unflinchingly maintains that a nonfoundationalist, fallibilist style of rational investigation is most prodigiously exemplified by the modern sciences.[319] Although often succumbing to scientism (the erroneous notion that anything real and important lies within the explanatory reach of the physical sciences) and occasionally downplaying the moral ambiguity of technology and the complex social processes involved in choosing between competing scientific paradigms, science is ultimately

> a cooperative venture that produces theories capable of winning unprecedented crosscultural agreement, that seeks out its mistakes and corrects its theories as needed, that makes exciting discoveries about the natural and human worlds, that inspires life-changing technological marvels from electricity to blood transfusions, and that effectively resists the arbitrary imposition of political and religious authority.[320]

In short, for Wildman, as for Soneson, Davaney, Kaufman, West, and their American pragmatist forebears, there is a via media between time- and chance-escaping Metaphysics and no metaphysics at all—that is, a nonfoundationalist, fallibilist, naturalistic metaphysics. And it is my contention that a healthy pragmatic historicism, a paleopragmatic historicism, should cultivate chastened metaphysicians, not antimetaphysicians, critical thinkers who speculate and generalize boldly, but publically, fallibilistically, and empirically.[321]

To recapitulate the central thesis of the foregoing excursus, pragmatic historicists stand with contemporary postmodernists in affirming nonfoundationalism, fallibilism, perspectivism, and the like. However, more a fellow traveler on classical pragmatism's late modern highroad around modernism than an errant nomad lost in the postmodern wilderness, pragmatic historicism refuses to throw the metaphysical baby out with the foundationalist bathwater. There is, according to many pragmatic historicists, such a thing as a pragmatic historicist metaphysics, speculatively ambitious, intellectually impressive, rationally defensible, and theoretically far-reaching generalizations that nevertheless (1) pertain not to eternal being or atemporal substances, but to the empirical world of human and natural history;[322] and (2) consist not of tradition-free Archimedean points, totalizing metanarratives, absolute truths, transcendental signifieds, detail-discounting simplifications, or indubitable certainties, but of contextually located, imaginatively constructed, situationally engendered, publically tested, and thoroughly fallibilized hypotheses.

In the eighth and concluding chapter of this book, I will venture that there is also such a thing as a pragmatic historicist metaphysics of *ultimate reality*—or at least there could be such a thing. But before I can do that, I need to demarcate and describe the paleopragmatic historicist theology that makes such a metaphysics possible in the first place.

Chapter 7

Theological Truth Reconsidered

Four Traits of a Paleopragmatic Historicist Theology

This chapter is an extension of the last one. Its aim is simple: to demonstrate that the pragmatic historicist theologians featured in this study—the early Chicago schoolers as well as Brown, Davaney, Dean, Kaufman, and McFague—are paleopragmatists, at least implicitly. Four traits, in particular, give their theologies a paleopragmatic flavor: (1) religious fallibilism, (2) theological liberalism, (3) constructive realism, and (4) probative pragmatism.

The First Trait: Religious Fallibilism

First, pragmatic historicist theologians are *fallibilists* of the highest order. Redolent of the classical pragmatists, they acknowledge that to know is to know fallibly—that is, in a provisional, incomplete, and hypothetical manner, through the mediation of language, culture, and ideology, and without foundations of certitude or indubitability. And such an acknowledgment leads them to cultivate a readiness both to come to terms with the adjustability, improvability, and potential mistakenness of our religious understandings and to subject every theological principle, even our loftiest and most venerable ones, to ongoing scrutiny, deconstruction, critical examination, analytical probing, and input from others.

Gerald Birney Smith, more than any of the other early Chicago schoolers, played up the scientific spirit and vocation of modern theology. And reminiscent of Peirce and Dewey, what Smith implored theologians to incorporate from science was, above all, its fallibilistic method (although, as we will see in the next chapter, the early Chicago schoolers also sought to square theological ideas with scientific conceptions of the universe).[1] As Davaney comments, the sciences, for Smith, modeled "an approach to human inquiry that is public, experimental, self-consciously critical, and empirically focused," a procedure that "yields not unassailable claims but tentative, revisable, and context-specific assertions about human and natural existence and their betterment."[2] Indeed, by Smith's count, religious concepts and images, far from displaying "finality of any sort," are "working hypotheses which may be altered as new discoveries warrant it."[3]

In the late 1980s, Sallie McFague reiterated (and updated) what Smith expressed at the turn of the century: theology is a "hypothetical, tentative, partial, open-ended, skeptical, and heuristic" affair. Accordingly, the theologian becomes an experimenter and a risk-taker, daring to think differently, to imagine novel possibilities, and to assess, criticize, renovate, reimagine, and sometimes discard time-honored religious symbols. No theological claim (not even a biblical one) is certain, absolute, uncritiqueable, irreplaceable, fixed, or infallible.[4] For that reason, a theology, not unlike any other human creation, must be constantly tested

> for its disclosive power, its ability to address and cope with the most pressing issues of one's day, its comprehensiveness and coherence, its potential for dealing with anomalies, and so forth. Theological constructions are "houses" to live in for a while, with windows partly open and doors ajar; they become prisons when they no longer allow us to come and go, to add a room or take one away—or if necessary, to move out and build a new house.[5]

Davaney's fallibilism is just as insistent as McFague's and Smith's. Our theories about the cosmos, human existence, religion, and the ultimate meaning of things are, however compelling, socially and imaginatively constructed, speculative in character, historically contingent and limited, hypothetical, open to reconsideration, contestation, and revision, and fated to be eventually supplanted. Such a recognition, Davaney asserts, "leads to an ongoing attitude of self-criticism that while continuing to hold strong assumptions nonetheless holds them a little less tightly, always acknowledging their fallible character."[6]

Smith, McFague, and Davaney, in short, exemplify the underlying fallibilism of a (paleo)pragmatic historicist theology. In religion, as in every other sphere of human life, our most deeply held beliefs are, in the words of James, "hypotheses liable to modification in the course of future experience."[7]

The Second Trait: Theological Liberalism

Second, having thoroughly fallibilized human religiousness, pragmatic historicist theologians take up a decidedly *liberal* theology. Classical pragmatism and liberal theology share a number of important characteristics in common: both are revisionistic enterprises, and both are committed to pursuing truth openly, critically, publically, and above all, freely (the word "liberal" comes from the Latin terms *liber* and *liberalis*, meaning "free" and "befitting a free person").

Gary Dorrien broadly defines theological liberalism as the idea of a theology that (1) argues "on the basis of reason and experience, not by appeal to external authority," and (2) strives to achieve rational and experiential credibility without capitulating to "the cultured despisers" of religion[8] or "the spiritless materialism of modern atheism." In other words, it sets out to reconcile faith and modernity in a way that does not compromise the integrity of either. A predominantly Protestant Christian enterprise,[9] liberal theology stretches back to Kant, Schleiermacher, Hegel, Ritschl, Baur, Harnack, Hermann, Troeltsch, and other German intellectuals. Roughly around the same time, a tradition of Christian liberalism developed in America through the work of several distinguished figures, from Horace Bushnell, Theodore Parker, and Washington Gladden to Theodore Munger, Charles Briggs, and Borden Parker Bowne. By the twentieth century, American liberal theology split into three distinctive factions, each of which found a leading academic home: evangelical liberalism (centered at Union Theological Seminary), personalist idealism (centered at Boston University), and naturalistic empiricism (centered at the University of Chicago Divinity School). Thus, theological liberalism is quite diverse, historically, culturally, and intellectually.

Still, in Dorrien's account, two broad factors earmark any theology as characteristically liberal: (1) the principle of antiauthoritarianism (cf. chapter 5), which refuses to allow an outside authoritative source, such as a sacred text (e.g., the Bible) or a religious institution (e.g., the church), to compel theological assent, and (2) the impulse toward "integrative mediation,"[10] which endeavors to forge a progressive "third way" between "orthodox over-belief" and "secular disbelief" (or, to put it in Wesley Wildman's terms, to balance "fidelity with plausibility"[11]). Liberalism's antiauthoritarian, mediating theologies, whatever their affiliation, generally tend to be "reformist" rather than "revolutionary" in both temperament and substance, attempting to rebuild religious faith on contemporary values (e.g., ethical humanism) and on "the verdicts of modern intellectual inquiry," especially the natural and social sciences and historical criticism (in this respect, the nineteenth- and twentieth-century liberal theologians thought of themselves as carrying on the work of the Reformers).[12] Wildman adds that most liberals also evince a hermeneutically sophisticated awareness of the symbolic, nonliteral, and myth-laden nature of theological notions; undercut premodern supernaturalism and superstition; assume that "knowledge is actually progressing" (i.e., that "we know better than the ancients did what . . . is likely to be true regarding history and nature"); and "share the Enlightenment hope for a peaceful future based on science, technology, medicine, the overcoming of tribalism, the rejection of ingroup-outgroup exclusion, the collapse of hierarchies, the refusal of fanatical aggression, and the affirmation of a moderate form of religious belief and practice that sustains people in meaningful lives while enhancing creative cultural expression."[13]

Another way of describing liberal theology is to contrast it with what Robert Neville (polemically but provocatively) dubs "identity theology," which conceives of the theological task as the assertion and explication of a community's "revelatory witness" or "deep grammar" by and for its believing adherents. The most famous and influential identity theologian was Karl Barth, who understood theology as "the narration of a history given in the Bible." Other prominent theologians of identity include the members of the neo-Barthian Yale School (e.g., Hans Frei, Stanley Hauerwas, and George Lindbeck) and proponents of the so-called "radical orthodoxy" movement (e.g., John Milbank). Typically, identity theologies regard theology as testimony, preaching, proclamation, or "faith seeking understanding" (Anselm) and tend to focus on whether or not beliefs are legitimately Christian or Jewish or Buddhist (i.e., conform to the authoritative revelation, established orthodoxy, founding narratives, or cultural-linguistic rules of the tradition). More often than not, outliers and dissenters are delegitimated rather than refuted, denied identification in the religion or, in extreme cases, dismissed as heretics, infidels, apostates, and so on.[14]

The opposite of identity theology is what Neville terms "truth-seeking" or "probating theology," according to which theology is about "the search for *truth* in theological matters," not the faithful articulation and arbitrary assertion[15] of a religious identity. Theology, stated otherwise, is normative instead of merely descriptive, concerned with what is true or false with respect to ultimate concerns and values and not simply with what is Christian or non-Christian (or Hindu or non-Hindu, Muslim or non-Muslim, etc.). The practice of theological truth-seeking is actually quite ancient:

> In the time of Thomas Aquinas, Christians were presumed to believe certain doctrines because they had reason to think the doctrines were true, not because believing them was part of their identity as Christians. The scholastics gave closely reasoned defenses of their theologies, working patiently to untangle confusions and find relevant evidence. When they argued with Jews and Muslims, they gave reasons for the positions and arguments against their opponents, never thinking to say "as Christians, we believe *x*."[16]

The quintessential modern probating theologian was Paul Tillich, who beckoned theologians to embark on the "pursuit of truth, wherever that might lead," and to reach out to "any domain of inquiry that might bear upon . . . systematic topics." Tillichian (as well as Peircean) in spirit, Neville's own theology of truth methodologically prioritizes inquiry over confession, answers to a global rather than just an ecclesial public, and draws not only on sources that are internal to a heritage (e.g., scriptural texts) but also on "a broad array of learned discourses," from the theologies of other religions to artistic insights, to all branches of secular learning (the sciences as well as the humanities). Such a theology is interdisciplinary, comparative, and utterly fallibilistic, continuously trying to "hunt up reasons to doubt" it, interacting "with as many domains of reality that might correct it," and allowing it to be "proved false or misguided as new evidence or perspectives for criticism are found." Its scope is nothing less than "the whole of human civilization," Neville dauntingly proposes; the audience to which it is responsible and against which it tests itself is made up not just of fellow believers but of anybody (e.g., a physicist, a grassroots organizer, a Confucian, a secular theorist, a literary critic, an artist, a double belonger, an outcast) who might root out, amend, or falsify its "biases, errors, or omissions." Admittedly, such vulnerability puts "religious identity at risk." The upside, however, is that theology is set "in a wider and wider context" and is exposed to as many "angles of criticism" as possible, thereby becoming much less "arbitrary" than it needs to be. The historical locatedness of all thought ensures that arbitrariness in theology can never be entirely eliminated, but globalizing and pluralizing theology's publics can considerably minimize it.[17]

By and large, theological liberals, I submit, are truth-seeking or probating theologians. In fact, although depicting the liberalisms and neoliberalisms of the past as "near misses," Neville characterizes his own brand of truth-seeking theology—"a theology of symbolic engagement"—as a pragmatically oriented liberal theology, a theology that "engages the world on its own terms, with vulnerability to a global public and dependence on the resources of the sciences, arts, and practical disciplines as well as religious traditions."[18] Committed to the same paleopragmatist virtues of fallibilism and open, self-correcting, honest, multidisciplinary, and interreligious inquiry, pragmatic historicist theologians, we will soon discover, are religious liberals of a very similar stripe. As Gordon Kaufman demands:

> The resources of the social sciences and the humanities, of the biological and physical sciences, of philosophical reflection and poetic insight, as well as of Christian and other religious traditions, will all need to be drawn upon as we try to gain a more adequate understanding of our common human nature and our situatedness in the world.[19]

Confessedly, many theological historicisms are identity theologies, not liberal theologies. Most obviously and famously, George Lindbeck's historicist theology prides itself on being *post*liberal. That is, rather than making doctrines and worldviews vulnerable to critique, improvement, alteration, and ceaseless correction, and building the theological enterprise around reason and critically interpreted experience, multidisciplinary and comparative inquiry, and the open-ended and candid search for truth in religious affairs, Lindbeck construes theology as the exploration of a religion's grammatical structures. I would even hazard that postliberalism (ironically) shares more in common with the atheistic neopragmatism of Richard Rorty than the paleopragmatist historicist theologies spotlighted in this book. That is, Lindbeck's theory (or at least the reception of it[20]) renders theology *nominalistic* (i.e., theology is not about "objective realities," but about words, signs, and concepts and their function within a story, a text, or a cultural-linguistic system); *relativistic* (i.e., religions are judged only by internal/confessional standards of applicability); *arbitrary* (i.e., theologians are in the fideistic business of "absorbing the universe into the biblical world" instead of listening to "the clamor of the religiously interested public for what is currently fashionable and immediately intelligible"); and even *ethnocentric* (i.e., the theological task is to be faithful to one's own religious community, culture, or tribe in all its "intratextual, untranslatable specificity").[21] Paleopragmatic theological historicisms are, by contrast, *realistic* (there is something outside of our texts, languages, perspectives, metaphors, constructions, and so on, even if that something is wholly natural and historical and is mediated to us by our texts, languages, perspectives, metaphors, constructions, and so on); *antirelativistic* (theologians are answerable to multiple publics and criteria); *nonarbitrary* (positions must be argued for rather than simply asserted, proclaimed, or witnessed to); and *pluralistic* (religions are not bound to parochial enclaves—cf. chapters 3 and 4).

Of course, pragmatic historicism, too, affirms identity theology in the loosest sense of the term, insisting that nobody theologizes from nowhere. Again and again, I have alleged that theological reasoning (like human reason in general) is always traditioned, situated in and funded by the particularities of concrete historical lineages (although theology need not, in a pragmatic historicist perspective, be monotraditional—see chapter 4). Even the most philosophical of theologies are, as Wildman discerns, "entangled historically" with the theological confessions and identities of the religions and are "in some way parasitic upon the vast streams of tradition that frame religious experience and guide thinking about ultimacy in each new generation of human beings." There is no such thing as pure, generic, institutionally and ideologically unlocated, and identity-less theology.[22] Still, there is a significant difference between a religiously identified, deeply traditioned liberal theology and what Wildman dubs "confessional theology," and the pragmatic historicists featured in this project clearly represent the former.[23] Like Neville, they do not so much deny a religious (or a multireligious) identity as much as they deploy truth-seeking and probation as a way of humbling, critically and constructively appropriating, and correcting it.[24] They view theology not simply as the "interiorization" of a religion's teachings, doctrines, practices, affections, narratives, and liturgies,[25] but as the *exteriorization* of them, as it were, calling on theologians to test them in public, to subject them to constant scrutiny and criticism, and to reinterpret them in fresh and contemporary ways.

To illustrate, for Gerald Birney Smith, theologizing, when carried out in a scientific (read: hypothetical, provisional, fallibilist, and inductive) manner, consists of investigation (i.e., truth-seeking) rather than advocacy (i.e., witness), of the activity of ongoing "empirical testing" rather than the invocation of "some absolute standard," "external authority," or "objective revelation of God." In point of fact, the final three tasks of a "scientifically formulated" theology (after conducting a thorough inventory and examination of a religious history) involve identifying and suggesting potential resolutions to the pressing problems of the day, reexpressing received ideas and practices in a "practically efficient and rationally defensible" idiom, and making an "apologetic" case for the tradition's newly refurbished convictions.[26] The second and third tasks comprise what Smith elsewhere dubbed "constructive dogmatics," the effort to actively, critically, and imaginatively reconstruct theological notions in a manner appropriate to the intellectual climate, changing situation, and social context of one's time and place.[27] For example, in the twentieth century, theological construction entails modifying and correcting "the older doctrines" in light of the modern worldview,

> with its belief in the uniformity of law in contrast to the older belief in miraculous interventions; with its consciousness of the ceaseless evolution of all things in the place of the older conception of finished creations; with its outlook on an indefinite future history of this world in the place of the older expectation of a sudden catastrophic ending; with its growing confidence in the possibility of scientific control of the conditions of life, in the place of the older attitude of helpless dependence on forces out of human control; with its confident faith in the natural power of man to achieve ideals of goodness, in the place of the older belief in human inability; with its consciousness of the intimate unity of the spiritual and the physical in our experience, in the place of the older belief in a "soul" with an independent existence of its own; with its growing certainty that all historic religions are positively but only relatively valuable, in the place of the older conviction that only a given form of the Christian religion was true, while others were false; with its honest agnosticism concerning things out of reach of any empirical testing, in the place of the older assumption as to the reality of angels and devils in heaven and hell.[28]

The fourth task of theology—apologetically defending the faith—is not synonymous with the uncritical promotion of a religion or with the special pleading typically undertaken to substantiate the "supernatural source" or authoritative status of a religious text, figure, or heritage. Rather, apologetics, in Smith's liberal theological methodology, has to do with arguing for and giving public reasons for our religious proposals—that is, making sure that they are "justified by the facts," consistent with "the conclusions of other sciences," verified by "repeated experiment," and pragmatically advantageous in the real world.[29]

Shailer Mathews joined Smith in the quest for a liberal-minded, non-dogmatic, intellectually appealing, and scientifically plausible theology. Even *The Faith of Modernism*—a transitional work in which evangelical liberalism was presented as a broad-church solution to the fundamentalist-liberal fracturing of the mainline denominations—favored liberal Christianity's Enlightenment-modernist heritage over the gospel norms of evangelicalism, holding out for a theology that was socially and religiously progressive, empirically driven, historically critical, and rationalistic, naturalistic, and humanistic in both tone and content.[30] Modernist Christians, counseled Mathews, anchor the faith in inductive methodology, higher criticism, creative reconstruction, and experimental science, not group authority, theological passivity, confessional conservatism, or biblical conformism. They "substitute persuasion for coercion," value "variation" more than "heredity," and emphasize "development" over "regularity." They "honor freedom of thought" and "the power of truth" and "accept the results of scientific research as data with which to think religiously." They regard dynamism and democracy as religious virtues and view the desire for intellectual and cultural relevance and the willingness to let go of archaic, outgrown, superstitious, supernatural dogmas as signs of spiritual maturity, not faithlessness. They refuse to protect any tenet from analytical scrutiny and adopt theological conclusions at the end, not the beginning, of inquiry.[31] They are, in a word, liberal theologians.

And so are present-day pragmatic historicist theologians, like Sheila Greeve Davaney and Delwin Brown. Sounding very Nevillian, Davaney surmises that the historicizing and fallibilizing of theology, far from resulting in the narrowing of discourse or the cloistering of traditions, "opens up the possibility of public, broad-based conversations in which multiple disciplines, none of them privileged, contribute to one another." Here, theologians enter into dialogue with "the broadest range of inquirers," appraising beliefs and practices against the claims of different cultural, literary, aesthetic, philosophic, and religious lineages and against the understandings of other fields of inquiry, "especially those that can force us to contend with that which we seem to leave out of our accounts." The ideal is not to erect new incontrovertible foundations, but to construct well-founded—that is, contemporary, multitraditioned, interdisciplinary, academically vetted—visions of reality and human life, "knowing full well that they are contingent and fallible and will, in the future, be superseded."[32] In this sense, pragmatic historicism, says Davaney, stands in continuity with the central mission of the liberal theological heritage, stipulating that theology "seek intellectual coherence with those contemporary interpretations of the world, generated within the natural and humanistic sciences, that have widespread credence if it is to make sense for many persons today. . . . We cannot separate the manifold worlds in which we live. . . . Our only choice is whether we live out of anachronistic interpretations of reality or ones that have gained currency in the world we inhabit."[33]

Brown is also a theological liberal of a certain type. In the closing pages of *Boundaries of Our Habitations*, he argues that liberal theology is, at bottom, an exercise in "evangelical modernism." The American liberal theologians of the nineteenth and twentieth centuries—Bushnell, Briggs, Rauschenbusch, and even the early Chicago schoolers—"believed that the future is to be created, and hence they were modernists, out of the resources of the past, and hence they were evangelicals. They believed in theology as the reconstruction of inherited symbols."[34] Nevertheless, theological liberalism (owing largely to its rootedness in the Enlightenment effort to undermine dogmatism and the tyranny of traditional authorities in the name of freedom and autonomy) too readily succumbs to the allure of momentary fads and often "looks like little more than a mimic of passing developments in the physical and social sciences," forgetting that human beings live in and out of particular historical traditions and that those traditions "form us, inform us, and are essential to our re-formation."[35] For that reason, a good deal of Brown's own scholarship has focused on formulating a more traditioned, historically conscious liberal theology (i.e., a "constructive historicism").[36]

But a more traditioned, historically conscious liberal theology is still a liberal theology, a theology that grows out of and continues to depend on the Enlightenment assumption that "reason, based on available evidence, should be the ultimate arbiter in questions of truth."[37] Like Davaney, Brown pushes back on the "intrasystematic" criteriology of certain theological models (e.g., postliberalism); he assures that "intersystematic reason giving is possible," even if there are no "universal norms." Theologians, no less than other scholars, need to give cross-contextual (i.e., multidisciplinary and comparative) warrants for their views. Brown explains:

> What is said in theology, as in other inquiries, must be tested in the varied arenas of contemporary knowledge and experience—across disciplinary divisions, across religious lines, across cultural

boundaries, across the lines of race, class, and gender. . . . No theology will ever be tested in all relevant alternative contexts. But no theology is entitled even tentatively to the claim of credibility if it is not tested in relation to at least some alternate perspectives.[38]

Indeed, what makes any liberal theology liberal—and what makes Brown a liberal theologian—is its unequivocal repudiation of "special pleading," its unflappable commitment to the "self-critical search for truth," and its unwavering insistence that religious beliefs be defended in the innumerable fields of modern discourse and defensible according to the best information available in the present. Theological criteria, that is to say, are "fallibly developed in the always difficult, always tentative process of reflection as it is conducted in conversation with our contemporaries." Theology, liberally conceived, is adjudicated by participating "in the same kinds of discussions, employing the same open rules of evaluation, that are used in making judgments about the claims of history, science, philosophy, and common sense."[39]

On one final note, both Brown and Davaney conceive of their liberal theological historicisms as types of *academic theology*.[40] Academic theology—which Brown traces back to Ernst Troeltsch and to the sociohistoricist theologians of the early Chicago school—conducts its business and stakes its claims (whether descriptive or constructive) principally in the milieu of the modern university (Davaney even sees it as a subset of the wider field of religious studies). Its subject matter are the dogmas, tenets, and convictions of a particular religion (or multiple religions), interpreted as natural, cultural, human phenomena. However, its (primary) sphere of accountability is not the "believing community" and "its own special criteria of adequacy," nor is its (chief) task "the propagation of inherited doctrine" or the "edification" of religious practitioners. On the contrary, the projects and proposals of the academic theologian (who may or may not belong to the tradition in which she specializes) are subjected to analysis and criticism from every disciplinary quarter and are evaluated and defended in relation to the criteriology (evidence, reasonableness, etc.), theories and methods, and canons of public argumentation debated within the academy.[41]

I would point out that the research program of academic theology is, more or less, comparable to the agenda Wildman sets for *religious philosophy*, putting a premium on multidisciplinarity and comparison in theological queries. Neither religious philosophers nor academic theologians serve "the institutional or intellectual interests" of any specific group or denomination (although either can help people of faith "gain a more sophisticated self-understanding"), submit to the authority structures or confessional witness of established religions, engage in "special pleading or favoritism," or honor presumptions of "supernaturally authorized revelatory information." Both, rather, are committed to "the morality of rational inquiry in a secular academic context," which involves pursuing open, honest inquiry regardless of where it leads (even if it conflicts with the traditional teachings of a religion); seeking out "sources of correction wherever they may be found" (the foremost duty of fallibilism); and making use of insights from multiple religions and wisdom traditions (cf. chapter 4), all relevant scholarly disciplines, and "every kind of naturally derived human knowledge as it bears on religious subject matters."[42]

The type of theology harbored within this multidisciplinary and comparative approach to religious inquiry is "transreligious theology"—or what Jerry Martin has very recently dubbed "theology without walls." Transreligious theology, according to Wildman, is *decidedly not* confessional theology." That is, it is "not in thrall to specific sacred texts" and does not do theology "on behalf of concrete religious traditions." Or, as Martin more positively puts it, transreligious theology theologizes *across* religious and disciplinary divides, taking into account "the total spiritual resources of humankind, every source of revelation and enlightenment and insight."[43] A pragmatic historicist theology, I would argue, is also a theology without walls. Or at the very least, pragmatic historicism's truth-seeking, self-critical, cross-contextual, nonparochial, academy-centered, and hyperfallibilistic species of theological liberalism should generate a theology whose walls (i.e., boundaries) are porous, malleable, and expansive (see chapter 5).

The Third Trait: Constructive Realism

Third, in addition to being religious fallibilists and theological liberals, pragmatic historicist theologians are, like their classical pragmatist forebears, *constructive realists*.

To begin with, from the early Chicago schoolers onward, theological historicists have adamantly maintained that truth claims in religion and theology (including ones about ultimate reality) are, to a considerable extent, constructed. As historicist theologians have variously expressed it, our religious beliefs, even our conceptions of the divine, are human projections (Foster),[44] social patterns (Mathews),[45] imaginative constructions (Kaufman),[46] metaphorical elaborations (McFague),[47] or sacred conventions (Dean).[48] Generally speaking, pragmatic historicism's theological constructivism rests on two principal arguments.

First of all, theology, as McFague reminds us, is created by and for human beings, and human beings (including the founders of our religions and the authors of our scriptures) always theologize within specific cultural and social contexts, through the "medium" and "indirection" of language, and from "particular perspectives influenced by a wide range of factors"—for example, "our class, race, and sex; our nationality, education, and family background; our interests, prejudices, and concerns."[49] Indeed, for all theological historicists, religious knowledge, not unlike every other kind of knowledge, is perspectival—"localized, relative to its time and place, shaped by its history, infused by interests and interpretive in character, and part of a historical strand of other interpretations."[50] In a pragmatic historicist outlook, nothing—be it divine revelations, prophetic injunctions, historic creeds, sacred writings, esteemed gurus, or ecstatic experiences—furnishes human beings with a God's-eye view of the universe, an acultural, neutral, impartial, or framework-independent view.

Kaufman, for instance, argues that what people believe about the beautiful, the true, the real, the important, and the ultimate, about the right way to treat their neighbors, about the virtues to be cultivated and the vices to be avoided, and so on, are always influenced, indeed defined, by our social and geographical locations, by the practices, taboos, habits, customs, and presuppositions of our societies, by a symbolic and mythic lineage already in place and passed down to us from our ancestors, and by "the interpretive schemes carried in language and culture." Likewise, religious symbols and theological concepts are not immediately known objects, but imaginative constructs created within a specific strand of human history for the purposes of orienting and imputing meaning and direction to existence. Hence, "we can have no way of knowing to just what they refer or how accurately they represent it," alleges Kaufman. To illustrate, there is "no way to jump out of our *idea* of God"—that is, "the God that we, with the help of a long tradition developing before us, construct in our imagination"—in order to perceive "God himself as an objective reality."[51] As he put it elsewhere, "We do not know how the images and metaphors in terms of which we conceive God apply, since they are always our own metaphors and images, infected with our limitations, interests, and biases."[52] Our religious knowing, then, has a historical and mediated connection with its intended referents, with the "things themselves," and, thus, does not "correspond" to them, at least "in any *straightforward* or *one-to-one*" fashion (this latter qualification is of signal importance because, as I will soon establish, pragmatic historicism defends a variant of theological realism, insisting that reality *does* place constraints on what is theologically admissible).[53]

Even our religious experiences are historically and perspectivally conditioned, in Kaufman's judgment. In fact, experience as such is structured, delimited, and even constituted by culture and the intricate vocabularies in which words gain meaning. With a nod to the later Wittgenstein, Kaufman urges that "there is no such thing as 'raw experience,' experience completely free of all symbolic and linguistic coloring and interpretation."[54] Moreover, the negation (or, better, complexification) of prelinguistic and preconceptual experience necessitates that *what* is experienced at any particular moment is not a "bare given" or a "pure-something-or-other," unaffected by the symbols, terms, and signs employed to comprehend and construe it. And since we never quite reach "some sort of reality-in-itself-wholly-independent-of-language," neither do we have access to "ultimate-reality-as-it-is-in-and-of-itself." Bristling against the empirical theologians of the third-generation Chicago school (especially Bernard Meland) and all *direct* realisms in theology (whether revelationally or empirically based), Kaufman proposes that human beings (and, by implication, the religions) are at least four steps removed from what is ultimately and transcendently real. There are our lived experiences and imaginatively constructed conceptual patterns, which are shaped by our languages, which are, in turn, formed by specific cultural histories and their "historical sedimentation of many generations of experience, reflective thought, and symbolization," which are all additionally relativized by the "inscrutability" of existence.[55]

Of course, as I have mentioned in previous chapters, several of the pragmatic historicist theologians with whom this volume deals identify as "radical empiricists." But all experiences, even the affective, inchoate, dim, bodily, and nonlinguistic experiences highlighted by radical empiricism, are contingent, concrete, relative to their locale, and not easily separated from language. Experience, as Davaney declares, is never decontextualized; it is "always from a particular perspective and that perspective shapes it."[56] Brown agrees, granting that even our preconscious affections are intertwined with sensation and reflection: "This interaction means that there is no such thing as 'pure experience' if that term suggests that a subject can take account of datum 'as it is.' All experience is perspectival."[57]

And all *religious* experience is perspectival. Trying to provide a corrective to Schleiermacherian liberalism, Smith contended that no experience, religious or otherwise, is universal or ahistorical, unconditioned by the specific, ever-evolving context in which it is had.[58] Foreshadowing today's postliberal theologians, Smith made the following pronouncement in 1910:

> A disciple of Schleiermacher declared that the theologian only had to look within himself for the material with which he was to deal. But further reflection showed that experience cannot be taken simply as a storehouse from which permanent conclusions may be drawn. Experience has a history; it is conditioned by historical circumstances; it varies with changing environment.[59]

Eighty years later, Brown expounded and expanded on Smith's strikingly prescient insight:

> There is no abiding "experience" which remains itself through varied contexts . . . . There is no essence such as "religious experience" which, once found, can be analyzed so as to "do theology" on the basis of it. . . . It is not an essence separable from a particular history; its meaning is what it has done in particular streams of space and time. If religious experience has a history, then what religious experience *is* includes that history, and what it *can* be for us—i.e., what it might mean and do, for example, in the modern Western, Christian context—can only be worked out in an analysis, critique, and development of that particular history. A truly empirical theology must be a socio-historical theology.[60]

In sum, it is, first and foremost, the humanness, the historical, cultural, and linguistic conditionedness, and the perspectivalness of our religious experience and knowledge that expose the constructedness of our theological convictions.

Secondly, though, the constructive nature of the theological enterprise is reinforced, even propelled, by the utter mysteriousness of that to which the religions are responding. To quote Kaufman: "At best, all of the concepts and images with which we seek to conceive God . . . are only analogies or metaphors, symbols or models, drawn from human experience and history; they are, therefore, never applicable literally. . . . God is beyond our every finite conception."⁶¹ Or, as he more plainly confessed some years later, "My piety toward the mystery *qua* mystery compels me to acknowledge that when we [theologize] we come up against the very limits of our language and our minds, we really do not know what we are saying."⁶²

McFague draws a very similar conclusion. Religion deals in parables, in fictions, in analogies, in myths, in stories—in metaphors and constructions—because it endeavors to relate to what humans do not, indeed cannot, grasp. Poets utilize metaphor in order to speak about "the great unknowns"—for example, mortality, love, hope, and so forth. "Religious language," McFague analogizes, "is deeply metaphorical for the same reason." Consequently, a constructive or heuristic theology, by necessity, sniffs and snuffs out literalisms, fundamentalisms, absolutisms, and idolatries of every ilk, cautioning against the "reification" and "petrification" of theological ideas and the collapsing of the "inevitable distance" between human understanding and sacred reality. In Christianity, the ultimate temptation is "bibliolatry," which equates the fallible, human, historically produced words of the Bible with the Word of God. Even Jesus sometimes becomes an idol; there is such a thing as "Jesusolatry," McFague admonishes. Theology, however, never furnishes "a literal or realistic representation of God's nature," of "the way God really is." Protestant and mystical in sensibility, McFague is iconoclastic to the core: "No finite thought, product, or creature can be identified with God and this includes Jesus of Nazareth, who . . . both 'is and is not' God."⁶³ Lest we forget that our constructions are constructions, we need to foreground the *via negativa*, experiment with a multiplicity of theological metaphors and models, and refuse to allow any authority, whether "scriptural status," "liturgical longevity," or "ecclesiastical fiat," to "decree that . . . some images . . . refer literally to God while others do not. None do."⁶⁴

In brief, pragmatic historicism argues for the constructedness of theology, not only because its creators are none other than historically situated and perspectivally limited human beings, but also because its subject matter is enshrouded in mystery.

Be that as it may, no historicist theologian presumes that we are just making it all up. The majority of pragmatic historicists, on the contrary, incorporate at least a modicum of realism into their otherwise constructive theologies. Foster and Mathews both averred that theological symbols, while human and social in origin, point at something objective in nature (i.e., the cosmos's "ideal-achieving capacity" and "personality-producing forces," respectively).⁶⁵ Even the Kantian Kaufman, although occasionally sounding antirealist (see chapter 8), alludes to theology's "real referent," to "an unfathomable depth of mystery and meaning."⁶⁶

Surprisingly, perhaps, the most explicitly, unabashedly, and consistently realist of the pragmatic historicist theologians is McFague, whose metaphorical theology is undergirded by a "critical realism." Theological ideas and images are, to be sure, metaphors—"human and indirect and hence relative." Yet our constructions, McFague presses, are not *merely* fictive, *merely* invented; they *do* point to realities, although never directly and always through a socially conditioned set of "interpretive glasses." Hence, as a *critical* realist, she lambastes all manifestations of "naive realism" in religion (e.g., dogmatism, literalism, fundamentalism), which pretend that doctrines are "replicas" or "copies" of the universe (or the ultimate) as it is in itself. But, as a critical *realist*, McFague is equally opposed to deconstructionism's pronouncement that there is *only* the play of metaphor, "interpretation upon interpretation, referring to nothing but other words, an endless spiral with no beginning or end." Deconstructionists, McFague grants, rightly and powerfully undercut "the metaphysics of presence," the desire for absoluteness, totality, certainty, and closure, and call attention to the partiality, relativity, and incompleteness of all our claims. Still, to say that "no construction is . . . better than any other" or "that language . . . is about only itself" is to verge on a deleterious relativism and an indefensible antirealism. There is, she persists, something outside the text, something to which our religious metaphors refer, "even though the only way we have of reaching it is by creating versions of it," by "redescribing" it. Even more daringly, McFague allows that theories and models (even in theology) are "created" as well as "discovered," illuminating (in a nonliteral, perspectival, historically mediated fashion) some aspect of the structure of things. Our cultural and linguistic paradigms and metaphorical theological constructs have a "negative" and a "positive," an "is not" and an "is" relationship with reality.⁶⁷ They are not simply mirrors in which we see our own reflection; they are "windows" (albeit not "transparent" ones) onto a real world.⁶⁸

The entirety of chapter 8 will be allotted to laying out a constructive realist theology (specifically, with respect to the question of religious ultimacy), so I will not further belabor the point here. For the time being, I want to make a few prefatory remarks about the nature and function of theological realism in a pragmatic historicist perspective.

For starters, not any theological realism will do. Principally, pragmatic historicism is incompatible with the supernatural realisms of traditional religion.⁶⁹ Pragmatic historicists, rather, are *naturalistic* realists. For Kaufman, Dean, and most pragmatic historicists, the sacred is a reality in nature and history or not at all.⁷⁰

Pragmatic historicism is also incompatible with naive or direct realisms and the evidentialist epistemologies that undergird them.⁷¹ Historicism's, instead, is an *apophatic* realism; as Kaufman puts it, theology's "real referent" is a "profound mystery," an "unknown X" that relativizes and limits what humanity claims to know religiously.⁷²

To further deepen these mystical intuitions, pragmatic historicists could again benefit from Wildman. Recall that in Wildman's pragmatic theory of inquiry, the world evidences a "feedback potential" (cf. chapter 6). And, for Wildman, to experience this "resistance to hypotheses," this "whence of correctability," is to brush up against *the other*, that which is "uncontrollably beyond us." Reality's otherness and pushback, that is, instill a profound and humbling sense of "something unquestionable, something that pushes back by questioning us." The experience of wonder, awe, and mystery that result from such an encounter is consistent with what Wildman calls the "mysticotheological tradition" of religious and philosophical thought, whose "fundamental intellectual instinct is that ultimacy surpasses absolutely the cognitive grasp of human beings," and that inquiry into ultimate reality "proceeds optimally when it registers awareness of its inevitable breakdown."⁷³ While capable of genuine engagement with ultimacy, our deepest theological symbols (e.g., our gods) are "misleading as literal descriptions of that which is our ultimate concern," breaking against the reality to which they perspectively point and at which they indirectly hint. *Apophasis*, then, remains a—if not the—primary manifestation of the feedback potential in religion, functioning to expose the constructedness of all "religious legitimators of cultural meaning making" and to deconstruct "claims to their definitive legitimacy."⁷⁴

What is more, realism, in a pragmatic historicist theology, functions to give direction to and place constraints on religious interpretations. As Dean realizes, theology will seem "merely arbitrary and random," nothing more than a "wild guess," unless its theological constructions are at least minimally guided by our experiences and knowledge of the real world.⁷⁵ Without a doubt, the world's hypothesis-correcting capability, as Wildman admits, does not always work optimally, sometimes because "subtle variations" in "social context and inquiry procedure" prevent human beings from utilizing "available corrective resources," and in other cases because certain spheres of experience and inquiry exhibit a veritable kaleidoscope of hermeneutical possibilities or even a "permanent aporia." For example, reality "rarely speaks clearly" in the area of ethics and aesthetic tastes, in the humanities, in the more speculative fields of the sciences (e.g., quantum cosmology), and in metaphysics. The feedback potential is especially weak in the domain of religion and theology, engendering a stunning mélange of religious meanings and sponsoring "numerous individually coherent but mutually inconsistent hypothetical interpretations of ultimate concerns and ultimate realities." Even so, theologians need not acquiesce to pure arbitrariness or hard relativism, Wildman confirms. Theology (like the humanities in general) can leverage reality (as it is disclosed to us through multidisciplinary, comparative inquiry) in order to limit, correct, or even eliminate particular lines of theological interpretation[76] and to render some religious ideas more plausible than others.[77] Religion, in other words, "profits here and there from empirical resources to prune the tangle of competing hypotheses and constrain the survivors."[78]

The Fourth Trait: Probative Pragmatism

Fourth, and finally, pragmatic historicist theologians are what I will label *probative pragmatists*, joining Peirce, James, and Dewey in negating whatever-works utilitarianisms.

It should be clear by now that pragmatism is a part of historicism's DNA, at least in the United States; as such, it has been a dominant characteristic of many American historicist theologies. As it happens, a traceable ancestral line runs from James and Dewey to the early Chicago schoolers, to Brown, Davaney, Dean, Kaufman, and McFague. In 1904, James boasted that "Chicago has a school of thought," an intellectual zeitgeist propelled, mostly, by Dewey's methods and theories: a naturalism and a "pure empiricism," a denunciation of some "Unknowable or Absolute behind or around the finite world," a rejection of substance ontology and static ways of thinking for a world in which "everything is process and change," and a functionalist, evolutionist, and instrumentalist conception of truth.[79] Indeed, ten years earlier (1894), Dewey became head of the philosophy department and, along with the sociologist George Herbert Mead, the psychologist James Rowland Angell, the philosopher James Hayden Tufts, and a few others (e.g., Edward Scribner Ames, Addison Webster Moore, and Harvey Carr), helped make the University of Chicago one of the two hotbeds of pragmatism in America.[80]

The wellsprings of "the pragmatic temper of mind," without a doubt, trickled down to the Divinity School, even though Foster, Case, Mathews, and Smith imbibed Jamesian and Deweyan pragmatism "primarily through osmosis."[81] As Dorrien recalls, while remaining generally ambivalent about philosophical speculation,[82] and rarely citing the pragmatists directly,[83] the early Chicago schoolers nevertheless

> believed that the best philosophy was the American pragmatic empiricism of Harvard philosopher William James and Chicago/Columbia philosopher John Dewey. . . . With James and Dewey, the Chicago schoolers taught that scientific empiricism deserves its superior standing in modern consciousness and that genuine knowledge in the field of religion is attained by disciplined empirical reflection on experience. . . . Epistemologically, they embraced the pragmatic empiricist doctrine that knowledge is best attained by observing objects and making inferences about what they do.[84]

And, whether explicitly or implicitly, contemporary pragmatic historicist theologians, as Davaney comments, have been influenced, more than anything else, by "the positions of the early Chicago School and the first American pragmatists." For them,

> historicism, when fully articulated, points in the direction of pragmatism and the pragmatic adjudication of claims to truth and adequacy. In particular, it suggests that human ideas and practices, forms of thought and ways of acting and being [including religious ones], emerge out of and are expressions of the human need to organize, give direction to, and endow human life with meaning and value. They are preeminently practical. . . . They are historically devised tools by which humans navigate life, interpret it, build on prior historical experiences and interpretations, and determine future directions for humans to pursue.[85]

Harking back to the pragmatic naturalism of the early pragmatists, both Foster and Smith conjectured that religion, similar to the eye, is natural in origin and instrumental in function, selected to aid in the evolutionary struggle for survival, to help *Homo sapiens* adapt to, and adapt, the vicissitudes of the surrounding environment.[86] And if religion is an instrument, a device invented by tool-making animals for the purposes of environmental adaptation, then the "validity and value" of religious constructions (including deities) depend not on their putative "supernatural cause," but on their functionality and workability, usefulness and serviceability, on the "practical advantages" yielded by them in concrete historical settings.[87] Smith put it the clearest and sharpest: "The glory and strength of any given theology is to be found in the fact that it successfully answered certain vital problems so that men were enabled to face the supreme tasks of life with courage and efficiency."[88]

Case was also a religious and theological pragmatist. As a New Testament scholar and church historian, he could acknowledge the *historical* truth and significance of worldviews and conceptualities no longer regarded as viable (e.g., supernaturalism), so long as the items in question functioned meaningfully and beneficially for the people who produced and promulgated them.[89] However, when donning his normative theological hat, Case, as I showed in chapter 5, made the present, not the past, the pragmatic testing ground for religion, willing to discard any idea or practice that contradicts modern knowledge and experience and that fails to engender useful social and intellectual consequences today, regardless of its previous believability or utility. Traditions and creeds are preserved if—and only if—they enhance human existence and understanding in the here and now and augur new possibilities for historical development in the future.[90]

Like Case, Mathews, according to William Lindsey, worked out "the significance of pragmatist insights for systematic theology," describing (in a "thoroughly Jamesian" fashion) "how doctrine functions in a given socio-cultural milieu."[91] And, echoing Foster and Smith, he surmised that "needs" are both the progenitor and the criterion of theology.[92] Theological method is largely "empirical and pragmatic," evaluating how well a religion's particular tenets and rituals satisfy the intellectual, economic, and political conditions facing the world in an actual context and era.[93] For example, what is important about "God" is not whether there is a being "corresponding to the pictures of his worshippers," but the extent to which our notions of divinity enable us "to live hopefully and morally in the midst of social change." To be sure, the metaphysical and objective content of theological notions matter, but the *primary* meaning of the idea of God, opined Mathews, "is found in the history of its usage in religious behavior."[94]

The religious pragmatisms of the early Chicago school of theology (and of the paleopragmatists) live on in the theologies of today's pragmatic historicists. Dean's acquaintance with the pragmatist lineage is particularly intimate.[95] Invoking the spirit of James's *The Varieties of Religious Experience* and Dewey's *A Common Faith*, Dean insists that theological thoughts, traditions, and conventions (e.g., God) "cannot be called true" or even "real" unless they show evidence of "psychological and social effectiveness" and "make a practical and beneficial difference" in a "secular history" and in the "public world" of a particular society.[96]

Although not as overtly dependent on the early pragmatists as Dean (and Davaney), Kaufman and McFague are still pragmatist theologians of a certain sort. Kaufman maintains that the imagination creates ideas such as "God" and "the world" ultimately to "orient" women and men to "the whole of reality" by providing a picture of "the overall context" or "fundamental order" within which human beings are situated. And if theology exists for the "essentially practical purposes" of orientation,[97] then the gauge for assessing theological claims is "in the last analysis . . . pragmatic and humanistic," seeing "how satisfactorily they do the intellectual and cultural work for which they have been constructed." They are deemed "true" if they confront the needs and problems of today (e.g., the environmental crisis), reflect "our best moral insight," resonate with "modern understandings of ourselves and the universe," and lead to a "fruitful" existence, "in the broadest and fullest and most comprehensive sense possible.[98] McFague concurs: the veracity of religious metaphors is ascertained pragmatically, "preferring those models of God that are most helpful in the praxis of bringing about fulfillment for living beings."[99] Indeed, McFague's entire project revolves around the assumption that the measure of sound and relevant theology is not timelessness (i.e., the distillation of "eternal truths"), but timeliness (i.e., the ability to address the most pressing issues, assumptions, quandaries, and circumstances of the present historical moment). And the "new sensibility" to which contemporary theological perspectives must become responsive and accountable includes, among other things, the ever-looming threat of a "nuclear holocaust," the "challenge that other religious options present to the Judeo-Christian tradition," the rise of the "dispossessed," and the ecological awareness of nature's "radical interdependence."[100]

Unfortunately, reminiscent of many neopragmatists, pragmatic theologians of both the past and the present tend to simplistically pit pragmatism against correspondence theories of truth, as if the latter is *automatically* precluded by the pragmatist (and historicist) rejection of naive realism, objectivism, and representationalist epistemologies.[101] I hope to have shown that it is not (see chapter 6). Indeed, one of the correctives this book seeks to supply to a contemporary American historicism is a recovery of paleopragmatism's nuanced conception of "corresponding" or "agreeing" with reality. In any event, with James, Dewey, and especially Peirce (and Wildman and Neville), the theological pragmatists under discussion do, for the most part, manage to at least avoid the subjectivistic, antirealist, unempirical, intellectually lethargic, ultraconstructivist, isolationist, hedonistic, anything-goes relativisms that often get mistaken for pragmatism. Theirs is a *probative* pragmatism.

The Chicago schoolers are illustrative. In his 1907 article "Pragmatism and Knowledge," Foster (sounding a lot like Peirce) berated a number of fellow pragmatists (the "new philosophers") for becoming mesmerized by a fashionable scientific nominalism, where "formula and law alike" are treated as "rule[s] of action," as "devices for the manipulation of phenomena and the achievement of practical results" instead of "for the intellectual apprehension of reality."[102] By Foster's reckoning, pragmatism without empiricism and realism is dead. Undeniably, Foster regarded science, art, ethical principles, the self, Euclidian space, sense impressions, and even the divine as human constructions. However, the "raw facts" human beings seek to constructively interpret are not; they are the stubborn empirical givens from which our inquires are derived, to which they are directed, and against which they are measured. He proceeded to spell out the implications for religion: "Let any functional psychologist try to act upon the idea of God, no matter how it arose, and at the same time disbelieve in his existence; he will find that no action will follow, if *ontological* reference be denied to the facts" (in Foster's case, the "ideal-achieving capacity" of the cosmos).[103] In other words, a pragmatically successful hypothesis—religious, scientific, or otherwise—needs to comport with what humans know and experience empirically; notions that blatantly misconstrue the real, external, objective world are, by definition, unpragmatic—that is, unable to function efficaciously.[104] As Dorrien observes, "Foster could not ask himself, 'Does this belief work for me?' or 'Is it in my best interest to hold this belief?' or 'Does this belief serve the common good?' without asking himself whether his beliefs about God or the good were metaphysically true."[105]

Smith struck a similar tone, admonishing any "irrational sort of pragmatism which would simply ask what it would be pleasant to believe." No doubt, the pragmatist thinks that "all conceptual knowledge must be functional to be meaningful so that any idea must be tested 'in the experience of living persons.'"[106] However, to pass the pragmatic test of functionality, a concept has to align with "the generally established conclusions of men" concerning what is true about reality. And, as for religion in particular, Smith wanted pragmatic theologians to take into account "what is and what is not rationally possible in the construction of religious beliefs." A theology whose "speculations" and "constructive imagination" remain "uncontrolled" and unverified by "observance of fact" is simply "inefficient" (read: pragmatically false), at least in the long run.[107] As Mathews confirmed, "No religious faith can be satisfactory that is out of harmony with what have been shown to be the facts of the universe."[108] For both Mathews and Smith, intellectual credibility (which, in the modern age, includes consistency with science, democracy, and religious pluralism) is one benchmark of pragmatic satisfactoriness.

McFague could not agree more. In most disciplines, "epistemic success" is determined pragmatically. But "a pragmatic or quasi-pragmatic criterion" itself utilizes a multiplicity of criteria, some internal and others external, assessing ideas for a whole range of results—for example, their "coherence" and "comprehensiveness," their "fruitfulness for living," their ability to "light up" human existence in "profound ways," their compatibility with contemporary knowledge, and their "empirical fit." Theologies, too, must evince "illuminating potential," which involves not only explaining and making sense of human experiences and events but also achieving a modicum of "isomorphism" (i.e., "similarity of structure") between the nature of reality and the models we use to interpret, redescribe, and construct it. Of course, no metaphor or concept ever refers *directly*—that is, in a perspective-free, nonideological, unmediated, ahistorical, incorrigible fashion. Nonetheless, deciding between theological options, even if not "absolute," is never purely "arbitrary" either. "Ghetto Christianity" (or ghetto Judaism or ghetto Buddhism) is the price theologians pay when they fail to put forward "evidence" in support of their proposals, when the pragmatic effects for which they test do not relate to different "ways of looking at the world" or line up with "other truths people hold to be significant."[109]

Davaney, too, articulates a pragmatic historicist theology that is intellectually rigorous, omnidisciplinary and comparative, rationally and empirically grounded, criteriologically wide-ranging, and committed to the honest pursuit of truth. As a pragmatist, Davaney calls us to test and revise our beliefs and practices (religious and otherwise) in accordance with "the ramifications they have for concrete lives" and "the forms of life they make possible." Hers, though, is a "procedural pragmatism" that invites theology to plead its case within "the public arena of conversation and debate." Obviously, humanity's various cultural inventions—science, the law, rituals, sporting competitions, religion, and so forth—perform different sorts of functions and serve vastly diverse purposes and, for that reason, require context-specific criteria for judgment. Even so, Davaney rebuffs postliberalism's proclivity for "communitarian retreat" as well as "the private nominalism of much postmodernism." The porous and reconfigurable nature of heritages, the multitraditioned character of individual and communal identities, and the "comprehensive thrust" of religious and theological visions oblige us to vet and assess our claims and proposals *publically*—that is, beyond their "locale of origin" and in relation to "the interconnected particularities that make up historical reality" and the broadest possible "range of material." In this connection, Davaney affirms Brown's bid for non-intrasystematic, cross-contextual "justificatory practices" (cf. the second trait). Such an "inclusive agenda" necessitates that theological argumentation and reason-giving take place within a plurality of publics, across myriad and overlapping disciplines, cultures, and perspectives, before several "interlocutors," and "in the face of multiple voices," especially the nonperson (i.e., groups or individuals "rendered invisible or denied access to the means of self-determination"), other religions (contra the postliberal inclination toward incommensurability and "ad hoc cooperation"), and the nonhuman natural world (in terms of both the account of nature emerging from contemporary science and the ethical demand of ecological responsibility).

In short, we must look to the consequences of our ideas, actions, and traditions for anyone or anything affected by them, actually or potentially—their adherents and detractors, their beneficiaries and victims, their insiders and outsiders. A procedurally pragmatic historicism, needless to say, does not bequeath "timeless or absolute truth." But it does, Davaney pledges, leave us with compelling and meaningful, albeit fragile and fallible, *truths*, provisional hypotheses that we "take to be warranted" and "defensible in light of what we know at the moment and are the result of open and free encounters with all relevant participants."[110]

Chapter 8

Sacred Conventions, Sacred Nature

Toward a Pragmatic Historicist Theology of the Divine

In the third volume of his magisterial trilogy on American theological liberalism, Gary Dorrien notes that pragmatic historicism has been long on "programmatic theorizing" but short on "constructive theologizing."[1] This concluding—and highly experimental—chapter is an attempt to fill that lacuna, to lay out *a pragmatic historicist theology of the divine.*

Of course, in order to fashion a constructive theology of the divine, pragmatic historicists need to first deal with their implicit atheism. To state the matter starkly, in the midst of naturalizing human religiosity and interpreting objects of worship and devotion (e.g., divine beings) as "sacred conventions" or "human imaginative constructions,"[2] pragmatic historicists advance a type of atheistic humanism and conventionalism, leaving religious believers to wonder whether religion refers, or at least points, to anything real. And so, quite understandably, some critics of historicism—and even a few conflicted historicists—question whether pragmatic historicist theologies are themselves pragmatically viable and theologically meaningful. Is not the very idea of a "pragmatic historicist theology" a contradiction in terms?

In what follows, I will hazard, along with William Dean,[3] that pragmatic historicism's is an *ironic* atheism. The desupernaturalizing, humanizing, and conventionalizing of the divine—that is, the realization that the gods are human creations, personifications and projections of our own needs and desires—can ironically set the conditions for a new kind of theism, for a realist, naturalistic, and even mystical metaphysics of ultimate reality. My strategy is to put forward a *multigenerational* Chicago-school theology, so to speak—that is, a theology that creatively fuses a theological humanism and conventionalism (characteristic of the early Chicago schoolers) with a religious empiricism and naturalism (characteristic of the later Chicago schoolers). I will proceed to argue that historicism—at least the bigger, more holistic version of historicism propounded in this book—is most compatible with what I will call "apophatic, pluralistic naturalism." Stitched together from the religious naturalisms of Dean and Gordon Kaufman, as well as a number of nonhistoricists, such as Bernard Loomer (a third-generation Chicago schooler), Wesley Wildman, and Donald Crosby, an apophatic, pluralistic naturalism imagines the divine in significant proximity to the whole of natural reality—natural reality in all its creativity, ambiguity, inexhaustible possibility, radical contingency, aesthetic and axiological fecundity, incalculable complexity of meaning, and ineffable mystery. In that sense, pragmatic historicism can become a way of lifting up (and naturalizing) the mystical and agnostic impulses, the *via negativa*, present in most traditions, which exist to critically relativize our theological imaginations and religious loyalties and to combat the idolatrous penchant to confuse finite images of the ultimate with the indeterminate unknown with which we are striving to come to grips. But then, in a final twist of irony, the awareness of the all-surpassing, incomprehensible mysteriousness of the ultimate, of nature in its spiritually breathtaking, ambiguous, and relativizing wholeness, compels us to return to the cataphatic and symbolic landscapes of our religious histories (including our humanly constructed deities), which alone can house our highest hopes and ideals and sustain our institutional, ethical, and cultural endeavors.

Naturalizing Religion, Humanizing Theology, Conventionalizing Divinity: Pragmatic Historicism and the Menace of Atheism

I want to open the chapter by making explicit something to which this project has recurrently alluded: the metaphysical worldview that underlies pragmatic historicism is what Dewey labeled "empirical naturalism or naturalistic empiricism."[4] In the main, empirical naturalists or naturalistic empiricists assert (1) that there is no reality above and beyond nature, (2) that knowledge is empirically grounded, and (3) that the legitimacy of one's beliefs is determined by appealing to, observing, and scrutinizing the data gleaned from experience. Put differently, empirical naturalism or naturalistic empiricism promulgates, according to Nancy Frankenberry, a cosmological, a genetic, and a justificational thesis. The cosmological thesis denies the existence of any and all supernatural, nonempirical spheres, causes, ideals, spirits, beings, souls, heavens, or forms. Positively stated, empirical naturalists or naturalistic empiricists maintain that the natural realm, and the natural realm alone, is the only realm that is real and experienceable. Whatever is, is in and of nature; there is nothing outside of it, nor anything that transcends it. The genetic thesis assumes that experience is the source and referent of ideas. "If the one world, with all its incalculable possibilities," is the only world there is, "then all principles, descriptions, and explanations must be understood to refer to events and their relations."[5] The justificational thesis, lastly, is that the best method of inquiry is experimental. A concept "is ultimately to be tested for its truth, soundness, or acceptability in terms of the evidence supplied by experience, where 'experience' is variously construed."[6]

Thus, to say that pragmatic historicists are empirical naturalists or naturalistic empiricists is to state that they (1) restrict both what is and what can be known to *this* world, the world of natural and human history, and (2) insist that every assertion, notion, and theory be *empirically founded and warranted*, based in and validated by experience.[7] As Dean puts it, the empiricist/naturalist/historicist evinces "an unblinking regard for what is sensed, without recourse to what is not sensed," which requires casting one's ontological and epistemological "lot with the contingencies of history."[8] She resists, in the words of Richard Rorty, "the Platonic urge" to break away from "the finitude of one's time and place," from "the contingent aspects of one's life," in the hopes of finding "something ahistorical and necessary to cling to."[9]

The classical pragmatists set pragmatic historicism on an empirical and naturalistic course. Again and again, John Dewey decried the Western philosophical penchant to treat natural and human experience as, at worst, transcendable and, at best, "merely phenomenal," that is, as shadowy "appearances" or "impressions" of something "non-natural" and "supra-empirical," something eternal and unchanging, stable and constant, certain and timeless. In the West, reality has been dualistically divided into two arenas of existence, with the empirical, historical sphere of contingency, chance, and change placed on a lower ontological plane than the "noumenal," "unmoving" domain of "ultimate Being," of "the Real in itself." The physical, material, natural realm was that from which philosophers needed to take refuge, and practical affairs and activities (e.g., morality and politics), by virtue of belonging to that "relatively real" realm, were disparaged. "Permanence, real essence, totality, order, unity, rationality, the *unum, verum et bonum*" thus became the "foundations" of any good philosophical system, and "remoteness from the concerns of daily life" one of philosophy's greatest assets. For Dewey, though, there is nothing supernatural, nothing "beyond the power of nature,"[10] and consequently, nothing more philosophically important or fundamental than "gross" and "ordinary" experience, experience in all its coarseness and crudity, precariousness and variability, heterogeneity and fullness, entanglement and complexity. Accordingly, rather than "withdrawing from the real world and cultivating fantasies," philosophers should try to shape history and attend to "the things of everyday experience, the things of action and affection and social intercourse."[11]

Hence, in a Deweyan naturalistic and historicist casting, philosophy is an empirically situated, scientifically informed, and utterly fallible, finite, and pragmatic mode of human inquiry, which proffers hypotheses rather than "finished facts" and enables people to adapt to the environment. It is willing to let go of atemporal truths and transcendent realities, "metaphysical absurdities and unverifiable speculations," and is, instead, intent on ameliorating suffering, on bolstering "fruitful interaction," on experimenting with and reconstructing the natural order, on nurturing individual and "social well-being," on resolving the ethical, intellectual, and cultural quandaries of the day, on working towards a more humane, intelligent, and democratic future, and on removing any obstruction in nature that impedes humanity's "most passionate desires and hopes."[12]

James shared Dewey's empiricism and naturalism. He captures it succinctly and memorably: "Everything real must be experienceable somewhere." There are no nonempirical, transcendental realities on which experience itself leans.[13] "The directly apprehended universe needs, in short, no extraneous transempirical connective support, but possesses in its own right a concatenated or continuous structure."[14] Or, as he writes in *Pragmatism*, "All 'homes' are in finite experience; finite experience as such is homeless."[15] And if all homes are in finite experience, then "the only things that shall be debatable among philosophers shall be definable in terms drawn from experience."[16] Consequently, empirical naturalists have no truck, metaphysically or methodologically, with the philosophical (and religious) search for the immutable, the nontemporal, the abiding, the supernatural, the absolute, the ahistorical, the extraempirical—in a word, for what James called "Reality with the big R":

> Something to support the finite many, to tie it to, to unify and anchor it. Something unexposed to accident, something eternal

and unalterable. The mutable in experience must be founded on immutability. Behind our *de facto* world, our world in act, there must be a *de jure* duplicate fixed and previous, with all that can happen here already there *in posse*, every drop of blood, every smallest item, appointed and provided, stamped and branded, without chance of variation.[17]

To be a naturalistic empiricist, on the contrary, is to be "tough-minded." It is to take to the "street," to turn toward "action," "power," and "the possibilities of nature." It is to be concerned with "the actual world of finite human lives," which is "multitudinous beyond imagination, tangled, muddy, painful and perplexed," and to focus on "this broad colossal universe of concrete facts, on their awful bewilderments, their surprises and cruelties, on the wildness which they show."[18]

Like James and Dewey, the pragmatic historicist theologians featured in this study, from Case, Foster, Mathews, and Smith to Brown, Davaney, Kaufman, and McFague, are all historically conscious empiricists and naturalists. At a minimum, none of them thinks that there is anything—at least anything knowable—above and beyond the confines of natural, historical experience. The religious is no exception. As Dean maintains, "Whatever might lie outside history lies outside religion, empirically considered."[19]

Among the earliest religious historicists to naturalize and historicize religion were the liberals of the Chicago school of theology. Gary Dorrien reports that one of the principal distinguishing marks of Chicago-school liberalism was a Jamesian and Deweyan pragmatism (see chapter 7) and, with it, a "commitment to a naturalistic empiricism." Case, Foster, Mathews, and Smith, observes Dorrien, followed the classical pragmatists in urging that the scientific method "deserves its superior standing in modern consciousness" and in teaching that "genuine knowledge in the field of religion is attained by disciplined empirical reflection on experience."[20] As Dean confirms, "The Chicago School theologians were influenced by the evolutionary and pragmatic naturalism of William James and John Dewey" and, as such, averred that "religious truths necessarily referred entirely and exclusively to the valuational events in natural and social history."[21]

The Chicago schoolers gave their naturalistic and empirical theology a historicist twist. I already established in chapter 5 that they were *Troeltschian* historicists. As Dorrien again chronicles, "With Ernst Troeltsch and other post-Ritschlian disciples of the *Religionsgeschichliche* approach to religion, the early Chicago schoolers emphasized the sociocultural development of

Christianity and the relation of its teaching and practices to other world religions."[22] Mathews, for his part, understood doctrines as culturally shaped and socially patterned products; a theological idea (e.g., the atonement), along with every aspect of a religion, "is a function of the religious life of a given period and this in turn is the expression of a social order conditioned not only by elements of culture, like philosophy, literature, and science, but also by the creative economic and political forces which engage in the production of the social order itself."[23]

The Chicago-school historicists were also *humanistic* historicists, however. Foster declared that religion, not unlike language, art, morality, and other "higher achievements of the soul," is an utterly human invention, a tool utilized by and for men and women to deal with the vicissitudes of existence.[24] Case added that "history may be said to make religion," where "history" is conceived in naturalistic and humanistic, as opposed to providential or dualistic, terms. In other words, history is neither "providentially supervised" nor infinitely distinct from something that is not history—for example, "the sphere of the superhistorical," "the outer world of eternity," or "the supernaturally mediated revelation" of a "totally other God." On the contrary, there is nothing deeper than history itself—that is, the "complexity of events," the "never ending stream of time," the "labyrinth of promiscuous happenings."[25] Prefiguring Dean by half a century,[26] Case put forward an ontology in which history alone—and not an "absolute spirit" or a "transcendental Deity"—makes history: "At least two distinct types of influence must be recognized in the making of history: it is a product of material existences belonging to a widely varied physical world, and it is also made by human beings who are something more than mere physical entities."[27] Such thoroughgoing historicism implies that religious (and cultural) phenomena, too, are the offspring of history, not vice versa. That is, the generator, or the "parent," of creeds, dogmas, communities, scriptures, and the like is none other than historical reconstruction and human initiative, the ongoing efforts of people to adjust inherited lineages to the stimuli of new environments:[28]

> Under the impact of circumstances subsequent generations of men lived and acted in the interests of certain values that seemed to them most worth while, and in this way they perpetuated and re-created that area of interest commonly termed "religion." While its institutions, its liturgies, its doctrines, its prescriptions for conduct, and the type of personal experience it nourished

embraced heritages from the past, all of these legacies had to be infused with new life in the experience of each new age. One of the most elemental lessons to be learned from history is the fact that religion is integral to the process of life itself. . . . Historical religion survives by being embodied in the experience and activity of actual persons living in specific situations within one or another area of the earth's surface. Thus religious living is definitely a human task. It always has been so in the past, and it must ever continue to be such in the future.[29]

In brief, neither Case nor any of the theologians of the Chicago school knew of any way of talking about Christianity or religion in general "except through ever-changing historical interpretations of previous historical interpretations."[30]

Neither do present-day pragmatic historicists. An heir of early Chicago-school religious humanism, historicism, and naturalism,[31] Dean suggests that religiousness is not the one area of human life that traffics with something supernatural, something that, at best, shines *through* history but is itself ahistorical—that is, infallible, absolute, unchanging, decontextualized, extraempirical, noncontingent, and so on. Rather, religion is, like everything else, formed and caught within the dynamics and limitations of historical happenings and is birthed in and through ordinary human experience. From Dean's monistic and naturalistic standpoint, there is only the one world, the world of "natural and social history," and "one experiences only what can be experienced within historical time and space." Hence, he chafes against metaphysical dualisms that bifurcate nature and spirit and locate religious objects in some "spiritual and nonhistorical dwelling place," in some "idealistic" or "supernaturalistic" realm beyond the spatiotemporal.[32] To quote Dean: "Historicism has had theology being pulled by history, so that theological ideas are abstractions derived from the concreteness of historical events and meaningful to the extent that they reflect those events. For most Christian theologians, history has been a time-bound fulfillment of or deviation from a universal and eternal reality described by theology."[33]

Davaney, too, picks up where the early Chicago schoolers left off, viewing religion as "one dimension of culture" and, thus, "interpretable by the same means" as any other culturally constructed artifact. Religious beliefs, religious practices, religious texts, religious communities, religious heritages, religious experiences, religious figures, and so on, are "elements within and products of cultural processes." Gone and ruled out, for Davaney (and for many historicists), are appeals to the sui generis character of religion, the notion that the religious is somehow exceptional—that is, in a class all by itself, different in kind from other spheres of existence, set off from the broader matrices of human history, and unbound by the conditions of historicity.[34] Historicism, therefore, swims in the much larger pool of "naturalistic" theories of religion now commonplace in the academic field of religious studies. Historicists, with most scholars of religion, assert that human religiosity is (at least partially) "explainable" in more mundane, natural, scientific, sociohistorical terms, without recourse to parochial authorities, privileged sources, special revelations, or supernatural causes.[35] And precisely because religion is natural and human in origin and sociocultural and historical in character, religious phenomena are assessable by the very same disciplines and procedures of analysis and criticism employed to illuminate any province and facet of society.[36]

If religion is natural and human in origin and sociocultural and historical in character, where exactly does this leave the sacred? Typically, as I pointed out in chapter 7, historicist theologians of both the past and the present purport that religions *construct* the realities—including the ultimate realities—with which they have to do.

Case, for instance, intimated that the always-shifting, ever-varied "theistic imagery" in which humans picture God is one more "child" of history's "generative energy." Indeed, the gods are "creations of our imagination" and, as such, "have always [been] made . . . in the image of man."[37] Foster also held out for a thoroughgoing religious humanism. In the spirit of atheists like Nietzsche and Feuerbach, he announced that "there is an element of illusion in religion" and that our faith in the divine "had its origin in human fantasy," in humanity's "God-making capacity." Human religiosity is exactly that—human. Men and women, that is, invented religions and deities for the purposes of coping with the environment, with "the impenetrable darkness of the future and the unconquerable might of hostile powers" (e.g., "over-mastering foes, ferocious beasts, storms, earthquakes, conflagration, famine, sickness . . . and, above all, inescapable death"). Fear was certainly not the source of every deity; some gods were fashioned out of "joy and the overflowing fulness of life." But in either case, the human organism created "the gods to do for him what he could not do for himself." Even the notion of "a personal God" is "symbolic" and "figurative," revealing more about the "appreciations of the subject" than "the nature of an object." The "subjectivity of [its] origin" in no way diminishes religion's value or veracity, Foster assured: "Are not our moral standards, are not our scientific formulae, are not our artistic creations, are not our languages, products of the subjective needs and activities of mankind? But do you discredit the reality and function of these because you made them?"[38] Still, he remained indefatigably humanistic (indeed effectively atheistic), adamant that gods and religions, akin to ethics, science, art, and even the number system, are constructs of the human imagination, produced by and for humans in order to "humanize" and "idealize" the world.[39]

Likewise, Mathews demonstrated that even the most ancient and revered religious doctrines, far from referring to extrahistorical, supernatural realities, are human constructs that arise in response to the problems of a specific cultural situation, grow over time, and stem from "social patterns" or "social processes" or "social minds" at work in a particular society.[40] Our concepts of the divine, to illustrate, never quite correlate, at least in an immediate, one-to-one manner, with an objective, "actually existent" entity. The idea of God is, well, an idea—that is, a humanly created, historically patterned theological construction that receives new content and undergoes reinterpretation whenever a community's needs, worldview, social psychology, or cultural experiences change.[41] Mathews concluded:

> The history of the usage of the term God shows that it is not strictly metaphysical or ontological. There is no existence exactly corresponding to the patterns with which the deity has been conceived. There was no Jahweh on Mount Sinai and no Zeus on Mount Olympus. No more is the God of the theologian a metaphysical being. He, too, is a reality conceived in patterns.[42]

Gerald Birney Smith made a comparable pronouncement just a few years earlier:

> Shamash was a very real figure in the religious life of the ancient Babylonians. Doubtless the theologians of that day regarded his existence as absolutely certain. Of the reality of Shamash *in Babylonian religious belief* there can be no question. But what about the ontological reality of Shamash? In the course of time those religious needs which had been satisfied by Shamash came to be satisfied by more convincing conceptions. We frankly say that Shamash was a symbol of religious hopes rather than an actual deity. . . . What would a modern theologian say concerning the ontological reality of Yahweh? Such a study of the history of religions suggests that religion has a way of outgrowing its

theologies. Christianity has outgrown many doctrines in the course of the centuries. Is it inconceivable that it should outgrow the traditional doctrine of God?[43]

The early Chicago schoolers, in brief, were constructive theologians decades before there was such a thing as "constructive theology." This is one reason why Dean pits them against the "pietistic liberals" of the nineteenth and twentieth century, from Schleiermacher and Emerson to Bushnell and Tillich. On Dean's reading, these liberal pietists rightly construed theology as "an evolving and interpreted record of human experience, set in history and reinterpreted for present history." But they were only half historicist, historicizing the religious subject but failing to recognize that the divine object, too, is historical. In contrast, Case, Foster, Mathews, and Smith, along with the theologians of the later Chicago schools (Wieman, Meland, and Loomer), were "empirical liberals," following through on their historicism and proclaiming that "whatever might be called spirit" either exists within history or it does not exist at all. For them (and for James, Dewey, and Whitehead), "history would contain all the values and all the Gods there ever would be."[44]

In the second half of the twentieth century, it has been McFague and especially Kaufman who, more than anyone else, have pushed theological historicism in a constructivist direction. McFague describes the constructedness of religion in terms of a *metaphorical* or *heuristic* theology. The ever-increasing awareness of both the "creative, interpretive character of human existence" and the mysteriousness of the sacred has led to the realization that our religions and their objects are social constructions. And McFague proposes that our religions are constructed, in large part, through the formation of metaphors. Metaphors, by definition, express the unfamiliar in the language of the familiar and exhibit an "is and is not" quality, thereby negating any presumption of identity or univocity between our conceptual imaginings and the phenomena they are striving to conceptualize. Metaphoricity is basic to human thinking as such; all concepts and images (not just poetic ones) are metaphors insofar as they are "indirect attempts to interpret reality, which can never be dealt with directly."[45] To understand *theology* as the elaboration of metaphors or as "heuristics" is, for McFague, to confess that every theological assertion is, without exception, an "imaginative construal," a "human construction" that "perforce 'misses the mark.'" And God-talk is particularly inadequate, uncertain, and, in some measure, improper, for no idea, picture, or name, no matter how august or antique, accurately depicts or defines the divine. By McFague's count, "Our concept of God is precisely that—*our concept* of God—and not God."[46] Thus, in a metaphorical or heuristic mode, theology becomes a mostly fictional, highly skeptical, and thoroughly experimental, hypothetical, pluralistic, and imagistic enterprise, engaging in constant "remythologization" and proceeding in an "as-if fashion."[47]

Since 1975, Kaufman, too, has declared that theology is primarily a human work, an activity of "imaginative construction" (as opposed to, say, the explication of divine revelation). Baldly and boldly put, "It emerges out of and interprets human historical events and experiences; it utilizes humanly created and shaped terms and concepts; it is carried out by human processes of mediation, reflection, ratiocination, speaking, writing and reading."[48] To be sure, all of our most fundamental symbols and notions (the self, time, etc.) are "our own constructions." They are, pronounces the Kantian Kaufman, the socially and linguistically constructed categories by which human beings give structure and order to experience and thought, not "objects" that are out there somewhere. The same thing applies to our most fundamental *theological* symbols and notions; Christ, creation, prayer, reconciliation, sin, and God (and their equivalents in other religious traditions) are productions of the imagination, cultural artifacts produced in a particular stream of human history "as the women and men in that historical movement gradually put together a world-picture which enabled them, with some measure of success, to come to terms with the exigencies of life."[49] To insist on their "objective reality" is to falsely "reify" them, to turn human, heuristic constructs into "things that are *really there*." As I discussed in chapter 3, religions, in Kaufman's pragmatic historicist theory, are not so much "maps" of the way the universe is in and of itself as they are "meaning-bestowing" heritages, providing the myths, stories, rituals, and comprehensive images (e.g., the idea of "God" and analogous conceptions of ultimacy) through which we comprehend our place within "the whole of reality," determine how we should live and act in the world, and orient ourselves "in face of the great mysteries" of existence.[50]

Kaufman adds that theology has *always* been a human, creative venture. Of course, Isaiah, Jesus, Paul, and Luther did not regard themselves as constructive theologians; it is only from our contemporary "vantage point, looking back (with the aid of several centuries of historical work increasingly informed by cross-cultural understanding) at the many great and diverse cultural traditions which have appeared in the course of human history, that we can see how much all of this must have been a product of human imaginative creativity."[51] Nonetheless, theological construction is precisely what has taken place throughout the entire history of Christianity (and indeed every religion), even though "this was seldom recognized until modern times." Our religious forebears, whether they knew it or not, reinterpreted the wisdom passed down to them by their ancestors, which in turn emerged from the interpretive ingenuity of still earlier generations, and so on indefinitely. For the most part, theology has moved from a first-order undertaking, which presupposes that theological constructs are "more or less adequate representations of objective realities," to a second-order one, which acknowledges that all positions, including our own, derive from the human imagination. Such a paradigm shift, Kaufman happily notes, puts present-day theologians in an unprecedented situation. In ways never before possible, we are now in a position to cultivate a *third-order* theology, to take full ownership of and responsibility for our imaginative constructions, carrying out the constructive theological task with critical self-consciousness and methodological deliberateness.[52]

Dean agrees with Kaufman, McFague, Smith, Mathews, Foster, and Case that religion deals in human constructions, historical interpretations, social patterns, metaphorical elaborations, and the like. But humanly constructed, historically interpreted, socially patterned, and metaphorically elaborated referents are not necessarily unreal, in Dean's account. In chapter 6, I introduced Dean's conventionalist ontology, which posits that cultural constructs (e.g., the American Constitution, universal human rights) sometimes turn into independent actualities by becoming conventions. By mid-career, Dean began espousing a *theological* conventionalism, referring to the sacred (i.e., gods and their counterparts in other faith traditions) as "conventions about what is ultimately important."[53] A major source of Dean's theological conventionalism is Dewey's *A Common Faith*. Here, Dewey conjectured that the divine, far from designating an antecedently extant "Personality" or a "Being . . . outside of nature," signifies "the unity of all ideal ends arousing us to desire and action." Ideals and their unification—symbolized by the word "God"—do not enjoy any sort of "supernatural or metaphysical . . . existence," but are "imaginative in origin." Even so, they are not "doubtful" or "fanciful," Dewey persisted. Quite the opposite, they are "the heritage of values" that exist not simply in the "mind," but "by grace of the doings and sufferings of the continuous human community in which we are a link." Their "reality" is "vouched for by their undeniable power in action," by their capacity to "stir and hold us."[54] For Dean, this makes Dewey a conventionalist (or, better, a protoconventionalist).[55]

Building on Dewey's incipient conventionalism, Dean contends that a sacred convention is a concrete embodiment of a historic community's profoundest imaginings and longings that, nevertheless, eventually becomes, to some degree, transcendent of the heritage that produced it. Like every convention, a sacred convention is neither an objective entity nor a subjective wish, but a third class of being, a "social habit" or an "active, living . . . tradition" that germinates from the soil of a local culture, but eventually assumes "an uncanny force of its own," accomplishing "what historical creatures cannot accomplish for themselves." Unable to be reduced to the sum total of interpretive causes out of which it emerges and grows, it takes initiatives and improvises, acting somewhat unpredictably and freely on the society that spawned it. It can be personally related to as "the spiritual and historical impetus that incites a community to act morally and religiously" and can even be considered a "spirit that people look to, not only with hushed anticipation but with fear and trembling, not quite knowing how it will speak in any new moment of history."[56] Thus, the gods and ultimates of the religions are not supernatural essences or beings, but neither are they mere fantasies or imaginary, momentary fads of human whimsy. Rather, Dean proposes that they are as solidly real "as any historical reality can be." In this connection, Dean likes to quote William James: "God is real because he produces real effects."[57] That is to say, sacred conventions begin as "fictions" but, sooner or later, exceed their human makers, acquiring a kind of "aseity" (i.e., ontological independence) and developing into autonomous, deeply entrenched sacred conventions that change lives, impart a sense of the whole, shape and create history, and even instill inspiration and awe.[58]

Dean surmises that a conventionalist perspective enjoys considerable advantages over the projectionism of the nineteenth-century atheist, Ludwig Feuerbach. Feuerbach (along with Emile Durkheim and most sociologists of religion) simply assumes that humanly projected phenomena (e.g., personal deities) are "figments of the personal or social imagination." But a sacred convention, Dean counters, "has a life of its own and affects societies in unexpected ways, so that by any pragmatic use of the term 'reality,' God is a living, historical reality."[59] Presumably, such realism[60] also distinguishes Dean's theological conventionalism from the more Feuerbachian historicisms of Foster and Kaufman. Foster, in *The Function of Religion in Man's Struggle for Existence*, appreciatively referenced "the great discovery" of Feuerbach, namely, "that man made God in his . . . own image."[61] And in his intellectual autobiography, Kaufman recalls that his conception of theology as imaginative construction was inspired not only by Kant's *Critique of Pure Reason* but also by Feuerbach's *The Essence of Christianity*, "which argued that what had hitherto been thought of as *theo*logy was really disguised *anthropology* (human studies). Feuerbach showed that all the major doctrines of Christian faith—including especially the doctrine of God—could be understood as expressions of an unconscious projection of human characteristics and qualities onto a non-existent external cosmic reality."[62]

Yet, for more moderately liberal (even if sympathetic) critics like Gary Dorrien, the differences between Foster's humanism, Kaufman's constructivism, and Feuerbach's projectionism, on the one hand, and Dean's conventionalism, on the other, are barely noticeable. After all, a sacred convention is still created by human beings and, as a result, is devoid of "any transcendent power over nonbeing." This is not much of a God, Dorrien opines. Dean's conventionalist reduction of the divine makes the continued usage of "God-language" seem, at best, "quaint" and, at worst, "dubious."[63] Indeed, to some, the very idea of a "historicist theology" is an oxymoron, for religion and its divine objects have become so naturalized, historicized, culturalized, and humanized that anything religions might recognize as theologically substantive and religiously real, to say nothing of spiritually nourishing, completely drops from view.

As it happens, a handful of historicists have voiced similar concerns over the years. In the 1910s, Foster exhibited an uneasy conscience about historicist religion. And at the dawn of our own century, Dean has begun to have "second thoughts"[64] about the religious viability of pragmatic historicism, suspecting that conventionalism terminates in atheism—or best-case scenario, in religious humanism. It is to their conflicted historicisms that I now turn.

Is "Historicist Theology" an Oxymoron? The Conflicted Historicisms of George Burman Foster and William Dean

George Burman Foster's 1909 humanist manifesto *The Function of Religion in Man's Struggle for Existence* approvingly cites Nietzsche's (in)famous epitaph: "God is dead!" Of course, Foster claimed to bask in "the sunnier side of doubt." Religion, he pledged, is a "necessary creation of human nature" since humankind has an "inextinguishable need . . . to create gods for itself." Although every deity will eventually be "retired," humanity's "God-forming impulse" will not, ensuring the ongoing demand "to replace old gods by new."[65] Foster hammered the point home with memorable candor and bluntness:

> The gods were created for the sake of the most vital practical interests. They were created in the interest of overcoming the evils that beset the human organism and of appropriating the good that would redound to the weal of that organism. Mindful of how help had been furnished in situations wherein superior adjustment had been achieved—water had saved him in time of conflagration, a comrade, in the extremity of war—primitive man created gods with which to meet emergencies that were beyond him. Need is the mother of the gods.[66]

Nevertheless, even if unwilling to capitulate to hard, combative atheism,[67] Foster completely humanized the source, function, and object of religion. W. Creighton Peden is correct to call him "the original 'Death-of-God' theologian in America."[68]

But for the next decade, he would equivocate about (or more accurately, agonize over) the religious implications of theological humanism—a struggle stirringly recounted by Douglas Clyde Macintosh (a doctoral student of Foster, who went on to develop a variant of realist empirical theology) and, more recently, by Gary Dorrien.[69] In 1912, Foster reflected on the sinking of the Titanic in the pages of the *Chicago Tribune*, seemingly contradicting the thesis of *The Function of Religion in Man's Struggle for Existence*: "The God of our making is a nonentity. . . . How may we attain not to a shadow-God, not to a God-idea merely, but to the real and living God? Not by calculation or stipulation, but by experience." Confused, Macintosh wrote to his teacher, asking him whether he had changed his mind about the metaphysical existence of the divine. Foster replied: "Yes, I have passed through the slough of epistemological subjectivity, and see more clearly and hold more firmly the objective and social reality of religion. . . . A real God, a real man, a real world—our need of these is too imperious to give them up." Later that year, he spoke at the annual meeting of the Baptist Congress, where he publically chastised his colleague, Edward Scribner Ames, for saying that God, much like Uncle Sam, "is not a being for himself." Foster pleaded that theology can neither abandon its "ontological philosophy of God" nor "allow itself to be reduced to a phenomenology of religion, to a branch of anthropology, and to the psychology of illusion," a plea he repeated in a number of subsequent writings.[70]

Be that as it may, by the very end of his life, Foster had stopped backsliding, rededicating himself to humanist religion. Already disillusioned by World War I, Foster lost a child, Harrison, to pneumonia in February 1918. Years before, the drowning of his eldest son drove him to confess to Shailer Mathews that "there must be a God somewhere in the universe." But the passing of his "brilliant soldier boy" was another matter, apparently reinforcing his earlier humanistic historicism and pragmatic functionalism. That summer, just months before his own death, Foster conceded to the students in his philosophy of religion course that Ames was right all along: "Is God like George Washington, the Father of his country, or is God like Uncle Sam, depending upon the people for whom he functions? He is like Uncle Sam; his reality is functional. . . . God is the personification of the ideals of man. . . . The supernatural world is an artificial projection. The religious man invents a 'real God,' which is but man's own self, immoderately enlarged."[71] In October, he made that sentiment known in his review of Ames's *The New Orthodoxy*, gesturing toward an antisupernaturalistic, post-theistic humanism:

> I, myself, think that we are witnessing the passing of theistic supernaturalism. Mankind is outgrowing theism in a gentle and steady way. . . . Religion is coming to mean, not other worldliness, but the valuing of human experiences and activities, the striving for their realization, loyalty to their call. . . . I value Dr. Ames' book as another good-spirited effort . . . to create loyalty to the values of human life here and now. These values are self-justifying and self-supporting. Worth while on their own account, they need no alien sanction, as they have no alien source and origin.[72]

The aging Foster grew more and more sympathetic not just to Ames, but to Nietzsche as well. Posthumously released in 1931, Foster's last volume was an appreciative study of Nietzsche's life and thought. Albert Eustace Haydon (a leading religious humanist and Foster's student and eventual successor at the University of Chicago) introduced the work by noting that the two thinkers shared quite a bit in common:

> Both knew the torture of spirit in wrestling in frank honesty with the problems of a world wrenched from its old, secure foundations on absolute truth. Both knew the sweet sadness of rejection by the good people still enfolded in untroubled security

of church and creed. "I speak as a man who has suffered as keen spiritual anguish for twenty-five years as one could well suffer and maintain his sanity and health." These, Foster's words to his brethren in religion, would apply equally well to Nietzsche. Both men made the pilgrimage out of orthodoxy unable to find rest on any plateau of compromise until they set their feet upon the adventurous and uncharted path of pure naturalism.[73]

Yet Foster, as Dorrien properly qualifies, was "double-minded" about how far to take that pure naturalism.[74] In my view, Haydon, along with a few other interpreters,[75] accurately read the late Foster as increasingly nontheistic and humanistic, as someone for whom "little by little, the man-agency takes the place of the god-agency."[76] In the penultimate chapter of the Nietzsche book, for instance, Foster describes the sweep of Nietzschean atheism admiringly, even if cautiously:

> And so God is dead! And Nietzsche would accept none of the historical traditional substitutes for this God that died. He repudiated world-ground, First Cause, Spinozistic Substance, moral order of the world. . . . He would have no vaporization of God into pure spirit, or system of values. He did not believe in our humanizing and teleologizing and ethicizing of nature. Nature was nature, not man with a conception of the distinction between right and wrong, good and evil. He warned us to be on our guard in speaking of the universe as either an organism or a mechanism—words which, by implication, point to a pale survival of the old God that is dead.[77]

However, although Foster came to accept humanism and the quasi-atheistic belief that the contemporary world is slowly beholding "the passing of theism,"[78] he probably remained conflicted about it until his final breath. As Dorrien judiciously concludes: "He was too influenced by Darwin, Strauss, Nietzsche, and Dewey to speak in Bowne's assured tones about the existence of divine personality, but he was too fervently religious to be satisfied with any form of secular reason. . . . He wanted to believe in something that antimetaphysical modern pragmatism could not secure, but he found pragmatist religion religiously wanting."[79]

The mature William Dean has also found pragmatist religion religiously wanting. In the opening chapter of *The American Spiritual Culture*, Dean decries the reductionism that dominates the academic study of religion.

Over the last century and a half, a wide range of theorists, from Emile Durkheim and Peter Berger (arguably the two most revered sociologists of religion) to Ludwig Feuerbach, Karl Marx, Friedrich Nietzsche, and Sigmund Freud (the so-called "masters of suspicion"), to Jacques Derrida and Richard Rorty (the icons of postmodernism), have reduced religious phenomena to sociological, anthropological, or psychological—in a word, human—processes.[80] Dean generalizes:

> For these thinkers, the claims of religion are like shouts in an empty canyon—nothing but human voices bouncing back, misinterpreted as divine voices. . . . Religion . . . and their constructions are effective, sometimes malignantly effective, because of the social forces they set loose. Those constructions remain powerful because they give societies enough social glue to avert anarchy, individuals enough psychological security to stave off mental illness, or both societies and individuals enough meaning to lend stature to their arbitrary desires. But in a mature and honest society . . . the constructions should be recognized for what they are: temporary, constructed palliatives or therapies rather than references to a reality that transcends society. In short, the gods, taken literally, are crutches for the immature and the dishonest.[81]

But it is not only secular academics who are beholden to reductionistic theories of religion. Dean regrets that post-1950s American liberal theologians have also "absorbed the postmodern ridicule and social-scientific dismissal of all that would ground theological truth," standing idly by as "neo-pragmatists, deconstructionists, hermeneuticists, and Religious-Studies scholars blithely trashed their truth-categories."[82] They have been so intent on becoming academically respectable that they have lost the ability to contribute anything "intellectually independent" or "religiously probing" to public discourse. They have been so preoccupied with mastering pluralist, pragmatist, constructivist, relativist, post-structuralist, and historicist methods that they have let go of distinctively "theological contents"—that is, "words about God, *logos* about *theos*." Worst of all, in Dean's Foster-esque assessment, they have been so enticed by reductionism, by the reduction of religious truth to what is explainable by contemporary learning and secular understanding, that they have given up the efforts of earlier theological liberals (e.g., Reinhold Niebuhr, Paul Tillich, and Henry Nelson Wieman) to speak compellingly about a divine reality that is both immanent *and* transcendent, mysterious, and somehow cosmic. They have, in short, forgotten that they are "theologians first and liberals second."[83]

Dean judges that pragmatic historicist theologians are definitely theologians second. When they "sit at the table of religion," he ruefully notices, "they tend to consume their host—and the partaking of the host is not exactly sacramental. As scholars should, they explain everything they possibly can with the instruments of their academic craft. . . . But, in the process, they make God their servant."[84] Dean even admits that his own theological conventionalism is, in effect, "an atheistic stance." A divine convention is so immanental and historical that it fails "to meet certain important religious expectations." Such a "God" is what the Foster of 1912 referred to as a "shadow-God," a "God-idea," a "God of our making" (as opposed to "the real and living God").[85] Such a God rises within ordinary human history and perishes within ordinary human history. Oxymoronically, then, conventionalist "theology" is rather atheological, ill-equipped to connect people "to what the religions call the sacred or the holy." Dean confesses that it can even "lead to atheism."[86]

Beyond Humanism: Atheistic Ironies and the Possibility of a Religious Naturalism

But Dean proceeds to show that there is something profoundly ironic about the atheism to which conventionalism leads: it can illumine a path to new, deeper theological riches, to "a sense of mystery."[87] I will go a step further and suggest that it can even pave the way for the development of a thoroughly naturalistic, but spiritually vigorous, theologically realist, and mystically inflected metaphysics of ultimate reality—a pragmatic historicist theology of the divine. The sublime, awesome, terrifying, ambiguous, transcendent, and mysterious depths of nature, I submit, are opened up to us *by* historicism and its reductive, atheistic conventionalizing. The way beyond humanistic religion is, ironically, *through* it.

From Convention to Mystery: The Irony of Atheism

"The irony of atheism," Dean stipulates, lies in its capacity to "set the conditions for a new theism." Dean clarifies that the referent of this newly acquired, this atheistically acquired, theism is not a "God-being" (which is what theistic terminology commonly connotes), but "something more like a spiritual presence . . . or a mystery." In fact, what makes an atheistic outlook ironic are the theistic treasures that emerge *from* the historicizing and humanizing of divine beings; that is, it is precisely when the gods are reduced to what secular thinking permits (e.g., wish fulfillments, projections or personifications of human ideals, imaginative and metaphorical constructions, social patterns, or sacred conventions) that something deeper—a spiritual presence, a mystery—is reached.[88]

Dean sees the irony of atheism nearly everywhere. He sees it, for example, in an aesthetic encounter with a musical masterwork. Precisely at the point when "the artistry of the performers and the particular structure of the composition" become everything, it can, ironically, "become anything but that; it can open the listener to what feels sacred, dwarfing the music itself." He also sees it in the poetry and fiction of Flannery O'Connor, according to whom "art transcends its limitations only by staying within them." A story, to illustrate, becomes "more than a story" only after it is construed as "nothing but a story." Similarly, O'Connor believed that a sense of "depth," "Mystery," and "religious meaning" appears just when "religion is reduced to its nonreligious and ordinary-historical causes." Dean even sees the irony of atheism in the Bible. The Apostle Paul insisted that salvation comes by despairing of any and all "means of self-salvation." Only after one has had "such atheistic despair, has abandoned efforts at works righteousness, and has known oneself to be doomed, can one discover true faith made possible through God's grace."[89] Even more strikingly, on the cross, Jesus accepted, indeed suffered, a form of atheism, crying out, "My God, why have you forsaken me?" But then the Gospels take "an ironic turn," and crucifixion yields resurrection. "By sacrificing himself to secular history," exegetes Dean, "Jesus became also the Christ of a sacred history."[90]

Dean, moreover, argues that a number of American religious thinkers herald the irony of atheism. To mention only a couple of examples, Paul Tillich maintained that after "the theistic idea of God"—the God-being whom "Nietzsche said had to be killed"—disappears in the anxiety of atheistic doubt, there appears "the God above the God of theism" (i.e., "the ground of being" or "the power of being-itself").[91] In a similar fashion, Ralph Waldo Emerson grew wary of Christian theology, calling on citizens to rely on themselves (rather than an eternal God) and to fully immerse themselves in the natural, historical world. "But, pursuing this humanistic, naturalistic, and historicist outlook to its end, Emerson," Dean observes, "arrived at a point where he affirmed that when human experience, nature, and history are truly plumbed, we find a Deep to which our own 'deep' must respond. . . . Emerson pushed secularity hard enough for it to reach spirituality."[92]

However, the quintessential ironic atheist, in Dean's telling, is William James. In the conclusion of *A Pluralistic Universe*, James discussed the Lutheran variety of religious experiences, "experiences of an unexpected life . . . succeeding on our most despairing moments" and emerging "in *spite* of certain forms of death, indeed *because* of certain forms of death." Luther (and Paul) realized that accepting the inevitable "bankruptcy" and "failure" of "self-sufficiency" ironically unleashes "possibilities that take our breath away," a "kind of happiness and power, based on giving up our own will and letting something higher work for us." To relinquish "one's conceit or hope of being good in one's own right is the only door to the universe's deeper reaches." Likewise, the experience of "godlessness" that ensues when the absolute, perfect, static, foreign, timeless "god of scholastic theology" is rendered "hollow" and "unreal" can "give way to a theism now seen to follow directly from that experience more widely taken." Such a theism points to a superhuman (but not superhistorical) "more," a "wider self," an "invisible spiritual environment from which help comes."[93] According to Dean, James eventually discovered that by entering "the darkness of atheism," one could return with a new awareness of something incomprehensible and mysterious, even if utterly finite.[94] As James's last-written essay, "A Pluralistic Mystic," stirringly concludes, "There is no complete generalisation, no total point of view, no all-pervasive unity, but everywhere some residual resistance to verbalisation, formulation, and discursification, some genius of reality that escapes from the pressure of the logical finger, that says 'hands off,' and claims its privacy, and means to be left to its own life."[95]

To Dean's communion of ironic atheist saints, I would add a few others. In *Radical Monotheism and Western Culture*, the mid-twentieth-century American historicist H. Richard Niebuhr talked about "the One beyond the many," "the great hidden mystery" that is dimly glimpsed precisely at the moment when the meanings, value-centers, and gods that humans wrongly and idolatrously absolutize "are revealed by time to be relative." Just as we acknowledge that "all our causes, all our ideas, all the beings on which we relied to save us from worthlessness are doomed to pass," something ineffable and abysmal appears on the horizon:

> We may not be able to give a name to it, calling it only the "void" out of which everything comes and to which everything

returns, though that is also a name. But it is there—the last shadowy and vague reality, the secret of existence by virtue of which things come into being, are what they are, and pass away. Against it there is no defense. This reality, this nature of things, abides when all else passes. It is the source of all things and the end of all. It surrounds our life as the great abyss into which all things plunge and as the great source whence they all come. What it is we do not know save that it is and that it is the supreme reality with which we must reckon.[96]

The irony of atheism is operative as well in the writings of many postmodernists. Drawing on some of the religious and theological motifs present in Jacques Derrida's later works,[97] theologian John Caputo points out that secularism ironically makes room for the advent of the "postsecular," modernist/postmodernist criticisms of religion for the resurgence of "religion without religion," the death of God for "the death of the death of God." To deconstruct "the idols of ontotheology"—that is, "the *ens supremum et deus omnipotens*" and even "the *hyperousios* of Neoplatonic mysticism"—is to "pass through a dark night and a mandatory atheism." But in so doing, deconstruction lets loose "the event" astir and harbored in the name of God—the "to come" (*à venir*), the "wholly other" (*tout autre*), the "messianic," the "undecidable" and the "undeconstructible," the "simmering potentiality" and the "inaccessible mystery."[98] Similarly, the postmodern philosopher Richard Kearney recently coined the neologism "anatheism" to signify "the return of God after the disappearance of God." Kearney ventures that secular, atheistic critiques of dogmatic theism (e.g., those of the so-called "new atheists," like Richard Dawkins, Daniel Dennett, and Christopher Hitchens[99]) exert a kind of (ironic) "emancipatory force," ushering in an "anatheist moment" in which "one can begin to recover the presence of holiness in the flesh of ordinary existence."[100]

To summarize, the irony of atheism is that new theological resources reside on the other side of atheistic desolation and disbelief. And it is my contention that there is something deeply mysterious and relativizing, something religiously, aesthetically, and spiritually probing, that is (or at least can be) released *by* pragmatic historicism's virtual atheism—its reductionism, constructivism, conventionalism, and humanism.

But to remain within a pragmatic historicist perspective, that "something" requires at least two additional qualifications. First, it is a *real* something. That is, "mystery" is both a negative and a positive designation. More than a linguistic placeholder for human unknowing, it refers as well to an unknown reality, a reality that transcends rational explanations. In this, I stand with Dean and against other historicists, hazarding that the divine mystery is not merely "the place where secular thought gives out," but is also "a rich and affirmative presence."[101]

Second, it is a *natural* something. The mysterious sacred, Dean insists, does not point to an "antinatural" or "nonhistorical" reality, but to the depths and mystery of *this* world, the empirical world.[102] As James indicated, "the more" signals "*the universe's* deeper reaches," something operative outside of human processes, but not outside of time, history, or nature.[103]

In short, the new theism, the sense of mystery, unloosed by pragmatic historicism's atheistic, humanistic reductions must be enfolded in a *theological realism* and a *religious naturalism*.

Constructive Historicism and the Receptive Side of Religion: Arguments for a Theological Realism

In chapter 7, I asserted that a pragmatic historicist theology is—or at least should be—not simply a constructive theology, but a *constructive realist* theology. Pragmatic historicism, that is to say, is at its best when it injects a healthy dose of theological realism into its otherwise domineering constructivism.

Most of the pragmatic historicists spotlighted in this study are religious constructivists *and* religious realists. Shirley Jackson Case believed that "the Deity" is humanly "devised." Be that as it may, "beyond these creations of our imaginations," Case continued, "there are the raw materials, so to speak, employed in the process of construction and the incentives that prompt us to create the imagery. The pictures, varying in form and quality, may be of our making; but the urge to produce and the elemental stuff with which we work are a more ultimate reality the apprehension of which constitutes our deepest knowledge of God."[104]

Dewey arrived at essentially the same position in *A Common Faith*. For Dewey, the ideals that are seized upon and imaginatively unified—the process for which the symbol "God" stands—"are not made out of imaginary stuff," but "out of the hard stuff of the world of physical and social experience." And "the ideal itself has its roots in natural conditions; it emerges when the imagination idealizes existence by laying hold of the possibilities offered to thought and action."[105] Thus, Dewey's concept of the divine, as Dean notes, was both humanistic and naturalistic, not only "pragmatically applied to nature but, in part, empirically derived from nature."[106] In fact, Dean himself shares Dewey's view: "The sacred is neither something objectively given nor something simply projected out of imagination; the sacred is the product of imagination in interaction with environment."[107] Delwin Brown is also a Deweyan—in spirit, if not in name. Brown professes that the activity of human construction (theological, religious, or whatever) always takes place within an "efficacious [and external] milieu," whose "complex of powers . . . give[s] rise to our constructings as much as our constructings give rise to our constructions." Ergo, the divine, like any construct, is both imagined and, in some measure, experientially received.[108]

In aligning myself with these constructive realist historicists, I necessarily distance myself from other pragmatic historicist theologians who place almost all of the emphasis on human construction. For instance, although never explicitly denouncing realism, Davaney completely "culturalizes" the theological enterprise. In my judgment, akin to her neopragmatist counterparts in philosophy (i.e., Rorty and West), she moves too precipitously from the (correct) premise that theology *is* a form of cultural analysis and criticism to the (incorrect) conclusion that theology is *about* cultural analysis and criticism. Philosophizing is a mode of conversing; but, as I argued in chapter 6, philosophers presumably have more to converse about than the conversation itself (e.g., the structure of language, overarching cosmological principles, the mind-body problem). Scientific research, too, is surely theory-laden and is a cultural activity undertaken by and for human beings; but, obviously, science studies something other than its paradigms (e.g., the cognitive machinery of mammals, the behavior of particles and societies, the origins and fate of the universe).

Likewise, religions (and their gods) are indeed "historical human constructions," and theology undoubtedly "involves . . . the treatment of religious beliefs, practices, and institutions as part of human culture and history that can and must be studied using the multiple approaches applicable to all other human realities." But are the humanly, culturally, and historically constructed beliefs *themselves* the lone subject matter of theology, as Davaney seems to suggest? If not, might theologians engage in something besides cultural analysis and criticism (for example, putting forward constructively adventurous, but empirically grounded, utterly fallibilized, publically argued, and academically scrutinized hypotheses about that to which the humanly, culturally, and historically constructed phenomena of religion are receptive)?[109] Ironically, for all of her incisive and sometimes biting critiques of postliberalism,[110] Davaney, much like Lindbeck (cf. chapter

7), tends to make theology self-referential and nominalistic; its tasks and even its *contents* are cultural without remainder. Put another way, Davaney perhaps falls prey to what Dean terms "methodologism," so bent on nailing down theology's critical, analytic, academic methods and "culturalizing" the data they investigate (worthwhile and indispensable undertakings, to be sure), that the methodological procedures themselves become the point of theology, and any realities to which human cultures and religions may be responding (e.g., the mystery and ambiguity of history) fall from the purview of theological analysis, critique, and construction.[111] This is the main reason why her pragmatic historicism is, according to Gary Dorrien, deficient in constructive theology—"interesting and relevant as cultural analysis and critique, not as speech about God."[112]

Kaufman is more overtly circumspect about the necessity of realism in religion and theology than Davaney. Actually, he tends to play the Rorty role in contemporary theological historicism. His neo-Kantian commitments, combined with his historical and pluralistic consciousness and his apophaticism—indeed agnosticism—with respect to the most fundamental questions of life and death, oblige him not only to underscore the constructive character of theology but also to rein in the realist impulse in human religiosity, "the overly optimistic belief that some sort of 'empirical' access to what is 'ultimately real' is available to humans." Theologians (including the liberal empiricists of the later Chicago school, Bernard Meland and Bernard Loomer) often presume that believers are "in direct epistemic touch with some sort of religious reality," with "what is *really the case*," and such a presumption too frequently leads to the "reification" of our most deeply held metaphors, to idolatry, and, worst of all, to the absolutizing of our religions.[113]

As a historicist and a religious pluralist, I relish and back Kaufman's efforts to keep the faith traditions honest about the highly speculative, historically conditioned, imaginatively constructed, and completely human, relative, partial, fallible, and metaphorical nature of all theological statements and, thus, about the need to "tread very cautiously in making claims about the ultimate, the universal, the really real."[114] Be that as it may, I think that Kaufman (analogous to Rorty) protests realism a bit too much. Kaufman is deeply suspicious of Bernard Meland's realist insistence that "ultimacy . . . inhere[s] in a ground of otherness to which man, in his subjectivity, relates himself,"[115] an assumption that characterized and fueled much of the theological work of the mid-twentieth century (e.g., neo-orthodoxy) but, he believes, no longer adequately reflects the contemporary zeitgeist.[116] I have the opposite intuition: the religious realism of which Meland speaks enjoys a heightened urgency and relevance in today's postmodern climate, a climate that emphasizes social constructions over the realities to which those constructions are seeking to connect.[117]

And yet, not even Kaufman can sustain antirealism for too long. Despite his (justifiable) theorizing about the imaginative genesis of religion and religious truths, he avers that "the overall context within which theological work is carried on is one of mystery."[118] Of course, Kaufman, as Dean realizes, often interprets "mystery" subjectivistically, even antirealistically, employing it to denote our cognitive limitations and "intellectual bafflements," not some experienced "object of arcane theological awareness or knowledge." It is a "grammatical or linguistic operator" that, far from telling us "anything specific about that which we are speaking" (including, presumably, that it is a mystery), simply "calls attention to something about ourselves: that we have reached a limit to our powers at this point, and we may, if we are not careful, easily become confused or misled."[119] Dean puckishly analogizes that Kaufman's construal of mystery "functions like a telephone directory used only as a door-stop: it may seem to be rich with meaning but, because it will not be read, 'the mystery of God' reveals nothing about an 'other.'"[120]

I prefer a more generous and expansive reading of Kaufman, however, viewing this mystical subjectivism as an unfortunate aberration in his overall theological program. Elsewhere, Kaufman, following H. Richard Niebuhr and Hans Frei, says that he does not wish to fall prey to a "merciless Kantian[ism]," according to which "the mind imagines or sets over against itself a transcendent 'other' for its own regulating and constructing purposes." Faith, he declares, is not just "creative of its object" but is, in some sense, responsive to something epistemologically inscrutable and ontologically extant.[121] For nearly his entire career, Kaufman told theologians that they can—and should—differentiate between "God" and God (sans the scare quotes), between theology's "available referent"—that is, the culturally created and historically particular symbolic constructs that developed over many centuries for the purposes of ordering and orienting human existence—and its "real referent"—that is, the hidden and mysterious "unknown" that relativizes our theological pictures and convictions.[122] As he later reassured in *In Face of Mystery*, the humanness and historicity of our concepts of the sacred "does not mean that God has no reality, is 'merely imaginary'; symbols such as 'tree' and 'I' and 'world' and 'light-year' have also been created by the human imagination, and that certainly does not imply either their falsity or emptiness."[123]

At this stage, it is of paramount importance to recall what a pragmatic historicist religious realism is and what it is not (cf. chapter 7). First, it is an apophatic realism, not a naive realism. As Dean professes, theological knowledge can never be "empirically grounded in any direct way," because "what is known," especially in religion, is "vague and murky," unfathomable and mysterious—and, I would interject, also because human and religious knowing is perspectivally, socially, and historically mediated.[124] Second, it is a naturalistic realism, not a supernaturalistic realism. In a pragmatic historicist outlook, ultimacy is something that transcends humankind and human culture, but not the historical, empirical, and natural world. This entails that the religions' postmortem soteriological scenarios, supernatural and anthropomorphic gods, and so on, are exactly what historicists (and others) have said they are—idealizations of human hopes and fears, mostly fictional metaphors, sacred conventions, socially patterned imaginative constructions created largely for the purposes of helping specific peoples, inhabiting discrete historical locales, find orientation amid the exigencies, contingencies, and mysteries of life and death. But perhaps these constructs, these "available referents" (to use Kaufmanian language), even if they are not themselves literally true, metaphysically real, or religiously ultimate, are, nonetheless, receptive to, engaged with, and even partially disclosive of the true, the real, and the ultimate. And the true/the real/the ultimate is none other than nature itself, whether in whole or in part (later, I will make a case for the former). Religious naturalists, as Wesley Wildman explains,

> comfortably argue for the social functions of religion . . . and for the possible reality of religious objects, for the potential authenticity of engagement with those objects, and for the genuine objective value of some aspects of religion. The religious naturalist would suggest that religious objects may not be what most religious people think they are; in particular, supernatural deities and personalized cosmic fates are not typically a part of the naturalist's theological scheme. Nevertheless, there are genuine religious objects—the valuational depths of nature, perhaps—and people can authentically engage them even under descriptions that are in some senses false and in other senses true.[125]

As it turns out, notwithstanding his reservations about religious and theological realism, Kaufman himself is a pragmatic historicist realist, an apophatic, naturalistic realist. In Kaufman's estimation, the religions are indeed responses to something that is real. But that "something" is not "God, as understood in the Christian tradition," nor is it any other supernatural religious ultimate. Rather, "human faiths everywhere" are responding (through the socially constructed and historically distinctive symbol systems furnished by their traditions) to the primordial mystery of things.[126] Dean keenly discerns that Kaufman's mature work is marked by a shift to a type of theological naturalism as well, where the divine signifies something that "lives outside the imagination," something that functions "not entirely in cultural and linguistic imaginative constructs, but also in natural events that could override any and all such constructions."[127] Humanity's widely diverse and culturally particular ultimates are created in response to "the heights and depths of experience," to "the surprises and calamities of history."[128] And the symbol "God," in particular, "suggests a reality, an ultimate tendency or power, which is working itself out in an evolutionary process."[129] Kaufman eventually came to describe that "ultimate tendency or power" as "creativity itself."[130] So, for Kaufman, our religious concepts *do* refer to "something objectively there," namely, the "cosmic evolutionary and historical processes on which we depend absolutely for our being."[131] Of course, referents are one thing, and reifications quite another:

> To regard a metaphor as *referring* (without reifying it) is to take it as indicating something real, something in some way significantly related to the metaphor's imagery . . . , but it is not to regard this reality as a straightforward instantiation of the content or imagery of the metaphor. . . . To understand our theological language as largely metaphorical in this way is to acknowledge that what is *really there* remains a mystery to us: it is something only dimly intimated in our symbols, never fully grasped.[132]

Still, religious metaphors and symbols, hazards Kaufman, can be properly said to "symbolize" and "represent" their intended realities. "Faith believes *that* they refer," even if "to what they refer remains in many respects a mystery."[133]

To summarize, a pragmatic historicist theology ought to—and usually does—remain candidly constructivist, conventionalist, and humanistic, without advocating constructivism, conventionalism, and humanism at the expense of realism. We have seen that even the neo-Kantian, Feuerbach-appreciating Kaufman is a constructive realist, not a radical constructivist—in practice, if not always in theory. What is more, pragmatic historicism's realist notes are apophatically and naturalistically inflected. Pragmatic historicists—Kaufman included—maintain that ultimate reality is both inscrutably mysterious and nonsupernatural (a point I shall flesh out in the sections to follow).

No historicist theologian embodies all of these aspects of a pragmatic historicist realism more consistently and elegantly than Dean. However, in a slew of recent articles, the now-retired Dean has vacillated about the religious value and desirability of pragmatist, historicist, conventionalist, naturalist religion.[134] In one breath, he expresses a desire to remain on "this side" of pragmatism, historicism, conventionalism, and naturalism.[135] Nevertheless, in the course of reprimanding American theological liberalism for having "over-learned the postmodern lesson" and, in so doing, sacrificing the ability to say anything academically persuasive or religiously meaningful about the divine,[136] he has reintroduced a number of antihistoricist, quasi-supernaturalistic, and frankly unmodern notions—for example, the sui generis character of religion, a version of "faith seeking understanding," and most spuriously, a God that is not just transcendent but "transhistorical," a God that "stands beyond" natural and social processes.[137] This is regrettable, in my opinion, for Dean already possesses the necessary tools for combatting a spiritually impotent, intellectually derivative, and effectively untheological liberal theology—that is, a historically conscious, radically empirical, and mystically tuned religious naturalism that provides an alternative to a disproportionate religious humanism, an ahistorical religious empiricism, and a premodern religious supernaturalism.[138] Dorrien is dead-on: Dean's greatest accomplishment has been his appropriation of the entire legacy of the Chicago school, his fusion of the sociohistoricism and pragmatism of the first generation with the empiricist and naturalist traditions of the second and third generations.[139] Dean, in brief, has always had the right project: *a full-orbed Chicago-school theology*, a theology that acknowledges both the humanness (or conventionality) of the divine and the divinity (or sacredness) of nature. This is a project that pragmatic historicists—Dean and all the rest—ought to hold on to and carry forward into the twenty-first century.

Radical Empiricism and Religious Naturalism as Sources of a Historicist Metaphysics of Ultimacy; or, Why Pragmatic Historicists Should Care about the Later Chicago School

In *History Making History*, Dean complains that postmodern historicists are wont to ignore the natural world, to obsess over method, to undervalue the fullness of experience and the valuational richness of nature, and to reduce all of reality—including the divine—to "a chain of linguistic tropes" (e.g., words, texts, signs, interpretations, social constructions). To find the antidote to this quasi-dualistic, neo-Kantian, antinaturalistic, language-centered, mono-humanistic historicism, America's new historicist theologians need look no further than their own oft-neglected history, to the radically empirical epistemology and religiously fecund naturalism of their predecessors—Dewey, James, Alfred North Whitehead, and the later Chicago-school theologians.[140]

Not every pragmatic historicist is as eager as Dean to revive these traditions of American theological and philosophical thought. Davaney is less than enthusiastic about radical empiricism (or at least Dean's criteriological deployment of it—cf. chapter 4),[141] while Kaufman challenges certain problematic (read: unhistoricist) tendencies in the empirical theologies of Meland and Loomer (chiefly, an insufficient attentiveness to the imaginative construction of religious "realities")[142] and voices reluctance about self-identifying as a religious naturalist (even though his idea of God as creativity is naturalistic, even Wiemanian).[143] In a similar vein, Brown mourns that the hiring of Henry Nelson Wieman in 1927 helped effect the collapse of historicism at the University of Chicago Divinity School, substituting the sociohistorical method with a dehistoricized empirical theology.[144]

Brown, Kaufman, and Davaney raise a number of vital red flags here. Still, I agree with Dean that a radical empiricist epistemology and a religious naturalist metaphysics, properly interpreted and duly historicized, are key sources of a pragmatic historicist model of ultimacy. More narrowly put, pragmatic historicists need a *multigenerational* Chicago-school theology, a theology that amalgamates the humanistic and historical consciousness of a Case, a Foster, a Mathews, and a Smith with the philosophically and metaphysically vigorous empiricism and naturalism of a Wieman, a Meland, and a Loomer.

Radical empiricism, to review, is a "revision and expansion of empiricism," a willingness to attend to everything that is experienced, "a studious effort not to be empirical in part but to be totally empirical."[145] Wieman alluded to "the surplusage of experience," to the "rich concrete . . . mass of experience," to the "experience which makes seven-eighths of the joy of living—a lover's kiss, the colors of the sunset, a child's soft little hands, the heart of a rose."[146] Or to use Jamesian terminology, beneath the surface of sensate awareness and clear, distinct, and precise thinking, there is a "fringe" of consciousness, a "felt-dimension," where reality's overtones, relations, transitions, and valuations are dimly adumbrated.[147] In brief, radical empiricists, Dean clarifies, stress "the whole of the creature's non-sensuous, affective, aesthetic, barely conscious, and largely physical ur-perception."[148] Or, as Meland tersely encapsulated it, "We live more deeply than we can think."[149]

For James and Dewey, a radical empiricism paves the way for a radical naturalism, even a *religious* naturalism, opening the experiencer to the depths of nature, a nature that is shrouded in mystery and that is relationally, aesthetically, and axiologically fecund. "The deeper features of reality," wrote James, "are found only in perceptual experience. Here alone do we acquaint ourselves with continuity, or the immersion of one thing in another, here alone with self, with substance, with qualities, with activity in various modes, with time, with cause, with change, with novelty, with tendency, and with freedom."[150] Elsewhere, James suggested that this form of perception is *religiously* significant. Religious experience is "that sense of the whole residual cosmos as an everlasting presence, intimate or alien, terrible or amusing, loving or odious," where the subject feels "fringed . . . by a *more*" that is "operative in the universe outside of him," a "something there" that "glimmers and twinkles and will not be caught, and for which reflection comes too late."[151]

Dewey made many of the very same arguments, and did so in roughly identical language. "What is really 'in' experience," asserted Dewey, "extends much further than that which at any time is *known*." An arbitrary philosophical "intellectualism" tries to reduce reality to that which is clear, evident, and penetrable by intelligence and reason. But "pure experience" reveals that, within nature, "the dark and twilight abound," possessing "obscurities," "hidden possibilities," and "potentialities which are not explicit."[152] In *Art as Experience* (1934), Dewey added that when a mundane object (e.g., an artwork) is "experienced with esthetic intensity . . . we are, as it were, introduced into a world beyond this world which is nevertheless the deeper reality of the world in which we live in our ordinary experiences." Such an experience rightly passes as a "religious feeling," for it "elicits and accentuates" an impression of "belonging to the larger, all-inclusive, whole."[153] This is why Dewey, in *A Common Faith* (also published in 1934), referred to this "whole," this "mysterious totality of being the imagination calls the universe," as "God."[154]

Akin to James and Dewey, the second- and third-generation Chicago schoolers also underscored the movement from a radical empiricism to a religious naturalism. Wieman insisted that taking account of the "intricacies and subtleties" of experience lays bare, even if only inchoately, indirectly, and obscurely, the "breadth" and "depth" of nature, "omitting, explaining away, flattening out, or truncating nothing." Wieman likened the structures accessed through sensation and conscious awareness to a "thin layer of oil" floating upon an infinitely massive ocean, a "deeper matrix" or a "creativity" that is "too complex and rich with quality for the human mind to comprehend."[155] "God" is the theological symbol of those oceanic depths, of that deeper matrix or creativity. Whitehead pictured God as that "actual entity" who "lures" the world's novel, creative advance, who "leads" and "saves" the processes of reality "by his vision of truth, beauty, and goodness."[156] Contrariwise, in Wieman's *naturalistic and empirical* process theology,[157] God *is* the creative event in nature that augments "qualitative meaning" or, simply, "the good" (human as well as cosmic), the tendency in the universe wherein "the several parts of life are connected in mutual support, vivifying and enhancing one another in the creation of a more inclusive unity of events and possibilities."[158]

Meland described "the subtleties of the fringe" (James) or the "dim, massive, and important" mode of perception (Whitehead) as "the appreciative consciousness." And the appreciative consciousness reaches down into "the subliminal depths" of nature, which, in turn, "opens up profound metaphysical and religious questions concerning the ultimate character of this depth discerned in concrete experience." The vague, unconscious, felt, bodily dimension of knowing to which radical empiricists point signals a "penumbra of mystery and meaning," quality and value, relationality and novelty that impinges on us, "an inexhaustible event" that remains irreducible to any predefined pattern, concept, framework, and category, an ungraspable "datum" or "given" that calls forth "intellectual humility, wonder, reverence, or simply open awareness," a "deeper stratum of organic being" that "operates more hiddenly" and "relates the individuated life with the fuller context of living."[159] Extending the Jamesian metaphor, Meland referenced "a *more* that is excluded by the reach for precision and . . . a *less* which must inevitably follow from the illusions of rationality where reason becomes assertive, mechanizing, and over-abstracting in its effect."[160] Our appreciative consciousness, moreover, connects us to "the Creative Passage," which is one of the several names Meland reserved for God.[161] And for Meland, as for Wieman, God is a wholly empirical and natural, but "higher-than-human working," which participates "in events which move toward qualitative attainment."[162] As he explained in *Fallible Forms and Symbols*, the "Creative Passage" (i.e., God) is "the Ultimate Efficacy attending all existence" or "the ever-present interplay of *creativity, sensitivity,* and *negotiability* that gives dynamic possibilities to each nexus of relationships imparting to each a creative intent, enabling it to live forward and to participate in the élan of existing."[163]

Loomer, like Meland and Wieman, was an empirical Whiteheadian who recognized that "primary" experience, which consists of physical feelings or perception in the mode of "cause efficacy,"[164] is where the "heights and depths" of reality are encountered—that is, "the processive and relational as well as the qualitative (especially the affectional and evaluative) dimensions of life," "the unmanageable and efficacious undertows" of nature, "the transformative energies of creative interchange," and "the ultimate mystery inherent within existence itself," which is symbolized by the appellation "God." Hence, with Wieman and Meland and against Whitehead, Loomer equated God not with a personal divine agent that is somehow distinct from creativity, but with the processes of the world itself, the world in all its transcendent and elusive meaning. However, against Wieman, Meland, and Whitehead (and virtually every process theologian since), Loomer divinized the *entirety* of the natural realm, even its destructive facets (a crucial difference to which we shall return later on in the chapter).[165]

To be sure, pragmatic historicism supplies a very important corrective to the radical empiricist heritage. Brown, as I mentioned above, considers the replacement of an early Chicago-school sociohistorical theology with a Wiemanian empiricism an uneven and unwelcome tradeoff. By Brown's lights, Wieman's approach to theological inquiry and religious experiencing was "thoroughly ahistorical." Indeed, for Wieman, the "unique datum of religious experience" is "that undefined awareness of the total passage of nature, the undiscriminated event."[166] Brown is right: Wieman failed to grasp that all our experiences, including our undefined awarenesses and our religious intuitions, have a history.[167] As I purported in chapter 7, there is no such thing as nonperspectival or universal experience, historically unconditioned or contextually uncircumscribed experience. Regardless, radical empiricism, I want to counsel, should be qualified and historicized, but not jettisoned (indeed, Brown himself was a radical historicist *and* a radical empiricist[168]).

For one thing, contemporary radical empiricists, such as Dean and Frankenberry, are much more historically conscious. Dean chides Wieman, Loomer, and Meland for ignoring history. Sounding a lot like Brown, Dean deems the historicist approach of Case and Mathews "an important moment in American religious empiricism," regretting that the sociohistorical method was "largely lost on the empirical process theologians who succeeded them at Chicago."[169] And Frankenberry, as forcefully and capably as any card-carrying historicist, balks at notions of "theory-free," "presuppositionless," or "uninterpreted" experience. Experience and language, in her perspective, exist in a "reciprocal and even codeterminate" relationship: experience "exerts its own subtle checks upon our socially mediated sign-systems," while language "is at once both the instrument of expression and largely also the conditioning medium of experience itself."[170] Echoing Brown, Frankenberry also repudiates any notion of a "*sui generis* religious experience." She acknowledges that there is no "cross-cultural single phenomenon called 'religious experience' . . . except as an invention of modern scholarship. Just as there is no 'essence' of religion for phenomenologists to capture, there is no *general* 'phenomenon' of religious experience for empirical philosophers of religion to explain."[171]

And yet, for Frankenberry (and for Dean), the philosophical tradition of radical empiricism does permit "a new *theory* concerning a set of experiences *interpreted* as religious."[172] Without a doubt, such a descriptive and explanatory paradigm (like any other) is socially constructed and culturally and historically limited, unable to adequately conceptualize the sheer mass of experiential data across religions and cultures. But American religious empiricists, Frankenberry ventures, do point to real "concrete experiencings" and, thus, could contribute to a new theoretical account of "the varieties, unities, and insistent particularities of religious experience."[173] Frankenberry, like Brown, has no truck with Wieman's grand pronouncements about "that totality of immediate experience which constantly flows over one" or the "total impact of the world."[174] Collectively, though, Wieman, Meland, Loomer, Dewey, James, and Whitehead hinted at a religiously distinguishable mode of experiencing that "begins in 'open awareness' and ends in an 'appreciable world' of much wider and deeper meaning," enabling the self, even if only momentarily and vaguely and always in a perspectival fashion, to become attentive, sensitive, and responsive to nature's "underlying richness"—its "amorphous 'More,'" its "aesthetic matrix of relations," its "valuational" fecundities, its "creative event," its "size," its "ultimate mystery."[175]

Since religious experiences are historically conditioned, Brown would prefer Frankenberry focus on the local historical traditions that give rise to them.[176] The drawback of this recommendation, by my reckoning, is that it threatens to bind theologians and philosophers of religion to the boundaries of their religious/cultural/social/human habitations (to paraphrase the title of Brown's magnum opus) and to insulate them from anything that might transcend those habitations. Even if a specific history is *included* in what a religious experience *is*, does it follow that *what* is experienced is *only* that history? Not that Brown necessarily crosses it, but there is a fine line between calling religious experiences interpretive (which they of course always are) and *reducing* them to human interpretations (of preceding interpretations, all the way down).[177] The advantage of radical empiricism is that it opens us to something that exists outside of the interpretations of a particular culture, language, or community (even though it is always and only mediated to us through the culturally and linguistically shaped specificities of our interpretive schemes and frameworks), something nonhuman and nonlocal but nonsupernatural, something empirical and natural.[178]

Wieman's theology is a case in point, providing a powerful alternative to both a religiously unsatisfying humanism and an antiquated Christian supernaturalism. The lecture that won Wieman an academic appointment at the Divinity School (delivered in the fall of 1926) aimed to convince the aging Chicago historicists to take Whitehead seriously, for a Whiteheadian philosophy of organism reveals that the existence and character of the divine are evident in the very structures and processes of nature. And for the next two decades—a time of increasing social-scientific apathy toward religion and theological sympathy for fundamentalism and Barthian and Niebuhrian crisis—Wieman continued to forge a liberal third way between the humanistic historicism of the early Chicago schoolers (and Dewey and Ames) and the supernaturalistic, revelational, science-dismissing neo-orthodoxy of Barth, Brunner, Niebuhr, and others. On the one hand, in opposition to Foster and Mathews, who waffled about God's objective actuality, he strenuously defended a theistic realism. He restored a sense of objectivity to theology, insisting that God is a present, potent, cosmic, ontological reality. Reared and educated in the tradition of Calvinism, Wieman also insisted that the salvation of the world depends on something sovereign, nonhuman, and divine, regarded God as the sole appropriate object of ultimate concern and commitment, and warned about giving allegiance to idols, to what he called "created goods" (e.g., technological advances, social programs, relative and achieved values, human efforts, aspirations, or ideals). On the other hand, like his predecessors, he belonged to the heritage of modernist liberalism, rejected prescientific theological conceptions, and held out for a naturalistic empiricism, alleging that the natural, empirical realm is the only realm there is; a genuinely modern theology should "have no recourse to any 'transcendental grounds, causes or purposes' beyond events, their qualities, and relations."[179]

Accordingly, God is suprahuman, but not supernatural, transhistorical, time-transcending, nonspatial, immaterial, or eternal, Wieman surmised. God is certainly real,[180] but is an empirically and even scientifically observable "part of the temporal, spatial, material world." God is the source, not the projection or personification, of human good; but the power that delivers us from evil is not a personal being who "resides beyond history" (e.g., the Judeo-Christian deity), but the "creative event" (the actual referent and empirical meaning of the mythological symbol "God"), the creativity within nature that generates value and promotes growth and transformation. God is functionally (and soteriologically) transcendent of human life (against the first-generation Chicago-school humanists), but is not metaphysically transcendent of the natural sphere (against traditional supernaturalists, neo-orthodox or otherwise).[181] Wieman's theological perspective, then, was theocentric rather than anthropocentric, realist rather than humanist, Reformed rather than Arminian, and yet, at the same time, empirical rather than otherworldly, nonpersonalistic rather than personalistic, naturalist rather than supernaturalist.[182]

Admittedly, from a pragmatic historicist standpoint, Wieman's radically empirical and religiously naturalistic theology is fraught with problems. Dean validly condemns the intractable ahistoricism of Wieman (and, to a lesser extent, Meland and Loomer). Wieman's theological empiricism is untempered by any sort of awareness of "cultural relativity" (and, I would add, of human/social construction), futilely striving to offer "context-independent," "universal," and "extrahistorical" truths about the divine.[183] And Frankenberry fairly questions whether any sort of "invariant structure"—for example, the four subevents that constitute the creative event[184]—"could ever be discerned empirically at all." Even more relentlessly, she detects a multitude of unempirical assumptions undergirding Wieman's empirical philosophy of religion, most notably, the claim that divine creativity is "entirely trustworthy" and "unqualified in its goodness."[185] Indeed, as I will argue below, a pragmatic historicist theological metaphysics should dispense with the idea that the sacred is unambiguously or absolutely good.

Despite these shortcomings, Wieman, along with Meland, Loomer, James, and Dewey, at the very least show how a radical empiricism might move theologians beyond an outdated religious supernaturalism, a shallow religious humanism, a reductive religious conventionalism, and a provincial religious historicism and toward a religiously compelling naturalism. And a religiously compelling naturalism, I propose, can lend to a pragmatic historicist theology of the divine a metaphysically robust and spiritually piercing model of ultimacy, a model that accounts not only for the pantheon of imaginatively constructed sacred conventions, but also for the reality that inspires their construction—the sublime and ambiguous, beautiful and terrifying, creative and destructive, incomprehensible and inexhaustible mystery faintly experienced at the fringe of consciousness, at the depths of nature.

Before laying out the specific contours and characteristics of pragmatic historicism's naturalistic metaphysics of ultimate reality, I need to first put forward a working, generic definition of religious naturalism.[186]

Religious naturalism, for starters, is a kind of naturalism. Charley Hardwick encapsulates the meaning of naturalism in four basic propositions:

> (1) that only the world of nature is real; (2) that nature is necessary in the sense of requiring no sufficient reason beyond itself to account either for its origin or ontological ground; (3) that nature as a whole may be understood without appeal to any kind of intelligence or purposive agency; and (4) that all causes are natural causes so that every natural event is itself a product of other natural events.[187]

Naturalism, in brief, stipulates that "for all we know and can know, what there is, and all there is, is the natural world."[188] Of course, the pragmatic historicist variant of naturalism fleshed out in this volume is characterized by a thoroughgoing pluralism—ontological, cosmological, cultural, and religious. Metaphysically, though, naturalists are monists.[189] Or to put it more polemically, the naturalist is radically antidualistic, refusing to "double up" the world into the natural and the supernatural.[190] As Robert Corrington clarifies, whatever is, is in and of the one nature. Nature is the only concept that has no "opposite" or "contrast term," no "outer shape or circumference," no "location" or exterior. To judge something "nonnatural" is metaphysically nonsensical, because the construct "nature" points to the "sheer availability" of whatever is, has been, or could ever be. Put differently, there is nothing in addition to, other than, or separate from nature. Nature is not "contained" in a domain beyond itself, in some putative supernature, but is all-inclusive, uncaused, self-sustaining, and given.[191] Michael Hogue sums it up well: "There is no going beneath or beyond nature to something that is qualitatively and ontologically different from, more than, or outside of nature."[192]

Naturalism necessitates four negations. First, naturalism rules out *supernaturalism*. For the naturalist, there are no supernatural entities or disembodied agents of any sort (angels, jinns, ancestor ghosts, personal gods, etc.), no otherworldly realms or destinies, such as Heavens, Hells, or Pure Lands, no cosmic teloi or World Spirits, no supreme deities that created nature ex nihilo, no miracles or special revelations, and no immortal souls that live on after death, whether through reincarnation, resurrection, or some other eschatological scenario.[193] In short, naturalism denies the existence of anything above, behind, or beyond nature, excluding all ostensible supernatural realities from its "ontological inventory."[194]

Second, naturalism denounces all species of *antinaturalism*. For example, I have intimated throughout the book that postmodernist, deconstructionist, and neopragmatist philosophies frequently exhibit antinaturalistic tendencies, construing some subaltern (and usually anthropocentric) category (textuality, language, writing, etc.) as all-encompassing. *Pace* Derrida,[195] it is nature, not the text, that is outsideless; texts, words, interpretations, and so forth, are, like everything else, complexes within the natural world, not the other way around (although historicists certainly agree that the *concept* of nature is a historical, linguistic, and culturally conditioned construction).[196]

Human beings are also natural complexes, which is why the third view that naturalism precludes is *nonnaturalistic humanism*. As Jerome Stone contends, "nature includes the worlds of culture and human history."[197] Corrington and other "descriptive naturalists" (e.g., Dewey[198]) make quick work of humanisms that fail to recognize human "littleness" vis-à-vis a natural realm that is utterly supreme, unimaginably vast, beyond our making, nonconscious, genuinely and often resistantly other, and indifferent—sometimes even inimical—to our desires and projects. Although partially amenable to human ends, nature, Corrington proclaims, always has "the final word."[199]

Fourth, and lastly, naturalism typically forecloses what Paul Tillich dubbed *supranaturalism*, the idea that ultimate reality is "a being, the highest being" which exists alongside of and above "all other beings."[200] As Wesley Wildman specifies, naturalists are antisupranaturalistic inasmuch as they oppose the widespread anthropomorphic (and idolatrous) penchant to conceive of the divine as a determinate entity with personality, conscious and benevolent intentions, and plans, purposes, and powers to act.[201]

Religious naturalisms, however, push back on the scientistic, value-allergic, spiritually dead, positivistic, and reductive materialisms that often get conflated with naturalism,[202] insisting that nature itself, whether part of it or all of it, is mysterious, wondrous, awesome, sustaining, multifarious, complex, deep, and transcendent enough to be religiously responded to and even to be considered sacred.[203] As the religious naturalist Ursula Goodenough exclaims: "Hosannah! Not in the highest, but right here, right now, this."[204] Or in the less poetic words of Wildman, naturalism "gains an ecstatic cast through an affirmation of the religious mystery of nature and history against reductionistic attempts to deny it, while embracing this-worldly accounts of nature and history through the full recognition of the social-psychological, natural-scientific, and critical-historical dimensions of interpretations of reality."[205] Against the so-called "secularization thesis," Hogue argues that the success of the sciences, the rise of naturalist modes of thinking, and other modernizing forces (industrialization, the emergence of nation-states, etc.) have radically metamorphosed rather than eclipsed religion, pulling religious phenomena into what philosopher Charles Taylor calls "the immanent frame."[206] And religious naturalism, Hogue goes on to reveal, is one of the new "post-traditional" and thoroughly immanentalized and naturalized forms of religiosity ushered in by Western modernity and secularity.[207]

To put it tautologically, religious naturalists are religious naturalists. As *naturalists*, they accept that "the natural sciences change the balance of plausibility, . . . and naturalism, though it flies in the face of virtually all of the great wisdom traditions of the world, has become . . . the working world view of everyday life in much of the modern Western world."[208] They are naturalistic because they recognize, with Owen Flanagan, that supranatural agents and supernatural powers, domains, and causes "cannot be seen, discovered, or inferred by way of any known and reliable epistemic methods."[209] But as *religious* naturalists, they are also convinced that the various matters with which religion typically deals—spirituality, ethics, salvation, meaning, purpose, transcendence, mystery, and even the divine—are capable of being interpreted and appreciated on a completely empirical basis and in a wholly naturalistic framework.

Dewey, for instance, refused to accept that "militant atheism" is the only alternative to "supernaturalism's reference to something beyond nature," holding out for a third, mediating option, for a "natural piety."[210] Foster felt the same way:

> It is evident that science, and any philosophy which undertakes to synthesize the results of natural knowledge in a self-consistent world-view, make for the overthrow of the old dualistic supernaturalism with which the religious world-view seemed so intimately related. But does the overthrow of this old theory necessarily involve the fall of religion? Both supernaturalism and naturalism think so. Our contention is that both are wrong. . . . It is for this reason, indeed, that we conceive it to be the modern thinker's foremost duty to disengage religion from supernaturalism and science from naturalism.[211]

Foster maintained that there is no supernatural deity active within the cosmos, just as there is no "self-dependent soul freely interactive within an organism." Such beliefs are vestiges of "primitive animism, which populated the whole world with spirits, demons, hobgoblins."[212] But there is, he exulted, such a thing as a nonsupernaturalistic religiosity, as a religion-friendly, even mystical, naturalism that reveres "the wonderful, the mysterious, the deep, hidden character of things, of all being—unsearchable mysteries over which we hover, abysmal depths by which we are upborne."[213]

Accordingly, I would characterize religious naturalism as a quintessential exemplification of liberal theology's principle of integrative mediation (cf. chapter 7),[214] navigating a via media between supernaturalistic and supranaturalistic overbelief and materialistic and scientistic disbelief. A religious naturalist hypothesizes that the natural sphere is metaphysically as well as religiously ultimate.[215] It is, to quote Hogue, not only "all that there is and all that can be known" but also "all that is necessary for meaningfully religious and purposefully moral lives and communities."[216] As Crosby illustrates, when we ponder nature's terrifying (and sometimes horrifying) sublimity, its daunting majesty and overwhelming vastness, we are filled with a sense of profound religious humility, realizing "how relatively small and insignificant we are in the whole scheme of things." When we venerate nature's sustaining power, its preeminence as the source and ground of all being, we are overcome by gratitude and a "feeling of absolute dependence" (à la Schleiermacher), thankful for "the privilege of being alive." When we consider nature's pervasive beauty, its unfathomable aesthetic marvels, we are called to "reverence, awe, and respect," being lifted "out of our narrow selves" and stretched beyond our parochial "horizons of appreciation and concern."[217] When we accept nature's temporal limits, ceaseless change, radical contingency, and unconquerable finitude, we are awakened to the preciousness of the here and now, reminded that *this* life enjoys "a special kind of urgency, vividness, value, and importance" precisely because it ends in death and does not last forever.[218] In a word, nature is enough[219]—enough to command our wholehearted religious commitment and concern and to arouse spiritual affections of wonder and gratefulness, amazement and devotion.

To sum up, religious naturalism can be defined as a broad family of philosophical and theological perspectives that regards nature as both exhaustive of reality and worthy of deep reverence and devotion. It is a way of responding—spiritually, ethically, theologically—to the perplexity, splendor, and power of *this* world, the only world there is.

Pragmatic Historicism and the Varieties of Religious Naturalism: Evaluating the Alternatives

Religious naturalism boasts an impressive pedigree within American philosophical and theological thought, stretching from the classical pragmatists (George Herbert Mead, William James, and especially John Dewey) to the radical and process empiricists of the later Chicago schools of theology (Henry Nelson Wieman, Bernard Meland, and Bernard Loomer), to a multitude of modern-day theologians and philosophers of religion, such as Robert Corrington, Donald Crosby, Nancy Frankenberry, Charley Hardwick, Jerome Stone, and Wesley Wildman.[220] Nearly all of the pragmatic historicists engaged in the present volume espouse religious naturalism in one form or another, although with varying degrees of consistency, radicality, and plausibility. In what follows, I will briefly and critically examine some of these pragmatic historicist varieties of religious naturalism and will ultimately opt for one position in particular, what I will term *apophatic, pluralistic naturalism*.

Truncated, Anthropocentric Naturalism: George Burman Foster, Shailer Mathews, Sallie McFague

I indicated above that Foster, in *The Finality of the Christian Religion*, castigated reductively materialistic naturalisms and championed, instead, a type of antisupernaturalistic mysticism, a naturalized piety that "is drawn toward the Hidden, the Un-understood, the Mysterious."[221] Even *The Function of Religion in Man's Struggle for Existence*—by far, Foster's most humanistic work—advances a religious naturalism. Foster, to reiterate, conceptualized the divine as an imaginative creation or a human projection. Be that as it may, the symbol "God" has an external referent, Foster qualified; its "roots strike deep into the soil of the real," because it designates something actual in the very "structure and function" of nature, namely, "the universe in its ideal-achieving capacity."[222] It is religious naturalism that makes religious humanism possible, not vice versa, for our values "are by us achievable, in virtue of our constitution *and of the constitution of that whole of which we are a part.*" For Foster, "the immanence of a . . . God-entity in the cosmos is unintelligible."[223] Nevertheless, the concept of God is subjective *and*, to some degree, objective; it symbolically personifies our own "yearnings" for "the true, the beautiful, and the good," but it also symbolizes the fact that *the universe* is such that those yearnings are attainable. To quote Foster, "The content of our God-faith is the conviction that in spite of much that is dark and inharmonious in the world, reality is on the side of the achievement of ideals such as ours."[224]

Commendably, Foster's theology is constructivist and realist, humanist and naturalist. As Jerome Stone suitably comments, "He unites the search for ideals and the capacities in the actual world to assist the pursuit of those ideals."[225] Even so, Stone goes on to suggest that Foster was only interested in *human* ideals, in "ideals such as ours," in "the ideal perfection of ourselves and of our kind."[226] I concur: whatever naturalistic sensibilities he had are curtailed and saddled by a deep-seated anthropocentrism. Religion reduces to "self-effectuation," and God to the parts of nature that ensure the "attainability" of *human* aspirations and aims.[227] A lingering left-Ritschlian personalism further truncates the version of religious naturalism championed by Foster: "Since personality is our highest idea, it must ever be on that account the word which most fittingly symbolizes our experience of the relation of reality to our ideal values. It is in our human personalities, and, so far as we know, in these alone, that this relation immediately comes to light."[228]

Following a comparable career curve, the mature Mathews also reinterpreted the divine naturalistically. Although continuing to defend the claim that the idea of God is a socially patterned human construct that evolves through history, the later writings of Mathews spoke as well of a theism that is "more than its patterns." The word "God" is surely "relative to the social process," is "our conception," and is completely "symbolic." Even so, it is symbolically representative of something "actual," something "objective," something that "expresses the ultimate reality on which human weal depends." And reminiscent of Foster, Mathews conceived of that actual, objective something, that ultimate reality, in natural but personalistic and anthropocentric terms, depicting the divine as "the personality-evolving and personally responsive elements of our cosmic environment with which we are organically related."[229] Mathews realized that supernatural notions of a "transcendentalized parent," an "Absolute Sovereign," or an "unknowable and unapproachable Being" are out of harmony with science and, thus, no longer feasible in the modern age. However, the ever-growing doctrine of God is capable of being repatterned to refer to "real . . . natural forces," forces that "can be discovered by scientific methods." Human life is produced by and reliant on the "personality-creating" powers of the universe, and "God" is the (imaginatively constructed and inevitably anthropomorphic) concept that enables men and women, both individually and collectively, to "adjust" to and "enter into personal and help-gaining relationships" with these powers.

Needless to say, there is no human-like divine person out there, nor is the cosmos itself personal. Regardless, there must be "environing activities" that "have made human personality and human society possible." And "as the symbol of such activity, God is *not* emeritus," Mathews surmised.[230]

Once again, Stone is spot-on: "Mathews' emphasis on personality is too narrow." In other words, Mathews tended to "gloss over" the nonpersonal and impersonal elements of the natural world, not to mention the "subpersonal" dimensions of human selfhood.[231] For Mathews, "God" is not just "pragmatic," but "metaphysical." The concept is obviously "born of social experience," but the processes to which it symbolically points are "as unlimited as the cosmos."[232] But that begs the question: Why limit its referential reach to the "personality-producing" activities of the universe? What about the rest of nature?

On the contemporary scene, McFague has posited an ecological and "cosmocentric" theology of nature in which the *whole* of the world is mythologized as "the body of God." The dynamic, evolving, continuing creation, in all its "teeming fecundity and variety," is the sacred embodiment of God, and God is the "source and vitality" of all existence, "enlivening each and every entity in the body of the universe." Hence, in McFague's panentheistic theological vision, the divine is embodied and sacramentally present in the entire fourteen-billion-year history of the cosmos—the sun and the moon, trees and rivers, stars and rocks, atoms and quarks, animals and people, even lichen and viruses—not merely "the personality-evolving and personally responsive elements of our cosmic environment" (Mathews) or "the universe in its ideal-achieving capacity" (Foster). As a Christian theologian, McFague is reluctant to let go of personal and agential language for God completely.[233] The key is to find a way of speaking about divinity personalistically that is not anthropocentric or incongruous with contemporary science. McFague's solution is at once metaphorical and pneumatological, proposing that "we think of God metaphorically as the spirit that is the breath, the life, of the universe."[234]

Oddly, though, McFague's panentheistic iteration of religious naturalism is, in some ways, even more anthropocentric than Mathews's or Foster's, her reputed "cosmocentrism" notwithstanding. While compellingly expanding divine embodiment and sacramental presence to encompass the totality of reality, McFague curiously proceeds to give the body of God a "Christic" shape and scope. Jesus, that is to say, is not a "surd," but the "paradigm or culmination of the divine way of enfleshment." And the notion of "the cosmic

Christ" allows theologians to extend "the liberating, healing, *and* suffering love of God" to "all of the natural world," to "all bodies in the universe," such that "the direction of creation" is toward liberation and justice for all, "especially the oppressed, the outcast, the vulnerable." In my judgment, to turn Jesus's identification with the poor, the marginalized, and the hurting into the soteriological "purpose" of the cosmos is arbitrarily selective, empirically untenable, confessionally motivated, and sadly fideistic. As even McFague admits, the "story of Jesus" and the "common creation story" are at loggerheads with one another; "the radical inclusiveness that is at the heart of Christian faith" is "not compatible" with scientific understandings of evolution, where "millions are wasted," "whole species are wiped out in the blinking of an eye," and "life, diversity, complexity, novelty" depend on "the randomness of natural selection" and even the "diminishment . . . and death of its processes." Thus, to make the nonhierarchical, destabilizing ministry and teachings of Jesus "paradigmatic of what we find everywhere" is, McFague concedes, "obviously a construction," a "modest, metaphorical statement," not a "fact." It is something that cannot be "read off evolutionary history," but only "back into natural, historical, and cultural evolution as its goal." Ultimately, it is a "wager of faith" that may "seem like an absurdity" but is, nonetheless, proclaimed "in the face of massive evidence to the contrary."[235]

Quite unfortunately, then, McFague, ends up undermining her own critical realism (see chapter 7) and her own liberal desire to construct a theology that is consistent with and answerable to (even if not dictated by) "postmodern science." Worse, by being *christocentric*, she ironically reinscribes the very *anthropocentrism* that she herself ardently condemns. McFague restricts the character and activity of God to "the principle of solidarity" that emerged in the "human, self-conscious stage" of evolutionary history and supposedly culminated in the life and death of Jesus, a principle that "counters the fang and claw of genetic evolution."[236] But if the *whole* universe is God's body, then must not the sacred not merely counteract (and suffer) but also somehow *participate in* "the inexorable caprices of natural selection" and the afflictions and "vagaries of random chance?" If the world that God embodies is one in which "the good of some will inevitably occur at the expense of others," then is it enough to affirm that human beings are not "the only creatures whose good is a matter of divine concern?"[237] Might not we also say (as I will in a little while) that the sacred is *morally ambiguous*, complicit in evils as well as goods? In her review of *The Body of God*, Rosemary Radford Ruether raises the troubling question of theodicy:

"How can the same God who creates a world in which so much cruelty exists also be the one who loves it and calls us to side with the most vulnerable? Not only sin but also the survival of the fittest through natural selection stand in tension with divine inclusive love. The unity of creation and redemption remains an affirmation of faith not easily reconciled with experience."[238] Or as Davaney more pungently queries:

> McFague repeatedly insists that the central motif of all her models is that God is on the side of life, seeking . . . enhancement and fulfillment for *all* living beings, a kind of cosmic justice, if you will. What this might mean in a universe of evolutionary process is utterly unclear. What does justice mean on a cosmic level? Does the evolutionary process have a purpose such as complexification of life, and what would this suggest for the "fulfillment" of a species that may, in the evolutionary schema of things, be replaced?[239]

Of course, McFague would respond by (rightly) admonishing that it is "elitist and self-indulgent" to "use natural evil as a smokescreen to hide the real ecological problem: human selfishness and greed. . . . It is not the Mount St. Helens eruptions or Hurricane Andrews that are threatening the planet . . . but the depletion of the ozone layer and the desertification of Africa."[240] All the same, I would retort that it is myopic, romantic, illiberal, antirealist, sectarian, anthropomorphic, and intellectually dishonest to allow the need for an ecofeminist theology (which I wholeheartedly embrace) to tempt theologians to project a Christian soteriology or teleology onto the cosmos or to sanitize, domesticate, and obscure the inescapable tragedies, brutalities, extinctions, and ambiguities of nature. Like McFague, I think pragmatic historicism should—indeed does—encourage the construction of ethically liberative theological metaphors, myths, and models; however, as I will contend in the final section of the chapter, these metaphors, myths, and models are constructed to humanistically (and ecologically) qualify and alter the divine cosmic life, not to read into it (in an act of blind faith) something that is not actually there (e.g., a salvific, healing telos).[241]

In brief, the religious naturalisms of Foster, Mathews, and McFague are too truncated, too anthropocentric or personalistic, too teleological, too romanticized and congenial to be suitable candidates for a pragmatic historicist metaphysics of ultimate reality.

Transitional, Cosmic Naturalism: Shirley Jackson Case and Gerald Birney Smith

The religious naturalisms of Shirley Jackson Case and Gerald Birney Smith are decidedly less prone to anthropomorphic truncation. Recognizing that theistic language and imagery continuously change over time, as interpreting communities adapt the idea of God to the conditions, needs, and worldviews of new sociohistorical environments, Case urged Christians of the twentieth century to go and do likewise. And radically reimagining the divine for the modern epoch means, first and foremost, allowing scientific knowledge "to displace or supplement even the most revered dogmas."[242]

That being said, science is not bad news for religion, Case pledged. While discrediting prescientific notions of a supernatural, omnipotent, miracle-working God, scientific understandings make room for a "vaster," if naturalistic, conception of divinity. Far from vanquishing the sacred or removing "all of the imponderables from religion," science actually increases their "immensity." Case illustrated: "The awesome reverence with which the ancient Psalmist saw in the heavens a display of God's glory and a manifestation of his handiwork is certainly not diminished by the majesty of that limitless star-spangled expanse of space revealed by the modern telescope."[243]

And so, akin to Mathews and Foster (and Dewey), Case hoped to find a "third form of thinking" in between supernaturalism, on the one hand, and strict materialism, on the other. The former pays little heed to the sciences and uncritically perpetuates the biblical image of an otherworldly deity who occasionally intervenes in the world to interrupt, thwart, or interfere with the physical laws of nature. The latter leaves "no room for any operation of spiritual forces inherent in the making of history or in individual experience." Steering a middle course between these extremes, Case unequivocally numbered himself among "the religious naturalists," discerning in "the normal processes of human living" and in "the natural world itself" ample "evidences" of a divine reality, a this-worldly power that, nevertheless, "seems . . . more tolerable, trustworthy, and significant than anything propounded by the traditional type of belief in revelation handed down from a transcendental realm."[244]

Like Foster and Mathews, Case linked God with that "force in nature" that inspires "the human race toward cultural advance and the pursuit of moral and spiritual ideals."[245] Yet, rather than confining divine reality to ideal-achieving capacities or personality-evoking processes, Case gestured toward "the unfathomable depths of the cosmos," toward "the magnificent *tremendum,*" and toward the "unlimited creative energy constantly operative in the maintenance of the universe." Humanity alone appreciates "higher values" and possesses "the incentive to struggle toward their attainment," but "*all* nature is shot through with the will to live."[246] Case's naturalistic theology is still somewhat limiting, especially in comparison to the more full-throated, ambiguity-acknowledging naturalisms we will explore shortly. Despite that, Case at least pointed in the direction of a more expansive religious naturalism, a less anthropocentric religious naturalism.

Smith inched even closer. In "Is Theism Essential to Religion?" and *Current Christian Thinking,* he set out to completely undercut the theistic conception of a divine creator, preserver, governor, and father. He also exposed the incompleteness of humanistic theologies. Of course, religious humanism is true as far as it goes. Ames's view "that the god of any people is the pictorial representation of the group spirit" is basically correct, in Smith's mind; indeed, every divinity, from the Babylonian Shamash to the Hebrew Yahweh, is an "anthropomorphic symbol" of "religious hopes" rather than "an actual deity." Be that as it may, humanists forget that religion exists to help men and women not only find "right adjustment" in a particular human society but also "feel at home" within "the non-human environment," that "vast mysterious realm" from which we evolved, on which we depend, and "into which we must pass at death." We cannot "ignore nature," even if "we have been partially protected from its ruthless hand by human devices during our life."

Therefore, in place of classical supernaturalism and modern religious humanism, Smith posited a kind of naturalistic mysticism,[247] which underscores the mystical import of the awesome and awful forces partially glimpsed by contemporary science—"the incalculable spaces disclosed by astronomy and the unimaginable stretches of time suggested by the doctrine of evolution and the almost incredible marvels of atomic structure and action." These cosmic, objective realities are "mysteries which we do not, and perhaps cannot, know." They "will not be pressed into exact theological descriptions" or into "the categories of human logic" and, as such, are best engaged through "poetry, symbolism, wordless adoration." They evoke a "sense of unutterable wonder" and, in so doing, stimulate "in us the experiences which we call religious." Smith refused to romanticize the cosmos, however. He favored James's "tough-minded" empiricism over religiously sentimental, theoretically optimistic, and scientifically indefensible idealisms, which grant God "ultimate control" over the world and brush aside "the problem of evil" and "the heartlessness of nature." Smith did make Foster- and Mathews- and Case-like assurances about a "quality" in the universe that undergirds, even blesses, our "highest ideals" and "supports and enriches humanity in its spiritual quest." Even so, evolutionary history unveils a nature that is shorn of a "clearly defined rational goal" and is "largely indifferent to human values."[248]

In the end, Smith, even more than Case, is a transitional figure. Although never fully developed (Smith died in 1929, the year after *Current Christian Thinking* was published), his breed of religious naturalism, with its dual emphasis on the "vast cosmic mystery" and on the ruthlessness, indifference, and teloslessness of nature, opened the door to what I want to label "apophatic, pluralistic naturalism." And apophatic, pluralistic naturalism is, I submit, the naturalistic ultimacy model most befitting of a contemporary pragmatic historicism—at least the bigger, more holistic species of pragmatic historicism set forth in this book (see especially chapter 2).[249]

Apophatic, Pluralistic Naturalism: Gordon Kaufman, William Dean, Bernard Loomer, Wesley Wildman, and Donald Crosby

Similar to all religious naturalisms, apophatic, pluralistic naturalism ventures that the relinquishment of supernaturalism and supranaturalism "does not entail the rejection of religion or religiosity or the dismissal of the religious categories of the divine, sacred, or transcendence."[250] Apophatic, pluralistic naturalism, however, envisions the divine, the sacred, the transcendent in relation to the *entirety* of natural, historical reality. For that reason, in addition to being antisupernaturalistic, nonsupranaturalistic, and proreligious, apophatic, pluralistic naturalism possesses two additional qualities.

First of all, to describe this class of naturalism as *apophatic* is to suggest that the ultimate reality vaguely experienced in the depths of nature—in its aesthetic and axiological richness, in its spectacular pluralism and near-infinite potentiality, in its inestimable complexity and density of meaning, in its exuding creativity and unpredictable contingency, in its unimaginable totality and sheer isness—is finally and utterly mysterious. Along with many others, Ursula Goodenough elegantly enunciates an apophatically charged religious naturalism, portraying the natural world as "the locus of Mystery"—the mystery evoked by its "impermanence" and "vastness," by the "apparent pointlessness" and "the *fact* of it all." To reflect on "the evolution of the cosmos," "the increase in biodiversity," and "the emergence of life," and indeed to ponder "why there is anything at all, rather than nothing," is to "join the saints and the visionaries in their experience of what they called the Divine" and to share in the sense of "wonder," "humility," and "awe" that it elicits. Today, however, nature itself, not a supernatural creator, "can take its place as a strange but wondrous given," as the context of "ultimacy" and of "the sacred," as the mystery with which we enter into "covenant."[251] Or, in the Anselmic words of Michael Hogue, "Nature is 'that than which nothing greater can be thought.'"[252]

The second qualifier, *pluralistic*, signifies that ultimate reality pertains to the natural sphere in its ambiguous totality, which distinguishes this naturalistic outlook from religious naturalisms that arbitrarily identify the sacred (or God) with the "good" elements of nature. According to Stone, whether all or only a part of the world is divine—or, posed somewhat differently, whether there is some aspect of nature that is profane—is a fiercely disputed matter within earlier and current discussions of religious naturalism.[253] Most of the later Chicago schoolers clearly took the latter position. Wieman insisted that God is none other than the empirically observable process within the natural realm that brings about "creative transformation" and the increase of good (especially human good).[254] The creative event, speculated Wieman, is "entirely trustworthy" and "good under all conditions and circumstances," without exception or qualification. "Life may be a valley of frustration, but nothing can prevent ultimate, absolute, and complete regnancy of supreme value, somehow, sometime, somewhere, although the human mind cannot know how this may be."[255] Likewise, Meland argued for divine omnibenevolence, for "a religious discernment which attends to the qualitative events within the concrete structures of experience giving intimation of God's grace and goodness."[256]

Jerome Stone (among others[257]) has kept the Wiemanian and Melandian tradition of religious naturalism alive. "The object of religious orientation," in Stone's perspective, is "axiologically determinate" and limited to those facets of nature that are "creative of the good," so that only "*some* things, like justice and human dignity, and the creativity of the natural world, are sacred."[258] Accordingly, "while life is ambiguous, the divine is not."[259] Although the ambiguous entirety of nature is *metaphysically* ultimate, only certain elements of it are *religiously* ultimate.

For religious naturalists across the aisle—from Charles Milligan, Brian Swimme, and Thomas Berry to Robert Corrington and Nancy Frankenberry, to (we will see) Bernard Loomer, William Dean, Wesley Wildman, and Donald Crosby—the very fact that life is ambiguous implies that the religious ultimate (or the divine) is as well.[260] As Frankenberry frankly remarks, "rain falls on the just and the unjust alike," and the natural environment "is often indifferent to human desires and deaf to our moral urgencies, a sign, perhaps, of the remorselessness of the divine nature."[261]

In my view, no one articulates the ambiguity side of this debate more evocatively, unflinchingly, deftly, and soberly than Robert Corrington. Corrington solemnly announces that, even if nature is metaphorized as "the great mother," she is anything but a mommy, known to nurture *and* maim, destroy, and even devour her offspring. By his reckoning, no sugarcoating strategy—be it an eschatological wish, a salvation history, an anthropocentric reading of evolution, an immortality-conferring divine consequent nature (à la Whitehead and panentheistic process theologians), an optimistic, romantic, utopic cosmology, or an upward-moving, value-increasing teleology—is able to neutralize nature's chaos, inertia, and "explosive violence," to shrug off its pervasive extinctions and predations, to discover providential design within its self-organizing processes, or to reverse its entropic descent toward heat loss and a lifeless biosphere. Following Emerson and other "honorific naturalists," Corrington appreciates the astonishing powers of "transformation" and "ecstatic renewal" welling up within the world. But he finds affinity, too, with the more "austere" naturalisms of Schelling, Dewey, Hobbes, Schopenhauer, and Darwin, which hold that nature is precarious, wasteful, and indifferent to our species, shorn of purpose and intention, and driven by nothing except natural selection and random variation. Ergo, nature's "sacred folds" are also fragmented and ambiguous, according to Corrington; they bring about "transfiguration and death," possess "much that is ugly and deformed" and even "demonic," and lack a rational logos, anthropomorphic meaning, or any indication that they are going somewhere or are aware of what they are doing.[262]

To summarize, apophatic, pluralistic naturalism imagines the sacred, the transcendent, or the divine in significant proximity to the *whole* of natural, historical reality, nature in all its mystery and ambiguous fullness. Negatively expressed, apophatic, pluralistic naturalists refuse to restrict the religious ultimate to those aspects of the world that we understand and like, that are penetrable by reason, reducible to the good, or amenable to human goals, interests, ends, and purposes (although the religious ultimate certainly *includes* these aspects, even if it is not *exhausted* by them).

Where does pragmatic historicism stand with respect to apophatic, pluralistic naturalism? To begin with, I have intimated throughout the chapter that an "appreciative awareness" of apophasis, of mystery, is a trademark of a pragmatic historicist naturalism. James spoke of "the 'inexplicable,' the 'mystery.' "[263] Smith portrayed modern theology as "a great mystic experiment," as "an experience of spiritual oneness with the cosmic mystery—an experience which gives to life unspeakable fullness and meaning."[264] Case alluded to the "mysterious power generating and sustaining the physical world and its life," and Foster talked about a piety that "seeks the deep in things" and stands in "humility" and "adoration" before the "mystery in the world of nature and of man."[265]

Fast-forwarding to our own era, Dean has very recently implored theological liberals to develop "a distinctly liberal concept of the mystery of God."[266] McFague has reminded us that "God is and remains a mystery" and, in response, has rehabilitated the *via negativa* in the form of a metaphorical, heuristic, iconoclastic, open-ended, hypothetical, and highly skeptical theology.[267] Brown has similarly clarified and foregrounded the never dominant but always present Christian apophatic tradition (which, positively stated, is "a way of naming the ultimate wonder of things" and the "mysterious givenness" of reality), has approved of Robert Neville's contention that ultimacy (i.e., "ontological creativity") is indeterminate (i.e., one can say nothing about it save that it "is the source and ground of all things determinate"), and has pledged that the (ancient and Nevillean) affirmation of the mystery of God is able to combat idolatry, infallibilism, and absolutism as well as their "attendant attitudes and actions—arrogance, intolerance, oppression, and the varied forms of the destruction of the other."[268] And Kaufman, finally, has reiterated time and again that "it is indeed *mystery* with which we humans ultimately have to do" and, like McFague and Brown, has maintained that the recognition of such mystery and a historicist theology are of a piece:

> Precisely because of the mystery, we must engage in relentless theological criticism of our faith and its symbols; precisely because of the mystery, we must give a prominent place in our vision of reality to forthright acknowledgement of our ultimate unknowing; precisely because of the mystery, we must undertake disciplined but imaginative construction of a vision of the world to which we can give ourselves, in faith, with confidence.[269]

Whereas virtually all pragmatic historicists have an apophatic streak, the question of divine ambiguity is a much more divisive issue (as it is among religious naturalists in general). Davaney's pragmatic historicism is, like Corrington's ecstatic naturalism, keyed in to both the hopeful and the tragic dimensions of reality, acknowledging that history is as much a theater for the absurd, the irrational, the fragmentary, the chaotic, and the catastrophic as it is for the orderly, the logical, the harmonious, the productive, and the healing. Davaney banks on history's "openness and generosity," on whatever "margin of creativity" it does have. Yet, she also accepts that history is not going anywhere. There is no palpable telos pushing the world along some foreordained route or toward some predestined end. History is "open" but "has no clear direction, . . . no promise of fulfillment, rest, or victory," Davaney concludes. The historical realm, "far from being a legacy of unrelenting progress, now appears marked by tragedy, loss, and ambiguity."[270] Davaney, though, has very little to say about *God's* relationship to history's tragedies, losses, and ambiguities. Actually, Davaney has very little to say about God, period.

Foster, Mathews, and Case, in contrast, have a lot to say about God. Still, similar to Wieman, Meland, and Stone, they reserve the symbol for that part of nature which is supportive of ideal values, productive of personality, or generative of the will to live.[271] McFague, in an instant of striking candor, confesses that "in a physical, biological, historicocultural evolutionary process as complex as the universe, much that is evil from various perspectives will occur, and if one sees this process as God's self-expression, then God is involved in evil." But evil, in McFague' model, "occurs *in and to* God's body." God, for her part, is always a saving, caring, and loving presence, wielding "a destabilizing, inclusive, nonhierarchical vision of fulfillment for all of creation." God is, metaphorically speaking, a "mother, lover, and friend."[272] The fact that there is so much evil and suffering in the world (both humanly caused and natural) is a sign that God is vulnerable, not ambiguous, limited in power, not goodness.[273]

Brown, akin to McFague, admits that God is at least characterized by an "ambiguity of condition." That is, like every other actual entity, "God cannot fully or unilaterally determine the quality of life—divine, human, or natural. The confusions and brokenness of the world are, to an unsurpassable degree, shaping forces within the life of God." However, "ambiguity of character" is a more complicated affair. For Brown, as for all Whiteheadians, the divine intentions are unambiguously good and pure. However, as a Whiteheadian "Scotist," he speculates that God's goodness and purity of intention are not metaphysically necessary (as Hartshornian "Thomists" presume), but are "rooted in divine will or freedom." In other words, "the structure of God's becoming . . . *could* give rise to vice as well as virtue, but *in fact* it does not." The divine nature is ambiguous *in principle*, but is unambiguous *in actuality*. McFague seems to infer that God is both unwilling *and unable* to choose evil (in that sense, she is a Hartshornian Thomist). Brown, on the contrary, believes that God is capable of choosing evil, although never does.[274]

In truth, only two pragmatic historicist theologians manage to promulgate a naturalistic theological metaphysics that is both apophatic and pluralistic, namely, Kaufman and Dean (though Smith, as I showed previously, prefigured this variation of religious naturalism). In chapter 2, I indicated that Kaufman adopts a holistic, or a naturalistic-humanistic, historicist anthropology, regarding human existence as "biohistorical," as a product of both the biological and evolutionary developments from which it arises and the diverse sociocultural networks in which it takes shape (and through which it exerts unmatched control over nature).[275] Holism and naturalism are distinguishing marks of Kaufman's concept of God as well. For Kaufman, the traditional anthropomorphic image of a supernatural, person-like, agential "Creator," of "a divine super-Self outside of or beyond the universe,"[276] is untenable in the modern age. In its stead, he puts forward a thoroughly naturalized, scientifically cogent theology in which *creativity itself* is the referent for the humanly constructed symbol "God." Creativity is displayed throughout the whole of nature and its varied and changing "historical trajectories," from the inexplicable appearance of the cosmos in the Big Bang some fourteen billion years ago (creativity$_1$), through the gradual unfolding of cosmic and earthly evolution and the emergence of truly novel realities and increasingly complex systems and life forms (creativity$_2$),[277] to the "directional movement" that led to language-using, self-conscious *Homo sapiens* and the spectacular array of social and imaginative worlds created by them (creativity$_3$). "There is," in short, "a powerful, awe-inspiring creativity manifest in our world." And "it is *creativity* that is God."[278]

The creativity that is God—the sheer enigma of why there is something rather than nothing, "the coming into being of the new" (cf. chapter 5), the eventuation of animals "with great symbolic facility"—is profoundly, amazingly, absolutely mysterious, Kaufman urges.[279] Kaufman draws on the venerable legacy of apophatic or negative theology within the Christian tradition, according to which God is (at least partially) concealed and inscrutable. The divine is an unseen reality (1 John 4:12), whose face remains hidden from view (Exodus 33:20, 23), whose thoughts and ways are higher than our thoughts and ways (Isaiah 55:9). God is "that than which nothing greater can be conceived" (Anselm), a mystery that can only be spoken of through analogy (Thomas Aquinas) and negation (Pseudo-Dionysius), a presence that is inaccessible to human knowing (Gregory of Nyssa), even beyond all understanding and comprehension (Meister Eckhart).[280] Naturally, apophatic mystics and negative theologians took Christianity's dualistic worldview for granted, positing a supernature outside of nature, an eternal life beyond this life, a God external and superior to the natural, historical realm. In a modern, scientific epoch, though, the postulation, literalization, and reification of an "other side" is no longer credible; there is only "the actual, factual empirical world." Be that as it may, the divine can be thoroughly naturalized, and yet still retain its critical function as the idol-smashing, agnosticism-requiring "relativizer of everything human and finite" (including our gods and other ultimacy metaphors). A naturalistic theology, Kaufman assures, clearly works with "a notion of transcendence," albeit a thoroughly immanentalized one. The reality symbolized by the word "God" (and possibly symbolic constructs in other religious traditions, such as Brahman and Sunyata)—"creativity," "the evolutionary and historical processes which produced us," "that which gives us humans our being and continues to sustain us in being," "the vastness and depths and mysteriousness of life"—is "truly *other* than we, different from us, mysterious, ultimately beyond our ken." Thus, no less than the almighty, absolute, supernatural Lord of traditional Christian faith, "the creative power at work throughout the universe" is "genuinely distinct from us and all our imaginings" and, as such, is able to provide "an ultimate point of reference" in terms of which "all human values, meanings, concepts, judgments, activities, practices and institutions can be called into question, assessed, and reconstructed." Analogous to Wieman's creative event, Kaufman's creativity is functionally transcendent, even if not metaphysically transcendent.[281]

Dorrien, accordingly, describes Kaufman's brand of theological naturalism as "Wiemanesque."[282] As a matter of fact, in portraying God as creativity, Kaufman explicitly allies himself with Wieman. At first blush, this alliance may appear to insinuate that Kaufman's God is unambiguously benign (as is Wieman's). For Kaufman, however, divine creativity is not always the source of good. "On this issue," he writes, "I depart significantly from Wieman."[283] Wesley Wildman suspects that Kaufman's accent on *serendipitous* creativity[284] may too easily distance "God from the nasty events that destroy harmony and peace." Wildman points to the several "competing trajectories" that "achieve a symbiotically creative" but "prodigiously destructive convergence," such as "asteroid collisions, which are an essential part of the process of planetary formation within a solar system," or "the often deadly yet vital symbiosis between bacterial and mammalian life on our own planet." At best, continues Wildman, what we have is "a fairly dangerous sort of serendipitous creativity, more like the good fortune of being in the right place at the right time than akin to the solicitous care of a doting parent."[285] But Kaufman actually agrees with Wildman here, conceding that "it would certainly be a mistake to argue that cosmic creativity always manifests love for all the creatures involved: that would be unintelligible, indeed absurd, in face of all we know about nature 'red in tooth and claw.'" Indeed, the same processes that generated Mennonite pacifists also bring forth "new realities through massive violent destruction"—for example, volcanic eruptions, earthquakes, floods, exploding stars, and black holes "that swallow up everything in their vicinity." And Kaufman (unlike Wieman) owns up to the theological implications of such a concession, speaking of "God's destructivity," of "God's bringing evils (as they seem to us) into being, as well as goods."[286] As Stone comments, Kaufman realizes that the serendipitous creative process produces "results which are not always happy or fortunate," which entails that "the cosmic and abstract scope of God is valuationally neutral to the human perspective" (even though only one of creativity's, or God's, trajectories is to be considered ethically normative—a qualification we will revisit in the final section).[287]

Unsurprisingly, Dean praises Kaufman's steady movement away from "a neo-Kantian subjectivism" and toward "a more naturalistic historicism." Convinced that the historical emergence of "unpredictable novelties" and "the tropism toward greater complexity" are, in fact, theologically suggestive, he finds particular affinity with the Kaufmanian notion that God is the "hidden creativity" working itself out in the evolutionary processes of nature and culture.[288]

But Dean has been even more dogged than Kaufman (and most theologians) about the thoroughgoing ambiguity of the divine, recognizing that creativity is supportive of the human good and, at the same time, inexorably leading to the extinction of our species.[289] He blasts other religious naturalists (including his beloved Dewey[290]) for hedging about the sacred's complicity in evil, for clinging to an omnibenevolent God far removed from "the dark side" of life. Such a God, as Dean recently reiterated, is fundamentally ahistorical, because "social and natural history evince nothing that is perfectly good. . . . In history . . . every 'good' is contextual and perspectival, so that, for example, what is good for a blood-sucking mosquito is bad for its victims."[291] In other words, if nonhuman nature and human society—with all their catastrophes, predations, genocides, inequities, injustices, oppressions, cruelties, and so on—are anything to go on, then the divine simply cannot be unambiguous. Rather than theologically honing in on the "better part" of reality and treating "the ambiguities of history as though the sacred does not relate to them," religious naturalists ought to take up a "historicist pantheism"—or what James once termed "pluralistic pantheism" or what I am more broadly designating "pluralistic naturalism"—accepting that "ultimate meanings refer to everything in history," even "history's evils." A pantheistic or pluralistic God is a God connected with, implicated in, and tainted by the entirety of nature, even its atrocities and tragedies.[292] As Dean searchingly asks:

> Must God not be . . . not only the fascinating but also the *tremendum*: the overpowering, the abyss, that which is repulsive to our moral sensibilities? We liberals believe that God is immanent in history. But where is the tipping point, where the immorality so pervasive in history suggests something about the morality of the God also pervasive in history?[293]

The ambiguity of the sacred is detectable in a number of sources, Dean hazards. The God of the Hebrew Bible, for instance, permits the Devil to wreak horrendous calamities on Job (Job 1–2); orders Abraham to sacrifice Isaac (Genesis 22:1–19); devours the sons of Aaron for inadvertently offering the wrong kind of sacrifice (Leviticus 10:1–3); hardens Pharaoh's heart and slays all of Egypt's firstborn (Exodus 10:1, 12:29); berates Saul for extending mercy to the Amalekites by refusing to "utterly destroy all that they have"—men, women, infants, and livestock (I Samuel 15:3); stands idly by as the unnamed concubine of a Levite is raped and dismembered (Judges 19); authorizes females to be taken as spoils of war (Numbers 31:17–18); takes the blame for the evil that befalls a city (Amos 3:6); and admits to both making "weal" and creating "woe" (Isaiah 45:7). Even in the New Testament, Jesus claims to "have come not to bring peace but a sword" (Matthew 10:34), and Ananias and Sapphira are struck dead after lying about selling a piece of property and keeping some of the proceeds for themselves (Acts 5:1–11). Scripture, Dean concludes, while indisputably affirming divine goodness, "offers little evidence to support the idea that God is *unambiguously* good."[294]

Luther and Calvin, too, acknowledged the ominousness of divine power, sovereignty, and election and "how this gave God a leading role in the dark side of history." And in the twentieth century, Judith Plaskow has maligned the "niceness" of feminist theology's stereotypically nurturing, healing, caretaking God.[295] Dean also mentions a number of liberationists, who implicate God in the injustices inflicted on the oppressed. For example, Native American theologian Robert Allen Warrior maintains that the liberating picture of God portrayed in the book of Exodus is one-sided and incomplete. When seen from the vantage point of dispossessed natives—whether Canaanite or American Indian—Yahweh is not a "deliverer" leading the "chosen people" into the so-called "promised land," but the genocidal "conqueror" of the conquest narratives, mercilessly annihilating the indigenous population.[296] Decades earlier, the liberal theological empiricists of the Chicago school (especially, we will very soon discover, Loomer) struck a tone of religious realism and pessimism. Dean sees great irony (and perhaps hypocrisy) in Barthian and Niebuhrian caricatures of liberalism's "naive optimism," for Barth, Niebuhr, and other neo-orthodox theologians "were actually optimists in the sense that they had believed that the Lord of the universe was so preoccupied with the welfare of the few worthy occupants of one planet that this Lord would do virtually anything to rescue them." The early and later Chicago schoolers, on the contrary, cast off all "extrahistorical securities" and resigned themselves to the fact that humanity "must live within an inescapable, inexorable, and insatiable history—which sooner or later eats everything alive."[297]

As a liberal, Dean even finds "evidence" for an ambiguous God in presumably secular or nonreligious contexts—for example, in the early poetry of Wallace Stevens, which is imbued with a sense of the destructive, even the "demonic" and the "satanic."[298] Stevens's 1942 "Esthétique du Mal" is a case in point, in which a man surmises "that there is 'a part of the sublime / From which we shrink,' symbolized by a Vesuvius that regularly threatens to consume us." The poem, Dean explicates, exposes the ways in which "we have blinded ourselves through our devotion to an 'over-human god.' . . . We have forgotten that 'Life is a bitter aspic.' . . . Our insistence in knowing that God is unambiguously good has virtually willed the death of Satan, and 'The death of Satan was a tragedy / for the imagination.'"[299] Therefore, Stevens, on Dean's reading, can contribute to progressive theology "a darker, a more realistic, and, finally a more plausible . . . stance," challenging, for example, Gustavo Gutiérrez's contention that God has a "predilection for those on the lowest rung of the ladder of history," or process theism's belief that the divine is an "ally in campaigns to lift public morality."[300]

Dean's naturalistic God is not only ambiguous but also mysterious. Earlier in the chapter, I examined his case for "the irony of atheism." Precisely at the moment when divine beings are conventionalized—that is, atheistically reduced to human projections or imaginative constructions or social patterns—a people can ironically become opened to "a 'more,' which is appreciated, finally, as a mystery that is irreducible to and transcendent of ordinary experience."[301] When he is not overcompensating for the "moribund" state of contemporary liberal theology,[302] Dean remains true to his own religious naturalism and (akin to Kaufman) maintains that this "more" is a "mystery that operates within the natural world." This is a mystery that is adumbrated by accepting the limits of a secular culture and the sacred conventions that rise and perish within it, a mystery that is "incarnate in . . . historical eventfulness and gives meaning *to* rather than *obliterates* its structures," a mystery that "remains within history more broadly understood."[303]

In sum, apophatic, pluralistic naturalism is the metaphysical and religious ultimacy model most adequate to a bigger and wider historicism (again, see chapter 2), a holistic and naturalistic-humanistic historicism, a historicism that takes nothing less than the *totality* of history—human and nonhuman, personal and impersonal, creative and destructive, intelligible and hidden—into theoretical and theological consideration. As Dean very persuasively contends, "Religious sympathies cannot be knit up with the finite world as such unless the sacred pertains to everything—not everything but the community, not everything but nature, not everything but ambiguity, but everything."[304]

Unfortunately, in refusing to exclude anything whatsoever from whatever is ultimate, Dean almost flies solo; only one other pragmatic historicist—Kaufman—conceives of the divine mysteriously *and* ambiguously. For that reason, pragmatic historicists, I want to advise, should look to a handful of nonhistoricist religious naturalists to shore up their apophatic, pluralistic naturalism.

There is, for starters, Dean's own teacher, Bernard Loomer, who might perhaps be christened the grandfather of apophatic, pluralistic naturalism. A self-avowed naturalist and empirical process theologian, he claimed that "the one world," the "experienceable," "interconnected" web of natural relations and events, is the only reality there is. God, it follows, must "be identified either with a part or with the totality of the concrete, actual world, including its possibilities." The mature Loomer chose the latter option, the *pantheistic* option: the divine is none other than "the organic restlessness of the whole body of creation."[305]

"Why deify this interconnected web of existence by calling it 'God'? Why not simply refer to the world and to the processes of life?"[306] Loomer replied:

> The justification for the identification is both ontological and pragmatic in the deepest Jamesian sense. In our traditions the term "God" is the symbol of ultimate values and meanings in all of their dimensions. It connotes an absolute claim on our loyalty. It bespeaks a primacy of trust, and a priority within the ordering of our commitments. . . . It signifies a richness of resources for the living of life at its depths. . . . It symbolizes a transcendent and inexhaustible meaning that forever eludes our grasp. The world is God because it is the source and preserver of meaning . . . and because it contains yet enshrouds the ultimate mystery inherent within existence itself. "God" symbolizes this incredible mystery. The existent world embodies it. The world in all the dimensions of its being is the basis for all our wonder, awe, and inquiry.[307]

Loomer, then, divinized the natural sphere, in part, because nature is metaphysically ultimate, deeply fecund, and profoundly mysterious. His *apophatic* naturalism led him to pantheism.

And his pantheism led him to a *pluralistic* naturalism. Loomer realized that nature "manifests a diversity of forces, many of which are either noncreative or destructive." And if God *is* the world, then the divine, reasoned the pantheistic Loomer, must embody all the ambiguity actually found therein, "all the evil, wastes, destructiveness, regressions, ugliness, horror, disorder, complacency, dullness, and meaninglessness, as well as their opposites."[308] Loomer took issue with the supranaturalism and panentheism of process theology, which serve to (ostensibly) circumvent the ambiguity that characterizes the concrete sphere of nature and to dissociate the divine from evil.[309] To illustrate, the abstract or "primordial" nature of God, in Whitehead's scheme, is ontologically separate from creativity, experienced as "an appetition toward conceptual novelty," as "an aesthetic form of persuasiveness that is pitted against the coercive and inertial powers of the world." And the receptive or "consequent" side of the divine life saves and preserves the world by everlastingly internalizing and synthesizing all actualities "into the unity of an experiential subject of experience." This "unambiguous structure or character can be derived only by a complex abstractive process, the end result of which has no counterpart in reality," Loomer harshly judged.[310]

Wieman fared a little better in Loomer's telling, correctly denying the existence of a supranatural agent or a divine person distinguishable from the creative process itself.[311] Wieman agreed with Whitehead that God is not the creator of the world; but neither is God the poet or the savior of the world.³¹² Rather, the divine is more like the *poetry* or the *salvation* of the world (i.e., the growth of qualitative meaning). As Frankenberry helpfully explains, Wieman's argument is not "that wherever God is manifest, there is creative transformation, but precisely the opposite—wherever one finds creative transformation, *there* one finds what has been meant by 'God.'"³¹³ Loomer concurred with Wieman that the divine is not an "enduring . . . individual with a sustained subjective life," that "the being of God is not other than the being of the world." However, Wieman stopped short of a pantheist theology, associating God only with "one aspect of the world or one kind of process," with the part of nature that is generative of good and worthy of worship. Thus, no less than Whitehead's (and Christianity's, more generally), Wieman's deity is defined by pure goodness and, as such, is too "clean" and "perfect," too "unsullied" and "orderly," to be concretely real; it is a bloodless, unempirical abstraction from a cosmos that is inescapably ambiguous. Loomer's Whiteheadian empiricism was much longer on empirical realism than Wieman's (or Meland's),³¹⁴ audaciously proclaiming that the sacred exemplifies not only "an expansive urge toward greater good" but also "a passion for greater evil." A God whose "stature" or "size" embraces nothing less than nature in its concrete wholeness must express itself as *both* creativity and destructivity, novelty and inertia, harmony and discord.³¹⁵

Wesley Wildman also accentuates the mysteriousness and ambiguity of the sacred, although he is a Tillichian instead of a Whiteheadian. Like Tillich, Wildman begins by mounting a sustained attack against supranaturalist metaphysics, the notion that God is a personal, active, intentional, benign, purposive being.³¹⁶ Supranaturalisms, or "determinate-entity theisms" (e.g., deism, the dualisms of Zoroastrianism and Manichaeism, intelligent design creationism and theistic evolution, Boston Personalism, and most process theologies), suffer at least two fatal flaws. First, anthropomorphic or personalistic models of divinity are often incompatible with the natural sciences. Darwinian biology, for example, casts doubt on the common liberal affirmation of a loving, personal deity who "creates through evolution." Wildman retorts, "Surely such a loving, personal deity would have created in another way, a way that involved less trial and error, fewer false starts, less mindless chance, fewer tragic species extinctions, less dependence on random symbiotic collaborations, fewer pointless cruelties, and less reliance on predation to sort out the fit and the unfit." In brief, Darwin's account of nature, and "the daunting theodicy challenges" it presents,³¹⁷ place serious plausibility constraints on the supranaturalist belief in a "God of endless love who cosuffers with us" and who would not "hurt a flea."[318] If evolutionary theory is true, then ultimate reality is probably not an all-benevolent divine being "with intentions and awareness, with feelings and intelligence, with plans and powers to act, and with a moral character that humans can recognize as good."[319]

Second, determinate-entity theisms and theological anthropomorphisms are susceptible to idolatry. More than anything else, Wildman is an apophaticist and an iconoclast, declaring that the mystics and negative theologians inhabiting the "undersides" of every religion are essentially correct: the ultimate is, in itself (*a se*), "absolute nothing," "empty of determinacy," "beyond all imagery," and, hence, finally ineffable, incomprehensible, and unspeakable. For that reason, if literalized, the anthropomorphic and personal divinities humans construct to "satisfy our personal needs, to make sense of our world, and to legitimate the exercise of social control" quickly become idolatrous distortions.[320]

If determinate entities or conscious and benevolent divine beings are not ultimate, what is? Wildman answers, the "power source in the depths of nature" that "hovers behind and beneath and beyond the symbolic Gods we create," the "cognitively all-surpassing," "aesthetically overwhelming," and "morally impenetrable" abyss that rumbles "in fecund creativity."[321] Fusing Tillich, Neville, and Corrington, Wildman pictures ultimacy as "the most basic ontological condition" and "self-transcending and ecstatic elements of the natural world," the natural world in all its imponderable beauty, fluxing intensity, axiological abundance, inaccessibility and wonder, incalculable density of meaning, and spiritual and sacred richness.[322]

Wildman's apophatically tinged and thoroughly naturalized ground-of-being theology subsumes rather than eliminates personalistic theisms, interpreting personal god-agents as myth-laden but religiously indispensable symbols; they "engage" ultimate reality, albeit brokenly rather than literally.[323] Although not referring to supernatural persons or worlds, deities and salvations are not without a referent, symbolically pointing to "the dimension of depth, horizon, scale, complexity, and mystery within natural reality," a dimension "that defies the grasping tentacles of religious understanding."[324] Or, as Wildman effuses elsewhere, religion involves

> the weaving of human dreams beneath the vastness of the cosmic sky and above the terrifying depths of possibility, a weaving not governed or regulated by anything except complex human desires and the measured and unmeasured exercise of power. This

godless world is not without an abysmal ground, however—or a Creative Dao, a God Beyond All Gods, or a One Beyond Comprehension. The name of God still testifies to this fact, and to the reality it hints at, so long as that name is wrested away from the religious legitimators of cultural meaning making. . . . Yet it insists with those strange theologians on the underside of large religious traditions that the fate of the religious philosopher who intends to speak of this unconditioned is apophasis. This does not mean utter silence, for apophasis is a complex form of indirect speech. Nor does it mean untelligibility, for apophasis involves intelligible trajectories of artful speech. But it does mean that creative trajectories of intelligible theological speech finally yield to silence and that the deepest theological truth is conjured in the echoes left behind after the collapse of words, and not finally expressed in their utterance.[325]

What is more, Wildman's religious naturalism is pluralistic; instead of positing a divinity that is "different from, higher, and certainly less ambiguous than . . . the world as we experience it," he suggests that "the moral ambiguity of reality is a natural outcome deriving from the character of ultimacy itself."[326] As the ground of reality, whatever determinate features ultimacy does have emerge in relation to "its expression in the valuational depth structures" of nature; and anything that is known about the divine character is acquired not via supernatural revelation but through "multidisciplinary, comparative inquiry" into what this world reveals to human experience in the "primal spring" of its axiological flows and possibilities. And the axiological flows and possibilities that nature actually discloses are emergently ordered yet fickle, chaotic, fierce, death-dealing, and totally ambiguous, leaving little, if any, empirical basis for attributing anthropocentric design, providence, intentionality, personality, perfection, and unambiguous goodness to ultimacy. When we curtail our "reality-evading biases toward the pleasant" and consider the natural world as a whole, what is glimpsed is something quite wild: the simultaneously awe-filled and awful ambiguities, the morally terrifying and untamable value-potentialities, that are encountered at the depths of nature. Ultimate reality is, for Wildman, at once "supportive of and hostile toward" our bodily, rational, cultural, and spiritual endeavors, the "partially intelligible ground" of being itself and "the abyss of infinite darkness" into which all beings—human and divine—end up plunging.[327]

Like Wildman's ground-of-being naturalism, Donald Crosby's "religion of nature" is both apophatic and pluralistic. But Crosby adds the Tillichian (and, presumably, the Wildmanian) postulation of a "God beyond God" to religious naturalism's catalogue of sweeping denials, wondering "why the power of being could not reside in nature itself."[328] Like the later Chicago schoolers, he is a process thinker of the empiricist variety,[329] affirming the central Whiteheadian maxim that becoming and change are more fundamental than being and pattern,[330] while jettisoning all nonempirical, ultraspeculative, and hyper-rationalistic components of Whitehead's cosmology.[331]

And he is a religious naturalist of the Loomerian variety, insisting that the entirety of nature enjoys both metaphysical and religious ultimacy. That is, there is nothing above, behind, or outside the dynamic, relational, everlasting matrix that is nature and, consequently, no object more suitable for the ultimate concerns and commitments of human beings, who are themselves natural creatures without remainder and whose origins, home, responsibilities, and destiny "lie here and not in some transcendent realm." However, although following Loomer in making the metaphysical ultimate (i.e., the whole of the natural sphere) religiously ultimate, Crosby dispenses with any form of theism, including pantheism: "Nature is sacred but not divine."[332] In Crosby's outlook, nature, regarded as bereft of deities, animating spirits, consciousness, personality, or purpose,[333] (1) comprises the only reality there is or ever will be, requiring no explanation beyond itself (e.g., a creator or even a ground) to account for its existence and sustenance,[334] and (2) contains enough grace and splendor to deserve the same sort of reverence and devotion typically reserved for supernatural entities.[335] But Crosby prefers not to call nature "God."[336]

In that sense, Crosby's religion of nature is atheistic. But it is certainly not the reductively positivistic, axiologically thin, "spiritually flat" atheism that Wildman thrashes.[337] Crosby bristles against scientism, which cedes unrivaled explanatory authority to the physical sciences, and shakes his head at eliminative materialisms.[338] His empiricism is generous and radical, his naturalism nonreductionistic and even apophatic, giving the arts and humanities their epistemological due, entertaining aesthetic, moral, existential, and religious experiences, and honoring nature's valuational fecundity, felt penumbra, unfathomable grandeur, and numinous depth. Most significantly, among the myriad features that make nature a legitimate candidate for religious faith and loyalty is its hiddenness,[339] the inexplicability of its "sheer givenness" and "creative ongoingness." It is "the secret wellspring of all that is," the stupefying "fringe of mystery" before which we stand in "reverential silence." It is "the most mysterious of all realities," which "can only be spoken of elliptically, with metaphors, analogies, and stories that point feebly beyond themselves."[340]

In addition, if Crosby's naturalism is not reductive or apophatically tone-deaf positivism, neither is it nature romanticism. Though *religiously* right, nature, he allows, is *morally* ambiguous, teeming with a mixture of value and disvalue, joy and suffering, creativity and destruction.[341] Crosby provides some useful examples:

> We would not be here were it not for the vast extinctions in evolutionary history that preceded us. Our solar system would not exist without the cataclysmic explosion of a supernova star. Many of earth's wonders have resulted from stupendous earthquakes, floods, storms, and fires. . . . Gravity mercifully holds us to the surface of the earth, but it can also kill us. . . . When we eat, we usually destroy some previously living thing.[342]

Even more to the point, "reality and ambiguity go necessarily together," since "good" and "evil" are often interdependent and always perspectival.[343] He elaborates: "It is good for predators to find their prey . . . because predation is necessary to preserve their lives and the lives of their progeny. But the process of being killed and eaten is evil from the perspective of the ones being preyed upon and from the standpoint of their progeny, now left defenseless and unprotected. Both perspectives are real or aspects of the real."[344]

To conclude, Loomer, Wildman, and Crosby, while differing with one another in several important respects, each epitomizes the generic theo-logic of an apophatic, pluralistic naturalism. And, together, these religious naturalists, I wish to suggest, give pragmatic historicism a firmer philosophical leg on which to stand and a richer metaphorical pool from which to draw when theologizing about the utterly mysterious and ambiguous depths of nature. Before moving on, though, three important clarifications are in order.

First, the objective of the foregoing analysis has not been to endorse any of these variants of religious naturalism.[345] Instead, I have simply tried to specify what a pragmatic historicist theological metaphysics would minimally require, namely, an apophatic, pluralistic naturalism. This model is intended to be as vague as possible, boasting enough latitude to include a plethora of alternatives, from a creativity theology (Kaufman and Dean) to a process pantheism (Loomer), to a ground-of-being naturalism (Wildman), to an atheistic religion of nature (Crosby). For my purposes here, whether a pragmatic historicist decides to view ultimate reality as the creative mystery within or the abysmal ground beneath the natural world, or opts to accord nature itself metaphysical and religious ultimacy, is of secondary importance; what matters is that the sacred or the divine be imagined *in significant proximity to* big history, human and natural history, history as we actually, concretely, empirically find it, history in its mysterious and ambiguous totality.

Second, naturalistic models of ultimacy, no less than supernaturalistic or supranaturalistic ones, are not read in a direct, objective fashion off the face of the natural world. Although responsive to the very real depths and axiological potentialities that nature manifests, they are still experiments in constructive theology—or to employ a term that seems to be gaining traction, *theopoetics*. Pragmatic historicism keeps us mindful of the fact that they are fallible, perspectival, metaphorical, and thoroughly human creations that arise in particular histories and reflect the contingencies, limitations, and distinctive colorations of those histories. For pragmatic historicist theologians, the density of nature is so immeasurable, the diversity of religion/culture so sweeping, the range of interpretation so variable, the scope of history so big, and the size of God so immense, that to reduce the sacred to *any* hypothesis or framework is tantamount to idolatry. To accept a historicism that is genuinely holistic, that is naturalistic *and* humanistic, is to remember, with William James, that the trail of the human serpent is truly over everything,[346] even religious naturalism, even apophatic, pluralistic naturalism.

Third, apophatic, pluralistic naturalism is not just intellectually plausible and compatible with pragmatic historicism; it is also a *religiously* compelling theology of the divine.

To begin with, in underscoring mystery, apophatic, pluralistic naturalists tap into what Wildman brands "the mysticotheological tradition," which is "more or less evenly represented" across religions, cultures, and philosophical schools and is held together by the remarkably common insight that ultimate reality is all-surpassing, that is, beyond all conceptions, conventions, beings, and divinities.[347] Delwin Brown agrees, arguing that apophatically oriented theologies, such as Robert Neville's (and I would append Kaufman's, Dean's, Loomer's, Wildman's, and Crosby's), are spiritually and religiously significant inasmuch as they connect directly with mystical experiences of "the ineffable" and, more generally, with the feeling of "contingency, dependence, and mysterious givenness that is frequently associated with religious moods, attitudes, and life forms." More than an intellectual category for theological debate, apophasis registers the phenomenological reality that some people "*feel* themselves and the world about them to be inexplicable," to be surrounded by a "cloud of unknowing." Brown adds that apophaticism "has enormous relevance for religion, society, and culture," because it opposes "every form of absolutism based on some version of the belief in the knowable nature or will of deity." The acknowledgment of ultimacy's utter mysteriousness undercuts any effort to conceal the fallibility and constructedness of our theological interpretations or, worse, to turn them into "weapons of destruction."[348]

Even the stress on ambiguity enjoys a certain kind of religious applicability and importance. For one thing, a pluralistic naturalism, as Crosby points out, furnishes a refreshing, if often painful, realism with respect to the tragic dimensions of life, offering "no pap, no panaceas, no empty promises." There is no heavenly paradise to compensate for the sufferings endured on earth, no purposive, active, personal deity to answer our prayers or to wipe away our tears, no eschatology or telos to ensure final resolution or ultimate victory, no theodicy to explain why bad things happen to good people or to exonerate the sacred from evil.[349] What Nancy Frankenberry says of empirical theologians in general is especially true of pluralistic naturalists:

> Empirical theologians, although not without natural piety, are willing to say with William James that the last word is not sweet, that all is not "yes, yes" in the universe, and that the very meaning of contingency is that ineluctable no's and losses form a part of it, with something permanently drastic and bitter always at the bottom of the cup.[350]

A pluralistic naturalism, then, keeps religion honest about the fact that nothing, not even the divine, evades the brutalities, the calamities, and the travesties—the ambiguities—of history.

What is more, the divine is just that: ambiguous, not unambiguously benign *or* unambiguously malicious. To Michael Zbaraschuk's charge that God's ambiguity removes any incentive for acting morally, Dean counters that "an ambiguous God is, by definition, both evil and good." And "to the extent that God is good, God certainly does provide a reason for religious critics to advocate moral action."[351] Crosby makes roughly the same point, minus the God-talk. Nature is, without a doubt, shot through with disvalues—"the universal system of kill or be killed," "grisly acts of cannibalism," "irremediable pain and loss," "organism prey[ing] upon organism in a macabre, unceasing dance of death," to name just a few. But nature's axiological ambiguity signals that the natural world is the locus of extinction *and* emergence, suffering *and* enjoyment, destruction *and* restoration.[352] Nature is not utterly indifferent and inimical to the human good, but is also, in some sense, supportive of it (albeit not consciously, deliberately, absolutely, exclusively, or unambiguously so):

> Our penchant for envisioning and striving for the attainment of values—moral, aesthetic, and religious; our possession of intelligence, consciousness, and freedom; our ability to fashion languages and diverse, ever-developing cultures—all of these things are nature's gifts to us. Here is no bland indifference to things human but moving testimony to nature's boundless creativity and continuing support.[353]

Finally, even though we cannot escape the ambiguity of nature (and the divine), we can, as Crosby avows, "find the courage to live in the face of it." And a religious naturalism supplies the motivation, encouragement, and stimulus for doing exactly that. We can draw on whatever goodness and restorative powers we and the rest of nature do have and "work together for their actualization and incorporation into our institutions and societies," even as we are "humbled and inspired" by the "vastness and splendor" of reality in its ambiguous entirety.[354] In a somewhat similar vein, the Jewish naturalist and pragmatist Henry Samuel Levinson suggests that an unflinching embrace of the vicissitudes, contingencies, tragedies, fragilities, and ambiguities of finite, historical existence, far from ruling out a religiously meaningful life, can actually generate a festive, celebratory, comic religious outlook:

> By "comic" I mean . . . a view that takes joy as seriously as it does meanness. Comedy, as I understand it, doesn't blink when it encounters suffering, absurdity, and evil. To the contrary, it insists on highlighting them. But it doesn't lend these things any romantic grandeur. Instead, it finds ways to celebrate "passing joys and victories in the world." Rather than revealing, or pretending to reveal, ways to triumph *over* finitude in some fantasy world of transcendent and eternal bliss, comic vision makes suffering, absurdity, and evil mean and tries to find festive ways to cope with them, ways geared to foster "more joyful life in a lasting world."[355]

In brief, one can live a religiously (and ethically) meaningful life as a naturalist,[356] even as an apophatic, pluralistic naturalist.

Yet there is a lurking suspicion that apophatic, pluralistic naturalism is still not quite sufficient for orienting human existence. As Brown grants, the conviction that the sacred is ultimately mysterious—to say nothing of ambiguous—"provides no positive frame of reference for understanding our world, our communities, our selves, and our actions. Thus apophatic religions . . . usually go on to assert that God takes some historical form . . . on the basis of which life is then to be lived." In a way, the very mystery and ambiguity that continuously unmask the idolatrous and anthropocentric nature of theological speech and thinking ironically make idols (e.g., personal gods, sacred conventions, human constructions) necessary.[357]

Qualifying, Engaging, and Transforming the Mystery and Ambiguity of History: The Irony of Theism and the Necessity of the Humanistic and the Cataphatic

Whatever religious sensibilities and spiritual affections an apophatic, pluralistic naturalism manages to occasion, a God (nature) that is too big to fathom or to limit to the human good is of meager use when it comes to directing cultural, institutional, and ethical projects. As Dean acknowledges, the experience of God's (nature's) mystery and ambiguity, while religiously humbling and spiritually sustaining, is not morally or practically sufficient. But Dean goes on to point to a "second ironic swing," to an "irony of theism," whereby the acceptance of God's (nature's) mystery and ambiguity sends us back—with renewed commitment and humility—to our ordinary, local histories.[358] Indeed, all apophatic, pluralistic naturalists realize that we cannot abide in the darkness of sacred ineffability and ambiguity forever; at some point, we must return to what Wildman calls the "brightly lit top-side traditions of religion and culture," which exist in large part "to hide from that terrifying divine visage."[359] Here, the humanizing myths, moral prescriptions, and cataphatic symbols of our religious or cultural traditions—including the pantheon of deities and other sacred conventions constructed over the ages—acquire a new kind of "sacred depth," qualifying, engaging, and even transforming different facets of ultimacy's mysterious and ambiguous landscape and, in the process, furnishing orientation in the world.

Kaufman, for instance, recognizes that creativity (God) "is utter mystery to us" and is generative of events that are "ambiguous in their consequences." As a result, except as a gauge for exposing idolatry, "the divine creativity as such" is unable to "provide much guidance on most of the issues with which we must come to terms as we seek to orient and order our lives."[360] Put differently, creativity itself—"creativity unqualified," "creativity per se," "abstract cosmic creativity in general"—cannot be emulated, first, because it is profoundly and vaguely mysterious, and second, because it is (as many of the scriptural writers acknowledged) creative of good *and* evil, ugliness, and devastation. Be that as it may, this very recognition demands that we place "qualifications on creativity" by restricting normativity to particular "historical trajectories." And the specific trajectory that is most suitable and helpful for norming human existence and activity in general is the productive creativity discernible in the evolutionary history of planet earth, which brought forth life, mammals and primates, and eventually self-conscious, morally responsible agents (creativity$_3$).[361]

Of special relevance to Christians (and perhaps to the entire world) is the fact that this same pattern of creativity also produced Jesus, and Jesus, in turn, opened up a historical trajectory grounded in forgiveness, nonviolence, generosity, peace, reconciliation, justice, and especially agapeic (self-giving) love.[362] In that sense, even though the Johannine confession that "God *is* love" (I John 4) is surely an anthropomorphic and anthropocentric exaggeration (given the massive amount of violent destruction evident throughout nature as a whole, it would be just as fitting to affirm that God is violence), we can at least say that, "in the course of bringing us humans into being," the creativity that is operative in our tiny, human corner of the universe "has also brought us to a point where we can entertain the possibility of living in a moral order that is nonviolent and loving."[363] God may be a mystery, and many (if not most) manifestations of creativity cannot be "regarded as either desirable or good *from our human point of view*." Despite that—or perhaps because of that—Jesus (among other religious images) has supplied a symbolic frame of reference through which the divine has received "humanizing and humane qualities,"[364] and those qualities become criteria by which humans can appraise and judge their own humanness and humaneness. In fact, in Kaufman's theology, the symbol "God" functions as both the relativizer of all things human (and conceiving of the sacred as the mysterious, ambiguous creativity at work throughout the universe serves this function quite well) *and* as the "humanizer" by which "women and men can and do measure themselves":[365]

> It sums up, unifies, and represents in a personification what are taken to be the highest and most indispensable human ideals and values, setting these before the minds of men and women

in what seems an almost visible standard for measuring human realization, an image/concept capable of attracting devotion and loyalty which can order and continuously transform individuals and societies toward fuller realization of their humanity.[366]

Christianity, almost from the outset, construed the life, teachings, and passion of the man Jesus as "the model in terms of which God was increasingly understood" (the real significance of viewing Christ as divine or as the second person of the trinity), as well as the norm "of what human life ought to be." And should we so choose, the images, stories, and radical ethics of Jesus—removed from the premodern, mythological, supernaturalistic, dualistic world-picture of antiquity (what Kaufman dubs "Jesus-trajectory$_1$") and reconceptualized as "the powerful stream of creativity (God) that has been manifest in and through Jesus and the Jesus-movement during the last two millennia," beginning with his baptism, ministry, death, and resurrection and developing through human history as a result of his steadily growing influence and extraordinary impact (what Kaufman dubs "Jesus-trajectory$_2$")—can continue to humanize (without anthropomorphizing) the divine and, thus, remain normative for orienting our moral actions, our social lives, and our ecological decisions in the twenty-first century.[367]

Crosby shares Kaufman's humanistically qualified naturalism, if not his Christian theism. A religion of nature relates human beings to the entirety of reality. And a religiosity or a spirituality oriented to the entire natural sphere combines a deep sense of amazement over the awesome and wondrous mysteries of nature—its unfathomable spatiotemporal scope, its incalculable complexity, its incredible diversity, its ongoing creative-destructive forces, its sheer givenness—with a "sober realism" with respect to the ambiguities, caprices, tragedies, and contingent happenstances of life. In a word, a religion of nature requires us to come clean about "the depth of our ignorance" and about the stubborn pervasiveness of evil, refusing to "minimize its extent, explain it away, or dismiss it as a delusion based upon the limitations of our human purview."[368]

But this is exactly why human beings need to "develop their own ways of thinking and acting" in the ethical and cultural domain. A religion of nature invites us to revere and sacralize the totality of the natural sphere; but our social life and our moral outlook cannot be based "on the whole of nature, only on some parts of it" (just as Jews and Christians should not view every act attributed to God in the Bible—for example, genocide—as morally or socially prescriptive). In other words, though just as ambiguous as the natural order to which we belong, we *Homo sapiens* must qualify (non-human and human) nature, not slavishly imitate it, critically distinguishing "those aspects of its functionings and potentialities that are worthy of our allegiance." We need to work to maximize that which is noble, exemplary, virtuous, healing, integrative, constructive, and saving, and to mitigate that which is ignoble, deplorable, bad, harmful, divisive, destructive, and death-dealing. After all, we are "a species with consciousness, intelligence, and freedom," and even if nature provides "context and support for moral living," it is up to us "to supply its specific precepts":[369]

> As human beings, we have the ability to think and choose, and thus to decide rationally how we shall live and what sorts of contribution we shall aspire to make to one another and to our other fellow creatures on earth. This ability means that we have the power to align ourselves with the forces for good in nature and in our own nature, forces that have produced so much that is undeniably exemplary and excellent in human life and experience.[370]

Like Crosby's, Kaufman's, and Dean's, Wildman's naturalistic metaphysics of the ultimate is scaled to the fullness of reality "in all its complexity and ambiguity."[371] Wildman does not mince words:

> Aristotle had it half right when he conceived God as the principle of natural order that knits together the natural purposes of every living creature into bodily, moral, social, and intellectual harmonies. The half he underplayed is that ultimacy is also the morally impenetrable chaos of mass feeding, the blind chance of random symbiotic events, and the heartless opportunism of viral parasitism. We can narrate one side of this great natural truth about the depths of nature and convince ourselves that we are telling the whole story. We can invent theodicies and other conceptual deflections to manage the painful cognitive dissonance that results. . . . But the whole story of ultimacy . . . is still there to be told. For nature manifests abysmal depths that pass understanding, that absorb mindlessly and hunt mercilessly, that defy moral taming and remain oblivious to the predictable interests of social orders. The apophatic mystics of all traditions have seen this.[372]

Yet Wildman also appreciates that there is a "real danger" in focusing on the incomprehensible whole of ultimate reality, including its dark and demonic aspects, as opposed to "the anthropomorphically intelligible bits" that we fathom and like, the bits that are supportive of our communities and amenable to our concerns.[373] He makes the point in Kaufmanian language: "God may be creativity itself, ultimately, but we can never meaningfully speak in face of mystery in these terms without forsaking our moral obligations to the world around us."[374] Therefore, Wildman, similar to Robert Neville and others,[375] merges a naturalistic, apophatic, and pluralistic metaphysics of ultimacy with a deep appreciation for the existentially, socially, and pragmatically orienting cataphatic symbols of practical and positive (and even personal) religion, which brokenly engage (rather than literally or propositionally describe) the mysterious and ambiguous ground of being.[376] Wildman points to the distinction Christian mystics and negative theologians (e.g., Pseudo-Dionysius) draw between the *via negativa* and the *via positiva* and to the "middle path" for which the Mādhyamaka school of Mahāyāna Buddhism is named. Central to Mādhyamaka thought are the various examples of *upāya* (artful means) that are necessarily employed to mediate between conventional and ultimate reality. Wildman illustrates:

> We rely on the *mudra*, the *mantra*, and the *mandala* (special gestures, sayings, and diagrams) to connect to ultimacy. We use song and ritual and formal discourse. We offer ourselves in *bhakti* devotion to a deity, we reach out to others in *karmic* good works, we fight for what we believe is right, we deploy spiritual yogic practices, and we strive for spiritual knowledge (*jñāna*) with all our might.... All of these actions and words and symbols are instances of *upāya*. They are means by which we engage effectively that which cannot be contained affectively or grasped cognitively or expressed actively.[377]

Of course, notwithstanding our attachments to particular *upāya*, none (including the Buddha) is essential for the attainment of enlightenment, "and thus all must be shed along the way." Nevertheless, *upāyic* conventions and constructions provide techniques for artfully engaging and participating in that which we are unable to finally comprehend.[378]

Wildman is a mystic at heart. "To see the face of God," he proclaims, is to be suffused with "a type of mystical awareness in which the cognitively all-surpassing, morally impenetrable, and aesthetically overwhelming qualities of ultimacy are spurs to worship." However, "when we draw close to this dark place," to this "impossibly profound abyss," to this "underside habitation" occupied by "spiritual beings in every religious and cultural tradition that has ever existed," we are almost immediately forced to come back to the "bright topsides" of our historical lineages, for here, and here alone, can stable institutions be built, moral actions pursued, civilizational ventures sustained, and ultimate reality engaged.[379]

It seems to me that pragmatic historicism ought to additionally maintain that the bright topsides of our historical lineages—that is, their cataphatic, conventional, symbolic, humanly constructed edifices—not only qualify (Kaufman and Crosby) and engage (Wildman and Neville) ultimacy, but also, in some measure, *transform* it. To revisit (and theologically apply) a basic motif of classical pragmatism (cf. chapter 6), human ideas—including, presumably, ideas of God—remake and "add to" (ultimate) reality. As James might put it, ultimacy, far from "ready-made and complete from all eternity," is "plastic" and "malleable" to the constructions humans "engender" upon it, "waiting to receive its final touches at our hands."[380] Or to state the matter in Deweyan terms, knowledge and reason have an instrumental and transformative quality, or "a creative, constructive function," which means that "the world"—or the sacred—"will be different from what it would have been if thought had not intervened."[381] Dewey highlighted the religious implications of such a position in *A Common Faith*:

> Natural piety is not of necessity either a fatalistic acquiescence in natural happenings or a romantic idealization of the world. It may rest upon a just sense of nature as the whole of which we are parts, while it also recognizes that we are parts that are marked by intelligence and purpose, having the capacity to strive by their aid to bring conditions into greater consonance with what is humanly desirable.[382]

Dean seems to pick up on this paleopragmatic humanism in *The Religious Critic in American Culture*. Any "mature philosophy of religion," in Dean's judgment, needs to come to grips with the ambiguity and mystery of God. But that is precisely what motivates *us* to take responsibility for our beliefs and practices, to actively conventionalize the sacred, and, in so doing, to alter "the deepest (the divine) character of history . . . through reinterpretation."[383] In this, Dean echoes his radical empiricist compatriot, Nancy Frankenberry, who defends pantheism against the charge that establishing criteria for the "ordering of values and commitments" is impossible "if nature as a whole is considered divine and known to contain evil as well as good, destruction as much as creation." With bold humanistic verve, she counters that ethics (and, I would add, ethically galvanizing conventions of the sacred) are "human, historical gift[s] to life on this planet"—that is, to God.[384]

Thus, I want to call on pragmatic historicists to take a cue from Charles Milligan and merge a religious naturalism with a "modest polytheism." Milligan rightly realizes that the difficulty of relating to "the All" or to "the universe at large" necessitates "lesser deities," which allow us to extrapolate from the ambiguous whole of existence particular strands of reality that "tie in with our interests" at a given time and regard them with "appreciative reverence." These deities are not God. On the contrary, they are "contrivances of human thought" that "come and go," that "inspire and expire." A pragmatic historicist like Dean would remind us that many of these deities evolve into sacred conventions, active, living traditions that take on a life of their own and act back on their human creators, often in unpredictable ways. In that sense, they are real.[385] But Milligan is right: it is we who construct them and enthrone them and feed them their lines—at least initially. It is also we who are responsible for bringing ethics (and art, religion, economic systems, etc.) into the world. We may succeed or fail, survive or perish. But in any case, it is given to humanity, and humanity alone, "to add justice and mercy to what nature hitherto has brought forth," and it is up to us to enlist the help of the gods—that is, conventions about what is ultimately important (Dean) or, as the early Chicago schoolers would put it, imaginative personifications of our own needs, desires, hopes, concerns, and ideals.[386]

What I am proposing, therefore, is a pragmatic historicist theology that weds a thoroughly naturalized radical monotheism with a radically historicized religious polytheism, a naturalistic and monistic metaphysics of ultimacy with a humanistic and pluralistic ontology of divinity. This is a theology that makes room for God *and* gods, sacred nature *and* sacred conventions, iconoclasm *and* theopoetics, realism *and* constructivism, mystery *and* metaphor, apophaticism *and* personalism, Ein Sof *and* sefirot, Loomerian "size" *and* Deweyan "ideal ends." This is a theology that deploys humanity's projected, provincial, and provisional gods to bring out the best in God, as it were, even as it insists on the relativizing indeterminateness and moral ambiguity of ultimate reality in its spiritually breathtaking entirety. As Stone stirringly remarks, "We need to be inspired by the elements of constructive goodness we select for devotion and also to humble ourselves in awe before the power of the entire creative process."[387] Wildman is dead-on: however misleading as literal depictions of ultimacy, "nothing in religion happens without . . . anthropomorphic constructions."[388] Our unavoidably anthropocentric, perspectivally mediated, historically constituted, socially patterned, and emergently real symbols, interpretations, traditions, habits, norms, salvations, and deities enable us to approach life with moral obligation and religious commitment; to cultivate the virtues necessary for the formation of character and culture; to personify our highest ideals, hopes, and values and mythologize our deepest longings, fears, and dreams; to fallibly register, discriminatingly navigate, and even creatively reshape different facets or potentialities of the world's multiaspected, inexhaustible richness and plenitude (see chapter 3); and to brokenly, contingently, and conditionally engage the mysterious, ambiguous creativity/ground/abyss dimly encountered in the depths of nature.[389]

And so, in a final twist of irony, the sense and taste of nature's abysmal, ambiguous mystery, which is ironically set loose by the social constructionism and quasi-atheistic humanism of historicist theologies, obliges us to eventually float back up to the historically conditioned surfaces of our particular religious heritages, where our "lesser deities" and other sacred conventions dwell. A theological historicism should gesture toward a ceaseless dialectic, or a cyclical back and forth, between apophasis and cataphasis, mystery and convention, indeterminacy and determinacy, monotheism and polytheism, emptiness and form, transcendence and immanence, deconstruction and reconstruction, naturalism and humanism. Appropriately, then, a pragmatic historicist theology of the divine ends in the same place it begins: in the particularities of history.

Conclusion

Pragmatic historicism is a significant intellectual tradition in the history of American religious and philosophical thought as well as a promising trajectory for academic theologians to pursue both now and into the future. It is a variety of historicism that is theologically liberal, religiously pluralist, wholly nonsupernaturalistic, and inextricably tied to empiricism, naturalism, and classical pragmatism. It is—at least if it follows the course I have charted in this study—a worldview that, among other things, (1) affirms the thoroughgoing historicity of human existence but also recognizes the historical character of existence as such; (2) embraces contextualism and particularism but also resists ethnocentrism, isolationism, and confessionalism; (3) puts a premium on traditionedness but also affirms the hybridity, malleability, and internal diversity of traditions; (4) acknowledges the religions' irreducible distinctiveness but also denies their claims to absoluteness and superiority and their inclinations toward exclusivism and sectarianism; (5) foregrounds the cultural-linguistic uniqueness of *Homo sapiens* but also takes account of the natural world, the natural sciences, and the natural embeddedness of human life; (6) appreciates the ways in which the present arises out of the givens of the past but also denounces authoritarianism and the essentializing, romanticizing, and deifying of religious heritages; (7) highlights the perspectival, fallible, relative, constructed, and instrumental nature of knowledge (including theological knowledge) but also defends a critical realism and even a correspondence theory of truth; (8) jettisons foundationalism but also refuses to give up on metaphysics; and (9) underscores the human imaginative creation of gods and other conventions of the sacred but also makes room for a radically empirical, apophatic, pluralistic, and naturalistic theology of the divine.

Nagging questions remain, however. In his review of *Pragmatic Historicism*, Donald Crosby asks Sheila Davaney whether a historicist perspective is *religiously* valuable, capable of sustaining a depth of religious commitment and satisfying the deepest spiritual longings and needs of human beings: "Why should we *stake our lives* on beliefs, outlooks, and practices" that are recognized as "fallible, contestable, restricted, and relative?"[1]

Davaney's reply to Crosby is short and sweet: pragmatic historicism is religiously wanting only if one first assumes that being religious necessitates believing in the "absoluteness, universality, and non-historical character" of one's convictions and values. But pragmatic historicists insist that we do not need to make overblown, untenable assumptions about our traditions and claims in order to fully commit ourselves to them. For instance, we are often willing to stake our lives on our political beliefs, even though most of us realize that they are "fallible, contestable, restricted, and relative."[2] Why, then, do our religious beliefs have to be regarded as absolute, universal, or ahistorical in order to warrant our assent? Besides, to believe things about our religions that flatly contradict the rest of our knowledge and experience is to lead a "bifurcated" existence, not a religiously authentic or harmonious one. On the contrary, conceiving of religion within the limits of history alone means that we no longer have to pretend that theological inquiry and religious practice somehow "play by different rules than other areas of human life."[3] For pragmatic historicists, that is *good* news.

What is more, there are many aspects of a pragmatic historicist vision that are religiously valuable in their own right. Take religious naturalism. From a traditional standpoint, religious naturalism may seem far too costly, dispensing with other worlds, omnibenevolent deities, supernatural causes, and so forth. But for religious naturalists like Crosby, the advantages of jettisoning supernaturalism and supranaturalism far outweigh the costs. For example, persons of faith are no longer obliged to brood over theodicy,[4] "to explain why a God of absolute power and perfect goodness should have created or wanted a world in which so much suffering and sorrow exist." Gone as well is the need to hold on to the "anthropomorphic" and "hubristic" view "that something closely resembling human personality must lie at the core of the universe." Religious naturalism, in contrast, disposes of such "pre-Copernican, pre-Darwinian, pre-galactic, and pre-ecological" notions, notions that undervalue "the diversity, immensity, and mystery of nature."[5]

Crosby proceeds to contend that supernaturalism is not a prerequisite of a religiously and spiritually meaningful existence, nor is the denial of supranatural, personal gods the same as an outright dismissal of religion;

there is, he assures, "a wide middle ground" between otherworldly dissembling and nihilistic despair, between "the absolute and the absurd."⁶ Ursula Goodenough concurs, adding that "religious naturalism . . . can yield deep and abiding spiritual experiences."⁷ She illustrates:

> Our story tells us of the sacredness of life, of the astonishing complexity of cells and organisms, of the vast lengths of time it took to generate their splendid diversity, of the enormous improbability that any of it happened at all. Reverence is the religious emotion elicited when we perceive the sacred. We are called to revere the whole enterprise of planetary existence, the whole and all of its myriad parts as they catalyze and secrete and replicate and mutate and evolve.⁸

Or in the soulful words of the pragmatic historicist Gordon Kaufman:

> This universe . . . is a universe of great beauty and of overwhelming displays of power; a universe populated by many utterly diverse kinds of beings; a universe within which, on planet Earth (and possibly elsewhere) living beings in countless varieties have been created—including our own human mode of existence. This is a universe and a creativity that call forth profound feelings of awe, appreciation, and gratitude—that is, basic modes of worship and prayer. . . . And we may find ourselves uttering prayers and singing songs of praise and thanksgiving to this wondrous God, this serendipitous creativity, and uttering prayers of contrition and penitence for marring this beautiful world by our faults and failures, our self-centeredness and greed, our sins against our fellow-humans, against the living environment in which we find ourselves, and against the creativity that has brought us forth in this magnificent world.⁹

Finally, there are ways of interpreting religion that are fully compatible with, even reflective of, a pragmatic historicist perspective. For example, the pragmatic naturalist George Santayana famously defined religion as "the love of life in the consciousness of impotence."¹⁰ A pragmatic historicist might similarly define religion as the love of life in the consciousness of historicity—in the consciousness of historical relativity, human finitude, unrelenting change, radical contingency, inevitable death, impenetrable mystery, and the inescapable ambiguities, tragedies, imperfections, and limitations of history. Drawing inspiration from Santayana, William Hart adds that pragmatic naturalists "affirm transitory joys amidst persistent-all-too-persistent sorrows" and "pursue justice in a world where many injustices are never acknowledged much less remedied and most victims die anonymously." Pragmatic naturalists also practice religion with ironic sincerity, that is, in full recognition of its human origins and superstitious distortions, and celebrate our highly distinctive, almost godlike, cognitive and moral capacities even while confessing that *Homo sapiens* are "gods who shit," animals who "succumb to disease, grow old, and die."[11] Pragmatic historicists share these pragmatic naturalist sensibilities.

I would go so far as to argue that pragmatic historicism has a kind of intrinsic religious quality. To be a pragmatic historicist is to embrace *this* world in all its limitation and possibility, ambiguity and serendipity, givenness and creativity, vastness and particularity, tragedy and beauty. To be a pragmatic historicist is to cultivate humility, gratitude, reverence, and metaphysical wonder. To be a pragmatic historicist is to accept one's fallibility and to admit that one is a lot lower than the angels. To be a pragmatic historicist is to don sackcloth and ashes, to beat one's breast, and to tame one's imperial ambitions, fundamentalist urges, and aspirations for certainty. To be a pragmatic historicist is to refuse to absolutize the relative (idolatry). To be a pragmatic historicist is to confront one's creatureliness and mortality and to be content with one's earthly, evolutionary origins. To be a pragmatic historicist is to acknowledge one's smallness and specialness in the vast sweep of space-time as well as one's absolute dependence on the interrelated web of existence of which we are a part. To be a pragmatic historicist is to contemplate the incalculable contingencies that had to occur to make this and every moment possible and to ponder the sheer mystery of why there is anything at all rather than nothing. To be a pragmatic historicist is to be vulnerable to change, to exercise whatever agency one has, and to take ownership of and constructive responsibility for one's profoundest claims and convictions—including one's *theological* claims and convictions. To be a pragmatic historicist is to appreciate the spectacular diversity of religious and nonreligious traditions and to lay bare the relativity, incompleteness, and humanness of all of them. To be a pragmatic historicist is to leave the safety of one's parochial enclave, to open oneself to critique and correction from other religions and secular points of view, and to engage in deep learning across religious, theological, and disciplinary borders. To be a pragmatic historicist is to tremble in awe and silence before the overwhelming, abysmal, and often terrifying power of nature, a nature of infinite depth and darkness. To be a pragmatic historicist is to be a mystic, to remember that whatever is ultimate is inscrutable and utterly mysterious, surpassing human understanding and always receding from one's theological advances, religious metaphors, moral expectations, and god-projections. Most of all, to be a pragmatic historicist is to be at home in history, which is indeed the only home we have.[12]

So, to return once more to Crosby's question: is pragmatic historicism capable of sustaining a depth of religious commitment and satisfying the deepest spiritual longings and needs of human beings? The wager of this book has been *yes*—at least for some people.

Notes

Introduction

1. Contemporary philosopher Frederick Beiser regards historicism as an "intellectual revolution" in Western thought, "because it replaced the older ahistorical ways of thinking, which had prevailed from antiquity throughout the Middle Ages, with a new historical way of thinking, which had begun in the middle of the eighteenth century." Frederick C. Beiser, *The German Historicist Tradition* (Oxford: Oxford University Press, 2011), 1.

2. For a very clear and concise account of the history of historicism, see Sheila Greeve Davaney, *Historicism: The Once and Future Challenge for Theology* (Minneapolis: Fortress, 2006).

3. To date, Sheila Greeve Davaney has written the most comprehensive and definitive work on the pragmatic historicist option in modern theology and philosophy. See Sheila Greeve Davaney, *Pragmatic Historicism: A Theology for the Twenty-First Century* (Albany: State University of New York Press, 2000).

4. See Davaney, *Historicism*, chs. 1 and 2.

5. For an illuminating study of German historicism, see Beiser, *The German Historicist Tradition*.

6. I should point out, however, that chapter 2 also contains an extended treatment of Johann Gottfried Herder's protohistoricism. "Without Herder," Karl Barth once wrote, "there would have been no Troeltsch" (and no Schleiermacher, de Wette, or history-of-religions school). Quoted in Marcia Bunge, introduction to *Against Pure Reason: Writings on Religion, Language, and History*, by Johann Gottfried Herder, trans. Marcia Bunge (Minneapolis: Fortress, 1993), 4.

7. Throughout the book, references to "American" thought will be used as shorthand for philosophical and theological traditions originating from the United States.

8. The complex relationship between historicism and pragmatism will be explored in chapters 6 and 7.

9. See Davaney, *Pragmatic Historicism*, x–xi.
10. Davaney, *Historicism*, 144.
11. See, for instance, Delwin Brown, *Boundaries of Our Habitations: Tradition and Theological Construction* (Albany: State University of New York Press, 1994); Davaney, *Pragmatic Historicism*; William Dean, *History Making History: The New Historicism in American Religious Thought* (Albany: State University of New York Press, 1988); Gordon D. Kaufman, *In Face of Mystery: A Constructive Theology* (Cambridge, MA: Harvard University Press, 1993); Sallie McFague, *Models of God: Theology for an Ecological, Nuclear Age* (Philadelphia: Fortress, 1987).
12. Davaney, *Historicism*, 148.
13. See Dean, *History Making History*; Davaney, *Historicism*.
14. See Davaney, *Pragmatic Historicism*, ch. 5.

Chapter 1

1. See Richard Rorty, *Contingency, Irony, and Solidarity* (Cambridge: Cambridge University Press, 1989), xiii, 16, 22.
2. See Sheila Greeve Davaney, *Pragmatic Historicism: A Theology for the Twenty-First Century* (Albany: State University of New York Press, 2000), 26; Davaney, "The Outsideless Life: Historicism, Theology and the Quest for Jesus," *Louvain Studies* 32, no. 1–2 (Spring–Summer 2007): 82.
3. William James, *Essays in Radical Empiricism, and A Pluralistic Universe* (New York: E. P. Dutton, 1971), 145.
4. See William Dean, "Deconstruction and Process Theology," *Journal of Religion* 64, no. 1 (January 1984): 12; Dean, *History Making History: The New Historicism in American Religious Thought* (Albany: State University of New York Press, 1988), 6.
5. William Dean, "Historical Process Theology: A Field in a Map of Thought," *Process Studies* 28, no. 3–4 (Fall–Winter 1999): 255.
6. Donald A. Crosby, *A Religion of Nature* (Albany: State University of New York Press, 2002), 20, 42.
7. See Dean, "Deconstruction and Process Theology," 14.
8. Larry E. Axel, "Process and Religion: The History of a Tradition at Chicago," *Process Studies* 8, no. 4 (Winter 1978): 232–34.
9. John Dewey, *Experience and Nature* (Chicago: Open Court, 1925), 61.
10. James, *Essays in Radical Empiricism, and A Pluralistic Universe*, 225, 233, 243–44.
11. George Burman Foster, *The Function of Religion in Man's Struggle for Existence* (Chicago: University of Chicago Press, 1909), 173.
12. Shirley Jackson Case, *Christianity in a Changing World* (New York: Harper, 1941), 1–2.

13. For example, from the very beginning of his career, Dean has sympathized, specifically, with the aesthetic and empirical side of Whitehead and with the Whiteheadian theological empiricists of the second- and third-generation Chicago schools (e.g., Henry Nelson Wieman, Bernard Meland, and Bernard Loomer), whom he distinguishes from the much larger group of rationalistic and speculative process theologians (e.g., Charles Hartshorne, Schubert Ogden, John Cobb, and David Ray Griffin). See William Dean, *American Religious Empiricism* (Albany: State University of New York Press, 1986), 30–36, 49, 89–96; Dean, "Deconstruction and Process Theology," 2, 7; Dean, "An American Theology," *Process Studies* 12, no. 2 (Summer 1982): 111–28; Dean, *Coming To: A Theology of Beauty* (Philadelphia: Westminster Press, 1972), 94–148. Later, Dean would differentiate his own "historical process theology" from the empirical process thought of Wieman, Meland, and Loomer. "Process historical thinkers," Dean explains, "turn to particular situations primarily to examine them for their particularity, not to open them up to generalities beyond their particularity. So, although the process historical thinkers are empiricists, they are atypical empiricists who focus on particularities in all their exceptionality, unrepeatability, and irreversibility—that is, on their historicity." Dean, "Historical Process Theology," 260.

14. Delwin Brown, "The Fall of '26: Gerald Birney Smith and the Collapse of the Socio-historical Framework of Theology," *American Journal of Theology and Philosophy* 11, no. 3 (September 1990): 201.

15. See Alfred North Whitehead, *Modes of Thought* (New York: Free Press, 1938), 138.

16. See Delwin Brown, *To Set at Liberty: Christian Faith and Human Freedom* (Maryknoll, NY: Orbis, 1981), 29.

17. Dean, "Deconstruction and Process Theology," 2.

18. Dean, *American Religious Empiricism*, 48–49; Dean, "Historical Process Theology," 256–57; Dean, "Deconstruction and Process Theology," 1–19.

19. Whitehead, *Modes of Thought*, 90.

20. Dean, *American Religious Empiricism*, 41–51; Dean, *History Making History*, ix–x, 1–22; William Dean, "A Present Prospect for American Religious Thought," *Journal of the American Academy of Religion* 60, no. 4 (Winter 1992): 740. Similar to Dean, Rorty reads Derrida as a type of historicist: "For Derrida, writing always leads to more writing, and more, and still more—just as history does not lead to Absolute Knowledge or the Final Struggle, but to more history, and more, and still more." Derrida, Rorty expounds, basically upholds "the horizontal character of Hegel's notion of philosophy without its teleology." That is, both philosophers understand truth as "the reinterpretation of our predecessors' reinterpretation of their predecessors' reinterpretation," except Derrida repudiates the Hegelian postulation of a "Last Reinterpretation." Richard Rorty, *Consequences of Pragmatism* (Minneapolis: University of Minnesota Press, 1982), 92–95.

21. Dean, *History Making History*, ix, 5.

22. Dean, "A Present Prospect for American Religious Thought," 740–41. Emphasis added. Throughout the book, added emphasis will be noted. Otherwise, emphasis is in the original.

23. See William Dean, *The Religious Critic in American Culture* (Albany: State University of New York Press, 1994), xx. In chapter 2, I will shed a little more light on what Dean means by "interpretation" and the extent to which nonhuman, nonconscious, and nonliving phenomena "interpret" their environments.

24. Crosby, *A Religion of Nature*, 89–114. See also Richard Rorty, *Philosophy and Social Hope* (London: Penguin, 1999), 68.

25. John Dewey, *Experience and Nature*, 85.

26. Rorty, *Contingency, Irony, and Solidarity*, xiii.

27. Gordon D. Kaufman, *In the Beginning . . . Creativity* (Minneapolis: Fortress, 2004), 44.

28. Clifford Geertz, *The Interpretation of Cultures* (New York: Basic Books, 1973), 49.

29. Simon S. Maimela, "Black Theology and the Quest for a God of Liberation," in *Theology at the End of Modernity: Essays in Honor of Gordon D. Kaufman*, ed. Sheila Greeve Davaney (Philadelphia: Trinity Press International, 1991), 142–45; Delwin Brown, "Limitation and Ingenuity: Radical Historicism and the Nature of Tradition," *American Journal of Theology and Philosophy* 24, no. 3 (September 2003): 208; Davaney, "The Outsideless Life," 82; Davaney, *Pragmatic Historicism*, 23–24.

30. Frederick C. Beiser, *The German Historicist Tradition* (Oxford: Oxford University Press, 2011), 2.

31. Brown, "Limitation and Ingenuity," 208.

32. Sheila Greeve Davaney, "Directions in Historicism: Language, Experience, and Pragmatic Adjudication," in *New Essays in Religious Naturalism*, ed. W. Creighton Peden and Larry E. Axel (Macon, GA: Mercer University Press, 1993), 57.

33. See Jeffrey Stout, *The Flight from Authority: Religion, Morality, and the Quest for Autonomy* (Notre Dame, IN: University of Notre Dame Press, 1981), 4–5.

34. Beiser, *The German Historicist Tradition*, 19.

35. Dean, *American Religious Empiricism*, 38.

36. Beiser correctly asserts that the fundamental principle of historicism is "self-reflexive, of course, applying to historicism itself. It too is intelligible only if we place it within its specific social and historical context." Beiser, *The German Historicist Tradition*, 19.

37. See Dean, *American Religious Empiricism*, 114, 117.

Chapter 2

1. Jeffrey Stout, *The Flight from Authority: Religion, Morality, and the Quest for Autonomy* (Notre Dame, IN: University of Notre Dame Press, 1981), 41.

2. René Descartes, *Selected Philosophical Writings*, trans. John Cottingham, Robert Stoothoff, and Dugald Murdoch (Cambridge: Cambridge University Press, 1988), 24–25.

3. Sheila Greeve Davaney, *Historicism: The Once and Future Challenge for Theology* (Minneapolis: Fortress, 2006), 3.

4. Descartes, *Selected Philosophical Writings*, 1–2.

5. Stout, *The Flight from Authority: Religion, Morality, and the Quest for Autonomy*, 1–7, 25–76, quote on 67. See also Richard J. Bernstein, *Beyond Objectivism and Relativism: Science, Hermeneutics, and Praxis* (Philadelphia: University of Pennsylvania Press, 1983), 16–20; Davaney, *Historicism*, 2–4.

6. See *Rules for the Direction of our Native Intelligence*, *Discourse on the Method*, and *Meditations on First Philosophy*, in Descartes, *Selected Philosophical Writings*, 1–19, 20–56, and 73–122.

7. Davaney, *Historicism*, 4–5.

8. Immanuel Kant, "What Is Enlightenment?," in *The Portable Enlightenment Reader*, ed. Isaac Kramnick (New York: Penguin, 1995), 1.

9. Frederick C. Beiser, *The German Historicist Tradition* (Oxford: Oxford University Press, 2011), 11, 12, 13.

10. Davaney, *Historicism*, 4–65, 148; Sheila Greeve Davaney, *Pragmatic Historicism: A Theology for the Twenty-First Century* (Albany: State University of New York Press, 2000), 5–11.

11. Davaney, *Historicism*, 62–63.

12. Ibid., 12.

13. For an in-depth, careful, and highly nuanced discussion of Herder's historicism, see Beiser, *The German Historicist Tradition*, 98–166.

14. Marcia Bunge, introduction to *Against Pure Reason: Writings on Religion, Language, and History*, by Johann Gottfried Herder, trans. Marcia Bunge (Minneapolis: Fortress, 1993), 1–3, 13–15; Davaney, *Historicism*, 16–17.

15. Davaney, *Historicism*, 16.

16. Johann Gottfried Herder, *Against Pure Reason: Writings on Religion, Language, and History*, trans. Marcia Bunge (Minneapolis: Fortress, 1993), 38–39. Emphasis removed.

17. Ibid., 48–54, quote on 50. Emphasis added.

18. Ibid., 58.

19. Ibid., 74.

20. Bunge, introduction, 17–18.

21. On this score, Herder took issue with thinkers such as Johann Peter Süssmilch, who conjectured that language originated from a divine source. Michael N. Forster, introduction to *Philosophical Writings*, by Johann Gottfried Herder, trans. Michael N. Forster (Cambridge: Cambridge University Press, 2002), xiv. See Herder, *Against Pure Reason*, 74; Herder, *Philosophical Writings*, 56–58.

22. Herder, *Against Pure Reason*, 63–77.

23. Herder, *Philosophical Writings*, 49–50.
24. Herder, *Against Pure Reason*, 38–48.
25. Herder, *Philosophical Writings*, 270.
26. Forster, introduction, xiv–xv.
27. Herder, *Philosophical Writings*, 247–56.
28. Davaney, *Historicism*, 16–19.
29. Bunge, introduction, 1.
30. Herder, *Against Pure Reason*, 57.
31. Ibid., 44.
32. See especially the excerpt from *Ideas toward a Philosophy of History* in ibid., 55–56.
33. Davaney, *Historicism*, 18–19; Forster, introduction, xxxi–xxxii; Georg G. Iggers, *The German Conception of History: The National Tradition of Historical Thought from Herder to the Present*, Rev. ed. (Middletown, CT: Wesleyan University Press, 1968), 41.
34. Herder, *Against Pure Reason*, 44, 46.
35. Bunge, introduction, 3, 19–20.
36. Herder, *Against Pure Reason*, 78–78.
37. Ibid., 106.
38. Ibid., 105.
39. Such a correlation is the focus of the subsequent chapter.
40. Herder, *Against Pure Reason*, 101.
41. Iggers, *The German Conception of History*, 30.
42. Delwin Brown, "Limitation and Ingenuity: Radical Historicism and the Nature of Tradition," *American Journal of Theology and Philosophy* 24, no. 3 (September 2003): 208.
43. Ursula Goodenough, *The Sacred Depths of Nature* (New York: Oxford University Press, 1998), 77–87.
44. Davaney, *Pragmatic Historicism*, 1. See also Clifford Geertz, *The Interpretation of Cultures* (New York: Basic Books, 1973), 49.
45. William Dean, *History Making History: The New Historicism in American Religious Thought* (Albany: State University of New York Press, 1988), 6–7; Richard Rorty, *Contingency, Irony, and Solidarity* (Cambridge: Cambridge University Press, 1989), 30, 40; Davaney, *Pragmatic Historicism*, 23.
46. Rorty, *Contingency, Irony, and Solidarity*, 32.
47. Brown, "Limitation and Ingenuity," 208; Sheila Greeve Davaney, *Divine Power: A Study of Karl Barth and Charles Hartshorne* (Philadelphia: Fortress, 1986), 235–39; Davaney, *Historicism*, 145, 148.
48. Gordon D. Kaufman, *In Face of Mystery: A Constructive Theology* (Cambridge, MA: Harvard University Press, 1993), 117.
49. Shailer Mathews, "The Historical Study of Religion," in *A Guide to the Study of the Christian Religion*, ed. Gerald Birney Smith (Chicago: University of

Chicago Press, 1916), 32; Mathews, *The Growth of the Idea of God* (New York: Macmillan, 1931), 16–17, 19, 25.

50. Davaney, *Pragmatic Historicism*, 23.

51. Dean, *History Making History*, 6. Dean actually echoes Herder here: "Every general picture, every generalization, is only an abstraction." See *Yet Another Philosophy of History*, in Herder, *Against Pure Reason*, 40.

52. William James, *Essays in Radical Empiricism, and A Pluralistic Universe* (New York: E. P. Dutton, 1971), 154, 214, 278. Emphasis removed. See also William James, *Pragmatism: A New Name for Some Old Ways of Thinking* (Cambridge, MA: Harvard University Press, 1978), 63–79.

53. Davaney, *Historicism*, 20.

54. To list but a few examples: embodiment, evolutionary origins, DNA-based genetics, sociality, and mortality. See Donald A. Crosby, *A Religion of Nature* (Albany: State University of New York Press, 2002), 89–101; Goodenough, *The Sacred Depths of Nature*, 143–51.

55. Philosopher Kwame Anthony Appiah contends that, even at the cultural level, humans, for all their splendid variety, also have "many deep things in common. Among them are practices like music, poetry, dance, marriage, funerals; values resembling courtesy, hospitality, sexual modesty, generosity, reciprocity, the resolution of social conflict; concepts such as good and evil, right and wrong, parent and child, past, present, and future." Appiah offers a historicist explanation of such shared cultural traits: "In culture, as in biology, our human environment presents similar problems; and societies, like natural selection, often settle on the same solution because it is the best available." Kwame Anthony Appiah, *Cosmopolitanism: Ethics in a World of Strangers* (New York: W. W. Norton, 2006), 96–97.

56. Brown, "Limitation and Ingenuity," 208.

57. Davaney, *Pragmatic Historicism*, 60.

58. Sallie McFague, "An Earthly Theological Agenda," in *Ecofeminism and the Sacred*, ed. Carol J. Adams (New York: Continuum, 1993), 85. See also McFague, "Cosmology and Christianity: Implications of the Common Creation Story for Theology," in *Theology at the End of Modernity: Essays in Honor of Gordon D. Kaufman*, ed. Sheila Greeve Davaney (Philadelphia: Trinity Press International, 1991), 19, 22.

59. See Iggers, *The German Conception of History*, ch. 2.

60. Forster, introduction, xxxi–xxxii.

61. See Davaney, *Historicism*, 18–19; Iggers, *The German Conception of History*, 40–41.

62. Iggers, *The German Conception of History*, 41.

63. See Herder, *Against Pure Reason*, 38, 77.

64. Ibid., 105.

65. Ibid., 46.

66. See especially *Fragments on Recent German Literature*, in Herder, *Philosophical Writings*, 50.

67. Davaney, *Historicism*, 17, 19.
68. Iggers, *The German Conception of History*, 7, 30–31, 33–37, 41–43.
69. Ibid., 3–28; Davaney, *Historicism*, 19–20.
70. Iggers, *The German Conception of History*, 11.
71. Ibid., 17.
72. Davaney, *Historicism*, 64.
73. Ibid., 18.
74. Herder, *Philosophical Writings*, 247.
75. Ibid., 256.
76. Davaney, *Historicism*, 17–18; Iggers, *The German Conception of History*, 8, 26, 35.

77. Herder, *Against Pure Reason*, 55–56. Herder, as Bunge points out, also grounded the historical unity of humankind in a doctrine of God's providence, believing that, amid the "individual scenes" of human history, men and women find glimpses of a divine plan and purpose. Bunge, introduction, 13–14. Iggers adds that most German historicists, although insisting on the historicity, individuality, and national conditionedness of all philosophy, understanding, and values, evinced a "deep faith in a metaphysical reality beyond the historical world. . . . They were convinced that each of the diverse cultures merely reflected the many aspects of this reality." Iggers, *The German Conception of History*, 13–14. As will become more and more obvious as this book unfolds, a pragmatic and naturalistic historicism negates any sort of providential superpurpose in history. And the reality of which the diverse cultures (and religions) of the world are aspects, far from transcending the historical plane, is none other than the metaphysically dense and multiaspected reality of history itself.

78. Iggers, *The German Conception of History*, 26, 37–38.
79. Forster, introduction, xxix–xxx.
80. Iggers, *The German Conception of History*, 13.
81. Herder, *Against Pure Reason*, 44, 43.
82. Davaney, *Historicism*, 18; Iggers, *The German Conception of History*, 8, 35.

83. Herder, *Against Pure Reason*, 106. Once more, according to Bunge, the mature Herder repudiated radical isolationism, understanding that cultural, national, and religious traditions emerge both out of their own historical inheritances and "in contact with other cultures." Bunge, introduction, 13. This is consistent with the pluralistic historicism that will be advanced in the final section of the present chapter.

84. Richard Rorty, "Solidarity or Objectivity?," in *Objectivity, Relativism, and Truth: Philosophical Papers* (Cambridge: Cambridge University Press, 1991), 22–23, 26, 29–30, 32; Rorty, "Postmodernist Bourgeois Liberalism," in *Objectivity, Relativism, and Truth*, 197–98, 202. See also David L. Hall, *Richard Rorty: Prophet and Poet of the New Pragmatism* (Albany: State University of New York Press, 1994), 175–76.

85. Richard Rorty, *Philosophy and Social Hope* (London: Penguin, 1999), 252–54; Rorty, "Introduction: Antirepresentationalism, Ethnocentrism, and Liberal-

ism," in *Objectivity, Relativism, and Truth*, 15–16; Rorty, "On Ethnocentrism: A Reply to Clifford Geertz," in *Objectivity, Relativism, and Truth*, 208. This appeal is given book-length consideration in Richard Rorty, *Achieving Our Country: Leftist Thought in Twentieth-Century America* (Cambridge, MA: Harvard University Press, 1998).

86. Rorty, "Solidarity or Objectivity?," 29–30.

87. Rorty, "Postmodernist Bourgeois Liberalism," 199.

88. Davaney, *Pragmatic Historicism*, 60–61. See also Davaney, *Historicism*, 186n68.

89. Although Davaney is quick to qualify that a pragmatic historicist conception of culture is derived mostly from *post-Geertzian* anthropological theories (e.g., the new ethnography of James Clifford). Davaney, *Pragmatic Historicism*, 200n22.

90. Clifford Geertz, *Available Light: Anthropological Reflections on Philosophical Topics* (Princeton, NJ: Princeton University Press, 2000), 68–75. See Rorty, "Postmodernist Bourgeois Liberalism," 200.

91. Geertz, *Available Light*, 71, 75–88.

92. Rorty, "Introduction," 14.

93. Rorty, "Postmodernist Bourgeois Liberalism," 201.

94. Hall, *Richard Rorty*, 180.

95. Geertz, *Available Light*, 81, 74.

96. Davaney, *Historicism*, 147, 163. In the next two chapters, I will spell out what this nonisolationist, particularity-sans-insularity mode of historicism portends for *interreligious* engagement.

97. Davaney, *Pragmatic Historicism*, 60.

98. See especially William Dean, "Humanistic Historicism and Naturalistic Historicism," in Davaney, *Theology at the End of Modernity*, 41–59; William Dean, *The Religious Critic in American Culture* (Albany: State University of New York Press, 1994), 55–67.

99. In my estimation, Dean's critique is applicable only to the *early* Mark C. Taylor. Taylor's later work is ambitiously interdisciplinary and breathtakingly expansive in scope, striving to take account of the varied aspects of human culture (e.g., politics, economics, art, technology, religion) *and* nonhuman systems of nature. In one of his most recent books (perhaps his magnum opus), Taylor describes reality as an "emergent self-organizing network of networks that extends from the natural and social to the technological and cultural dimensions of life." Such networks are coevolving and radically interconnected, codetermining each other and complexly interrelating to form "the infinite fabric of life." Mark C. Taylor, *After God* (Chicago: University of Chicago Press, 2007), 346, 343, 314.

100. Dean, *History Making History*, 123–44.

101. William Dean, *American Religious Empiricism* (Albany: State University of New York Press, 1986), 50.

102. Robert S. Corrington, *Ecstatic Naturalism: Signs of the World* (Bloomington: Indiana University Press, 1994), 4–5; Corrington, "Beyond Experience:

Pragmatism and Nature's God," *American Journal of Theology and Philosophy* 14, no. 2 (May 1993): 147–49.

103. Robert S. Corrington, *Nature and Spirit: An Essay in Ecstatic Naturalism* (New York: Fordham University Press, 1992), 3–4.

104. Robert S. Corrington, review of *American Religious Empiricism* and *History Making History: The New Historicism in American Religious Thought*, by William Dean, *Journal of Speculative Philosophy*, n.s., 3, no. 3 (1989): 229–30. See also Corrington, *Ecstatic Naturalism*, 4; Corrington, "Beyond Experience," 147–48.

105. See Dean, *The Religious Critic in American Culture*, 63–67.

106. I will consider the *theological* implications of such an alliance in chapter 8.

107. The most historically thorough and philosophically and theologically sophisticated exposition of radical empiricism is Nancy Frankenberry, *Religion and Radical Empiricism* (Albany: State University of New York Press, 1987).

108. Dean, *American Religious Empiricism*, 36.

109. Ibid., 1, 9, 19–36; Dean, *History Making History*, 101–22.

110. John Dewey, *Reconstruction in Philosophy*, enl. ed. (Boston: Beacon, 1957), xxxi.

111. Dean, *American Religious Empiricism*, 48, 50; William Dean, "Deconstruction and Process Theology," *Journal of Religion* 64, no. 1 (January 1984): 8. See also Richard J. Bernstein, *The Pragmatic Turn* (Cambridge: Polity, 2010), ix, 8, 18; Tyron L. Inbody, "History of Empirical Theology," in *Empirical Theology: A Handbook*, ed. Randolph Crump Miller (Birmingham, AL: Religious Education Press, 1992), 35.

112. See especially Delwin Brown, *Boundaries of Our Habitations: Tradition and Theological Construction* (Albany: State University of New York Press, 1994), ch. 2.

113. Delwin Brown, "Marginalizing the Life of Language: Radical Empiricism as a Critique of Gadamer," in *New Essays in Religious Naturalism*, ed. W. Creighton Peden and Larry E. Axel (Macon, GA: Mercer University Press, 1993), 31.

114. Ibid., 21–32; Brown, *Boundaries of Our Habitations*, 46–53, 106–7.

115. John Dewey, *Experience and Nature* (Chicago: Open Court, 1925), 1, 4.

116. Robert Neville cleverly invented the term "paleopragmatism" to differentiate the classical pragmatist lineage from the postmodern neopragmatism of Rorty and others. See Robert Cummings Neville, "A Paleopragmatic Philosophy of History of Philosophy," in *Pragmatism, Neo-pragmatism, and Religion: Conversations with Richard Rorty*, ed. Charley D. Hardwick and Donald A. Crosby (New York: Peter Lang, 1997), 43–60. I will argue for a "paleopragmatic historicism" in chapters 6 and 7.

117. Dean, *History Making History*, 125–26, 130.

118. Dean, *American Religious Empiricism*, 48. See also Dean, *History Making History*, 130–33.

119. Dean, *History Making History*, 75–76, 90–97, quote on 97. See also Brown, *Boundaries of Our Habitations*, 46.

120. Davaney, *Pragmatic Historicism*, 77, 80.

121. George A. Lindbeck, *The Nature of Doctrine: Religion and Theology in a Postliberal Age* (Philadelphia: Westminster Press, 1984), 16–17, 20–21, 23, 30–32.
122. Ibid., 17–25, 30–41.
123. Ibid., 118.
124. Ibid., 112–24; George A. Lindbeck, "The Gospel's Uniqueness: Election and Untranslatability," *Modern Theology* 13, no. 4 (October 1997): 426–34, 440.
125. Linell E. Cady, "Resisting the Postmodern Turn: Theology and Contextualization," in Davaney, *Theology at the End of Modernity*, 81–90.
126. Lindbeck, *The Nature of Doctrine*, 124–35; Lindbeck, "The Gospel's Uniqueness," 426–27.
127. See also Cady, "Resisting the Postmodern Turn," 88.
128. Lindbeck, *The Nature of Doctrine*, 62–63.
129. Dean, "Humanistic Historicism and Naturalistic Historicism," 41–59; Dean, *The Religious Critic in American Culture*, 55–67.
130. See Davaney, *Pragmatic Historicism*, 59–65.
131. Ibid., 113, 172.
132. Ibid., 108–16. See also Sheila Greeve Davaney, "Between the One and the Many: A Response to Delwin Brown's Theology of Tradition," *American Journal of Theology and Philosophy* 18, no. 2 (May 1997): 141–45.
133. Davaney, *Historicism*, 154.
134. Davaney, *Pragmatic Historicism*, 108–9.
135. Delwin Brown, "Refashioning Self and Other: Theology, Academy, and the New Ethnography," in *Converging on Culture: Theologians in Dialogue with Cultural Analysis and Criticism*, ed. Delwin Brown, Sheila Greeve Davaney, and Kathryn Tanner (New York: Oxford University Press, 2001), 43.
136. Brown, *Boundaries of Our Habitations*, 76–77; Davaney, *Historicism*, 148–53.
137. Davaney, *Pragmatic Historicism*, 109.
138. Ibid., 109–10.
139. Kaufman, *In Face of Mystery*, 119–20.
140. See Talal Asad, *Genealogies of Religion: Discipline and Reasons of Power in Christianity and Islam* (Baltimore: Johns Hopkins University Press, 1993), 27–54; David Chidester, *Savage Systems: Colonialism and Comparative Religion in Southern Africa* (Charlottesville: University Press of Virginia, 1996), xi–xvi, 219–66; Tomoko Masuzawa, *The Invention of World Religions; or, How European Universalism Was Preserved in the Language of Pluralism* (Chicago: University of Chicago Press, 2005), 1–206; Russell T. McCutcheon, *Manufacturing Religion: The Discourse on Sui Generis Religion and the Politics of Nostalgia* (New York: Oxford University Press, 2003), 3–6; Jonathan Z. Smith, *Imagining Religion: From Babylon to Jonestown* (Chicago: University of Chicago Press, 1982), xi; J. Z. Smith, *Relating Religion: Essays in the Study of Religion* (Chicago: University of Chicago Press, 2004), 179–96; Wilfred Cantwell Smith, *The Meaning and End of Religion* (Minneapolis: Fortress, 1991),

15–79, 119–53. This compressed summation of the current scholarship on genealogies of "religion" and "religions" is also supplemented by John Thatamanil and Kevin Schilbrack. See John J. Thatamanil, "Comparative Theology after 'Religion,'" in *Planetary Loves: Spivak, Postcoloniality, and Theology*, ed. Stephen D. Moore and Mayra Rivera (New York: Fordham University Press, 2010), 242–43; Kevin Schilbrack, "Religions: Are There Any?," *Journal of the American Academy of Religion* 78, no. 4 (December 2010): 1112–17.

141. Thatamanil, "Comparative Theology after 'Religion,'" 243–44.

142. W. C. Smith, *The Meaning and End of Religion*, 43, 51, 57.

143. For its part, "Hinduism," as Jeffrey Long points out, was also constructed to serve imperialistic interests. Referencing Edward Said's *Orientalism* and Ronald Inden's *Imagining India*, Long notes that the term was "developed first by Muslim and then by European Christian conquerors in order to facilitate their dominion over the Indian subcontinent. The power to define a thing is a power that imperialist forces have utilized throughout history in order to shape the world according to their own ends. . . . The concept of 'Hinduism' has helped enable Westerners for centuries to divest the people of India of agency by teaching them that they are benighted victims of an inescapable prison of superstition and otherworldly spirituality." Jeffrey D. Long, "Anekanta Vedanta: Toward a Deep Hindu Religious Pluralism," in *Deep Religious Pluralism*, ed. David Ray Griffin (Louisville: Westminster John Knox Press, 2005), 147.

144. W. C. Smith, *The Meaning and End of Religion*, 60–76, 141–69, 195, quote on 60, 65.

145. In the famous and tantalizing (and misleading) words of Jonathan Z. Smith: "Religion is solely the creation of the scholar's study. . . . Religion has no independent existence apart from the academy." J. Z. Smith, *Imagining Religion*, xi.

146. Chidester, *Savage Systems*, 238, 259. Process theologian John Cobb agrees: when the concept "religion" is essentialized and reified, "each tradition's more distinctive elements tend to be depreciated." Be that as it may, there is "a variety of phenomena that the word evokes in common usage." John B. Cobb, Jr., "Some Whiteheadian Assumptions about Religion and Pluralism," in Griffin, *Deep Religious Pluralism*, 244, 246.

147. Schilbrack, "Religions: Are There Any?," 1112–35.

148. Brown, *Boundaries of Our Habitations*, 75–77; Brown, "Refashioning Self and Other," 45.

149. Brown, "Refashioning Self and Other," 43.

150. W. C. Smith, *The Meaning and End of Religion*, 195.

151. John J. Thatamanil, "Defining the Religious: Comprehensive, Qualitative Orientation" (unpublished manuscript, 2012), Microsoft Word file. This manuscript is from a very early draft of Thatamanil's most recent book, *Circling the Elephant*. See John J. Thatamanil, *Circling the Elephant: A Comparative Theology of Religious Diversity* (New York: Fordham University Press, 2020), ch. 5. See also Schilbrack, "Religions: Are There Any?," 1117, 1131, 1135.

152. Thatamanil, "Comparative Theology after 'Religion,'" 247–48, 250–52.
153. Thatamanil, "Defining the Religious."
154. Thatamanil, "Comparative Theology after 'Religion,'" 247–48.
155. Davaney, *Historicism*, 148–49; Brown, *Boundaries of Our Habitations*, 76–77, 79. The Catholic theologian Peter Phan drives the point home forcefully: "No one with a modicum of historical knowledge would deny that all religious traditions—including Christianity, or more accurately, Christianities—are porous to each other, and, in this sense, each religion is intrinsically religiously multiple." But we need to be careful not to discount "the stubborn facts of social, doctrinal, liturgical, ethical, and institutional boundaries and barriers among religions, which religious and political authorities have not refrained from exploiting to their advantages." Peter C. Phan, "Response to Premawardhana," *Journal of Ecumenical Studies* 46, no. 1 (Winter 2011): 103.
156. Thatamanil, "Comparative Theology after 'Religion,'" 244.
157. Chidester, *Savage Systems*, 260.
158. I have described the theoretical contours and theological implications of a holistic historicism in Demian Wheeler, "Big History and the Size of God: Holistic Historicism as a Pathway to Religious Naturalism," *American Journal of Theology and Philosophy* 34, no. 3 (September 2013): 226–47.
159. Beiser, *The German Historicist Tradition*, 3.
160. Ibid., 3–4.
161. Iggers, *The German Conception of History*, 4–5.
162. See Dean, "Humanistic Historicism and Naturalistic Historicism," 41–59; Dean, *The Religious Critic in American Culture*, 55–67.
163. Rorty, "Solidarity or Objectivity?," 33–34; Richard Rorty, "Science as Solidarity," in *Objectivity, Relativism, and Truth*, 35–45.
164. See Dean, "Humanistic Historicism and Naturalistic Historicism," 52–55; Cady, "Resisting the Postmodern Turn," 88.
165. Davaney, *Pragmatic Historicism*, 59–60.
166. Dean, "Humanistic Historicism and Naturalistic Historicism," 52, 54, 59.
167. Davaney, *Pragmatic Historicism*, 177.
168. Davaney, *Historicism*, 145; Davaney, *Pragmatic Historicism*, 80.
169. McFague, "Cosmology and Christianity," 25, 31.
170. Kaufman, *In Face of Mystery*, 133.
171. Davaney, *Pragmatic Historicism*, 24, 61, 77–79, 142; Davaney, *Historicism*, 145–46, 155.
172. Davaney calls West a "philosophical fellow traveler" and appreciates the way in which he "thickens" historicist analysis by "politicizing it and tracing its formation in material culture." See Davaney, *Pragmatic Historicism*, 142.
173. Cornel West, *The American Evasion of Philosophy: A Genealogy of Pragmatism* (Madison: University of Wisconsin Press, 1989), 3–4, 206–39; West, *Keeping Faith: Philosophy and Race in America* (New York: Routledge, 1993), 119–34,

135–41. See also "Nietzsche's Prefiguration of Postmodern American Philosophy" in West, *The Cornel West Reader* (New York: Basic Civitas Books, 1999), 188–210.

174. Gordon D. Kaufman, *In the Beginning . . . Creativity* (Minneapolis: Fortress, 2004), 44–46. For example, the raw chemical materials from which we—and all living things—are made, as well as the energy that fuels the biosphere, are derived from stars. As David Christian elaborates: "The heavier elements scattered throughout the galaxy were first formed in stars and in supernovae. As the universe aged, the proportion of new elements (other than hydrogen and helium) has steadily increased. Without the chemically rich environment created by stars and supernovae, our earth could not have been born, and life could not have evolved . . . In addition, many important processes on the earth are driven by the earth's internal heat engine, whose heat was generated partly during the formation of our sun and comes partly from radioactive elements created in supernovae. In all these ways, *the life histories of stars are a vital component of the story of life on Earth*"—nonhuman and human. Indeed, without stars and supernovae, "we could not exist." David Christian, *Maps of Time: An Introduction to Big History* (Berkeley: University of California Press, 2011), 51–52. Emphasis added.

175. Crosby, *A Religion of Nature*, 89–114. See also Rorty, *Philosophy and Social Hope*, 68.

176. Kaufman, *In Face of Mystery*, 14, 112.

177. Davaney, *Pragmatic Historicism*, 176–77. See also Davaney, *Historicism*, 155.

178. Dean, "Humanistic Historicism and Naturalistic Historicism," 41–47; Dean, *The Religious Critic in American Culture*, 65.

179. Richard J. Bernstein, "Pragmatism, Pluralism, and the Healing of Wounds," in *Pragmatism: A Reader*, ed. Louis Menand (New York: Vintage, 1997), 388–89.

180. William James, *The Will to Believe, and Other Essays in Popular Philosophy* (New York: Dover, 1956), 145–83.

181. Bernstein, *The Pragmatic Turn*, 7, 144–50; Rorty, *Philosophy and Social Hope*, 30. That Dewey never totally abandoned Hegelian historicism but, instead, naturalized it in light of Darwin's theory of evolution is, according to Bernstein, evident in the following passage: "For life is no uniform uninterrupted march or flow. It is a thing of histories, each with its own plot, its own inception and movement toward its close, each having its own particular rhythmic movement; each with its own unrepeated quality pervading it throughout." Quoted in Bernstein, *The Pragmatic Turn*, 147.

182. John Dewey, *The Influence of Darwin on Philosophy, and Other Essays* (Amherst, NY: Prometheus, 1997), 7–12, quote on 11–12.

183. Dewey, *Experience and Nature*, 38.

184. James, *Pragmatism*, 142.

185. See Bernstein, "Pragmatism, Pluralism, and the Healing of Wounds," 389.

186. See Dean, *American Religious Empiricism*, 75–76; Dean, *The Religious Critic in American Culture*, 123.

187. James, *The Will to Believe, and Other Essays in Popular Philosophy*, 216–54.

188. Ibid., 226.

189. Undeniably, human history, as David Christian demonstrates, "marks the appearance of new rules of historical change." As humanity acquired the capacity for symbolic language and collective learning and gradually developed the lifeways, complex social/cultural/political structures, and technological innovations (e.g., agriculture) that enabled the species to have a greater and greater impact on the biosphere and to intensively extract more and more energy and ecological resources from local environments, the scale and pace of historical change accelerated exponentially. Indeed, in the last millennium, and especially in the past two or three centuries (i.e., the modern period), the rate and scope of transformation have been more rapid and thoroughgoing than at any other time in the history of the world. See Christian, *Maps of Time*, pts. 3, 4, and 5, quote on 144. See also David Christian, "World History in Context," *Journal of World History* 14, no. 4 (December 2003): 444–56.

190. Dewey, *Reconstruction in Philosophy*, 86, 94–97.

191. Ibid., 84–85.

192. See Dean, *American Religious Empiricism*, 75–76; Dean, *History Making History*, 100; Dean, *The Religious Critic in American Culture*, 123.

193. William Dean, "Historical Process Theology: A Field in a Map of Thought," *Process Studies* 28, no. 3–4 (Fall–Winter 1999): 256–57.

194. Dean, *The Religious Critic in American Culture*, 65.

195. Ibid., 121–25.

196. Dean, *History Making History*, 100. See also William Dean, "A Present Prospect for American Religious Thought," *Journal of the American Academy of Religion* 60, no. 4 (Winter 1992): 740–41.

197. Dean, *American Religious Empiricism*, 52.

198. Dean, *The Religious Critic in American Culture*, 115–21; Dean, *American Religious Empiricism*, 51–55.

199. Dean, *The Religious Critic in American Culture*, 114.

200. Davaney, *Pragmatic Historicism*, 201n41.

201. Dean, *History Making History*, 131–32. Brown also works from within a Whiteheadian perspective and suggests that *every* actual occasion, although dependent on "the actualities and latent possibilities given in the past," possesses "at least some minuscule measure of self-directedness." And, akin to Dean, Brown enthuses that in contemporary physics "the deterministic model" has been replaced with "a looser, more dynamic conception of physical relationships," thereby lending credence to the (panpsychist) theory that creativity and even freedom and agency are ingredient in the *entire* natural order, even if only "in some very embryonic form." Delwin Brown, *To Set at Liberty: Christian Faith and Human Freedom* (Maryknoll, NY: Orbis, 1981), 30.

202. Corrington, *Ecstatic Naturalism*, 57.

203. Drawing on the scholarship of the biological anthropologist and neuroscientist Terrence Deacon, Kaufman points out that even the *natural history* of

Homo sapiens has been affected by the uniquely cultural and linguistic character of our historicity: "It was the emergence of symbolic behaviors—such as language, a central feature in the historical unfolding of human cultural life—that brought about the very evolution of our unusually large brains." And through ongoing research in genetics and medicine, we will most likely impact our evolutionary *future* as well. See Kaufman, *In the Beginning . . . Creativity*, 44–45.

204. Kaufman, *In Face of Mystery*, 97–193.

205. Kaufman, *In the Beginning . . . Creativity*, 45. Shirley Jackson Case came to the same exact conclusion in 1943: "While man is a natural animal, he is also possessed of spiritual capacities; he has powers of thought and choice and decision that the oak has never acquired. . . . Thus, by means of nurture he can transcend or transform nature. It is this spiritual freedom of man—his pursuit of choice, the exercise of his will, the determinative effect of his decisions, his susceptibility to ideals, his response to envisaged values, his feeling of communion with unseen forces, his yearning for larger knowledge, his restless quest for new experiences—that constitutes his chief significance for the making of human history." Shirley Jackson Case, *The Christian Philosophy of History* (Chicago: University of Chicago Press, 1943), 155–56.

206. Dean, *The Religious Critic in American Culture*, 123–25. Emphasis added.

207. Ibid., 121, 124.

208. My synopsis of Gould is heavily reliant on Richard York and Brett Clark, *The Science and Humanism of Stephen Jay Gould* (New York: Monthly Review Press, 2011), 11–91.

209. Stephen Jay Gould, *Wonderful Life: The Burgess Shale and the Nature of History* (New York: W. W. Norton, 1989), 14–15.

210. Ibid., 300–301.

211. Stephen Jay Gould, *Full House: The Spread of Excellence from Plato to Darwin* (New York: Three Rivers Press, 1996), 4; Gould, "The Wheel of Fortune and the Wedge of Progress," *Natural History* 98, no. 3 (March 1989): 16, 18; Gould, "Modified Grandeur," *Natural History* 102, no. 3 (March 1993): 18–19; Gould, *Wonderful Life*, 306–8, 319–21.

212. Gould, *Full House*, 29.

213. Other important studies in big history include the following: Cynthia Stokes Brown, *Big History: From the Big Bang to the Present* (New York: New Press, 2007); Eric J. Chaisson, *Epic of Evolution: Seven Ages of the Cosmos* (New York: Columbia University Press, 2006); Fred Spier, *The Structure of Big History: From the Big Bang until Today* (Amsterdam: Amsterdam University Press, 1996); Fred Spier, "Big History: The Emergence of a Novel Interdisciplinary Approach," *Interdisciplinary Science Reviews* 33, no. 2 (2008): 141–52.

214. See Christian, *Maps of Time*, 79–105.

215. David Christian, "The Return of Universal History," *History and Theory* 49, no. 4 (December 2010): 19.

216. David Christian, "The Case for 'Big History,'" *Journal of World History* 2, no. 2 (Fall 1991): 225. Christian reports that, as the cosmos continues to expand, star formation will cease, entropy will increase, and the universe will get "simpler, colder, and lonelier in an infinitely slow diminuendo," leaving behind "a colossal galactic graveyard" and a "depressingly thin sprinkling of photons and subatomic particles." Christian, *Maps of Time*, 486–91. Some physicists (e.g., John Wheeler and Andrei Linde) speculate that our universe may eventually come to an end in a kind of "Big Crunch." Crosby, *A Religion of Nature*, 39.

217. Christian, "The Case for 'Big History,'" 223–38; Christian, "The Return of Universal History," 6–27; Christian, *Maps of Time*.

218. McFague, "Cosmology and Christianity," 25.

219. Ibid., 32.

220. Davaney, *Pragmatic Historicism*, 66.

221. Beiser, *The German Historicist Tradition*, 4.

222. Christian, "The Return of Universal History," 26.

223. Davaney, *Pragmatic Historicism*, 80.

224. McFague, "Cosmology and Christianity," 32–33.

Chapter 3

1. Ernst Troeltsch, "Historical and Dogmatic Method in Theology," in *Religion in History*, ed. and trans. James Luther Adams and Walter F. Bense (Minneapolis: Fortress, 1991), 31, 15, 16.

2. Ernst Troeltsch, "Christianity and the History of Religion," in *Religion in History*, 77–78.

3. See Ernst Troeltsch, *Der Historismus und seine Probleme* (Berlin: R. Heise, 1924).

4. Sheila Greeve Davaney, *Historicism: The Once and Future Challenge for Theology* (Minneapolis: Fortress, 2006), 61–62.

5. Gary Dorrien, *Kantian Reason and Hegelian Spirit: The Idealistic Logic of Modern Theology* (Malden, MA: Wiley-Blackwell, 2012), 365.

6. Ibid., 334.

7. Troeltsch, "Christianity and the History of Religion," 77–78.

8. Ernst Troeltsch, *The Christian Faith*, trans. Garrett E. Paul (Minneapolis: Fortress, 1991), 82.

9. Ernst Troeltsch, *The Absoluteness of Christianity and the History of Religions*, trans. David Reid (Eugene, OR: Wipf and Stock, 2003), 46–48.

10. Ernst Troeltsch, "The Place of Christianity among the World Religions," in *Christianity and Plurality: Classic and Contemporary Readings*, ed. Richard J. Plantinga (Oxford: Blackwell, 1999), 214.

11. Troeltsch, *The Absoluteness of Christianity and the History of Religions*, 45–83, 100–101, quotes on 53, 64, 66, 69, 71; Davaney, *Historicism*, 59–60; Hans-Georg Drescher, "Ernst Troeltsch's Intellectual Development," in *Ernst Troeltsch and the Future of Theology*, ed. John Powell Clayton (New York: Cambridge University Press, 1976), 16; Dorrien, *Kantian Reason and Hegelian Spirit*, 350–52; Wesley J. Wildman, *Fidelity with Plausibility: Modest Christologies in the Twentieth Century* (Albany: State University of New York Press, 1998), 68–69. See also Troeltsch, "The Place of Christianity among the World Religions," 213–14.

12. Elsewhere, Troeltsch referred to such a principle as "the religious a priori." Indeed, for all his skewering of Hegelianism, he, too, detected "an active presence of the absolute spirit in the realm of the finite." In *The Christian Faith* (*Glaubenslehre*), he deemed Christianity "the highest revelation," even while pointing to a "supra-historical" and universal "divine seizure" that is "found everywhere" in history (again redolent of Hegel). Troeltsch, "On the Question of the Religious A Priori," in *Religion in History*, 41; Troeltsch, *The Christian Faith*, 10, 81–82.

13. Georg G. Iggers, *The German Conception of History: The National Tradition of Historical Thought from Herder to the Present*, rev. ed. (Middletown, CT: Wesleyan University Press, 1968), 179.

14. Troeltsch, *The Absoluteness of Christianity and the History of Religions*, 26, 30–31, 89–91, 94–96, 100–101, 105–6, 112, 114–15; Davaney, *Historicism*, 60–61; Drescher, "Ernst Troeltsch's Intellectual Development," 11, 17; Wildman, *Fidelity with Plausibility*, 70–71; Dorrien, *Kantian Reason and Hegelian Spirit*, 348–49, 352–53. See also Troeltsch, *The Christian Faith*, 9–10, 26.

15. Troeltsch, *The Absoluteness of Christianity and the History of Religions*, 92–93, 109, 112, 114, 117, 121, 131–63; Dorrien, *Kantian Reason and Hegelian Spirit*, 352–53; Wildman, *Fidelity with Plausibility*, 70–71; Drescher, "Ernst Troeltsch's Intellectual Development," 17–18; Michael Pye, "Ernst Troeltsch and the End of the Problem about 'Other' Religions," in J. P. Clayton, *Ernst Troeltsch and the Future of Theology*, 176–82. See also Troeltsch, "Christianity and the History of Religion," 81–84.

16. Iggers, *The German Conception of History*, 179, 195.

17. Pye, "Ernst Troeltsch and the End of the Problem about 'Other' Religions," 175–76, 179, 182–88.

18. Troeltsch, *The Christian Faith*, 10.

19. Troeltsch, *The Absoluteness of Christianity and the History of Religions*, 71, 85.

20. Ibid., 114–15; Wildman, *Fidelity with Plausibility*, 69.

21. Troeltsch, "The Dogmatics of the History-of-Religions School," in *Religion in History*, 87–88, 92, final quotes on 94–95. Emphasis added.

22. Wildman, *Fidelity with Plausibility*, 107.

23. Troeltsch, "Modern Philosophy of History," in *Religion in History*, 293; Iggers, *The German Conception of History*, 179.

24. Troeltsch, "Christianity and the History of Religion," 84.

25. See Troeltsch, "Modern Philosophy of History," 273–320.

26. Wildman, *Fidelity with Plausibility*, 71–72, 104–14, 124, 137–39.

27. Troeltsch, "The Place of Christianity among the World Religions," 218.

28. Ibid., 211–19; Wildman, *Fidelity with Plausibility*, 69–74; Davaney, *Historicism*, 61–62. The latter point—that Christianity (and every other religion) "presents no historical uniformity," but alters over time, in accordance with the varying circumstances and changing contexts in which it has been located and by which it has been conditioned (Troeltsch, "The Place of Christianity among the World Religions," 214, 217)—became expressly and abundantly clear to Troeltsch after he befriended the sociologist Max Weber and completed his massive work, *The Social Teaching of the Christian Churches* (1911). Wildman, *Fidelity with Plausibility*, 121–25. See Ernst Troeltsch, *The Social Teaching of the Christian Churches*, trans. Olive Wyon, 2 vols. (Louisville: Westminster John Knox Press, 1992).

29. Troeltsch, "The Place of Christianity among the World Religions," 212, 215, final quotes on 219. Emphasis added.

30. Tomoko Masuzawa, *The Invention of World Religions; or, How European Universalism Was Preserved in the Language of Pluralism* (Chicago: University of Chicago Press, 2005), 320.

31. Ibid., 312.

32. Paul F. Knitter, *No Other Name? A Critical Survey of Christian Attitudes toward the World Religions* (Maryknoll, NY: Orbis, 1985), 23, 24, 29. See also Masuzawa, *The Invention of World Religions*, 310–14.

33. Dorrien, *Kantian Reason and Hegelian Spirit*, 349, 354.

34. Troeltsch, "Historical and Dogmatic Method in Theology," 18.

35. See ibid., 27.

36. Dorrien, *Kantian Reason and Hegelian Spirit*, 349, 345, 364.

37. Iggers, *The German Conception of History*, 179–80, 182, 190–94, quote on 192–93.

38. Troeltsch, "The Place of Christianity among the World Religions," 221.

39. Ibid., 219–22.

40. Sheila Greeve Davaney, *Pragmatic Historicism: A Theology for the Twenty-First Century* (Albany: State University of New York Press, 2000), 11. See also Davaney, *Historicism*, 61–62.

41. Dorrien, *Kantian Reason and Hegelian Spirit*, 364–65. Emphasis added.

42. Troeltsch, "The Place of Christianity among the World Religions," 218–19.

43. See Dorrien, *Kantian Reason and Hegelian Spirit*, 365.

44. Troeltsch, "The Place of Christianity among the World Religions," 218–19.

45. See Masuzawa, *The Invention of World Religions*, ch. 9.

46. See Troeltsch, "The Place of Christianity among the World Religions," 219–22. Emphasis added.

47. See Kenneth Rose, *Pluralism: The Future of Religion* (New York: Bloomsbury, 2013), 37n9.

48. Masuzawa, *The Invention of World Religions*, 326, 327.

49. See ibid., 325.

50. For the best—and fairest—introduction to the modal options and major issues in the theology of religions, see Paul F. Knitter, *Introducing Theologies of Religions* (Maryknoll, NY: Orbis, 2002).

51. Perry Schmidt-Leukel, "Pluralisms: How to Appreciate Religious Diversity Theologically," in *Christian Approaches to Other Faiths*, ed. Alan Race and Paul M. Hedges (London: SCM Press, 2008), 85.

52. Although beginning as a predominantly intra-Christian enterprise, theology of religions, as Kristin Beise Kiblinger notices, now occurs in non-Christian traditions as well. Kristin Beise Kiblinger, "Relating Theology of Religions and Comparative Theology," in *The New Comparative Theology: Interreligious Insights from the Next Generation*, ed. Francis X. Clooney (London: T. and T. Clark, 2010), 25–26. For instance, Kiblinger herself has made a case for a *Buddhist* inclusivism. See Kristin Beise Kiblinger, *Buddhist Inclusivism: Attitudes towards Religious Others* (Aldershot, UK: Ashgate, 2005). For Hindu, Sikh, Buddhist, Muslim, and Jewish variants of a pluralist theology of religions, see Paul F. Knitter, ed., *The Myth of Religious Superiority: A Multifaith Exploration* (Maryknoll, NY: Orbis, 2005).

53. Assembled from James L. Fredericks, introduction to Clooney, *The New Comparative Theology*, xiii–xiv; Kiblinger, "Relating Theology of Religions and Comparative Theology," 21; John J. Thatamanil, "God as Ground, Contingency, and Relation: Trinitarian Polydoxy and Religious Diversity," in *Polydoxy: Theology of Multiplicity and Relation*, ed. Catherine Keller and Laurel C. Schneider (London: Routledge, 2011), 240; Veli-Matti Kärkkäinen, *An Introduction to the Theology of Religions: Biblical, Historical and Contemporary Perspectives* (Downers Grove, IL: IVP Academic, 2003), 20; Alan Race, *Christians and Religious Pluralism: Patterns in the Christian Theology of Religions* (Maryknoll, NY: Orbis, 1982), ix.

54. Alan Race was the first scholar to describe theologies of religions as modally exclusivist, inclusivist, or pluralist. See Race, *Christians and Religious Pluralism*. A host of recent critics, such as Gavin D'Costa, Wesley Ariarajah, Terrence Tilley, S. Mark Heim, and many others, have raised several objections to this (now standard) way of classifying the different positions within the field. However, with Perry Schmidt-Leukel, I do not believe that the "tripolar typology" has outlived its usefulness, so long as the models are interpreted in a careful and capacious manner. For that reason, this book retains (though carefully and capaciously reinterprets) the designations exclusivism, inclusivism, and pluralism. See Perry Schmidt-Leukel, "Exclusivism, Inclusivism, Pluralism: The Tripolar Typology—Clarified and Reaffirmed," in Knitter, *The Myth of Religious Superiority*, 13–27.

55. John Hick, *God Has Many Names: Britain's New Religious Pluralism* (London: Macmillan, 1980), 43.

56. Diana L. Eck, *Encountering God: A Spiritual Journey from Bozeman to Banaras* (New York: Penguin, 1996), 168, 170–78; Paul F. Knitter, preface to *The*

Myth of Christian Uniqueness: Toward a Pluralistic Theology of Religions, ed. John Hick and Paul F. Knitter (Maryknoll, NY: Orbis, 1987), viii; Knitter, *Introducing Theologies of Religions*, 19, 23, 27–29; John Hick, *A Christian Theology of Religions: The Rainbow of Faiths* (Louisville: Westminster John Knox Press, 1995), 19, 82–87, 113; Hick, "The Non-absoluteness of Christianity," in Hick and Knitter, *The Myth of Christian Uniqueness*, 16–17; Schmidt-Leukel, "Exclusivism, Inclusivism, Pluralism," 19–21; Rose, *Pluralism*, 8.

57. Schmidt-Leukel, "Exclusivism, Inclusivism, Pluralism," 19.

58. Rose, *Pluralism*, 8.

59. Although, as Paul Knitter notes, inclusivism represents the majority opinion of mainline Protestantism as well. Knitter, *Introducing Theologies of Religions*, 63. There is even a growing contingency of evangelicals, most notably Clark Pinnock, John Sanders, and Amos Yong, who have begun to develop markedly evangelical or pentecostal versions of inclusivism. See Clark H. Pinnock, *A Wideness in God's Mercy: The Finality of Jesus Christ in a World of Religions* (Grand Rapids, MI: Zondervan, 1992); John Sanders, *No Other Name: An Investigation into the Destiny of the Unevangelized* (Grand Rapids, MI: Eerdmans, 1992); Amos Yong, *Beyond the Impasse: Toward a Pneumatological Theology of Religions* (Grand Rapids, MI: Baker Academic, 2003).

60. See *Nostra Aetate* ("Declaration on the Relationship of the Church to Non-Christian Religions") and *Lumen Gentium* ("Dogmatic Constitution on the Church") in Austin Flannery, ed., *Vatican Council II: Constitutions, Decrees, Declarations* (Northport, NY: Costello, 1996), 569–74, 1–95.

61. Ibid., 571.

62. See Karl Rahner, "Christianity and the Non-Christian Religions," in Plantinga, *Christianity and Plurality*, 288–303.

63. Hick, *A Christian Theology of Religions*, 20.

64. Knitter, *Introducing Theologies of Religions*, 63–79; Knitter, preface, viii; Eck, *Encountering God*, 168, 178–85; Hick, *A Christian Theology of Religions*, 20–23; Terrence W. Tilley et al., *Religious Diversity and the American Experience: A Theological Approach* (New York: Continuum, 2007), 64–73. To this day, most Roman Catholic theologians of religions continue to align themselves with some form of inclusivism. See especially Gavin D'Costa, *The Meeting of Religions and the Trinity* (Maryknoll, NY: Orbis, 2000); Jacques Dupuis, *Toward a Christian Theology of Religious Pluralism* (Maryknoll, NY: Orbis, 1997).

65. Knitter, preface, vii–viii; Rose, *Pluralism*, 8–9.

66. Diana L. Eck, "Dialogue and Method: Reconstructing the Study of Religion," in *A Magic Still Dwells: Comparative Religion in the Postmodern Age*, ed. Kimberley C. Patton and Benjamin C. Ray (Berkeley: University of California Press, 2000), 135.

67. Perry Schmidt-Leukel, *Religious Pluralism and Interreligious Theology: The Gifford Lectures*, extended ed. (Maryknoll, NY: Orbis, 2017), 1.

68. Knitter, *No Other Name?*, 6. For more on the difference between plural*ity* and plural*ism*, see Eck, *Encountering God*, 191.

69. Eck, *Encountering God*, 190–99; Knitter, *No Other Name?*, 6–7, 16–20; Knitter, *Introducing Theologies of Religions*, 1–15.

70. See Knitter, preface, viii–ix; Rose, *Pluralism*, 28–29. More recently, Knitter has gestured toward "the possibility of an interreligious crossing of the Rubicon." People of *all* faiths, he reassuringly remarks, have "found it increasingly difficult to stand before the entire world and claim that theirs was the only or the best religion." Paul F. Knitter, introduction to *The Myth of Religious Superiority*, vii–viii.

71. Knitter, introduction, viii.

72. Schmidt-Leukel, "Pluralisms," 86.

73. Hick, *A Christian Theology of Religions*, ix.

74. See John Hick, *An Interpretation of Religion: Human Responses to the Transcendent* (New Haven, CT: Yale University Press, 1989), 235.

75. Gordon D. Kaufman, *God—Mystery—Diversity: Christian Theology in a Pluralistic World* (Minneapolis: Fortress, 1996), 164.

76. Karl Barth, "The Revelation of God as the Abolition of Religion," in *Attitudes toward Other Religions: Some Christian Interpretations*, ed. Owen C. Thomas (London: SCM Press, 1969), 96–112.

77. Sheila Greeve Davaney, *Divine Power: A Study of Karl Barth and Charles Hartshorne* (Philadelphia: Fortress, 1986), 237–39; Kaufman, *God—Mystery—Diversity*, 18.

78. Robert Cummings Neville, *On the Scope and Truth of Theology: Theology as Symbolic Engagement* (New York: T. and T. Clark, 2006), 16. Emphasis added.

79. Hick, *A Christian Theology of Religions*, 8.

80. Harold A. Netland, *Dissonant Voices: Religious Pluralism and the Question of Truth* (Grand Rapids, MI: William B. Eerdmans, 1991), 151–95, summary of principles on 192–93.

81. Gavin D'Costa, "Whose Objectivity? Which Neutrality? The Doomed Quest for a Neutral Vantage Point from Which to Judge Religions," *Religious Studies* 29, no. 1 (March 1993): 84. Emphasis added.

82. Ibid., 88–89.

83. Ibid., 87–88.

84. Ibid., 81, 89.

85. Netland, *Dissonant Voices*, 261–62.

86. John Hick, "A Pluralist View," in *Four Views on Salvation in a Pluralistic World*, ed. Dennis L. Okholm and Timothy R. Phillips (Grand Rapids, MI: Zondervan, 1996), 43.

87. Kaufman, *God—Mystery—Diversity*, 167–68, 173–74, 177.

88. Gerald Birney Smith, *Current Christian Thinking* (Chicago: University of Chicago Press, 1928), 155–56.

89. Rose, *Pluralism*, 8.

90. Hick, "The Non-absoluteness of Christianity," 22.

91. Eck, *Encountering God*, 184. Or to mention but one of many possible Christian examples, the contemporary Catholic inclusivist, Jacques Dupuis, seeks to move beyond the fulfillment agenda of most classical inclusivisms, where religious others "have at best been considered as provisional 'stepping-stones' for 'things to come,' useful, no doubt, yet transitory by nature and in any event rendered obsolete and abrogated by the advent of the reality to which they pointed or of which they were 'partial anticipations.'" On the contrary, the other religions enjoy "a lasting role and a specific meaning in the overall mystery of divine-human relationships" and even "mediate salvation for their followers." Still, Dupuis upholds "the constitutive uniqueness and universality of Jesus Christ." That is to say, "Christ's risen humanity," and nothing else, "is the guarantee of God's indissoluble union with humankind." As such, non-Christian faiths are construed as "true interventions and authentic manifestations of God in the history of peoples; they form integral parts of one history of salvation that culminates in the Jesus Christ–event." Dupuis, *Toward a Christian Theology of Religious Pluralism*, 211, 303, 315, 387. See also Knitter, *Introducing Theologies of Religions*, 89–93; Rose, *Pluralism*, 54–56.

92. Gordon D. Kaufman, "Religious Diversity, Historical Consciousness, and Christian Theology," in Hick and Knitter, *The Myth of Christian Uniqueness*, 4–5, 8, 14.

93. Eck, *Encountering God*, 184.

94. Langdon Gilkey, "Plurality and Its Theological Implications," in Hick and Knitter, *The Myth of Christian Uniqueness*, 42.

95. See Knitter, *Introducing Theologies of Religions*, 103.

96. Hick, *A Christian Theology of Religions*, 22.

97. Kaufman, *God—Mystery—Diversity*, 18.

98. Ibid., 12.

99. Davaney, *Pragmatic Historicism*, 20, 25, 172.

100. See ibid., 171–72.

101. Kaufman, *God—Mystery—Diversity*, 164.

102. Kaufman, "Religious Diversity, Historical Consciousness, and Christian Theology," 4.

103. For my review of this important book, see Demian Wheeler, review of *Pluralism: The Future of Religion*, by Kenneth Rose, *American Journal of Theology and Philosophy* 38, no. 2–3 (May–September 2017): 238–44.

104. Rose, *Pluralism*, 68, 1.

105. Ibid., 2, 5, 68.

106. Ibid., 2–3, 8–10, 13, 50, 65–70, 73–82.

107. Ibid., 2–4, 6–7, 25–30, 56, 68, 145.

108. Rose condenses the classical tripolar typology into a binary one. In this taxonomy, exclusivism and inclusivism, as two sides of the same coin, are brought together under the broader umbrella term "particularism," which treats one particular

religion as superior, universal, and unsurpassable (i.e., as the replacement or the fulfillment of the others), and pluralism is defined as "nonparticularism," which "holds that no contextually shaped body of religious teachings can justify a claim that it is final, normative, and universally binding." Ibid., 8. While I find his simplified classification economic and helpful, I prefer the labels "absolutism" and "nonabsolutism" to "particularism" and "nonparticularism," since pragmatic historicism (as I will soon show) makes possible a particularist theology of religions that is genuinely pluralistic (i.e., nonabsolutist—or nonparticularistic in Rose's sense).

109. Ibid., 147.

110. Hick famously drew the following analogy. Like Ptolemaic astronomers who, in the face of increasing evidence for a heliocentric picture of the universe, tried to save geocentricity by positing smaller planetary orbits (i.e., epicycles) "revolving with their centres on the original circles," Christian inclusivists, when confronted with members of other religions, attempt to preserve the finality of Christianity by adding "an epicycle of theory to the effect that although they are consciously adherents of a different faith, nevertheless they may unconsciously or implicitly be Christians." Hick surmised that these sorts of epicyclical maneuvers—whether astronomical or theological—will likely appear "artificial, implausible and unconvincing" to "anyone who is not firmly committed to the original dogma." John Hick, *God and the Universe of Faiths: Essays in the Philosophy of Religion* (London: Macmillan, 1973), 124–25.

111. Rose, *Pluralism*, 2–4, 10, 26, 31, 46–47, 51–52, 54, 56–57, 66, 70, 143–44, 147.

112. Namely, Kaufman, "Religious Diversity, Historical Consciousness, and Christian Theology."

113. Knitter, preface, vii–viii.

114. The U-turn in the theology of religions began as early as 1990, the year Gavin D'Costa released a collection of essays entitled, *Christian Uniqueness Reconsidered: The Myth of a Pluralistic Theology of Religions*. This book served as a kind of counter-volume to Hick and Knitter's earlier anthology. As D'Costa states in the preface, the different contributors—ranging from theologians and philosophers to indologists, sociologists, and hermeneutic specialists—are "united by their varying degrees of dissatisfaction at the pluralist project as so defined by *The Myth of Christian Uniqueness*" as well as by their shared desire "to affirm the importance and significance of Christian uniqueness." Gavin D'Costa, preface to *Christian Uniqueness Reconsidered: The Myth of a Pluralistic Theology of Religions* (Maryknoll, NY: Orbis, 1990), x.

115. Rose, *Pluralism*, 1, 5, 25–29, 35, 45–46, quote on 45. See also Kenneth Rose, "Toward an Apophatic Pluralism: Beyond Confessionalism, Epicyclism, and Inclusivism in Theology of Religions," *Journal of Ecumenical Studies* 46, no. 1 (Winter 2011): 67–75.

116. Terrence Tilley employs the appellation "particularism" to describe the stance taken by these thinkers. See Tilley et al., *Religious Diversity and the American Experience*, chs. 7 and 8.

117. Rose, *Pluralism*, 5, 25–27, 46.

118. Kenneth Surin, "A 'Politics of Speech': Religious Pluralism in the Age of the McDonald's Hamburger," in D'Costa, *Christian Uniqueness Reconsidered*, 200, 204.

119. See the essays "The Copernican Revolution in Theology" and "The New Map of the Universe of Faiths" in Hick, *God and the Universe of Faiths*, 120–47.

120. Knitter, *No Other Name?*, 165–67.

121. Hick, *God Has Many Names*, 51–53; Knitter, *Introducing Theologies of Religions*, 114.

122. Hick, *An Interpretation of Religion*, 235–36.

123. John Hick, "The Next Step beyond Dialogue," in Knitter, *The Myth of Religious Superiority*, 12.

124. Hick, *A Christian Theology of Religions*, 11–16.

125. Ibid., 16–23, 106–07.

126. Hick, *An Interpretation of Religion*, 279.

127. Ibid., 234.

128. Hick, "The Next Step beyond Dialogue," 11.

129. Hick, *An Interpretation of Religion*, 233–96; Hick, *A Christian Theology of Religions*, 23–30, 51–52, 65, 67–69; Knitter, *Introducing Theologies of Religions*, 115–17.

130. See Knitter, *Introducing Theologies of Religions*, 134–48.

131. Knitter, "Toward a Liberation Theology of Religions," 178–90. Emphasis removed.

132. Knitter recently renamed pluralism "mutualism," chiefly because pluralists, more than anything else, endeavor to forge "relationships of mutuality" between the religions. Paul F. Knitter, "Is the Pluralist Model a Western Imposition? A Response in Five Voices," in *The Myth of Religious Superiority*, 33. See Knitter, *Introducing Theologies of Religions*, pt. 3.

133. J. A. DiNoia, "Pluralist Theology of Religions: Pluralistic or Non-pluralistic?," in D'Costa, *Christian Uniqueness Reconsidered*, 119–34; DiNoia, *The Diversity of Religions: A Christian Perspective* (Washington, DC: Catholic University of America Press, 1992), 48–49, 51–53.

134. Thatamanil, "God as Ground, Contingency, and Relation," 242.

135. S. Mark Heim, *Salvations: Truth and Difference in Religion* (Maryknoll, NY: Orbis, 1995), 23–43.

136. Ibid., 6.

137. Ibid., 83–98, 115–16, 195–210.

138. Ibid., 195, 206.

139. Ibid., 102.

140. This is why Knitter refers to particularism as "the acceptance model." See Knitter, *Introducing Theologies of Religions*, pt. 4.

141. Ibid., 173–78; Peter C. Phan, *Being Religious Interreligiously: Asian Perspectives on Interfaith Dialogue* (Maryknoll, NY: Orbis, 2004), xvii–xx; Tilley et al., *Religious Diversity and the American Experience*, 110–24.

142. Knitter, *Introducing Theologies of Religions*, 178–83.

143. George A. Lindbeck, *The Nature of Doctrine: Religion and Theology in a Postliberal Age* (Philadelphia: Westminster Press, 1984), 31, 33, 37, 39, 41.

144. Ibid., 40. Lindbeck's viewpoint lines up with the "contextualist" approach within the philosophy of mysticism. Steven Katz and Wayne Proudfoot, for instance, have both argued that all experiences, including mystical encounters, are conditioned and mediated by the epistemic categories, hermeneutical frameworks, linguistic structures, moral predispositions, historical backgrounds, religious beliefs, and cultural traditions of the experiencer and are, for that reason, multifarious, variegated, and particular. See Steven T. Katz, "Language, Epistemology, and Mysticism," in *Mysticism and Philosophical Analysis*, ed. Steven T. Katz (New York: Oxford University Press, 1978), 22–74; Katz, "The 'Conservative' Character of Mystical Experience," in *Mysticism and Religious Traditions*, ed. Steven T. Katz (Oxford: Oxford University Press, 1983), 3–60; Wayne Proudfoot, *Religious Experience* (Berkeley: University of California Press, 1985), 119–54 and passim.

145. See Stephen Kaplan, *Different Paths, Different Summits: A Model for Religious Pluralism* (Lanham, MD: Rowman and Littlefield, 2002).

146. Heim, *Salvations*, 4–10, 129–31, 211–21; S. Mark Heim, *The Depth of the Riches: A Trinitarian Theology of Religious Ends* (Grand Rapids, MI: William B. Eerdmans, 2001), 1–45.

147. Heim, *The Depth of the Riches*, 2.

148. See Sheila Greeve Davaney, "Rethinking Theology and Religious Studies," in *Religious Studies, Theology, and the University: Conflicting Maps, Changing Terrain*, ed. Linell E. Cady and Delwin Brown (Albany: State University of New York Press, 2002), 147; Davaney, *Historicism*, 159.

149. Kaufman, *God—Mystery—Diversity*, 189–90. Kaufman accuses Hick of playing down the significance of difference, of advancing a paradoxically "monolithic" framework which "takes up into itself *all* religious conceptions, however diverse," and presumes that the faiths "all come down to *essentially the same thing*" (225n2).

150. See Heim, *The Depth of the Riches*, 38.

151. Rose, *Pluralism*, 33.

152. Rose, "Toward an Apophatic Pluralism" 69; Rose, *Pluralism*, 5, 27, 45.

153. DiNoia, "Pluralist Theology of Religions," 119–24. See also DiNoia, *The Diversity of Religions*, 49–50, 75–82.

154. DiNoia, *The Diversity of Religions*, 49–50.

155. Paul J. Griffiths, "The Properly Christian Response to Religious Plurality," *Anglican Theological Review* 79, no. 1 (Winter 1997): 3–26.

156. Ibid., 13–26.

157. Heim, *The Depth of the Riches*, 29, 30.

158. Heim, *Salvations*, 3, 124–60, 219–29; Heim, *The Depth of the Riches*, 2, 6, 24, 27, 29, 31–32, 43–44.

159. See Kiblinger, "Relating Theology of Religions and Comparative Theology," 28; Rose, *Pluralism*, 46–47.

160. Lindbeck, *The Nature of Doctrine*, 61, 114–15, 57.

161. DiNoia, *The Diversity of Religions*, 47–48, 94–108, quotes on 48 and 107.

162. Gavin D'Costa, *Christianity and World Religions: Disputed Questions in the Theology of Religions* (Malden, MA: Wiley-Blackwell, 2009), 165–80, 188–94. See Rose, "Toward an Apophatic Pluralism," 70; Rose, *Pluralism*, 51–52.

163. Heim, *The Depth of the Riches*, 8–9.

164. S. Mark Heim, "God's Diversity: A Trinitarian View of Religious Pluralism," *Christian Century* 118, no. 3 (January 24, 2001): 14–18, quotes on 14–15, 18. See also Heim, *The Depth of the Riches*, pt. 3.

165. Lindbeck, *The Nature of Doctrine*, 118.

166. Griffiths, "The Properly Christian Response to Religious Plurality," 14–15.

167. This is one of John Thatamanil's major objections to Heim's view and other "extant trinitarian approaches." Thatamanil, "God as Ground, Contingency, and Relation," 244.

168. Rose, *Pluralism*, 25, 45; Rose, "Toward an Apophatic Pluralism," 69–71.

169. Heim, "God's Diversity," 18.

170. Heim, *The Depth of the Riches*, 2, 24, 30, 32, 43–44.

171. Masuzawa, *The Invention of World Religions*, 325.

172. See, for example, Hick, *An Interpretation of Religion*, 233–51.

173. See Troeltsch, "The Place of Christianity among the World Religions," 219–22. Emphasis added.

174. Rose, *Pluralism*, 33–34, 66. Pluralists have long seen a "causal link" between claims to possess the absolute truth, the highest revelation, the only way, the ultimate enlightenment, the divine word, the holy land, and so on, and instances of religious injustice and violence (e.g., colonialism, the crusades, witch burnings, anti-Semitism, suicide bombings, the caste system). See Knitter, introduction, ix; Hick, "The Non-absoluteness of Christianity," 16–20, 29–30. In the sobering words of Hick: "We are acutely aware that throughout history almost all human conflicts have been validated and intensified by a religious sanction. God has been claimed to be on both sides of every war. This has been possible because each of the great world faiths has either assumed or asserted its own unique superiority as the one and only true faith and path to the highest good. . . . These exclusive claims to absolute truth have exacerbated the division of the human community into rival groups, and have repeatedly been invoked in support of oppression, slavery, conquest, and exploitation." Quoted in Knitter, introduction, x.

175. Heim, *Salvations*, 153, 227.

176. See Knitter, *Introducing Theologies of Religions*, 233–34. Heim appears to concede this point in regards to ultimacy: "Whether we are theists or not, we all tend to participate in a monotheistic consciousness: there is only one religious ultimate." Heim, *The Depth of the Riches*, 33.

177. Knitter, *Introducing Theologies of Religions*, 234.

178. Heim, *Salvations*, 141–42, 212.

179. Rose, *Pluralism*, 46.

180. Knitter, *Introducing Theologies of Religions*, 233–35.

181. Kaufman, "Religious Diversity, Historical Consciousness, and Christian Theology," 5–6, 15n2.

182. Ibid., 8.

183. Ibid., 5–13; Kaufman, *God—Mystery—Diversity*, 55–65.

184. Heim, *The Depth of the Riches*, 37, 42.

185. See Heim, *Salvations*, 219–29.

186. Ibid., 226.

187. Davaney, *Pragmatic Historicism*, 25.

188. David Ray Griffin, "Religious Pluralism: Generic, Identist, and Deep," in *Deep Religious Pluralism*, ed. David Ray Griffin (Louisville: Westminster John Knox Press, 2005), 24, 3.

189. Ibid., 3–38.

190. Delwin Brown, "History, Country, Academy, and God: On the Role of the Religious Critic," *American Journal of Theology and Philosophy* 16, no. 1 (January 1995): 86.

191. Knitter, introduction, xi.

192. Paul F. Knitter, "Key Questions for a Theology of Religions," *Horizons* 17, no. 1 (Spring 1990): 93–94.

193. Knitter, "Is the Pluralist Model a Western Imposition?," 39.

194. The historicizing and naturalizing of religion in pragmatic historicism certainly predates Kaufman, stretching back to the liberal theologians of the early Chicago school. See, for example, George Burman Foster, *The Function of Religion in Man's Struggle for Existence* (Chicago: University of Chicago Press, 1909), 35, 44–60, 63, 79–88, 90–91; Shirley Jackson Case, *The Christian Philosophy of History* (Chicago: University of Chicago Press, 1943), 163–76. Here, I will concentrate exclusively on Kaufman's historicist and naturalistic theory of the origins and function of human religiousness, mainly because it takes up and expands upon most of the key claims of these earlier historicists and, even more, because it explicitly engages the issue of religious pluralism. I will, however, revisit the religious historicism, naturalism, and humanism of the early Chicago schoolers in later chapters.

195. Kaufman, *God—Mystery—Diversity*, 56, 74–75, 172–73, 189–90.

196. Gordon D. Kaufman, *In Face of Mystery: A Constructive Theology* (Cambridge, MA: Harvard University Press, 1993), 477n3. See Peter Berger, *The Sacred*

Canopy: Elements of a Sociological Theory of Religion (New York: Anchor, 1967); Clifford Geertz, *The Interpretation of Cultures* (New York: Basic Books, 1973), 87–125.

197. Kaufman, *In Face of Mystery*, 35–37, 225–34; Kaufman, *God—Mystery—Diversity*, 6, 19, 35–37, 57–59, 64, 173, 191–95.

198. Kaufman, *In Face of Mystery*, 232.

199. Kaufman, *God—Mystery—Diversity*, 190.

200. Even though this theory of religion stems from Kaufman, it harkens back to John Dewey's conception of "the religious." Dewey rebutted any notion of "religion in the singular." And, as for the *religions*, "the differences among them are so great and so shocking that any common element that can be extracted is meaningless." There is, though, a ubiquitous dimension of human experience that the *adjective* "religious" sufficiently describes. The "religious," states Dewey, does not capture a distinctive, *sui generis* experience that "can exist by itself" (i.e., apart from aesthetic, political, moral, or scientific modes of existence) or "validate a belief in some special kind of object" (e.g., God), but connotes a *quality of ordinary human experience* in which the self seeks to cultivate "a sense of an extensive and underlying whole," a "comprehensive attitude" that engenders "an orientation" or "a better, deeper, and enduring adjustment in life." See John Dewey, *A Common Faith* (New Haven, CT: Yale University Press, 1934), 8–23; Dewey, *Art as Experience* (New York: Perigee, 1934), 194–95.

201. See Kaufman, *God—Mystery—Diversity*, 172–73, 224n1.

202. Working within a Whiteheadian philosophical scheme, Cobb and Griffin conjecture that there are three ultimates: (1) being itself (what Whitehead calls "creativity" and religions have called Emptiness, Dharmakaya, Nirguna Brahman, the Godhead, etc.); (2) the supreme being (what Whitehead calls "God" and religions have called Yahweh, Saguna Brahman, Christ, Allah, Ishvara, Amida Buddha, etc.); and (3) the universe (what Whitehead calls "the world" or "the totality of things" and religions have called the sacred cosmos, etc.). See Griffin, "John Cobb's Whiteheadian Complementary Pluralism," 44–51.

203. Thatamanil, "God as Ground, Contingency, and Relation," 243.

204. Hick, *A Christian Theology of Religions*, 69. Emphasis added.

205. Heim, *The Depth of the Riches*, 34. See also Heim, *Salvations*, 137. Schmidt-Leukel agrees with Thatamanil, Hick, and Heim: "The idea of several 'ultimates' seems to be to a significant extent counterintuitive. If 'ultimate reality' refers to an 'unlimited' reality or a reality 'greater than anything else,' it is even logically impossible that more than one such reality exists. For if there were a second 'ultimate,' both would 'limit' each other and none of them would be 'greater than anything else.'" Schmidt-Leukel, "Pluralisms," 97.

206. Thatamanil, "God as Ground, Contingency, and Relation," 244; Heim, *The Depth of the Riches*, 35–36.

207. Heim, *The Depth of the Riches*, 36.

208. Hick, *An Interpretation of Religion*, 242.

209. See, for instance, Hick, *A Christian Theology of Religions*, 41.

210. Thatamanil, "God as Ground, Contingency, and Relation," 244; Heim, *The Depth of the Riches*, 39, 243–69; Heim, *Salvations*, 163–71. Before Heim and Thatamanil, Raimundo (Raimon) Panikkar famously insisted that divine reality is *itself* pluralistic, diverse, and multiaspected. Raimundo Panikkar, "The Jordan, the Tiber, and the Ganges: Three Kairological Moments of Christic Self-consciousness," in Hick and Knitter, *The Myth of Christian Uniqueness*, 109; Panikkar, *The Unknown Christ of Hinduism: Towards an Ecumenical Christophany* (Maryknoll, NY: Orbis, 1981), 19. See also Knitter, *Introducing Theologies of Religions*, 128–30.

211. See Thatamanil, "God as Ground, Contingency, and Relation," 245–57. Thatamanil justly criticizes Heim for presupposing the superiority of Christianity: "Only Christians have arrived at a trinitarian vision whereas other traditions, however legitimate, manage to access only one dimension of the divine life" (245). Regardless, is not Thatamanil subject to the same critique (even if to a lesser degree)? Although the Christian faith has "a long history of erring on the side of personalism under the weight of contingency" (254), and every religion has access to all three aspects of the trinity (246), Christianity still has a metaphysical advantage over the other religions since it is the only tradition that speaks of ultimate reality as triune. Does not the very appeal to a trinity ipso facto privilege Christianity? Furthermore, the polydoxic threefold, Thatamanil admits, is "richly resonant" with traditional trinitarianism (i.e., father, son/logos, and spirit roughly approximate ground, particularity, and relation), which again seems to give Christians a head start (albeit not a position of supremacy) when speaking of ultimacy (246). Do non-Christian religions possess equivalent built-in categories for just as seamlessly registering all three facets of this trinity? If not, are they not in some sense inferior?

212. Heim, *The Depth of the Riches*, 32, 34.

213. Heim, "God's Diversity," 18. Emphasis added.

214. Thatamanil, "God as Ground, Contingency, and Relation," 244. As I stated earlier, Heim himself concedes that Buddhists, Hindus, Muslims, Daoists, and so on, would never themselves comprehend their ultimates as features of Christianity's triune God. See Heim, "God's Diversity," 18.

215. Hick, *An Interpretation of Religion*, 234–35; Hick, *A Christian Theology of Religions*, 43, 51–53.

216. See Shailer Mathews, *The Growth of the Idea of God* (New York: Macmillan, 1931).

217. Sallie McFague, *Metaphorical Theology: Models of God in Religious Language* (Philadelphia: Fortress, 1982), vii, 1, 16–17, 26–28, 32–42; McFague, *Models of God: Theology for an Ecological, Nuclear Age* (Philadelphia: Fortress, 1987), xi–xii, 21–23, 31–39.

218. See William Dean, *The Religious Critic in American Culture* (Albany: State University of New York Press, 1994), 131–39; Dean, *The American Spiritual*

Culture: And the Invention of Jazz, Football, and the Movies (New York: Continuum, 2002), 70–86.

219. See Gordon D. Kaufman, *An Essay on Theological Method*, 3rd ed. (Atlanta: Scholars Press, 1995), ix, 25–49; Kaufman, *In Face of Mystery*, ix, 3–17, 39–40.

220. See Gordon D. Kaufman, "Empirical Realism in Theology: An Examination of Some Themes in Meland and Loomer," in *New Essays in Religious Naturalism*, ed. W. Creighton Peden and Larry E. Axel (Macon, GA: Mercer University Press, 1993), 135–51.

221. Hick, *A Christian Theology of Religions*, 69.

222. Of course, in a historicist perspective, even if that reality is ontologically superhuman and noncultural, it is known and experienced through, and even shaped by, linguistically and culturally constituted patterns of human meaning.

223. See William Dean, *History Making History: The New Historicism in American Religious Thought* (Albany: State University of New York Press, 1988), 124–26, 140–42.

224. William James, *The Varieties of Religious Experience: A Study in Human Nature* (New York: Penguin, 1902), 508–15; Dewey, *A Common Faith*, 19; Case, *The Christian Philosophy of History*, 210; Gordon D. Kaufman, *In the Beginning . . . Creativity* (Minneapolis: Fortress, 2004), ix–x; Dean, *The American Spiritual Culture*, 87–110.

225. See Hick, *A Christian Theology of Religions*, 67–69, 102–3; Hick, *An Interpretation of Religion*, 1, 111–18.

226. I would actually postulate an ontological *fourfold*—a *quaternity*, as it were. To "being, contingent being, and being in relation," one might add *nonbeing*. Nonbeing alludes to the wonderment of *finitude*, of the fact that being, both in its contingent singularity and its relational depth, is impermanent, transitory, and vulnerable, spiraling, inexorably, toward death, nonexistence, oblivion, entropy, nothingness—what Paul Tillich dubbed "the abyss." An array of theological symbols across the traditions—for example, the Hindu god Shiva, the ambiguous, capricious, and often destructive deity of the Hebrew scriptures, the Christian doctrine of Hell—appear to be attuned to this feature of reality, as is the variant of religious naturalism that I will lay out in chapter 8.

227. See Thatamanil, "God as Ground, Contingency, and Relation," 245–55.

228. Rose, *Pluralism*, 36n3.

229. Gavin D'Costa, "The Impossibility of a Pluralist View of Religions," *Religious Studies* 32, no. 2 (June 1996): 229, 232, 226.

230. D'Costa, *Christianity and World Religions*, 10, 18.

231. Aimee Upjohn Light, "Harris, Hick, and the Demise of the Pluralist Hypothesis," *Journal of Ecumenical Studies* 44, no. 3 (Summer 2009): 468.

232. Heim, *Salvations*, 102.

233. Ibid., 16, 29–30, 99–126, 141–43. A similar allegation is made by Kenneth Surin. See Surin, "A 'Politics of Speech.'"

234. S. Wesley Ariarajah, "Power, Politics, and Plurality: The Struggles of the World Council of Churches to Deal with Religious Plurality," in Knitter, *The Myth of Religious Superiority*, 191.

235. Rose, *Pluralism*, 5, 25–27, 36–37nn3–8.

236. Ibid., 3–4, 25–26. As it happens, Rose both acknowledges and supports the *cataphatic* dimension of pluralism as well, namely, "the reasonable and philosophically noncontroversial attempt to discover common intentions in human religious movements, which . . . can be filled out through comparative study and contemplative practice." See Rose, "Toward an Apophatic Pluralism," 68–69, 70–71, quote on 70. Pragmatic historicists, I showed earlier, also take up the pluralist mantle of discovering "common intentions" across religious traditions (e.g., the quest for direction and meaning in face of the mystery and vicissitudes of existence, the imaginative construction of unifying worldviews). I even suggested that pragmatic historicism can (and should) adopt a nonperennialistically, pluralistically, and naturalistically reconfigured version of Hick's most debatable speculative claim—that is, that the various faiths are historically conditioned responses to "the Real." In the next chapter, I will contend that the substantive aim of Knitter's pluralist theology of religions—the building of an "ethical-practical bridge" between the traditions—is not just defensible, but obligatory.

237. Knitter, introduction, xi. Emphasis removed.

238. Rose, *Pluralism*, 89–138, quotes on 99–100, 128, 130.

239. Quoted in Hick, *An Interpretation of Religion*, 238.

240. Rose, *Pluralism*, 145, 28.

241. Schmidt-Leukel, "Pluralisms," 94, 101.

242. Ibid., 88–89.

243. Hick, *An Interpretation of Religion*, 236–39; Hick, *A Christian Theology of Religions*, 57–58; Rose, *Pluralism*, 28, 69, 145, 161; Schmidt-Leukel, "Pluralisms," 93.

244. D'Costa, *Christianity and World Religions*, 18.

245. Rose, *Pluralism*, 127, 82, 28. Emphasis added.

246. See especially Lindbeck, *The Nature of Doctrine*, 73–96.

247. Griffiths, "The Properly Christian Response to Religious Plurality," 8–9, 13–16. Lindbeck also equates the "permanent" and "normative" nucleus of the Christian faith with the "selfsame" story found in the canonical scriptures, the narrative "that stretches from creation to eschaton and culminates in Jesus' passion and resurrection." Lindbeck, *The Nature of Doctrine*, 84.

248. Paul J. Griffiths, "The Uniqueness of Christian Doctrine Defended," in D'Costa, *Christian Uniqueness Reconsidered*, 170.

249. Ibid., 158.

250. Knitter, *Introducing Theologies of Religions*, 232. Emphasis added.

251. A principle that Lindbeck (wrongly) takes to be "unconditionally and permanently necessary to mainstream Christian identity." Lindbeck, *The Nature of Doctrine*, 96.

252. Knitter, *Introducing Theologies of Religions*, 233.

253. Knitter, introduction, vii, x.

254. Paul F. Knitter, *Jesus and the Other Names: Christian Mission and Global Responsibility* (Maryknoll, NY: Orbis, 1996), 67–83. Hick also avers that accepting the pluralist vision entails making substantial revisions to traditional christological dogma. In Hick's view, there is an inextricable link between the notion that Christianity is the one true divinely established religion, intended to supersede all the others, and the belief that Christ is literally God incarnate. Consequently, Hick proceeds to reimagine the incarnation and divinity of Jesus as *metaphors* of his openness and obedience to the Spirit. This "inspiration christology" (which, although suppressed by Christendom, is implicit in the New Testament) sees Jesus as a "spiritual leader" and "prophet," an inspirational "model" for incarnating "the divine purpose on earth." In that sense, incarnation "has occurred and is occurring in many different ways and degrees in many different persons." Hick, "A Pluralist View," 51–59; Hick, "The Non-absoluteness of Christianity," 30–32. See also John Hick, *The Metaphor of God Incarnate: Christology in a Pluralistic Age* (Louisville: Westminster John Knox Press, 1993). Incidentally, Hick and Knitter are prefigured by Troeltsch. For Troeltsch, the fact that there is "an infinite plurality of spiritual worlds," all of which have "their own redeemers and paradigmatic figures," renders it "impossible to deify Jesus and to assign him an absolutely central position." Foreshadowing Hick, Troeltsch placed the christological emphasis on the "inspiration," "impact," and "great example" of Jesus and on the "influence" of his "God-consciousness." See Troeltsch, "On the Possibility of a Liberal Christianity," 347–49; Ernst Troeltsch, "The Significance of the Historical Existence of Jesus for Faith," in *Writings on Theology and Religion*, ed. Robert Morgan and Michael Pye (Louisville: Westminster John Knox Press, 1977), 182–207; Troeltsch, *The Christian Faith*, 24–25, 76, 85–107.

255. Heim, *Salvations*, 105–6, 124, 138, 141–42; Heim, *The Depth of the Riches*, 32. Although to the criticism that pluralism is "the elaboration of a particular perspective," Hick retorts, "Of course it is; and so is every other theory about anything!" Hick, *A Christian Theology of Religions*, 50.

256. Hick, *A Christian Theology of Religions*, 40–50, quote on 48. Emphasis added.

257. See Heim, *The Depth of the Riches*, 30, 32, 9; Hick, *An Interpretation of Religion*, 242, 249.

258. Hick, *A Christian Theology of Religions*, 50.

259. Troeltsch, "Christianity and the History of Religion," 77.

Chapter 4

1. The phrase "being religious interreligiously" comes from the title of one of Peter Phan's most influential books. See Peter C. Phan, *Being Religious Interreligiously: Asian Perspectives on Interfaith Dialogue* (Maryknoll, NY: Orbis, 2004).

2. Perry Schmidt-Leukel, "Pluralisms: How to Appreciate Religious Diversity Theologically," in *Christian Approaches to Other Faiths*, ed. Alan Race and Paul M. Hedges (London: SCM Press, 2008), 102.

3. See George A. Lindbeck, *The Nature of Doctrine: Religion and Theology in a Postliberal Age* (Philadelphia: Westminster Press, 1984), 112–35; Lindbeck, "The Gospel's Uniqueness: Election and Untranslatability," *Modern Theology* 13, no. 4 (October 1997): 426–34, 440.

4. Paul J. Griffiths, "The Properly Christian Response to Religious Plurality," *Anglican Theological Review* 79, no. 1 (Winter 1997): 17.

5. Lindbeck, "The Gospel's Uniqueness," 426–27.

6. Ernst Troeltsch, "The Place of Christianity among the World Religions," in *Christianity and Plurality: Classic and Contemporary Readings*, ed. Richard J. Plantinga (Oxford: Blackwell, 1999), 220. Emphasis added.

7. Sheila Greeve Davaney, *Historicism: The Once and Future Challenge for Theology* (Minneapolis: Fortress, 2006), 163.

8. Lindbeck, *The Nature of Doctrine*, 53–55.

9. Paul F. Knitter, *Introducing Theologies of Religions* (Maryknoll, NY: Orbis, 2002), 224–25.

10. Griffiths, "The Properly Christian Response to Religious Plurality," 19.

11. Lindbeck, *The Nature of Doctrine*, 61–62. Emphasis added. For example, Christians may "encourage Marxists to become better Marxists, Jews and Muslims to become better Jews and Muslims, and Buddhists to become better Buddhists" (54).

12. J. A. DiNoia, *The Diversity of Religions: A Christian Perspective* (Washington, DC: Catholic University of America Press, 1992), 31. Emphasis added.

13. Terrence W. Tilley et al., *Religious Diversity and the American Experience: A Theological Approach* (New York: Continuum, 2007), 118. Emphasis added.

14. "Other religions have resources for speaking truths and referring to realities, even highly important truths and realities, of which Christianity as yet knows nothing and by which it could be greatly enriched." Lindbeck, *The Nature of Doctrine*, 61.

15. Griffiths, "The Properly Christian Response to Religious Plurality," 19–21.

16. Paul J. Griffiths, *An Apology for Apologetics: A Study in the Logic of Interreligious Dialogue* (Eugene, OR: Wipf and Stock, 1991), xii.

17. Paul J. Griffiths, "Why We Need Interreligious Polemics," *First Things* 44 (June–July 1994): 31–37; Knitter, *Introducing Theologies of Religions*, 185–87. See also Griffiths, *An Apology for Apologetics*.

18. Sheila Greeve Davaney, *Pragmatic Historicism: A Theology for the Twenty-First Century* (Albany: State University of New York Press, 2000), 171.

19. Ibid., 172.

20. Ibid.; Gordon D. Kaufman, "Religious Diversity, Historical Consciousness, and Christian Theology," in *The Myth of Christian Uniqueness: Toward a Pluralistic Theology of Religions*, ed. John Hick and Paul F. Knitter (Maryknoll, NY: Orbis, 1987), 12.

21. See Raimon Panikkar, *The Intrareligious Dialogue*, rev. ed. (New York: Paulist Press, 1999), xviii–xix.

22. Kaufman, "Religious Diversity, Historical Consciousness, and Christian Theology," 12–14.

23. Gordon D. Kaufman, *God—Mystery—Diversity: Christian Theology in a Pluralistic World* (Minneapolis: Fortress, 1996), 202–3; Davaney, *Pragmatic Historicism*, 172; Davaney, *Historicism*, 163.

24. Catherine Cornille, *The Im-possibility of Interreligious Dialogue* (New York: Herder and Herder, 2008), 4. Yet, despite her "pluralist" and "apophatic sense of epistemological and theological modesty," Cornille, Kenneth Rose regretfully notices, "throws a backward glance toward muted forms of inclusivism." Kenneth Rose, *Pluralism: The Future of Religion* (New York: Bloomsbury, 2013), 50. Indeed, for Cornille, it is "a matter of hermeneutical necessity" that "religions judge the truth of the other, either implicitly or explicitly, on the basis of their own particular worldview and norms." What is more, "commitment to the truth of one religion logically excludes recognition of the equal truth of others." Cornille, *The Im-possibility of Interreligious Dialogue*, 79, 84.

25. Davaney, *Pragmatic Historicism*, 171.

26. See Griffiths, "Why We Need Interreligious Polemics," 31–37.

27. Davaney, *Historicism*, 163.

28. Griffiths, "Why We Need Interreligious Polemics," 36.

29. Knitter, *Introducing Theologies of Religions*, 187. See also Lindbeck, "The Gospel's Uniqueness," 430.

30. Davaney, *Historicism*, 163. Emphasis added.

31. Such a view seems to necessarily follow from the particularist maxim that a religion "cannot be encompassed" but "can only encompass." Griffiths, "Why We Need Interreligious Polemics," 35.

32. Kaufman, *God—Mystery—Diversity*, 196–203.

33. Ibid., 201.

34. A. Bagus Laksana, "Comparative Theology: Between Identity and Alterity," in *The New Comparative Theology: Interreligious Insights from the Next Generation*, ed. Francis X. Clooney (London: T. and T. Clark, 2010), 18.

35. Francis X. Clooney, *Comparative Theology: Deep Learning across Religious Borders* (Malden, MA: Wiley-Blackwell, 2010), 11.

36. Ibid., 9–11, 43, 47, 57–60, 64, 67; James L. Fredericks, *Faith among Faiths: Christian Theology and Non-Christian Religions* (New York: Paulist Press, 1999), 167–71; Fredericks, introduction, to Clooney, *The New Comparative Theology*, ix–xix.

37. Clooney, *Comparative Theology*, 60.

38. Fredericks, *Faith among Faiths: Christian Theology and Non-Christian Religions*, 9.

39. Ibid., 165–66; Fredericks, introduction, xiii–xv.

40. Francis X. Clooney, "Response," in *The New Comparative Theology: Interreligious Insights from the Next Generation*, 196. See also Clooney, *Comparative Theology*, 14–15.

41. For example, Kaufman's understanding of religious plurality was informed, funded, and deepened by a sustained dialogue with Japanese and American Buddhists. See Kaufman, *God—Mystery—Diversity*, pt. 3.

42. See Clooney, *Comparative Theology*, 15; Fredericks, *Faith among Faiths*, 8–11, 165–66.

43. Kristin Beise Kiblinger, "Relating Theology of Religions and Comparative Theology," in Clooney, *The New Comparative Theology*, 21–23, 25–28, 31.

44. Stephen J. Duffy, "A Theology of Religions and/or a Comparative Theology?," *Horizons* 26, no. 1 (1999): 107.

45. Knitter, *Introducing Theologies of Religions*, 235.

46. Kiblinger, "Relating Theology of Religions and Comparative Theology," 29.

47. Ibid., 22, 24–25, 28–33, 42.

48. Clooney, *Comparative Theology*, 14.

49. Kiblinger, "Relating Theology of Religions and Comparative Theology," 37–38.

50. In his latest book, Perry Schmidt-Leukel shows that a pluralistic understanding of religious diversity opens up the prospect of *doing theology interreligiously*. As he boldly remarks in the first chapter: "If religiously relevant truth is understood as being no longer confined to one's own religion, any theological reflection that looks for truth can no longer be satisfied with drawing only on the sources of one's own religious tradition. . . . In the future it will also draw on other religions when reflecting on the major questions of human life and will reconsider, and further develop, the answers that have been given in one's own tradition in a fresh comparative light. It will also reflect on one's own tradition in order to see what possible contribution might be made to the issues on the agenda of a global interreligious theological inquiry." Perry Schmidt-Leukel, *Religious Pluralism and Interreligious Theology: The Gifford Lectures*, extended ed. (Maryknoll, NY: Orbis, 2017), 8.

51. John J. Thatamanil, "God as Ground, Contingency, and Relation: Trinitarian Polydoxy and Religious Diversity," in *Polydoxy: Theology of Multiplicity and Relation*, ed. Catherine Keller and Laurel C. Schneider (London: Routledge, 2011), 245.

52. John J. Thatamanil, *The Immanent Divine: God, Creation, and the Human Predicament* (Minneapolis: Fortress, 2006), 1–26, 169–207, quotes on 21–23.

53. Ibid., xii–xiii, 9, 24.

54. Fredericks asserts that "the inclusivist (or fulfillment) theology model is the most adequate to the demands of Christian faith." And Clooney admits to standing in "the great tradition" of Karl Rahner and Jacques Dupuis, trying to "balance claims to Christian uniqueness with a necessary openness to learning from other religions." Fredericks, introduction, xv; Clooney, *Comparative Theology*, 16.

55. Clooney, *Comparative Theology*, 112. See also Fredericks, *Faith among Faiths*, 167.

56. Clooney, *Comparative Theology*, 65–66, 121–23. See Francis X. Clooney, *The Truth, the Way, the Life: Christian Commentary on the Three Holy Mantras of the Srivaisnavas* (Leuven, Belgium: Peeters, 2008).

57. Fredericks, *Faith among Faiths*, 169.

58. Clooney, *Comparative Theology*, 12.

59. Knitter, *Introducing Theologies of Religions*, 237.

60. See Thatamanil, "God as Ground, Contingency, and Relation," 242.

61. Clooney, *Comparative Theology*, 58, 67.

62. Sheila Greeve Davaney, "Theology and the Turn to Cultural Analysis," in *Converging on Culture: Theologians in Dialogue with Cultural Analysis and Criticism*, ed. Delwin Brown, Sheila Greeve Davaney, and Kathryn Tanner (Oxford: Oxford University Press, 2001), 6, 8–9. See also Davaney, *Pragmatic Historicism*, 77–79.

63. Delwin Brown, "Limitation and Ingenuity: Radical Historicism and the Nature of Tradition," *American Journal of Theology and Philosophy* 24, no. 3 (September 2003): 209–10.

64. Delwin Brown, *Boundaries of Our Habitations: Tradition and Theological Construction* (Albany: State University of New York Press, 1994), 53, 92–109, 145–47. The historically "thick" historicism of Brown and Davaney also lines up well with the recent work of Manuel Vásquez, whose "materialist theory of religion" seeks to bring much-needed balance to the regnant textualisms and linguisticisms of postmodern and social constructionist paradigms and to the anthropocentric and anatural approaches that continue to dominate religious studies. Vásquez calls attention to religion's performative, embodied, and nonliterary practices; to its emplacement and navigation of sacred spaces; and above all, to its embeddedness in the material and natural world, in transnational markets and political systems, and in intricately interconnected cultural, biophysical, ecological, and virtual networks. See Manuel A. Vásquez, *More than Belief: A Materialist Theory of Religion* (New York: Oxford University Press, 2011).

65. Clooney, *Comparative Theology*, 58.

66. See Michelle Voss Roberts, "Religious Belonging and the Multiple," *Journal of Feminist Studies in Religion* 26, no. 1 (2010): 49–51, 60–61. On the contrary, Clooney allows that his approach to comparative theology—"peering deeply into difficult texts"—necessarily involves a kind of elitism. See Clooney, *Comparative Theology*, 67–68.

67. Michelle Voss Roberts, "Gendering Comparative Theology," in Clooney, *The New Comparative Theology*, 126. See also Tracy Sayuki Tiemeier, "Comparative Theology as a Theology of Liberation," in Clooney, *The New Comparative Theology*, 129–49.

68. Thatamanil, *The Immanent Divine*, xii–xiii; John J. Thatamanil, "Comparative Theology after 'Religion,'" in *Planetary Loves: Spivak, Postcoloniality, and*

Theology, ed. Stephen D. Moore and Mayra Rivera (New York: Fordham University Press, 2010), 247, 250.

69. Catherine Cornille, "Introduction: The Dynamics of Multiple Belonging," in *Many Mansions? Multiple Religious Belonging and Christian Identity*, ed. Catherine Cornille (Maryknoll, NY: Orbis, 2002), 1.

70. Cornille is very cautious: "It is true that many of us have benefited from the experiences and struggles of pioneers or 'liminal figures' who have experimented with double religious belonging. But that does not necessarily mean that it should or could be advocated as an ideal." Catherine Cornille, "Double Religious Belonging: Aspects and Questions," *Buddhist-Christian Studies* 23 (2003): 49.

71. Phan, *Being Religious Interreligiously*, 60–81.

72. Devaka Premawardhana, "The Unremarkable Hybrid: Aloysius Pieris and the Redundancy of Multiple Religious Belonging," *Journal of Ecumenical Studies* 46, no. 1 (Winter 2011): 98.

73. See Jeffrey Carlson, "Responses," *Buddhist-Christian Studies* 23 (2003): 77–83; Jeannine Hill Fletcher, *Monopoly on Salvation? A Feminist Approach to Religious Pluralism* (New York: Continuum, 2005), 82–101; Premawardhana, "The Unremarkable Hybrid," 76–101; Roberts, "Religious Belonging and the Multiple," 60; Thatamanil, "Comparative Theology after 'Religion,' " 238, 244.

74. Carlson, "Responses," 78–79.

75. Fletcher, *Monopoly on Salvation?*, 88.

76. Ibid., 82–101.

77. Thatamanil, "Comparative Theology after 'Religion,' " 238.

78. Premawardhana, "The Unremarkable Hybrid," 98.

79. In addition to Christianity (which resulted from "the combination of Greek philosophy and the Hebrew tradition"), Davaney lists ancient Manichaeism, modern Santería, and myriad forms of popular religion as prominent instances of religious syncretism. Davaney, *Pragmatic Historicism*, 109.

80. Ibid., 108–16, 174–76.

81. Delwin Brown, "Knowing the Mystery of God: Neville and Apophatic Theology," in *Interpreting Neville*, ed. J. Harley Chapman and Nancy K. Frankenberry (Albany: State University of New York Press, 1999), 190.

82. For Davaney's critique of Brown's monotraditionalism, see especially Sheila Greeve Davaney, "Between the One and the Many: A Response to Delwin Brown's Theology of Tradition," *American Journal of Theology and Philosophy* 18, no. 2 (May 1997): 141–45.

83. Davaney, *Pragmatic Historicism*, 173–76.

84. Griffiths, "The Properly Christian Response to Religious Plurality," 11.

85. Paul F. Knitter, *One Earth, Many Religions: Multifaith Dialogue and Global Responsibility* (Maryknoll, NY: Orbis, 1995), 55.

86. Knitter, *Introducing Theologies of Religions*, 134–37.

87. Knitter, *One Earth, Many Religions*, 54–67, 70–72, 79–80, 89. Emphasis removed. See also Paul F. Knitter, "Religion and Globality: Can Interreligious Dialogue Be Globally Responsible?," in *A Dome of Many Colors: Studies in Religious Pluralism, Identity, and Unity*, ed. Arvind Sharma and Kathleen M. Dugan (Harrisburg, PA: Trinity Press International, 1999), 104–36.

88. S. Mark Heim, *Salvations: Truth and Difference in Religion* (Maryknoll, NY: Orbis, 1995), 207.

89. John Milbank, "The End of Dialogue," in *Christian Uniqueness Reconsidered: The Myth of a Pluralistic Theology of Religions*, ed. Gavin D'Costa (Maryknoll, NY: Orbis, 1990), 181–82.

90. Heim, *Salvations*, 94.

91. Knitter, *Introducing Theologies of Religions*, 134.

92. Knitter, *One Earth, Many Religions*, 67–70, 79–82, 88–90, 97–117, 124–25.

93. See Paul F. Knitter, "Is the Pluralist Model a Western Imposition? A Response in Five Voices," in *The Myth of Religious Superiority: A Multifaith Exploration*, ed. Paul F. Knitter (Maryknoll, NY: Orbis, 2005), 28–30.

94. Anselm Kyongsuk Min, "Dialectical Pluralism and Solidarity of Others: Towards a New Paradigm," *Journal of the American Academy of Religion* 65, no. 3 (Fall 1997): 600. Emphasis altered.

95. Quoted in Knitter, *One Earth, Many Religions*, 90.

96. Kaufman, *God—Mystery—Diversity*, 23, 65–66, 76–80, 133.

97. I am very grateful to Michael Hogue for reminding me of this crucial point.

98. Sallie McFague, "An Earthly Theological Agenda," in *Ecofeminism and the Sacred*, ed. Carol J. Adams (New York: Continuum, 1993), 87.

99. See Heim, *Salvations*, 87, 185–210.

100. See Kaufman, *God—Mystery—Diversity*, 199–200.

101. See Sallie McFague, "Cosmology and Christianity: Implications of the Common Creation Story for Theology," in *Theology at the End of Modernity: Essays in Honor of Gordon D. Kaufman*, ed. Sheila Greeve Davaney (Philadelphia: Trinity Press International, 1991).

102. Although far from a totally novel occurrence in history, human interconnectedness and cultural and religious interpenetration have certainly assumed greater magnitude and importance in the new millennium. See Veli-Matti Kärkkäinen, *An Introduction to the Theology of Religions: Biblical, Historical and Contemporary Perspectives* (Downers Grove, IL: IVP Academic, 2003), 17; Peter Berger and Anton Zijderveld, *In Praise of Doubt: How to Have Convictions without Becoming a Fanatic* (New York: HarperOne, 2009), 1–24.

103. Gordon D. Kaufman, *In Face of Mystery: A Constructive Theology* (Cambridge, MA: Harvard University Press, 1993), 116–20, quote on 119.

104. Ibid., 112.

105. See Kaufman, *God—Mystery—Diversity*, 78. Of course, Kaufman's naturalistic conception of universality differs markedly from that of the particularists (DiNoia, Griffiths, Heim, et al.), who universalize their particular religions and parochial notions of ultimacy and salvation. As Kaufman admonishes: "We no longer dare conceive the universal simply in terms of ourselves—our belief, our traditions, even our God. Rather, the other way around: we must learn to see our traditions, our beliefs, our God, in terms of the universal world-process of which we all are part. Our way of thinking (whether Christian or Jewish or something else), our beliefs and practices, our religious traditions with their conception of God, all emerged in the great cosmic evolutionary-historical process which is the context of all life and being, and thus of all human existence." Kaufman, *In Face of Mystery*, 137.

106. Ursula Goodenough, *The Sacred Depths of Nature* (New York: Oxford University Press, 1998), xvi.

107. Knitter, *One Earth, Many Religions*, 122–23.

108. McFague, "Cosmology and Christianity," 31, 33.

109. Kaufman, *God—Mystery—Diversity*, 79; Kaufman, *In Face of Mystery*, 123.

110. See Jerome A. Stone, *Religious Naturalism Today: The Rebirth of a Forgotten Alternative* (Albany: State University of New York Press, 2008), xi, 1; Donald A. Crosby, *A Religion of Nature* (Albany: State University of New York Press, 2002), pt. 3.

111. Michael S. Hogue, *The Promise of Religious Naturalism* (Lanham, MD: Rowman and Littlefield, 2010), xx, 37–38, 203–4.

112. Ibid., xx, 25, 27–29, 38, 94–95, 128, 136, 138, 204, 223–24.

113. Loyal Rue, *Nature Is Enough: Religious Naturalism and the Meaning of Life* (Albany: State University of New York Press, 2011), 123.

114. Ibid., 122–29, quote on 128. See also Loyal Rue, *Religion Is Not about God: How Spiritual Traditions Nurture Our Biological Nature and What to Expect When They Fail* (New Brunswick, NJ: Rutgers University Press, 2005), 360–67.

115. Goodenough, *The Sacred Depths of Nature*, xvi, xx–xxi, 172–74; Hogue, *The Promise of Religious Naturalism*, 28–29, 128.

116. Goodenough, *The Sacred Depths of Nature*, 173–74.

117. According to Jerome Stone, several twentieth- and twenty-first-century theologians, from George Burman Foster, Gerald Birney Smith, Edward Scribner Ames, and Shailer Mathews to Henry Nelson Wieman, Bernard Meland, and Bernard Loomer, to Karl Peters, Gordon Kaufman, William Dean, Wesley Wildman, and Charley Hardwick, have articulated a decidedly *Christian* naturalism (i.e., a naturalism that retains the symbol "God" and highlights the "positive significance of Christ"). Stone also to points to a trajectory of naturalistic *Judaism*, which includes Samuel Alexander, Mordecai Kaplan, Jack Cohen, Henry Levinson, and David Oler, among others. Jerome A. Stone, "Is a 'Christian Naturalism' Possible? Exploring the Boundaries of a Tradition," *American Journal of Theology and Philosophy* 32, no. 3 (September 2011): 205–20. For Stone's analysis of the Jewish naturalists, see Stone, *Religious Naturalism*

Today, 37–44, 111–20, 179–82, 221–22. For very recent efforts to develop Jewish and Christian as well as Buddhist, Shawnee, Daoist, Hindu, and Confucian forms of religious naturalism, see Donald A. Crosby and Jerome A. Stone, eds., *The Routledge Handbook of Religious Naturalism* (London: Routledge, 2018), pt. 5.

118. Wesley J. Wildman, "Religious Naturalism: What It Can Be, and What It Need Not Be," *Philosophy, Theology and the Sciences* 1, no. 1 (2014): 41.

119. Crosby, *A Religion of Nature*, 156.

120. Wildman, "Religious Naturalism," 41, 44, 49–51.

121. However, it should be noted that, by Brown's standards, even Kaufman is insufficiently historicist. His naturalist "reconstruction of the Christian mythos is," Brown pronounces, "simply too frail to be efficacious. It does too little to reconstruct the rich reservoir of Christian symbols that still dominate, if sometimes only as a whisper, the cultural and religious scene, the symbols that must be renegotiated if alternatives are to be viable, changes are to last, and worthy achievements are to be sustained. If the postmodern cultural theorists are right, any theology that fails to reconstruct a tradition's symbolic complex in its depth and breadth is doomed to cultural and religious impotence." Delwin Brown, "Mystery and History in Kaufman's Theology," review of *In Face of Mystery: A Constructive Theology*, by Gordon D. Kaufman, *Journal of the American Academy of Religion* 62, no. 4 (Winter 1994): 1215–16.

122. See Brown, "Knowing the Mystery of God," 190.

123. Crosby, *A Religion of Nature*, 123, 155–56, quote on 155.

124. See Rue, *Religion Is Not about God: How Spiritual Traditions Nurture Our Biological Nature and What to Expect When They Fail*, 360–68.

125. William Dean, *History Making History: The New Historicism in American Religious Thought* (Albany: State University of New York Press, 1988), 102, 105.

126. John Dewey, *Experience and Nature* (Chicago: Open Court, 1925), 5, 343–44.

127. William James, *Essays in Radical Empiricism, and A Pluralistic Universe* (New York: E. P. Dutton, 1971), 72–80.

128. Dean, *History Making History*, 75–122; William Dean, *American Religious Empiricism* (Albany: State University of New York Press, 1986), 19–39.

129. Brown, *Boundaries of Our Habitations*, 51.

130. See also Nancy Frankenberry, "Major Themes of Empirical Theology," in *Empirical Theology: A Handbook*, ed. Randolph Crump Miller (Birmingham, AL: Religious Education Press, 1992), 41.

131. John Dewey, *Art as Experience* (New York: Perigee, 1934), 16.

132. Knitter, *One Earth, Many Religions*, 55.

133. Dean, *History Making History*, 83.

134. Davaney, *Pragmatic Historicism*, 183.

135. Richard Rorty, *Philosophy and Social Hope* (London: Penguin, 1999), 85, 76.

136. Dean, *History Making History*, 101, 110, 118–22.

137. William James, *The Will to Believe, and Other Essays in Popular Philosophy* (New York: Dover, 1956), 61.

138. John Dewey, *A Common Faith* (New Haven, CT: Yale University Press, 1934), 47.

139. Crosby, *A Religion of Nature*, 85–87.

140. Bernard Loomer, "The Size of God," in *The Size of God: The Theology of Bernard Loomer in Context*, ed. William Dean and Larry E. Axel (Macon, GA: Mercer University Press, 1987), 20–51.

141. Donald A. Crosby, *Living with Ambiguity: Religious Naturalism and the Menace of Evil* (Albany: State University of New York Press, 2008), 64.

142. In chapter 6, I will declare that interactionism or constructive realism is—or at least should become—the governing principle of pragmatic historicism's epistemology and theory of truth.

143. Crosby, *A Religion of Nature*, 74–78.

144. Dewey, *Experience and Nature*, 321, 330, 348–49, 354. See also Dean, *History Making History*, 107–10.

145. Davaney, *Pragmatic Historicism*, 182–84.

146. Dean, *History Making History*, 82–83.

147. Heim, *Salvations*, 207, 87.

148. See Knitter, *One Earth, Many Religions*, 58–67.

149. James, *Essays in Radical Empiricism, and A Pluralistic Universe*, 75.

150. Dean, *History Making History*, 102, 104.

151. Ibid., 6–7.

152. John Dewey, *Reconstruction in Philosophy*, enl. ed. (Boston: Beacon, 1957), 156.

153. Davaney, *Historicism*, 157.

154. See Kaufman, *God—Mystery—Diversity*, 187, 194.

155. Dean, *History Making History*, 82.

156. In good historicist fashion, Kaufman adds that each religion should formulate such a criterion in the idiom and symbol system of its own heritage. For example, Christians might construe the work of humanization as an expression and extension of Christianity's "ministry of reconciliation" (cf. 2 Corinthians 5:17–20), which endeavors to build "community where there is dissension" and to promote "understanding and acceptance where there has been estrangement and rejection." Kaufman, *God—Mystery—Diversity*, 37–39.

157. Ibid., 24–43, 80–85, 93. See also Kaufman, *In Face of Mystery*, 125–40.

Chapter 5

1. Delwin Brown, *Boundaries of Our Habitations: Tradition and Theological Construction* (Albany: State University of New York Press, 1994), 2.

2. Sheila Greeve Davaney, *Historicism: The Once and Future Challenge for Theology* (Minneapolis: Fortress, 2006), 148.
3. See ibid., 13–15, 23–32, 49–51, 63.
4. Ibid., 21–32.
5. Van A. Harvey, *The Historian and the Believer: The Morality of Historical Knowledge and Christian Belief* (Urbana: University of Illinois Press, 1996), 4.
6. Ibid., 5.
7. Ernst Troeltsch, "Historical and Dogmatic Method in Theology," in *Religion in History*, ed. and trans. James Luther Adams and Walter F. Bense (Minneapolis: Fortress, 1991), 16, 12.
8. Gary Dorrien, *Kantian Reason and Hegelian Spirit: The Idealistic Logic of Modern Theology* (Malden, MA: Wiley-Blackwell, 2012), 315–21, 333–37; Gary Dorrien, *The Word as True Myth: Interpreting Modern Theology* (Louisville: Westminster John Knox Press, 1997), 45–52. See also Hans-Georg Drescher, "Ernst Troeltsch's Intellectual Development," in *Ernst Troeltsch and the Future of Theology*, ed. John Powell Clayton (New York: Cambridge University Press, 1976), 3–4, 6–8.
9. Troeltsch, "Historical and Dogmatic Method in Theology," 11–12, 19–21 29–31; Dorrien, *Kantian Reason and Hegelian Spirit*, 333–41, 344, 349–50; Davaney, *Historicism*, 56–57.
10. Troeltsch, "Historical and Dogmatic Method in Theology," 19.
11. Dorrien, *Kantian Reason and Hegelian Spirit*, 344–50. See Troeltsch, "Christianity and the History of Religion," 77–78.
12. Troeltsch, "Historical and Dogmatic Method in Theology," 14–15, 18–19; Davaney, *Historicism*, 58–59. See also Ernst Troeltsch, "The Dogmatics of the History-of-Religions School," in *Religion in History*, 89. Dorrien notes that the members of the *religionsgeschichtliche Schule* saw most religions as "syncretistic blends of various sources and traditions." Dorrien, *Kantian Reason and Hegelian Spirit*, 334. Indeed, by Troeltsch's reckoning: "Christianity is by no means the product of Jesus alone. Plato, the Stoa and immeasurable popular religious forces from the ancient world are involved in it." Even Jesus himself, declared Troeltsch, was "tied to the popular world picture of antiquity, to Jewish and oriental notions and to apocalyptic eschatological ideals." Ernst Troeltsch, "The Significance of the Historical Existence of Jesus for Faith," in *Writings on Theology and Religion*, ed. Robert Morgan and Michael Pye (Louisville: Westminster John Knox Press, 1977), 189, 183.
13. Troeltsch, "Historical and Dogmatic Method in Theology," 18.
14. Ibid., 13–14.
15. Of course, decades earlier (1835, to be exact), another German historicist, David Friedrich Strauss, already showed that the gospel stories consist largely of mythological and legendary constructions rather than history (whether supernatural or natural). A watershed in the quests for the historical Jesus and in New Testament criticism generally, Strauss's fifteen-hundred-page magnum opus, *Das Leben Jesu, kritisch bearbeitet*, provides a meticulous, comprehensive, methodical, and comprehensive commentary on Matthew, Mark, Luke, and John, divulging that the evangelists

neither reliably described miraculous contraventions of the processes of nature (as orthodox supernaturalists and literalists believed) nor misapprehended ordinary, mundane occurrences (as most rationalist interpreters presumed), but couched the sayings and deeds of Jesus in "the rich pictorial and imaginative mode of thought and expression of the primitive ages." Unwilling to either take the fantastical and spectacular events of the canonical gospels at face value (which is scientifically and historically untenable) or to give naturalistic explanations of these obviously premodern narratives (which is exegetically contrived), Strauss powerfully argued that Jesus, similar to other "celebrated personages," was mythologized, receiving "many and wondrous amplifications in the legends of a wonder-loving people." See David Friedrich Strauss, *The Life of Jesus Critically Examined*, ed. Peter C. Hodgson, trans. George Eliot (Philadelphia: Fortress, 1972), li, 52–59. See also Sheila Greeve Davaney, "The Outsideless Life: Historicism, Theology and the Quest for Jesus," *Louvain Studies* 32, no. 1–2 (Spring–Summer 2007): 97.

16. Harvey, *The Historian and the Believer*, 86–88.

17. Troeltsch, "Historical and Dogmatic Method in Theology," 13–14; Harvey, *The Historian and the Believer*, 14–15, 68–101; Roger Haight, *Dynamics of Theology* (Maryknoll, NY: Orbis, 2001), 172–73; Davaney, *Historicism*, 58; Dorrien, *Kantian Reason and Hegelian Spirit*, 349.

18. Troeltsch, "Historical and Dogmatic Method in Theology," 31, 29.

19. Ernst Troeltsch, *The Absoluteness of Christianity and the History of Religions*, trans. David Reid (Eugene, OR: Wipf and Stock, 2003), 70. Emphasis added.

20. Incidentally, one of Troeltsch's most important essays, "The Dogmatics of the History-of-Religions School," originally appeared in *American Journal of Theology*, the University of Chicago Divinity School's flagship periodical. See Ernst Troeltsch, "The Dogmatics of the *Religionsgeschichtliche Schule*," *American Journal of Theology* 17 (January 1913): 1–21. That same year, the journal's editors, Shirley Jackson Case and Gerald Birney Smith, published articles by two other history of religionists, Johannes Weiss and Hugo Gressmann. William J. Hynes, *Shirley Jackson Case and the Chicago School* (Chico, CA: Scholars Press, 1981), 101.

21. Gary Dorrien, *Idealism, Realism, and Modernity, 1900–1950*, vol. 2 of *The Making of American Liberal Theology* (Louisville: Westminster John Knox Press, 2003), 151.

22. See George Burman Foster, *The Function of Religion in Man's Struggle for Existence* (Chicago: University of Chicago Press, 1909), 68–72.

23. George Burman Foster, *The Finality of the Christian Religion*, 2nd ed. (Chicago: University of Chicago Press, 1906), 144.

24. See ibid., 4–6.

25. Ibid., 6.

26. Ibid., 115–42, quote on 131.

27. Hynes, *Shirley Jackson Case and the Chicago School*, 99–106. See especially Shirley Jackson Case, "New *Religionsgeschichtliche* Studies on Christian Origins," *American Journal of Theology* 18 (1914): 440–45.

28. Shirley Jackson Case, "Education in Liberalism," in *Contemporary American Theology*, ed. Vergilius Ferm (New York: Roundtable, 1932), 113.

29. Hynes, *Shirley Jackson Case and the Chicago School*, 99. See Shirley Jackson Case, *The Evolution of Early Christianity: A Genetic Study of First-Century Christianity in Relation to Its Religious Environment* (Chicago: University of Chicago Press, 1914), 191–92.

30. Hynes, *Shirley Jackson Case and the Chicago School*, 26.

31. Dorrien, *Idealism, Realism, and Modernity, 1900–1950*, 196.

32. Case developed this argument further in *The Social Origins of Christianity* and *The Social Triumph of the Ancient Church*. See Shirley Jackson Case, *The Social Origins of Christianity* (Chicago: University of Chicago Press, 1923); Case, *The Social Triumph of the Ancient Church* (New York: Harper, 1933). See also Hynes, *Shirley Jackson Case and the Chicago School*, 42; William Dean, *History Making History: The New Historicism in American Religious Thought* (Albany: State University of New York Press, 1988), 53.

33. Case, *The Evolution of Early Christianity*, 45.

34. Dorrien, *Idealism, Realism, and Modernity, 1900–1950*, 195.

35. See Case, *The Evolution of Early Christianity*, chs. 3–10.

36. Ibid., v–vii, 7, 26–47.

37. Ibid., 35.

38. Shirley Jackson Case, *The Origins of Christian Supernaturalism* (Chicago: University of Chicago Press, 1946), 1.

39. Ibid., 69–94, 145–72.

40. Ibid., 233–34.

41. Ibid., v–vi, 2, 13, 21, 163, 170–72, 220–26, 233–34.

42. Shirley Jackson Case, *Jesus: A New Biography* (Chicago: University of Chicago Press, 1927), 70; Case, *Jesus through the Centuries* (Chicago: University of Chicago Press, 1932), 350.

43. Case, *Jesus through the Centuries*, 9–10. Fellow Chicago schooler, Gerald Birney Smith, adds that modern interpretations of Jesus, no different than antique ones, "are expressions of faith, in which the believer attributes to Jesus those traits which are deemed by him to be essential to salvation." Gerald Birney Smith, "The Christ of Faith and the Jesus of History," *American Journal of Theology* 18, no. 4 (October 1914): 538.

44. Shirley Jackson Case, "The Religion of Jesus," in *The Chicago School of Theology—Pioneers in Religious Inquiry: The Early Chicago School, 1906–1959*, ed. W. Creighton Peden and Jerome A. Stone (Lewiston, NY: Edwin Mellen, 1996), 249.

45. Case, *Jesus: A New Biography*, 1–159; Case, *Jesus through the Centuries*, 1–16; Hynes, *Shirley Jackson Case and the Chicago School*, 24, 35–50, 55; Davaney, *Historicism*, 107–9. See also Case, *The Evolution of Early Christianity*, 40–41, 332–33.

46. Case, *Jesus: A New Biography*, 115.

47. Shirley Jackson Case, *The Christian Philosophy of History* (Chicago: University of Chicago Press, 1943), 179.

48. Ibid., 59–63.

49. See Gordon D. Kaufman, *In Face of Mystery: A Constructive Theology* (Cambridge, MA: Harvard University Press, 1993), 259.

50. William Dean, *American Religious Empiricism* (Albany: State University of New York Press, 1986), 41.

51. Dean, *History Making History*, 1, 7.

52. Historicism's dialectic of givenness and agency is at least as old as Herder. In *Ideas toward a Philosophy of History*, he called them the principles of "tradition" (*Bildung*) and "organic powers." On the one hand, humans are "imitators," the products of the inherited cultures into which they are born and the given circumstances into which they are thrown. "Tradition takes hold of them, forms their minds, and fashions their limbs. They become what they are . . . according to tradition." On the other hand, "imitators must have powers . . . to receive what has and can be transmitted and to convert it. . . . Accordingly, their own receptive powers determine what and how much they receive, from whom they acquire it, and how much they make it their own, use it, and apply it." Johann Gottfried Herder, *Against Pure Reason: Writings on Religion, Language, and History*, trans. Marcia Bunge (Minneapolis: Fortress, 1993), 51–52.

53. Sheila Greeve Davaney, *Pragmatic Historicism: A Theology for the Twenty-First Century* (Albany: State University of New York Press, 2000), 1.

54. Delwin Brown, "Limitation and Ingenuity: Radical Historicism and the Nature of Tradition," *American Journal of Theology and Philosophy* 24, no. 3 (September 2003): 208–9.

55. Ibid., 208–10; Delwin Brown, *To Set at Liberty: Christian Faith and Human Freedom* (Maryknoll, NY: Orbis, 1981), 29–30, 31–36; Kaufman, *In Face of Mystery*, 127–30; Davaney, *Historicism*, 145–47.

56. See Richard Rorty, *Philosophy and Social Hope* (London: Penguin, 1999), 47–71; Davaney, *Pragmatic Historicism*, 23–25, 51–52; Dean, *History Making History*, 6–7.

57. The number 17, Rorty illustrates, is shorn of some static essence that is ascertainable "apart from its relationship to other numbers." It can be described as "less than 22, more than 8, the sum of 6 and 11, the square root of 289, the square of 4.123105, the difference between 1,678,922 and 1,678,905. . . . None of these descriptions seems to give you a clue to the intrinsic seventeenness of 17—the unique feature which makes it the very number that it is." Rorty, *Philosophy and Social Hope*, 52–53.

58. Ibid., 47, 50, 53–55, 57.

59. John Dewey, *Reconstruction in Philosophy*, enl. ed. (Boston: Beacon, 1957), 60–61.

60. See John Dewey, "The Postulate of Immediate Empiricism," in *The Essential Dewey*, vol. 1, *Pragmatism, Education, Democracy*, ed. Larry A. Hickman and Thomas M. Alexander (Bloomington: Indiana University Press, 1998), 115–20;

Dewey, *Reconstruction in Philosophy*, viii–ix, xiv, xvii, xxx; 28–43, 68–69, 84–95, 113–17; Dewey, *The Quest for Certainty: A Study in the Relation of Knowledge and Action* (New York: Pedigree, 1929), 37–39, 49–50, 78–90, 98–107, 112–39, 173–74, 178, 204, 299.

61. Dewey, *Reconstruction in Philosophy*, 94–95.

62. See Davaney, *Historicism*, 148; Gordon D. Kaufman, *In the Beginning . . . Creativity* (Minneapolis: Fortress, 2004), 75.

63. Davaney, *Pragmatic Historicism*, 66.

64. Sallie McFague, "Cosmology and Christianity: Implications of the Common Creation Story for Theology," in *Theology at the End of Modernity: Essays in Honor of Gordon D. Kaufman*, ed. Sheila Greeve Davaney (Philadelphia: Trinity Press International, 1991), 32.

65. Kaufman, *In Face of Mystery*, 259; Kaufman, *In the Beginning . . . Creativity*, 86–93; Dean, *American Religious Empiricism*, 74–77.

66. Kaufman, *In the Beginning . . . Creativity*, 56, 70.

67. Of course, for Whitehead, the ongoing emergence of historical novelty presupposes that the universe includes a theistic source of unactualized ideals (i.e., God). See Alfred North Whitehead, *Modes of Thought* (New York: Free Press, 1938), 101–4. In *Process and Reality*, Whitehead speculates that the divine "primordial nature" is the conceptual storehouse and "envisagement" of these unactualized ideals, of "pure potentials" or "eternal objects," which God uses (via an "initial aim") to "lure" the world's "novel" and "creative advance." See Alfred North Whitehead, *Process and Reality: An Essay in Cosmology*, corr. ed. (New York: Free Press, 1978), 7, 21, 31–34, 39–60, 343–44. For pragmatic historicists, on the contrary, there are no "eternal objects" (i.e., "abstract possibilities" or "pure potentials"), only what Whitehead, elsewhere in *Process and Reality*, calls "real potentialities," potentialities that are "conditioned by the data provided by the actual world" (65; cf. 80, 220). When all is said and done, pragmatic historicism, akin to Donald Crosby and contra Whitehead, adopts an Aristotelian rather than a Platonist philosophy of potentialities. That is, although awesome and bafflingly mysterious, the new and the possible are empirical and natural, latent within the processes and actualities of history itself. Instead of having a separate, extrahistorical, enduring existence (say, in a realm of immutable forms or in God's timeless primordiality), novel possibilities stem from history's indeterminate, contingent, open, and agential character and change with the potentialities that become concretely realized in time and space. See Donald A. Crosby, *A Religion of Nature* (Albany: State University of New York Press, 2002), 34–36.

68. Brown, *To Set at Liberty*, 28–31; Brown, *Boundaries of Our Habitations*, 102–5.

69. See Brown, "Limitation and Ingenuity," 207–8; Brown, *Boundaries of Our Habitations*, 4.

70. Davaney, *Historicism*, 150. See also Jonathan R. Herman, "The Contextual Illusion: Comparative Mysticism and Postmodernism," in *A Magic Still Dwells:*

Comparative Religion in the Postmodern Age, ed. Kimberly C. Patton and Benjamin C. Ray (Berkeley: University of California Press, 2000), 97; Diana L. Eck, "Dialogue and Method: Reconstructing the Study of Religion," in Patton and Ray, *A Magic Still Dwells*, 137.

71. Troeltsch, "The Dogmatics of the History-of-Religions School," 103–4. Emphasis added.

72. Brown, *Boundaries of Our Habitations*, 59–67. See also Delwin Brown, "Refashioning Self and Other: Theology, Academy, and the New Ethnography," in *Converging on Culture: Theologians in Dialogue with Cultural Analysis and Criticism*, ed. Delwin Brown, Sheila Greeve Davaney, and Kathryn Tanner (New York: Oxford University Press, 2001), 45–50; Brown, "Limitation and Ingenuity," 200–202.

73. Brown, "Limitation and Ingenuity," 201.

74. Brown, *Boundaries of Our Habitations*, 74, 4.

75. Quoted in ibid., 40.

76. On this issue, Brown, as I critically pointed out in chapter 2, does tend to slip into a "monotraditionalism." As Davaney admonishes, Brown fails to address the "multitraditionedness" of human identity and "neglects to appreciate fully what might be termed the hybrid or composite or even syncretistic character of many traditions." Davaney, *Pragmatic Historicism*, 108–9.

77. Brown, *Boundaries of Our Habitations*, 2, 9–27, 31–54, 87, 113.

78. Brown, "Limitation and Ingenuity," 205.

79. Brown, *Boundaries of Our Habitations*, 80.

80. Ibid., 78.

81. Ibid., 28–29, 75–92; Brown, "Refashioning Self and Other," 45–46.

82. Brown, *Boundaries of Our Habitations*, 86, 88.

83. Brown, "Limitation and Ingenuity," 194–99, 206. Here, Brown, far from engaging in mere armchair theorizing, grounds a historicist conceptualization of tradition in a number of case studies. To illustrate the varied ways in which religious adherents refashion their inherited traditions, Brown describes how Native Americans elevated Mother Earth, a previously undeveloped and peripheral symbol of Indian piety, to the status of a deity, thereby giving the different tribes a "unified ideology on the basis of which to oppose white aggression" and European conquest; how ancient Hebrews, exiled in Babylon and needing to maintain Jewish identity away from the promised land, actually altered the ending of the Torah, replacing the narrative of Israel's conquest of Canaan with the legal code contained in the book of Deuteronomy; and how black slaves, desiring exodus, gradually made Moses the primary figure in the African pantheon, which, in turn, eventually prompted "the Mosaic assimilation of Christ" and, thus, the transformation of traditional African religion into an Africanized version of Christianity.

84. William Dean, *The American Spiritual Culture: And the Invention of Jazz, Football, and the Movies* (New York: Continuum, 2002), 140–41. See also Dean, *History Making History*, 45–46.

85. See Shailer Mathews, "Theology and the Social Mind," *Biblical World* 46, no. 4 (October 1915): 201–48.

86. Shailer Mathews, *The Atonement and the Social Process* (New York: Macmillan, 1930); Mathews, *The Growth of the Idea of God* (New York: Macmillan, 1931). To mention one among many possible examples, Mathews notes that, early on, the ancient Hebrews depicted "Jahweh" primarily as a desert "warrior-god," who was responsible for Israel's exodus and for the vanquishing of its enemies. However, after obtaining Canaan, "the land flowing with milk and honey," these tribal nomads became concerned with the raising of crops and herds. As a result, God "acquired traits which he did not possess before he led his people through the Jordan." The Jews were surrounded by a myriad of local fertility divinities, who proved to be "particularly competent in agriculture." However, they were loyal to Jahweh, who had delivered them from Egypt and guided them through the wilderness. Accordingly, instead of following the standard practice of "adopting special gods" for particular ends, "they discovered *in Jahweh* the qualities which the god of an agricultural people should possess if he were to help them face difficulties and satisfy their needs as farmers." Jahweh was offered "the first fruits of the field," and decidedly agrarian elements were incorporated into old festivals (e.g., Passover). So, like the Hebrews who invented him, Jahweh was "naturalized." That is, "the conception of Jahweh was enlarged and . . . he became a more settled deity living in the midst of a people who now had homes and farms." Mathews, *The Growth of the Idea of God*, 53–54. Emphasis added.

87. Shailer Mathews, *Is God Emeritus?* (New York: Macmillan, 1940), 26–27. See Dean, *History Making History*, 54–58; Dorrien, *Idealism, Realism, and Modernity, 1900–1950*, 208–12; Larry E Axel, "Process and Religion: The History of a Tradition at Chicago," *Process Studies* 8, no. 4 (Winter 1978): 235–36.

88. Shirley Jackson Case, *Christianity in a Changing World* (New York: Harper and Brothers Publishers, 1941), vii–viii, 1–41. See also Case, *The Evolution of Early Christianity*, 1–2, 7, 25.

89. Case, *Christianity in a Changing World*, 39–40.

90. Case, *Jesus through the Centuries*, quotes on 3–5, 16, 348; Hynes, *Shirley Jackson Case and the Chicago School*, 24, 49–55. Brown also believes that Christianity's striking christological variations attest to the dynamism and diversity of religious traditions. Drawing on the historical scholarship of William Clebsch, Brown states that when "the actual history of that stream known as Christianity" is surveyed, what comes into view is not a single, definitive, harmonious, or consistent portrayal of Jesus Christ. Rather, "the Jesus who endured throughout appeared in such varied roles amidst such diverse experiences that . . . one should really speak of different 'Christs' and different 'Christianities.'" Brown, *Boundaries of Our Habitations*, 23, 19.

91. Case, *The Evolution of Early Christianity*, 2.

92. Ibid., 25.

93. Case, *Christianity in a Changing World*, 29–39.

94. See Adolf von Harnack, *What Is Christianity?* (San Diego: Book Tree, 2006). This book, which began as a series of lectures given by Harnack at the University of Berlin in 1899 and 1900, became one of the classic statements of liberal Protestant theology.

95. Case, *Christianity in a Changing World*, 29; Case, *The Evolution of Early Christianity*, 1–25. See Hynes, *Shirley Jackson Case and the Chicago School*, 55, 82–83, 133–34; Dorrien, *Idealism, Realism, and Modernity, 1900–1950*, 196–97.

96. Mathews, *The Atonement and the Social Process*, 179–80; Mathews, *The Growth of the Idea of God*, 18; Dean, *History Making History*, 56.

97. Shailer Mathews, "Theology as Group Belief," in Ferm, *Contemporary American Theology*, 180. See also Mathews, *Is God Emeritus?*, 171; and Mathews, *The Growth of the Idea of God*, 20.

98. Foster, *The Finality of the Christian Religion*, 279–324. See Dean, *History Making History*, 61–62.

99. Foster, *The Finality of the Christian Religion*, 324.

100. See ibid., 301–2.

101. Troeltsch, "What Does 'Essence of Christianity' Mean?," 124–79; Troeltsch, "The Dogmatics of the History-of-Religions School," 95–97. See also S. W. Sykes, "Ernst Troeltsch and Christianity's Essence," in J. P. Clayton, *Ernst Troeltsch and the Future of Theology*, 139–71.

102. Troeltsch, "What Does 'Essence of Christianity' Mean?," 162–63.

103. "In the case of Christianity," writes Lindbeck, "the framework is supplied by the biblical narratives interrelated in certain specified ways (e.g., by Christ as center)." George A. Lindbeck, *The Nature of Doctrine: Religion and Theology in a Postliberal Age* (Philadelphia: Westminster Press, 1984), 80–81.

104. Ibid., 80–81, 83.

105. Davaney, *Pragmatic Historicism*, 23–25, 30–40, 112–16, 148, 150; Davaney, *Historicism*, 142–43, 148–49.

106. Davaney, *Pragmatic Historicism*, 112.

107. Brown, *Boundaries of Our Habitations*, 137, 136.

108. Like, to provide a couple examples of my own, claiming that the love of God and neighbor is the *heart* of the Christian message and then dismissing the Crusades or the Salem Witch Trials or the Moral Majority as deviations of "true Christianity." Or insisting that the terrorists of al-Qaeda or ISIS are not "real Muslims" because Islam is *essentially* a religion of peace.

109. Brown, *Boundaries of Our Habitations*, 120–27, 132–37. As it happens, Davaney adds that even pragmatic historicists sometimes succumb to essentialism, citing (and chiding) Kaufman's efforts to catalogue Christianity's "categorical scheme" (i.e., God, Christ, humanity, and the world) and McFague's contention that Jesus of Nazareth is the "root-metaphor" or "paradigmatic embodiment" of the Christian faith. See Davaney, *Pragmatic Historicism*, 89, 95–98.

110. See the essay, "Fences and Neighbors: Some Contours of Early Judaism," in Jonathan Z. Smith, *Imagining Religion: From Babylon to Jonestown* (Chicago:

University of Chicago Press, 1982), 1–18. See also J. Z. Smith, *Relating Religion: Essays in the Study of Religion* (Chicago: University of Chicago Press, 2004), 22–23.

111. Davaney, *Historicism*, 150–53, quote on 152–53.

112. Case, *Christianity in a Changing World*, 18.

113. See Brown, "Limitation and Ingenuity," 207–8.

114. Davaney, *Pragmatic Historicism*, 97; Brown, *Boundaries of Our Habitations*, 116.

115. Delwin Brown and Clark H. Pinnock, *Theological Crossfire: An Evangelical/Liberal Dialogue* (Grand Rapids, MI: Zondervan, 1990), 24. See also Delwin Brown, "Struggle till Daybreak: On the Nature of Authority in Theology," *Journal of Religion* 65, no. 1 (January 1985): 15–19.

116. Brown, *Boundaries of Our Habitations*, 114–16; Brown, "Limitation and Ingenuity," 202, 206; Davaney, *Pragmatic Historicism*, 112.

117. Brown, *Boundaries of Our Habitations*, 116–19; Brown, "Limitation and Ingenuity," 205–7, 211; Davaney, *Pragmatic Historicism*, 112–15.

118. Case, *The Christian Philosophy of History*, 167.

119. See Davaney, *Historicism*, 158.

120. Foster, *The Finality of the Christian Religion*, 100.

121. Ibid., 112; Foster, *The Function of Religion in Man's Struggle for Existence*, 7–8, 129, 143, 163–64, 277–78.

122. Dorrien, *Idealism, Realism, and Modernity, 1900–1950*, 164, 157.

123. Foster, *The Finality of the Christian Religion*, 196–97; Foster, *The Function of Religion in Man's Struggle for Existence*, 76–115, 169–70, 221–23, 255. See Dorrien, *Idealism, Realism, and Modernity, 1900–1950*, 156–68.

124. Gerald Birney Smith, *Social Idealism and the Changing Theology: A Study of the Ethical Aspects of Christian Doctrine* (New York: Macmillan, 1913), 94–95.

125. Gerald Birney Smith, "The Task and Method of Systematic Theology," *American Journal of Theology* 14, no. 2 (April 1910): 216–22, 224; G. B. Smith, "Systematic Theology and Ministerial Efficiency," *American Journal of Theology* 16, no. 4 (October 1912): 589–605; G. B. Smith, *Current Christian Thinking* (Chicago: University of Chicago Press, 1928), 1–4, 14–15, 22–25, 40–46, 61; G. B. Smith, *Social Idealism and the Changing Theology*, viii–ix, 1–46, 156–57, 170, 185, 211; final quote from G. B. Smith, *Current Christian Thinking*, 44. See Dorrien, *Idealism, Realism, and Modernity, 1900–1950*, 257–59; Davaney, *Historicism*, 97, 99; Delwin Brown, "The Fall of '26: Gerald Birney Smith and the Collapse of the Socio-historical Framework of Theology," *American Journal of Theology and Philosophy* 11, no. 3 (September 1990): 186.

126. For instance, the trinity, according to Smith, "is a doctrine which grew up in order to solve peculiarly Hellenistic problems—problems which would have been unintelligible to the Christians of New Testament times." G. B. Smith, *Current Christian Thinking*, 43.

127. G. B. Smith, "The Task and Method of Systematic Theology," 221–23. See Davaney, *Historicism*, 100–101; Dean, *History Making History*, 58–60.

128. Gerald Birney Smith, "Christianity and the Spirit of Democracy," *American Journal of Theology* 21, no. 2 (April 1917): 346–50; G. B. Smith, *Social Idealism and the Changing Theology*, 190–204, 217–19. The contemporary theological historicist Sallie McFague makes a similar observation. To see the Bible as a "prototype" or "model" of *how* to do theology is to stop treating it as "the authority dictating the terms in which it is done." McFague elaborates: "If we take the form of Scripture seriously, the plurality of interpretive perspectives that it is, we will have to do the same risky, adventuresome thing that it does: interpret the salvific love of God in ways that can address our crises most persuasively and powerfully. . . . It is precisely the patchwork, potpourri character of the Hebraic and Christian Scriptures with their rich flood of images, stories, and themes—some interweaving and mutually supportive, and others disparate, presenting alternative possibilities—that gives Christian theologians 'authority' to experiment." To be truly biblical, in other words, is to do what the writers of the Bible actually did: reimagine the "demonstrable continuities" of the tradition from within the givens and metaphors of *our* time, place, and situation rather than sacralize, petrify, or render normative those of another. Sallie McFague, *Models of God: Theology for an Ecological, Nuclear Age* (Philadelphia: Fortress, 1987), 30, 40–45, quote on 44.

129. G. B. Smith, "Christianity and the Spirit of Democracy," 350.

130. G. B. Smith, "The Task and Method of Systematic Theology," 224–26; G. B. Smith, *Social Idealism and the Changing Theology*, 185.

131. G. B. Smith, *Current Christian Thinking*, 40–43, 46; G. B. Smith, "Christianity and the Spirit of Democracy," 346–50. See Davaney, *Historicism*, 98, 100–101.

132. Brown, "The Fall of '26," 186–87; Dorrien, *Idealism, Realism, and Modernity, 1900–1950*, 257.

133. G. B. Smith, "The Task and Method of Systematic Theology," 220.

134. Case, *The Christian Philosophy of History*, 163.

135. See Shirley Jackson Case, "The Historical Study of Religion," *Journal of Religion* 1 (January 1921): 14.

136. Davaney, "The Outsideless Life," 100.

137. Shirley Jackson Case, "The Religious Meaning of the Past," *Journal of Religion* 4, no. 6 (November 1924): 576–91; Case, *The Christian Philosophy of History*, 2–6, 88–91, 143–48, 157–63, 185–87. See Davaney, *Historicism*, 104–6; Hynes, *Shirley Jackson Case and the Chicago School*, 70–81.

138. Linell E. Cady, "Resisting the Postmodern Turn: Theology and Contextualization," in Davaney, *Theology at the End of Modernity*, 95.

139. Gordon D. Kaufman, *An Essay on Theological Method*, 3rd ed. (Atlanta: Scholars Press, 1995), 40; Kaufman, *The Theological Imagination: Constructing the Concept of God* (Philadelphia: Westminster Press, 1981), 23.

140. Gordon D. Kaufman, *Theology for a Nuclear Age* (Philadelphia: Westminster Press, 1985), 16–29; Kaufman, *In Face of Mystery*, xi.

141. Kaufman, *In Face of Mystery*, 43–44.

142. Sheila Greeve Davaney, "A Historicist Model for Theology," in *Jesus and Faith: A Conversation on the Work of John Dominic Crossan*, ed. Jeffrey Carlson and Robert A. Ludwig (Maryknoll, NY: Orbis, 1994), 55; Davaney, *Historicism*, 158.

143. Mordecai Kaplan, *Judaism without Supernaturalism: The Only Alternative to Orthodoxy and Secularism* (New York: Reconstructionist Press, 1967), 28. Quoted in Davaney, *Historicism*, 112.

144. Davaney, *Pragmatic Historicism*, 63, 150–53; Davaney, *Historicism*, 158.

145. Davaney, "A Historicist Model for Theology," 55.

146. See Brown, *Boundaries of Our Habitations*, ix.

147. Namely, Hannah Arendt, "What Was Authority?," in *Authority*, ed. Carl J. Friedrich (Cambridge, MA: Harvard University Press, 1958).

148. Brown, "Struggle till Daybreak," 15–26, quote on 25.

149. Brown, *Boundaries of Our Habitations*, 113. Emphasis added.

150. Brown and Pinnock, *Theological Crossfire*, 28; Brown, "Struggle till Daybreak," 26–29.

151. Brown and Pinnock, *Theological Crossfire*, 28; Brown, *Boundaries of Our Habitations*, 113–16.

152. Brown, *Boundaries of Our Habitations*, x, 137, 140–41, 144; Brown, "Struggle till Daybreak," 31.

153. In the case of the latter, postmodern "a/theologians," like Mark C. Taylor, underestimate the potency of inherited lineages and overestimate their perniciousness. Brown admonishes, "To say that humans are historical means that our futures are built through the reconstruction of our pasts." What is more, "traditions are not only culprits; they also have goods to give—judgments and alternatives, as yet unnoticed, worthy of consideration, capable of transformation. To neglect tradition is to neglect its power for good as well as ill." Brown, *Boundaries of Our Habitations*, 131–132. See Mark C. Taylor, *Erring: A Postmodern A/theology* (Chicago: University of Chicago Press, 1984).

154. Brown, *Boundaries of Our Habitations*, 113–14, 116–32, 137–38, 141–50, quotes on 137–38, 116–17.

155. Ibid., 148.

156. Frederick C. Beiser, *The German Historicist Tradition* (Oxford: Oxford University Press, 2011), 17.

157. Davaney, "The Outsideless Life," 106.

158. Kaufman, *In Face of Mystery*, 43. Ellipses in original.

159. Lindbeck, *The Nature of Doctrine*, 73–96, quotes on 74, 81. See Brown, *Boundaries of Our Habitations*, 124–26.

160. For example, if "Christological maximalism" is a part of Christianity's abiding and authoritative grammar, then whence and whither low—but ostensibly no less Christian—christologies? See Lindbeck, *The Nature of Doctrine*, 92–96.

161. Davaney, *Pragmatic Historicism*, 181.

162. Davaney, "The Outsideless Life," 109–10.

163. Case, *Jesus through the Centuries*, 346–76.

164. Ibid., 351–52, 354.

165. Ibid., 349.

166. W. Montgomery translated the book into English in 1910 under the title *The Quest of the Historical Jesus: A Critical Study of Its Progress from Reimarus to Wrede*. Gregory W. Dawes, *The Historical Jesus Question: The Challenge of History to Religious Authority* (Louisville: Westminster John Knox Press, 2001), 122, 128.

167. Albert Schweitzer, *The Quest of the Historical Jesus: A Critical Study of Its Progress from Reimarus to Wrede* (Baltimore: Johns Hopkins University Press, 1998), 398.

168. Ibid., 398–403.

169. See especially ibid., chs. 15, 16, and 19.

170. Ibid., 399.

171. Shailer Mathews, *The Social Teaching of Jesus: An Essay in Christian Sociology* (New York: Macmillan, 1897), 51, 54, 61–64, 130, 201.

172. Shailer Mathews, *The Messianic Hope in the New Testament* (Chicago: University of Chicago Press, 1905), 82.

173. Mathews, *The Social Teaching of Jesus*, 40.

174. Foster, *The Finality of the Christian Religion*, 249. Smith made the same exact point in 1914: "For a time, it seemed as if the process of criticism might reveal to us behind the doctrinal statements of the New Testament the figure of one who was interested primarily in the social questions which are so vital to us. But as historical criticism has proceeded, it has led many scholars to feel that it is probable that Jesus entertained an apocalyptic view of the course of history which puts miraculous deliverance in the foreground, and which is therefore not compatible with the ideal of social evolution so familiar to us. While it would be too much to say that the view of Schweitzer has come to be taken seriously by many scholars, nevertheless it is at present impossible for us to be historically certain that Jesus actually held the religious ideals which the advocates of the 'social gospel' today demand." G. B. Smith, "The Christ of Faith and the Jesus of History," 535.

175. Mathews, *The Growth of the Idea of God*, 8–9, 15, 18, 21, 23–24.

176. Dorrien, *Idealism, Realism, and Modernity, 1900–1950*, 192.

177. Mathews, *Is God Emeritus?*, 72, 82.

178. See Dorrien, *Idealism, Realism, and Modernity, 1900–1950*, 166–67, 185–99.

179. G. B. Smith, "The Christ of Faith and the Jesus of History," 543–44.

180. Schweitzer, *The Quest of the Historical Jesus*, 400.

181. Others include Bart Ehrman and E. P. Sanders. See Bart D. Ehrman, *Jesus: Apocalyptic Prophet of the New Millennium* (New York: Oxford University Press, 1999); E. P. Sanders, *Jesus and Judaism* (Minneapolis: Fortress, 1985).

182. Marcus Borg enthuses that a "renaissance in Jesus studies," a "third quest," has been well underway since the mid-1970s. Marcus J. Borg, *Jesus in Contemporary Scholarship* (Valley Forge, PA: Trinity Press International, 1994), ix, 1–17.

183. Founded by Robert Funk and the Westar Institute in 1985, the Jesus Seminar is the primary institutional locus of the third quest. The organization consists of a group of "Fellows" (the most distinguished of whom are Marcus Borg, John Dominic Crossan, Burton Mack, and Hal Taussig) who have studied, debated, and voted on the historical authenticity of all the words and acts ascribed to Jesus in the gospels and other early Christian sources. See Robert W. Funk, ed., *The Acts of Jesus: The Search for the Authentic Deeds of Jesus* (San Francisco: Harper SanFrancisco, 1998); Robert W. Funk and Roy W. Hoover, eds. *The Five Gospels: The Search for the Authentic Words of Jesus* (New York: HarperCollins, 1993). Perhaps more noteworthy than its (mostly) "black letter" editions of Matthew, Mark, Luke, John, and Thomas, in which less than twenty percent of the utterances and deeds attributed to Christ are deemed authentic, is its "sapiential" depiction of Jesus. For the vast majority of these third questers, the portrait that emerges from the earliest, and most historically trustworthy, layer of the gospel traditions (which consists predominantly of terse aphorisms and parables) is that of an itinerate, anti-imperial, countercultural *sage* trading in socially, politically, and religiously subversive wisdom, not an eschatological prophet foretelling gloom and doom. Borg, *Jesus in Contemporary Scholarship*, 9–10; Tyron L. Inbody, *The Many Faces of Christology* (Nashville: Abingdon Press, 2002), 30–32.

184. Paula Fredriksen, "What You See Is What You Get: Context and Content in Current Research on the Historical Jesus," *Theology Today* 52, no. 1 (April 1995): 75–76, 94, 97.

185. Luke Timothy Johnson, *The Real Jesus: The Misguided Quest for the Historical Jesus and the Truth of the Traditional Gospels* (New York: HarperOne, 1996), vii–xiii, 1–27, 29–44, 46, 49–50, 54–55. See also Walter Wink, "Response to Luke Timothy Johnson's *The Real Jesus*," *Bulletin for Biblical Research* 7 (1997): 236–38.

186. Here, I refer specifically to the scholarship of John Dominic Crossan. See John Dominic Crossan, *The Historical Jesus: The Life of a Mediterranean Jewish Peasant* (New York: HarperCollins, 1991); Crossan, *Jesus: A Revolutionary Biography* (New York: HarperCollins, 1994).

Chapter 6

1. See Robert Cummings Neville, "A Paleopragmatic Philosophy of History of Philosophy," in *Pragmatism, Neo-pragmatism, and Religion: Conversations with Richard Rorty*, ed. Charley D. Hardwick and Donald A. Crosby (New York: Peter Lang, 1997), 43–60.

2. William James, *Essays in Radical Empiricism, and A Pluralistic Universe* (New York: E. P. Dutton, 1971), 248.

3. William James, *Pragmatism: A New Name for Some Old Ways of Thinking* (Cambridge, MA: Harvard University Press, 1978), 34–35, 82–83, 107–8, 116.

4. Donald A. Crosby, *Living with Ambiguity: Religious Naturalism and the Menace of Evil* (Albany: State University of New York Press, 2008), 67–68, 72.

5. See Delwin Brown, *Boundaries of Our Habitations: Tradition and Theological Construction* (Albany: State University of New York Press, 1994), 104.

6. James, *Pragmatism*, 11–13, 104, 118.

7. William James, *The Meaning of Truth: A Sequel to Pragmatism* (Cambridge, MA: Harvard University Press, 1978), 135.

8. The translation cited here comes from Walter Kaufmann, ed., *The Portable Nietzsche* (New York: Penguin, 1982), 458.

9. Friedrich Nietzsche, *The Will to Power*, ed. Walter Kaufmann, trans. Walter Kaufmann and R. J. Hollingdale (New York: Vintage, 1968), secs. 259, 272, 481, 552, 616.

10. Friedrich Nietzsche, *On the Genealogy of Morals*, in *Basic Writings of Nietzsche*, ed. and trans. Walter Kaufmann (New York: Modern Library, 2000), 555.

11. Charles Sanders Peirce, "Some Consequences of Four Incapacities," in *The Essential Peirce: Selected Philosophical Writings*, vol. 1, *1867–1893*, ed. Nathan Houser and Christian Kloesel (Bloomington: Indiana University Press, 1992), 28–29; Richard J. Bernstein, *The Pragmatic Turn* (Cambridge, UK: Polity, 2010), 32–34; Robert Cummings Neville, *The Highroad around Modernism* (Albany: State University of New York Press, 1992), 25–26.

12. Charles Sanders Peirce, "What Pragmatism Is," in *The Essential Peirce: Selected Philosophical Writings*, vol. 2, *1893–1913*, ed. Peirce Edition Project (Bloomington: Indiana University Press, 1998), 336.

13. In fact, Peirce uses the neologism "interpretant" to signal that "there is something which the sign in its significant function essentially determines in its interpreter." Charles Sanders Peirce, "Pragmatism," in *The Essential Peirce*, 2:409. See also Peirce, "Excerpts from Letters to Lady Welby," in *The Essential Peirce*, 2:478.

14. Charles Sanders Peirce, "Questions concerning Certain Faculties Claimed for Man," in *The Essential Peirce*, 1:11–27; Peirce, "Some Consequences of Four Incapacities," 28–55. See Neville, *The Highroad around Modernism*, 25–27; Bernstein, *The Pragmatic Turn*, 39–46.

15. Ludwig Wittgenstein, *Philosophical Investigations*, trans. G. E. M. Anscombe, 3rd ed. (Englewood Cliffs, NJ: Prentice Hall, 1953), 193–229.

16. See Thomas S. Kuhn, *The Structure of Scientific Revolutions*, 3rd ed. (Chicago: University of Chicago Press, 1996), viii, 44–45.

17. Ibid., x–xii, 1–22.

18. Ibid., 50–51.

19. Ibid., 111.

20. Ibid., 6, 17–19, 111–35.

21. Steven Best and Douglas Kellner, *Postmodern Theory: Critical Interrogations* (New York: Guilford Press, 1991), 4.

22. See Wesley J. Wildman, *Religious Philosophy as Multidisciplinary Comparative Inquiry: Envisioning a Future for the Philosophy of Religion* (Albany: State University of New York Press, 2010), 63–68.

23. Michel Foucault, *Power/Knowledge: Selected Interviews and Other Writings, 1972–1977*, ed. Colin Gordon, trans. Colin Gordon et al. (New York: Pantheon, 1980), 131, 133.

24. Michel Foucault, *Discipline and Punish: The Birth of the Prison*, trans. Alan Sheridan, 2nd ed. (New York: Vintage, 1995), 27–28.

25. Jacques Derrida, *Of Grammatology*, trans. Gayatri Chakravorty Spivak (Baltimore: John Hopkins University Press, 1974), 158.

26. Ibid., 7, 159.

27. John D. Caputo, *Deconstruction in a Nutshell: A Conversation with Jacques Derrida* (New York: Fordham University Press, 1997), 79.

28. Ibid., 80.

29. Derrida states that "Peirce goes very far in the direction that I have called the de-construction of the transcendental signified, which, at one time or another, would place a reassuring end to the reference from sign to sign." Derrida, *Of Grammatology*, 49.

30. Ibid., 7–26, 44–50, 158–60. See Caputo, *Deconstruction in a Nutshell*, 79–80; Stanley J. Grenz, *A Primer on Postmodernism* (Grand Rapids, MI: William B. Eerdmans, 1996), 140–42, 150; William Dean, *American Religious Empiricism* (Albany: State University of New York Press, 1986), 43–45.

31. Richard Rorty, *Consequences of Pragmatism* (Minneapolis: University of Minnesota Press, 1982), 160.

32. For instance, throughout *Consequences of Pragmatism*, Rorty points out all sorts of interesting philosophical similarities that Nietzsche, Heidegger, Wittgenstein, Quine, Sellars, Davidson, Gadamer, Derrida, Kuhn, Deleuze, and Foucault shared with one another and with James and Dewey (without overlooking the crucial differences in emphasis, tone, style, outlook, argument, and even content). See ibid., xviii, xx, 19–36, 37–59, 148–59, 203–8, 211–30, and passim. To cite just one of many possible examples, Rorty concludes that "Dewey and Foucault make exactly the same criticism of the tradition. They agree, right down the line, about the need to abandon traditional notions of rationality, objectivity, method, and truth. . . . They agree that rationality is what history and society make it—that there is no overarching ahistorical structure (the Nature of Man, the laws of human behavior, the Moral Law, the Nature of Society) to be discovered. They share the . . . Kuhnian notion of Galilean science—as exemplifying the power of new vocabularies rather than offering the secret of scientific success. . . . Foucault's vision of discourse as a network of power-relations isn't very different from Dewey's vision of it as instrumental, as one element in the arsenal of tools people use for gratifying, synthesizing, and harmonizing their desires" (204, 208). Rorty later

argues in *Philosophy and Social Hope* that, in general, "post-Nietzschean European philosophy" (which includes Heidegger, Sartre, Gadamer, Derrida, and Foucault) and "post-Darwinian American philosophy" (which includes James, Dewey, Kuhn, Quine, Putnam, and Davidson) unite under the banner of *antidualism*, casting aspersions on the entire repository of Platonic-Cartesian-Kantian binaries (appearance-reality, matter-mind, accident-essence, subject-object, etc.). Richard Rorty, *Philosophy and Social Hope* (London: Penguin, 1999), xii, xix–xx, 47.

33. Rorty, *Consequences of Pragmatism*, xx. Rorty also puts Sellars, Gadamer, and Heidegger in the same perspectivist (or "linguistic") camp, and, later in the book, mentions both Nietzsche's and Kuhn's perspectivism as well. "James and Nietzsche . . . developed the same criticism of traditional notions of truth, and the same 'pragmatic' (or 'perspectivalist') alternative." And Kuhn, for his part, demonstrated that during any period of "normal science," theories are justified "in terms of a determinate observation-language, a list of meaning-rules, and some canons of theory-choice" (104, 205). See also "Thomas Kuhn, Rocks and the Laws of Physics," in Rorty, *Philosophy and Social Hope*, 175–89.

34. Rorty, *Consequences of Pragmatism*, xviii–xxi, xxvi, xxxvii, 140.

35. Richard Rorty, *Philosophy and the Mirror of Nature* (Princeton, NJ: Princeton University Press, 1979), 368.

36. Ibid., 3–13, 357–94. Fellow neopragmatist, Jeffrey Stout, also assures that a thoroughly historicized, antirepresentationalist philosophy still has a lot to do: "Maybe we can discover, in the difference between old sentences and new ones, what it is to be situated in history as we are. Such a discovery, while it would not help much with the [post-Cartesian] quest for autonomy from history, might at least make connection with Socrates' injunction to seek self-understanding or with Aristotle's conviction that philosophy begins in the surprised wonder at everything that is as it is. If philosophy is, as Wittgenstein and Socrates could agree, a kind of therapy, it will be natural to wonder what kind of therapy historical insight into our language might provide. Perhaps it will be a kind that does not leave everything as it is. The ancient city, after all, is ours to repair and renew." Jeffrey Stout, *The Flight from Authority: Religion, Morality, and the Quest for Autonomy* (Notre Dame, IN: University of Notre Dame Press, 1981), 21.

37. See Rorty, *Consequences of Pragmatism*, 194, 202.

38. Ibid., 139.

39. Ibid., 67, 100. Emphasis added.

40. Ibid., 154.

41. Richard Rorty, "Inquiry as Recontextualization: An Anti-dualist Account of Interpretation," in *Objectivity, Relativism, and Truth: Philosophical Papers* (Cambridge: Cambridge University Press, 1991), 102.

42. Richard Rorty, "Introduction: Antirepresentationalism, Ethnocentrism, and Liberalism," in *Objectivity, Relativism, and Truth*, 1–17; Rorty, "Inquiry as Recontextualization," 97–102; Rorty, *Philosophy and Social Hope*, 48, 50.

43. Richard Rorty, *Contingency, Irony, and Solidarity* (Cambridge: Cambridge University Press, 1989), xvi.

44. William Dean, *History Making History: The New Historicism in American Religious Thought* (Albany: State University of New York Press, 1988), 6.

45. Sheila Greeve Davaney, *Pragmatic Historicism: A Theology for the Twenty-First Century* (Albany: State University of New York Press, 2000), 23–24; Davaney, *Historicism: The Once and Future Challenge for Theology* (Minneapolis: Fortress, 2006), 155–56. See also Davaney, "Mapping Theologies: An Historicist Guide to Contemporary Theology," in *Changing Conversations: Religious Reflection and Cultural Analysis*, ed. Dwight N. Hopkins and Sheila Greeve Davaney (New York: Routledge, 1996), 26–27.

46. See especially Cornel West, *The American Evasion of Philosophy: A Genealogy of Pragmatism* (Madison: University of Wisconsin Press, 1989), 3–4, 206–39; West, *Keeping Faith: Philosophy and Race in America* (New York: Routledge, 1993), 119–34, 135–41. For Davaney's (appreciative) analysis of Cornel West, see Davaney, *Pragmatic Historicism*, 141–45.

47. Davaney, *Pragmatic Historicism*, 24, 61, 77–79, 142; Davaney, *Historicism*, 145–46, 155.

48. Davaney, *Historicism*, 155.

49. Rorty, *Philosophy and Social Hope*, xvii.

50. James, *Pragmatism*, 108.

51. William James, *The Will to Believe, and Other Essays in Popular Philosophy* (New York: Dover, 1956), 25.

52. James, *Pragmatism*, 33, 37, 93, 104, 108, 111, 115, 117, 123. See also Davaney, *Historicism*, 70–71, 74; Dean, *American Religious Empiricism*, 54–55, 60–61. Even the worthwhileness of life is, for James, a human construction. "Visible nature is all plasticity and indifference," he candidly declares. Far from manifesting a "man-loving Deity" or a supernatural "unseen order," this "awful power . . . neither hates nor loves, but rolls all things together meaninglessly to a common doom." Yet reality may still be *made* meaningful, ethically purposive, and worthy of living if we the "livers," by means of our faith, ideals, and redemptive influence, choose to render it so. To quote James at length: "This life *is* worth living, we can say, *since it is what we make it, from the moral point of view*; and we are determined to make it from that point of view, so far as we have anything to do with it, a success. . . . If this life be not a real fight, in which something is eternally gained for the universe by success, it is no better than a game of private theatricals from which one may withdraw at will. But it *feels* like a real fight—as if there were something really wild in the universe which we, with all our idealities and faithfulness, are needed to redeem." James, *The Will to Believe, and Other Essays in Popular Philosophy*, 32–62, quote on 61.

53. James, *Pragmatism*, 122.

54. William James, "Remarks on Spencer's Definition of Mind as Correspondence," in *Writings 1878–1899*, ed. Gerald E. Myers (New York: Library of America, 1992), 908.

55. John Dewey, "The Development of American Pragmatism," in *The Essential Dewey*, vol. 1, *Pragmatism, Education, Democracy*, ed. Larry A. Hickman and Thomas M. Alexander (Bloomington: Indiana University Press, 1998), 11.

56. John Dewey, *The Quest for Certainty: A Study in the Relation of Knowledge and Action* (New York: Pedigree, 1929), 17, 23, 44, 69, 91–95, 102–3, 128, 136–38, 140–94, 195–222, 231–46, 291, 298–99; Dewey, *Reconstruction in Philosophy*, enl. ed. (Boston: Beacon, 1957), 51, 91, 95–102, 112–13, 134–38, 145. See also Dewey, "The Development of American Pragmatism," 8, 10.

57. Rorty, *Philosophy and Social Hope*, 266.

58. Ibid. 48–49, 72–73, 77–78, 85–86; Rorty, *Contingency, Irony, and Solidarity*, 23–69.

59. Rorty, *Contingency, Irony, and Solidarity*, 3.

60. See ibid., 5, 21.

61. Rorty, "Inquiry as Recontextualization," 101; Rorty, *Philosophy and Social Hope*, 58; Rorty, *Contingency, Irony, and Solidarity*, 5; Rorty, "Introduction," 10.

62. See the previous treatment of Rorty's perspectivism.

63. Rorty, *Contingency, Irony, and Solidarity*, 5.

64. Ibid., 3–7; Rorty, "Inquiry as Recontextualization," 96–101; Rorty, *Philosophy and Social Hope*, 33.

65. Rorty, *Philosophy and Social Hope*, xvii; Rorty, *Consequences of Pragmatism*, 166; Rorty, *Contingency, Irony, and Solidarity*, 3–6; Rorty, *Philosophy and the Mirror of Nature*, 375; Dean, *History Making History*, 6.

66. René Descartes, *Selected Philosophical Writings*, trans. John Cottingham, Robert Stoothoff, and Dugald Murdoch (Cambridge: Cambridge University Press, 1988), 76.

67. Richard J. Bernstein, *Beyond Objectivism and Relativism: Science, Hermeneutics, and Praxis* (Philadelphia: University of Pennsylvania Press, 1983), 16.

68. Descartes, *Selected Philosophical Writings*, 80.

69. Stout, *The Flight from Authority*, 4.

70. See Dean, *History Making History*, 6–7.

71. See Davaney, *Historicism*, chs. 1 and 2.

72. Peirce, "Questions concerning Certain Faculties Claimed for Man," 11–27; Peirce, "Some Consequences of Four Incapacities," 28–30, 51–52; Peirce, "The Fixation of Belief," in *The Essential Peirce*, 1:119; Peirce, "How to Make Our Ideas Clear," in *The Essential Peirce*, 1:124–25; Peirce, "What Pragmatism Is," 336. See Richard J. Bernstein, "Pragmatism, Pluralism, and the Healing of Wounds," in *Pragmatism: A Reader*, ed. Louis Menand (New York: Vintage, 1997), 385–86; Bernstein, *The Pragmatic Turn*, 17–18, 34–39.

73. West, *The American Evasion of Philosophy*, 43–45.

74. Ibid., 56.

75. James, *The Will to Believe, and Other Essays in Popular Philosophy*, 14–17.

76. Dewey, *Reconstruction in Philosophy*, xii–xiii.

77. Dewey, *The Quest for Certainty*, 6–8, 14–25, 34–37, 140–41, 165, 167, 193, 277, 288–92, 307, 310–11; Dewey, *Reconstruction in Philosophy*, 21–22, 107–13, 157–60; Dewey, "The Development of American Pragmatism," 8.

78. Davaney, *Pragmatic Historicism*, 23.

79. See the essay, "Nietzsche's Prefiguration of Postmodern American Philosophy," in Cornel West, *The Cornel West Reader* (New York: Basic Civitas Books, 1999), 198–205.

80. Ibid., 198.

81. Ibid., 201–2. See also West, *The American Evasion of Philosophy*, 201–2.

82. Rorty, *Consequences of Pragmatism*, 186; Rorty, *Philosophy and the Mirror of Nature*, 159, 163.

83. Rorty, *Philosophy and the Mirror of Nature*, 6, 315.

84. Rorty, *Philosophy and Social Hope*, 151–52; Rorty, *Philosophy and the Mirror of Nature*, 157, 159.

85. Bernstein, *Beyond Objectivism and Relativism*, 8.

86. Bernstein, "Pragmatism, Pluralism, and the Healing of Wounds," 387; Robert Cummings Neville, *On the Scope and Truth of Theology: Theology as Symbolic Engagement* (New York: T. and T. Clark, 2006), x.

87. Quoted in Lawrence E. Cahoone, *The Ends of Philosophy* (Albany: State University of New York Press, 1995), 105.

88. Neville, *The Highroad around Modernism*, 31.

89. Peirce, "Some Consequences of Four Incapacities," 29, 33–36, 52; Peirce, "The Fixation of Belief," 114, 120–22; Peirce, "How to Make Our Ideas Clear," 137–41; Peirce, "What Pragmatism Is," 331–33, 339–41. See Bernstein, "Pragmatism, Pluralism, and the Healing of Wounds," 387; Bernstein, *The Pragmatic Turn*, 36–37.

90. Peirce, "Some Consequences of Four Incapacities," 29.

91. Peirce, "What Pragmatism Is," 333.

92. James, *Pragmatism*, 34–35, 82–83, 108, 116–17.

93. James, *The Will to Believe, and Other Essays in Popular Philosophy*, vii; James, *Pragmatism*, 83, 89, 94. The pragmatist philosopher Wesley Wildman reaches a similar conclusion about the principles of logic and mathematics, which only appear "indubitable" and "beyond question." In truth, they are "excellent abstractions," abstractions that are derived from experience but are "rarely or never contradicted in experience." On the whole, a pragmatic theory of inquiry, Wildman maintains, is "radically empiricist" insofar as it "discerns no basis or need for synthetic a priori propositions" and treats "their seeming definitiveness as an artifact of habits built around relatively stable generalizations." Yet even these generalizations, however empirically consistent, are simply "promising hypotheses." As such, we must "test them in every way we can imagine, using the best social organization we can devise

for the task." Wildman, *Religious Philosophy as Multidisciplinary Comparative Inquiry*, 179, 197, 215–16.

94. See Dewey, *The Quest for Certainty*, 6–8, 14–25, 34–37, 140–41, 165, 167, 193, 277, 288–92, 307, 310–11; Dewey, *Reconstruction in Philosophy*, 21–22, 107–13, 157–60; Dewey, "The Development of American Pragmatism," 8.

95. Dewey, *Reconstruction in Philosophy*, 96.

96. Cornel West, *Prophetic Fragments: Illuminations of the Crisis in American Religion and Culture* (Grand Rapids, MI: William B. Eerdmans, 1988), 267–70; West, *The Cornel West Reader*, xvii.

97. Davaney, *Pragmatic Historicism*, 189–90.

98. Ibid., 189.

99. Rorty, "Solidarity or Objectivity?," 23.

100. See Bernstein, *The Pragmatic Turn*, 8.

101. See, for example, John Dewey, *The Influence of Darwin on Philosophy, and Other Essays* (Amherst, NY: Prometheus, 1997).

102. Louis Menand, *The Metaphysical Club: A Story of Ideas in America* (New York: Farrar, Straus and Giroux, 2001), 357, 361, 364.

103. James, *Pragmatism*, 94.

104. William James, *The Principles of Psychology*, authorized ed. (New York: Dover, 1950), 2:618, 626, 629, 631, 661–62, 677, 683.

105. Peirce, "How to Make Our Ideas Clear," 129–31; Dewey, "The Development of American Pragmatism," 9–10.

106. Menand, *The Metaphysical Club*, xi–xii.

107. Rorty, *Philosophy and Social Hope*, xxii–xxiii, xxvi, 64–65, 263–69. See also Rorty, *Philosophy and the Mirror of Nature*, 359, 375; Rorty, "Introduction," 10; Rorty, *Consequences of Pragmatism*, xviii–xix.

108. William James, "Philosophical Conceptions and Practical Results," in *The Writings of William James: A Comprehensive Edition*, ed. John J. McDermott (Chicago: University of Chicago Press, 1977), 348.

109. Peirce, "How to Make Our Ideas Clear," 129–32, quote on 132.

110. James, "Philosophical Conceptions and Practical Results," 349.

111. Ibid., 360.

112. Ibid., 347–52; James, *Pragmatism*, 27–44, 45–62, 95–113; James, *The Meaning of Truth*, 37–60; William James, *The Varieties of Religious Experience: A Study in Human Nature* (New York: Penguin, 1902), 443–45; Davaney, *Historicism*, 72–73.

113. James, *The Meaning of Truth*, 48.

114. See, especially, Dewey, "The Development of American Pragmatism," 3–13.

115. Dewey took "warranted assertibility" to be the proper end of inquiry. See John Dewey, *Logic: The Theory of Inquiry* (New York: Henry Holt, 1938), 9, 11, 16, passim.

116. Dewey, *The Quest for Certainty*, 129, 135, 277–78; Dewey, *Reconstruction in Philosophy*, 145. See also Dewey, *The Influence of Darwin on Philosophy, and Other Essays*, 143.

117. Dewey, "The Development of American Pragmatism," 10.
118. Dewey, *The Quest for Certainty*, 129, 136, 184–85, 260–61, 271–73, 277–78, 284–85; Dewey, *Reconstruction in Philosophy*, 48, 145–46, 154–57; Dewey, *The Influence of Darwin on Philosophy, and Other Essays*, 126–53.
119. Rorty, *Philosophy and Social Hope*, 72.
120. Rorty, *Consequences of Pragmatism*, 191–95; Rorty, "Solidarity or Objectivity?," 29; Rorty, *Philosophy and Social Hope*, 27, 270.
121. Rorty, *Consequences of Pragmatism*, xliii.
122. Dean, *History Making History*, 6–7.
123. Bernstein, *The Pragmatic Turn*, 29, 109, 111.
124. Dean, *History Making History*, 11.
125. See Rorty, *Consequences of Pragmatism*, 3–18. Rorty qualifies that the world that is well lost is none other than "the true realistic believer's notion of 'the world,'" the world as it is "in itself," the world that is isolatable from our theories about it, from the "different conceptual schemes" that "carve up the world differently" (16, 14). Robert Neville puts it more pejoratively (though not inaccurately): "The world is any sense of 'reality' that philosophy should be about." Robert Cummings Neville, "Pragmatism, Metaphysics, Comparison, and Realism," in *The Philosophy of Richard Rorty*, ed. Randall E. Auxier and Lewis Edwin Hahn, Library of Living Philosophers (Chicago: Open Court, 2010), 152–53n4.
126. Rorty, *Consequences of Pragmatism*, xvii, 165.
127. Due to space constraints, there are several other important present-day pragmatic realists with whom I will not deal, most notably, Joseph Margolis and Hilary Putnam. See Joseph Margolis, *Pragmatism without Foundations: Reconciling Realism and Relativism* (Oxford: Blackwell, 1986); Hilary Putnam, *Reason, Truth and History* (New York: Cambridge University Press, 1981).
128. This reading of the pragmatist tradition differs from that of Lawrence Cahoone, who maintains that pragmatism is antirealist by nature. See Cahoone, *The Ends of Philosophy*, 8–9, 61, 65, 70–73, 99–155. In Cahoone's telling, even Peircean pragmaticism "cannot succeed in justifying the possibility of realist philosophical knowledge." Besides a slew of unmistakably antirealist notions (e.g., fallibilism, the critique of Cartesian foundationalism and of immediacy in epistemology, the semiotic theory that all thought is in signs), Peirce, akin to virtually all pragmatic thinkers (including, startlingly, the most un-Peircean of pragmatists, Rorty, who reduces justification to "solidarity" with members of one's own society or culture), adopted a form of conventionalism, venturing that the true and the real "refer, respectively, to the opinion fated to be ultimately agreed to by the community of inquirers in the indefinite future and to the object of that belief" (a position I will explore later on). But this conventionalist doctrine, Cahoone counters, is incompatible with realism, for it is none other than the view "that the validity of our judgments is relative to the community, whether it be a definite, actual, and local community [e.g., Rorty's ethnos], or an indefinite, possible, and universal community." Even more antirealistically still, reality itself "is defined idealistically as the object of the

community's opinion" (100, 115, 128; for Cahoone's appraisal of Rorty's more "ethnocentric" conventionalism, see 306–7).

129. Brown, *Boundaries of Our Habitations*, 51.

130. See Peter Berger and Thomas Luckmann, *The Social Construction of Reality: A Treatise in the Sociology of Knowledge* (New York: Anchor 1967); Steinar Kvale, "Themes of Postmodernity," in *The Truth about the Truth: De-confusing and Re-constructing the Postmodern World*, ed. Walter Truett Anderson (New York: Jeremy P. Tarcher/Putnam, 1995).

131. Bernstein, *Beyond Objectivism and Relativism*, 4.

132. William Dean, "A Present Prospect for American Religious Thought," *Journal of the American Academy of Religion* 60, no. 4 (Winter 1992): 739.

133. Gary Dorrien, *Kantian Reason and Hegelian Spirit: The Idealistic Logic of Modern Theology* (Malden, MA: Wiley-Blackwell, 2012), 14–18, 38–45.

134. See Immanuel Kant, *Critique of Pure Reason*, trans. Werner S. Pluhar, unified ed. (Indianapolis, IN: Hackett, 1996), A77–130, B102–69 (129–203). "A" denotes the first edition (1781), and "B" the second edition (1787). Kant's "pure concepts of understanding" include twelve categories under four headings: (1) unity, plurality, and allness (the categories of *quantity*); (2) reality, negation, and limitation (the categories of *quality*); (3) subsistence, causality, and community (the categories of *relation*); and (4) possibility/impossibility, existence/nonexistence, and necessity/contingency (the categories of *modality*). See Dorrien, *Kantian Reason and Hegelian Spirit*, 39.

135. Kant, *Critique of Pure Reason*, B369 (401).

136. Ibid., A491, B519 (506).

137. Likewise, Rorty lifts up some of the striking similarities between Kant and post-Kantian idealists, on the one hand, and twentieth-century "textualists" (e.g., post-structuralists, such as Derrida and Foucault), on the other. Whereas the former conjectured "that nothing exists but ideas," the latter "write as if there were nothing but texts." Rorty, *Consequences of Pragmatism*, 139–59.

138. Dean, "A Present Prospect for American Religious Thought," 738–39, 747–49. Gordon Kaufman is the contemporary pragmatic historicist most beholden to Kant. In *An Essay on Theological Method* (originally published in 1975), Kaufman bases the entire enterprise of theology as "imaginative construction" on Kant's revolutionary claim that concepts like "God" and "world" are "regulative ideas" or "intra-mental" constructs "by means of which the mind orders its own contents but the objective referent for which we have no way of discovering." Gordon D. Kaufman, *An Essay on Theological Method*, 3rd ed. (Atlanta: Scholars Press, 1995), 29–30. To get a sense of the place of Kant in Kaufman's lifelong theological development, see Gordon D. Kaufman, *In the Beginning . . . Creativity* (Minneapolis: Fortress, 2004), 107–27, especially 109 and 113.

139. Davaney, *Pragmatic Historicism*, 7.

140. Dean, "A Present Prospect for American Religious Thought," 739, 749–50.

141. Ibid., 738, 749–50.

142. West, *The American Evasion of Philosophy*, 201; West, *Prophetic Fragments*, 269.

143. Dean, *History Making History*, 8, 23. See Rorty, *Consequences of Pragmatism*, xxxv–xxxvii.

144. See, for example, Rorty, "Solidarity or Objectivity?," 23; Rorty, *Philosophy and Social Hope*, 58.

145. Rorty, *Philosophy and the Mirror of Nature*, 176.

146. Richard Rorty, "Cultural Politics and the Question of the Existence of God," in *Philosophy as Cultural Politics: Philosophical Papers* (Cambridge: Cambridge University Press, 2007), 6–7.

147. See Rorty, *Consequences of Pragmatism*, 169–75.

148. Ibid., xiv, 191–193; Rorty, *Contingency, Irony, and Solidarity*, 7–9, 16, 20.

149. See Rorty, "Inquiry as Recontextualization," 96; Rorty, "Solidarity or Objectivity?," 21–22; Rorty, *Contingency, Irony, and Solidarity*, xv.

150. Rorty, *Consequences of Pragmatism*, xxvi.

151. Ibid., xxxix, 165.

152. See Bernstein, *The Pragmatic Turn*, 211–16.

153. Quoted in ibid., 211–212. See Richard Rorty, "Science as Solidarity," in *Objectivity, Relativism, and Truth*, 39–42.

154. Rorty, *Consequences of Pragmatism*, xiv, 166; Rorty, *Contingency, Irony, and Solidarity*, 5–6.

155. Rorty, "Inquiry as Recontextualization," 101.

156. Rorty, *Philosophy and the Mirror of Nature*, 157, 159.

157. Rorty, *Contingency, Irony, and Solidarity*, 6. Rorty illustrates: "The fact that Newton's vocabulary lets us predict the world more easily than Aristotle's does not mean that the world speaks Newtonian."

158. Rorty, *Philosophy and the Mirror of Nature*, 157–59.

159. Even Kuhn realizes that "what a man sees depends both upon what he looks at and also upon what his previous visual-conceptual experience has taught him to see." Kuhn, *The Structure of Scientific Revolutions*, 113.

160. Rorty, "Inquiry as Recontextualization," 101.

161. Ibid., 101; Rorty, *Consequences of Pragmatism*, xxxix, 165. See Bernstein, *The Pragmatic Turn*, 215.

162. Neville, "Pragmatism, Metaphysics, Comparison, and Realism," 150–52.

163. Douglas R. Anderson and Carl R. Hausman, *Conversations on Peirce: Reals and Ideals* (New York: Fordham University Press, 2012), 59–60.

164. John McDowell, "Towards Rehabilitating Objectivity," in *Rorty and His Critics*, ed. Robert B. Brandom (Malden, MA: Blackwell, 2000), 109–21, final quote on 110.

165. See, among numerous other works, Rorty, *Consequences of Pragmatism*.

166. See James, *Pragmatism*, 33, 37, 93, 104, 108, 111, 115–19, 123.

167. Ibid., 37.

168. See ibid., 115–29; James, *The Meaning of Truth*, 99–119.
169. Michael R. Slater, *William James on Ethics and Faith* (New York: Cambridge University Press, 2009), 184–85, 187–88, 197–216, quote on 197.
170. James, *Pragmatism*, 91.
171. Ibid., 119–20.
172. Ibid., 117–18.
173. James, *The Meaning of Truth*, 56.
174. See James, *The Will to Believe, and Other Essays in Popular Philosophy*, 97.
175. James, *The Meaning of Truth*, 106.
176. Ibid., 105.
177. Ibid., 145.
178. Ibid., 107.
179. Dewey, *The Quest for Certainty*, 210–11.
180. John Dewey, *Experience and Nature* (Chicago: Open Court, 1925), 10–11.
181. Jerome A. Stone, *Religious Naturalism Today: The Rebirth of a Forgotten Alternative* (Albany: State University of New York Press, 2008), 45. See also Dewey, *Experience and Nature*, 102–242, 352.
182. Dewey, *Experience and Nature*, 15, 309.
183. Rorty, "Inquiry as Recontextualization," 96.
184. Dewey, *Experience and Nature*, 4, 13, 285, 341.
185. Anderson and Hausman, *Conversations on Peirce*, 60–67, 71–72.
186. Ibid., 71.
187. Ibid., 63, 59.
188. Donald A. Crosby, *A Religion of Nature* (Albany: State University of New York Press, 2002), 22–26.
189. Nancy Frankenberry, "Major Themes of Empirical Theology," in *Empirical Theology: A Handbook*, ed. Randolph Crump Miller (Birmingham, AL: Religious Education Press, 1992), 54. While Frankenberry's point is well-taken, it is very important not to overgeneralize or parody postmodernism in the process of critiquing it. John Caputo, for example, takes umbrage with critics who unfairly portray the post-structuralist Jacques Derrida as an enemy of reason, knowledge, and truth or as a purveyor of an "anarchistic relativism in which 'anything goes,' " or a linguistic subjectivism, where "language is a prison, just a game of signifiers signifying nothing." Derridean deconstruction, according to Caputo, is "acutely sensitive . . . to the deeply historical, social, and linguistic 'constructedness' of our beliefs and practices." But it does not "bury the idea of 'objectivity,' " propagate the "stupidity" and "stupefying nonsense" that reality is reducible to "words without reference," or "turn everything—the great Greeks, Plato and Aristotle, mathematical physics and the law of gravity included—into fiction." Even Derrida's notorious phrase, "there is nothing outside the text," is not intended to "wipe out the real world," but to affirm "the irreducible alterity of the world we are trying to construe." Derrida is

simply calling for "referential humility" and acknowledging that "existence claims cannot be disentangled from the web of discourse that makes them possible to begin with." Caputo, *Deconstruction in a Nutshell*, 36–38, 52, 55, 74, 80; John D. Caputo, *More Radical Hermeneutics: On Not Knowing Who We Are* (Bloomington: Indiana University Press, 2000), 253–54.

190. Frankenberry, "Major Themes of Empirical Theology," 44–48; Nancy Frankenberry, *Religion and Radical Empiricism* (Albany: State University of New York Press, 1987), 67–68, 143–44.

191. John Ryder, *The Things in Heaven and Earth: An Essay in Pragmatic Naturalism* (New York: Fordham University Press, 2013), 25.

192. Ibid., 5–6, 15–36, 47.

193. Wildman gives a mundane, but helpful, illustration: "To reach out for the handle on a photo-realistic painting of a door, expecting to open the door and pass through, fails to produce an affordance that matches organism interest. This in turn refines perception, modifies action, and rectifies understanding." Wildman, *Religious Philosophy as Multidisciplinary Comparative Inquiry*, 186.

194. Here, Wildman is building on a key idea of classical pragmatism. For instance, Peirce, as I will further expound shortly, surmised that "what anything really is . . . is what it may finally come to be known to be in the ideal state of complete information. . . . In this way, the existence of thought now, depends on what is to be hereafter; so that it has only a potential existence, dependent on the future thought of the community." Peirce, "Some Consequences of Four Incapacities," 54–55.

195. Wildman, *Religious Philosophy as Multidisciplinary Comparative Inquiry*, 78, 170, 181–89, 203–5, 216, 221–24, 230–34.

196. Wesley J. Wildman, *Science and Religious Anthropology: A Spiritually Evocative Naturalist Interpretation of Human Life* (Farnham, UK: Ashgate, 2009), 194.

197. Ibid., 194, 198–201.

198. See Wildman, *Religious Philosophy as Multidisciplinary Comparative Inquiry*, 169–70, 200–201.

199. Peirce, "What Pragmatism Is," 342–43.

200. Bernstein helpfully clarifies that Peirce is "not speaking about a datable time in the future when inquiry ends, but rather about the end of inquiry as a regulative ideal." Bernstein, *The Pragmatic Turn*, 112.

201. Peirce, "Some Consequences of Four Incapacities," 52–55; Peirce, "The Fixation of Belief," 120; Peirce, "How to Make Our Ideas Clear," 136–39; Peirce, "What Pragmatism Is," 339, 342–43. See Neville, *The Highroad around Modernism*, 31.

202. Peirce, "The Fixation of Belief," 120.

203. Peirce, "An American Plato: Review of Royce's *Religious Aspect of Philosophy*," in *The Essential Peirce*, 1:233–34; Peirce, "On Phenomenology," in *The Essential Peirce*, 2:150–51, 154; Peirce, "The Seven Systems of Metaphysics," in *The*

Essential Peirce, 2:182–83; Peirce, "Sundry Logical Conceptions," in *The Essential Perice*, 2:268. See Bernstein, *The Pragmatic Turn*, 46–51, 131–36; Anderson and Hausman, *Conversations on Peirce*, 62; Cahoone, *The Ends of Philosophy*, 124, 128.

204. Neville, *The Highroad around Modernism*, 25–31; Cahoone, *The Ends of Philosophy*, 102.

205. Cahoone, *The Ends of Philosophy*, 62, 100, 105–6.

206. Peirce, "Some Consequences of Four Incapacities," 40; Peirce, "What Pragmatism Is," 345; Peirce, "The Categories Defended," in *The Essential Peirce*, 2:160; Peirce, "The Seven Systems of Metaphysics," 183; Peirce, "Sundry Logical Conceptions," 269. See Bernstein, *The Pragmatic Turn*, 132–36. In addition to secondness and thirdness, Peirce also talked about *firstness*, which designates the *qualitative* aspects of things. See Peirce, "The Categories Defended," 160; Peirce, "Sundry Logical Conceptions," 268–69. See also Bernstein, *The Pragmatic Turn*, 130–31.

207. Peirce, "Sundry Logical Conceptions," 268.

208. Rorty, *Consequences of Pragmatism*, 160–61.

209. Frankenberry, *Religion and Radical Empiricism*, 67.

210. Davaney lists the neopragmatists Rorty, Stout, and West as pragmatic historicism's primary "philosophical fellow travelers." Elsewhere, she traces the history of American historicism back to the paleopragmatist philosophies of James and Dewey. See Davaney, *Pragmatic Historicism*, ch. 5; Davaney, *Historicism*, 68–92. I do not necessarily wish to displace any of these philosophers (especially James and Dewey), but only to bring pragmatists of a more realist bent along for the journey.

211. Berger and Luckmann, *The Social Construction of Reality*, 60–61.

212. See ibid., 88–89.

213. Ibid., 60–61.

214. Dean, "A Present Prospect for American Religious Thought," 741–43; William Dean, *The Religious Critic in American Culture* (Albany: State University of New York Press, 1994), 101–7; Dean, *The American Spiritual Culture: And the Invention of Jazz, Football, and the Movies* (New York: Continuum, 2002), 70–78.

215. Dean, "A Present Prospect for American Religious Thought," 742.

216. Dean, *The American Spiritual Culture*, 72–73, 85.

217. Wildman, *Religious Philosophy as Multidisciplinary Comparative Inquiry*, 199–201, 203–4.

218. Neville, *The Highroad around Modernism*, 32.

219. Rorty, *Consequences of Pragmatism*, xvii, 166.

220. Rorty, *Philosophy and Social Hope*, xxiii, xxvi, 27, 65, 269.

221. For an illuminating discussion of early pragmatism's (specifically, Peirce's) convergence theory of truth and reality, see Cahoone, *The Ends of Philosophy*, 115–16, 124–29.

222. Peirce, "How to Make Our Ideas Clear," 139; Peirce, "Some Consequences of Four Incapacities," 52–55. See also Peirce, "What Pragmatism Is," 340.

223. James, *The Meaning of Truth*, 143.

224. James, *Pragmatism*, 106–7; James, *The Meaning of Truth*, 143.
225. See Peirce, "Some Consequences of Four Incapacities," 52–55.
226. Quoted in West, *The American Evasion of Philosophy*, 51–52.
227. Peirce accepted the "nominal definition" of truth as "the correspondence of a representation with its object." Peirce, "The Basis of Pragmaticism in the Normative Sciences," in *The Essential Peirce*, 2:379. Years earlier, he put it more aggressively, assuring that "there is nothing to prevent knowing outward things as they really are, and it is most likely that we do thus know them in numberless cases." Peirce, "Some Consequences of Four Incapacities," 52.
228. Peirce, "What Pragmatism Is," 334–35; Peirce, "A Sketch of Logical Critics," in *The Essential Peirce*, 2:457. See Anderson and Hausman, *Conversations on Peirce*, 59–60.
229. Although a defender rather than a decrier of it, Rorty, similar to Wildman and Peirce, mistakenly interprets the Jamesian notion that the true is "what is good for *us* to believe" as an anti-correspondence theory of truth. See Rorty, "Solidarity or Objectivity?," 22. Rorty, Wildman, and Peirce all miss the fact that, for James, ideas are good for us to believe *only if* they "'agree' in the widest sense with a reality." James, *Pragmatism*, 102.
230. James, *The Meaning of Truth*, 104, 117.
231. Slater, *William James on Ethics and Faith*, 183–199, 204–16, quote on 183–84.
232. James, *The Meaning of Truth*, 112.
233. See West, *The American Evasion of Philosophy*, 67; Slater, *William James on Ethics and Faith*, 190–191.
234. James, *Pragmatism*, 38, 96–97; James, *The Meaning of Truth*, 110. Emphasis added.
235. James, *Pragmatism*, 95–113; James, *The Meaning of Truth*, 104–19.
236. Slater, *William James on Ethics and Faith*, 207.
237. Ibid., 221.
238. James, *Pragmatism*, 23, 26, 31, 40, 43–44, 131, quote on 40.
239. James, *The Varieties of Religious Experience*, 1–25, 217–429, 485–519.
240. Ibid., 20.
241. Ibid., 506.
242. James, *Pragmatism*, 143.
243. Ibid., 54–55.
244. James, *The Varieties of Religious Experience*, 445–47, 508.
245. Ibid., 329, 331.
246. James, *Pragmatism*, 43.
247. Slater, *William James on Ethics and Faith*, 180–82, 185.
248. James, *The Varieties of Religious Experience*, 15; James, *Pragmatism*, 43.
249. This does not mean, according to Slater, that James defended a coherence theory of truth, only that "coherence is one of the properties which makes an idea or theory *satisfactory*." Slater, *William James on Ethics and Faith*, 192n44.

250. James, *Pragmatism*, 74–79.
251. James, *The Varieties of Religious Experience*, 163.
252. Peirce, "What Pragmatism Is," 335, 341. See, for example, James, *The Meaning of Truth*, 102–3, 111–14, 145.
253. James, *Pragmatism*, 34, 43, 97, 101–4, 111–12; James, *The Meaning of Truth*, 99–119, 142–45.
254. Slater, *William James on Ethics and Faith*, 207.
255. Dewey, "The Development of American Pragmatism," 8.
256. Dewey, *The Influence of Darwin on Philosophy, and Other Essays*, 155.
257. Ibid., 154–68; Dewey, *The Quest for Certainty*, 226–28, 262, 274–75; Dewey, *Reconstruction in Philosophy*, 157–60; John Dewey, "What Pragmatism Means by 'Practical,'" in *The Essential Dewey*, vol. 2, *Ethics, Logic, Psychology*, ed. Larry A. Hickman and Thomas M. Alexander (Bloomington: Indiana University Press, 1998), 377, 383–84; Dewey, "Philosophy and Democracy," in *The Essential Dewey*, 1:74.
258. See Wildman, *Religious Philosophy as Multidisciplinary Comparative Inquiry*, 200–201, 203–4.
259. Dewey, *Experience and Nature*, 46.
260. Rorty, *Contingency, Irony, and Solidarity*, xvi.
261. Ibid., xiii, xv.
262. Jean-François Lyotard, *The Postmodern Condition: A Report on Knowledge*, trans. Geoff Bennington and Brian Massumi (Minneapolis: University of Minnesota Press, 1984), xxiii.
263. Ibid., xxiv–xxv, 73, 81–82.
264. Caputo, *Deconstruction in a Nutshell*, 31–105. See Derrida, *Of Grammatology*, 7–26, 44–73, 158–60, as well as the essay "Différance" in Jacques Derrida, *Margins of Philosophy*, trans. Alan Bass (Chicago: University of Chicago Press, 1982), 3–27.
265. Caputo, *Deconstruction in a Nutshell*, 51–52, 70.
266. Davaney, *Pragmatic Historicism*, 3, 11; Davaney, *Historicism*, 131–32.
267. Wildman, *Religious Philosophy as Multidisciplinary Comparative Inquiry*, 57. Emphasis added.
268. See Neville, *The Highroad around Modernism*, xi.
269. Neville notes that contemporary Chinese neo-Confucianism, although not at all historically connected with European modernity, also intersects with American philosophy's highroad around modernism at several important junctures (both, for example, undertake speculative metaphysics and challenge monolithic readings of the Western tradition). See ibid., xii.
270. Ibid., xi–xiv, 1–21. See also Wildman, *Religious Philosophy as Multidisciplinary Comparative Inquiry*, 169–70.
271. Bernstein, *The Pragmatic Turn*, 29.
272. See Davaney, *Historicism*, 132, 185n30.
273. Jacques Derrida, *Writing and Difference*, trans. Alan Bass (Chicago: University of Chicago Press, 1978), 279–80.

274. Wildman, *Religious Philosophy as Multidisciplinary Comparative Inquiry*, 11.
275. Neville, "Pragmatism, Metaphysics, Comparison, and Realism," 141.
276. Ibid., 143–44.
277. See Peirce, "The Doctrine of Necessity Examined," in *The Essential Peirce*, 1:298–311; Peirce, "Evolutionary Love," in *The Essential Peirce*, 1:352–71; Peirce, "The Seven Systems of Metaphysics," 179–95. See also Neville, *The Highroad around Modernism*, 25–52; Robert S. Corrington, *Ecstatic Naturalism: Signs of the World* (Bloomington: Indiana University Press, 1994), 5.
278. See James, *Essays in Radical Empiricism*, and *A Pluralistic Universe*; Dewey, *Experience and Nature*.
279. Dean, *History Making History*, 84, 88–97; Jerome Paul Soneson, *Pragmatism and Pluralism: John Dewey's Significance for Theology* (Minneapolis: Fortress, 1993), 164.
280. Dewey, *Experience and Nature*, 48.
281. See Dean, *American Religious Empiricism*, 64; Neville, *The Highroad around Modernism*, 138–39.
282. James, *Pragmatism*, 31, 38, 40. Here, James prefigured Whitehead, who, in *Process and Reality*, compared metaphysics with an airplane trip: "It starts from the ground of particular observation; it makes a flight in the thin air of imaginative generalization; and it again lands for renewed observation rendered acute by rational interpretation." And the metaphysical categories that result from such a journey are not dogmatically final or "severally clear, distinct, and certain," but are "tentative formulations of the ultimate generalities." In his own way, then, Whitehead, like the American pragmatists, was a nonfoundationalist, fallibilistic metaphysician: "Speculative boldness must be balanced by complete humility before logic, before fact." Alfred North Whitehead, *Process and Reality: An Essay in Cosmology*, corr. ed. (New York: Free Press, 1978), 5, 8, 17.
283. Neville, "Pragmatism, Metaphysics, Comparison, and Realism," 144; Neville, *Realism in Religion*, 24–25; Dean, *American Religious Empiricism*, 64.
284. Rorty, *Consequences of Pragmatism*, 161, 213–14. Dean bemoans that Rorty, as a rule, "systematically deprives James and Dewey of everything except their pragmatism," dismissing their radical empiricist metaphysics, axiology, and epistemology. See Dean, *History Making History*, 84.
285. Rorty, *Consequences of Pragmatism*, 72–89.
286. Johann Gottfried Herder, *Against Pure Reason: Writings on Religion, Language, and History*, trans. Marcia Bunge (Minneapolis: Fortress, 1993), 38.
287. Mathews, *Is God Emeritus?*, 31.
288. Neville, *Realism in Religion*, 24.
289. Davaney, *Pragmatic Historicism*, 52.
290. Dean, *American Religious Empiricism*, 65; Dean, *History Making History*, 84–85.
291. See Rorty, *Contingency, Irony, and Solidarity*, xvi, 20.
292. Jerome Paul Soneson, "Rorty's Final Vocabularies and the Possibility of a Historicist Metaphysics," in Hardwick and Crosby, *Pragmatism, Neo-pragmatism,*

and Religion, 300; Kaufman, *In Face of Mystery*, 240–41; Davaney, *Pragmatic Historicism*, 51–53, 55, 61.

293. Davaney, *Pragmatic Historicism*, 51–52.

294. Brown, "The Fall of '26," 199–201.

295. Kaufman, *In Face of Mystery*, 250–52, 259, quote on 252.

296. Rorty, *Contingency, Irony, and Solidarity*, xiii.

297. See Soneson, "Rorty's Final Vocabularies and the Possibility of a Historicist Metaphysics," 295–96.

298. Dean, *History Making History*, 85. Soneson also notes that Rorty's vision of a "liberal utopia" is achievable only under a certain set of metaphysical conditions. Specifically, the world must be (1) "plastic," "historical," and "open-ended" as opposed to "fixed," "final," and "complete," and (2) capable of transforming history's "limits" and "constraints" from "impediments into the enrichment of life, into dynamic and evolving social orders which increasingly encourage a diversification of new vocabularies, new ways of being human, the flourishing of new self-constructions in and through the creation of new narratives." Soneson, "Rorty's Final Vocabularies and the Possibility of a Historicist Metaphysics," 304.

299. Rorty, *Contingency, Irony, and Solidarity*, xiii.

300. Rorty, *Philosophy and Social Hope*, 262.

301. Mathews, *Is God Emeritus?*, 31; Dorrien, *Idealism, Realism, and Modernity, 1900–1950*, 212.

302. Robert S. Corrington, *Nature and Spirit: An Essay in Ecstatic Naturalism* (New York: Fordham University Press, 1992), 4.

303. Soneson, "Rorty's Final Vocabularies and the Possibility of a Historicist Metaphysics," 293–307.

304. Soneson, *Pragmatism and Pluralism*, 164–82.

305. Davaney, *Pragmatic Historicism*, 126–27.

306. Ibid., 52, 55–56, 58, 61–62, 64, 79–80, 191.

307. Kaufman, *In Face of Mystery*, 240–41, 250–63.

308. West, *The American Evasion of Philosophy*, 5.

309. Robert S. Corrington, "Beyond Experience: Pragmatism and Nature's God," *American Journal of Theology and Philosophy* 14, no. 2 (May 1993): 148.

310. Robert S. Corrington, "The Emancipation of American Philosophy," *Newsletters on the Black Experience* 90, no. 3 (Fall 1991): 23–26. See also Corrington, *Ecstatic Naturalism*, 4–5.

311. West, *Prophetic Fragments*, 267–70.

312. West, *The American Evasion of Philosophy*, 96.

313. Ibid., 207–8.

314. See Ryder, *The Things in Heaven and Earth*, 18.

315. See Soneson, "Rorty's Final Vocabularies and the Possibility of a Historicist Metaphysics," 293–307.

316. Ayer was a representative of logical positivism, which held that every meaningful and valid statement is either analytic or synthetic, a priori or demonstrable and falsifiable by empirical, observable facts. Accordingly, the logical positivists restricted philosophy to the analysis, clarification, and organization of language and thought and dispensed with metaphysical, ontological, and religious abstraction. See, for example, A. J. Ayer, *Language, Truth, and Logic* (New York: Dover, 1952). And Kant significantly limited the role of metaphysics in philosophical (and theological) discourse by talking about "the antinomy of pure reason," showing that antithetical positions on traditional metaphysical questions—for example, whether the world has a beginning, whether freedom or a necessary Supreme Being exists—proffer equally strong arguments and, thus, ultimately lie beyond the reach of experience and rational proof. Wildman, *Religious Philosophy as Multidisciplinary Comparative Inquiry*, 8–10; Dorrien, *Kantian Reason and Hegelian Spirit*, 47. See Kant, *Critique of Pure Reason*, A406–567, B433–595 (442–559).

317. Wildman, *Religious Philosophy as Multidisciplinary Comparative Inquiry*, 4–13, 57–61, 63–74.

318. For example, Wildman notes that Kant's first antinomy (whether or not "the world has a beginning in time and is also enclosed within bounds as regards space"), far from being a perpetually irresolvable dispute, "may prove to be tractable." Physical cosmologists "are finding ways to test the claims that the universe has a finite age and that it is spatially finite. . . . Neither of the two opposed arguments in the first antinomy is as compelling as Kant claimed, and the question may eventually be decidable, if not based on direct observation then indirectly and probabilistically within the framework of quantum cosmologies." The moral of the story, for Wildman, is that even if some "big-question inquiries" may turn out to be futile in the long run, we cannot "easily determine where these dead ends are without trying" and seeing what happens. Ibid., 10, 12, 74. For Kant's discussion of the first antinomy, see Kant, *Critique of Pure Reason*, A426–32, B454–60 (458–64).

319. Wildman, *Religious Philosophy as Multidisciplinary Comparative Inquiry*, 4–13, 46–47, 60–68, 71–77, 177–78, 198, 216.

320. Ibid., 60.

321. See Davaney, *Pragmatic Historicism*, 64, 79–80, 191.

322. See Dean, *American Religious Empiricism*, 64.

Chapter 7

1. See Gerald Birney Smith, *Social Idealism and the Changing Theology: A Study of the Ethical Aspects of Christian Doctrine* (New York: Macmillan, 1913), 167.

2. Sheila Greeve Davaney, *Historicism: The Once and Future Challenge for Theology* (Minneapolis: Fortress, 2006), 97.

3. Gerald Birney Smith, "Systematic Theology and Ministerial Efficiency," *American Journal of Theology* 16, no. 4 (October 1912): 609.

4. Sallie McFague, *Models of God: Theology for an Ecological, Nuclear Age* (Philadelphia: Fortress, 1987), 22, 25, 26–27, 36–40.

5. Ibid., 27.

6. Sheila Greeve Davaney, *Pragmatic Historicism: A Theology for the Twenty-First Century* (Albany: State University of New York Press, 2000), 55–56, 80.

7. William James, *The Will to Believe, and Other Essays in Popular Philosophy* (New York: Dover, 1956), vii.

8. The subtitle of Schleiermacher's masterpiece, *On Religion* (1799), is *Speeches to Its Cultured Despisers*. This book is often hailed as the founding work of liberal theology. See Friedrich Schleiermacher, *On Religion: Speeches to Its Cultured Despisers*, trans. John Oman (Louisville: Westminster John Knox Press, 1994).

9. Wesley Wildman, however, identifies analogues to liberal Christianity in Reform movements within Judaism and, more recently, in Islamic modernism. Wesley J. Wildman, "The Ambiguous Heritage and Perpetual Promise of Liberal Theology," *American Journal of Theology and Philosophy* 32, no. 1 (January 2011): 45.

10. This is why the early liberal movement in Germany referred to itself as "mediating theology" (*Vermittlungstheologie*). See Gary Dorrien, *Kantian Reason and Hegelian Spirit: The Idealistic Logic of Modern Theology* (Malden, MA: Wiley-Blackwell, 2012), 4.

11. See Wesley J. Wildman, *Fidelity with Plausibility: Modest Christologies in the Twentieth Century* (Albany: State University of New York Press, 1998).

12. Gary Dorrien, *Imagining Progressive Religion, 1805–1900*, vol. 1 of *The Making of American Liberal Theology* (Louisville: Westminster John Knox Press, 2001), xiii–xxv; Gary Dorrien, "The Crisis and Necessity of Liberal Theology," *American Journal of Theology and Philosophy* 30, no. 1 (January 2009): 3–4, 21; Dorrien, *Kantian Reason and Hegelian Spirit*, 4–5.

13. Wildman, "The Ambiguous Heritage and Perpetual Promise of Liberal Theology," 45–50, quote on 45.

14. See Robert Cummings Neville, *On the Scope and Truth of Theology: Theology as Symbolic Engagement* (New York: T. and T. Clark, 2006), ch. 1.

15. Neville argues that arbitrariness is the major drawback of all identity theologies. See Neville, *On the Scope and Truth of Theology*, 16–19. For instance, Barthian theology, for all its beauty, appears completely arbitrary from the outside. After all, "it simply did not engage the stories of the Buddhists and Hindus, Confucians and Daoists, and hardly the Jews and Muslims. From their standpoint, Barth's story looks both parochial and uninteresting except as perhaps giving clues for understanding colonialism." Even from the inside, a narrated theology will seem revelatory merely to those inclined (for mostly historical or personal reasons) to identify with it. To a fundamentalist dispensationalist, or even to an Anglican Thomist like John Milbank, Barth's telling of the Christian narrative may smack more of Reformed Protestantism than of the gospel. Neville concludes that narrative always "lends itself to the

arbitrariness of the narrator's own stresses and internal interpretations" (and so do its postmodern counterparts—texts, grammars, languages, regulative doctrines, etc.). Robert Cummings Neville, *Realism in Religion: A Pragmatist's Perspective* (Albany: State University of New York Press, 2009), 10.

16. Neville, *Realism in Religion*, 23.

17. Neville, *On the Scope and Truth of Theology*, ix–xviii, 1–28; Neville, *Realism in Religion*, 9–21, 75–86.

18. Neville, *Realism in Religion*, 27–34, quote on 34.

19. Gordon D. Kaufman, *In Face of Mystery: A Constructive Theology* (Cambridge, MA: Harvard University Press, 1993), 42.

20. According to Neville, the Lindbeckian program "can be dragged from the legacy of Barth to that of Tillich." Still, like me, he worries that the postliberal approach is in danger of nominalism (doctrines are about language and narrative rather than their "purported real subjects"), fideism ("pick your community and you've got your truth"), and relativism (theology has no "normative context" for theological critique, other than the intratextualist one of discerning whether or not a religion is being true to its "basic grammar"). Most of all, the cultural-linguistic model falls prey to severe arbitrariness, Neville laments, reducing theology to the way particular communities talk about religious topics as opposed to the intended referents of those topics (resembling, I would add, Rorty's efforts to make philosophy about philosophical conversation rather than that which philosophers are conversing about—e.g., the nature of reality). See Neville, *Realism in Religion*, 2, 35, 49, 77–78, 82; Neville, *On the Scope and Truth of Theology*, 17–18.

21. George A. Lindbeck, *The Nature of Doctrine: Religion and Theology in a Postliberal Age* (Philadelphia: Westminster Press, 1984), ch. 6, quote on 134–35.

22. Wesley J. Wildman, *Religious Philosophy as Multidisciplinary Comparative Inquiry: Envisioning a Future for the Philosophy of Religion* (Albany: State University of New York Press, 2010), 26–34, 236.

23. According to Dorrien, Case, Foster, Mathews, Smith, Brown, Davaney, Dean, Kaufman, and McFague are all characters in the larger story of American liberal theology. See Gary Dorrien, *Idealism, Realism, and Modernity, 1900–1950*, vol. 2 of *The Making of American Liberal Theology* (Louisville: Westminster John Knox Press, 2003), chs. 3 and 4; Gary Dorrien, *Crisis, Irony, and Postmodernity, 1950–2005*, vol. 3 of *The Making of American Liberal Theology* (Louisville: Westminster John Knox Press, 2006), chs. 5, 6, and 8. Incidentally, Troeltsch, whose historicism was analyzed in chapters 3 and 5, also belongs to the tradition of Christian theological liberalism. See especially Ernst Troeltsch, *The Christian Faith*, trans. Garrett E. Paul (Minneapolis: Fortress, 1991); Ernst Troeltsch, "On the Possibility of a Liberal Christianity," in *Religion in History*, ed. and trans. James Luther Adams and Walter F. Bense (Minneapolis: Fortress, 1991), 343–59. In some ways, the debates between Troeltschian and Ritschlian historicists in the late nineteenth and early twentieth century (see chapter 5) prefigure the liberal-postliberal divide in contemporary historicist theology.

24. See Neville, *Realism in Religion*, 18.
25. See Lindbeck, *The Nature of Doctrine*, 32–39.
26. Gerald Birney Smith, "The Task and Method of Systematic Theology," *American Journal of Theology* 14, no. 2 (April 1910): 219–33.
27. G. B. Smith, "Systematic Theology and Ministerial Efficiency," 605–11. See also Gerald Birney Smith, *Current Christian Thinking* (Chicago: University of Chicago Press, 1928), 46.
28. G. B. Smith, "Systematic Theology and Ministerial Efficiency," 608–9.
29. G. B. Smith, "The Task and Method of Systematic Theology," 232–33; G. B. Smith, "Systematic Theology and Ministerial Efficiency," 611–13. See Davaney, *Historicism*, 102. Neville develops a comparable approach to religious apologetics and philosophical argumentation. See Neville, *Realism in Religion*, ch. 5.
30. Dorrien, *Idealism, Realism, and Modernity, 1900–1950*, 203–07.
31. Shailer Mathews, *The Faith of Modernism* (New York: Macmillan, 1924), 1–53, 83, 169–82.
32. Davaney, *Pragmatic Historicism*, 58, 61, 64, 79–80.
33. Ibid., 167–68. Of course, Davaney, akin to Gustavo Gutiérrez and other liberation theologians, is not uncritical of theological liberalism, rebuking it for failing "to include or provide the means of contributing to the struggles of the world's nonpersons" (167). Hers is a liberal *and a liberationist* historicism.
34. Delwin Brown, *Boundaries of Our Habitations: Tradition and Theological Construction* (Albany: State University of New York Press, 1994), 148–49. Wildman comes to a similar conclusion, alleging that the proper contrasts are between liberalism and conservatism (or fundamentalism), not liberalism and evangelicalism: "Contrary to more recent narrow usage, the word 'evangelical' is shared property within the Christian heritage. As the nineteenth-century Protestant battles between modernists and conservatives indicate, most on both sides thought of themselves as evangelicals and the relevant questions were the meanings of engagement with contemporary cultural wisdom and fidelity to extant traditions of belief and practice." Wildman, "The Ambiguous Heritage and Perpetual Promise of Liberal Theology," 46.
35. Delwin Brown and Clark H. Pinnock, *Theological Crossfire: An Evangelical/Liberal Dialogue* (Grand Rapids, MI: Zondervan, 1990), 26, 31–32. Neville fairly reports (though with a hint of exaggeration) that even the sociohistorical theologians of the Chicago school "left very little of the distinctive Christian heritage in play," thereby succumbing to "religious boredom and banality." They were "famous for focusing so much on method that it was never used." Neville, *Realism in Religion*, 28, 33.
36. See Brown, *Boundaries of Our Habitations*, ch. 5.
37. Brown and Pinnock, *Theological Crossfire*, 25.
38. Brown, *Boundaries of Our Habitations*, 6.
39. Brown and Pinnock, *Theological Crossfire*, 24–25, quote on 28–29.
40. As does Kaufman. Kaufman sponsors a "critical theology" that, unlike "authoritarian Christian theologies," ought to become "a legitimate discipline even in entirely secular institutions" (e.g., the modern academy). Critical theologians (Roman

Catholic, Buddhist, feminist, Jewish, or whatever) engage in "critical examination of the faith-orientations of the communities with which they identify themselves, and in conversation with each other, and with others in the university, about the whole spectrum of positions they are collectively exploring." Gordon D. Kaufman, "Critical Theology as a University Discipline," in *Theology and the University: Essays in Honor of John B. Cobb, Jr.*, ed. David Ray Griffin and Joseph C. Hough (Albany: State University of New York Press, 1991), 36, 42–43.

41. See Delwin Brown, "Academic Theology in the University; or, Why an Ex-Queen's Heir Should Be Made a Subject," in *Religious Studies, Theology, and the University: Conflicting Maps, Changing Terrain*, ed. Linell E. Cady and Delwin Brown (Albany: State University of New York Press, 2002), 126–39; Sheila Greeve Davaney, "Rethinking Theology and Religious Studies," in *Religious Studies, Theology, and the University: Conflicting Maps, Changing Terrain*, ed. Linell E. Cady and Delwin Brown (Albany: State University of New York Press, 2002), 140–54.

42. Wildman, *Religious Philosophy as Multidisciplinary Comparative Inquiry*, xv, 232–33, 236–37, 307–14.

43. Wesley J. Wildman, "Theology without Walls: The Future of Transreligious Theology," *Open Theology* 2, no. 1 (January 2016): 243; Jerry L. Martin, "Introduction to the Topical Issue 'Is Transreligious Theology Possible?,'" *Open Theology* 2, no. 1 (January 2016): 261.

44. See George Burman Foster, *The Function of Religion in Man's Struggle for Existence* (Chicago: University of Chicago Press, 1909).

45. See Shailer Mathews, *The Atonement and the Social Process* (New York: Macmillan, 1930); Mathews, *The Growth of the Idea of God* (New York: Macmillan, 1931); Mathews, "Theology and the Social Mind," *Biblical World* 46, no. 4 (October 1915): 201–48.

46. See Gordon D. Kaufman, *An Essay on Theological Method*, 3rd ed. (Atlanta: Scholars Press, 1995); Kaufman, *In Face of Mystery*.

47. See Sallie McFague, *Metaphorical Theology: Models of God in Religious Language* (Philadelphia: Fortress Press, 1982); McFague, *Models of God*.

48. See William Dean, *The Religious Critic in American Culture* (Albany: State University of New York Press, 1994); Dean, *The American Spiritual Culture: And the Invention of Jazz, Football, and the Movies* (New York: Continuum, 2002).

49. McFague, *Metaphorical Theology*, 2–3, 34.

50. Davaney, *Pragmatic Historicism*, 23.

51. Kaufman, *An Essay on Theological Method*, 36, 32–33.

52. Gordon D. Kaufman, "Mystery, Critical Consciousness, and Faith," in *The Rationality of Religious Belief: Essays in Honour of Basil Mitchell*, ed. William J. Abraham and Steven W. Holtzer (Oxford: Clarendon Press, 1987), 67.

53. Kaufman, *In Face of Mystery*, 32–34, 37–40; Kaufman, *An Essay on Theological Method*, 28–42. Emphasis added.

54. Gordon D. Kaufman, "Empirical Realism in Theology: An Examination of Some Themes in Meland and Loomer," in *New Essays in Religious Naturalism*,

ed. W. Creighton Peden and Larry E. Axel (Macon, GA: Mercer University Press, 1993), 142.

55. Ibid., 135–46; Kaufman, *An Essay on Theological Method*, 5–10.

56. Sheila Greeve Davaney, "Directions in Historicism: Language, Experience, and Pragmatic Adjudication," in Peden and Axel, *New Essays in Religious Naturalism*, 59. See William Dean, "Empirical Theology: A Revisable Tradition," *Process Studies* 19, no. 2 (Summer 1990): 87.

57. Brown, *Boundaries of Our Habitations*, 51–52.

58. It should be pointed out, however, that Schleiermacher had a historically conscious side, a side that many of his past and present critics have tended to disregard. As James Livingston notes: "Related to this discovery of the religious feeling prior to all thought is Schleiermacher's sense of religion as a historical, social phenomenon which can be best described in terms of an empirical or experiential representation of a community's self-consciousness at a given time. Here we can see a similarity between Schleiermacher and Herder's historicist conception of religion." James C. Livingston, *Modern Christian Thought: The Enlightenment and the Nineteenth Century*, 2nd ed. (Minneapolis: Fortress, 2006), 100. For a short but insightful analysis of Schleiermacher's neglected historicism, see Davaney, *Historicism*, 32–37.

59. G. B. Smith, "The Task and Method of Systematic Theology," 217.

60. Delwin Brown, "The Fall of '26: Gerald Birney Smith and the Collapse of the Socio-historical Framework of Theology," *American Journal of Theology and Philosophy* 11, no. 3 (September 1990): 195, 200–201.

61. Gordon D. Kaufman, *Theology for a Nuclear Age* (Philadelphia: Westminster Press, 1985), 25.

62. Kaufman, *In Face of Mystery*, xii.

63. McFague, *Metaphorical Theology*, 19.

64. Ibid., 1–2, 4–5, 9–10, 13–29, 38, 40–41; McFague, *Models of God*, xii, 22–23, 34–40, final quote from 35.

65. See Foster, *The Function of Religion in Man's Struggle for Existence*, 109; Shailer Mathews, *Is God Emeritus?* (New York: Macmillan, 1940), 34–38, 85; Mathews, *The Growth of the Idea of God*, 226. Incidentally, I consider the naturalistic theisms of both Foster and Mathews too personalistic and human-centered. I include them in my discussion here only to indicate that their constructive historicisms had a realist component (however problematic). What I will endeavor to do in chapter 8 is to fuse the methodology of the early Chicago school with the theological content of the later Chicago school, combining the first generation's emphasis on the social construction of the religions' diverse ultimates with the third generation's (primarily Loomer's) less anthropocentric religious naturalism.

66. Gordon D. Kaufman, *God the Problem* (Cambridge, MA: Harvard University Press, 1972), 85.

67. As I will point out in the next chapter, Davaney, in her review of *Models of God*, questions the extent to which McFague's own theological metaphors (e.g., a

God that seeks "enhancement and fulfillment for *all* living beings") relate to modern understandings of reality (e.g., evolutionary theory). See Sheila Greeve Davaney, review of *Models of God: Theology for an Ecological, Nuclear Age*, by Sallie McFague, *Religious Studies Review* 16, no. 1 (January 1990): 40. The version of religious naturalism I lay down in this book jettisons nature romanticism, teleology, cosmological optimism, unambiguously just and loving deities, and anthropomorphisms of all stripes and flavors (cf. chapter 8), and so I resonate entirely with Davaney's concerns. Nevertheless, I welcome McFague's critical realist epistemology, even if the realism of her own theology is wanting.

68. McFague, *Metaphorical Theology*, 131–37; McFague, *Models of God*, 22–28.

69. Pragmatic historicism departs, as well, from a number of traditional realist theologies on the contemporary scene, such as that of Francesca Aran Murphy. Refreshingly, Murphy argues that narrative theologians (e.g., George Lindbeck, Robert Jenson, and Herbert McCabe) make theology self-referential by construing both its method *and its content* narratively (and in the postmodern epoch, linguistically). In the process of "describing the relations between God and humanity as a story," they end up intimating that "God *is* a story." See Francesca Aran Murphy, *God Is Not a Story: Realism Revisited* (Oxford: Oxford University Press, 2007). However, whereas Murphy "revisits realism" primarily to reassert (albeit in careful and sophisticated manner) the reality of classical Christian doctrines, a pragmatic historicist like Kaufman differentiates between "God," the doctrinal symbol imaginatively constructed by particular human beings for the purpose of providing orientation and direction in life—which, in some sense, is indeed a story—and God, the impenetrable mystery, the relativizer of all our constructs and stories (including the Christian God). See Kaufman, *God the Problem*, 85–115. By late career, Kaufman came to view theology's "real referent" (the God who is not a story, as it were) not only apophatically but also naturalistically, as "creativity itself." See Gordon D. Kaufman, *In the Beginning . . . Creativity* (Minneapolis: Fortress, 2004).

70. William Dean, "The Persistence of Experience: A Commentary on Kaufman's Theology," in Peden and Axel, *New Essays in Religious Naturalism*, 72. See also Dean, *History Making History: The New Historicism in American Religious Thought* (Albany: State University of New York Press, 1988), 124–26.

71. Dean, "The Persistence of Experience," 77.

72. Kaufman, *God the Problem*, 85–86.

73. Wildman, *Religious Philosophy as Multidisciplinary Comparative Inquiry*, 294.

74. Ibid., 78, 80–83, 170, 181–89, 203–5, 216, 221–24, 230–34; Wildman, *Science and Religious Anthropology*, 198.

75. Dean, "The Persistence of Experience," 73–76.

76. To illustrate, the stubborn fact of religious diversity, as I demonstrated in chapter 3, severely militates against exclusivist and inclusivist conceptions of the ultimate and salvation. In chapter 8, I will suggest that supernaturalism and what Tillich called "supranaturalism" conflict with modern, scientific understandings of reality.

77. Wildman, *Religious Philosophy as Multidisciplinary Comparative Inquiry*, 221–24, 230–34.

78. Ibid., 230.

79. Recounted in Larry E. Axel, "Process and Religion: The History of a Tradition at Chicago," *Process Studies* 8, no. 4 (Winter 1978): 232–34. See also William James, *Pragmatism: A New Name for Some Old Ways of Thinking* (Cambridge, MA: Harvard University Press, 1978), 34.

80. The other was Columbia University, to which Dewey emigrated in 1904.

81. Bernard E. Meland, "Reflections on the Early Chicago School of Modernism," *American Journal of Theology and Philosophy* 5, no. 1 (January 1984): 3; Tyron Inbody, "History of Empirical Theology," in *Empirical Theology: A Handbook*, ed. Randolph Crump Miller (Birmingham, AL: Religious Education Press, 1992), 19. For more on how the members of the Divinity School assimilated (albeit often indirectly) the university's pragmatist philosophical orientation, see William J. Hynes, *Shirley Jackson Case and the Chicago School* (Chico, CA: Scholars Press, 1981), 118–25; Dorrien, *Idealism, Realism, and Modernity, 1900–1950*, 6, 172–73, 262; and Darnell Rucker, *The Chicago Pragmatists* (Minneapolis: University of Minnesota Press, 1969).

82. A carryover, perhaps, of the antimetaphysical proclivities of the Ritschlians by whom they were influenced.

83. Another example, according to Dean, of historicism's ironic neglect of its own history. See Dean, *History Making History*, 64, ix.

84. Dorrien, *Crisis, Irony, and Postmodernity, 1950–2005*, 59–60.

85. Davaney, *Historicism*, 144, 156–57.

86. Foster, *The Function of Religion in Man's Struggle for Existence*, 35, 44–47, 57–60, 79–88; G. B. Smith, *Current Christian Thinking*, 142–43, 156, 165.

87. Foster, *The Function of Religion in Man's Struggle for Existence*, 84, 88, 100–110, 112–13; George Burman Foster, *The Finality of the Christian Religion*, 2nd ed. (Chicago: University of Chicago Press, 1906), 146–47; G. B. Smith, "The Task and Method of Systematic Theology," 222–23, 229; G. B. Smith, "Systematic Theology and Ministerial Efficiency," 597, 599–601, 605.

88. G. B. Smith, "The Task and Method of Systematic Theology," 222–23.

89. Shirley Jackson Case, *The Origins of Christian Supernaturalism* (Chicago: University of Chicago Press, 1946), 220–21, 233–34; Case, "The Religious Meaning of the Past," *Journal of Religion* 4, no. 6 (November 1924): 586–87; Case, *The Evolution of Early Christianity: A Genetic Study of First-Century Christianity in Relation to Its Religious Environment* (Chicago: University of Chicago Press, 1914), 24; Case, *The Christian Philosophy of History* (Chicago: University of Chicago Press, 1943), 43; Case, "Education in Liberalism," in *Contemporary American Theology*, ed. Vergilius Ferm (New York: Roundtable, 1932), 112–15.

90. Case, *The Christian Philosophy of History*, 172, 183–84; Case, "The Religious Meaning of the Past," 587–91.

91. William Lindsey, "'Somebody, Somehow, Somewhere, and Somewhen': Shailer Mathews and the Socio-historical Interpretation of Doctrine," *American Journal of Theology and Philosophy* 20, no. 3 (September 1999): 192, 196.

92. See Mathews, *The Faith of Modernism*, 2, 282.

93. Mathews, "Theology and the Social Mind," 245; Mathews, *The Atonement and the Social Process*, 12, 37.

94. Mathews, *The Growth of the Idea of God*, 25–26, 138–40, 186, 195, 210.

95. See especially Dean, *History Making History*.

96. William Dean, "Pragmatism, History, and Theology," in *Pragmatism and Religion*, ed. Stuart Rosenbaum (Urbana: University of Illinois, 2003), 166, 159–60, 171.

97. Kaufman elaborates: "The central question for theology is not merely, or even preeminently, who or what God is, . . . nor is it what humanity is, and what the central problems of human existence are. It is not primarily a speculative question, a problem of knowledge, at all. Most fundamentally, it is a *practical* question: How are we to live? To what should we devote ourselves?" Kaufman, *In Face of Mystery*, 15.

98. Kaufman, *An Essay on Theological Method*, 35, 38–39, 88–89; Kaufman, *In Face of Mystery*, xi–xii; Gordon D. Kaufman, *God—Mystery—Diversity: Christian Theology in a Pluralistic World* (Minneapolis: Fortress, 1996), 23, 31.

99. McFague, *Models of God*, 196n13.

100. Ibid., ix–xii, 3–21, 41.

101. To list but a few examples, see Mathews, *The Growth of the Idea of God*, 26, 213; Davaney, *Historicism*, 158; Dean, *History Making History*, 18; Kaufman, *An Essay on Theological Method*, 87–89; McFague, *Models of God*, 26.

102. George Burman Foster, "Pragmatism and Knowledge," *American Journal of Theology* 11, no. 4 (October 1907): 591–92.

103. Ibid., 596.

104. See Dean, *History Making History*, 63, 88.

105. Dorrien, *Idealism, Realism, and Modernity, 1900–1950*, 231. Regrettably, very late in his career, Foster gave in to a cruder utilitarianism, instrumentalism, and functionalism. As he lectured to his students in 1918 (the year of his death): "Utility is not truth. Beliefs may be useful because they are true, yet they may be useful even if they are not true. . . . What do you mean by saying that an idea is true? That it copies some ontological reality? No, but that it does its job." Quoted in Douglas Clyde Macintosh, *The Problem of Religious Knowledge* (New York: Harper, 1940), 116.

106. G. B. Smith, *Current Christian Thinking*, 147.

107. G. B. Smith, "The Task and Method of Systematic Theology," 229–30, 233. See also G. B. Smith, "Systematic Theology and Ministerial Efficiency," 599–601, 608–9.

108. Mathews, *Is God Emeritus?*, 28.
109. McFague, *Metaphorical Theology*, 107, 134, 137–44.
110. Davaney, *Pragmatic Historicism*, 153–89.

Chapter 8

1. Gary Dorrien, *Crisis, Irony, and Postmodernity, 1950–2005*, vol. 3 of *The Making of American Liberal Theology* (Louisville: Westminster John Knox Press, 2006), 486.
2. See William Dean, *The Religious Critic in American Culture* (Albany: State University of New York Press, 1994), 131–39; Gordon D. Kaufman, *In Face of Mystery: A Constructive Theology* (Cambridge, MA: Harvard University Press, 1993), ix, 3–17, 39–40.
3. See William Dean, *The American Spiritual Culture: And the Invention of Jazz, Football, and the Movies* (New York: Continuum, 2002), 91–97.
4. John Dewey, *Experience and Nature* (Chicago: Open Court, 1925), 1.
5. Nancy Frankenberry, "Major Themes of Empirical Theology," in *Empirical Theology: A Handbook*, ed. Randolph Crump Miller (Birmingham, AL: Religious Education Press, 1992), 39.
6. Nancy Frankenberry, *Religion and Radical Empiricism* (Albany: State University of New York Press, 1987), 37.
7. William Dean, *American Religious Empiricism* (Albany: State University of New York Press, 1986), 1, 8, 19; Tyron L. Inbody, "History of Empirical Theology," in Miller, *Empirical Theology*, 11–12; Frankenberry, "Major Themes of Empirical Theology," 37–40; Frankenberry, *Religion and Radical Empiricism*, ix, 37–38.
8. Dean, *American Religious Empiricism*, x–xii, 70.
9. Richard Rorty, *Consequences of Pragmatism* (Minneapolis: University of Minnesota Press, 1982), xix, 165.
10. John Dewey, *A Common Faith* (New Haven, CT: Yale University Press, 1934), 1.
11. Dewey, *Experience and Nature*, 1, 9–10, 13–14, 25–27, 31–36; John Dewey, *The Quest for Certainty: A Study in the Relation of Knowledge and Action* (New York: Pedigree, 1929), 232.
12. John Dewey, *Reconstruction in Philosophy*, enl. ed. (Boston: Beacon, 1957), 20–22, 24–27, 49–52; Dewey, *The Quest for Certainty*, 36–37, 102, 173, 287–99, 309–13; Dewey, "Philosophy and Democracy," in *The Essential Dewey*, vol. 1, *Pragmatism, Education, Democracy*, ed. Larry A. Hickman and Thomas M. Alexander (Bloomington: Indiana University Press, 1998), 71–78; Dewey, *The Influence of Darwin on Philosophy and Other Essays* (Amherst, NY: Prometheus, 1997), 177–278, 298–99, 303. See Sheila Greeve Davaney, *Historicism: The Once and Future Challenge for Theology* (Minneapolis: Fortress, 2006), 82–88.

13. William James, *Essays in Radical Empiricism, and A Pluralistic Universe* (New York: E. P. Dutton, 1971), 84, 102–3. See Frankenberry, *Religion and Radical Empiricism*, 86.

14. William James, *The Meaning of Truth: A Sequel to Pragmatism* (Cambridge, MA: Harvard University Press, 1978), 7.

15. William James, *Pragmatism: A New Name for Some Old Ways of Thinking* (Cambridge, MA: Harvard University Press, 1978), 125.

16. James, *The Meaning of Truth*, 6.

17. James, *Pragmatism*, 125–26.

18. Ibid., 13, 17–18, 31.

19. Dean, *American Religious Empiricism*, x.

20. Gary Dorrien, *Crisis, Irony, and Postmodernity, 1950–2005*, 59–60.

21. William Dean, *History Making History: The New Historicism in American Religious Thought* (Albany: State University of New York Press, 1988), 46.

22. Dorrien, *Crisis, Irony, and Postmodernity, 1950–2005*, 59.

23. Shailer Mathews, *The Atonement and the Social Process* (New York: Macmillan, 1930), 11.

24. George Burman Foster, *The Function of Religion in Man's Struggle for Existence* (Chicago: University of Chicago Press, 1909), 35, 44–60, 63, 79–88, 90–91.

25. See Shirley Jackson Case, *The Christian Philosophy of History* (Chicago: University of Chicago Press, 1943), chs. 2, 4, and 5, quote on 164.

26. See Dean, *History Making History*.

27. Case, *The Christian Philosophy of History*, 154.

28. Ibid., 56, 88–91, 132, 148–49, 163–74. See Dean, *History Making History*, 52.

29. Case, *The Christian Philosophy of History*, 164, 176.

30. Dean, *History Making History*, 46–47.

31. See especially ibid., ch. 3.

32. Dean, *American Religious Empiricism*, 5–12, 67–72; Dean, *History Making History*, 2, 6.

33. William Dean, "Theological Historicism's Missing Historicity: A Commentary on *Boundaries of Our Habitations*," *American Journal of Theology and Philosophy* 18, no. 2 (May 1997): 109.

34. Sheila Greeve Davaney, "Theology and the Turn to Cultural Analysis," in *Converging on Culture: Theologians in Dialogue with Cultural Analysis and Criticism*, ed. Delwin Brown, Sheila Greeve Davaney, and Kathryn Tanner (Oxford: Oxford University Press, 2001), 3–16; Sheila Greeve Davaney, "Rethinking Theology and Religious Studies," in *Religious Studies, Theology, and the University: Conflicting Maps, Changing Terrain*, ed. Linell E. Cady and Delwin Brown (Albany: State University of New York Press, 2002), 140–54; Davaney, *Historicism*, 158–60.

35. See J. Samuel Preus, *Explaining Religion: Criticism and Theory from Bodin to Freud* (Atlanta: Scholars Press, 1996), ix–xxi.

36. Davaney, "Theology and the Turn to Cultural Analysis," 7, 12. This does not mean that historicists are necessarily yoked to monocausal explanations of religion. In fact, historicism's allergy to foundationalism ought to refuse any attempt to squeeze the complexity, breadth, and diversity of religious phenomena into a homogenized metascheme. Moreover, the antidualistic, expansive, and naturalistic-humanistic construal of history championed in this volume should enable pragmatic historicists (at least in principle) to remain thoroughly historicist, while still recognizing that human religion is, as Manuel Vásquez indicates, multicausal—generated and shaped by a "complex interplay" of sociological, psychological, economic, existential, evolutionary, and biological factors. See Manuel A. Vásquez, *More than Belief: A Materialist Theory of Religion* (New York: Oxford University Press, 2011), 4–5, 10, 13. I would argue that a holistic historicism can even be open to new developments in the scientific study of religion, which seeks to explain religious experiences and aspects of religiosity that are cross-cultural and species-wide (e.g., the ubiquitous penchant to ascribe intentionality and causal powers to invisible supernatural beings). See Wesley J. Wildman, *Science and Religious Anthropology: A Spiritually Evocative Naturalist Interpretation of Human Life* (Farnham, UK: Ashgate, 2009), 89–91. These universal features of religion, a holistic historicist could affirm, are *transhistorical* but not *ahistorical*, emerging from prior and wider, but no less contingent, historical circumstances (e.g., supernatural agents are so religiously prevalent because, some time in our evolutionary past, "it was . . . adaptive for human beings to have overactive cognitive capacities for recognizing patterns, detecting causes, and attributing intentions"; 91). Indeed, the very centerpiece of a historicist theory of religion—that is, the social construction of all-encompassing, life-orienting, culture-specific, ever-developing world-pictures (cf. chapter 3)—is one such universal feature, constitutive of religious activity always and everywhere, yet emergent from and rooted in the *natural* history of *Homo sapiens*.

37. Case, *The Christian Philosophy of History*, 163–74, 188–200, 208–9.

38. Foster, *The Function of Religion in Man's Struggle for Existence*, 102–3.

39. Ibid., 44, 49–50, 58–60, 63–64, 83–84, 90–91, 102–4, 109, 114–15, 149. See Jerome A. Stone, *Religious Naturalism Today: The Rebirth of a Forgotten Alternative* (Albany: State University of New York Press, 2008), 60–64, 67–68, 128; Dean, *History Making History*, 62–63.

40. See Shailer Mathews, "Theology and the Social Mind," *Biblical World* 46, no. 4 (October 1915): 201–48; Mathews, *The Atonement and the Social Process*, 13; Mathews, *The Growth of the Idea of God* (New York: Macmillan, 1931), 3–11, 212.

41. Mathews, *The Growth of the Idea of God*, 1–26, 212.

42. Ibid., 212.

43. Gerald Birney Smith, *Current Christian Thinking* (Chicago: University of Chicago Press, 1928), 155.

44. Dean, *American Religious Empiricism*, 5–12, 67–72, final quote on 71. See also Dorrien, *Crisis, Irony, and Postmodernity, 1950–2005*, 474. Dorrien actually pushes back on Dean's way of parsing the liberal tradition. Neither pietists nor empiricists have "an exclusive claim to empiricism," Dorrien writes. "From Schleiermacher and Ritschl to the present day, liberals on the 'transhistorical spirit' side of the field have claimed to practice an empirical approach to religion by virtue of their emphasis on, and study of, religious experience." Gary Dorrien, *Idealism, Realism, and Modernity, 1900–1950*, vol. 2 of *The Making of American Liberal Theology* (Louisville: Westminster John Knox Press, 2003), 13.

45. Sallie McFague, *Metaphorical Theology: Models of God in Religious Language* (Philadelphia: Fortress, 1982), 16, 26.

46. Sallie McFague, *Models of God: Theology for an Ecological, Nuclear Age* (Philadelphia: Fortress, 1987), 37.

47. McFague, *Metaphorical Theology*, vii, 1, 16–17, 26–28, 32–42; McFague, *Models of God*, xi–xii, 21–23, 31–39.

48. Gordon D. Kaufman, *An Essay on Theological Method*, 3rd ed. (Atlanta: Scholars Press, 1995), ix, 4.

49. Kaufman, *In Face of Mystery*, 39.

50. Kaufman, *An Essay on Theological Method*, 3–4, 14, 28–30, 32–41; Kaufman, *In Face of Mystery*, ix, 32, 42, 49–53; Gordon D. Kaufman, *Theology for a Nuclear Age* (Philadelphia: Westminster Press, 1985), 19, 22–26.

51. Kaufman, *In Face of Mystery*, 37.

52. Kaufman, *An Essay on Theological Method*, 42–47; Kaufman, *In Face of Mystery*, ix, 41; Kaufman, *Theology for a Nuclear Age*, 27–28.

53. William Dean, *The Religious Critic in American Culture* (Albany: State University of New York Press, 1994), 133.

54. Dewey, *A Common Faith*, 42–49, 85–87.

55. See Dean, *The Religious Critic in American Culture*, 141–42.

56. Dean, *The American Spiritual Culture*, 75, 78.

57. William James, *The Varieties of Religious Experience: A Study in Human Nature* (New York: Penguin, 1902), 516–17.

58. Dean, *The American Spiritual Culture*, 70–86; Dean, *The Religious Critic in American Culture*, 131–39.

59. Dean, *The American Spiritual Culture*, 72.

60. According to Dean, "conventionalism explains how religious critics can be relativistic, pluralistic, and historicist and yet be realists." Dean, *The Religious Critic in American Culture*, 106.

61. Foster, *The Function of Religion in Man's Struggle for Existence*, 66. Incidentally, later on in the book, Foster appears to endorse a watered-down version of conventionalism: "While all our values are first human achievements, and then transferred to the world of the divine, it is also true that the values once lodged

there react into the human in a way that is indispensible to the idealizing and transfiguring of the human. Human fatherliness, for example, is transferred to the world of the gods, but on that account it reacts into the experience of our fatherhood here for its ennoblement and beauty and sacredness" (149).

62. Gordon D. Kaufman, "My Life and My Theological Reflection: Two Central Themes," *American Journal of Theology and Philosophy* 22, no. 1 (January 2001): 8–10, quote on 10.

63. Dorrien, *Crisis, Irony, and Postmodernity, 1950–2005*, 482.

64. See William Dean, "Second Thoughts," *American Journal of Theology and Philosophy* 29, no. 3 (September 2008): 289–303.

65. Foster, *The Function of Religion in Man's Struggle for Existence*, 57, ix, 88, 139. See Dorrien, *Idealism, Realism, and Modernity, 1900–1950*, 170–72.

66. Foster, *The Function of Religion in Man's Struggle for Existence*, 59–60.

67. See ibid., 139.

68. W. Creighton Peden, "The Radical Tradition: Paine and Foster," *American Journal of Theology and Philosophy* 5, no. 1 (January 1984): 28.

69. See Douglas Clyde Macintosh, *The Problem of Religious Knowledge* (New York: Harper, 1940), 97–119; Dorrien, *Idealism, Realism, and Modernity, 1900–1950*, 170–81.

70. Synopsis as well as quotations included in Macintosh, *The Problem of Religious Knowledge*, 105–10. See also Dorrien, *Idealism, Realism, and Modernity, 1900–1950*, 175–77.

71. Macintosh, *The Problem of Religious Knowledge*, 111–15; Dorrien, *Idealism, Realism, and Modernity, 1900–1950*, 177–78.

72. George Burman Foster, review of *The New Orthodoxy*, by Edward Scribner Ames, *Christian Century* 35, no. 41 (October 24, 1918): 17–18.

73. In George Burman Foster, *Friedrich Nietzsche* (New York: Macmillan, 1931), ix.

74. Dorrien, *Idealism, Realism, and Modernity, 1900–1950*, 180.

75. Dorrien alludes to a division in the secondary literature on Foster. Most mainline Protestants (e.g., Macintosh, Mathews, and Edgar Towne) have "claimed him for liberal Christianity," while a larger contingency of Unitarians and naturalists (e.g., Charles Harvey Arnold, Larry Axel, Alan Gragg, and W. Creighton Peden) have interpreted him as a "forerunner of their brand of religious humanism." Ibid., 180–81.

76. In Foster, *Friedrich Nietzsche*, x.

77. Ibid., 225.

78. Foster made the latter observation in a letter he wrote to Ames on October 9, 1918. See Macintosh, *The Problem of Religious Knowledge*, 113–14.

79. Dorrien, *Idealism, Realism, and Modernity, 1900–1950*, 180. Macintosh reached a similar conclusion, surmising that Foster continuously "alternated between honest philosophic doubt and an equally sincere and fervent religious faith; and it is difficult indeed to believe that he ever finally ceased to be religious in the

essentially Christian and theistic way that was so deeply ingrained in his mind and character. . . . Even at those times when his thought was a-theistic, his feeling was by no means anti-theistic." Macintosh, *The Problem of Religious Knowledge*, 111, 115.

80. Dean, *The American Spiritual Culture*, 34–39.

81. Ibid., 34.

82. William Dean, "Dorrien the Historian," *American Journal of Theology and Philosophy* 29, no. 2 (May 2008): 170.

83. Ibid., 170–73; William Dean, "Can Liberal Theology Recover?," *American Journal of Theology and Philosophy* 30, no. 1 (January 2009): 41–47; Dean, "Second Thoughts," 300–301; Dean, *The American Spiritual Culture* 40–41, 90.

84. Dean, *The American Spiritual Culture*, 89.

85. Quoted in Macintosh, *The Problem of Religious Knowledge*, 105.

86. Dean, *The American Spiritual Culture*, 108–9.

87. Ibid., 88, 109.

88. Ibid., 91–92.

89. Ibid., 107.

90. Ibid., 95–97, 104–7, final quote on 107.

91. Ibid., 95. See Paul Tillich, *The Courage to Be* (New Haven, CT: Yale Nota Bene, 2000), 182–90.

92. Dean, *The American Spiritual Culture*, 94.

93. James, *Essays in Radical Empiricism, and A Pluralistic Universe*, 265–72.

94. Dean, *The American Spiritual Culture*, 87–88, 94, 100.

95. William James, "A Pluralistic Mystic," in *Writings, 1902–1910*, ed. Bruce Kuklick (New York: Library of America, 1987), 1312–13.

96. H. Richard Niebuhr, *Radical Monotheism and Western Culture* (Louisville: Westminster John Knox Press, 1960), 31–37, 122–26, quote on 122.

97. See especially Jacques Derrida, "How to Avoid Speaking: Denials," in *Derrida and Negative Theology*, ed. Harold Coward and Toby Foshay (Albany: State University of New York Press, 1992); Jacques Derrida, *On the Name*, ed. Thomas Dutoit, trans. David Wood, John P. Leavey, and Ian McLeod (Stanford, CA: Stanford University Press, 1993).

98. John D. Caputo and Gianni Vattimo, *After the Death of God* (New York: Columbia University Press, 2007), 47–85, 114–60. See also John D. Caputo, *The Prayers and Tears of Jacques Derrida: Religion without Religion* (Bloomington: Indiana University Press, 1997).

99. See Richard Dawkins, *The God Delusion* (Boston: Mariner, 2006); Daniel C. Dennett, *Breaking the Spell: Religion as a Natural Phenomenon* (New York: Penguin, 2006); Christopher Hitchens, *God Is Not Great: How Religion Poisons Everything* (New York: Twelve, 2007).

100. Richard Kearney, *Anatheism: Returning to God after God* (New York: Columbia University Press, 2010), 5, 16.

101. Dean, *The American Spiritual Culture*, 97.

102. Ibid., 96, 98.

103. James, *Essays in Radical Empiricism, and A Pluralistic Universe*, 266–67, 272–73. Emphasis added.

104. Case, *The Christian Philosophy of History*, 209.

105. Dewey, *A Common Faith*, 48–49.

106. Dean, *History Making History*, 142.

107. Dean, *The Religious Critic in American Culture*, 149.

108. Delwin Brown, "History, Country, Academy, and God: On the Role of the Religious Critic," *American Journal of Theology and Philosophy* 16, no. 1 (January 1995): 72. On this score, pragmatic historicists line up well with the critical realism of Wesley Wildman. From Wildman's standpoint, sacredness (like truth, value, and beauty—cf. chapter 6) is "a collaborative hermeneutical achievement," with the human interpreter and the interpreted world each making an indispensable contribution. Looking to the social scientific study of religion, Wildman argues that our religious and spiritual engagements with the real are mediated, even constituted, by our culturally distinctive histories and heritages and our socially embedded "habits of living and seeing." But there is a realistic and receptive side of religion, too. The sacred, and indeed many theological symbols (e.g., salvations), are both constructed *and* confronted, made *and* found, produced *and* encountered, created "in concert with" ultimate reality. And ultimate reality in Wildman's (and pragmatic historicism's) religiously naturalistic theology is nature's "axiological potentials," its "depth structures and flows." See Wesley J. Wildman, "Corrington's Ecstatic Naturalism in Light of the Scientific Study of Religion," *American Journal of Theology and Philosophy* 34, no. 1 (January 2013): 3–16. In this article, Wildman is attempting to bring equilibrium to Robert Corrington's ecstatic naturalism, which underplays the social construction of sacred realities. Nevertheless, Wildman's critical realism can also be used to critique positions that err in the other direction, that overemphasize humanity's "reality-constituting" powers.

109. Davaney, "Rethinking Theology and Religious Studies," 140–54, quote on 150.

110. See especially Sheila Greeve Davaney, *Pragmatic Historicism: A Theology for the Twenty-First Century* (Albany: State University of New York Press, 2000), 30–41.

111. See Dean, *History Making History*, 126–34.

112. Dorrien, *Crisis, Irony, and Postmodernity, 1950–2005*, 486.

113. Gordon D. Kaufman, "Empirical Realism in Theology: An Examination of Some Themes in Meland and Loomer," in *New Essays in Religious Naturalism*, ed. W. Creighton Peden and Larry E. Axel (Macon, GA: Mercer University Press, 1993), 135–39.

114. Gordon D. Kaufman, "Response to Hans Frei," in *The Legacy of H. Richard Niebuhr*, ed. Ronald F. Thiemann (Minneapolis: Fortress, 1991), 27–32.

115. Bernard E. Meland, *Fallible Forms and Symbols: Discourses on Method in a Theology of Culture* (Philadelphia: Fortress, 1976), 21.

116. Kaufman, "Empirical Realism in Theology," 136–39.

117. Dean also looks favorably on Meland's bid for a "new realism in religious inquiry." See Dean, "Can Liberal Theology Recover?," 42.

118. Kaufman, *In Face of Mystery*, 60.

119. Ibid., 60–61; Gordon D. Kaufman, *God—Mystery—Diversity: Christian Theology in a Pluralistic World* (Minneapolis: Fortress, 1996), 97.

120. Dean, "Can Liberal Theology Recover?," 44.

121. Kaufman, "Response to Hans Frei," 29.

122. See "God as Symbol" in Gordon D. Kaufman, *God the Problem* (Cambridge, MA: Harvard University Press, 1972), 82–115. Written in 1970, this is Kaufman's "turning-point essay," according to Gary Dorrien, marking his move from a revelation-based neo-orthodox historicism (influenced, chiefly, by his teacher H. Richard Niebuhr) to a full-blown neo-Kantian constructivist theology. Dorrien, *Crisis, Irony, and Postmodernity, 1950–2005*, 307–8, 313.

123. Kaufman, *In Face of Mystery*, 39–40.

124. William Dean, "The Persistence of Experience: A Commentary on Kaufman's Theology," in Peden and Axel, *New Essays in Religious Naturalism*, 77.

125. Wildman, *Science and Religious Anthropology*, 67.

126. Kaufman, "Response to Hans Frei," 28–30.

127. Dean, "The Persistence of Experience," 71–72; Dean, *History Making History*, 141.

128. Kaufman, "Response to Hans Frei," 29.

129. Kaufman, *Theology for a Nuclear Age*, 43.

130. See Gordon D. Kaufman, *In the Beginning . . . Creativity* (Minneapolis: Fortress, 2004); Kaufman, "Biohistorical Naturalism and the Symbol 'God,'" *Zygon* 38, no. 1 (March 2003): 95–100.

131. Kaufman, *In Face of Mystery*, 320.

132. Ibid., 331.

133. Ibid., 330–31.

134. Dorrien, *Crisis, Irony, and Postmodernity, 1950–2005*, 483.

135. Dean, "Second Thoughts," 302–3.

136. Dean, "Dorrien the Historian," 170.

137. Dean, "Can Liberal Theology Recover?," 36, 41, 43, 47. See also Dean, *The American Spiritual Culture*, 35, 89.

138. See Dean, *History Making History*, 126, 143–44.

139. Dorrien, *Crisis, Irony, and Postmodernity, 1950–2005*, 482–83. Henry Nelson Wieman's twenty-year stint on the faculty (1927–1947), which marks the second period of Chicago modernism, pushed empirical theology in a more metaphysical, philosophical, and naturalistic direction. Although becoming more and more critical of the overly speculative, rationalistic, and abstract features of Whitehead's system, Wieman essentially replaced the pragmatism, historicism, and humanism of

the first-generation Chicago schoolers with an empirically grounded Whiteheadian theology. In the 1940s, 1950s, and 1960s, Wieman protégés Bernard Meland and Bernard Loomer continued to champion versions of radical empiricism and religious naturalism, but quickly tired of the perceived sterility of the school's Wiemanian phase. For that reason, Meland and Loomer, along with theologian Daniel Day Williams and philosopher Charles Hartshorne, brought about a third-generation shift at the University of Chicago, turning the Divinity School into the center of process theology. See Dorrien, *Idealism, Realism, and Modernity, 1900–1950*, 262–85; Dorrien, *Crisis, Irony, and Postmodernity, 1950–2005*, 60–132.

140. Dean, *History Making History*, ix–xi, 45.
141. See Davaney, *Pragmatic Historicism*, 181–83.
142. See Kaufman, "Empirical Realism in Theology."
143. See Kaufman, "Biohistorical Naturalism and the Symbol 'God.'"
144. Delwin Brown, "The Fall of '26: Gerald Birney Smith and the Collapse of the Socio-historical Framework of Theology," *American Journal of Theology and Philosophy* 11, no. 3 (September 1990): 195–96.
145. Dean, *American Religious Empiricism*, 21–22, 35.
146. Henry Nelson Wieman, *Religious Experience and Scientific Method* (Carbondale: Southern Illinois University Press, 1971), 186–87.
147. See William James, *The Principles of Psychology*, authorized ed. (New York: Dover, 1950), 1:224–90; James, *Essays in Radical Empiricism, and A Pluralistic Universe*, 25–34, 37–39, 46, 49–64, 84. See also Frankenberry, *Religion and Radical Empiricism*, 83–93.
148. Dean, "Second Thoughts," 293.
149. Meland, *Fallible Forms and Symbols*, 24.
150. James, "Some Problems in Philosophy," 1031.
151. James, *The Varieties of Religious Experience*, 35, 58, 456–57, 508, 512; James, *Essays in Radical Empiricism, and A Pluralistic Universe*, 39. See Dean, *The American Spiritual Culture*, 102.
152. Dewey, *Experience and Nature*, 20–21. See Donald A. Crosby, *A Religion of Nature* (Albany: State University of New York Press, 2002), 71–72.
153. John Dewey, *Art as Experience* (New York: Perigee, 1934), 195.
154. Dewey, *A Common Faith*, 85, 19, 42–43, 52–54. See Dean, *The American Spiritual Culture*, 103.
155. Henry Nelson Wieman, *The Source of Human Good* (Atlanta: Scholars Press, 1995), 6, 66–67.
156. Alfred North Whitehead, *Process and Reality: An Essay in Cosmology*, corr. ed. (New York: Free Press, 1978), 342–51, quote on 346.
157. According to Bernard Lee, over against the "rational school" of Whiteheadian theology (whose representatives include David Ray Griffin, John Cobb, Lewis Ford, Norman Pittenger, and Schubert Ogden, among others), the empirical

process theologians (Wieman, Meland, and Loomer, as well as Dean and Daniel Day Williams) read Whitehead with James as opposed to Hartshorne standing over their shoulders. They uphold Whitehead's radical empiricism and empiricist accent on "adequacy and applicability" and emphasize the "broad strokes" of a processive and relational paradigm over scholastic fealty to the technical and often overreaching categories of *Process and Reality*. Most important, they refuse all empirically baseless abstractions. Bernard J. Lee, "The Two Process Theologies," *Theological Studies* 45, no. 2 (June 1984): 313–16. Wieman, for his part, became disillusioned with Whitehead's turn toward the abstract and the speculative. As Dorrien comments, even though he never left Whitehead completely behind, and "his theology remained a religious philosophy of creative process," Wieman concluded that Whiteheadianism was "essentially a castle of abstractions," "a 'wholly groundless' piece of speculation," virtually none of which "was based on empirical demonstration." Dorrien, *Idealism, Realism, and Modernity, 1900–1950*, 269–70.

158. Wieman, *The Source of Human Good*, 7, 56. See Frankenberry, *Religion and Radical Empiricism*, 122–24.

159. Bernard E. Meland, *Essays in Constructive Theology: A Process Perspective*, ed. Perry LeFevre (Chicago: Exploration, 1988), 225–49.

160. Ibid., 237.

161. Ibid., 228, 241. Among the other names were "Creative Order," "Creative Matrix," "Matrix of Sensitivity," "Sensitive Nature within Nature," "Depth of Mystery," "Cosmic Presence and Intent," and "Ultimate Efficacy within Relationships." Dorrien, *Crisis, Irony, and Postmodernity, 1950–2005*, 127.

162. Bernard E. Meland, *Higher Education and the Human Spirit* (Chicago: University of Chicago Press, 1953), 162.

163. Meland, *Fallible Forms and Symbols*, 45.

164. See Bernard Loomer, "Empirical Theology within Process Thought," in *The Future of Empirical Theology*, ed. Bernard E. Meland (Chicago: University of Chicago Press, 1969), 160.

165. Bernard Loomer, "The Size of God," in *The Size of God: The Theology of Bernard Loomer in Context*, ed. William Dean and Larry E. Axel (Macon, GA: Mercer University Press, 1987), 24, 41–43.

166. Wieman, *Religious Experience and Scientific Method*, 38.

167. Brown, "The Fall of '26," 196.

168. See especially Delwin Brown, "Marginalizing the Life of Language: Radical Empiricism as a Critique of Gadamer," in Peden and Axel, *New Essays in Religious Naturalism*, 21–32; Delwin Brown, "Limitation and Ingenuity: Radical Historicism and the Nature of Tradition," *American Journal of Theology and Philosophy* 24, no. 3 (September 2003): 210–13.

169. Dean, *American Religious Empiricism*, 36–39.

170. Frankenberry, *Religion and Radical Empiricism*, 131, 143–44.

171. Ibid., 154, 192.

172. Ibid., 190. Emphasis added. Against Frankenberry and Dean (and myself), Brown alleges that "radical empiricism has no special relevance to the accrediting of religion or religious sensibilities." Brown, "Marginalizing the Life of Language," 31n35.

173. Frankenberry, *Religion and Radical Empiricism*, 190, 192.

174. Wieman, *Religious Experience and Scientific Method*, 38, 368. See Frankenberry, *Religion and Radical Empiricism*, 118.

175. Frankenberry, *Religion and Radical Empiricism*, 84–98, 109, 120, 152, 190–91.

176. Brown, "The Fall of '26," 199.

177. See ibid., 200, 199.

178. Frankenberry renders a similar verdict: "It is precisely the suitability of this type of religious experiencing to naturalistic categories of explanation that frees it from the parochial apologetics of one religion or another and at the same time is the source of the complaint that it seems indistinguishable from what could be said in strictly nonreligious terms. But this is exactly what one should expect from a theory that prescinds from the dichotomy religious-nonreligious. The distinction between religious experience and other kinds of experience is, after all, a poor one." Frankenberry, *Religion and Radical Empiricism*, 191.

179. Wieman, *The Source of Human Good*, 6–7.

180. See Wieman, *Religious Experience and Scientific Method*, 9, 289. Brown comments that "Wieman's promise of certitude" was one of the reasons why the Chicago theologians found him so appealing: "A liberal who claimed to be able to demonstrate that God's existence could not be doubted was not a liberal to be ignored." Brown, "The Fall of '26," 195.

181. Frankenberry astutely observes that Wieman's idea of functional (as opposed to metaphysical) transcendence served a "heuristic" purpose, allowing him to view all ideals, values, and current structures of knowledge as "conjectural, tentative, provisional—unremittingly fallibilistic." Even more than that, it is a "naturalistic version of the old theological idea that human sinfulness and despair puts us in need of a power not our own that makes for creativity." That is, "the distinction between the creat*ive* event and creat*ed* good" is, according to Frankenberry, simply his way of describing "what Tillich called the 'Protestant principle,' an injunction not to absolutize the relative." Frankenberry, *Religion and Radical Empiricism*, 127–28.

182. Wieman, *The Source of Human Good*, chs. 1–3, 10. See Dorrien, *Idealism, Realism, and Modernity, 1900–1950*, 262–85; Brown, "The Fall of '26," 183–98; Frankenberry, *Religion and Radical Empiricism*, 113–29.

183. Dean, *History Making History*, 143–44; William Dean, "Empiricism and God," in Miller, *Empirical Theology*, 120–28.

184. See Wieman, *The Source of Human Good*, 58–69.

185. Frankenberry, *Religion and Radical Empiricism*, 125–27.

186. For my recent efforts to define religious naturalism and to catalogue the different varieties of it (including my own), see Demian Wheeler, "*Deus sive Natura*: Pantheism as a Variety of Religious Naturalism," in *The Routledge Handbook of Religious Naturalism*, ed. Donald A. Crosby and Jerome A. Stone (London: Routledge, 2018), 106–17.

187. Charley D. Hardwick, *Events of Grace: Naturalism, Existentialism, and Theology* (Cambridge: Cambridge University Press, 1996), 5–6.

188. Owen Flanagan, "Varieties of Naturalism," in *The Oxford Handbook of Religion and Science*, ed. Philip Clayton (Oxford: Oxford University Press, 2006), 437. Emphasis removed.

189. See Arthur C. Danto, "Naturalism," in *The Encyclopedia of Philosophy*, ed. Paul Edwards (New York: Macmillan, 1967), 5:448.

190. Robert S. Corrington, "Deep Pantheism," *Journal for the Study of Religion, Nature and Culture* 1, no. 4 (December 2007): 503.

191. Robert S. Corrington, *A Semiotic Theory of Theology and Philosophy* (Cambridge: Cambridge University Press, 2000), 10, 23, 217; Corrington, *Nature's Religion* (Lanham, MD: Rowman and Littlefield, 1997), 3; Corrington, "Empirical Theology and Its Divergence from Process Thought," in *Introduction to Christian Theology: Contemporary North American Perspectives*, ed. Roger A. Badham (Louisville: Westminster John Knox Press, 1998), 169. See also John Ryder, *The Things in Heaven and Earth: An Essay in Pragmatic Naturalism* (New York: Fordham University Press, 2013), 37–41.

192. Michael S. Hogue, *The Promise of Religious Naturalism* (Lanham, MD: Rowman and Littlefield, 2010), 52. See also Crosby, *A Religion of Nature*, xi, 12, 17, 20, 36, 122.

193. Adapted and assembled from Wildman, *Science and Religious Anthropology*, 23–24; Stone, *Religious Naturalism Today*, xi, 1–2; and Donald A. Crosby, *Living with Ambiguity: Religious Naturalism and the Menace of Evil* (Albany: State University of New York Press, 2008), ix–x, 1–4.

194. Wesley J. Wildman, "Religious Naturalism: What It Can Be, and What It Need Not Be," *Philosophy, Theology and the Sciences* 1, no. 1 (2014): 41–43.

195. See Jacques Derrida, *Of Grammatology*, trans. Gayatri Chakravorty Spivak (Baltimore: John Hopkins University Press, 1974), 163.

196. See Robert S. Corrington, *Nature and Spirit: An Essay in Ecstatic Naturalism* (New York: Fordham University Press, 1992), ix; Corrington, *Ecstatic Naturalism: Signs of the World* (Bloomington: Indiana University Press, 1994), 9; Corrington, "Empirical Theology and Its Divergence from Process Thought," 169; Corrington, *A Semiotic Theory of Theology and Philosophy*, 10; Corrington, "My Passage from Panentheism to Pantheism," *American Journal of Theology and Philosophy* 23, no. 2 (May 2002): 137; Corrington, "Deep Pantheism," 503.

197. Stone, *Religious Naturalism Today*, 1.

198. Dewey dismissed any perspective "which attributes human achievement and purpose to man in isolation from the world of physical nature. . . . Our successes are dependent upon the cooperation of nature." Dewey, *A Common Faith*, 25.

199. See Robert S. Corrington, "Ecstatic Naturalism and the Transfiguration of the Good," in Miller, *Empirical Theology*, 204–6, 208, 213; Corrington, *Nature and Spirit*, 13; Corrington, *Ecstatic Naturalism*, 8, 19–20, 25, 61; Corrington, *Nature's Religion*, 2–3, 53, 77; Corrington, *A Semiotic Theory of Theology and Philosophy*, 25–26; Corrington, "My Passage from Panentheism to Pantheism," 136.

200. Paul Tillich, *Systematic Theology*, vol. 2 (Chicago: University of Chicago Press, 1957), 6.

201. See Wesley J. Wildman, "Ground-of-Being Theologies," in P. Clayton, *The Oxford Handbook of Religion and Science*, 616, 628–29; Wesley J. Wildman, "The Ambiguous Heritage and Perpetual Promise of Liberal Theology," *American Journal of Theology and Philosophy* 32, no. 1 (January 2011): 52; Wesley J. Wildman, *Religious and Spiritual Experiences* (New York: Cambridge University Press, 2011), xii; Wildman, *Science and Religious Anthropology*, 19–25. Likewise, Hardwick infers that any theology which affirms a naturalistic worldview can no longer assume "(1) that God is personal, (2) that some form of cosmic teleology is metaphysically true, and (3) that there is a cosmically comprehensible conservation of value." Hardwick, *Events of Grace*, 8.

202. See Robert S. Corrington, "Evolution, Religion, and an Ecstatic Naturalism," *American Journal of Theology and Philosophy* 31, no. 2 (May 2010): 124; Wildman, *Science and Religious Anthropology*, 21.

203. See Stone, *Religious Naturalism Today*, xi, 1; Crosby, *A Religion of Nature*, pt. 3.

204. Ursula Goodenough, *The Sacred Depths of Nature* (New York: Oxford University Press, 1998), 169.

205. Wesley J. Wildman, *Fidelity with Plausibility: Modest Christologies in the Twentieth Century* (Albany: State University of New York Press, 1998), 360–61.

206. See Charles Taylor, *A Secular Age* (Cambridge: Belknap Press of Harvard University Press, 2007).

207. Hogue, *The Promise of Religious Naturalism*, 1–2, 9–15.

208. Wildman, *Fidelity with Plausibility*, 360.

209. Flanagan, "Varieties of Naturalism," 433. Often, supernaturalistic and supranaturalistic convictions are epistemologically grounded in an alleged authority or revelation. The problem, of course, is that there are many different authorities and several conflicting revelations, and choosing among them usually comes down to arbitrary assent, a leap of faith, or deferential submission. As Donald Crosby contends, the only option we are left with "is to surrender to what someone or something tells us is the truth." However, in order to genuinely believe something is true, one must have convincing reasons (e.g., evidence and rational intelligibility) for doing so, Crosby counters: "And it is hard to understand how one could be

convinced if the belief in question does not have plausibility or convincingness in its own right, apart from the authoritative source or sources to which appeal is made." Crosby, *Living with Ambiguity*, 44–45, 103.

210. Dewey, *A Common Faith*, 52–53.

211. George Burman Foster, *The Finality of the Christian Religion*, 2nd ed. (Chicago: University of Chicago Press, 1906), 206–7.

212. Foster, *The Function of Religion in Man's Struggle for Existence*, 21.

213. Foster, *The Finality of the Christian Religion*, 9, 20–22, 198–275, quote on 259.

214. See Gary Dorrien, *Imagining Progressive Religion, 1805–1900*, vol. 1 of *The Making of American Liberal Theology* (Louisville: Westminster John Knox Press, 2001), xxi–xxiii.

215. See Stone, *Religious Naturalism Today*, xi, 1; Crosby, *A Religion of Nature*, pt. 3; Hogue, *The Promise of Religious Naturalism*, xx, 37–38, 203–4.

216. Hogue, *The Promise of Religious Naturalism*, 37.

217. Crosby, *A Religion of Nature*, 160–61, 169.

218. Crosby, *Living with Ambiguity*, 99, 100. On this final point, Crosby echoes Nancy Frankenberry: "Is it necessary that something must endure forever in order for its significance to matter? Is it not sufficient that our fragile, novel, risk-filled acts of radical contingency can strut and fret their hour across the stage, even if they are heard no more? Is not death the mother of beauty rather than of tales signifying nothing?" Frankenberry, "Classical Theism, Panentheism, and Pantheism," 38.

219. See Loyal Rue, *Nature Is Enough: Religious Naturalism and the Meaning of Life* (Albany: State University of New York Press, 2011).

220. For a very helpful historical survey of religious naturalism, as well as a concise and clear analysis of some of the key issues facing religious naturalists in the twenty-first century, see especially Stone, *Religious Naturalism Today*.

221. Foster, *The Finality of the Christian Religion*, 211.

222. Foster, *The Function of Religion in Man's Struggle for Existence*, 109.

223. Ibid., 22.

224. Ibid., 107–10, 178–79, final quote on 108.

225. Stone, *Religious Naturalism Today*, 60. See Foster, *The Function of Religion in Man's Struggle for Existence*, 108–10.

226. Stone, *Religious Naturalism Today*, 62.

227. Foster, *The Function of Religion in Man's Struggle for Existence*, 110, 108.

228. Ibid., 109–10.

229. Mathews, *The Growth of the Idea of God*, 226.

230. Ibid., 192–234; Shailer Mathews, *Is God Emeritus?* (New York: Macmillan, 1940), v, 7, 10–11, 19–68, 85–93, final quote on 93. For early intimations of Mathews's theistic and personalistic naturalism, see Shailer Mathews, *The Faith of Modernism* (New York: Macmillan, 1924), 108–20.

231. Jerome A. Stone, *The Minimalist Vision of Transcendence: A Naturalist Philosophy of Religion* (Albany: State University of New York Press, 1992), 52.

232. Mathews, *The Growth of the Idea of God*, 230, 226.

233. In this connection, McFague rebukes naturalist theologians like Gordon Kaufman for ceding too much control to science and failing to "suggest new personal metaphors in place of traditional ones." Sallie McFague, *The Body of God: An Ecological Theology* (Minneapolis: Fortress, 1993), 251n14. As will become clearer below, I share Kaufman's strong allergy to personalism, although I also applaud McFague's efforts to retain—and reimagine—personalistic language for God at the metaphorical, conventional, or symbolic level.

234. McFague, *The Body of God*, 131–57, final quote on 144. See also McFague, *Models of God*, 69–78; Sallie McFague, "An Earthly Theological Agenda," in *Ecofeminism and the Sacred*, ed. Carol J. Adams (New York: Continuum, 1993), 95–96.

235. McFague, *The Body of God*, 133, 135, 157, 159–91. I cannot help but wonder if all of this is a holdover from McFague's erstwhile Barthianism. See Dorrien, *Crisis, Irony, and Postmodernity, 1950–2005*, 358–60.

236. McFague, *The Body of God*, 171.

237. Ibid., 175.

238. Rosemary Radford Ruether, review of *The Body of God: An Ecological Theology*, by Sallie McFague, *Interpretation* 48 (July 1994): 315.

239. Sheila Greeve Davaney, review of *Models of God: Theology for an Ecological, Nuclear Age*, by Sallie McFague, *Religious Studies Review* 16, no. 1 (January 1990): 40.

240. McFague, *The Body of God*, 178, 177.

241. See ibid., 181.

242. Case, *The Christian Philosophy of History*, 189–204. See Dean, *History Making History*, 53–54.

243. Case, *The Christian Philosophy of History*, 204–5.

244. Shirley Jackson Case, *The Origins of Christian Supernaturalism* (Chicago: University of Chicago Press, 1946), 231–32.

245. Case, *The Christian Philosophy of History*, 206. See also Case, *The Origins of Christian Supernaturalism*, 232.

246. Case, *The Christian Philosophy of History*, 205–7, 210. Emphasis added.

247. Inbody, "History of Empirical Theology," 22.

248. G. B. Smith, *Current Christian Thinking*, 131, 142–43, 146–70; Gerald Birney Smith, "Is Theism Essential to Religion?," *The Journal of Religion* 5, no. 4 (1925): 356–77. See Stone, *Religious Naturalism Today*, 64–66; Dorrien, *Idealism, Realism, and Modernity, 1900–1950*, 261.

249. Portions of the following sections adapt and expand arguments introduced in Demian Wheeler, "Big History and the Size of God: Holistic Historicism as a Pathway to Religious Naturalism," *American Journal of Theology and Philosophy* 34, no. 3 (September 2013): 226–47.

250. Hogue, *The Promise of Religious Naturalism*, 203.

251. Goodenough, *The Sacred Depths of Nature*, xx, 10–13, 29, 167–68.

252. Hogue, *The Promise of Religious Naturalism*, 204.
253. See Stone, *Religious Naturalism Today*, 194–208.
254. Wieman, *The Source of Human Good*, 54–83.
255. Ibid., 79–82, quote on 81–82.
256. Meland, *Higher Education and the Human Spirit*, 166. Dorrien notes that Meland did emphasize tragedy, ambiguity, and dissonance. In Meland's estimation, "There is no human life of any depth or vigor that is without its tragic sense." But Meland never went as far as Loomer in affirming that God's being includes the world's evil, exclaiming on one occasion that he was not willing "to make a devil out of God." Dorrien, *Crisis, Irony, and Postmodernity, 1950–2005*, 128–31.
257. For example, Charley Hardwick. See Hardwick, *Events of Grace*, 115–57.
258. Stone, *Religious Naturalism Today*, 194–95.
259. Stone, *The Minimalist Vision of Transcendence*, 20.
260. Stone, *Religious Naturalism Today*, 196–203.
261. Nancy Frankenberry, "Classical Theism, Panentheism, and Pantheism: On the Relation between God Construction and Gender Construction," *Zygon* 28, no. 1 (March 1993): 40.
262. See Corrington, "Ecstatic Naturalism and the Transfiguration of the Good," 213; Corrington, *Ecstatic Naturalism*, 6, 19–22, 39, 51–52, 63; Corrington, *Nature's Religion*, 8–9, 17–18, 21, 26–28, 32, 56–57, 61, 97, 99, 102–3, 131; Robert S. Corrington, "A Unitarian Universalist Theology for the Twenty-First Century: Toward an Ecstatic Naturalism," *Voice* 3, no. 3 (Fall 1997): 4, 8–9; Corrington, "Empirical Theology and Its Divergence from Process Thought," 172, 175–76; Corrington, *A Semiotic Theory of Theology and Philosophy*, 14, 28–29, 40, 48, 138, 207; Corrington, "My Passage from Panentheism to Pantheism," 130; Corrington, "Three Conventional Notions Ignore the Fullness of Nature," *Research News and Opportunities* 3, no. 10 (June 2003): 20; Corrington, "Evolution, Religion, and an Ecstatic Naturalism," 125–28, 134–35; Robert S. Corrington and Leon J. Niemoczynski, "An Introduction to Ecstatic Naturalism: An Interview with Robert S. Corrington," *Kinesis* 36, no. 1 (Spring 2009): 66, 74, 77–78, 91–92. I discuss this aspect of Corrington's ecstatic naturalism further in Demian Wheeler, "American Religious Empiricism and the Possibility of an Ecstatic Naturalist Process Metaphysics," *Journal for the Study of Religion, Nature and Culture* 8, no. 2 (June 2014): 157–58, 165–67.
263. James, "A Pluralistic Mystic," 1313.
264. G. B. Smith, *Current Christian Thinking*, 169, 166.
265. Case, *The Christian Philosophy of History*. 210; Foster, *The Finality of the Christian Religion*, 210–11.
266. Dean, "Can Liberal Theology Recover?," 44.
267. See McFague, *Models of God*, 192n37, 21–40.
268. Delwin Brown, "Knowing the Mystery of God: Neville and Apophatic Theology," in *Interpreting Neville*, ed. J. Harley Chapman and Nancy K. Frankenberry (Albany: State University of New York Press, 1999), 190–202; Delwin Brown, "Four Gods of the Christian Faith," in *The Evolution of Rationality: Interdisciplinary*

Essays in Honor of J. Wentzel van Huyssteen, ed. F. LeRon Shults (Grand Rapids, MI: William B. Eerdmans, 2006), 296. See also Delwin Brown, "Locating God for the Twenty-First Century," *Quarterly Review* 22, no. 2 (Summer 2002): 114–16.

269. Kaufman, *In Face of Mystery*, 63.

270. Davaney, *Pragmatic Historicism*, 189, 191, 26.

271. See Foster, *The Function of Religion in Man's Struggle for Existence*, 107–10; Mathews, *The Growth of the Idea of God*, 218–34; Case, *The Christian Philosophy of History*, 206.

272. See McFague, *Models of God*, pt. 2.

273. McFague, *The Body of God*, 69–87, quotes on 75 and 78. Emphasis added.

274. Delwin Brown, "The Ambiguity of Ambiguity: A Response to Loomer's 'Size of God,'" in Dean and Axel, *The Size of God*, 57–58. Emphasis added. See Dorrien, *Crisis, Irony, and Postmodernity, 1950–2005*, 130.

275. See Kaufman, *In Face of Mystery*, 97–111; Kaufman, *In the Beginning . . . Creativity*, 42–52; Kaufman, "Biohistorical Naturalism and the Symbol 'God,'" 96–97.

276. Kaufman, *In Face of Mystery*, 305 (cf. 329).

277. Today, discussions about emergent complexity and novelty are happening in a number of disciplinary quarters, from evolutionary biology and physics to mathematics and big history. For instance, the biologist (and religious naturalist) Ursula Goodenough contends that the origination of life from "the underlying chemistry of biomolecules" is a powerful example of "emergence," of "something more" coming from "nothing but." She expounds: "Once these molecules came to reside inside cells, they began to interact with one another to generate new processes, like motility and metabolism and perception, processes that are unique to living creatures, processes that have no counterpart at simpler levels. These new, life-specific functions are referred to as emergent functions." Goodenough, *The Sacred Depths of Nature*, 28. David Christian theorizes that the existence of emergent functions—that is, novel features that are not intrinsic in the component parts of things but appear (unpredictably) only when those component parts are arranged and assembled in larger structures—is evidence of history's "increasing complexity" (which, according to the astrophysicist Eric Chaisson, can be measured by calculating the density of "energy flows" through complex things). Christian concedes that, on average, the earth and indeed most of the cosmos have remained very simple. And, even more foreboding yet, everything succumbs to chaos, to disorder, to entropy in due course. Be that as it may, at particular corners of the universe there seem to be "creative forces" that momentarily and locally counteract the second law of thermodynamics (i.e., the dissipation of usable energy over time) and allow "complex entities" (e.g., stars, living organisms, human societies) to come into being, entities with emergent and novel properties. David Christian, "The Case for 'Big History,'" *Journal of World History* 2, no. 2 (Fall 1991): 237; Christian, "The Return of Universal History," *History and Theory* 49, no. 4 (December 2010): 22–23; Christian, *Maps*

of Time: An Introduction to Big History (Berkeley: University of California Press, 2011), 505–11. See also Eric J. Chaisson, *Cosmic Evolution: The Rise of Complexity in Nature* (Cambridge, MA: Harvard University Press, 2001).

278. Kaufman, *In the Beginning . . . Creativity*, ix–x, 53–106, quotes on 70, 73; Kaufman, "Biohistorical Naturalism and the Symbol 'God,'" 98–99.

279. Kaufman, *In the Beginning . . . Creativity*, 55–60, 71–74, 80, 87–88, 90, 100–103; Kaufman, "Biohistorical Naturalism and the Symbol 'God,'" 98.

280. Kaufman, *In the Beginning . . . Creativity*, 5–6, 22–26.

281. Kaufman, *In Face of Mystery*, 55–59, 301–40, quotes on 314, 310. See also Kaufman, *In the Beginning . . . Creativity*, 59–60.

282. Dorrien, *Crisis, Irony, and Postmodernity, 1950–2005*, 308.

283. Kaufman, *In the Beginning . . . Creativity*, 59–60.

284. See Kaufman, *In Face of Mystery*, 264–80; Kaufman, *In the Beginning . . . Creativity*, 53–70.

285. Wesley J. Wildman, "Nature, God, Jesus, and Creativity," *American Journal of Theology and Philosophy* 29, no. 1 (January 2008): 57–58. In his rejoinder to Wildman, Kaufman says that such exhibitions of creativity, although far from beneficial to human beings, "may still be serendipitous in many respects—for other living creatures; for the long-range future of life on planet Earth; for developing features of the universe beyond our understanding or knowledge; and so on." Gordon D. Kaufman, "Response to Critics," *American Journal of Theology and Philosophy* 29, no. 1 (January 2008): 98.

286. Kaufman, *In the Beginning . . . Creativity*, 63–64, 104, 60.

287. Stone, *Religious Naturalism Today*, 203, 205. See Kaufman, *In the Beginning . . . Creativity*, 60–64.

288. Dean, *American Religious Empiricism*, 59–63, 74–77; Dean, *History Making History*, 140–41; Dean, *The Religious Critic in American Culture*, 90–92.

289. Dean, "Second Thoughts," 301.

290. See Dean, *The Religious Critic in American Culture*, 141–43.

291. William Dean, "Dean Replies to Zbaraschuk," *American Journal of Theology and Philosophy* 31, no. 3 (September 2010): 262.

292. Dean, *The Religious Critic in American Culture*, 69–70, 75–79, 82–83, 140–48.

293. Dean, "Second Thoughts," 302.

294. Dean, *The American Spiritual Culture*, 161–65. Emphasis added. See also Kaufman, *In the Beginning . . . Creativity*, 60.

295. Dean, *The Religious Critic in American Culture*, 144–45.

296. Dean, *The American Spiritual Culture*, 165. See Robert Allen Warrior, "Canaanites, Cowboys, and Indians," *Christianity and Crisis* 41 (September 11, 1989): 261–65. In addition to Warrior, Dean cites the gay theologian Gary Comstock, who forthrightly condemns the homophobia and heterosexism of several scriptural passages, as well as the womanist theologian Delores Williams, who points out that the same

God who brought the enslaved Hebrews out of Egypt did not liberate Hagar and other non-Jewish slaves from bondage. See Gary Comstock, *Gay Theology without Apology* (Cleveland: Pilgrim, 1993); Delores Williams, *Sisters in the Wilderness: The Challenge of Womanist God-Talk* (Maryknoll, NY: Orbis, 1993).

297. Dean, *History Making History*, 65. See also Dean, *American Religious Empiricism*, 69.

298. William Dean, "Even Stevens: A Poet for Liberal Theologians," *Journal of Religion* 92, no. 2 (April 2012): 178, 189.

299. Ibid., 189.

300. Ibid., 198, 188.

301. Dean, *The American Spiritual Culture*, 108.

302. Dorrien jocularly (and pugnaciously) references a "depressing talk" Dean gave several years ago at an American Theological Society meeting, in which he repeatedly (four times, to be exact) used the adjective "moribund" to describe the current condition of liberal theology. See Gary Dorrien, "Liberal Method, Postmodernity, and Liberal Necessity: On *The Making of American Liberal Theology*," *American Journal of Theology and Philosophy* 29, no. 2 (May 2008): 177.

303. Dean, *The American Spiritual Culture*, 96, 98, 109.

304. Dean, *The Religious Critic in American Culture*, 83.

305. Loomer, "The Size of God," 20–21, 41.

306. Ibid., 41.

307. Ibid., 42.

308. Ibid., 40, 42.

309. Dorrien astutely notices that the panentheistic God of Whitehead (and, to a lesser extent, Wieman) is unambiguous by virtue of being both more and less than nature in its concrete totality. As more than the world, God is the creative, saving power that shapes and pervades it; and, as less than the world, God excludes its evils. Dorrien, *Idealism, Realism, and Modernity, 1900–1950*, 268. Incidentally, McFague's panentheism—which is partly inspired by process theism—similarly allows her to retain an unambiguously good deity. As a panentheist, McFague can argue that evil (along with everything that is) is *in* God, but that God is somehow more than, other than, and better than the universe in its ambiguous entirety—that is, a personal spirit (metaphorically speaking) luring "all of creation in a particular salvific direction, toward the liberation, healing, and fulfillment of all bodies." McFague, *The Body of God*, 140–50, 160. See also McFague, *Models of God*, 72.

310. Loomer, "The Size of God," 50, 39, 38.

311. See Wieman, *The Source of Human Good*, 265–66. Dorrien comments that Wieman considered theological personalism "anthropocentric on its face." Therefore, "he pressed hard on the theme that God is not a personality." Dorrien, *Idealism, Realism, and Modernity, 1900–1950*, 271.

312. See Whitehead, *Process and Reality*, 346.

313. Frankenberry, *Religion and Radical Empiricism*, 124.

314. See Dorrien, *Crisis, Irony, and Postmodernity, 1950–2005*, 129.
315. Loomer, "The Size of God," 40–51.
316. See Wildman, "Ground-of-Being Theologies," 616, 628–29; Wildman, *Science and Religious Anthropology*, 20–21; Wesley J. Wildman, "Behind, between, and beyond Anthropomorphic Models of Ultimate Reality," *Philosophia* 35, no. 3–4 (2007): 421–24.
317. See Wildman, "Behind, between, and beyond Anthropomorphic Models of Ultimate Reality," 421.
318. Similarly, Kaufman remarks that it is hard to square literalistic notions of God as an "all-powerful, all-knowing, absolutely righteous and merciful Person" with the world's rampant and horrific evils. It is more reasonable to think of "the difficulties encountered in life" as "arising out of the complexity of the patterns of nature and history in which we are living—with a good deal of human bungling and malevolence added to the mix; they are not a direct intentional expression of some 'will' thought to be divine." Kaufman, *In Face of Mystery*, 335–36.
319. Wildman, "The Ambiguous Heritage and Perpetual Promise of Liberal Theology," 51–55, quotes on 52 and 54. Theologian Andrew Irvine echoes Wildman's sentiments and applies them to another popular supranatural god, the divine liberator of liberation theology. Irvine avers that the "cultural physics" of late modernity, including evolutionary explanations of natural history, severely militate against a "metaphysics that insists there is a divine person who intervenes in the world so as to advance the cause of the oppressed in relation to others." He goes on: "Theologians who affirm that God has a special concern for humankind need to reckon with the realization that the universe was and will be devoid of human worries and delights for all but a tiny sliver of its temporal extension. Much more must theologians who affirm God has an exceptional concern for the victims of humanity's inhumanity reflect that the flourishing of all kinds of life evidently depends upon processes that also waste and destroy life." Andrew B. Irvine, "Liberation Theology in Late Modernity: An Argument for a Symbolic Approach," *Journal of the American Academy of Religion* 78, no. 4 (December 2010): 946, 936.
320. Wildman, "The Ambiguous Heritage and Perpetual Promise of Liberal Theology," 50, 54; Wildman, "Behind, between, and beyond Anthropomorphic Models of Ultimate Reality," 424; Wildman, *Science and Religious Anthropology*, 20–21, 23–25; Wildman, "Ground-of-Being Theologies," 612–13, 615, 618–19.
321. Wildman, "The Ambiguous Heritage and Perpetual Promise of Liberal Theology," 54–55, 60–61.
322. Wildman, *Science and Religious Anthropology*, 21, 24; Wildman, *Religious and Spiritual Experiences*, 264–65.
323. Wildman, "Behind, between, and beyond Anthropomorphic Models of Ultimate Reality," 423; Wildman, "The Ambiguous Heritage and Perpetual Promise of Liberal Theology," 50. Here, Wildman is drawing heavily on Robert Neville's understanding of religious symbolism (which is pieced together from Paul Tillich's

theory of symbols and Charles Sanders Peirce's pragmatic semiotics). For Neville, our theological symbols authentically engage and participate in the divine realities to which they refer, yet remain "broken" so as to avoid idolatry. See Robert Cummings Neville, *The Truth of Broken Symbols* (Albany: State University of New York Press, 1996). Prayer, according to Wildman, nicely illustrates Neville's theory. To assume that there really is a deity "who hears," and that "the world is different from how it would be otherwise if this divine entity chooses to act in response" to human petitions, is obviously "mistaken," at least "at the level of literalized metaphysics." Nonetheless, prayer can be "profoundly meaningful if we interpret it non-literally, as a symbolic expression of human dependence on a ground of being and the sometimes happy way that the creative flux of events sometimes works out for human beings." Wildman, "Ground-of-Being Theologies," 623–24.

324. Wildman, *Religious and Spiritual Experiences*, 264–65.

325. Wildman, *Religious Philosophy as Multidisciplinary Comparative Inquiry*, 83.

326. Wildman, "Ground-of-Being Theologies," 618.

327. Wildman, "Behind, between, and beyond Anthropomorphic Models of Ultimate Reality," 410, 421–24; Wildman, "Ground-of-Being Theologies," 612–31; Wildman, "The Ambiguous Heritage and Perpetual Promise of Liberal Theology," 54, 60–61; Wildman, *Science and Religious Anthropology*, 19–25, 194–98, 200–206; Wildman, *Religious and Spiritual Experiences*, 264–65.

328. Crosby, *A Religion of Nature*, 9.

329. In his intellectual autobiography, Crosby reflects that his philosophical naturalism pivots on one "basic principle"—empiricism (more exactly, Whiteheadian and Jamesian radical empiricism)—and two "supporting principles"—processism and pluralism. Donald A. Crosby, "Finite Is All Right! Confessions of a Slow Learner," in *Pragmatism, Neo-pragmatism, and Religion: Conversations with Richard Rorty*, ed. Charley D. Hardwick and Donald A. Crosby (New York: Peter Lang, 1997), 360.

330. See especially Crosby, *A Religion of Nature*, 26–42.

331. See Crosby, "Finite Is All Right!," 361–62.

332. Crosby, *Living with Ambiguity*, 63.

333. Crosby allows that consciousness, personality, and purpose exist *in* nature (e.g., in *Homo sapiens*), even if nature itself is not conscious, personal, and purposive. Curiously, though, he does not make the same allowance for God, gods, goddesses, and animating spirits, negating even metaphorical or symbolic usages of these concepts. Crosby, *A Religion of Nature*, 148; Crosby, *Living with Ambiguity*, 5. It seems to me that a more consistent approach would be to maintain that God, gods, goddesses, and animating spirits, like consciousness, personality, and purpose, inhere *in* nature (i.e., in the social constructions, symbol systems, sacred conventions, and cultural traditions of humans), even if such beings are not metaphysically or literally real or located beyond or behind nature.

334. Crosby's case for the metaphysical ultimacy of nature itself (as opposed to a creator or a ground of nature) rests on four principal arguments. First, the ques-

tions typically raised to establish that nature needs a more ultimate source to explain it—"Where did nature come from? Why do some things exist rather than nothing? Why do these particular things exist rather than some other things?"—can be pushed back a step and applied just as easily to God—"Where did God come from? Why does God exist rather than no God at all? Why this particular God rather than some other God?" Second, avoiding an "infinite regress of explanations" requires that something be "accepted as given," and "there is no compelling reason not to conclude that the given is nature itself." Third, "nature as we presently experience it (*natura naturata*) is admittedly contingent," but "the creative power (*natura naturans*) underlying and producing all the systems of nature that ever have been or ever will be" is not. Fourth, nature, unlike a divine being or a ground of being, is open to scientific inquiry and has an existence that is "beyond debate." Crosby, *A Religion of Nature*, 153–55.

335. Ibid., ix, 11–12, 17, 18, 20–21, 34, 42, 53–54, 89–114, 117–18, 141, 145–55, 159–64, 168–69.

336. Crosby, *Living with Ambiguity*, 64.

337. Wildman names names, targeting the so-called "new atheists." Christopher Hitchens, Daniel Dennett, Richard Dawkins, and Sam Harris, in particular, shred popular "supra/supernaturalist religion" yet posit, in its place, a reductionistic, materialistic, and metaphysically depleted physicalism that is equally dubious. They attack the "straw man" of "highly anthropomorphic theism" but never seriously grapple with more respectable, albeit minority, ultimacy models, such as religious naturalism, which is simultaneously anti-super/supranaturalistic and pro-religion (or, more precisely, convinced that *certain elements* of religion are valuable, disclosive, and worth preserving). Although just as vehement in their eschewing of human-like divine beings, angels and demons, supernatural revelation, life after death, and other superstitions, religious naturalists, unlike the new atheists, are able to account for reality's valuational and aesthetic depths and to ponder "legitimate questions about the ultimate origins and meaning of nature"—all while still operating within a fully naturalistic worldview. In fact, "one of the great discoveries of modern philosophy of religion," Wildman confidently asserts, is "that consistent non-religious naturalism, or equivalently, ontologically and axiologically flattened-out atheism, is intellectually untenable." Wildman, *Science and Religious Anthropology*, 21, 24, 89; Wildman, *Religious and Spiritual Experiences*, 23–25, 262; Wildman, "Behind, between, and beyond Anthropomorphic Models of Ultimate Reality," 422–23; Wildman, "Ground-of-Being Theologies," 626–27, final quote on 626.

338. Crosby qualifies that religious naturalists can be *noneliminative* materialists, however, "a position affirming the irreducible reality and indispensable functions of life, mind, and spirit." Donald A. Crosby, "Religious Naturalism," in *The Routledge Companion to Philosophy of Religion*, ed. Chad Meister and Paul Copan (London: Routledge, 2007), 672.

339. The others are uniqueness, primacy, pervasiveness, rightness, and permanence. See Crosby, *A Religion of Nature*, 118–30.

340. Ibid., 12, 21, 34, 46–50, 57–85, 111, 120–22, 125–26, 130. See also Crosby, *Living with Ambiguity*, 55–56, 88; Donald A. Crosby, "A Case for Religion of Nature," *Journal for the Study of Religion, Nature and Culture* 1, no. 4 (December 2007): 491–92, 495; Crosby, "Religious Naturalism," 672–73.

341. Crosby goes so far as to avow that nature is "religiously right" (i.e., deserving of our utmost trust, faith, and devotion) *because of* its ambiguity. See Crosby, *Living with Ambiguity*, ix, 22–33, 79–90.

342. Crosby, "A Case for Religion of Nature," 499.

343. Crosby, *A Religion of Nature*, 85–87, 124, 132–45; Crosby, *Living with Ambiguity*, ix, 22–33, 36, 79–90.

344. Crosby, *Living with Ambiguity*, 27, 36. In chapter 4, Crosby demonstrates how the ambiguity of nature and a perspectivist metaphysics inexorably presuppose one another.

345. Elsewhere, however, I have developed and defended a pantheistic variant of religious naturalism. See Wheeler, "*Deus sive Natura*," 108–16; Demian Wheeler, "Bernard Loomer as a Bridge between Whitehead and Tillich: Towards a Ground-of-Being Process Theology," *Bulletin of the North American Paul Tillich Society* 44, No. 1 (January 2018): 22–29; Wheeler, "Seizing a Whiteheadian Alternative: A Retrieval of the Empirical Option in Process Thought," in *Conceiving an Alternative: Philosophical Resources for an Ecological Civilization*, ed. Demian Wheeler and David E. Conner (Anoka, MN: Process Century Press, 2019), 128–33.

346. See James, *Pragmatism*, 37.

347. Wildman, *Religious Philosophy as Multidisciplinary Comparative Inquiry*, 294–304.

348. Brown, "Knowing the Mystery of God," 199–201.

349. Crosby, *Living with Ambiguity*, 108, 93.

350. Frankenberry, "Major Themes of Empirical Theology," 52.

351. Dean, "Dean Replies to Zbaraschuk," 263.

352. Crosby, *A Religion of Nature*, 134–41.

353. Ibid., 141.

354. Crosby, *Living with Ambiguity*, 107, 111–12.

355. Henry Samuel Levinson, "Rorty, Diggins, and the Promise of Pragmatism," in Hardwick and Crosby, *Pragmatism, Neo-pragmatism, and Religion*, 40.

356. See Stone, *Religious Naturalism Today*, 225–29.

357. Brown, "History, Country, Academy, and God," 76–77.

358. Dean, *The American Spiritual Culture*, 109–10.

359. Wildman, "The Ambiguous Heritage and Perpetual Promise of Liberal Theology," 60–61.

360. Kaufman, *Jesus and Creativity*, 7, 18, 26.

361. Kaufman, *In the Beginning . . . Creativity*, 60–61, 105; Kaufman, *Jesus and Creativity*, 21–23, 25–26, 46, 50.

362. In emphasizing the (serendipitous) trajectory that led to life, to *Homo sapiens*, and finally to Jesus of Nazareth, Kaufman betrays a kind of teleological

hangover. In *In Face of Mystery*, he alludes to a "directionality in the cosmic process," where "God's activity in history and nature will be thought of as working toward justice, righteousness, merciful and loving communities, ecological sensitivity, and so forth." Kaufman, *In Face of Mystery*, 318–19. In *Jesus and Creativity*, he suggests that the image/story of Jesus imparts "a sense of the direction in which creativity may be moving in our human world." Lest he fall prey to the very anthropocentrism (and christocentrism) that he has so stridently denounced, Kaufman (unlike McFague) is quick to qualify that "these Christian concerns" do not "reveal much to us about that wider creativity in the universe at large." Still, he is hopeful that "future creativity" will move "the human trajectory on planet Earth" further down this path. Of course, Kaufman considers all of this a "matter of (Christian) faith, not knowledge." I consider it, at best, wishful thinking and, at worst, a loss of naturalist nerve, especially given today's grave (and possibly irreversible) ecological concerns—which, as Kaufman confesses later on, could very well bring the human story to an abrupt conclusion. I would contend that the very fact of the ecological crisis (among other things, such as the inevitable extinction of our species and the eventual solar vaporization of our globe) casts serious doubt on any sort of christological or ecojustice-directed telos, even in creativity$_3$. Kaufman, *Jesus and Creativity*, 53–54, 103.

363. Kaufman, *Jesus and Creativity*, 46–47.
364. Kaufman, *God—Mystery—Diversity*, 114.
365. Kaufman, *In Face of Mystery*, 310.
366. Ibid., 311.
367. Kaufman, *In the Beginning . . . Creativity*, 64, 105; Kaufman, *Jesus and Creativity*, xii–xiii, 16–17, 24–61.
368. Crosby, *Living with Ambiguity*, 54–56, 82, 89.
369. Crosby, *A Religion of Nature*, 138–39, 165–66, 169; Crosby, *Living with Ambiguity*, 85–86.
370. Crosby, *A Religion of Nature*, 165.
371. Wildman, "Ground-of-Being Theologies," 625.
372. Wildman, *Science and Religious Anthropology*, 204.
373. Ibid., 204; Wildman, "Nature, God, Jesus, and Creativity," 60.
374. Wildman, "Nature, God, Jesus, and Creativity," 60.
375. See, for example, Robert Cummings Neville, *On the Scope and Truth of Theology: Theology as Symbolic Engagement* (New York: T. and T. Clark, 2006), 11 (cf. chs. 2, 3, and 4). See also Neville, "Naturalism: So Easily Wrong," *American Journal of Theology and Philosophy* 34, no. 3 (September 2013): 209–13. Even the metaphysically antipersonalistic Wieman, for whom God "cannot be a person but is so much more," concluded that "the mythological symbol" of a divine personality "may be indispensable for the practice of worship and personal devotion to the creative power." Wieman, *The Source of Human Good*, 266–67.
376. See Wildman, "Ground-of-Being Theologies," 623–24.
377. Wildman, *Religious Philosophy as Multidisciplinary Comparative Inquiry*, 301.

378. Ibid., 301; Wildman, "Nature, God, Jesus, and Creativity," 60.

379. Wildman, "The Ambiguous Heritage and Perpetual Promise of Liberal Theology," 60–61.

380. James, *Pragmatism*, 117, 123.

381. Dewey, "The Development of American Pragmatism," in *The Essential Dewey*, vol. 1, *Pragmatism, Education, Democracy*, ed. Larry A. Hickman and Thomas M. Alexander (Bloomington: Indiana University Press, 1998), 8–9.

382. Dewey, *A Common Faith*, 25.

383. Dean, *The Religious Critic in American Culture*, 78–79, 143.

384. Frankenberry, "Classical Theism, Panentheism, and Pantheism," 39–40.

385. Sacred conventions taking on a life of their own is an instance of the larger phenomenon of "emergence." According to the sociologist of religion Christian Smith, the social worlds that human beings invent "become real themselves and bring into being with them new causal capacities and powers. The latter remain completely dependent on the human activities that, through emergence, give rise to them. But, once they have come into being, they are then themselves entirely real, possessing their own new capacities and features that are *irreducible* to the activities that gave and continually give rise to their existence." These emergently real powers significantly influence "the lower-level entities that brought them into being through their relations or interactions," a process Smith terms "downward causation." Religion is one such emergently real power. It is "born of humanity's incapacities and limits of power." However, once it exists among humans, religion comes to possess "a host of new causal capacities and powers"—for example, sacred conventions—that act "back upon" their human makers. Christian Smith, *Religion: What It Is, How It Works, and Why It Matters* (Princeton, NJ: Princeton University Press, 2017), 84–87.

386. Charles S. Milligan, "The Eco-religious Case for Naturalistic Pantheism," in *Religious Experience and Ecological Responsibility*, ed. Donald A. Crosby and Charley D. Hardwick (New York: Peter Lang, 1996), 244, 247–52.

387. Stone, *Religious Naturalism Today*, 208.

388. Wildman, "Behind, between, and beyond Anthropomorphic Models of Ultimate Reality," 425.

389. See Wildman, *Science and Religious Anthropology*, 198–201; Wildman, *Religious Philosophy as Multidisciplinary Comparative Inquiry*, 294–304; Wildman, "Ground-of-Being Theologies," 624; Wildman, "Nature, God, Jesus, and Creativity," 60.

Conclusion

1. Donald A. Crosby, "Commentary and Questions," review of *Pragmatic Historicism: A Theology for the Twenty-First Century*, by Sheila Greeve Davaney, *Journal of Religion and Society* 4 (2002).

2. In *Contingency, Irony, and Solidarity*, Richard Rorty speaks of "liberal ironists," that is, "people who [combine] commitment with a sense of the contingency of their own commitment." Richard Rorty, *Contingency, Irony, and Solidarity* (Cambridge: Cambridge University Press, 1989), 61.

3. Sheila Greeve Davaney, "Response to My Interlocutors," *Journal of Religion and Society* 4 (2002).

4. See Donald A. Crosby, *Living with Ambiguity: Religious Naturalism and the Menace of Evil* (Albany: State University of New York Press, 2008), 52–54.

5. Donald A. Crosby, *A Religion of Nature* (Albany: State University of New York Press, 2002), 146–51.

6. Crosby, *Living with Ambiguity*, 8, 92–105.

7. Ursula Goodenough, *The Sacred Depths of Nature* (New York: Oxford University Press, 1998), 174.

8. Ibid., 170.

9. Gordon D. Kaufman, *Jesus and Creativity* (Minneapolis: Fortress, 2006), 60.

10. Quoted in William Hart, "One Percenters: Black Atheists, Secular Humanists, and Naturalists," *South Atlantic Quarterly* 112, no. 4 (Fall 2013): 689.

11. Ibid., 689–93.

12. See Sheila Greeve Davaney, *Pragmatic Historicism: A Theology for the Twenty-First Century* (Albany: State University of New York Press, 2000), 26.

Bibliography

Anderson, Douglas R., and Carl R. Hausman. *Conversations on Peirce: Reals and Ideals*. New York: Fordham University Press, 2012.
Appiah, Kwame Anthony. *Cosmopolitanism: Ethics in a World of Strangers*. New York: W. W. Norton, 2006.
Arendt, Hannah. "What Was Authority?" In *Authority*, edited by Carl J. Friedrich, 81–112. Cambridge, MA: Harvard University Press, 1958.
Ariarajah, S. Wesley. "Power, Politics, and Plurality: The Struggles of the World Council of Churches to Deal with Religious Plurality." In Knitter, *The Myth of Religious Superiority*, 176–93.
Asad, Talal. *Genealogies of Religion: Discipline and Reasons of Power in Christianity and Islam*. Baltimore: Johns Hopkins University Press, 1993.
Axel, Larry E. "Process and Religion: The History of a Tradition at Chicago." *Process Studies* 8, no. 4 (Winter 1978): 231–39.
Ayer, A. J. *Language, Truth, and Logic*. New York: Dover, 1952.
Barth, Karl. "The Revelation of God as the Abolition of Religion." In *Attitudes toward Other Religions: Some Christian Interpretations*, edited by Owen C. Thomas. 96–112. London: SCM Press, 1969.
Beiser, Frederick C. *The German Historicist Tradition*. Oxford: Oxford University Press, 2011.
Berger, Peter. *The Sacred Canopy: Elements of a Sociological Theory of Religion*. New York: Anchor, 1967.
Berger, Peter, and Thomas Luckmann. *The Social Construction of Reality: A Treatise in the Sociology of Knowledge*. New York: Anchor, 1967.
Berger, Peter, and Anton Zijderveld. *In Praise of Doubt: How to Have Convictions without Becoming a Fanatic*. New York: HarperOne, 2009.
Bernstein, Richard J. *Beyond Objectivism and Relativism: Science, Hermeneutics, and Praxis*. Philadelphia: University of Pennsylvania Press, 1983.
———. *The Pragmatic Turn*. Cambridge, UK: Polity, 2010.

———. "Pragmatism, Pluralism, and the Healing of Wounds." In *Pragmatism: A Reader*, edited by Louis Menand, 382–401. New York: Vintage, 1997.
Best, Steven, and Douglas Kellner. *Postmodern Theory: Critical Interrogations*. New York: Guilford Press, 1991.
Borg, Marcus J. *Jesus in Contemporary Scholarship*. Valley Forge, PA: Trinity Press International, 1994.
Brown, Cynthia Stokes. *Big History: From the Big Bang to the Present*. New York: New Press, 2007.
Brown, Delwin. "Academic Theology in the University; or, Why an Ex-Queen's Heir Should Be Made a Subject." In Cady and Brown, *Religious Studies, Theology, and the University*, 126–39.
———. "The Ambiguity of Ambiguity: A Response to Loomer's 'Size of God.'" In Dean and Axel, *The Size of God*, 56–58.
———. *Boundaries of Our Habitations: Tradition and Theological Construction*. Albany: State University of New York Press, 1994.
———. "The Fall of '26: Gerald Birney Smith and the Collapse of the Socio-historical Framework of Theology." *American Journal of Theology and Philosophy* 11, no. 3 (September 1990): 183–201.
———. "Four Gods of the Christian Faith." In *The Evolution of Rationality: Interdisciplinary Essays in Honor of J. Wentzel Van Huyssteen*, edited by F. LeRon Shults, 294–305. Grand Rapids, MI: William B. Eerdmans, 2006.
———. "History, Country, Academy, and God: On the Role of the Religious Critic." *American Journal of Theology and Philosophy* 16, no. 1 (January 1995): 69–86.
———. "Knowing the Mystery of God: Neville and Apophatic Theology." In *Interpreting Neville*, edited by J. Harley Chapman and Nancy K. Frankenberry, 189–204. Albany: State University of New York Press, 1999.
———. "Limitation and Ingenuity: Radical Historicism and the Nature of Tradition." *American Journal of Theology and Philosophy* 24, no. 3 (September 2003): 194–211.
———. "Locating God for the Twenty-First Century." *Quarterly Review* 22, no. 2 (Summer 2002): 113–24.
———. "Marginalizing the Life of Language: Radical Empiricism as a Critique of Gadamer." In Peden and Axel, *New Essays in Religious Naturalism*, 21–32.
———. "Mystery and History in Kaufman's Theology." Review of *In Face of Mystery: A Constructive Theology*, by Gordon D. Kaufman. *Journal of the American Academy of Religion* 62, no. 4 (Winter 1994): 1209–18.
———. "Refashioning Self and Other: Theology, Academy, and the New Ethnography." In Brown, Davaney, and Tanner, *Converging on Culture*, 41–55.
———. "Struggle Till Daybreak: On the Nature of Authority in Theology." *Journal of Religion* 65, no. 1 (January 1985): 15–32.
———. *To Set at Liberty: Christian Faith and Human Freedom*. Maryknoll, NY: Orbis, 1981.

Brown, Delwin, Sheila Greeve Davaney, and Kathryn Tanner, eds. *Converging on Culture: Theologians in Dialogue with Cultural Analysis and Criticism.* New York: Oxford University Press, 2001.
Brown, Delwin, and Clark H. Pinnock. *Theological Crossfire: An Evangelical/Liberal Dialogue.* Grand Rapids, MI: Zondervan, 1990.
Bunge, Marcia. Introduction to Herder, *Against Pure Reason,* 1–37.
Cady, Linell E. "Resisting the Postmodern Turn: Theology and Contextualization." In Davaney, *Theology at the End of Modernity,* 81–98.
Cady, Linell E., and Delwin Brown, eds. *Religious Studies, Theology, and the University: Conflicting Maps, Changing Terrain.* Albany: State University of New York Press, 2002.
Cahoone, Lawrence E. *The Ends of Philosophy.* Albany: State University of New York Press, 1995.
Caputo, John D. *Deconstruction in a Nutshell: A Conversation with Jacques Derrida.* New York: Fordham University Press, 1997.
———. *More Radical Hermeneutics: On Not Knowing Who We Are.* Bloomington: Indiana University Press, 2000.
———. *The Prayers and Tears of Jacques Derrida: Religion without Religion.* Bloomington: Indiana University Press, 1997.
Caputo, John D., and Gianni Vattimo. *After the Death of God.* Edited by Jeffrey W. Robbins. New York: Columbia University Press, 2007.
Carlson, Jeffrey. "Responses." *Buddhist-Christian Studies* 23 (2003): 77–83.
Case, Shirley Jackson. *Christianity in a Changing World.* New York: Harper, 1941.
———. *The Christian Philosophy of History.* Chicago: University of Chicago Press, 1943.
———. "Education in Liberalism." In Ferm, *Contemporary American Theology,* 107–22.
———. *The Evolution of Early Christianity: A Genetic Study of First-Century Christianity in Relation to Its Religious Environment.* Chicago: University of Chicago Press, 1914.
———. "The Historical Study of Religion." *Journal of Religion* 1 (January 1921): 1–17.
———. *Jesus: A New Biography.* Chicago: University of Chicago Press, 1927.
———. *Jesus through the Centuries.* Chicago: University of Chicago Press, 1932.
———. "New *Religionsgeschichtliche* Studies on Christian Origins." *American Journal of Theology* 18 (1914): 440–45.
———. *The Origins of Christian Supernaturalism.* Chicago: University of Chicago Press, 1946.
———. "The Religion of Jesus." In *The Chicago School of Theology—Pioneers in Religious Inquiry: The Early Chicago School, 1906–1959,* edited by W. Creighton Peden and Jerome A. Stone. Lewiston, NY: Edwin Mellen, 1996.
———. "The Religious Meaning of the Past." *The Journal of Religion* 4, no. 6 (November 1924): 576–91.

———. *The Social Origins of Christianity*. Chicago: University of Chicago Press, 1923.
———. *The Social Triumph of the Ancient Church*. New York: Harper, 1933.
Chaisson, Eric J. *Cosmic Evolution: The Rise of Complexity in Nature*. Cambridge, MA: Harvard University Press, 2001.
———. *Epic of Evolution: Seven Ages of the Cosmos*. New York: Columbia University Press, 2006.
Chidester, David. *Savage Systems: Colonialism and Comparative Religion in Southern Africa*. Charlottesville: University Press of Virginia, 1996.
Christian, David. "The Case for 'Big History.'" *Journal of World History* 2, no. 2 (Fall 1991): 223–38.
———. *Maps of Time: An Introduction to Big History*. Berkeley: University of California Press, 2011. 2004.
———. "The Return of Universal History." *History and Theory* 49, no. 4 (December 2010): 6–27.
———. "World History in Context." *Journal of World History* 14, no. 4 (December 2003): 437–58.
Clayton, John Powell, ed. *Ernst Troeltsch and the Future of Theology*. New York: Cambridge University Press, 1976.
Clayton, Philip, ed. *The Oxford Handbook of Religion and Science*. Oxford: Oxford University Press, 2006.
Clooney, Francis X. *Comparative Theology: Deep Learning across Religious Borders*. Malden, MA: Wiley-Blackwell, 2010.
———, ed. *The New Comparative Theology: Interreligious Insights from the Next Generation*. London: T. and T. Clark, 2010.
———. "Response." In *The New Comparative Theology*, 191–200.
———. *The Truth, the Way, the Life: Christian Commentary on the Three Holy Mantras of the Srivaisnavas*. Leuven, Belgium: Peeters, 2008.
Cobb, John B., Jr. "Some Whiteheadian Assumptions about Religion and Pluralism." In Griffin, *Deep Religious Pluralism*, 243–62.
Comstock, Gary. *Gay Theology without Apology*. Cleveland: Pilgrim, 1993.
Cornille, Catherine. "Double Religious Belonging: Aspects and Questions." *Buddhist-Christian Studies* 23 (2003): 43–49.
———. *The Im-possibility of Interreligious Dialogue*. New York: Herder and Herder, 2008.
———. "Introduction: The Dynamics of Multiple Belonging." In *Many Mansions? Multiple Religious Belonging and Christian Identity*, edited by Catherine Cornille, 1–6. Maryknoll, NY: Orbis, 2002.
Corrington, Robert S. "Beyond Experience: Pragmatism and Nature's God." *American Journal of Theology and Philosophy* 14, no. 2 (May 1993): 147–60.
———. "Deep Pantheism." *Journal for the Study of Religion, Nature and Culture* 1, no. 4 (December 2007): 503–7.
———. "Ecstatic Naturalism and the Transfiguration of the Good." In Miller, *Empirical Theology*, 203–21.

---. *Ecstatic Naturalism: Signs of the World*. Bloomington: Indiana University Press, 1994.

---. "The Emancipation of American Philosophy." *Newsletters on the Black Experience* 90, no. 3 (Fall 1991): 23–26.

---. "Empirical Theology and Its Divergence from Process Thought." In *Introduction to Christian Theology: Contemporary North American Perspectives*, edited by Roger A. Badham, 166–79. Louisville: Westminster John Knox Press, 1998.

---. "Evolution, Religion, and an Ecstatic Naturalism." *American Journal of Theology and Philosophy* 31, no. 2 (May 2010): 124–35.

---. "My Passage from Panentheism to Pantheism." *American Journal of Theology and Philosophy* 23, no. 2 (May 2002): 129–53.

---. *Nature and Spirit: An Essay in Ecstatic Naturalism*. New York: Fordham University Press, 1992.

---. *Nature's Religion*. Lanham, MD: Rowman and Littlefield, 1997.

---. Review of *American Religious Empiricism* and *History Making History: The New Historicism in American Religious Thought*, by William Dean. *Journal of Speculative Philosophy*, n.s., 3, no. 3 (1989): 223–30.

---. *A Semiotic Theory of Theology and Philosophy*. Cambridge: Cambridge University Press, 2000.

---. "Three Conventional Notions Ignore the Fullness of Nature." *Research News and Opportunities* 3, no. 10 (June 2003): 20–21.

---. "A Unitarian Universalist Theology for the Twenty-First Century: Toward an Ecstatic Naturalism." *Voice* 3, no. 3 (Fall 1997): 1–9.

Corrington, Robert S., and Leon J. Niemoczynski. "An Introduction to Ecstatic Naturalism: An Interview with Robert S. Corrington." *Kinesis* 36, no. 1 (Spring 2009): 64–94.

Crosby, Donald A. "A Case for Religion of Nature." *Journal for the Study of Religion, Nature and Culture* 1, no. 4 (December 2007): 489–502.

---. "Commentary and Questions." Review of *Pragmatic Historicism: A Theology for the Twenty-First Century*, by Sheila Greeve Davaney. *Journal of Religion and Society* 4 (2002).

---. "Finite Is All Right! Confessions of a Slow Learner." In Hardwick and Crosby, *Pragmatism, Neo-pragmatism, and Religion*, 357–82.

---. *Living with Ambiguity: Religious Naturalism and the Menace of Evil*. Albany: State University of New York Press, 2008.

---. "Naturism as a Form of Religious Naturalism." *Zygon* 38 (March 2003): 117–20.

---. *A Religion of Nature*. Albany: State University of New York Press, 2002.

---. "Religious Naturalism." In *The Routledge Companion to Philosophy of Religion*, edited by Chad Meister and Paul Copan, 672–81. London: Routledge, 2007.

Crosby, Donald A., and Jerome A. Stone, eds. *The Routledge Handbook of Religious Naturalism*. London: Routledge, 2018.

Crossan, John Dominic. *The Historical Jesus: The Life of a Mediterranean Jewish Peasant*. New York: HarperCollins, 1991.
———. *Jesus: A Revolutionary Biography*. New York: HarperCollins, 1994.
D'Costa, Gavin. *Christianity and World Religions: Disputed Questions in the Theology of Religions*. Malden, MA: Wiley-Blackwell, 2009.
———, ed. *Christian Uniqueness Reconsidered: The Myth of a Pluralistic Theology of Religions*. Maryknoll, NY: Orbis, 1990.
———. "The Impossibility of a Pluralist View of Religions." *Religious Studies* 32, no. 2 (June 1996): 223–32.
———. *The Meeting of Religions and the Trinity*. Maryknoll, NY: Orbis, 2000.
———. Preface to *Christian Uniqueness Reconsidered*, viii–xxii.
———. "Whose Objectivity? Which Neutrality? The Doomed Quest for a Neutral Vantage Point from Which to Judge Religions." *Religious Studies* 29, no. 1 (March 1993): 79–95.
Danto, Arthur C. "Naturalism." In *The Encyclopedia of Philosophy*, edited by Paul Edwards, 5:448–50. New York: Macmillan, 1967.
Davaney, Sheila Greeve. "Between the One and the Many: A Response to Delwin Brown's Theology of Tradition." *American Journal of Theology and Philosophy* 18, no. 2 (May 1997): 135–45.
———. "Directions in Historicism: Language, Experience, and Pragmatic Adjudication." In Peden and Axel, *New Essays in Religious Naturalism*, 49–65.
———. *Divine Power: A Study of Karl Barth and Charles Hartshorne*. Philadelphia: Fortress, 1986.
———. *Historicism: The Once and Future Challenge for Theology*. Minneapolis: Fortress, 2006.
———. "A Historicist Model for Theology." In *Jesus and Faith: A Conversation on the Work of John Dominic Crossan*, edited by Jeffrey Carlson and Robert A. Ludwig, 44–56. Maryknoll, NY: Orbis, 1994.
———. "Mapping Theologies: An Historicist Guide to Contemporary Theology." In *Changing Conversations: Religious Reflection and Cultural Analysis*, edited by Dwight N. Hopkins and Sheila Greeve Davaney. 25–41. New York: Routledge, 1996.
———. "The Outsideless Life: Historicism, Theology and the Quest for Jesus." *Louvain Studies* 32, no. 1–2 (Spring–Summer 2007): 81–110.
———. *Pragmatic Historicism: A Theology for the Twenty-First Century*. Albany: State University of New York Press, 2000.
———. "Response to My Interlocutors." *Journal of Religion and Society* 4 (2002).
———. "Rethinking Theology and Religious Studies." In Cady and Brown, *Religious Studies, Theology, and the University*, 140–54.
———. Review of *Models of God: Theology for an Ecological, Nuclear Age*, by Sallie McFague. *Religious Studies Review* 16, no. 1 (January 1990): 36–40.
———. "Theology and the Turn to Cultural Analysis." In Brown, Davaney, and Tanner, *Converging on Culture*, 3–16.

———, ed. *Theology at the End of Modernity: Essays in Honor of Gordon D. Kaufman.* Philadelphia: Trinity Press International, 1991.
Dawes, Gregory W. *The Historical Jesus Question: The Challenge of History to Religious Authority.* Louisville: Westminster John Knox Press, 2001.
Dawkins, Richard. *The God Delusion.* Boston: Mariner, 2006.
Dean, William. *American Religious Empiricism.* Albany: State University of New York Press, 1986.
———. *The American Spiritual Culture: And the Invention of Jazz, Football, and the Movies.* New York: Continuum, 2002.
———. "An American Theology." *Process Studies* 12, no. 2 (Summer 1982): 111–28.
———. "Can Liberal Theology Recover?" *American Journal of Theology and Philosophy* 30, no. 1 (January 2009): 24–47.
———. *Coming To: A Theology of Beauty.* Philadelphia: Westminster Press, 1972.
———. "Dean Replies to Zbaraschuk." *American Journal of Theology and Philosophy* 31, no. 3 (September 2010): 259–63.
———. "Deconstruction and Process Theology." *Journal of Religion* 64, no. 1 (January 1984): 1–19.
———. "Dorrien the Historian." *American Journal of Theology and Philosophy* 29, no. 2 (May 2008): 166–74.
———. "Empirical Theology: A Revisable Tradition." *Process Studies* 19, no. 2 (Summer 1990): 85–102.
———. "Empiricism and God." In Miller, *Empirical Theology*, 107–28.
———. "Even Stevens: A Poet for Liberal Theologians." *Journal of Religion* 92, no. 2 (April 2012): 177–98.
———. "Historical Process Theology: A Field in a Map of Thought." *Process Studies* 28, no. 3–4 (Fall–Winter 1999): 255–66.
———. *History Making History: The New Historicism in American Religious Thought.* Albany: State University of New York Press, 1988.
———. "Humanistic Historicism and Naturalistic Historicism." In Davaney, *Theology at the End of Modernity*, 41–59.
———. "The Persistence of Experience: A Commentary on Kaufman's Theology." In Peden and Axel, *New Essays in Religious Naturalism*, 67–81.
———. "Pragmatism, History, and Theology." In *Pragmatism and Religion*, edited by Stuart Rosenbaum, 153–74. Urbana: University of Illinois Press, 2003.
———. "A Present Prospect for American Religious Thought." *Journal of the American Academy of Religion* 60, no. 4 (Winter 1992): 737–55.
———. *The Religious Critic in American Culture.* Albany: State University of New York Press, 1994.
———. "Second Thoughts." *American Journal of Theology and Philosophy* 29, no. 3 (September 2008): 289–303.
———. "Theological Historicism's Missing Historicity: A Commentary on *Boundaries of Our Habitations*." *American Journal of Theology and Philosophy* 18, no. 2 (May 1997): 109–19.

Dean, William, and Larry E. Axel, eds. *The Size of God: The Theology of Bernard Loomer in Context*. Macon, GA: Mercer University Press, 1987.
Dennett, Daniel C. *Breaking the Spell: Religion as a Natural Phenomenon*. New York: Penguin, 2006.
Derrida, Jacques. "How to Avoid Speaking: Denials." In *Derrida and Negative Theology*, edited by Harold Coward and Toby Foshay, 73–142. Albany: State University of New York Press, 1992.
———. *Margins of Philosophy*. Translated by Alan Bass. Chicago: University of Chicago Press, 1982.
———. *Of Grammatology*. Translated by Gayatri Chakravorty Spivak. Baltimore: John Hopkins University Press, 1974.
———. *On the Name*. Translated by David Wood, John P. Leavey and Ian McLeod. Edited by Thomas Dutoit. Stanford, CA: Stanford University Press, 1993.
———. *Writing and Difference*. Translated by Alan Bass. Chicago: University of Chicago Press, 1978.
Descartes, René. *Selected Philosophical Writings*. Translated by John Cottingham, Robert Stoothoff, and Dugald Murdoch. Cambridge: Cambridge University Press, 1988.
Dewey, John. *Art as Experience*. New York: Perigee, 1934.
———. *A Common Faith*. New Haven, CT: Yale University Press, 1934.
———. "The Development of American Pragmatism." In *The Essential Dewey*, 1:3–13.
———. *The Essential Dewey*, Vol. 1, *Pragmatism, Education, Democracy*, edited by Larry A. Hickman and Thomas M. Alexander. Bloomington: Indiana University Press, 1998.
———. *The Essential Dewey*, Vol. 2, *Ethics, Logic, Psychology*, edited by Larry A. Hickman and Thomas M. Alexander. Bloomington: Indiana University Press, 1998.
———. *Experience and Nature*. Chicago: Open Court, 1925.
———. *The Influence of Darwin on Philosophy, and Other Essays*. Amherst, NY: Prometheus, 1997.
———. *Logic: The Theory of Inquiry*. New York: Henry Holt, 1938.
———. "Philosophy and Democracy." In *The Essential Dewey*, 1:71–78.
———. "The Postulate of Immediate Empiricism." In *The Essential Dewey*, 1:115–20.
———. *The Quest for Certainty: A Study in the Relation of Knowledge and Action*. New York: Pedigree, 1929.
———. *Reconstruction in Philosophy*. Enl. ed. Boston: Beacon, 1957.
———. "What Pragmatism Means by 'Practical.'" In *The Essential Dewey*, 2:377–86.
DiNoia, J. A. *The Diversity of Religions: A Christian Perspective*. Washington, DC: Catholic University of America Press, 1992.
———. "Pluralist Theology of Religions: Pluralistic or Non-pluralistic?" In D'Costa, *Christian Uniqueness Reconsidered*, 119–34.

Dorrien, Gary. "The Crisis and Necessity of Liberal Theology." *American Journal of Theology and Philosophy* 30, no. 1 (January 2009): 3–23.
———. *Crisis, Irony, and Postmodernity, 1950–2005*. Vol. 3 of *The Making of American Liberal Theology*. Louisville: Westminster John Knox Press, 2006.
———. *Idealism, Realism, and Modernity, 1900–1950*. Vol. 2 of *The Making of American Liberal Theology*. Louisville: Westminster John Knox Press, 2003.
———. *Imagining Progressive Religion, 1805–1900*. Vol. 1 of *The Making of American Liberal Theology*. Louisville: Westminster John Knox Press, 2001.
———. *Kantian Reason and Hegelian Spirit: The Idealistic Logic of Modern Theology*. Malden, MA: Wiley-Blackwell, 2012.
———. "Liberal Method, Postmodernity, and Liberal Necessity: On *The Making of American Liberal Theology*." *American Journal of Theology and Philosophy* 29, no. 2 (May 2008): 175–83.
———. *The Word as True Myth: Interpreting Modern Theology*. Louisville: Westminster John Knox Press, 1997.
Drescher, Hans-Georg. "Ernst Troeltsch's Intellectual Development." In J. P. Clayton, *Ernst Troeltsch and the Future of Theology*, 3–32.
Duffy, Stephen J. "A Theology of Religions and/or a Comparative Theology?" *Horizons* 26, no. 1 (1999): 105–15.
Dupuis, Jacques. *Toward a Christian Theology of Religious Pluralism*. Maryknoll, NY: Orbis, 1997.
Eck, Diana L. "Dialogue and Method: Reconstructing the Study of Religion." In Patton and Ray, *A Magic Still Dwells*, 131–49.
———. *Encountering God: A Spiritual Journey from Bozeman to Banaras*. New York: Penguin, 1996.
Ehrman, Bart D. *Jesus: Apocalyptic Prophet of the New Millennium*. New York: Oxford University Press, 1999.
Ferm, Vergilius, ed. *Contemporary American Theology*. New York: Roundtable, 1932.
Flanagan, Owen. "Varieties of Naturalism." In P. Clayton, *The Oxford Handbook of Religion and Science*, 430–52.
Flannery, Austin, ed. *Vatican Council II: Constitutions, Decrees, Declarations*. Northport, NY: Costello, 1996.
Fletcher, Jeannine Hill. *Monopoly on Salvation? A Feminist Approach to Religious Pluralism*. New York: Continuum, 2005.
Forster, Michael N. Introduction to Herder, *Philosophical Writings*, vii–xxxv.
Foster, George Burman. *The Finality of the Christian Religion*. 2nd ed. Chicago: University of Chicago Press, 1906.
———. *Friedrich Nietzsche*. New York: Macmillan, 1931.
———. *The Function of Religion in Man's Struggle for Existence*. Chicago: University of Chicago Press, 1909.
———. "Pragmatism and Knowledge." *American Journal of Theology* 11, no. 4 (October 1907): 591–96.

———. Review of *The New Orthodoxy*, by Edward Scribner Ames. *Christian Century* 35, no. 41 (October 24, 1918): 17–18.

Foucault, Michel. *Discipline and Punish: The Birth of the Prison*. Translated by Alan Sheridan. 2nd ed. New York: Vintage, 1995.

———. *Power/Knowledge: Selected Interviews and Other Writings, 1972–1977*. Edited by Colin Gordon and translated by Colin Gordon, Leo Marshall, John Mepham, and Kate Soper. New York: Pantheon, 1980.

Frankenberry, Nancy. "Classical Theism, Panentheism, and Pantheism: On the Relation between God Construction and Gender Construction." *Zygon* 28, no. 1 (March 1993): 29–46.

———. "Major Themes of Empirical Theology." In Miller, *Empirical Theology*, 36–56.

———. *Religion and Radical Empiricism*. Albany: State University of New York Press, 1987.

Fredericks, James L. *Faith among Faiths: Christian Theology and Non-Christian Religions*. New York: Paulist Press, 1999.

———. Introduction to Clooney, *The New Comparative Theology*, ix–xix.

Fredriksen, Paula. "What You See Is What You Get: Context and Content in Current Research on the Historical Jesus." *Theology Today* 52, no. 1 (April 1995): 75–97.

Funk, Robert W., ed. *The Acts of Jesus: The Search for the Authentic Deeds of Jesus*. San Francisco: HarperSanFrancisco, 1998.

Funk, Robert W., and Roy W. Hoover, eds. *The Five Gospels: The Search for the Authentic Words of Jesus*. New York: HarperCollins, 1993.

Geertz, Clifford. *Available Light: Anthropological Reflections on Philosophical Topics*. Princeton, NJ: Princeton University Press, 2000.

———. *The Interpretation of Cultures*. New York: Basic Books, 1973.

Gilkey, Langdon. "Plurality and Its Theological Implications." In Hick and Knitter, *The Myth of Christian Uniqueness*, 37–50.

Goodenough, Ursula. *The Sacred Depths of Nature*. New York: Oxford University Press, 1998.

Gould, Stephen Jay. *Full House: The Spread of Excellence from Plato to Darwin*. New York: Three Rivers Press, 1996.

———. "Modified Grandeur." *Natural History* 102, no. 3 (March 1993): 14–20.

———. "The Wheel of Fortune and the Wedge of Progress." *Natural History* 98, no. 3 (March 1989): 14–21.

———. *Wonderful Life: The Burgess Shale and the Nature of History*. New York: W. W. Norton, 1989.

Grenz, Stanley J. *A Primer on Postmodernism*. Grand Rapids, MI: William B. Eerdmans, 1996.

Griffin, David Ray, ed. *Deep Religious Pluralism*. Louisville: Westminster John Knox Press, 2005.

———. "John Cobb's Whiteheadian Complementary Pluralism." In *Deep Religious Pluralism*, 39–66.

———. "Religious Pluralism: Generic, Identist, and Deep." In *Deep Religious Pluralism*, 3–38.
Griffiths, Paul J. *An Apology for Apologetics: A Study in the Logic of Interreligious Dialogue*. Eugene, OR: Wipf and Stock, 1991.
———. "The Properly Christian Response to Religious Plurality." *Anglican Theological Review* 79, no. 1 (Winter 1997): 3–26.
———. "The Uniqueness of Christian Doctrine Defended." In D'Costa, *Christian Uniqueness Reconsidered*, 157–73.
———. "Why We Need Interreligious Polemics." *First Things* 44 (June–July 1994): 31–37.
Haight, Roger. *Dynamics of Theology*. Maryknoll, NY: Orbis, 2001.
Hall, David L. *Richard Rorty: Prophet and Poet of the New Pragmatism*. Albany: State University of New York Press, 1994.
Hardwick, Charley D. *Events of Grace: Naturalism, Existentialism, and Theology*. Cambridge: Cambridge University Press, 1996.
Hardwick, Charley D., and Donald A. Crosby, eds. *Pragmatism, Neo-pragmatism, and Religion: Conversations with Richard Rorty*. New York: Peter Lang, 1997.
Harnack, Adolf von. *What Is Christianity?* San Diego: Book Tree, 2006.
Hart, William. "One Percenters: Black Atheists, Secular Humanists, and Naturalists." *South Atlantic Quarterly* 112, no. 4 (Fall 2013): 675–96.
Harvey, Van A. *The Historian and the Believer: The Morality of Historical Knowledge and Christian Belief*. Urbana: University of Illinois Press, 1996.
Heim, S. Mark. *The Depth of the Riches: A Trinitarian Theology of Religious Ends*. Grand Rapids, MI: William B. Eerdmans, 2001.
———. "God's Diversity: A Trinitarian View of Religious Pluralism." *Christian Century* 118, no. 3 (January 24, 2001): 14–18.
———. *Salvations: Truth and Difference in Religion*. Maryknoll, NY: Orbis, 1995.
Herder, Johann Gottfried. *Against Pure Reason: Writings on Religion, Language, and History*. Translated by Marcia Bunge. Minneapolis: Fortress, 1993.
———. *Philosophical Writings*. Translated by Michael N. Forster. Cambridge: Cambridge University Press, 2002.
Herman, Jonathan R. "The Contextual Illusion: Comparative Mysticism and Postmodernism." In Patton and Ray, *A Magic Still Dwells*, 92–100.
Hick, John. *A Christian Theology of Religions: The Rainbow of Faiths*. Louisville: Westminster John Knox Press, 1995.
———. *God and the Universe of Faiths: Essays in the Philosophy of Religion*. London: Macmillan, 1973.
———. *God Has Many Names: Britain's New Religious Pluralism*. London: Macmillan, 1980.
———. *An Interpretation of Religion: Human Responses to the Transcendent*. New Haven, CT: Yale University Press, 1989.
———. *The Metaphor of God Incarnate: Christology in a Pluralistic Age*. Louisville: Westminster John Knox Press, 1993.

———. "The Next Step Beyond Dialogue." In Knitter, *The Myth of Religious Superiority*, 3–12.

———. "The Non-absoluteness of Christianity." In Hick and Knitter, *The Myth of Christian Uniqueness*, 16–36.

———. "A Pluralist View." In *Four Views on Salvation in a Pluralistic World*, edited by Dennis L. Okholm and Timothy R. Phillips, 27–91. Grand Rapids, MI: Zondervan, 1996.

Hick, John, and Paul F. Knitter, eds. *The Myth of Christian Uniqueness: Toward a Pluralistic Theology of Religions*. Maryknoll: Orbis, 1987.

Hitchens, Christopher. *God Is Not Great: How Religion Poisons Everything*. New York: Twelve, 2007.

Hogue, Michael S. *The Promise of Religious Naturalism*. Lanham, MD: Rowman and Littlefield, 2010.

Hynes, William J. *Shirley Jackson Case and the Chicago School*. Chico, CA: Scholars Press, 1981.

Iggers, Georg G. *The German Conception of History: The National Tradition of Historical Thought from Herder to the Present*. Rev. ed. Middletown, CT: Wesleyan University Press, 1968.

Inbody, Tyron L. "History of Empirical Theology." In Miller, *Empirical Theology*, 11–35.

———. *The Many Faces of Christology*. Nashville: Abingdon Press, 2002.

Irvine, Andrew B. "Liberation Theology in Late Modernity: An Argument for a Symbolic Approach." *Journal of the American Academy of Religion* 78, no. 4 (December 2010): 921–60.

James, William. *Essays in Radical Empiricism, and a Pluralistic Universe*. New York: E. P. Dutton, 1971.

———. *The Meaning of Truth: A Sequel to Pragmatism*. Cambridge, MA: Harvard University Press, 1978.

———. "Philosophical Conceptions and Practical Results." In *The Writings of William James: A Comprehensive Edition*, edited by John J. McDermott, 345–62. Chicago: University of Chicago Press, 1977.

———. "A Pluralistic Mystic." In *Writings, 1902–1910*, 1294–313.

———. *Pragmatism: A New Name for Some Old Ways of Thinking*. Cambridge, MA: Harvard University Press, 1978.

———. *The Principles of Psychology*. Authorized ed. 2 vols. New York: Dover, 1950.

———. "Remarks on Spencer's Definition of Mind as Correspondence." In *Writings 1878–1899*, edited by Gerald E. Myers, 893–909. New York: Library of America, 1992.

———. "Some Problems in Philosophy: A Beginning of an Introduction to Philosophy." In *Writings, 1902–1910*, 979–1106.

———. *The Varieties of Religious Experience: A Study in Human Nature*. New York: Penguin, 1902.

———. *The Will to Believe, and Other Essays in Popular Philosophy*. New York: Dover, 1956.

———. *Writings, 1902–1910*, edited by Bruce Kuklick. New York: Library of America, 1987.

Johnson, Luke Timothy. *The Real Jesus: The Misguided Quest for the Historical Jesus and the Truth of the Traditional Gospels*. New York: HarperOne, 1996.

Kant, Immanuel. *Critique of Pure Reason*. Translated by Werner S. Pluhar. Unified ed. Indianapolis: Hackett, 1996.

———. "What Is Enlightenment?," In *The Portable Enlightenment Reader*, edited by Isaac Kramnick, 1–7. New York: Penguin, 1995.

Kaplan, Mordecai. *Judaism without Supernaturalism: The Only Alternative to Orthodoxy and Secularism*. New York: Reconstructionist Press, 1967.

Kaplan, Stephen. *Different Paths, Different Summits: A Model for Religious Pluralism*. Lanham, MD: Rowman and Littlefield, 2002.

Kärkkäinen, Veli-Matti. *An Introduction to the Theology of Religions: Biblical, Historical and Contemporary Perspectives*. Downers Grove, IL: IVP Academic, 2003.

Katz, Steven T. "The 'Conservative' Character of Mystical Experience." In *Mysticism and Religious Traditions*, edited by Steven T. Katz, 3–60. Oxford: Oxford University Press, 1983.

———. "Language, Epistemology, and Mysticism." In *Mysticism and Philosophical Analysis*, edited by Steven T. Katz, 22–74. New York: Oxford University Press, 1978.

Kaufman, Gordon D. "Biohistorical Naturalism and the Symbol 'God.'" *Zygon* 38, no. 1 (March 2003): 95–100.

———. "Critical Theology as a University Discipline." In *Theology and the University: Essays in Honor of John B. Cobb, Jr.*, edited by David Ray Griffin and Joseph C. Hough, 35–50. Albany: State University of New York Press, 1991.

———. "Empirical Realism in Theology: An Examination of Some Themes in Meland and Loomer." In Peden and Axel, *New Essays in Religious Naturalism*, 135–60.

———. *An Essay on Theological Method*. 3rd ed. Atlanta: Scholars Press, 1995.

———. *God—Mystery—Diversity: Christian Theology in a Pluralistic World*. Minneapolis: Fortress, 1996.

———. *God the Problem*. Cambridge, MA: Harvard University Press, 1972.

———. *In Face of Mystery: A Constructive Theology*. Cambridge, MA: Harvard University Press, 1993.

———. *In the Beginning . . . Creativity*. Minneapolis: Fortress, 2004.

———. *Jesus and Creativity*. Minneapolis: Fortress, 2006.

———. "My Life and My Theological Reflection: Two Central Themes." *American Journal of Theology and Philosophy* 22, no. 1 (January 2001): 3–32.

———. "Mystery, Critical Consciousness, and Faith." In *The Rationality of Religious Belief: Essays in Honour of Basil Mitchell*, edited by William J. Abraham and Steven W. Holtzer, 53–70. Oxford: Clarendon Press, 1987.

———. "Religious Diversity, Historical Consciousness, and Christian Theology." In Hick and Knitter, *The Myth of Christian Uniqueness*, 3–15.

———. "Response to Critics." *American Journal of Theology and Philosophy* 29, no. 1 (January 2008): 76–117.

———. "Response to Hans Frei." In *The Legacy of H. Richard Niebuhr*, edited by Ronald F. Thiemann, 25–32. Minneapolis: Fortress, 1991.

———. *The Theological Imagination: Constructing the Concept of God*. Philadelphia: Westminster Press, 1981.

———. *Theology for a Nuclear Age*. Philadelphia: Westminster Press, 1985.

Kaufmann, Walter, ed. *The Portable Nietzsche*. New York: Penguin, 1982.

Kearney, Richard. *Anatheism: Returning to God after God*. New York: Columbia University Press, 2010.

Kiblinger, Kristin Beise. *Buddhist Inclusivism: Attitudes towards Religious Others*. Aldershot, UK: Ashgate, 2005.

———. "Relating Theology of Religions and Comparative Theology." In Clooney, *The New Comparative Theology*, 21–42.

Knitter, Paul F. *Introducing Theologies of Religions*. Maryknoll, NY: Orbis, 2002.

———. Introduction to *The Myth of Religious Superiority*, vii–xi.

———. "Is the Pluralist Model a Western Imposition? A Response in Five Voices." In *The Myth of Religious Superiority*, 28–42.

———. *Jesus and the Other Names: Christian Mission and Global Responsibility*. Maryknoll, NY: Orbis, 1996.

———. "Key Questions for a Theology of Religions." *Horizons* 17, no. 1 (Spring 1990): 92–102.

———, ed. *The Myth of Religious Superiority: A Multifaith Exploration*. Maryknoll, NY: Orbis, 2005.

———. *No Other Name? A Critical Survey of Christian Attitudes toward the World Religions*. Maryknoll, NY: Orbis, 1985.

———. *One Earth, Many Religions: Multifaith Dialogue and Global Responsibility*. Maryknoll, NY: Orbis, 1995.

———. Preface to Hick and Knitter, *The Myth of Christian Uniqueness*, vii–xii.

———. "Religion and Globality: Can Interreligious Dialogue Be Globally Responsible?" In *A Dome of Many Colors: Studies in Religious Pluralism, Identity, and Unity*, edited by Arvind Sharma and Kathleen M. Dugan, 104–36. Harrisburg, PA: Trinity Press International, 1999.

———. "Toward a Liberation Theology of Religions." In Hick and Knitter, *The Myth of Christian Uniqueness*, 178–200.

Kuhn, Thomas S. *The Structure of Scientific Revolutions*. 3rd ed. Chicago: University of Chicago Press, 1996.

Kvale, Steinar. "Themes of Postmodernity." In *The Truth about the Truth: De-confusing and Re-constructing the Postmodern World*, edited by Walter Truett Anderson, 18–25. New York: Jeremy P. Tarcher/Putnam, 1995.

Laksana, A. Bagus. "Comparative Theology: Between Identity and Alterity." In Clooney, *The New Comparative Theology*, 1–20.
Lee, Bernard J. "The Two Process Theologies." *Theological Studies* 45, no. 2 (June 1984): 307–19.
Levinson, Henry Samuel. "Rorty, Diggins, and the Promise of Pragmatism." In Hardwick and Crosby, *Pragmatism, Neo-pragmatism, and Religion*, 25–42.
Light, Aimee Upjohn. "Harris, Hick, and the Demise of the Pluralist Hypothesis." *Journal of Ecumenical Studies* 44, no. 3 (Summer 2009): 467–70.
Lindbeck, George A. "The Gospel's Uniqueness: Election and Untranslatability." *Modern Theology* 13, no. 4 (October 1997): 423–50.
———. *The Nature of Doctrine: Religion and Theology in a Postliberal Age*. Philadelphia: Westminster Press, 1984.
Lindsey, William. "'Somebody, Somehow, Somewhere, and Somewhen': Shailer Mathews and the Socio-historical Interpretation of Doctrine." *American Journal of Theology and Philosophy* 20, no. 3 (September 1999): 191–215.
Long, Jeffrey D. "Anekanta Vedanta: Toward a Deep Hindu Religious Pluralism." In Griffin, *Deep Religious Pluralism*, 130–57.
Loomer, Bernard. "Empirical Theology within Process Thought." In *The Future of Empirical Theology*, edited by Bernard E. Meland, 149–73. Chicago: University of Chicago Press, 1969.
———. "The Size of God." In Dean and Axel, *The Size of God*, 20–51.
Lyotard, Jean-François. *The Postmodern Condition: A Report on Knowledge*. Translated by Geoff Bennington and Brian Massumi. Minneapolis: University of Minnesota Press, 1984.
Macintosh, Douglas Clyde. *The Problem of Religious Knowledge*. New York: Harper, 1940.
Maimela, Simon S. "Black Theology and the Quest for a God of Liberation." In Davaney, *Theology at the End of Modernity*, 141–59.
Margolis, Joseph. *Pragmatism without Foundations: Reconciling Realism and Relativism*. Oxford: Blackwell, 1986.
Martin, Jerry L. "Introduction to the Topical Issue 'Is Transreligious Theology Possible?'" *Open Theology* 2, no. 1 (January 2016): 261.
Masuzawa, Tomoko. *The Invention of World Religions; or, How European Universalism Was Preserved in the Language of Pluralism*. Chicago: University of Chicago Press, 2005.
Mathews, Shailer. *The Atonement and the Social Process*. New York: Macmillan, 1930.
———. *The Faith of Modernism*. New York: Macmillan, 1924.
———. *The Growth of the Idea of God*. New York: Macmillan, 1931.
———. "The Historical Study of Religion." In *A Guide to the Study of the Christian Religion*, edited by Gerald Birney Smith, 19–79. Chicago: University of Chicago Press, 1916.
———. *Is God Emeritus?* New York: Macmillan, 1940.

———. *The Messianic Hope in the New Testament*. Chicago: University of Chicago Press, 1905.

———. *The Social Teaching of Jesus: An Essay in Christian Sociology*. New York: Macmillan, 1897.

———. "Theology and the Social Mind." *Biblical World* 46, no. 4 (October 1915): 201–48.

———. "Theology as Group Belief." In Ferm, *Contemporary American Theology*, 163–96.

McCutcheon, Russell T. *Manufacturing Religion: The Discourse on Sui Generis Religion and the Politics of Nostalgia*. New York: Oxford University Press, 2003.

McDowell, John. "Towards Rehabilitating Objectivity." In *Rorty and His Critics*, edited by Robert B. Brandom, 109–23. Malden, MA: Blackwell, 2000.

McFague, Sallie. *The Body of God: An Ecological Theology*. Minneapolis: Fortress, 1993.

———. "Cosmology and Christianity: Implications of the Common Creation Story for Theology." In Davaney, *Theology at the End of Modernity*, 19–40.

———. "An Earthly Theological Agenda." In *Ecofeminism and the Sacred*, edited by Carol J. Adams, 84–98. New York: Continuum, 1993.

———. *Metaphorical Theology: Models of God in Religious Language*. Philadelphia: Fortress, 1982.

———. *Models of God: Theology for an Ecological, Nuclear Age*. Philadelphia: Fortress, 1987.

Meland, Bernard E. *Essays in Constructive Theology: A Process Perspective*. Edited by Perry LeFevre. Chicago: Exploration, 1988.

———. *Fallible Forms and Symbols: Discourses on Method in a Theology of Culture*. Philadelphia: Fortress, 1976.

———. *Higher Education and the Human Spirit*. Chicago: University of Chicago Press, 1953.

———. "Reflections on the Early Chicago School of Modernism." *American Journal of Theology and Philosophy* 5, no. 1 (January 1984): 3–12.

Menand, Louis. *The Metaphysical Club: A Story of Ideas in America*. New York: Farrar, Straus and Giroux, 2001.

Milbank, John. "The End of Dialogue." In D'Costa, *Christian Uniqueness Reconsidered*, 174–91.

Miller, Randolph Crump, ed. *Empirical Theology: A Handbook*. Birmingham, AL: Religious Education Press, 1992.

Milligan, Charles S. "The Eco-religious Case for Naturalistic Pantheism." In *Religious Experience and Ecological Responsibility*, edited by Donald A. Crosby and Charley D. Hardwick, 235–55. New York: Peter Lang, 1996.

Min, Anselm Kyongsuk. "Dialectical Pluralism and Solidarity of Others: Towards a New Paradigm." *Journal of the American Academy of Religion* 65, no. 3 (Fall 1997): 587–604.

Murphy, Francesca Aran. *God Is Not a Story: Realism Revisited*. Oxford: Oxford University Press, 2007.
Netland, Harold A. *Dissonant Voices: Religious Pluralism and the Question of Truth*. Grand Rapids, MI: William B. Eerdmans, 1991.
Neville, Robert Cummings. *The Highroad around Modernism*. Albany: State University of New York Press, 1992.
———. "Naturalism: So Easily Wrong." *American Journal of Theology and Philosophy* 34, no. 3 (September 2013): 199–213.
———. *On the Scope and Truth of Theology: Theology as Symbolic Engagement*. New York: T. and T. Clark, 2006.
———. "A Paleopragmatic Philosophy of History of Philosophy." In Hardwick and Crosby, *Pragmatism, Neo-pragmatism, and Religion*, 43–60.
———. "Pragmatism, Metaphysics, Comparison, and Realism." In *The Philosophy of Richard Rorty*, edited by Randall E. Auxier and Lewis Edwin Hahn, 139–54. Library of Living Philosophers. Chicago: Open Court, 2010.
———. *Realism in Religion: A Pragmatist's Perspective*. Albany: State University of New York Press, 2009.
———. *The Truth of Broken Symbols*. Albany: State University of New York Press, 1996.
Niebuhr, H. Richard. *The Meaning of Revelation*. Louisville: Westminster John Knox Press, 1941.
———. *Radical Monotheism and Western Culture*. Louisville: Westminster John Knox Press, 1960.
Nietzsche, Friedrich. *On the Genealogy of Morals*. Translated and edited by Walter Kaufmann. In *Basic Writings of Nietzsche*, 437–599. New York: Modern Library, 2000.
———. *The Will to Power*. Edited by Walter Kaufmann, and translated by Walter Kaufmann and R. J. Hollingdale. New York: Vintage, 1968.
Panikkar, Raimon. *The Intrareligious Dialogue*. Rev. ed. New York: Paulist Press, 1999.
———. "The Jordan, the Tiber, and the Ganges: Three Kairological Moments of Christic Self-consciousness." In Hick and Knitter, *The Myth of Christian Uniqueness*, 89–116.
———. *The Unknown Christ of Hinduism: Towards an Ecumenical Christophany*. Maryknoll, NY: Orbis, 1981.
Patton, Kimberly C., and Benjamin C. Ray, eds. *A Magic Still Dwells: Comparative Religion in the Postmodern Age*. Berkeley: University of California Press, 2000.
Peden, W. Creighton. "The Radical Tradition: Paine and Foster." *American Journal of Theology and Philosophy* 5, no. 1 (January 1984): 25–32.
Peden, W. Creighton, and Larry E. Axel, eds. *New Essays in Religious Naturalism*. Macon, GA: Mercer University Press, 1993.
Peirce, Charles Sanders. "An American Plato: Review of Royce's *Religious Aspect of Philosophy*." In *The Essential Peirce*, 1:229–41.

———. "The Basis of Pragmaticism in the Normative Sciences." In *The Essential Peirce*, 2:371–97.
———. "The Categories Defended." In *The Essential Peirce*, 2:160–78.
———. "The Doctrine of Necessity Examined." In *The Essential Peirce*, 1:298–311.
———. *The Essential Peirce: Selected Philosophical Writings*. Vol. 1, *1867–1893*, edited by Nathan Houser and Christian Kloesel. Bloomington: Indiana University Press, 1992.
———. *The Essential Peirce: Selected Philosophical Writings*. Vol. 2, *1893–1913*, edited by Peirce Edition Project. Bloomington: Indiana University Press, 1998.
———. "Evolutionary Love." In *The Essential Peirce*, 1:352–71.
———. "Excerpts from Letters to Lady Welby." In *The Essential Peirce*, 2:477–91.
———. "The Fixation of Belief." In *The Essential Peirce*, 1:109–23.
———. "How to Make Our Ideas Clear." In *The Essential Peirce*, 1:124–41.
———. "On Phenomenology." In *The Essential Peirce*, 2:145–59.
———. "Pragmatism." In *The Essential Peirce*, 2:398–433.
———. "Questions concerning Certain Faculties Claimed for Man." In *The Essential Peirce*, 1:11–27.
———. "The Seven Systems of Metaphysics." In *The Essential Peirce*, 2:179–95.
———. "A Sketch of Logical Critics." In *The Essential Peirce*, 2:451–62.
———. "Some Consequences of Four Incapacities." In *The Essential Peirce*, 1:28–55.
———. "Sundry Logical Conceptions." In *The Essential Peirce*, 2:267–88.
———. "What Pragmatism Is." In *The Essential Peirce*, 2:331–45.
Phan, Peter C. *Being Religious Interreligiously: Asian Perspectives on Interfaith Dialogue*. Maryknoll, NY: Orbis, 2004.
———. "Response to Premawardhana." *Journal of Ecumenical Studies* 46, no. 1 (Winter 2011): 103–04.
Pinnock, Clark H. *A Wideness in God's Mercy: The Finality of Jesus Christ in a World of Religions*. Grand Rapids, MI: Zondervan, 1992.
Plantinga, Richard J., ed. *Christianity and Plurality: Classic and Contemporary Readings*. Oxford: Blackwell, 1999.
Premawardhana, Devaka. "The Unremarkable Hybrid: Aloysius Pieris and the Redundancy of Multiple Religious Belonging." *Journal of Ecumenical Studies* 46, no. 1 (Winter 2011): 76–101.
Preus, J. Samuel. *Explaining Religion: Criticism and Theory from Bodin to Freud*. Atlanta: Scholars Press, 1996.
Proudfoot, Wayne. *Religious Experience*. Berkeley: University of California Press, 1985.
Putnam, Hilary. *Reason, Truth and History*. New York: Cambridge University Press, 1981.
Pye, Michael. "Ernst Troeltsch and the End of the Problem about 'Other' Religions." In J. P. Clayton, *Ernst Troeltsch and the Future of Theology*, 172–95.
Race, Alan. *Christians and Religious Pluralism: Patterns in the Christian Theology of Religions*. Maryknoll, NY: Orbis, 1982.

Rahner, Karl. "Christianity and the Non-Christian Religions." In Plantinga, *Christianity and Plurality*, 288–303.
Roberts, Michelle Voss. "Gendering Comparative Theology." In Clooney, *The New Comparative Theology*, 109–28.
———. "Religious Belonging and the Multiple." *Journal of Feminist Studies in Religion* 26, no. 1 (2010): 43–62.
Rorty, Richard. *Achieving Our Country: Leftist Thought in Twentieth-Century America*. Cambridge, MA: Harvard University Press, 1998.
———. *Consequences of Pragmatism*. Minneapolis: University of Minnesota Press, 1982.
———. *Contingency, Irony, and Solidarity*. Cambridge: Cambridge University Press, 1989.
———. "Cultural Politics and the Question of the Existence of God." In *Philosophy as Cultural Politics: Philosophical Papers*, 3–26. Cambridge: Cambridge University Press, 2007.
———. "Inquiry as Recontextualization: An Anti-dualist Account of Interpretation." In *Objectivity, Relativism, and Truth*, 93–110.
———. "Introduction: Antirepresentationalism, Ethnocentrism, and Liberalism." In *Objectivity, Relativism, and Truth*, 1–17.
———. *Objectivity, Relativism, and Truth: Philosophical Papers*. Cambridge: Cambridge University Press, 1991.
———. "On Ethnocentrism: A Reply to Clifford Geertz." In *Objectivity, Relativism, and Truth*, 203–10.
———. *Philosophy and Social Hope*. London: Penguin, 1999.
———. *Philosophy and the Mirror of Nature*. Princeton, NJ: Princeton University Press, 1979.
———. "Postmodernist Bourgeois Liberalism." In *Objectivity, Relativism, and Truth*, 197–202.
———. "Science as Solidarity." In *Objectivity, Relatvism, and Truth*, 35–45.
———. "Solidarity or Objectivity?" In *Objectivity, Relativism, and Truth*, 21–34.
Rose, Kenneth. *Pluralism: The Future of Religion*. New York: Bloomsbury, 2013.
———. "Toward an Apophatic Pluralism: Beyond Confessionalism, Epicyclism, and Inclusivism in Theology of Religions." *Journal of Ecumenical Studies* 46, no. 1 (Winter 2011): 67–75.
Rucker, Darnell. *The Chicago Pragmatists*. Minneapolis: University of Minnesota Press, 1969.
Rue, Loyal. *Nature Is Enough: Religious Naturalism and the Meaning of Life*. Albany: State University of New York Press, 2011.
———. *Religion Is Not about God: How Spiritual Traditions Nurture Our Biological Nature and What to Expect When They Fail*. New Brunswick, NJ: Rutgers University Press, 2005.
Ruether, Rosemary Radford. Review of *The Body of God: An Ecological Theology*, by Sallie McFague. *Interpretation* 48 (July 1994): 314–15.

Ryder, John. *The Things in Heaven and Earth: An Essay in Pragmatic Naturalism.* New York: Fordham University Press, 2013.
Sanders, E. P. *Jesus and Judaism.* Minneapolis: Fortress, 1985.
Sanders, John. *No Other Name: An Investigation into the Destiny of the Unevangelized.* Grand Rapids, MI: Eerdmans, 1992.
Schilbrack, Kevin. "Religions: Are There Any?" *Journal of the American Academy of Religion* 78, no. 4 (December 2010): 1112–38.
Schleiermacher, Friedrich. *On Religion: Speeches to Its Cultured Despisers.* Translated by John Oman. Louisville: Westminster John Knox Press, 1994.
Schmidt-Leukel, Perry. "Exclusivism, Inclusivism, Pluralism: The Tripolar Typology—Clarified and Reaffirmed." In Knitter, *The Myth of Religious Superiority*, 13–27.
———. "Pluralisms: How to Appreciate Religious Diversity Theologically." In *Christian Approaches to Other Faiths*, edited by Alan Race and Paul M. Hedges, 85–110. London: SCM, 2008.
———. *Religious Pluralism and Interreligious Theology: The Gifford Lectures.* Extended ed. Maryknoll, NY: Orbis, 2017.
Schweitzer, Albert. *The Quest of the Historical Jesus: A Critical Study of Its Progress from Reimarus to Wrede.* Baltimore: Johns Hopkins University Press, 1998.
Slater, Michael R. *William James on Ethics and Faith.* New York: Cambridge University Press, 2009.
Smith, Christian. *Religion: What It Is, How It Works, and Why It Matters.* Princeton, NJ: Princeton University Press, 2017.
Smith, Gerald Birney. "Christianity and the Spirit of Democracy." *American Journal of Theology* 21, no. 2 (April 1917): 339–57.
———. "The Christ of Faith and the Jesus of History." *American Journal of Theology* 18, no. 4 (October 1914): 521–44.
———. *Current Christian Thinking.* Chicago: University of Chicago Press, 1928.
———. "Is Theism Essential to Religion?" *Journal of Religion* 5, no. 4 (1925): 356–77.
———. *Social Idealism and the Changing Theology: A Study of the Ethical Aspects of Christian Doctrine.* New York: Macmillan, 1913.
———. "Systematic Theology and Ministerial Efficiency." *American Journal of Theology* 16, no. 4 (October 1912): 589–613.
———. "The Task and Method of Systematic Theology." *American Journal of Theology* 14, no. 2 (April 1910): 215–33.
Smith, Jonathan Z. *Imagining Religion: From Babylon to Jonestown.* Chicago: University of Chicago Press, 1982.
———. *Relating Religion: Essays in the Study of Religion.* Chicago: University of Chicago Press, 2004.
Smith, Wilfred Cantwell. *The Meaning and End of Religion.* Minneapolis: Fortress, 1991.
Soneson, Jerome Paul. *Pragmatism and Pluralism: John Dewey's Significance for Theology.* Minneapolis: Fortress, 1993.

———. "Rorty's Final Vocabularies and the Possibility of a Historicist Metaphysics." In Hardwick and Crosby, *Pragmatism, Neo-pragmatism, and Religion*, 293–307.
Spier, Fred. "Big History: The Emergence of a Novel Interdisciplinary Approach." *Interdisciplinary Science Reviews* 33, no. 2 (2008): 1–12.
———. *The Structure of Big History: From the Big Bang until Today*. Amsterdam: Amsterdam University Press, 1996.
Stone, Jerome A. "Is a 'Christian Naturalism' Possible? Exploring the Boundaries of a Tradition." *American Journal of Theology and Philosophy* 32, no. 3 (September 2011): 205–20.
———. *The Minimalist Vision of Transcendence: A Naturalist Philosophy of Religion*. Albany: State University of New York Press, 1992.
———. *Religious Naturalism Today: The Rebirth of a Forgotten Alternative*. Albany: State University of New York Press, 2008.
Stout, Jeffrey. *The Flight from Authority: Religion, Morality, and the Quest for Autonomy*. Notre Dame, IN: University of Notre Dame Press, 1981.
Strauss, David Friedrich. *The Life of Jesus Critically Examined*. Edited by Peter C. Hodgson and translated by George Eliot. Philadelphia: Fortress, 1972.
Surin, Kenneth. "A 'Politics of Speech': Religious Pluralism in the Age of the McDonald's Hamburger." In D'Costa, *Christian Uniqueness Reconsidered*, 192–212.
Sykes, S. W. "Ernst Troeltsch and Christianity's Essence." In J. P. Clayton, *Ernst Troeltsch and the Future of Theology*, 139–71.
Taylor, Charles. *A Secular Age*. Cambridge, MA: Belknap Press of Harvard University Press, 2007.
Taylor, Mark C. *After God*. Chicago: University of Chicago Press, 2007.
———. *Erring: A Postmodern A/theology*. Chicago: University of Chicago Press, 1984.
Thatamanil, John J. *Circling the Elephant: A Comparative Theology of Religious Diversity*. New York: Fordham University Press, 2020.
———. "Comparative Theology after 'Religion.'" In *Planetary Loves: Spivak, Postcoloniality, and Theology*, edited by Stephen D. Moore and Mayra Rivera, 238–57. New York: Fordham University Press, 2010.
———. "Defining the Religious: Comprehensive, Qualitative Orientation." Unpublished manuscript, 2012. Microsoft Word file.
———. "God as Ground, Contingency, and Relation: Trinitarian Polydoxy and Religious Diversity." In *Polydoxy: Theology of Multiplicity and Relation*, edited by Catherine Keller and Laurel C. Schneider, 238–57. London: Routledge, 2011.
———. *The Immanent Divine: God, Creation, and the Human Predicament*. Minneapolis: Fortress, 2006.
Tiemeier, Tracy Sayuki. "Comparative Theology as a Theology of Liberation." In Clooney, *The New Comparative Theology*, 129–49.

Tilley, Terrence W., Louis T. Albarran, Ernest W. Durbin, II, Coleman Fannin, Lora M. Robinson, Daniel E. Martin, and Matthew G. Minix. *Religious Diversity and the American Experience: A Theological Approach*. New York: Continuum, 2007.
Tillich, Paul. *The Courage to Be*. New Haven, CT: Yale Nota Bene, 2000.
———. *Systematic Theology*. Vol. 2. Chicago: University of Chicago Press, 1957.
Troeltsch, Ernst. *The Absoluteness of Christianity and the History of Religions*. Translated by David Reid. Eugene, OR: Wipf and Stock, 2003.
———. *The Christian Faith*. Translated by Garrett E. Paul. Minneapolis: Fortress, 1991.
———. "Christianity and the History of Religion." In *Religion in History*, 77–86.
———. *Der Historismus und seine Probleme*. Berlin: R. Heise, 1924.
———. "The Dogmatics of the History-of-Religions School." In *Religion in History*, 87–108.
———. "The Dogmatics of the *Religionsgeschichtliche Schule*." *American Journal of Theology* 17 (January 1913): 1–21.
———. "Historical and Dogmatic Method in Theology." In *Religion in History*, 11–32.
———. "Modern Philosophy of History." In *Religion in History*, 273–320.
———. "On the Possibility of a Liberal Christianity." In *Religion in History*, 343–59.
———. "On the Question of the Religious A Priori." In *Religion in History*, 33–45.
———. "The Place of Christianity among the World Religions." In Plantinga, *Christianity and Plurality*, 209–22.
———. *Religion in History*. Edited and translated by James Luther Adams and Walter F. Bense. Minneapolis: Fortress, 1991.
———. "The Significance of the Historical Existence of Jesus for Faith." Translated by Robert Morgan. In *Writings on Theology and Religion*, 182–207. Louisville: Westminster John Knox Press, 1977.
———. *The Social Teaching of the Christian Churches*. Translated by Olive Wyon. 2 vols. Louisville and London: Westminster John Knox Press, 1992.
———. "What Does 'Essence of Christianity' Mean?" Translated by Michael Pye. In *Writings on Theology and Religion*, 124–79. Louisville: Westminster John Knox Press, 1977.
———. *Writings on Theology and Religion*. Edited by Robert Morgan and Michael Pye. Louisville: Westminster John Knox Press, 1977.
Vásquez, Manuel A. *More than Belief: A Materialist Theory of Religion*. New York: Oxford University Press, 2011.
Warrior, Robert Allen. "Canaanites, Cowboys, and Indians." *Christianity and Crisis* 41 (September 11, 1989): 261–65.
West, Cornel. *The American Evasion of Philosophy: A Genealogy of Pragmatism*. Madison: University of Wisconsin Press, 1989.
———. *The Cornel West Reader*. New York: Basic Civitas Books, 1999.
———. *Keeping Faith: Philosophy and Race in America*. New York: Routledge, 1993.
———. *Prophetic Fragments: Illuminations of the Crisis in American Religion and Culture*. Grand Rapids, MI: William B. Eerdmans, 1988.

Wheeler, Demian. "American Religious Empiricism and the Possibility of an Ecstatic Naturalist Process Metaphysics." *Journal for the Study of Religion, Nature and Culture* 8, no. 2 (June 2014): 156–81.

———. "Bernard Loomer as a Bridge between Whitehead and Tillich: Towards a Ground-of-Being Process Theology," *Bulletin of the North American Paul Tillich Society* 44, No. 1 (January 2018): 22–29.

———. "Big History and the Size of God: Holistic Historicism as a Pathway to Religious Naturalism." *American Journal of Theology and Philosophy* 34, no. 3 (September 2013): 226–47.

———. "*Deus sive Natura*: Pantheism as a Variety of Religious Naturalism." In Crosby and Stone, *The Routledge Handbook of Religious Naturalism*, 106–17. London: Routledge, 2018.

———. Review of *Pluralism: The Future of Religion*, by Kenneth Rose. *American Journal of Theology and Philosophy* 38, nos. 2–3 (May–September 2017): 238–44.

———. "Seizing a Whiteheadian Alternative: A Retrieval of the Empirical Option in Process Thought." In *Conceiving an Alternative: Philosophical Resources for an Ecological Civilization*, edited by Demian Wheeler and David E. Conner, 115–47. Anoka, MN: Process Century Press, 2019.

Whitehead, Alfred North. *Modes of Thought*. New York: Free Press, 1938.

———. *Process and Reality: An Essay in Cosmology*. Edited by David Ray Griffin and Donald W. Sherburne. Corr. ed. New York: Free Press, 1978.

Wieman, Henry Nelson. *Religious Experience and Scientific Method*. Carbondale: Southern Illinois University Press, 1971.

———. *The Source of Human Good*. Atlanta: Scholars Press, 1995.

Wieman, Henry Nelson, and Bernard E. Meland. *American Philosophies of Religion*. Chicago: Willett, Clark, 1936.

Wildman, Wesley J. "The Ambiguous Heritage and Perpetual Promise of Liberal Theology." *American Journal of Theology and Philosophy* 32, no. 1 (January 2011): 43–61.

———. "Behind, between, and beyond Anthropomorphic Models of Ultimate Reality." *Philosophia* 35, no. 3–4 (2007): 407–25.

———. "Corrington's Ecstatic Naturalism in Light of the Scientific Study of Religion." *American Journal of Theology and Philosophy* 34, no. 1 (January 2013): 3–16.

———. *Fidelity with Plausibility: Modest Christologies in the Twentieth Century*. Albany: State University of New York Press, 1998.

———. "Ground-of-Being Theologies." In P. Clayton, *The Oxford Handbook of Religion and Science*, 612–32.

———. "Nature, God, Jesus, and Creativity." *American Journal of Theology and Philosophy* 29, no. 1 (January 2008): 44–60.

———. *Religious and Spiritual Experiences*. New York: Cambridge University Press, 2011.

———. "Religious Naturalism: What It Can Be, and What It Need Not Be." *Philosophy, Theology and the Sciences* 1, no. 1 (2014): 36–58.

---. *Religious Philosophy as Multidisciplinary Comparative Inquiry: Envisioning a Future for the Philosophy of Religion.* Albany: State University of New York Press, 2010.
---. *Science and Religious Anthropology: A Spiritually Evocative Naturalist Interpretation of Human Life.* Farnham, UK: Ashgate, 2009.
---. "Theology without Walls: The Future of Transreligious Theology." *Open Theology* 2, no. 1 (January 2016): 242–247.
Williams, Delores. *Sisters in the Wilderness: The Challenge of Womanist God-Talk.* Maryknoll, NY: Orbis, 1993.
Wink, Walter. "Response to Luke Timothy Johnson's *The Real Jesus*." *Bulletin for Biblical Research* 7 (1997): 233–47.
Wittgenstein, Ludwig. *Philosophical Investigations.* Translated by G. E. M. Anscombe. 3rd ed. Englewood Cliffs, NJ: Prentice Hall, 1953.
Yong, Amos. *Beyond the Impasse: Toward a Pneumatological Theology of Religions.* Grand Rapids, MI: Baker Academic, 2003.
York, Richard, and Brett Clark. *The Science and Humanism of Stephen Jay Gould.* New York: Monthly Review Press, 2011.

Index

agape, 63, 240, 345
Ames, Edward Scribner, 269, 291, 292, 323
"anatheism," 298
Anderson, Douglas, 218–19, 221–22
Angell, James Rowland, 269
"anonymous Christians," 74, 82, 86, 97–98
Anselm of Canterbury, 38, 254, 325, 329
anthropocentric naturalism, 317–21
antiauthoritarianism, 141, 145, 171–81, 253–54; Jesus and, 181–87
antiessentialism, 114, 141, 145, 156–71; of Brown, 159–62, 168–69; of Chicago schoolers, 163–66; of Davaney, 167–69, 169–70; naturalism and, 138; Rorty on, 157, 404n57; of Troeltsch, 166–67
antihistoricism, 29, 305
antinaturalism, 33, 306, 314; Dean on, 33–35, 299; Iggers on, 48
antirealism, 45, 197, 216–17
antirepresentationalism, 196–97, 200, 217, 416n36
antisupernaturalism, 145, 153–56, 170–81, 324; of Case, 153; of Foster, 292, 315–16; of Wildman, 314
apologetics, 38, 63–64, 66, 120, 258–59; Frankenberry on, 450n178;

Neville on, 434n29; Smith on, 258–59
apophasis, 62, 268, 326–27, 350; Dean on, 295–99; Kaufman on, 265–66, 268, 301, 327, 437n69; McFague on, 266; Wildman on, 139, 268, 337–38, 341, 347, 348
apophatic pluralism, 84–85, 111–13
apophatic pluralistic naturalism, 278, 317, 324–44, 353
apophatic realism, 268, 303–4
Appiah, Kwame Anthony, 365n55
Aquinas, Thomas, 255, 328, 329, 432n15
Arendt, Hannah, 178, 411n147
Ariarajah, S. Wesley, 111, 378n54
Aristotle, 211, 347, 405n67, 423n157
Arnold, Charles Harvey, 444n75
atheism, 69, 277–95, 351, 444n79; humanistic, 277, 292, 298–99; ironic, 277, 295–99, 333–34; militant, 315; neopragmatic, 256; "new," 298, 461n337
a/theology, 33, 411n153
authority, 171–81; of Jesus, 181–87; supernaturalistic, 148, 452n209. *See also* antiauthoritarianism
Axel, Larry, 9, 444n75
Ayer, A. J., 247, 248, 431n316

Barth, Karl, 38, 254, 333; fideism of, 76–77; Herder and, 359n6; Lindbeck and, 37; McFague and, 454n235; neo-orthodoxy of, 311; Neville on, 76–77, 432n15, 433n20

Beiser, Frederick, 48; on Enlightenment, 17–18; on historicism, 60, 359n1, 362n36; on historicization, 13, 14

Berger, Peter, 105, 227–28, 294

Bernstein, Richard, 212, 214, 217; on Peirce, 425n200; on postmodernism, 238

Best, Steven, 193–94

"bibliolatry," 266

Big Bang theory, 58–59, 329

"big history," 58–59, 341, 371n158, 374n213, 456n277

Borg, Marcus J., 412n181

Bousset, Wilhelm, 63, 147

Bowne, Borden Parker, 253, 293

Briggs, Charles, 253, 260

Brown, Delwin, 3, 46, 129, 140, 156–57; on apophatic tradition, 327, 341–42, 344; on authority, 179–80; on christology, 407n90; on constructivism, 213–14, 300; Davaney and, 42–43, 132, 178, 260–61, 275, 406n76; on Enlightenment, 145–46; on Gadamer, 161; on historicism, 13, 23, 104, 159–60, 242; Kaufman and, 158, 399n121; liberal theology of, 260–61; Lindbeck and, 168; materialist historicism of, 129; radical empiricism of, 35–36, 450n172; on religious experience, 265, 310–11; on traditions, 46–47, 159–62, 180, 406n83; Whitehead and, 9–10, 129, 328, 373n201; Wieman and, 306, 309, 450n180

Buchler, Justus, 223

Buddhism, 80; Christianity and, 107, 392n11; *Dhammapada* of, 72; Dharma in, 72–73, 95; Dharmakaya in, 88, 89, 387n202; Hick on, 74; Hinduism and, 46, 114; Mādhyamaka, 348; Neville on, 432n15; Nirvana in, 89, 90, 93, 95, 99; Sunyata in, 88, 89, 111, 112, 330; Troeltsch on, 65; Zen, 79, 83, 90

Bunge, Marcia, 20, 366n77, 366n83

Bushnell, Horace, 253, 260, 286

Cady, Linell, 39, 177

Cahoone, Lawrence, 226, 421n128

Calvin, John, 332

Caputo, John, 195, 237–38, 298, 424n189

Carlson, Jeffrey, 131

Carr, Harvey, 269

Case, Shirley Jackson, 109, 170–71, 176, 374n205; apophatic naturalism and, 327; on authority of the past, 175–76; on change, 9; on comparative history of religion school, 151; constructive realism and, 299; on cosmic naturalism, 322–24; on historical Jesus, 153–55, 164–65, 182–83; on religious humanism, 284; on supernaturalism, 153–54, 155, 322–23; on theological pragmatism, 271

Case, Shirley Jackson, works of: *Christianity in a Changing World*, 164; *The Christian Philosophy of History*, 282–83; *The Evolution of Early Christianity*, 151–52, 165; *Jesus through the Centuries*, 164

cataphasis, 84, 111, 278, 344, 348–51, 390n236

Chaisson, Eric, 456n277

Chicago school of theology, 150, 183–84, 260, 269–71; antiauthoritarianism of, 172, 175, 176; Dean on, 281, 286, 305; Dorrien on, 270, 281–82, 305; early, 1–3, 9, 145, 277–78, 309, 386n194; later, 5, 34, 277–78, 301; modernism and, 238; multigenerational, 277–78, 306, 307, 447n139; naturalistic empiricism of, 253, 281, 325; pragmatism of, 273, 281; sociohistorical method of, 14, 163, 261, 434n35; Troeltsch and, 281–82
Chidester, David, 45
Christian, David, 58–60, 372n174, 373n189, 375n216; on emergent functions, 456n277
Christological maximalism, 114, 181, 411n160
christologies, 85, 154, 186–87; Brown on, 407n90; Case on, 164, 183; Hick on, 391n254; "inspiration," 391n254; Kaufman on, 462n362; Knitter on, 114–15
Clebsch, William, 407n90
Clifford, James, 160
Clooney, Francis, 123–28
Cobb, John, 103, 370n146, 448n157
"cognitive propositionalism," 37
comparative history of religion, 61–72, 116, 145; Case on, 151; Dorrien on, 147–48, 281–82, 401n12; Foster on, 150; method of, 61, 64–66; naturalistic empiricism and, 150; scholars of, 147; Troeltsch and, 61–72, 116, 145, 147–50. *See also* theology of religions
comparative theology, 123–30. *See also* theology of religions
Comstock, Gary, 457n296
Confucianism, 82, 84, 88, 432n15

constructive historicism, 260, 299–305
constructive realism, 213–29, 262–69, 299
constructivism, 286; of Dean, 263, 288; of Dewey, 199–200, 220–21; historicism and, 198–201, 213–29; of Kant, 215; of Kaufman, 263–68, 272, 287–88; radical, 222; of Rorty, 199–200, 216–19
conventionalism, 108, 228–29, 263, 277, 288–90, 443n60
Cornille, Catherine, 122, 130, 393n24, 396n70
correspondence theory of truth, 229–36
Corrington, Robert, 55; on ambiguity, 326; on Dean, 34, 55; on metaphysics, 243–44; on naturalism, 313–14, 326–27, 446n108; on neopragmatism, 34; on West, 245
cosmology, 8–12, 156; Frankenberry on, 278–79; McFague on, 158; panpsychist, 55; Wildman on, 431n318
cosmopolitanism, 18, 21, 26–27, 32
Crosby, Donald A., 51, 138, 141, 222–23, 357; constructive realism of, 222–23; Davaney and, 354; on empiricism, 460n329; religious naturalism of, 278, 316, 339–43, 346, 354–55, 462n341; on nature, 8; on perspectivism, 190–91
Crosby, Donald A., works of: *Living with Ambiguity*, 452n209, 453n218; *A Religion of Nature*, 405n67
Crossan, John Dominic, 413n186
Cyprian of Carthage, 73

Daoism, 84, 88, 89, 113, 138, 337, 432n15
Darwin, Charles, 52–53, 208–9, 336; Dean on, 11, 54; Dewey on, 52, 372n181; Gould on, 57–58; James

Darwin, Charles *(continued)* on, 52–53; Rorty on, 209; Wildman on, 336–37

Davaney, Sheila Greeve, 2–5, 242; on agency, 157; on antiessentialism, 167–69; on authority of the past, 177–78; Barth and, 76; Brown and, 42–43, 132, 178, 260–61, 275, 406n76; criteriological pragmatism and, 143; Crosby and, 354; on Descartes, 16; Dorrien on, 301; on Enlightenment, 17–19; on ethnocentrism, 30–31; on fallibilism, 206–7; Geertz and, 33; on German nationalism, 27; on Herder's particularism, 21, 25, 26; on historicized naturalism, 55; holistic historicism and, 50–51, 283–84; on interreligious engagement, 119–23; on Kant, 215; on Kaufman, 82, 408n109; on Lindbeck, 167–68; materialist historicism of, 50, 129; on McFague, 321, 408n109, 436n67; metaphysics and, 245, 246; on modernism, 237; on multitraditionedness, 42–43, 131–32; on nature-human dichotomies, 33; Neville and, 259; perspectivism of, 197–98, 264; on popular religion, 129; on postliberalism, 300–301; on pragmatic historicism, 2, 4–5, 260, 270, 274–75, 301, 327–28, 408n109, 426n210; on radical empiricism, 140, 306; on religious heritages, 177–78, 180; on religious pluralism, 62, 82, 103; on Smith, 252–53; on syncretism, 43; theological realism and, 300–1; on traditions, 47, 146, 169; on Troeltsch, 70; on West, 371n172, 417n46

Davaney, Sheila Greeve, works of: *Historicism*, 3–4; *Pragmatic Historicism*, 3–4

Dawkins, Richard, 298, 461n337

D'Costa, Gavin, 79, 86, 98, 110, 382n114

Deacon, Terrence, 373n203

Dean, William, 108, 109, 140–43; on ambiguity of God, 331–33; apophatic naturalism and, 327, 333–34; on Bernstein, 212; on Chicago school, 281, 286, 305; on communalism, 40; on conventionalism, 108, 228–29, 263, 277, 288–90, 443n60; on Derrida, 10–11, 33, 35; on Dewey, 53–54, 56, 288–89, 299–300; Dorrien on, 305; on Emerson, 296–97; on generalizations, 24; Herder and, 365n51; on historical process theology, 361n13; historicism of, 14, 40–41, 156, 283–84, 293–95; on ironic atheism, 277, 295–99; on ironic theism, 344; on James, 289, 297; on Kant, 214–16; Kaufman and, 302, 304, 331–32, 334; on liberal theology, 294–95, 333; on Locke, 214–16; on metaphysical speculation, 243, 268; on "methodologism," 33, 301; on mystery, 295–97, 299; on naive realism, 197; naturalism of, 36, 268, 278, 279, 334; naturalistic-humanistic historicism of, 11, 48–49, 281; nonfoundationalism of, 202; on O'Connor, 296; on pantheism, 350; pluralistic naturalism of, 329; pragmatism of, 34, 39–40, 212, 271–72; on radical empiricism, 34–35, 140, 303, 306, 309; on Rorty, 429n284; on

Stevens, 333; on Taylor, 367n99; on theodicy, 332; theological constructivism of, 263, 288; on uncertainty principle, 54–55; on U.S. Constitution, 228; Whitehead and, 9–10, 55, 361n13, 449n157
Dean, William, works of: *The American Spiritual Culture*, 293–97; *History Making History*, 305–6; *The Religious Critic in American Culture*, 349
Dennett, Daniel, 298, 461n337
Derrida, Jacques, 33, 238–39, 242, 294; Brown on, 162; Caputo on, 195, 237–38, 298, 424n189; Dean on, 10–11, 33, 35; Hegel and, 361n20; McFague on, 267; Peirce and, 195, 415n29; perspectivism of, 194–95; Rorty on, 361n20, 195–96
Descartes, René, 16–17, 201–5, 225; on intuition, 17, 192, 196, 202, 226; Peirce on, 192, 205, 226
desupernaturalization, 61, 145–56, 173, 277
Dewey, John, 51–56, 108, 140–41; Bernstein on, 212; constructivism of, 199–200, 220–21, 299–300; constructive realism of, 220–21; conventionalism and, 288–89; correspondence theory of truth and, 234–35; on Darwinism, 52, 372n181; Dean on, 53–54, 56, 288–89, 299–300; Dorrien on, 270; on empirical naturalism, 36, 240, 278–80; on experimental empiricism, 157–58; fallibilism of, 206, 238; Hegel and, 372n181; instrumentalism of, 208, 210–11; James on, 269; metaphysics of, 240, 244, 246; naturalism of, 52, 279–80, 314, 315, 452n198; nonfoundationalism of, 203, 238; Peirce and, 227; Plato and, 203, 241; pragmatism of, 189, 213; on "the religious," 387n200; Rorty on, 221, 241, 415n32; on "succession of histories," 11; West on, 246
Dewey, John, works of: *Art as Experience*, 307; *A Common Faith*, 271, 288, 299, 307, 349, 387n200, 452n198; *Experience and Nature*, 240, 241; *The Quest for Certainty*, 220
Dharma, 72–73, 95
Dharmakaya, 88, 89, 387n202
Dieterich, Albrecht, 147
Dilthey, Wilhelm, 48
DiNoia, J. A., 86, 90–92, 95, 98, 99, 120
Dorrien, Gary, 253, 277, 290; on Case, 151, 152; on Chicago school, 270, 281–82; on Davaney, 301; on Dean, 305; on Foster, 172, 273, 291, 293, 444n75; on Kant, 214; on Kaufman, 447n122; on Mathews, 184–85; on Meland, 455n256; on Troeltsch, 63, 69–71, 147, 148
Droysen, Johann Gustav, 146
Duffy, Stephen, 126
Duns Scotus, John, 225–26, 328
Dupuis, Jacques, 381n91, 394n54
Durkheim, Emile, 289, 294

ecology. *See* environmentalism
Eck, Diana L., 74, 81
Eckhart, Meister, 113, 330
Ehrman, Bart, 412n181
Emerson, Ralph Waldo, 30, 286, 296–97, 326
empiricism: experimental, 157–58; liberal, 286; Lockean, 215; naturalistic, 36, 133–36, 240, 253,

empiricism *(continued)*
278–81; theological, 265, 281, 291, 306, 308, 309–10, 312, 333, 334, 335–36, 342, 361n13, 447n139. *See also* radical empiricism

Enlightenment, 110; Beiser on, 17–18; Brown on, 145–46; cosmopolitanism of, 18; Kant on, 17; liberal theology and, 260; Lyotard on, 237; modernity and, 237; particularist theology and, 92; scientism of, 49; Stout on, 15–16; universalism of, 23, 202

environmentalism, 89, 133–37, 139, 144, 247, 272, 275, 319–21, 463n362

epistemological perspectivism, 191

eros, 63

ethnocentrism: Geertz on, 31–33; Rorty on, 29–32

exclusivism, 72, 102; "anonymous," 110; covert, 110–16; inclusivism and, 81–86, 110–17; Kaufman on, 76, 80; universalism and, 113–14

"experiential expressivism," 37

fallibilism, 189, 204–7, 236, 243; definitions of, 204–5; nonfoundationalist, 248; of Peirce, 205–6, 238, 239; religious, 251–53; West on, 246; Wieman on, 450n181; Wildman on, 248

feminist theology, 2, 72, 321, 332–33, 434n40

Feuerbach, Ludwig, 284, 289–90, 294, 304

fideism, 76–79, 118, 433n20; of Barth, 76–77; of Heim, 100; of Lindbeck, 38–40; of McFague, 320

Fiorenza, Francis, 134

Flanagan, Owen, 315, 452n209

Fletcher, Jeannine Hill, 131

Ford, Lewis, 448n157

Forster, Michael N., 21, 26, 29

Foster, George Burman, 166; anthropocentric naturalism and, 317–19, 321; antisupernaturalism of, 292; on apophatic naturalism, 327; on authoritarianism, 172–73; Dorrien on, 172, 273, 291, 293, 444n75; historicist theology of, 290–95; humanistic historicism of, 282; Macintosh on, 291, 444n79; on miracles, 151; naturalism of, 150, 315, 436n65; Nietzsche and, 290, 292–93; probative pragmatism of, 273; religious humanism of, 284–85, 290–93, 295; Stone on, 318; theological constructivism of, 262–63, 266; theological pragmatism of, 270–71, 439n105

Foster, George Burman, works of: *The Finality of the Christian Religion*, 150–51, 166, 317; *The Function of Religion in Man's Struggle for Existence*, 289–91, 317–18

Foucault, Michel, 50, 238, 248; Dean on, 35; *Discipline and Punish*, 194; Rorty on, 195–96, 415n32

foundationalism, 201–2, 219, 239–40; historicism and, 442n36. *See also* nonfoundationalism

Frankenberry, Nancy, 223, 424n189; constructive realism of, 227; Crosby and, 453n218; on empirical theology, 309–10, 312, 342; on naturalistic empiricism, 278–79, 325–26; on pantheism, 349–50; radical empiricism of, 223, 309–10; on religious experience, 310, 450n178; Rorty and, 223; on Wieman, 312, 336, 450n181

Fredericks, James, 123–25, 127, 394n54

Frei, Hans, 39, 254
Freud, Sigmund, 294
functionalism, 232, 269, 292, 439n105
Funk, Robert W., 413n183

Gadamer, Hans Georg, 160–61, 196, 416n33
Galileo, 211
Geertz, Clifford, 12, 105, 159–60; on ethnocentrism, 31–33; Lindbeck and, 37
Gilkey, Langdon, 82, 134
Gladden, Washington, 253
Goodenough, Ursula, 23, 137, 138; on emergence, 456n277; on religious naturalism, 138, 314, 324–25, 355
Gould, Stephen Jay, 57–58
Gragg, Alan, 444n75
Gregory of Nyssa, 112, 329
Griffin, David Ray, 103, 448n157
Griffiths, Paul, 96, 99; on apologetics, 120–23; on inclusivism, 86, 132; on noncompossibility, 118–20; on universalism, 113–14, 120
"group subjectivism," 40
Gunkel, Hermann, 63, 147
Gutiérrez, Gustavo, 333, 434n33

Hall, David, 32
Hamann, Johann Georg, 19
"hamartiocentrism," 134–36
Hardwick, Charley D., 313, 452n201
Harnack, Adolf von, 147, 165, 408n94
Harris, Sam, 461n337
Hart, William, 356
Hartshorne, Charles, 328–29, 448n139
Harvey, Van A., 146–47, 149
Hauerwas, Stanley, 254
Haydon, Albert Eustace, 292–93
Hegel, Georg Wilhelm Friedrich, 63–64, 214, 247; Darwin and, 52; Derrida and, 361n20; Dewey and, 372n181; Troeltsch and, 63–64, 66–67, 376n12
Heidegger, Martin, 35, 196, 416n33
Heim, S. Mark, 103, 120; Hick and, 91, 107–8, 115–16; on inclusivism, 86, 96–100, 102, 103, 110; on justice, 91–92; on liberation theology, 92; on particularism, 93–94, 98–103, 106–8, 115; on pluralistic salvations, 93–96, 116, 118; Rose on, 95; Thatamanil on, 385n167, 388n211; trinitarianism of, 98–99, 107; Troeltsch and, 99–100
Hellenism, 131, 151–54, 409n126. See also Roman Empire
Heraclitus, 13
Herbert of Cherbury, 112
Herder, Johann Gottfried von, 20–29; Barth on, 359n6; Bunge on, 20, 366n77, 366n83; Dean and, 365n51; on human nature, 20–21; nationalism of, 21, 26–27; particularism of, 21, 25; relativism of, 28–29; on religion, 22–23; Schleiermacher and, 436n58; Süssmilch and, 363n21
Herder, Johann Gottfried von, works of: *First Dialogue concerning National Religions*, 22–23, 26, 29; *Ideas toward a Philosophy of History*, 19–20, 28, 30, 404n52; *On the Change of Taste*, 21, 28; *Yet Another Philosophy of History*, 19–22, 241
Hermann, Wilhelm, 147
Hick, John, 71, 103; on critical realism, 108; D'Costa on, 110; DiNoia on, 90–91; on epicycles, 85–86, 382n110; Heim and, 91, 107–8, 110–11, 115–16; inclusivism and, 382n110; Kantianism of,

Hick, John *(continued)*
  88–89, 110; Kaufman on, 384n149; pluralism of, 73–77, 84, 110–11, 115, 391n254; pluralistic hypothesis of, 87–92, 96–97, 110, 117; on "the Real," 87–89, 92, 106–9; on religious superiority, 385n174; on salvation, 80, 91; Troeltsch and, 391n254; on ultimacy, 88–89, 106–9, 386n176
Hick, John, works of: *An Interpretation of Religion*, 87; *The Myth of Christian Uniqueness*, 86, 388n210
Hinduism, 80–82, 88; Brahman in, 79, 88, 89, 98, 113, 330; Buddhism and, 46, 114; Christianity and, 107; Clooney on, 127–28; Hick on, 74; Long on, 370n143; Neville on, 432n15; Rig Veda of, 180; Srivaisnava, 127; Thatamanil on, 107, 127; Troeltsch on, 65; Upanishads of, 112
historical process, 10, 190; Dean on, 361n13; flux of, 81, 148, 156–71; Kaufman on, 398n105; relativism and, 67
historicism, 145–56; as anthropology, 12–13; Beiser on, 60, 359n1, 362n36; bigger, 15, 41–60; Brown on, 13, 23, 104, 159–62; constructive, 159–62, 260; Dean on, 14, 40–41, 156, 283; definitions of, 7, 146; dynamic, 41–48; fallibilism of, 204–7; foundationalism and, 17–18, 201–4, 442n36; humanistic, 39–40, 145–56, 282, 292; without insularity, 41–48; isolationism and, 25–36; Masuzawa on, 71–72; metaphysics and, 236–49; as methodology, 13–14; naturalism and, 11–12, 34, 48–49, 55, 281–82, 284; "new," 202; as ontology, 7–12, 156, 190; origins of, 1–5, 9, 17; postliberal, 37–41; relativism and, 21, 28–29, 62, 64, 70, 212; of Troeltsch, 62–72; universal, 25, 60. *See also* holistic historicism; pragmatic historicism
historicist theology, 2, 4, 290–95; hermeneutics of nature and, 49; liberal theology and, 2–3, 41, 150, 168, 172, 178, 181, 183–87, 253–62, 433n23; postliberalism and, 36, 41, 118
history of religions. *See* comparative history of religion
Hitchens, Christopher, 298, 461n337
Hogue, Michael, 137–38, 313, 315, 316
holistic historicism, 12, 36, 47–60, 90, 341, 442n36; Davaney and, 50–51, 283–84; definitions of, 41, 48–49; perspectivism and, 191. *See also* naturalistic-humanistic historicism
humanism, 25, 88, 344–51; atheistic, 277, 292, 298–99; of Dewey, 299–300, 311, 312; ethical, 254; of Foster, 282, 284–85, 290–93, 295; of James, 198, 219–20, 222, 227, 231; of Kaufman, 272; Marxism and, 105; of Mathews, 259; nonnaturalistic, 34, 48, 314; of Rorty, 217; of Smith, 323; theological, 278, 291, 295, 345–46. *See also* humanistic historicism; naturalistic-humanistic historicism
humanistic historicism, 36–40, 145–56, 213, 282–85, 290–93, 306, 341
Humanitätsideal, 28
human nature, 25, 170, 242; Beiser on, 48; Davaney on, 168; Foster on, 290; Herder on, 19–21; Kaufman on, 24, 50–51, 82, 256; nonhuman nature and, 49, 50–51, 53–60, 331; Rorty on, 243–44

Humboldt, Wilhelm von, 146
Hume, David, 21, 151
Hynes, William, 151

identism, 103, 106–7
identity theology, 254–57, 432n15
Iggers, Georg, 366n77; on antihistoricism, 29; on historicism, 23, 48; on nationalism, 26, 27; on Troeltsch, 64, 65, 69
inclusivism, 73–74; Catholic theology and, 73–74, 381n91, 394n54; DiNoia on, 86, 120; exclusivism and, 81–86, 110–17; Griffiths on, 86, 132; Heim on, 86, 96–100, 102, 103, 110; Hick on, 382n110; Kaufman on, 81, 82; Knitter on, 128, 379n59; pentecostal, 379n59; Rahner and, 74, 86, 97; Rose on, 85–86, 99, 393n24
incommensurability, 25–26, 31–32, 41–42, 117–18, 125–27; Davaney on, 33, 275; Dean on, 243; Griffiths on, 133; Knitter on, 90, 120; Kuhn on, 193; Lindbeck on, 38–39, 118–19; Thatamanil on, 46–47
Inden, Ronald, 370n143
instrumentalism, 5, 189, 207–12, 269, 439n105
insularity, 15, 25–29, 36, 59, 118, 133; historicism without, 41–48
integrative mediation, 253–54, 316
interactionism, 141, 221, 223, 400n142
interreligious engagement, 47, 83, 89–90, 117–44; Hogue on, 137–38; Kaufman on, 144, 256; Knitter on, 133, 134, 380n70; particularism and, 143; Phan on, 391n1; Schmidt-Leukel on, 394n50
Irvine, Andrew, 459n319
Islam, 72–73, 80, 180, 408n108; Christianity and, 392n11; exclusivism of, 72, 114; Hick on, 74; liberal theology and, 432n9; Neville on, 432n15; Sufi, 113; Troeltsch on, 65; Wildman on, 432n9
isolationism, 41, 273, 353, 366n83; historicism and, 25–36; relativistic, 62. *See also* insularity

Jainism, 44, 72, 73, 82
James, William, 52–53, 56, 108, 190; apophatic naturalism and, 326–27; Chicago school and, 269, 270; constructive realism of, 219–20; constructivism of, 198–99; correspondence theory of truth and, 231–34; Dean on, 289, 297; on Dewey, 269; epistemological perspectivism of, 191; fallibilism of, 206, 238; functionalism of, 232; on God's existence, 289; humanism of, 198, 219–20, 222, 227, 231; instrumentalism of, 208–11; on life's worthwhileness, 417n52; naive realism and, 220; naturalism of, 280; Nietzsche and, 416n33; nonfoundationalism of, 202, 238; Peirce and, 226–27, 230–31; pragmatism of, 51, 189, 209–10, 213, 240; radical empiricism of, 140–42, 240–41, 299, 307, 460n329; Rorty and, 427n229; Slater on, 219–20, 231–34; Whitehead and, 9, 429n282; Wildman and, 231, 419n93
James, William, works of: "A Pluralistic Mystic," 297; *A Pluralistic Universe*, 8, 9, 24, 297; *Pragmatism*, 209–10, 232, 280–81; *The Principles of Psychology*, 208; "Remarks on Spencer's Definition of Mind as Correspondence," 199; *The Varieties*

James, William, works of *(continued)*
of Religious Experience, 232, 234–36, 271; *The Will to Believe*, 202, 417n52
Jastrow, Joseph, 192–93
Jesus, 82, 112, 153, 166, 266, 287, 296, 332; authority of, 168, 173, 174, 176, 179, 181–87; Case on 154–55, 164, 182–83; christology and, 85, 154, 164, 391n254, 403n43, 407n90, 411n160; "Jesusolatry" and, 266; historical, 154–55, 182, 183–87, 401n12, 401n15, 412n174, 412n182, 413n183; Kaufman on, 345–46, 462n362; Knitter on, 114–15; Mathews on, 184–85; McFague on, 266, 319–21; Schweitzer on, 183; uniqueness of, 73–74, 79–80, 87, 95–98, 114–15, 128, 381n91
Johnson, Luke Timothy, 186, 187
Judaism, 72, 80, 88, 178–79; Christianity and, 61, 71, 83, 151, 392n11; Kabbalist, 113; liberal theology and, 432n9; naturalistic, 398n117; Noahic Covenant of, 85; Smith on, 169; Torah of, 406n83; Troeltsch on, 65; Wildman on, 432n9
justice, 30, 88, 142, 143, 345, 350; Hart on, 356; Heim on, 91–92, 110; Kaufman on, 462n362; McFague on, 272, 320, 321; Milbank on, 133, 134; Min on, 134; Stone on, 325. *See also* "hamartiocentrism"; liberation theology; Marxism

Kaftan, Julius, 148
Kant, Immanuel, 112, 240–41, 247, 248; Davaney on, 215; Dean on, 214–16; Dorrien on, 214; dualism and, 33; Hick and, 88–89, 110; Kaufman and, 302, 422n138; historicism and, 19, 215, 216; liberal theology and, 253; metaphysics and, 241, 247, 248; Nietzsche and, 191; on phenomenal/noumenal worlds, 88–89; Ritschl and, 147; subjective idealism and, 214–15; Wildman on, 431n318
Kant, Immanuel, works of: *Critique of Pure Reason*, 240, 290, 422n134, 431n316; "What Is Enlightenment?," 17
Kaplan, Mordecai, 178, 398n117
Kaplan, Stephen, 93
Katz, Steven T., 384n144
Kaufman, Gordon, 3, 43, 50, 137, 355, 373n203; on antiauthoritarianism, 176–77; Barth and, 76; Berger and, 105; Brown and, 158, 399n121; constructivism of, 287–88, 304–5; on creativity, 109, 158; on critical theology, 434n40; Davaney on, 82, 408n109; Dean and, 302, 304, 331–32; on emergent truth, 123; on empirical theology, 306; Geertz and, 105; on God as creativity, 304, 329–31, 344–45; hamartiocentrism and, 134–36; on Hick, 384n149; on historicity, 143–44, 242, 400n156; humanism of, 345–46; on human nature, 24, 56, 256; on inclusivism, 81; on interreligious engagement, 119–23; Kant and, 301, 422n138; McFague and, 454n233, 463n362; metaphysics and, 245, 246; on mystery, 105–6, 265–66, 268, 304, 329–30; naturalism of, 50–51, 104–6, 278, 329–31; on naturalistic universality, 398n105; as particularist mutualist, 101–2, 104–5; on

pluralism, 62, 75–76, 80, 82, 86, 94, 102–3; pluralistic naturalism of, 278, 329, 330–31; pragmatic historicism of, 104–6, 108, 287–88, 303–5, 386n194, 439n97; theory of religion of, 104–6; on religious tradition, 181; Rorty and, 301; on theodicy, 331, 459n318; theological constructivism of, 263–68, 272, 287–88; on theological naturalism, 330; theological realism and, 301–2, 303–5; Wieman and, 330, 331; Wildman and, 330–31, 457n285; Wittgenstein and, 264

Kaufman, Gordon, works of: *In Face of Mystery*, 301, 327, 459n318, 463n362; *Jesus and Creativity*, 463n362

Kearney, Richard, 298

Kellner, Douglas, 193–94

Kiblinger, Kristin Beise, 125–26, 378n52

Knitter, Paul, 103, 114–15, 137; D'Costa on, 110; on inclusivism, 128, 379n59; liberation theology of, 89–92, 111, 134; mutualism of, 91, 104, 383n132; on particularism, 100, 122, 384n140; on pluralism, 75, 92, 100–1, 110–11, 390n236; on religious unity, 89, 111; on Troeltsch, 68–69

Knitter, Paul, works of: *Introducing Theologies of Religions*, 101; *The Myth of Christian Uniqueness*, 86, 388n210; *One Earth, Many Religions*, 133

Kuhn, Thomas, 40, 193, 415nn32–33, 423n159

Laksana, A. Bagus, 123

Lee, Bernard, 448n157

Leibniz, Gottfried Wilhelm, 69

Lessing, Gotthold Ephraim, 112

Levinson, Henry Samuel, 343

Lévi-Strauss, Claude, 31

liberal theology, 253–62, 286, 333, 433n23; historicist theology and, 2–3, 41, 150, 168, 172, 178, 181, 183–87, 253–62, 433n23; in Islam, 432n9; in Judaism, 432n9; postliberalism versus, 37–41, 181, 256–57, 274–75, 300–1; religious naturalism and, 316, 327

liberation theology, 332–33, 434n33; Heim on, 91–92; historicism and, 2, 275, 434n33; of Knitter, 89–92, 111, 134. *See also* "hamartiocentrism"; justice; Marxism

Light, Aimee Upjohn, 86, 110

Lindbeck, George, 33, 37–41, 92–93, 99, 167; on authority, 181; Brown on, 168; Cady on, 39; Davaney and, 42, 121, 167–68, 300–1; identity theology of, 254; mysticism and, 384n144; Neville on, 254, 256, 433n20; *The Nature of Doctrine*, 37–40, 119, 390n247, 392n11; postliberalism of, 113, 167–69, 256–57; on Rahner, 97–98; on religious particularity, 37–38, 92–93, 97, 99, 118–20. *See also* postliberal historicism; postliberal theology

Lindsey, William, 271

linguicentrism, 35, 36, 306

Livingston, James C., 436n58

Locke, John, 214–16

logical positivism, 431n316

logocentrism, 195, 237, 238

Long, Jeffrey, 370n143

Loomer, Bernard, 141, 301, 448n157; on ambiguity of God, 309, 325, 334–36; Dorrien on, 455n256; pantheism of, 334–35; process theology of, 23, 34, 309, 341,

Loomer, Bernard *(continued)* 361n13, 447n139; radical empiricism of, 306, 447n139; religious naturalism of, 278, 334–36; Whitehead and, 309, 335–36
Lotze, Rudolf Hermann, 69
Luckmann, Thomas, 227–28
Luther, Martin, 287, 297, 332
Lyotard, Jean-François, 236, 238

Macintosh, Douglas Clyde, 291, 444n75, 444n79
Manichaeism, 336, 396n79
Margolis, Joseph, 421n127
Martin, Jerry, 262
Marxism, 91, 105, 110, 111, 294, 392n11. *See also* liberation theology
Masuzawa, Tomoko, 68, 70–72
Mathews, Shailer, 24, 108, 163–66, 282; anthropocentric naturalism and, 318–19, 321; antiessentialism of, 163–64, 165–66, Dorrien on, 184–85; on Foster, 444n75; on historical Jesus, 184–85; on liberal theology, 184, 259; on metaphysical speculation, 243; naturalistic empiricism of, 150; naturalistic theism of, 241, 318–19, 436n65; theological constructivism of, 262, 266; theological pragmatism of, 271, 274
Mathews, Shailer, works of: *The Atonement and the Social Process*, 163; *The Faith of Modernism*, 259; *The Growth of the Idea of God*, 163, 285, 407n86; *The Messianic Hope in the New Testament*, 184; *The Social Teaching of Jesus*, 184
McDowell, John, 218, 219
McFague, Sallie, 49, 60, 108, 137; anthropocentric naturalism and, 319–21; Barth and, 454n235; on contextuality, 26; on cosmology, 158; critical realism of, 267; Davaney on, 321, 408n109, 436n67; ecological theology of, 49, 59–60, 272, 319–21; Kaufman and, 454n233, 463n362; metaphorical theology of, 108, 263, 266–67, 272, 274, 286–87, 319, 320, 321, 327, 328, 410n128, 454n233; panentheism of, 458n309; on scripture, 410n128; on theodicy, 328–29; theological constructivism of, 263, 266, 272, 286–87; on theological pragmatism, 274; on *via negativa*, 266, 327
Mead, George Herbert, 269, 317
Meinecke, Friedrich, 146
Meland, Bernard, 264, 307, 325, 448n157; on "appreciative consciousness," 308; Dorrien on, 455n256; on radical empiricism, 306, 448n139; on theological realism, 301–2
Menand, Louis, 208
Merleau-Ponty, Maurice, 129
Merton, Thomas, 112
metaphors, 285–87, 304
metaphysics, 3, 4, 10, 11–12, 24, 52, 67, 112, 224, 232, 431n316; Derrida on, 195, 237, 239; historicism and 10, 11–12, 55, 189, 236–49, 353, 356, 430n298, 438n82; perspectivism and, 190–91, 462n344; pragmatism and, 237–41, 429n284; radical empiricism and, 306–12, 447n139; religious naturalism and, 313–16, 452n201; Whitehead on, 429n282; Wildman on, 247–49; of ultimacy, 41, 106, 109, 118, 250, 277, 295, 305–6, 317–44, 348, 350, 459n319, 460n334

"methodologism," 33, 301
Milbank, John, 133–34, 254, 432n15
Millennium Development Goals, 135–36
Milligan, Charles, 350
Min, Anselm, 134
miracle stories, 149–51, 266, 401n15
Mithraism, 153
modernism, 18; Brown on, 260; Davaney on, 237; Lyotard on, 236; Neville on, 238–40; Wildman on, 237–38
Moore, Addison Webster, 269
Moses (prophet), 82, 178, 406n83
Mother Earth (Native American deity), 406n83
multiculturalism, 30–31, 130–33; Davaney on, 42, 103. *See also* pluralism
multiple religious belonging, 42, 130–33, 396n70
Munger, Theodore, 253
Murphy, Francesca Aran, 437n69
mutualism, 90; of Knitter, 91, 104, 383n132; particularist, 61–62, 101–9. *See also* pluralism
mysterium tremendum, 37, 268, 322–23, 332
mysticism, 297, 329, 341, 347–49; naturalistic, 316, 323, 324–35, 326–27, 329–30, 333–34, 335, 339–40, 348–49, 353, 357; Neoplatonic, 298; philosophy of, 384n144
myths, 149–51, 266, 401n15

nationalism, 26–30; cosmopolitan, 21, 26–27; of Herder, 21, 26–27; Rorty on, 30
Native American religions, 30, 74, 132, 138, 333, 406n83
naturalism, 102, 461n337; anthropocentric, 317–21, 344; cosmic, 322–24; definition of, 313–14; ecstatic, 327, 446n108; empirical, 36, 240, 253, 278–81; historicism and, 11–12, 34, 48–49, 55, 284; pluralistic, 278, 317, 324–44, 353; pragmatic, 224, 355–56; religious, 108–9, 136–39, 312–44, 350–51, 353, 354–55, 436n65, 437n67, 461n337, 462n345
naturalistic-humanistic historicism, 11, 48–49, 59, 329, 334, 341, 442n36
naturalistic realism, 267–68, 303
naturalistic theism, 241
Neoplatonism, 298
neopragmatism, 2, 34, 36, 272–73; atheistic, 256; Corrington on, 34; nominalism and, 4, 189, 212–13, 217–18, 221; nonfoundationalism and, 203–4; paleopragmatic historicism and, 4, 212–36, 241; postmetaphysical, 189, 236; of Rorty, 189, 229–30, 241, 246–47; of West, 50, 206, 216, 245
Nestorians, 112
Netland, Harold, 77–80
Neville, Robert Cummings, 218, 229; on Barth, 76–77, 432n15, 433n20; Davaney and, 259; on identity theology, 254, 257, 432n15, 433n20; on metaphysics, 240–41; on modernism, 238–40, 428n269; on "ontological creativity," 327; on paleopragmatism, 189, 229, 368n116; on Peirce, 205, 239–40; on realism, 218, 421n125; on Rorty, 218, 368n116, 421n125; on sociohistorical theologians, 434n35; on symbols, 459n323; on "truth-seeking theology," 254–56; Wildman and, 459n323
Newton, Isaac, 423n157
Nicene Creed, 181

Nicholas of Cusa, 112
Niebergall, Friedrich, 148
Niebuhr, H. Richard, 1, 297–98, 302; Dorrien and, 447n122; neo-orthodoxy of, 311, 333
Nietzsche, Friedrich, 191–92, 203, 284, 294; Foster and, 290, 292–93; James and, 416n33; perspectivism of, 191–92; Rorty and, 416n33; Tillich and, 296
Nirvana, 89, 90, 93, 95, 99
Noahic Covenant, 85
nominalism, 4, 189, 212–13, 217–18, 221, 225, 231, 256, 274–75, 301, 433n20
nonbeing, 389n226
nonfoundationalism, 189, 201–4, 236, 243–48
nonhuman nature, 48–60, 331
normativity of the past, 171–81
nostalgia, 145
noumenal/phenomenal worlds: Dewey on, 279–80; Hick and, 88–89, 91, 106, 108, 110; Kant on, 88–89

O'Connor, Flannery, 296
Ogden, Schubert, 168, 448n157
"ontological creativity," 327
ontology, 103, 282, 288; antirealist, 216; historicist, 7–12, 156, 190
onto-theology, 244
Otto, Rudolf, 37, 147

paleopragmatic historicism, 4–5, 36, 212–13, 235–36; constructivism and, 198–201, 213–29; elements of, 189–90; fallibilism and, 204–7; instrumentalism and, 207–12; metaphysics and, 237–38, 239–42; neopragmatism and, 212–36; nonfoundationalism and, 201–4, 236; perspectivism and, 190–98;

relativism and, 229–36. *See also* pragmatic historicism
paleopragmatic historicist theology, 251–53, 269–75
paleopragmatic humanism, 349
panentheism, 319, 326, 335, 458n309
Panikkar, Raimon, 121, 388n210
panpsychism, 55, 373n201
pantheism, 332, 462n345; Crosby on, 339; Dean on, 332; Frankenberry on, 349–50, 453n218; Loomer on, 334–35, 341; Milligan on, 350; Wieman and, 336
Parker, Theodore, 253
particularism, 99–100, 103; contextual, 15–25, 25–26, 31–32; "departicularization" and, 83–85; of Heim, 93–95, 96–97, 98–101, 102, 106, 107–8; of Herder, 21, 25; interreligious dialogue and, 143; Kaufman and, 94, 101–2; Knitter on, 384n140; of Lindbeck, 38, 92–93; mutualism and, 61–62, 101–9; nonparticularism and, 381n108; pluralism and, 85, 90, 92–94, 100–1, 104; relativistic, 28
particularist mutualism, 118; of Kaufman, 101–2, 104–5; pragmatic historicism and, 61–62, 72–75, 86–104, 123–30
Paul (apostle), 174, 287, 296, 297
Peden, W. Creighton, 291, 444n75
Peirce, Charles Sanders, 5; Bernstein on, 425n200; Cahoone on, 226, 421n128, 426n221; Corrington and, 34; Derrida on, 195, 415n29; on Descartes, 192, 205, 226; on Duns Scotus, 225–26; fallibilism of, 205–6, 238, 239; on "interpretant," 414n13; James and, 230, 231; Neville on, 205, 239–40; on "nominal definition" of truth,

427n227; nonfoundationalism of, 202, 238; perspectivism of, 192; "pragmaticism" of, 222, 231, 234; pragmatism of, 51, 189, 208–10, 213, 218–19; realism of, 221, 225–27; Rorty on, 195–96, 226; semiotics of, 192, 241; West on, 245–46; Wildman and, 225, 231, 425n194

Pentecostalism, 84, 379n59

perennialism, 87–90, 94, 102–3, 117–18; of Hick, 87–89; particularist critique of, 90–104; soteriocentric, 89

personal god(s), 88–89, 98, 284–85, 313, 314, 319, 344, 350–51, 452n201; Crosby on, 342, 354–55, 460n333; Dean on, 289, 295–96; Kaufman on, 329; Loomer on, 309; McFague on, 319, 454n233; Wieman on, 312, 335–36; 458n311, 463n375; Wildman on, 336–37

perspectivism, 190–98, 264–65

Phan, Peter C., 371n155, 391n1

phenomenal/noumenal worlds: Dewey on, 279–80; Hick and, 88–89, 91, 106, 108, 110; Kant on, 88–89

Pinnock, Clark, 168, 379n59

Pittenger, Norman, 448n157

Plaskow, Judith, 332

Plato, 63, 168, 201, 204, 298; Dewey and, 203, 241; Rorty and, 244, 279; Troeltsch and, 401n12; West and, 245

pluralism, 110; as covert exclusivism, 110–16; definitions of, 75, 83, 325; "differential," 103; Eck on, 74; Heim on, 91–92; Hick on, 71–77, 84, 87–92, 110–11, 115, 117, 391n254; Kaufman on, 62, 75–76, 80, 82, 86, 94; Knitter on, 75, 92, 100–1, 383n132, 390n236;

nonparticularism and, 381n108; particularism and, 85, 90, 92–94, 100–101, 104; without perennialism, 86–87; Rose on, 83–87, 111, 112–13, 385n174, 390n236; Schmidt-Leukel on, 112–13, 117, 394n50; syncretism and, 84; Thatamanil on, 90; Troeltsch on, 70–72. *See also* multiculturalism; mutualism

polytheism, 64–65, 90, 350, 351

postliberal historicism, 25, 37–41, 48, 92–93, 181; Davaney on, 42, 121, 167–68, 300–1; Dean and, 40–41; Lindbeck and, 37–41, 119. *See also* postliberal theology

postliberal theology, 167–68, 256–57, 274–75, 300–1. *See also* Lindbeck, George; postliberal historicism

postmodernism, 97–98, 320; Bernstein on, 238; ironic atheism and, 298; late modernism and, 237–39, 249 Lyotard on, 236–37; metaphysics and, 236–37; Neville on, 189, 238, 368n116; particularism and, 92; perspectivism of, 191, 194–95; Ryder on, 223; Wildman on, 225, 247–48

pragmatic historicism, 15, 181, 186–87, 353; atheism and, 278–91; of Bernstein, 212; constructive realism of, 213–29, 262–69, 446n108; of Davaney, 260, 270, 274–75, 301, 408n109, 426n210; Dorrien on, 277, 301; fallibilism and, 204–7, 251–53; identity theology and, 257; incommensurability and, 41–42; for interreligious engagement, 117–19; of Kaufman, 105–6, 108, 287–88, 303–5, 386n194, 439n97; liberal theology and, 2–3, 41, 150, 168, 172, 178, 181, 183–87, 253–62, 433n23; naturalistic empiricism and,

pragmatic historicism *(continued)*
279–81; nonfoundationalism of, 201–4, 246; particularist mutualism and, 61–62, 72–75, 86–109, 123–30; probative pragmatism of, 269–75; religious naturalism and, 108–9, 317–44; religious pluralism and, 62, 75–86, 118; religious realism and, 303; theological realism and, 299; ultimate reality in, 278–79, 317–44, 353, 357, 446n108. *See also* historicist theology; holistic historicism; humanistic historicism; naturalistic-humanistic historicism; paleopragmatic historicism

"pragmaticism," 222, 231, 234

pragmatic naturalism, 224

pragmatic realism, 225

pragmatism, 2, 235; of Chicago School, 273, 281, 269–74; correspondence theory of truth and, 229–36; criteriological, 142–44; fallibilism of, 205–7; instrumentalism of, 207–12; naturalism and, 51–53; nonfoundationalism of, 202–4; postmodernism and, 237–41; probative, 269–75. *See also* neopragmatism; paleopragmatic historicism

Premawardhana, Devaka, 131

process theology, 103, 309, 447n139; of Brown, 9–10, 129, 328, 373n201; of Cobb, 370n146; of Dean, 9–10, 55, 361n13, 448n157; empirical, 34, 308, 334, 447n139, 448n157; historical, 361n13; of Loomer, 23, 34, 309, 334, 335, 341, 361n13, 447n139; panentheistic, 326, 458n309; speculative, 361n13; of Wieman, 308, 448n157; Wildman and, 336

Proudfoot, Wayne, 384n144
Pseudo-Dionysius, 329, 348
Putnam, Hilary, 421n127
Pye, Michael, 65

Quine, Willard Van Orman, 196, 203

Rabinow, Paul, 160
Race, Alan, 378n54
radical empiricism, 2, 139–42, 264; of Brown, 35–36, 310–11, 450n172; Davaney on, 140, 306; of Dean, 34–35, 303, 306–7, 309; definition of, 34, 306; of Frankenberry, 223, 309–10; of James, 140–42, 240, 299, 307, 460n329; of Loomer, 306, 447n139; of Meland, 306, 308, 447n139; religious naturalism and, 305–12; of Whitehead, 35, 460n329; of Wieman, 312, 447n139
radical orthodoxy, 254
Rahlfs, Alfred, 63, 147
Rahner, Karl, 74, 97–98, 394n54
Randall, John Herman, 223
Ranke, Leopold von, 146
Rauschenbusch, Walter, 260
realism: apophatic, 268, 303; constructive, 213–29, 262–69, 299; critical, 108, 267, 446n108; direct, 222; "dynamic," 221; naive, 45, 197, 216, 220, 224, 268, 303; naturalistic, 267–68, 303; pragmatic, 225; theistic, 311; theological, 267–68, 299–305, 437n69
recontextualization, 3, 161, 179–80, 197
relativism, 212, 219, 225, 227, 229, 234, 248, 256, 267, 269, 273, 278, 297, 318, 354, 356, 424n189; of Foster, 150; of Herder, 28–29; Kaufman and, 118, 264, 268, 302, 330, 345, 437n69; Neville and, 433n20; of Rorty, 29, 213, 216–18,

229; of Troeltsch, 62, 64, 67–70, 100; West and, 245–46
religionsgeschichtliche Schule. See comparative history of religion
religio perennis, 89, 102. See also perennialism
religious experience, 103, 265, 310; Brown on, 264–65; Dewey on, 307; Frankenberry on, 310, 450n178; James on, 232, 234–36, 271, 297, 307; Loomer on, 308; Meland on, 307; Smith on, 265; Wieman on, 307–8, 309
religious naturalism, 108–9, 136–39, 312–44, 350–51, 353, 354–55, 436n65, 436n67, 461n337, 462n345; Christianity and, 398n117; of Crosby, 138–39, 316, 338–40, 346–47, 354–55; of Dean, 331–34, 349; of Dewey, 307, 315, 349; of early Chicago schoolers, 316, 317–19, 322–24, 327, 328, 436n65; of Goodenough, 138, 314, 324, 355; of Hogue, 137–38, 313, 315, 316, 325; of James, 307; Judaism and, 398n117; of Kaufman, 139, 329–31, 344–46, 355; liberal theology and, 316; of Loomer, 309, 334–36; of Meland, 308, 325, 328; of McFague, 319–21, 328; of Stone, 325, 328, 350–51; theology of religions and, 108–9; of Wieman, 307–8, 311–12, 328; of Wildman, 138–39, 314, 336–38, 347–49; world religions and, 137–39, 398n117. See also naturalism
Rig Veda, 180
Ritschl, Albrecht, 63, 69
Ritschlianism, 147–48; gospel-centered, 150; liberal theology and, 433n23
Roman Empire, 61, 83, 131, 148, 151–54, 178

Rorty, Richard, 12, 242–43, 294, 433n20; Anderson on, 219, 221–22; on antiessentialism, 157, 404n57; antirepresentationalism of, 196–97, 200, 217; atheistic neopragmatism of, 256; Bernstein on, 212; constructivism of, 199–200, 216–19; conventionalism and, 421n128; on Darwin, 209; Dean on, 35, 429n284; on Derrida, 361n20; Dewey and, 221, 241; on ethnocentrism, 29–32; fallibilism of, 207; Frankenberry and, 223; on historical contingencies, 7–8; on human nature, 243; instrumentalism of, 211–12; on irony, 465n2; on James, 427n229; Kaufman and, 301; on metaphysics, 243–46; on nationalism, 30; neopragmatism of, 189, 229–30, 241, 246–47; Neville on, 218, 368n116, 421n125; nonfoundationalism of, 204; on particularism, 24; on Peirce, 195–96, 226–27; perspectivism of, 195–97; on "Platonic urge," 279; on postfoundationalism, 236; on relativism, 29, 213, 216–18, 229; on scientism, 49; Soneson on, 430n298; West and, 50, 204, 245–47
Rorty, Richard, works of: *Consequences of Pragmatism*, 415n32, 421n125; *Contingency, Irony, and Solidarity*, 197, 423n157; *Philosophy and Social Hope*, 415n32; *Philosophy and the Mirror of Nature*, 196, 217
Rose, Kenneth, 81; on apophatic pluralism, 113; on cataphatic pluralism, 390n236; on Cornille, 393n24; on "departicularization," 83–84; on Heim, 95; on inclusivism, 85–86, 99, 393n24; on Merton, 112; on particularism, 95,

Rose, Kenneth *(continued)*
  381n108; on pluralism, 83–87, 111, 112–13, 385n174, 390n236; on theology of religions, 86
Rue, Loyal, 138
Ruether, Rosemary Radford, 168, 320
Ryder, John, 223–24

sacred conventions. *See* conventionalism
Sahlins, Marshall, 160
Said, Edward, 370n143
Salem Witch Trials, 408n108
salvation. *See* soteriologies
Sanders, E. P., 412n181
Sanders, John, 379n59
Santayana, George, 196, 355–56
Santería, 396n79
Schilbrack, Kevin, 45, 370n140
Schleiermacher, Friedrich, 37, 38, 112, 316; historicism of, 436n58; liberalism of, 38, 253, 265, 286, 443n44; *On Religion*, 432n8; Troeltsch on, 66
Schmidt-Leukel, Perry, 72, 112–13; on inclusivism, 73, 117; on interreligious theology, 394n50; on pluralism, 112–13, 117, 394n50; on "tripolar typology" in theology of religions, 378n54; on ultimacy, 387n205
Schweitzer, Albert, 183–85, 187, 412n174
scientism, 247, 249, 314, 316; Crosby on, 339; Rorty on, 49; Wildman on, 249
"secularization thesis," 315
Sellars, Wilfred, 196, 204, 416n33
semiotics, 34, 38, 39, 43, 213, 215; of Derrida, 10; of Frankenberry, 223; Geertz on, 32; of Lindbeck, 38, 119; of Peirce, 192, 226, 241, 459n323
shamanism, 84
Shinto, 42, 83–84, 138
Sikhs, 73, 88
Slater, Michael R., 232–34, 427n249
slavery, 30, 385n174, 406n83, 457n296
Smith, Christian, 464n385
Smith, Gerald Birney, 80–81, 173–75, 185; on apologetics, 258–59; cosmic naturalism of, 322–24; mystical naturalism of, 323–24, 327; pluralistic naturalism and, 329; on religious experience, 265; religious fallibilism of, 251–53; on tasks of theology, 257–58; on theological construction, 285–86; theological pragmatism of, 271, 273–74; on theology and science, 251–52
Smith, Gerald Birney, works of: "The Christ of Faith and the Jesus of History," 403n43, 412n174; *Current Christian Thinking*, 323; "The Task and Method of Systematic Theology," 258–59; "Is Theism Essential to Religion?," 323
Smith, Jonathan Z., 44, 169, 370n145
Smith, Wilfred Cantwell, 44–46, 101
sociohistorical theology, 2, 13–14, 151–52, 163, 261, 265, 305, 306, 309, 434n35
Soneson, Jerome, 243, 244, 246, 430n298
soteriocentrism, 89, 91, 134
soteriologies, 46, 73, 93, 118, 148, 168, 303, 328; DiNoia on, 90, 98; Heim on, 91, 93–97, 102–3, 107, 116; Hick on, 80, 85, 88, 90; Kaufman on, 134, 144, 345–46, 400n156; McFague on, 319–21
South Korean Pentecostalism, 84

Spencer, Herbert, 53
Spinoza, Benedict de, 151, 293
Stevens, Wallace, 333
Stoics, 401n12
Stone, Jerome, 221, 314, 398n117; on Dewey, 221; on Foster, 318; on Kaufman, 331; on Mathews, 319; religious naturalism of, 325, 350–51; on religious naturalism in Christianity and Judaism, 398n117
Stout, Jeffrey, 2, 14; on antirepresentationalist philosophy, 416n36; on Cartesianism, 16, 202; on Enlightenment, 15–16
Strauss, David Friedrich, 401n15
Suchocki, Marjorie, 101
Sunyata, 88, 89, 111, 112, 330
supernaturalism, 303, 313–14, 323; antisupernaturalism and, 145–56, 153–56, 171–81, 292, 313–14, 437n76; authority and, 148, 172, 173, 176, 452n209; Case on, 153–54, 155, 176, 322–24; Dean on, 40–41, 283; Dewey on, 280, 315; Foster on, 292, 315–16; origins of, 153–54, 442n36; religious realism and, 303; religious traditions and, 145–56; Wieman on, 311
supranaturalism, 314, 315, 324, 335–36, 341, 354, 437n76, 459n319; Tillich on, 314, 437n76; Wildman on, 336–38
Surin, Kenneth, 86, 87, 92
Süssmilch, Johann Peter, 363n21
syncretism, 83–84, 132; Davaney on, 42, 43, 396n79; Rose on, 83–84; Troeltsch on, 401n12

Taylor, Charles, 315
Taylor, Mark C., 33; Brown on, 411n153; Dean on, 367n99

Thatamanil, John, 5, 130–31; on comparative theology, 127, 130; on Heim, 107, 385n167, 388n211; on Hick, 90–91; on "polydoxic" trinity, 107, 109, 127, 388n211; on "religion" and "religions," 44, 46–47; on ultimacy, 106–9, 127
theodicy: Davaney on, 321; Dean on, 331–33; Kaufman on, 331, 459n318; McFague on, 320–21, 328–29; Ruether on, 320; Wildman on, 336–37, 338, 347–48
theological realism, 267–68, 299–305, 437n69. *See also* realism
theology of religions, 61–62, 72–75, 114–16; comparative theology and, 124–27; definitions of, 72; exclusivist, 72–73, 75–81; inclusivist, 73–74, 81–82, 85–86, 378n52, 379nn59–60, 379n64, 381n91, 382n110; particularist, 86–87, 90–104, 110–11, 118–23, 381n108, 382n114, 383n116, 384n140; pluralist, 74–75, 82–86, 87–92, 110–116, 380n70, 383n132, 385n174, 390n236, 391n254; pragmatic historicist, 72, 82, 97–109; tripolar typology of, 378n54. *See also* comparative history of religion
"theopoetics," 341, 350
Tilley, Terrence, 120, 383n116
Tillich, Paul, 38, 127, 133, 389n226; Crosby and, 339; Dean on, 296; liberalism of, 286; Neville on, 433n20; on Protestant principle, 450n181; on supranaturalism, 314, 437n76; Wildman and, 336
Towne, Edgar, 444n75
transreligious theology, 262
trinity, 79, 89, 98, 409n126; Heim on, 98–99, 107; nonbeing and,

trinity *(continued)*
  389n226; "polydoxic," 107, 109, 127, 388n211; Thatamanil on, 107, 109, 388n211
Troeltsch, Ernst: academic theology of, 261; on antiessentialism, 167; biblical criticism of, 147; Chicago school and, 150–51, 281–82; on Christianity's changeability, 159, 166–67; on Christianity's syncretism, 401n12; comparative history of religion and, 61, 62–68, 116, 145, 147–150; Dilthey and, 48; Dorrien on, 63, 69, 70–71, 147, 148; Hegel and, 63–64, 66–67, 376n12; Heim and, 99–100; Hick and, 391n254; historicism of, 2, 62–72, 149–50; liberal theology and, 433n23; Masuzawa on, 68, 70–72; relativism of, 62, 64, 67–70, 100; Wildman on, 66–67. *See also* comparative history of religion
Troeltsch, Ernst, works of: *The Absoluteness of Christianity and the History of Religions*, 63, 66; "The Dogmatics of the History-of-Religions School," 66, 402n20; *Glaubenslehre*, 63, 65; *Der Historismus und seine Probleme*, 13, 62, 67, 69; *Der Historismus und seine Überwindung*, 70; "The Place of Christianity among the World Religions," 68–71
Tufts, James Hayden, 269
"tychism," 240

ultimacy, 90, 118, 250, 295, 303, 305–44, 386n176, 459n319; Crosby on, 339, 460n334; Hick on, 88–89, 106–9; historicist metaphysics of, 295, 305–16, 350–51, 353, 357; Mathews on, 318; Neville on, 327; religious naturalism and, 317–44; Schmidt-Leukel on, 387n205; Thatamanil on, 106–9, 127; Tillich on, 314; Whitehead and, 387n202; Wildman on, 268, 337–38, 347–49, 446n108
uncertainty principle, 54–55
Union Theological Seminary, 253
Unitarianism, 444n75
United States Constitution, 228
Universal Declaration on Human Rights, 135–36
universalism, 59, 60, 71, 72, 104, 109, 136–37; Enlightenment and, 23, 202; Griffiths on, 113–14, 120–21; hamartiocentrism and, 134–36; Kaufman on, 76, 104–6, 143–44, 398n105; naturalistic, 398n105; religious naturalism and, 137–39; Rose on, 100, 111, 390n236; Troeltsch and, 70–72
Upanishads, 112
utilitarianism, 233, 269, 439n105

Vásquez, Manuel A., 395n64, 442n36
Vatican Council, Second, 73–74
via negativa, 327, 329, 348
Voltaire, 21
von Balthasar, Hans Urs, 38
Voss Roberts, Michelle, 130, 131

Wagner, Roy, 160
Warrior, Robert Allen, 332–33
Weber, Max, 377n28
Weiss, Johannes, 63, 147, 183–84, 187
West, Cornel, 2, 50; on antirealist ontology, 216; Corrington on, 245–46; Davaney on, 371n172, 417n46; on Dewey, 246; on metaphysics, 245–47; on nonfoundationalism, 202–4; on Peirce, 245–46; on Rorty, 50, 204, 246–47

Westar Institute, 413n183
Wheeler, John, 54–55
Whitehead, Alfred North, 308; Brown and, 9–10, 129, 328, 373n201; cosmology of, 10; Crosby and, 339; Dean and, 9–10, 55, 361n13, 448n157; James and, 9, 429n282; Lee and, 448n157; Loomer and, 309, 335–36; Merleau-Ponty and, 129; panpsychism and, 55; *Process and Reality*, 9–10, 405n67, 429n282, 448n157; radical empiricism of, 35, 460n329; ultimates of, 387n202; Wieman and, 311, 447n139, 448n157
Whorf, Benjamin Lee, 193
Wieman, Henry Nelson, 307–12, 325, 463n375; Brown on, 306, 309, 450n180; Calvin and, 311; Frankenberry on, 336, 450n181; Kaufman and, 330, 331; Loomer and, 335–36; on personal God, 312, 335–36; 458n311, 463n375; radical empiricism of, 312, 447n139; on religious experience, 307–8, 309; religious naturalism of, 307–8, 311–12, 328; Whitehead and, 308, 311, 447n139, 448n157
Wilamowitz-Moellendorff, Ulrich von, 147
Wildman, Wesley, 66–67, 138–39, 224–25; on Buddhism, 348; on confessional theology, 257, 262; on correspondence theory of truth, 229–31, 235–36; critical realism of, 224–25, 446n108; on "feedback potential," 224–25, 268–69; on foundationalism, 239; on James, 231, 419n93; on Kant, 431n318; Kaufman and, 330–31, 457n285; on mathematical principles, 419n93; on modernism, 237–38; on mysticotheological tradition, 341, 347–49; Neville and, 459n323; on nonfoundationalist fallibilism, 247–49; on "new atheists," 461n337; Peirce and, 225, 231, 425n194; on postmodernism, 225, 247–48; religious naturalism of, 138–39, 278, 303, 314–15, 336–38, 347–49; on religious philosophy, 261–62, 351; *Religious Philosophy as Multidisciplinary Comparative Inquiry*, 247–50; on theodicy, 347–48; on theological liberalism, 254, 432n9, 434n34; Tillich and, 336, 337; on transreligious theology, 262, 432n9; on Troeltsch, 66–67
Williams, Daniel Day, 448n139, 448n157
Williams, Delores, 457n296
Williams, Raymond, 160
Wittgenstein, Ludwig, 192–93, 196, 416n36; Kaufman and, 264; Lindbeck and, 37; Rorty on, 195–96, 415n32
Woodbridge, F. J. E., 223
World Council of Churches, 120–21
Wrede, Wilhelm, 63, 147

Yahweh, 285–86, 323, 407n86
Yong, Amos, 379n59

Zbaraschuk, Michael, 342
Zen Buddhism, 79, 83, 90
Zoroastrianism, 82, 83, 336

www.ingramcontent.com/pod-product-compliance
Lightning Source LLC
Chambersburg PA
CBHW022005300426
44117CB00005B/46